AF270308

The Kissinger Tapes

The Kissinger Tapes

Inside His Secretly Recorded Phone Conversations

Tom Wells

OXFORD
UNIVERSITY PRESS

Oxford University Press is a department of the University of Oxford.
It furthers the University's objective of excellence in research, scholarship,
and education by publishing worldwide. Oxford is a registered trade mark of
Oxford University Press in the UK and in certain other countries.

Published in the United States of America by Oxford University Press
198 Madison Avenue, New York, NY 10016, United States of America.

CIP data is on file at the Library of Congress

ISBN 9780190933340

DOI: 10.1093/oso/9780190933340.001.0001

Printed by Sheridan Books, Inc., United States of America

The manufacturer's authorized representative in the EU for product safety is
Oxford University Press España S.A. of Parque Empresarial San Fernando de Henares,
Avenida de Castilla, 2 – 28830 Madrid (www.oup.es/en or product.safety@oup.com).
OUP España S.A. also acts as importer into Spain of products made by the manufacturer.

CONTENTS

Cast of Characters   x
Acknowledgments   xiv

Introduction: Kissinger's Personal Trove   1

1. The Secret Cambodia Bombing and Vietnam
   Peace Talks: January–March 1969   16

2. North Korea's Shootdown of a U.S. Spy Plane, Leaks,
   and Vietnam Withdrawals: April–June 1969   23

3. Secret Vietnam Peace Talks, the Green Beret Murder Scandal, a B-52
   Stand-Down, and Golda Meir's First Visit: July–September 1969   32

4. The Moratorium and Mobilization Protests, Nixon's
   November 1 Ultimatum to Hanoi, the My Lai Massacre,
   and Warsaw Talks with China: October–December 1969   40

5. French Plane Sales to Libya, B-52s over Laos, Japanese Textile
   Negotiations, Hitting SAM Sites in North Vietnam, Danielle
   Hunebelle, and Thai Troops in Laos: January–March 1970   51

6. Arms to General Lon Nol, Beecher Leaks, the Invasion of
   Cambodia and the Hunt for Supplies and COSVN, an Explosion
   of Protest, and the Heaviest Bombing of North
   Vietnam Since 1968: April–May 1970   65

7. Brian McDonnell, Cambodia and the Press, U.S. Air Strikes and
   South Vietnamese in Cambodia, Frictions with State, and a Tenuous
   Middle East Cease-Fire and Clashes over Credit: June–August 1970   84

8. *60 Minutes* Debut, Subverting Allende in Chile, Jordan on the Brink and Intervention Planning with Israel, and a Trumped-Up Soviet Facility in Cuba: September–October 1970 101

9. The Son Tay Prison Raid and Heavy Bombing of North Vietnam, Charles de Gaulle's Funeral, South Vietnamese Operations and U.S. Bombing in Cambodia, and Laos Planning: November–December 1970 122

10. Laird's Vietnam Machinations; More Strains with State; Planning a Meeting with the Kidnapping Plotters; the Ill-Fated U.S.-Supported South Vietnamese Invasion of Laos, the News Blackout and PR; and Slowing and Toning Down State on the Middle East: January–February 1971 140

11. The Laos Invasion—Tchepone, the Hasty South Vietnamese Retreat, Rout Stories and Bad Press, the PR Offensive, Upbeat Military Reports, and Whistling in the Dark; Kissinger's Meeting with the Kidnapping Plotters, Cover Stories, and Lies; and Another Round of Bombing of North Vietnam and "Protective Reaction" Claims: March 1971 154

12. My Lai; More Troop Withdrawals; U.S. "Moral Bankruptcy" in Pakistan; the Opening and Invitation to China, the Soviet Game, and Picking an Envoy; Creighton Abrams's Indiscretion on Laos; Allen Ginsberg's Overture; and an Ambiguous SALT Announcement Negotiated in the Back Channel: April–May 1971 179

13. Secret Senate Sessions on Laos; Retreat at Snuol; Pinning Laos on Kennedy; the Pentagon Papers—"This Is Treason," Kissinger's Distancing ("I Didn't Know the Thing Existed"), and Appealing to Lyndon Johnson; Kissinger's Secret Trip to China; Announcing Nixon's Visit to China and the New Public Mood; More Secret Vietnam Talks and the Impasse over Thieu; the Upcoming Rigged South Vietnamese Election; and Bypassing State on Berlin: June–August 1971 201

14. Defense Leaks on U.S. Withdrawal from Vietnam and More Unguarded Remarks from Abrams, Another Round of Heavy Bombing in Southern North Vietnam (Nixon—"I Am Not So Goddamned Concerned About the Civilian Population"), Egyptian–Israeli Clashes and Retaliations, Upheaval in China and the China Summit, Kissinger's Second Trip to China, Reining in State on the Middle East, and SALT: September–October 1971 224

15. The Pakistan–India Conflict—the United Nations, a "Soviet–Indian Naked Power Play," Border Clashes and Escalation, Cutting Off Aid to India, Disputes with State, Pakistan's Surprise Attack, Blaming India, Illegal Arms Shipments, Preventing "a Dismemberment of West Pakistan," Coordinating with China, Pakistan's Surrender and Gandhi's Cease-fire; a Cuban Attack on a Suspect Freighter; and Massive Bombing of North Vietnam: November–December 1971 242

16. Relations with India and Bangladesh, the Radford Leaks and JCS Spying Operation, in Nixon's Doghouse and Under Attack in the Press, Bemoaning Rogers and Talk of Resigning, Haldeman's Incendiary *Today* Show Charge, Preparing for the Enemy Offensive and Intensified Bombing in the South, and the China Summit and Shanghai Communiqué: January–February 1972 260

17. The Enemy Offensive in South Vietnam—U.S. Bombing and Shelling of the North, Weather Delays, Bombing in the South, Discord with Abrams and Laird, Expanding the Bombing Northward, Rolling Out the B-52s, and the Heavy Weekend Bombing of Haiphong and Hanoi; Kissinger's Secret Trip to Moscow; and Nixon's Threats to Cancel the Summit and Blockade the North: March–April 1972 275

18. A Futile Meeting in Paris; Prodding the South Vietnamese; Soviet Summit in the Balance; Mining North Vietnam's Ports, Bombing Its Rail Lines, Resuming Heavy Bombing in the Hanoi–Haiphong Area, and Internal Dissent; a Supreme Commander in Vietnam?; the Battle and B-52s in South Vietnam; the SALT Agreements; and Danielle Hunebelle's *Dear Henry*: May–June 1972 298

19. The Disturbed Bobby Fischer; the Cockamamie Jimmy Hoffa Pardon and POW Scheme; George McGovern, Pro-Nixon Democrats, and the Thomas Eagleton Debacle; Bombing Dikes; the Nixon Campaign and Fundraising; Swifty Lazar's Pursuit of Kissinger's Memoirs; and the Jackson Amendment on SALT: July–August 1972 319

20. Maligning and Attacking George McGovern; Nixon's Backing of the Jackson SALT Amendment; Connally and Resignation Rumors; *Kissinger: The Adventures of Super-Kraut*; the October Peace Agreement—Leaning on Thieu, His Rejection and "Suicide," Hanoi's Demand That It Be Upheld and Signed, "Peace Is at Hand," and Fear of a Blow-Up: September–October 1972 337

21. McGovern—"He's an Awful Man," Pressuring and Appeasing Thieu and Reneging on a Peace Agreement That Was "Good Enough," Moving Without and Threatening Thieu, the Connally Problem—"He's a Total

Lightweight," Nixon's Distancing, Visit of a Thieu Emissary, Breakdown in Paris, and the Christmas Bombing: November–December 1972   359

22. PR on the Christmas Bombing; Agreement in Paris; Facing Down and "Turning the Screw" on Thieu, Threatening a Separate Peace and an Aid Cutoff, and Contingency Planning for a "Tragedy"; Initialing and Signing the Agreement; "Peace with Honor"; Memoirs and Interviews: January 1973   386

23. Israel's Shootdown of a Civilian Libyan Airliner; Flacking Kissinger's Hanoi and China Visits; POW Releases, Peace Agreement Violations, and the Paris Conference; Diplomatic Killings in Sudan; Cambodia and Laos Bombing; and Aid to Pakistan: February–March 1973   403

24. "Trouble-Making" Cables; Stepped-Up Bombing in Cambodia and Two Days of Air Raids in Laos; Watergate Explodes, Getting "Blood Flowing" and "Total Disassociation," Plotting with Garment and Shultz, and Pleading Ignorance of Watergate; the Wiretapping Breaks and Kissinger's Evasions and Lies; and Kalb Book Intrigues: April–May 1973   420

25. Watergate, the Wiretaps, and the Plumbers; the Brezhnev Summit; Another Grain Deal; the Looming Cambodia Bombing Cutoff; Morton Halperin's Wiretapping Lawsuit; Memoirs; Nixon's Pneumonia; Dan Rather's Report on Kissinger's Move to State; the Butterfield Taping Revelation; and the Uncovering of the Secret Cambodia Bombing: June–July 1973   445

26. The Safire Wiretap and Safire's Angry Crusade; Nixon's Watergate Speech and Statement; Senate Hearings and Pentagon Releases on the Secret Cambodia Bombing; Legal Pleadings on the Halperin Wiretap; Nixon's Press Conference on Kissinger's Nomination as Secretary of State; Kissinger's Confirmation Hearings and the Wiretap Problem; Kissinger as Wiretap Victim?; the Coup Against Allende; and the Joe Kraft Wiretap: August–September 1973   471

27. The Yom Kippur War—Egypt's and Syria's Surprise Attacks, Restraining Israel and Egypt, the Soviets and the UN, Regaining the Prewar Lines, Warplanes, Tanks, and Ammo to Israel, Israel's Counterattacks, the Cease-Fire and Its Collapse, Israel's Strangulation of Egypt's Third Army, and Brezhnev's Threat of Unilateral Action; the Watergate Tapes; and Elliot Richardson's Resignation: October 1973   501

28. Golda Meir's Visit, Middle East Negotiations, the Arab
Oil Embargo, and Wiretapping of Kissinger
Revisited: November–December 1973 527

29. Kissinger's Shuttle Diplomacy and Israeli–Egyptian Disengagement,
More Resignation Threats, the JCS Spying Operation Breaks,
and the Oil Embargo in Limbo: January–February 1974 535

30. The Lifting of the Oil Embargo, Israeli–Syrian Disengagement, Tensions with Schlesinger, Israeli Raids in Lebanon,
and More Wiretap Questioning: March–June 1974 545

31. The Greek Coup in Cyprus—the Ousting of Makarios, Consulting and Excluding the Soviets, the Unsavory Nikos
Sampson, Collaboration and Conflict with Britain, Sisco's Mis-
sions, and Keeping U.S. Options Open; the Turkish Invasion
of Cyprus—the Clerides Solution, Preventing War with Greece, Frustrations with Sisco and Underlings at State, Schlesinger's Arms Cutoff
and Dissociation from Greece, and Threatening a Turkey
Arms Cutoff; and More Wiretap Testimony: July 1974 559

32. Nixon's Resignation and Kissinger's Role, and
Memoirs: August 1974 581

Abbreviations 587
Notes 588
Bibliography 597
Index 599

CAST OF CHARACTERS

Abrams, Creighton, commander of U.S. forces in Vietnam, then army chief
    of staff
Agnew, Spiro, vice president
Anderson, Jack, columnist
Beecher, William, *New York Times* reporter
Bernstein, Robert, president of Random House
Brandon, Henry, British journalist
Brezhnev, Leonid, general secretary of Soviet Communist Party
Buckley, William F., public intellectual
Bunker, Ellsworth, U.S. ambassador to South Vietnam
Bush, George H. W., U.S. ambassador to United Nations
Buzhardt, Fred, Nixon's chief Watergate counsel
Callaghan, James, British foreign secretary
Chou En-lai, Chinese premier
Clements, William, deputy secretary of defense
Colby, William, CIA director
Colson, Charles, special counsel to Nixon and outside liaison
Connally, John, secretary of the treasury, then outside Nixon adviser and
    supporter
Davidson, Daniel, National Security Council staffer
Dayan, Moshe, Israeli defense minister
Dean, John, Nixon counsel
Dinitz, Simcha, Israeli ambassador to United States
Dobrynin, Anatoly, Soviet ambassador to United States
Ehrlichman, John, counsel and assistant to Nixon for domestic affairs
Evans, Rowland, columnist
Fahmy, Ismail, Egyptian foreign minister
Flanigan, Peter, Nixon aide on business and economic issues

Frankel, Max, head of Washington bureau of *New York Times*

Friedheim, Jerry, Pentagon spokesman

Fulbright, J. William, senator and chairman of Senate Foreign Relations Committee

Gandhi, Indira, Indian prime minister

Garment, Leonard, special consultant to Nixon, then counsel

Gromyko, Andrei, Soviet foreign minister

Haig, Alexander, military assistant to Kissinger, then deputy to Kissinger, then army vice chief of staff, then White House chief of staff

Haldeman, H. R., White House chief of staff

Halperin, Morton, National Security Council staffer

Harlow, Bryce, Nixon assistant for legislative affairs and counselor

Helms, Richard, CIA director, then U.S. ambassador to Iran

Hersh, Seymour, *New York Times* reporter

Hoover, J. Edgar, FBI director

Hunebelle, Danielle, French journalist

Hussein, king of Jordan

Ingersoll, Robert, deputy secretary of state

Ismail, Hafiz, Egyptian national security adviser

Johnson, U. Alexis, undersecretary of state

Kalb, Marvin, *CBS News* correspondent

Keating, Kenneth, U.S. ambassador to India, then Israel

Kendall, Donald, CEO and president of PepsiCo

Kissinger, Henry, national security adviser and secretary of state

Klein, Herb, White House communications director

Kleindienst, Richard, deputy attorney general, then attorney general

Kosygin, Alexei, Soviet premier

Kraft, Joseph, columnist

Laird, Melvin, secretary of defense, then Nixon counsel on Watergate

Lazar, Irving (Swifty), Hollywood agent

Lodge, Henry Cabot, Nixon's first head of U.S. delegation at Paris peace talks

Makarios, archbishop and president of Cyprus overthrown in coup

Maw, Carlyle, legal adviser to Kissinger

McCloskey, Robert, State Department spokesman

McDonnell, Brian, antiwar protester who Kissinger befriended

McGovern, George, senator and 1972 Democratic presidential candidate

Meir, Golda, Israeli prime minister

Mitchell, John, attorney general, then chairman of Nixon's reelection campaign

Moorer, Thomas, chairman of Joint Chiefs of Staff

Nasser, Gamal Abdel, Egyptian president

Nol, Lon, Cambodian prime minister, then head of state

Packard, David, deputy secretary of defense

Peterson, Peter, secretary of commerce

Phouma, Souvanna, Laotian prime minister

Pursley, Robert, Laird's top military assistant

Rabin, Yitzhak, Israeli ambassador to United States

Rather, Dan, *CBS News* correspondent

Raza, N. A. M., Pakistani ambassador to United States

Reston, James (Scotty), *New York Times* vice president and columnist

Richardson, Elliot, undersecretary of state, then secretary of HEW, then
    secretary of defense, then attorney general

Rockefeller, David, president and chairman of Chase Manhattan Bank

Rockefeller, Nelson, governor of New York

Rogers, William, secretary of state

Rush, Kenneth, U.S. ambassador to West Germany, then deputy secretary
    of defense, then deputy secretary of state

Sadat, Anwar, president of Egypt

Safire, William, White House speechwriter, then columnist

Sato, Eisaku, Japanese prime minister

Scali, John, Nixon adviser on PR and foreign affairs, then U.S. ambassador
    to United Nations

Schlesinger, James, CIA director, then secretary of defense

Schreiber, Taft, MCA executive and Nixon fundraiser

Scowcroft, Brent, deputy national security adviser

Shultz, George, secretary of labor, then budget director, then treasury
    secretary

Sihanouk, Prince Norodom, Cambodian head of state

Sisco, Joseph, assistant secretary of state, then undersecretary of state

Smith, Gerard, head of U.S. delegation at SALT talks and Arms Control and
    Disarmament Agency

Smith, Hedrick, *New York Times* reporter

Stennis, John, senator and chairman of Senate Armed Services Committee

Thieu, Nguyen Van, president of South Vietnam

Tho, Le Duc, senior North Vietnamese negotiator at Paris peace talks

Thuy, Xuan, North Vietnamese negotiator at Paris peace talks

Timmons, William, Nixon assistant for legislative affairs

Vogt, John, director of Joint Staff, then commander of air war in Southeast
    Asia

Vorontsov, Yuli, Soviet chargé d'affaires

Waldheim, Kurt, secretary-general of United Nations

Warren, Gerald, White House deputy press secretary
Westmoreland, William, former commander of U.S. forces in Vietnam, army chief of staff
Wheeler, Earle, chairman of Joint Chiefs of Staff
Yahya Khan, Agha Muhammad, Pakistani president
Yoshida, Mr. (pseudonym), Japanese emissary on textile negotiations
Young, David, member of Plumbers and former Kissinger personal aide
Zayyat, Mohamed El-, Egyptian foreign minister
Ziegler, Ronald, White House press secretary

ACKNOWLEDGMENTS

I wish to thank my agent, John Wright (now deceased), who placed the book with Oxford, knew the Kissinger era well, encouraged me to write the book, and provided advice on the proposal; David McBride, my acquisitions editor at Oxford, who smartly kept the book at a reasonable length; acquisitions editor Gabriel Kachuck at Oxford, who handled the book, including developing marketing plans, after McBride left Oxford; William Burr, who encouraged me to undertake the book and gave me feedback on the introduction; Emily Benitez, senior project editor at Oxford, who gracefully and skillfully coordinated the production process; my copyeditor Judith Hoover, who, though I thought I'd identified all of the many characters in the book and explained every issue, flagged some I had not; and Swetha Kodimari, senior project manager at Integra, who adeptly kept the production process on track.

INTRODUCTION

Kissinger's Personal Trove

Henry Kissinger is one of the most polarizing figures in recent American history, both celebrated and reviled. He is hailed by many as a master in the art of diplomacy and realpolitik who adroitly pursued the U.S. national interest while maintaining a stable balance of international power, and for orchestrating détente with the Soviet Union, negotiating the first arms control agreement with the Soviets, and opening relations with communist China. His diplomacy during the 1973 Yom Kippur War and subsequent "shuttle diplomacy" in the Middle East also have many admirers. All required extraordinary diplomatic skills and fortitude.

But many critics consider his diplomacy overhyped and some condemn him for committing war crimes and other violations of law, or being complicit in them. These crimes, they argue, were committed during the Vietnam War, through the genocide in East Pakistan perpetrated by the Pakistani military dictatorship supported by the Nixon administration, by the undermining and overthrow of Chilean President Salvador Allende and backing of the murderous Pinochet dictatorship afterward, and in other countries. Many also denounce his central role in the 17 secret and illegal FBI wiretaps of officials and journalists ordered by the Nixon White House.

Kissinger's fiercest critics believe he should have been prosecuted for his crimes. But his most ardent admirers, and there is no shortage of them, consider him one of the United States' greatest statesmen. There is not a lot of middle ground.

This book consists of Kissinger's phone conversations that he had secretly monitored or recorded (mainly recorded) when he was national security adviser

(1969–1974) and secretary of state (1973–1974) in the Nixon administration.*
They were selected from thousands of such conversations. I found them the most
illuminating of the issues Kissinger dealt with and of Kissinger, though some I
included primarily for entertainment value.

They were not intended for public use or scrutiny. Rather, they were intended
for Kissinger's own use and to be under his control.

Kissinger's motivations for recording his phone conversations ranged from
recordkeeping, which he needed, given his disorderliness—"he was so busy that
if somebody did not police up after him, his commitments on the phone, and
keep a specific record of these things, he would have been in great administrative
trouble," his former assistant Alexander Haig recalled—to providing material for
his memoirs. When a *Washington Post* reporter got wind of a few transcripts and
asked Kissinger if he planned to use them for writing his memoirs, he replied,
"These notes are strictly for the president's files. I have no intention of writing a
book." But their use is frequently evident in his memoirs. In fact, he used them
heavily, with some whole sections of his memoirs paralleling the transcripts,
which is strong evidence of his motive. He told Assistant Attorney General
Robert Mardian, after President Nixon directed Mardian to transfer FBI records
of the secret FBI wiretaps to the White House, to prevent disclosure and keep
FBI Director J. Edgar Hoover from potentially blackmailing him with them,
that he had been keeping records of his phone conversations for his memoirs,
then laughed and said he no longer did. He probably also had in mind wield-
ing the transcripts, if needed, against his bureaucratic rivals—getting them on
the record and holding them to account—or covering himself against internal
charges or leaks. "I should record every conversation I have with *those* people,"
he remarked to an aide after talking over the phone with Nixon adviser John
Ehrlichman and kidding him about his recording system before installing his
own equipment. The National Archives says "the purpose of the telcons was to
follow up on promises that Dr. Kissinger made and understandings he reached,"
which is Kissinger's own explanation and only a partial one. (His aides would
later remark, perhaps half-joking, that he needed to keep track of which lie he
told to whom.)[1]

Initially, Kissinger had secretaries and aides listen to his phone conversations
on extensions, take notes, and write memos on them. But he refined his system over time, with secretaries then preparing transcripts based on their notes.
The people Kissinger spoke with could not hear his secretaries or aides pick
up the phone extensions to listen to their conversations. Soon, Kissinger had

---

* Kissinger also recorded his phone conversations during his tenure in the Ford administration,
but only those from the Nixon administration are included in this book. All uncited quoted material
in the introduction is from his conversations that appear later in the book.

recording equipment installed, resulting in full records of his conversations and much higher-quality transcripts. Ultimately, nearly verbatim transcripts were produced. Kissinger's secretaries might work until late at night transcribing their notes or the recordings.[2]

Kissinger kept the transcripts in his personal files, not his official files. The tapes themselves were destroyed, he testified, right after being transcribed.[3]

For a good while, only a handful of people knew that Kissinger was keeping records of his phone conversations. Eventually, however, other people Kissinger spoke with probably came to know or suspect that they were being taped. Officials understood the ways of Washington, or got wind of Kissinger's taping, and Kissinger sometimes shared transcripts with his aides, President Nixon, or other officials to prove a point, advance his agendas, demonstrate his loyalty to Nixon, stress Nixon's orders, or assail foes. Before providing one phone transcript to White House Chief of Staff H. R. Haldeman, he edited it to express stronger support for Nixon; that was surely not an isolated occurrence. He was also fond of gesturing to aides to pick up the phone extensions and mocking, through his facial expressions or movements, what Nixon and rivals like Secretary of Defense Melvin Laird were saying. His aides, too, sometimes shared transcripts or tidbits with others. Haig, whom Kissinger often asked to monitor his phone conversations and was "constantly under the lash" of Kissinger for sharing the transcripts too widely, occasionally showed Haldeman transcripts to demonstrate Kissinger's questionable loyalty (while Kissinger questioned Haig's loyalty). Nixon was aware that Kissinger was keeping a record of their talks and collecting other materials for his memoirs, which could compete with his own record. Nixon sought in part through his own taping system to document that he rather than Kissinger was the chief strategist behind his administration's foreign policy initiatives and achievements.[4]

But most people Kissinger spoke to over the phone were unaware that their words were being recorded. George Shultz, who held three cabinet posts in the Nixon administration, was startled when a Kissinger aide related to him details of a phone conversation he'd had with Kissinger earlier that day; afterward, Shultz was more guarded with Kissinger over the phone.[5]

When people Kissinger talked to occasionally raised the possibility that they were being monitored or recorded, Kissinger denied it or fobbed off the query, although sometimes he ordered his secretary to get off the phone. He wanted his taping to remain as confidential as possible. Yet, on occasion he asked other officials if *they* had someone else on the line.

Kissinger spoke over the phone with many colleagues in the upper reaches of the Nixon administration, along with midlevel and lower officials. They include a pantheon of notables—President Nixon, secretaries of defense and state, treasury and commerce and agriculture and HEW secretaries, the two vice presidents, CIA directors, attorneys general, senior White House staff, budget directors, military commanders, assistant secretaries, deputy secretaries, undersecretaries, the White House press secretary, the deputy press secretary, and so on down the line. Along, of course, with his many aides and spokesmen.

He talked frequently with journalists. "He spent more time on the phone with journalists than with the rest of the government," Roger Morris of his National Security Council staff recalled.[6] He seduced and manipulated reporters, who were largely deferential to him. Many sought "guidance" from him; they were grateful for the access he gave them and for seemingly taking them into his confidence. That access, along with his wit, affected intimacy, and brilliance, were part of his seduction of them. They were conduits for his views and agendas. (One cannot examine newspaper stories of this period without getting a profound sense of the extent to which the press was often a mouthpiece of government officials.) Most journalists Kissinger spoke with were admirers, and a few were sycophants and consistent conduits. Some of the biggest admirers and conduits were Bernard Gwertzman of the *New York Times*, Jerrold Schecter and Hugh Sidey of *Time* magazine, CBS's Marvin Kalb ("I'm the president of the Henry Kissinger fan club"), and David Kraslow of the *Los Angeles Times* and the Washington *Evening Star*. (One who was not, Seymour Hersh of the *New York Times*, nonetheless played up to Kissinger full-on for a story on the administration's wiretapping, calling him a "national asset," sympathizing with the wiretapping, saying "you had a terrific problem," and even advising on PR. He did the same for a story on the secret Cambodia bombing.) It surprised John Ehrlichman that veteran journalists let Kissinger use them the way they did.[7]

Kissinger often flirted with female journalists, such as Barbara Walters—who was not interested and was disturbed by stories linking them but wanted continued access—and Marilyn Berger of the *Washington Post*. He enjoyed and drew people's attention to his playboy reputation (and commented that he wished the men he dealt with were prettier).

Kissinger spoke with many celebrities and powerbrokers in Hollywood. He relished his relations with them. (He seemed to perk up when Frank Sinatra came on the line.) But it incensed him when actresses he dated used him for publicity.

Of course, he spoke on numerous occasions with foreign officials—prime ministers, presidents, foreign ministers, defense ministers, and ambassadors. His relationship with the Soviet ambassador to the United States, Anatoly Dobrynin, an amiable man who was adept and perceptive about people (he would report to Moscow early in their relationship that Kissinger was "smart and erudite" but "extremely vain . . . boasting of his influence") and who appreciated Kissinger's sense of humor, was a warm, joking, and affectionate one when they weren't at odds over issues. "I don't know whether one can have a feeling of personal friendship with a Communist diplomat but I have it," he told Dobrynin after the ambassador applauded Nixon's reelection in 1972.[8] In pursuit of détente or other objectives with the Soviets, Kissinger sometimes conspired with Dobrynin against his own bureaucracy or railed about colleagues to show Dobrynin what he was up against.

Kissinger had many talks with members of Congress and other prominent people, including corporate executives, whom he largely scorned as he did congressmen. ("American businessmen are certified morons," he snapped, though his brother was one.)[9] He also spoke with many officials from the Kennedy and Johnson administrations. His conversations with his former patron Nelson Rockefeller, the governor of New York, often took on the character of a mutual admiration society (as did his conversations with Hubert Humphrey, whom he disparaged as a "coward" and "weakling" behind his back).[10] And he had numerous talks with academics, particularly those at Harvard, where he'd previously taught (many of whom he did not think much of either).

Kissinger's phone conversations offer a rich and sweeping portrait of the man and his era. They show him in action on a daily, even hourly or minute-by-minute basis in a way that other histories do not. They offer a different level of history, compressed into shorter time spans (particularly during crises, with frequent phone calls), more detailed and intimate at times, providing another look behind the scenes, but often lacking broader context. They capture blunt words, invective, and scheming the participants wouldn't put on paper, while at other times evince guardedness about speaking on tape, or possibly on tape.

They show Kissinger barking orders and consulting with colleagues during pressure-packed crises. Sometimes he appears remarkably unruffled, with his sense of humor still intact, other times highly agitated, enraged, and snapping derisively or sarcastically at aides. The conversations not only provide many revelations on his role in events but throw his personality and character into sharp relief. They offer a wealth of insight into both Kissinger the person and the many matters in which he was involved as the U.S. government's top foreign policy adviser and its second most powerful man (though a full accounting of these matters, of course, requires consulting meeting transcripts, memos, and many other documents). As Kissinger wrote, his conversations "convey the mood in which major decisions were made," and certainly the stress.[11]

They cover a broader period than the more famous Nixon tapes. Kissinger began keeping records of his phone conversations as soon as he started working at the White House, in January 1969—two years before Nixon's taping system was installed in February 1971—and he continued taping for over three years (through his time in the Ford administration) after Nixon's system was dismantled in July 1973 after its existence was revealed.

Kissinger's conversations bear on a wide range of issues. They include, of course, the Vietnam War—the overriding and endlessly frustrating foreign policy issue of the day—including U.S. strategizing and threats, troop withdrawals, the U.S. invasion of Cambodia, and the disastrous U.S.-supported South Vietnamese invasion of Laos. They also include U.S. bombing campaigns, such as the secret and then more extensive public bombing of Cambodia, the brutal campaigns against North Vietnam, and the heavy bombing of Laos. Plus the conversations take up Nixon's November 1 ultimatum to Hanoi and planning for an all-out assault, the failed Son Tay prison camp raid (and simultaneous heavy bombing that officials baldly lied about), the enemy offensive in 1972, and the mining of Haiphong harbor. They also go into the earlier My Lai massacre, the Green Beret murder scandal, and antiwar protesters.

In addition, Kissinger's conversations discuss Nixon's Vietnam peace proposals and the Paris negotiations (and a crazy scheme by Jimmy Hoffa to obtain the release of American POWs that required a presidential pardon for his past crimes). They also get into Kissinger's infamous "peace is at hand" announcement, his strains with Nixon in the weeks that followed, their infuriating struggle to get South Vietnam's president on board with their peace agreement, and threats to proceed without him and cut off his aid if he didn't sign it. Kissinger's talks also discuss disputes with the North Vietnamese over POWs and cease-fire violations after the Paris peace agreement, and the U.S. bombing of Laos and Cambodia that followed it and the Laotian cease-fire. His conversations show his extensive direct dealings with U.S. military leaders, particularly Chairman of the Joint Chiefs of Staff Thomas Moorer, in part to try to circumvent Secretary of Defense Laird, with whom he had a running conflict over prerogatives and authority.[12] And they discuss the JCS spying operation against Kissinger, who, when the operation surfaced, denied it and called the allegation against Chairman Moorer "absurd."

Further, Kissinger's conversations cover the Nixon administration's first big crisis—North Korea's shootdown of a U.S. spy plane in April 1969, which killed all 31 men aboard. Kissinger, who thought it was a deliberate act (though it was probably a shaky decision by a single pilot), wanted to retaliate forcefully and even raised the specter of using tactical nuclear weapons. His talks also take up the horrendous 1971 slaughter in East Pakistan (later Bangladesh) and U.S. support for the Pakistani military dictatorship that committed it, including through illegal arms sales. Nixon and Kissinger castigated India and its prime minister, Indira Gandhi, whom they blamed for the India-Pakistan war that followed the massacre and the resulting refugee crisis in India; they were indifferent to the genocide in East Pakistan. Kissinger's conversations evidence his frictions with Secretary of State William Rogers over their pro-Pakistan policy.

The administration's undermining of socialist President Salvador Allende in Chile also comes up.

Moreover, Kissinger's conversations get into the administration's momentous rapprochement with China, including its strategizing vis-à-vis the Chinese, the Soviets, and the public—"We have got to have a diversion from Vietnam in this country," Kissinger told Nixon—Kissinger's trips to China, and the earthshaking China summit. U.S. relations with the Soviet Union, the first SALT arms control agreement, the long-thorny issue of Berlin, Soviet Jewish emigration, and the Soviet summits are covered too. So is Kissinger's trumped-up claim that the Soviets were constructing a nuclear-submarine base in Cuba.

The endless search for a peace settlement in the Middle East features abundantly in Kissinger's talks. As do relations with Israel and Egypt, U.S. military aid to Israel, the Palestinian threat in Jordan in 1970 and U.S.-Israel planning in response to Syrian involvement there (with the administration nervously green-lighting Israeli ground intervention), and Israel's attacks in neighboring countries. The 1973 Yom Kippur War is covered at length, from the Egyptian and Syrian surprise attacks to the cease-fire and its collapse to Israel's strangulation of Egypt's Third Army to the negotiations for disengagement on both fronts. Kissinger's frustrations with the Israelis—their inflexibility in peace talks, their aggressiveness and inclination to take more territory, their nonstop requests for weapons, particularly jet fighters (for which he and Nixon sought more flexibility in peace negotiations), their cross-border strikes at inopportune times ("You know those guys are primitive"), and their provocative public remarks—are evident. As is his displeasure with Jewish groups at home for their unrelenting lobbying in support of Israel's agenda.

The Greek coup in Cyprus in 1974 and subsequent Turkish invasion of Cyprus are also covered. Kissinger opposed reinstating Cyprus's ousted president (a member of the nonaligned movement) but faced a quandary over who to now back and worried about communist influence on the island. After Turkey's invasion, Kissinger strove to stave off war between Turkey and Greece while engaged in a delicate collaboration with Great Britain and clashing angrily with his underlings at State over their resistance to carrying out his orders.

Plus there are foreign side stories—Israel's shocking shootdown of a Libyan civilian airliner, the killings of American diplomats in Sudan, Kissinger's exasperating back-channel negotiations to limit exports of Japanese textiles to the United States, and more.

Kissinger's conversations also get into the secret and unlawful FBI wiretaps of officials and journalists following the disclosure of them and inquiries into Kissinger's role in them. (The wiretaps were later found by courts and the House Judiciary Committee to have violated the Fourth Amendment; the committee and a federal appeals court also found that they violated 1968 wiretapping legislation.) The conversations show a nervous Kissinger, who had been a key impetus to the initiation of the wiretapping and pivotal to the whole wiretapping program, acting evasively with journalists who asked him about the taps, lying repeatedly to them and others about his role, and, above all, minimizing his culpability—"I had nothing to do with it," "I did not request any wiretaps at all." A potential criminal indictment could not have failed to occur to him. He had recognized from the get-go that the wiretapping could be "explosive" and was a "dangerous game," former attorney general John Mitchell recalled; he wanted it done quietly. His military assistant, Alexander Haig, in requesting the start of the wiretapping on his behalf, told the FBI it was "so sensitive it demands handling on a need-to-know basis, with no record maintained," FBI Director J. Edgar Hoover recorded. (The FBI held the wiretapping closely inside the bureau, on a strictly need-to-know basis, and kept minimal records of it, which were subsequently destroyed, outside regular FBI files since it was an extremely sensitive "special project" that could embarrass the bureau. A wary Hoover, who insisted on Attorney General Mitchell's authorizations for each of the wiretaps, worried that they would be uncovered and damage him and the FBI. He and others at the FBI sought to discontinue the taps.)[13] Kissinger ensured that he and then–White House Chief of Staff Haig, who as his assistant and liaison to the FBI earlier had requested wiretaps from the FBI on his behalf, were on the same page in Senate testimony about them. He also claimed that he too was wiretapped. His talks get into his former aide Morton Halperin's lawsuit over his wiretapping as well.

Kissinger's conversations also take up the Watergate scandal—a multipart corruption scandal that was "less an event than a way of life for the Nixon administration," as Garrett Graff aptly put it, but included most prominently the break-ins at the Democratic National Committee headquarters and Daniel Ellsberg's psychiatrist's office, other illegalities and abuses of power, and the White House cover-up—that ultimately toppled Nixon. The conversations show a great deal of concern on the part of Kissinger and his colleagues about the scandal as it deepened. Worried about his reputation, Kissinger strove to distance himself from both Watergate and the wiretaps (which became part of the Watergate Special Prosecution Force's investigation and the impeachment articles against Nixon). "Look, you probably know more than I do," he told the columnist Rowland Evans about Watergate—he was in the dark. "I don't know a damn bit more than you do," he declared to HEW Secretary Caspar Weinberger.[14] He repeatedly denied any knowledge of the White House Plumbers extralegal investigations unit, though he was well aware of its formation, knew its purposes, and was apprised of some of its activities (though he probably wouldn't have known it as the Plumbers). He offered advice to Nixon and other officials on how to respond to the Watergate revelations, save Nixon, and contain the damage, often taking a hard line. (Nixon should get "blood flowing . . . up to the neck," he told Nixon counsel Leonard Garment, and launch "a frontal attack on these guys saying 'I was betrayed by my closest friends'. . . . But we'd need a guy who would be willing to set up them." "He shouldn't be groveling," he advised Haig about a Nixon statement on Watergate he helped shape. No "'True Confession' crap.") However, he claimed not to be involved in any such discussions to journalists. He was also duplicitous internally—praising Elliot Richardson as a "guarantee of virtue" after he resigned as U.S. attorney general rather than carry out Nixon's order to fire Watergate special prosecutor Archibald Cox, only to tell Nixon hours afterward that Richardson "stabbed you in the back."

Kissinger also denied any complicity in the false-reporting system employed in the administration's secret bombing of Cambodia that also became part of the Watergate inquiries. Though he had ordered the system to keep the bombing secret and had approved it, and had worked with an air force officer on it (mainly through Haig), he lied repeatedly about it in conversations with journalists and others after the bombing was uncovered, professing no knowledge of it. He denied participating in any discussions about false reporting.

Leaks, and who might be responsible for them, are a never-ending issue in Kissinger's conversations. They emerged as a colossal irritant early in the Nixon administration and consumed a large amount of time and energy: Who was behind the latest one? That question bred a certain amount of paranoia. Nixon was on the warpath over leaks soon after assuming office, demanding depositions from possible culprits and ranting about treason. Kissinger complained endlessly about leaks, hurling accusations while concealing his own leaks (a game he played with some regularity with Melvin Laird, a master leaker; they were a match for devious behavior and seemed to come to respect each other for it). It was not unusual for Kissinger and people he spoke with to complain about a leak that one of them had committed; when he was responsible, Laird sometimes phoned Kissinger to blame him.[15] Kissinger might condemn a news story that bore his fingerprints as "a disgrace" or "outrageous." It was quite the game being played. Kissinger also grumbled often about leaks by other governments (like Israel's). Kissinger and his colleagues leaked to undermine their rivals, promote their agendas, scuttle policies, curry favor with reporters, send messages overseas, enhance their reputations, and wield influence, among other reasons. Kissinger, an adroit serial leaker (though he told the journalist Mary McGrory, in a hell of a whopper, "he does not leak anything"), was frequently enraged by leaks. The ire over leaks that played a role in Nixon's downfall was in part Kissinger's doing. The massive leak in 1971 of the Top Secret Pentagon study on Vietnam that became known as the Pentagon Papers is a concern in numerous conversations, where officials debated the fallout and ways to respond (including with the Lyndon Johnson camp in Texas). Kissinger claimed repeatedly in these conversations that he never knew the study existed, at least in final form, though he knew about it nearly from the start, had consulted on it, and had been sent a copy after it was completed.

Other subjects in Kissinger's conversations include his female companions (including those in show business and the smitten French journalist Danielle Hunebelle, who became "a nightmare" to him), his other friends in the entertainment world, his many rivalries and animosities inside the government—the disdain was acerbic, the contempt virtually nonstop—his potential return to Harvard, his acute sensitivity to what his former Harvard colleagues thought of him, and his continual threats to resign from the government ("I am not going to wind up as an Ehrlichman—an errand boy in the White House"). His coveted appointment as secretary of state (which he professed not to want), particularly his preparations for his confirmation hearings (the wiretaps, and what, precisely, to say about them and his involvement, being the leading worry), is featured in his talks too. So are his memoirs, including the famous Hollywood agent Irving "Swifty" Lazar's and Random House's pursuits of them.

Kissinger appears in his phone conversations as, at turns, brilliant, with an exceptionally quick, powerful, and wide-ranging mind, possessing an impressive wit and sense of humor ("well-timed" to break tension), equipped with boundless stamina, capable of withstanding an endless series of headaches while working long hours, and an adept bureaucratic infighter. He is also arrogant, caustic about the "idiots," "maniacs," "lightweights," and mindless PR flacks he worked around, controlling, a highly demanding and at times abusive boss, and intolerant of those who did not carry out his orders. He threatens showdowns before Nixon to bring people into line. And he is charming, self-deprecating, and a false flatterer. Plus, he is a habitual and easy liar. He appears to have had little hesitation about lying. "Henry does not lie because it is in his interest," the NSC staffer Helmut Sonnenfeldt, who worked closely with him, said. "He lies because it is in his nature." "The man lied the way most people breathed," Seymour Hersh observed. He lies frequently to his colleagues and journalists. He sometimes misrepresents previous conversations or even denies they took place. (Yet CBS's Dan Rather would say that Kissinger "has the reputation that he never lies," and Kissinger would complain about other people's dishonesty, such as Senator Edward Kennedy's "complete lack of moral character, a deep lack of integrity.") The former Pentagon official Leslie Gelb would aptly describe Kissinger as "devious with his peers, domineering with his subordinates, obsequious to his superiors."[16] He was invariably deferential to Nixon, whom he, without a single exception over the phone during their nearly six years together, addressed as "Mr. President," though he grew to resent the requirement for deference (and being trotted out to serve Nixon's PR purposes).

Kissinger seduced more than a few people, not just journalists, with his charm, humor, flattery, feigned forthrightness, and sharing of intimacies. ("I'm talking to you as a friend.") "I have never met a person with greater powers of seduction when he chooses to exercise them," wrote former chief of naval operations Elmo Zumwalt, who grew to dislike Kissinger mainly for his deceit, secrecy, and dishonesty. Kissinger has been described as secretive so many times that it has become almost a cliché, but it is well-deserved. ("He never tells anybody anything, ever," his former deputy Brent Scowcroft would say with a thin smile and emphasizing his words.) And he was a backstabber and two-faced. Few colleagues in the government escaped his barbed tongue behind their backs. Plus, "He was able to give a conspiratorial air to even the most minor of things," his assistant Lawrence Eagleburger later said. "It was rather adolescent at times."[17]

Kissinger also comes off in his phone conversations as worried about his public reputation and standing inside the government, sensitive to criticism in the press, and stunningly callous to the deaths and suffering wrought by his Vietnam policies. Both he and Nixon treated American casualties as largely a political problem, while Vietnamese deaths were just body counts and measures of military success, ones that brought them gratification. They exulted over all the dead bodies piled up following bombing strikes. When Nixon said in April 1972 that they were going to "starve them out if necessary," Kissinger replied, "I couldn't agree more." He derided the North Vietnamese to Nixon as Soviet Ambassador Dobrynin's "little yellow friends." Seymour Hersh wrote that by the spring of 1972 Nixon was "conducting the war by temper tantrum," and Kissinger appeared to do so at times too.[18] His anger at North Vietnamese negotiators in Paris fueled his orders to JCS Chairman Thomas Moorer and encouragement to Nixon to take the gloves off when bombing the North. Kissinger was forever disposed to demonstrate his "toughness" to his colleagues and placed great value on being "tough." (There are also references in his conversations to acting "brutally," or being "strong" or "manly," and disdain for "pansy" language.)

Kissinger logged more hours over the phone with Nixon than anyone else, and their conversations provide a window into their relationship. They engaged in endless scheming and plotting—about their goals and means for reaching them, threats to their success, their colleagues, their domestic and foreign adversaries and their intentions, how to handle and manipulate or counter them, the press, members of Congress, and their allies at home and overseas (and how to play them too). Often, they sound no different than anyone else seeking to get what they want from people, coordinating their moves, deciding what to conceal, what lies to offer, and when to speak to people. They brooded frequently about their enemies and castigated other government agencies. They both relished foreign policy, Nixon being "the grand strategist, Kissinger the great tactician," as Tim Weiner wrote, and they chewed over all the big international issues of the day, Vietnam at the greatest length, and the latest foreign crises. Kissinger was often forced to remain on the line and listen to his boss's musings far longer than he had time for. (Listening for hours to Nixon in the Oval Office, Kissinger would find himself "praying for some crisis to bring relief.")[19] Nixon would call him at all hours. When events went south for them, as they did with Vietnam or Watergate, the two did a lot of whistling in the dark and bucking each other up.

Kissinger lavished praise on Nixon, though Nixon recognized it was often phony. He doubted Kissinger's sincerity and thought he talked down to him. Nixon also doubted Kissinger's loyalty, giving rise to a good deal of tension between them. He knew Kissinger leaked in his own interest. "It was impossible to talk to Nixon without wondering afterward what other game he might be engaged in at the moment," Kissinger wrote, and Nixon surely thought the same about him. "I resented being constantly manipulated," Kissinger recalled. It was not an easy relationship and they never fully trusted each other. "Both were talented liars," Weiner observed. But while Nixon could be short with him, Kissinger was rarely short with Nixon. He couldn't afford to be: his standing with his boss and pleasing him were always paramount concerns. Nixon had him by the short hairs. He was somewhat insecure about their relationship, which Nixon fed, and had to stomach a certain amount of abuse. Nixon felt "Kissinger should never be allowed to forget his subordinate status," as Michael Dobbs wrote. He regularly held his tongue when Nixon made dubious claims or requests (including some pretty wild ones, though he might laugh or rant about them behind Nixon's back or otherwise disparage him—"a raging beast," he would call Nixon).[20] He was quite disciplined about acting deferential and subservient.

Nixon valued Kissinger's enormous intellect, analytical abilities, extraordinarily hard work, diplomatic and PR skills, and coldness in the pursuit of their goals, and figured he could use him for his own purposes. He concluded that Kissinger was worth the considerable price he had to pay in "emotional drain" and all the headaches (such as Kissinger's constant, time-wasting, and often petty complaints about Secretary of State William Rogers, whom he disliked with a vehemence that was "startling" and thought was "out to get him," "psychopathic" efforts to subvert Rogers, blowing up issues, repeated threats to resign, need for public acclaim, and desire to control things). "He's a goddamn hard man to deal with," Nixon complained to his aides H. R. Haldeman and John Ehrlichman. But he was "indispensable to the president, and both he and the president know it," Haldeman told Kissinger.[21] Nixon and Kissinger understood each other's strengths and weaknesses well. Both were ruthless men unimpeded by morality who believed in the importance of power for advancing American interests in the world and thought the ends of their policies justified the means.

And Kissinger sometimes played to Nixon's darker side (though Kissinger's own dark side when it came to the application of power was dark indeed).

In the fall of 1976, shortly before the end of the Ford administration, Kissinger, no longer national security adviser but still secretary of state, had his phone summaries and transcripts along with other materials moved from his State Department office to the estate of his longtime friend Vice President Nelson Rockefeller in New York. He did not seek the approval of any government agency responsible for the preservation of government records; a State Department legal adviser had judged his phone transcripts to be personal papers. Kissinger had already secretly moved some 30 crates of files, including telephone transcripts, to the bomb shelter at Rockefeller's estate several years earlier when he was considering resigning from the Nixon administration; he'd then had them surreptitiously moved back to the White House after he decided to stay, partly because it was prohibited for an official to store government records in a private location. But he kept the most sensitive telephone transcripts at Rockefeller's luxurious estate, surrounded by lavish gardens and sculptures. His shipment of files to the Rockefeller property had started during his second year in the Nixon administration.[22]

Kissinger maintained that his phone transcripts were his personal property. He donated them to the Library of Congress under provisions that gave him control over them. Researchers could not examine them for 25 years, or five years after his death, whichever came later, unless he granted them permission. And authorization of a committee appointed by him was required to look at them after his death.

Kissinger, his assistant Lawrence Eagleburger, and others "sanitized" some of the transcripts. They removed the names of some people "to protect their privacy" and deleted other material they did not want researchers to read. They made many deletions. It is safe to assume that some were made to show Kissinger in a more favorable light or to avoid embarrassing him. Secretary of Defense Melvin Laird "knew Kissinger had a habit of doctoring" the records of his phone conversations "to make himself look better," Laird's biographer wrote.[23]

In 1977, after fending off inquiries from a congressional committee and the U.S. archivist into the propriety of his arrangement with the Library of Congress, Kissinger faced three lawsuits to gain access to his phone transcripts. One of the plaintiffs was William Safire, the former Nixon speechwriter, who had been wiretapped and believed Kissinger had requested the tap. (Kissinger told Safire he was unaware of it, though his assistant Alexander Haig had requested it from the FBI. Haig testified later that he never submitted a name for wiretapping that he did not get from Kissinger or from Nixon with Kissinger's knowledge. When questioned about the Nixon administration's wiretaps, Safire wrote later, Kissinger "gets visibly upset; he lies in an unstudied, amateurish way that can be found out.")[24] Another plaintive was a reporters organization. However, a U.S. Supreme Court ruling on the lawsuits declared that the remedy lay with government authorities, not the court, a big win for Kissinger.

Then, in 1999, the National Security Archive, an organization dedicated to fighting government secrecy and increasing public access to government records, wrote to the National Archives and the State Department disputing Kissinger's control of the transcripts. It asked the National Archives to obtain their return and raised the possibility of "more forceful measures." It also filed a legal complaint to compel the two government agencies to recover the transcripts and directly threatened litigation.[25] As a result, both agencies asked Kissinger to turn over the transcripts to them.

Based on legal advice, and perhaps wary of a lawsuit by the National Security Archive and the media attention it might attract, Kissinger complied in the early 2000s. (In his book *Crisis*, he wrote that he turned over the transcripts "to enable these agencies to process them with a view to their general availability," without mentioning that he'd been compelled to do so.)[26]

Kissinger was undoubtedly nervous about releasing his phone transcripts. He'd been worried about the release of Nixon's own tapes. He was distressed when Haig told him about Nixon's taping system in 1973 (which Nixon had not wanted him to know about); he realized the tapes could be damaging to him. "He felt violated, and raged at the horror of the secret taping system," his biographer Walter Isaacson wrote. He was rankled, too, when H. R. Haldeman's former assistant Alexander Butterfield disclosed the existence of Nixon's taping system to the Senate Watergate Committee. "There's no need to volunteer anything," he complained. He advised destroying the tapes. When Nixon was fighting for custody of his presidential papers after he resigned in August 1974, "it was Henry who called him and insisted on Nixon's right to destroy the tapes," Haldeman wrote. Kissinger "was adamant that this had to be done." But Nixon's claim that he had a right to eventually destroy the tapes effectively killed a deal he had struck with the General Services Administration over his tapes and papers, one that permitted their destruction, as Congress then enacted legislation giving the government custody of them. Nixon told Haldeman that "Kissinger was really the one who had the most to lose from the tapes becoming public," Haldeman recounted. "Henry apparently felt that the tapes would expose a lot of things he had said that would be very disadvantageous to him publicly."[27]

In 2004, the National Archives released the bulk of Kissinger's phone records from the Nixon administration. The National Security Archive filed a Freedom of Information Act request for those held by the State Department covering the period when Kissinger was secretary of state. Most of these were also subsequently released, though the National Security Archive had to fight for the release of many others. (My own Mandatory Declassification Review requests for declassification of transcripts or redacted material in transcripts with the Nixon Library are still in limbo a half-dozen years after filing them, but David Fort of the National Declassification Center at the National Archives helped get many other transcripts declassified, and I have included some of them and declassified portions of others in this book.)

There are over 15,000 Kissinger phone records, some 20,000 pages for the Nixon years, and the task of culling them, converting them to editable files, correcting the many errors in the transcripts and those resulting from the conversions, editing and trimming them, and determining their context and thus their precise meaning (which could be a puzzle) was long, arduous, and at times maddening. But it was rarely boring.

Greetings, pleasantries, and minor small talk at the beginning and end of conversations have been largely omitted.

1

The Secret Cambodia Bombing and Vietnam Peace Talks

January–March 1969

In February 1969, the North Vietnamese and National Liberation Front launched an offensive in South Vietnam. In March, the Nixon administration began secretly bombing with B-52s enemy bases in Cambodia along the South Vietnamese border. Renewing the bombing of North Vietnam was politically untenable at the start of the administration, but failing to react to the enemy offensive would send the wrong signal to Hanoi, one of weakness. Nixon and Kissinger, who both would have liked to have bombed the North, and hard, felt the timing was not right. But they needed to show Hanoi they were capable of escalation. The Defense Department's David Packard, cofounder of Hewlett-Packard, was a strong advocate of the secret Cambodia bombing. Peace talks in Paris were going nowhere.*

President Nixon
February 4, 1969, 5:35 p.m.
Kissinger passes on appreciation from CIA Director Richard Helms.

President asked what meeting they had on Thursday. Kissinger said it was the 303 [covert operations] briefing. Kissinger said Helms had reported that nothing had given his staff such a shot in the arm—first time a president took him seriously in eight years.

Richard Helms
February 15, 1969, 12:50 p.m.
Helms says the CIA has no control over coup plotters in Peru, where the military government had earlier seized the holdings of the International Petroleum Company.

---

* Quoted material in the chapter introductions in this book comes from the phone transcripts in the chapters or (in several cases) sources cited in the prefaces to the transcripts in the chapters; other material in the introductions is also either in the transcripts or sourced in the prefaces.

Kissinger said president has been reading about a possible coup in Peru, and do we have any control over this? Helms said none, none whatsoever; these are not people we've been in touch with, and they are elements of a community hard to control. Kissinger asked, "We can't accelerate it?" Helms said he didn't think so, but he would take another reading on this. . . .

David Packard
March 8, 1969, 9:30 a.m.
Deputy Defense Secretary Packard advocates going ahead with the secret Cambodia bombing.

Packard said that he would support it if Kissinger wanted to call the president. If we do nothing, it looks as if we are afraid of escalation. Packard said we ought to be quiet and then give them a little bang.

Kissinger said when you have a weak poker hand, you shouldn't be too cautious. We shouldn't be afraid that they will walk out in Paris. We shouldn't sit here and do nothing. . . .

Kissinger said he thought maybe some of our colleagues would start a vendetta. Packard wasn't worried about that. He thought the president should tell Rogers what he plans to do and that he had considered the alternatives. . . .

H. R. Haldeman
March 8, 1969, 10:10 a.m.
White House Chief of Staff Haldeman and Kissinger talk over the Cambodia bombing and sentiments on whether to go ahead. Kissinger stresses Packard's strong advocacy and says while he can understand Secretary of State William Rogers's opposition, he thinks it will hasten the end of the war.

Kissinger told Haldeman he canceled yesterday evening "that thing we discussed in Belgium" [the bombing], and that Packard went through the roof, calling again this morning saying he wanted to call the president, but Kissinger said no, that was his job, and that if the president wants to talk about it further to Packard he will do so. Packard feels very strongly that we are making Laird the fall guy; that we are looking terribly weak; that it is not such a big thing to do; that after the next attack on us it will be too little. He is very, very strong about it. . . .

> KISSINGER: He [Nixon] feels the way to handle the other end of town is to say this is the decision, and he expects full support. I don't think you negotiate with a cabinet officer after you have given him a chance to make his case.
> HALDEMAN: You still have that risk problem.
> KISSINGER: That risk problem will not be diminished. . . . As of now, it is canceled by my orders based on full discussion with the president. [Head U.S.

negotiator in Paris Henry Cabot] Lodge is meeting today with Hanoi—let's see what he gets out of that. In the meantime, why don't you tell the president what Packard thinks. Tell him I am not yet prepared to make a recommendation, but I will call you after I know what Paris reports, and I will then see whether he wants to talk to me. Just tell him Packard feels very strongly . . . and I didn't want him to be in a position where he had to overrule Packard.

HALDEMAN: Does the president know how the sides are drawn? In other words, the only opposition is Rogers—the rest of you are in agreement to go ahead?

KISSINGER: . . . I can see Rogers's argument, but my view is that what will determine the president's position in public opinion will be whether the war is wound up 15 months from now. If it isn't, having received a favorable editorial now will do him no good; if it is, having been clobbered by the *New York Times* this week won't harm him. My feeling is we ought to consider where we will be a year from now rather than next week. In terms of immediate reaction, there's no question but that Rogers is right. . . .

President Nixon
March 8, 1969, 10:45 a.m.
Nixon and Kissinger discuss the secret Cambodia bombing and enlisting Packard to persuade Rogers to support it. They also consider retaliation against North Vietnam for its offensive with the NLF in South Vietnam and revealing the Cambodia bombing if needed.

NIXON: I talked to Haldeman. My general feeling is, as you know, strongly along the lines of Packard's. The problem is not one of Rogers's veto, which has nothing to do with it. But you know the little State boys will start squealing, and then having Rogers not going along on a major decision. It occurred to me that it could be useful if you would get Rogers and Packard together. Packard is a strong man and I'd like to see Packard work Rogers over a little on this. I am glad that he is willing to step up to a tough one. I am certainly willing to do it—and in fact I'm leaning toward it—and we may have to tell them. . . .

KISSINGER: I am gradually coming to the point of view that our original idea . . . which was really to think of doing it as quite independent from . . . the offensive, it's really the right thing.

NIXON: Your whole point is you want to influence the Soviets—

KISSINGER: My feeling is we lean over backward not to hit the North. . . . After we have done this, I would keep taking things for a long time and then do something very drastic.

NIXON: If they continue to go along [with their offensive] we crack the North and crack it good. . . .

KISSINGER: My overall judgment is if the war is settled in a year, it doesn't make any difference if you get attacked now. So the really key question is how can one bring it to a conclusion more quickly?

NIXON: State, I guess, is traditionally opposed—they don't think it would have any effect to hit them.

KISSINGER: State believes it's a negotiation game. I think that may work but it's also a very time-consuming strategy and time is not on our side. . . .

NIXON: . . . Do you think, if Packard feels that strongly, that he will stand up to Bill? I was thinking if you and Packard and Bill could talk. . . . Basically, Rogers has to go along on this. I think Packard ought to work him over a little. . . .

KISSINGER: Packard and I both think that if we do it, and if silence about it doesn't help, we have to step up and say what we did.

NIXON: . . . We remain silent and let heat build up. . . . And then say, yes, I ordered the attack on the border for those reasons. . . . The attacks originated from that area; it was a thinly populated area; we had to hit them from both sides, so we did. I wouldn't fudge it at all.

KISSINGER: Packard agrees. Everyone agrees that the target is important.

NIXON: Helms says he is not so sure they are all there. . . . That doesn't bother me too much there. So we'll hit something. . . . Tell Packard to be strong and firm. . . . This is not the time to hit the North; I think we've got to threaten it by physically having a movement [of ships]. But if we hit the North we have to hit something worthwhile.

KISSINGER: Then as a seeming retaliation hit something way off in another direction. . . . But we can wait a few days [on the Cambodia bombing]; it can't be done over the weekend.

NIXON: Do you think we can wait? I understand Packard would like to do it Monday. I would like to do it tomorrow, for that matter. I think the pressure for hitting the North—this is the alternative. I don't want to hit the North, but I'm going to do something. . . .

KISSINGER: . . . For the first time we can start pounding away at the infrastructure. . . .

NIXON: . . . If we can bring Rogers along, it would be infinitely better. . . . The thing with Bill is that I really believe there must be a response because of the bargaining table situation, and on that score we can't give the impression that we're just sitting here. The main thing is Packard must hold up the specter of pressures for hitting the North. . . .

President Nixon

March 8, 1969, 6:25 p.m.

Nixon and Kissinger worry that they can't really bomb Cambodia after private peace talks begin in Paris. Nixon is also concerned about being "boxed in" against hitting the North, demands to see the instructions to U.S. negotiators in Paris, and threatens swift reprisal to enemy attacks.

> ... NIXON: Once we are in private talks, we are virtually dead as far as strong action is concerned. If done, it has to be before.
>
> KISSINGER: Hit them and then ask for private talks. . . . I think myself we have now wound up, in this first testing period, in a weak posture in a tough sequence of events. My concern is they will now feel free to press us along in these private talks.
>
> NIXON: We can't be boxed in where we are at the mercy of the fact that we can't hit the North. . . . We will have no bargaining position. . . .
>
> KISSINGER: I don't believe it will be easy for you to attack Cambodia while the private talks are going on and not much is being done in South Vietnam.
>
> NIXON: My point is if while the private talks are going on and they are kicking us, we are going to do something.
>
> KISSINGER: The Communist objective will be to push you to the left. They will be much less cautious when this is achieved.
>
> NIXON: Get [Paris negotiator Philip] Habib in and we will see what's going on. . . . I want to see those cables next time myself—any cables of instruction on these talks. I have strong feelings and I will personally dictate them on any instructions. . . . I have to see them! . . . There is not going to be any de-escalation. . . . We are just going to keep giving word to [Chairman of the Joint Chiefs of Staff Earle] Wheeler to knock the hell out of them. . . . We cannot stand back and not hit them. . . . If they hit us again, we will hit them with no warning. . . .

President Nixon

March 15, 1969, 3:35 p.m.

Nixon tells Kissinger he has ordered the secret bombing of Cambodia. The first strikes were code-named Breakfast.

President ordered immediate implementation of Breakfast plan. State is to be notified only after the point of no return. Lodge is to make no complaint. The order is not appealable. [U.S. Ambassador to South Vietnam Ellsworth] Bunker is to be told there is to be no complaint, but only after the operation is beyond recall.

President Nixon

March 15, 1969, 3:44 p.m.

Nixon orders that no comments be made on enemy rocket attacks on Saigon that day, which spurred his order to begin Operation Breakfast.[1]

President said what he wants is an order to go out to the State Department. He wants one to go to Lodge, to Bunker in Vietnam, and one to Defense. All officials of this government for 72 hours are not to comment on this attack without express direction from the president. No comment, no warnings, no complaints, no protests.

President said to put that out as an order from him and not from Kissinger.... President said, "I mean it, not one thing to be said to anyone publicly or privately, on or off the record, about this new attack on Saigon for 72 hours." President then changed 72 hours to "without my prior approval."

President Nixon

March 15, 1969, 3:45 p.m.

President said everything that will fly is to get over to North Vietnam. President said there is to be no appeal from that either. He will let them know who is boss around here.

Melvin Laird

March 15, 1969, 5:40 p.m.

Kissinger informs Secretary of Defense Laird that Nixon has ordered the secret Cambodia bombing and stresses the importance of Laird's support.

Kissinger said he just talked to president and he would like to order this thing. Laird said fine. Kissinger said we are assuming that you are also in favor of it, and Laird said yes. . . . Kissinger said the president may want to have a meeting between Laird, Kissinger, and Bill [Rogers] tomorrow afternoon, and president is counting on Laird to be firm at that meeting. Laird said he does not have to worry about that, he will be firm. . . . Kissinger said not to change anything—should follow normal activities. Kissinger said there is to be no public comment at all from anyone at any level either complaining or threatening. . . .

President Nixon

March 17, 1969, 1:20 p.m.

Kissinger tells Nixon that the bombing of Cambodia, which he was quite excited about,[2] will start shortly and that North Vietnam agreed to private peace talks.

President asked whether that thing was about done now. Kissinger said another hour it will start. . . . Kissinger said it is all in order—he checked it all through again this morning. President said what pleases him is that he is glad the fellow agreed to private talks right away. President thinks the two are closely related. Kissinger agreed. President said this was a token of our intent and they think we really mean business. Otherwise, they were about to conclude that we were being pressured and starting again on same cycle that we had gone through before. . . .

Earle Wheeler
March 18, 1969, 8:00 p.m.
General Wheeler, the chairman of the Joint Chiefs of Staff, reports to Kissinger on the start of Operation Breakfast and they discuss targeting. "Psychologically, the impact must have been something," Kissinger, who had been "beaming" about a report on it earlier, surmises. A week later, a Cambodian radio news broadcast reported many civilian casualties from the bombing.[3]

Wheeler said he thought things worked out well. Kissinger wanted to know about the military point of view. Wheeler said he didn't know if we really hit prime areas, but they were highly important because of the secondary [explosion] factor. He mentioned that since the secondaries were four to seven times the normal bomb burst, this was significant. He explained that the secondary is measured over and above the initial bomb blast and isn't just the second plane seeing what the first plane hit. . . .

Kissinger said they should put in two or three more hits along the whole area, if we can get the right intelligence. There was one target he had grave reservations about because of the civilian reports, but he was checking that out for truth. He is also looking into the other area that was mentioned.

Kissinger said if they [the North Vietnamese] retaliate without any diplomatic screaming, we are in the driver's seat. Psychologically, the impact must have been something. Wheeler said they probably already had their speech written for Paris. He added that they have recalled their MiGs from North Vietnam to go to China. They are in a high state of alarm. Kissinger said now they have to go back to the drawing board since the expected didn't happen.

Wheeler said all would go well as long as something doesn't leak. Kissinger said our friend [probably referring to Melvin Laird] is probably so scared of the whole thing he wouldn't say a word to anyone. Kissinger said the president felt strongly and felt that Wheeler did a fine job.

Wheeler said this was mostly Abe's [General Creighton Abrams's] idea. Kissinger said it was great whoever figured it out.

2

North Korea's Shootdown of a U.S. Spy Plane, Leaks, and Vietnam Withdrawals

April–June 1969

In April 1969, a North Korean jet fighter shot down a U.S. spy plane off the coast of North Korea in international waters, killing all 31 men aboard. It was the administration's first big crisis, and Kissinger advocated a tough response, even raising the possibility of using tactical nuclear weapons if it escalated. "All hell will break loose for two months, but at end of road there will be peace in Asia," he told Nixon. He thought there would be enormous benefit in "taking on toughest character in Communist camp and facing him down." Though Nixon and Kissinger both believed that the North Koreans were "testing" them and Nixon's first reaction was to retaliate (if only by seizing a North Korean ship or blockading a port), Nixon ultimately decided against it. Meanwhile, a series of leaks roiled the administration.

Mary McGrory
April 4, 1969, 4:15 p.m.
Kissinger tells the Washington Evening Star *columnist that he never leaks.*

McGrory said she had read [James] Reston's column and wondered if Kissinger would comment on it. Kissinger said no, he does not comment on troop withdrawals in any sense. McGrory said she assumes Kissinger is not the source of the story. Kissinger said he was not—he does not leak anything. . . .

President Nixon
April 15, 1969, 5:40 p.m.
The North Korean shootdown had taken place the night before, and Kissinger confers with Nixon on how to respond. Nixon was disposed to retaliate with an air strike, as was Kissinger, who wanted to bomb the North Korean airfield where the jet that shot down the U.S. spy plane took off.[1]

NIXON: Anything further on the plane?

KISSINGER: Nothing further yet, no.

NIXON: It should be daylight there pretty soon.

KISSINGER: We should be getting word within two hours. . . . Strong probability no survivors. We are getting reports on North Korean assets abroad
and they're very discouraging. One Korean ship which is sailing with
Dutch registry and Dutch crew and flag—so it's almost impossible to seize
that.

NIXON: Check with the Dutch; they ought to want to help us. It's a question
of doing that or something else. Why not pick up a half dozen fishing boats?

KISSINGER: They don't come out in the open seas.

NIXON: No North Korean ships on the high seas at all?

KISSINGER: The largest ship is the [USS] *Pueblo* and of course they're keeping
that in the port. It hasn't been out at all since they captured it [in January
1968].[2]

NIXON: Well, the more I think about it—there has to be some reaction here.
I have a feeling they're testing us.

KISSINGER: That's clearly true. . . . Domestically, there will be among the intellectuals considerable heat if we do the other thing [referring to some form
of military retaliation]. Curiously enough, some of the members of my staff
feel we ought to do what you and I were talking about earlier. They feel
to let this one go again will be taken very seriously. There was an intelligence report of [Egypt President Gamal Abdel] Nasser's conversation with
[Jordan's King] Hussein to the effect, "After all, it isn't so risky to defy the
United States—look at North Korea and the *Pueblo*."

NIXON: . . . No, I think that's right. Okay, I certainly lean in that direction. . . .

President Nixon
April 15, 1969, 6:30 p.m.
*Nixon advises violating international law to seize a North Korean ship with a Dutch
crew and raises the possibility of doing a second round of the secret Cambodia bombing
and "getting caught." (They thought it would be seen as a response to the shootdown.)
Kissinger says the North Koreans deliberately shot down the plane, though it may have
been an error by a single North Korean plane.[3]*

The president wanted to know what the situation on the Dutch ship and crew
was. Kissinger said they still haven't located it yet. It has been reported to be on
the high seas. . . . The president said his view would be to pick up the ship. . . .
The president said it was impossible to pick up the *Pueblo* too but they did. We
should pick up the crew and take them back to Holland. When they give us the
Pueblo, we'll give them their ship. . . . He said he would be willing to take heavy
criticism for this.

Kissinger said he had already put this on a high-priority basis. The president said to find a way that international law can be breached. The U.S. became a great nation by breaking international law. The president said we certainly have concluded that we won't just sit here and do nothing. Kissinger agreed. The president said even if the peaceniks on Kissinger's staff didn't agree. Kissinger said he didn't have any peaceniks on his staff. The president said he was just kidding. . . . The president said the price is too high to pay not to do anything. . . . If we don't face up to the Dutch, we have to face the navy action. . . .

The president said someone is trying to pursue the line that recon planes are fair game. This was not a regular recon plane, was it? Kissinger said it definitely was not. This plane has been doing the same thing for 15 years without protest. It had been a deliberate plan to get it. . . .

The president said that ship must not get to North Korea. . . . He has determined in his own mind that we are going to do something "even if I have to overrule everybody in the State Department."

Kissinger said when we move the carrier to another position, we should make it public. . . . We should look dangerous. The president said how about doing the Lunch plan [the next phase of the secret Cambodia bombing following Operation Breakfast] and getting caught? They took the ship, so we get Cambodia. . . .

President Nixon
April 15, 1969, 10:00 p.m.
Nixon suggests a naval blockade and possibly bombing North Korean airfields not too close to the Soviet border.

President said another option had occurred to him with greater symbolic meaning—a navy blockade of the one port of significance. Kissinger said he was sure it could be done. President referred to Cuban blockade and said question is how long can it be maintained. Kissinger said that is the problem. President said he was thinking of the impact. President said people say it does not mean anything, but it means a lot to a lot of people. . . . President said it would not take a lot to blockade that place. Kissinger said on the other hand there is not much going in or out either, so it may be an empty gesture. President said they have to live, so there is something going in and out. President referred to three Polish ships which have to come in—they could be kept out. Kissinger said they could unload elsewhere and ship down by train. . . .

President said he wants to get something that has symbolism—that is what we are talking about. President said it could be a signal of what we are going to do down below [in Vietnam]. President said we could keep it for a few months and then lift it but not say anything. Kissinger said if they wanted to play it nastily, we could get hit with it every day—harassing us, etc. . . .

Kissinger said we have assigned State to come up with a legal opinion supporting president if he decides to seize ship. President said throw the blockade one at them too. . . . Kissinger said the Cuban blockade worked because they thought we were heading for an invasion. . . .

President said he was just looking over military plans. They want to hit two other airfields because they are not so close to the Soviet border. President said there is something to be said about fields not so close to Soviet border. . . .

President Nixon
April 17, 1969, 8:00 p.m.
In response to the shootdown, Nixon had decided to resume reconnaissance flights—which had been suspended by the Defense Department without informing the White House (Defense Secretary Laird, who concluded from intelligence that the shootdown was probably a mistake by a nervous pilot, "didn't think it necessary")—with armed escorts. He also ordered two aircraft carriers into the area for possible retaliatory attacks. Kissinger raises the possible use of tactical nuclear weapons if a ground war resulted. (John Ehrlichman recalled Kissinger saying, "It could go nuclear.")[4] Nixon had not foreclosed military retaliation either.

. . . President said he is still affirmative [on a military response]. He has to be sure we are leading the charge, with other people coming along a bit. Kissinger said it is about the boldest course president can take. In long run it may turn out not to be so risky. President said when you come right down to it here's the Soviet Union finally flushing Czech revolution down the drain and no one gives a damn; here we are on isolated basis and we do not do a thing with 31 lives missing. . . .

Kissinger said if we do this, we have to be ready to go very, very far in case it leads to ground action. . . . That is a very tough one to bite early in administration and I owe it to you to say that. Kissinger said his judgment is that it will not come to that.

President said he trusts Mel is not backing off. Kissinger said he is uneasy about it. Kissinger said if president says he wants to do it, Mel would agree to do it and take public responsibility for it. President said Rogers would not. Kissinger said he believes to do this will make or break president's administration—they owe it to president and must stand behind him.

President said take the people on the other side—take [Senator Edward] Kennedy. Country will be strongly against him. Kissinger said they will say president risked another ground war in Asia. Kissinger said president will have to say we will not tolerate another ground war in Asia—to Dobrynin we will have to say more. When it happens, we might have to go to tactical nuclears and clean it up. All hell will break loose for two months, but at end of road there will be peace in Asia. Kissinger said that is something that is easy for him to say.

. . . Kissinger said this is low-risk course [resuming reconnaissance flights with armed escorts] and he would favor it if there were no Vietnam war going on and if we had not slipped back so much in last 10 years. Because there is Vietnam and because there is general erosion of moral fiber of country, president said a bold move is indicated. Kissinger said in his view we may be forced into an even bolder move a year from now if we do not do this one. . . .

President said if question comes up tomorrow, should he indicate that we are going to continue reconnaissance? Kissinger said absolutely. President said he thought he should say too that we can't expect Americans to take these activities when they are in open sea and open air unless government backs them up. . . . President said with option one [military retaliation] the gains are great and risks very great. President said with option two [resuming the reconnaissance flights] there are no gains and no risk except perhaps down the road. Kissinger said the risk in option two over a period of time, which will be cumulative, will be greater than risk in option one, which will be enormous in brief period. President agreed. President said every time U.S. fails to react, it encourages some pipsqueak to do something.

President said not to let Laird move off now—when they meet Saturday morning he does not want him wobbling around. . . . President speculated about effect this action would have on averting another Korean confrontation—can't brush off fact that they say they will take us on. Kissinger agreed they might do it. Kissinger talked of gain of taking on toughest character in Communist camp and facing him down—this would be enormous. . . .

President Nixon
May 13, 1969, 7:45 p.m.
Nixon instructs Kissinger to tell dovish senators he will end the Vietnam war "one way or the other."

President said the point he thought was very important to have in mind when Kissinger meets with dovish senators is to not play it too dovish—go overboard in terms of saying we have done everything. . . . President said tell them this president will end the war one way or the other. President said this will frighten some and shake up others. President said the ones that will be frightened and go fluttering off we would not get anyway. President said Kissinger should say they have known this president, have seen him, and one way or the other he will end the war. President said they will ask how, but Kissinger should not talk about that. President said they are a bunch of peaceniks. President said Kissinger should do this with the press too.

Melvin Laird
June 3, 1969, 11:10 a.m.

The New York Times *had run a front-page story by Hedrick Smith that morning that Nixon had decided to remove U.S. nuclear weapons from Okinawa as part of negotiations with Japan over the reversion of Okinawa to Japanese rule, undermining the U.S. bargaining position. (Kissinger told Nixon he set up a plan for wiretapping suspected leakers on his NSC staff.)*[5]

Laird said president had given him a note about his concern over the story today in the *New York Times*. Kissinger said "concern" is no expression—he is climbing walls. Laird said he is sure it [the leak] is not out of his shop. Kissinger said Laird will get an official request by president to conduct an investigation. Kissinger said we have a pretty good idea where it came from, but in order to be fair we are going to ask every senior official to make an investigation. Laird said it was the worst thing that could have happened over there. . . . Kissinger said it was disastrous.

Melvin Laird
June 4, 1969, 9:00 a.m.
Kissinger and Laird complain about another story by Smith in that morning's New York Times, *one in the* Evening Star, *and another by* Los Angeles Times *reporter Robert Donovan that Nixon and South Vietnamese President Nguyen Van Thieu would announce the first U.S. troop withdrawals from Vietnam at their upcoming conference on Midway Island. (That morning, Kissinger had the FBI begin wiretapping Smith's phone.)*[6]

Laird was very upset about the *Times* story by Rick Smith this morning, as was Kissinger. Laird thought they were speculative and didn't understand how it happened. Kissinger pointed out the *Star* story of yesterday which pointed to a State Department source saying there would be an announcement after Midway.

The Donovan and Smith stories are directly attributable to State since both these men write from there. . . . Kissinger said the president's reaction is to say that we won't announce anything now at Midway. . . . Kissinger wanted to know Laird's view on how this got out. Laird thought someone was handed a paper but he didn't know where. . . . Maybe State was disappointed that Laird cut the reductions to 50,000 instead of 82,000. . . .

H. R. Haldeman
June 4, 1969, 5:40 p.m.
Nixon was "convinced of treason" by the latest leak and Kissinger says he will try to ferret out the culprit.

Haldeman said the president now has the answer to the leak on Midway—someone gave a deliberate backgrounder. It has now appeared in the *Star*, the *New York Times*, and there is a definitive piece in the *Los Angeles Times* by Bob Donovan. These people all obviously had the same source or they could not have come up with the same piece. Haldeman said the president is convinced of treason, and asked Haldeman to get in touch with Kissinger right away and have him call State and make the point to Rogers that it is clear to the president someone put this story out. We have to find out who did it.

Kissinger said considering how beautifully the secret was held, this is unforgiveable. He thought it might die after the *Star* article on Tuesday, but it is now the headline in every paper he sees—even the *Boston Globe.* Kissinger told Haldeman to tell the president he would ask each department to give him a list of backgrounders given this week and by whom. . . .

H. R. Haldeman
June 4, 1969, 5:50 p.m.
Haldeman tells Kissinger that Nixon was "building up a head of steam at a rapid rate" on the leaks, but Kissinger cautions against overreacting.

Kissinger said he thought it would be best if Haldeman called [Rogers] but not to make accusation. Kissinger said just to say president has requested list of backgrounders, who gave them and who attended—Kissinger said he would not say we know it [the Midway leak] was done at a backgrounder; let them fret, they will get the point. Kissinger said he would call both State and Defense and tell both he is asking the other department for the same thing.

Haldeman said president is building up a head of steam at a rapid rate. Because of leak [on SALT], there will be no NSC meeting at any time on SALT, and there will be no NSC meetings at all until further notice from president. Haldeman said president will decide on basis of discussion with Kissinger. Kissinger said he better have a talk with the president. Haldeman said this is not the time to do it. President had said he wanted it understood there is no appeal on this. Kissinger said he just cannot do this—he will be cut to ribbons if there is no NSC on SALT; they will say he is delaying deliberately. Haldeman said this was not the time to argue with him and if the president calls him again, he will tell him Kissinger has been given the message.

Haldeman said president has asked him what he was doing on other matter and Haldeman told president that Kissinger felt it would be better for Haldeman to make contact with departments and not say we know backgrounder was source—just to get list of backgrounders, etc. He said he agreed and then told Haldeman to write down the following: "You are to call [Undersecretary of State Elliot] Richardson and tell him we have learned from one of reporters present at backgrounder this week that there was a discussion of this whole thing at backgrounder. We know this now and therefore the president wants in two hours a report back on this." . . . Kissinger said he really would not do it. . . . If he makes a flat charge which does not stick for some reason, this would be bad. . . .

President Nixon

June 13, 1969, 7:55 p.m.

Nixon wants to recognize a so-called provisional government of Cuba that had earlier been instigated by the CIA.[7]

The president said he wanted Kissinger to get State on the telephone right away and tell them that the president is going to recognize the provisional government for Cuba. President said he saw the picture in the newspaper of [Soviet Premier Alexei] Kosygin receiving the others [the Provisional Revolutionary Government of South Vietnam]. President said get State on the telephone tonight and say we are going to recognize the provisional government for Cuba and the president wants a recommendation on his desk by 8:00 o'clock Monday morning. President said this is very important. President said we can't allow the Russians to recognize a provisional government—if they do, we are going to also. Kissinger said it is going to be a little harder for us to make it stick. President said he wanted to worry the hell out of State and CIA and he said Kissinger knew what he meant. . . . President said for Kissinger to follow up on this very hard.

Elliot Richardson

June 13, 1969, 8:25 p.m.

Kissinger tells Undersecretary of State Richardson he doesn't want Nixon's order on Cuba to get out.

Kissinger said he has problem which requires delicate handling. President has felt generally aggrieved today about a variety of things and then read in evening papers that Russia has recognized provisional government in Vietnam. Kissinger said president wants to now recognize provisional government in Cuba. Kissinger said we have to have a plan ready by Monday but we must not have any leak on this. . . . Kissinger said he knows the objections Richardson will raise and Kissinger considers it his duty to bring them to president's attention. Nothing will be done until they look at it, but Kissinger has been ordered to get started on this. Kissinger said for everyone's sake it should be done in smallest channel possible. . . .

John Mitchell

June 18, 1969, 3:35 p.m.

A New York Times *article that morning had revealed a report of the U.S. Intelligence Board that the Soviets neither had nor were pursuing a first-strike nuclear capability, undermining the U.S. position on antiballistic missiles in the upcoming SALT talks and obtaining congressional support for them.*

Mitchell forgot to mention to Kissinger that the president discussed with him the *New York Times* front-page story. Mitchell has dissuaded the president from using the FBI to find out how the story leaked; however, he is to contact Helms,

Laird, and Rogers (and it might be better to do this by memo for record purposes) and tell them the president asked him to investigate this and to obtain the names of the people in the three establishments who had access to the information. Kissinger thought this was good because it will scare them. Mitchell agreed—with the FBI in his department, they won't know if that is the next step. Mitchell asked Kissinger what his thought was on where the leak occurred. Kissinger said it had to be either CIA or State and nowhere else. It was against the interests of Defense. . . .

Kissinger said [reporter Peter] Grose probably was not the recipient of the information; it was probably given to someone else on the *Times* who relayed it. He suggested that Mitchell ask the three agencies for a list of all *New York Times* contacts with their people.

Mitchell asked if Kissinger could recommend any other action besides the polygraph. Kissinger said that had been discussed, too, but that action is too humiliating. . . .

3

Secret Vietnam Peace Talks, the Green Beret Murder Scandal, a B-52 Stand-Down, and Golda Meir's First Visit

July–September 1969

In August 1969, Kissinger had his first secret meeting with the North Vietnamese in Paris. The same month, the administration faced a scandal in Vietnam: Green Berets had executed, on the advice of the CIA, they said, their Vietnamese interpreter who they'd concluded was a double agent. In September, Kissinger temporarily suspended B-52 strikes over South Vietnam during an enemy-declared cease-fire without telling either Secretary of Defense Melvin Laird or the State Department. Later that month, Golda Meir made her first visit to Washington as Israel's prime minister, where she expressed consternation over news reports that Nixon was pressuring her to be more flexible in Middle East peace negotiations in return for weapons.

President Nixon
August 5, 1969, 6:50 p.m.
Kissinger tells Nixon about his secret meeting in Paris with North Vietnamese negotiator Xuan Thuy, which accomplished little. The "deadline" he mentions refers to a threat he made that if no progress was made by November 1, they would have to consider "steps of grave consequence," meaning execute a plan for major escalation of the war code-named Duck Hook.[1]

. . . Kissinger said he wanted to give president brief rundown on his talk—spent three and a half hours with their chief negotiator. . . . Kissinger said he laid down deadline on them very hard. Kissinger said they asked eight clarifying questions and then launched into usual line. Kissinger said he told them if they had nothing new to say, they were speaking in wrong forum and he would leave. Kissinger said in every case when he got tough, he moved back. . . .

Kissinger said one of his assistants who was present feels this was the most conciliatory they have ever been. Kissinger said while none of this proves anything, before he would have said the chances were one in ten, and now he thinks they are one in four or three that this thing will work. . . . Kissinger said they had a number of modifications in their negotiating position, but it is not enough for us yet. President said this movement has not been made to [lead U.S. negotiator in Paris Henry Cabot] Lodge? . . . President said not to tell them a thing about it. . . .

President said it looks to him as though they will try to diddle us along, but this also proves that Lodge has not been tough enough. Kissinger said he told them president will not withdraw troops unilaterally and will not replace [South Vietnamese President] Thieu. . . . Kissinger said he suggested that they do normal negotiation in Paris and if they reach point where they want to tell us something quite new, they get in touch with Kissinger. Kissinger said he told them he did not want to come over there to hear the same old thing. President said he agreed completely with this. Kissinger said if they get in touch and ask to see him it would be the first time in 18 months that they have asked to see us—the other meetings have been at our request. President said he wants Lodge instructed to that effect and to stop begging. . . .

Melvin Laird
August 15, 1969, 1:40 p.m.
Two of the Green Berets who had executed their Vietnamese translator said they had acted on the advice of the CIA,[2] but the U.S. Army charged their commander, Colonel Robert Rheault, and six others with murder and conspiracy.

. . . Laird said the colonel has admitted the whole thing in letters. He should not have written letters. My problem is I don't think it is in our interest to have a court-martial. [General Creighton] Abrams called the colonel in and the colonel lied to Abrams and said he did not do it. . . . This is the thing Abrams did not like—the fact that he was lied to. This is a problem. The colonel could have gotten this guy disposed of by the South Vietnamese. CIA advised him to do it that way. If that all comes out, the fact that they were told to not do it this way—it will be bad. Kissinger said what we would like to do is avoid a court-martial. Laird said here is my problem. Before they make a decision on the court-martial, they will be in touch with me. If they can make a charge that higher authority is intervening, this will not be good. . . . Laird said I am getting those boys out of jail—they can stay in their house under house arrest. . . .

Laird said Congressman [Peter] Rodino has the letter that the man sent his wife in which he admits doing it. He should never have written the letter and his wife should not have sent it to the congressman. . . .

Earle Wheeler

September 10, 1969, 9:11 p.m.

JCS Chairman Wheeler and Kissinger discuss standing down a military action in Vietnam during an enemy-declared 72-hour cease-fire to mark the death of North Vietnamese President Ho Chi Minh, probably to appease the public and so that the resumption of full-scale fighting afterward could be blamed on North Vietnam. They decide to suspend B-52 strikes over South Vietnam. Kissinger doesn't want the State Department told until it was done.[3]

Kissinger said he just spoke to the president and the president said after the end of cease-fire, in his judgment, they are going to start clobbering us again. Wheeler said that's right. Kissinger said the president would like to be in a position that he has done something. He would like to know what we could stand down for 24 hours. Wheeler said the only thing he could stand down is the B-52 strikes. Wheeler said with regard to any other operation he doesn't know what is going on or the details. He said it would be difficult to get instructions out like that. . . .

Kissinger said he wouldn't want to tell State until it is done—we could tell Secretary Laird, Laird can be informed—but we don't want to tell State until it is done.

Kissinger said he knows this makes Wheeler climb walls. Wheeler said you're right. . . . Wheeler said do it on the B-52 basis because I know I can do that, but I am not sure I can do anything else. Wheeler said he was trying to think how he could formulate an order to the commander in the field that would not be construed as telling him to go on the defensive. . . . That's my problem. . . .

Earle Wheeler

September 10, 1969, 9:22 p.m.

. . . Kissinger asked if we could do this without State knowing. Wheeler said yes, we can. Kissinger said he would tell Mel Laird tomorrow. . . . Kissinger said he would tell Mel that we did this when he was out of town. . . .

Melvin Laird

September 11, 1969, 9:30 a.m.

Laird is angry about not being told about the suspension of the B-52 bombing.

. . . In answer to query from Laird, Kissinger said the president called last night about 9:30 and said to get a job done. Kissinger told him Laird was away, and the president told Kissinger to get with Wheeler. (They didn't want Packard in on it, and they didn't want State to know.) Laird was upset because the first he knew of it was by an inquiry from the chief of staff of the air force. He said this is why the Johnson administration got screwed up—they didn't keep to the lines of communication. . . .

Kissinger reiterated that he was under the misapprehension that Laird was out of town; Kissinger had planned to talk with Laird upon his return. . . . Kissinger said it was a complete goof-up which was his fault. . . .

President Nixon

September 18, 1969, 11:30 p.m.

The U.S. Army had announced that it would try six of the Green Berets accused of killing the Vietnamese double agent. The White House had opposed court-martials. Kissinger and Nixon disparage Secretary of the Army Stanley Resor, who supported court-martials. Resor said he'd been pressured to dismiss the charges (which he later did when the CIA refused to testify).[4]

The president asked what the score was on the Green Beret thing. Kissinger said that is one hot potato that Laird pushed into our lap in a way that we could not refuse to handle. . . . Kissinger said the problem was . . . the trial would be disastrous. On the other hand, Resor . . . because Laird had washed his hands of it, had come full speed ahead recommending a trial and wrote a memo saying he would fight anyone that tried to stop it. Since they already have the confessions, since they were going to leak the confessions, and [Nixon aide Bryce] Harlow said there will be a congressional investigation—president asked what about Resor, what is going to be done about him? President said I don't like that fellow. President said just tell Laird that I don't want him around. I don't have confidence in him. President said I am going to ask him for his resignation. Kissinger said Resor acted very poorly—everyone was saving his own hide. . . .

President Nixon

September 24, 1969, 7:05 p.m.

They take up a prospective Time *magazine article saying that they want to overthrow South Vietnamese President Nguyen Van Thieu and how to kill the article.*

. . . Hugh Sidey was in—said *Time* wanted to do an article next week about wanting to overthrow Thieu. Kissinger gave him hell. President asked Kissinger to call [*Time* President James] Shepley. He could ask Shepley to come down; Kissinger could see him and then president would see him and tell him he would personally attack *Time* if they printed such an article. President said this would admit defeat! . . . President said if they did such a thing he would blast them like they have never been blasted. He said don't worry—people would be on our side. *Time* would get 100,000 cancellations.

Kissinger said if Hanoi is considering which way to go, as we now have some reason to believe, this would certainly be most unhelpful. President said we haven't agreed to throw Thieu aside. He recalled that people from *Time* had come in for a session in the fairly recent past. He told Kissinger to tell Shepley that he had had *Time*'s meeting with us recorded and he will not hesitate to print it all.

President said he is going to play a very rough game with them. . . . President said for Kissinger to tell Shepley he was "calling for the president. The president couldn't reach him, but he was shocked." President said they can't do this when these delicate things are in process. . . .

James Shepley
September 25, 1969, 10:15 a.m.
Kissinger protests the prospective Time *article to a receptive* Time *President Shepley.*
. . . Shepley should assume that Kissinger is speaking for the president. Hugh Sidey was in yesterday and said that *Time* was taking the editorial position that we should disassociate ourselves from Thieu and move further in making peace overtures. . . . Shepley said that disturbed him very much. . . . Kissinger asked if he could speak very frankly. . . . We are way beyond the point that we are trying to impose our terms. There has been an unbelievable amount of concessions and there hasn't been the slightest response from the other side. To say there has been a lack of imagination is preposterous. It shows a collapse of the leadership group that is appalling. . . . It is totally against the national interest now to give them additional ammunition against settling. There are reasons to believe that this would be an inopportune time for them to see a publication which used to be hard line—that even they are turning on the president. . . . Shepley again said he was on Kissinger's side and would do all he could to see what could be done. . . .

President Nixon
September 27, 1969, 4:40 p.m.
Kissinger recounts for Nixon his conversation with Soviet Ambassador Anatoly Dobrynin about, among other topics, Vietnam and Soviet Foreign Minister Andrei Gromyko's desire for a meeting with Nixon. They also contemplate a "tough move" in Vietnam, that is, Operation Duck Hook, the plan for a massive attack on the North, which Nixon would prefer to make before a big Vietnam Moratorium antiwar protest on October 15th. But Kissinger is concerned that it might preempt an overture from Hanoi.
. . . Kissinger told Dobrynin his call was providential—as far as the White House is concerned, we have no great incentives. . . . The train has left the station. The Soviets have a choice of believing the president or the *New York Times,* and Kissinger, if he could advise him, would recommend that they believe the president. . . . Dobrynin had said we may not believe it, but the Soviets have a real interest in ending this war, but for different reasons than ours. Kissinger told him we have no evidence of this. . . . Kissinger gave no encouragement here and wasn't really very pleasant. . . .

Kissinger said he thinks Dobrynin came to see him to let him know they knew about Kissinger's Paris meeting and to fix an invitation for Gromyko to see the president. Dobrynin had said in all previous administrations Gromyko had been received by the president. Kissinger told Dobrynin that Gromyko hadn't asked for a meeting. Kissinger told the president if Gromyko asks for a meeting formally, the president will have to see him, but if he doesn't Kissinger doesn't think we should invite him. . . .

He thinks events of the last two or three weeks show the long route [in Vietnam] cannot possibly work. The president agreed, especially with our 60,000-man withdrawal, reduction of the draft by 50,000, and Ho Chi Minh's death. The doves and the public are making it impossible to happen. He asked Kissinger if in his planning he could pick this up so that we make the tough move before the 15th of October. Kissinger said yes. President said he . . . doesn't want to appear to be making the tough move after the 15th just because of the rioting at home. Kissinger said there is a problem, however. . . . If we want them to make the move, we should give them time—two weeks. His only worry is that if we went ahead with the tough move before the 15th—and there is a 10 percent chance Hanoi might want to move—if we hit them before they have a chance to make the move, it will look as if we tricked them. . . . President would like to nip it before the first demonstration, because there will be another one on November 15. . . .

Golda Meir
September 27, 1969, 5:20 p.m.
Israeli Prime Minister Meir, who was in Washington, complains about a leak in the Washington Evening Star, *one that Kissinger attributed to the State Department, on Nixon's proposal to trade "hardware for software"—be responsive to Israel's requests for weapons from the United States if Israel was more flexible in peace negotiations. Meir sought continued delivery of Phantom jet fighters.*[5]

. . . Meir said she was much disturbed and wanted to speak with Kissinger about it. She referred to the *Star* article of September 26 and said her Israeli newspaper people tell her that there is news and rumors that actually there was pressure on her to change her attitude and that of the Israeli government to the discussion of the "two and four" [the two superpowers, the United States and the Soviet Union, and the so-called Big Four in the UN Security Council that also included the British and the French]. Kissinger said he could assure her that nothing like this came from the White House. Meir said she was assured that it had not come from our president or Kissinger, that Kissinger did not have to assure her of this. She said the newspaper people say their source is "high officials"; some say State; some say the White House. She would be most grateful to Kissinger if he would do something about it. . . . The Israeli newspaperman tried to press her on whether there had been pressure applied on her. She had denied any pressure. But she said what worried her was this formula—hardware—which was mentioned by the newspaperman. Kissinger said he now had an idea where it came from, and asked her if she were sure this precise phrase had been used. Meir said exactly. Kissinger said he thought this was an outrage. It is true the formula was used, but in the strictest confidence—only two people knew about it. Meir said she wouldn't accept this formula if it meant a deal whereby they get arms if they give up their stance on the two and four. She said she hadn't been so disturbed in a long, long time—she doesn't know what she is going home with.

Kissinger said we would never do anything like this—the president or he. We told her our view and she told us hers. There was no intention of embarrassing her or putting her into a difficult position by using cheap newspaper stories to pressure her. He said if the formula was used, it helps identify where it must have come from, and he regrets it very much.

Meir asked if she were right in saying there has been no condition put on the question of the president's consideration of their request for planes. Kissinger said there has been no condition put on it. . . . Meir said there is no hope of their getting out [of the occupied territories]. She said yesterday she said to the president, "What shall I tell my government?" He told her the first shipment of Phantoms will go on. As to the other request, the president is considering it and he has an understanding for it. She asked Kissinger if this were not right. Kissinger said it was absolutely correct. Meir said the president didn't ask her to give up their stance in order to get arms. She said she is glad there is no difference between her and Kissinger on what happened. . . .

President Nixon
September 27, 1969, 5:45 p.m.
Kissinger reports to Nixon on his conversation with Meir and the leak he ascribed to State.

Kissinger said he was sorry to disturb the president, but just in case Rogers calls him on the Middle East, Golda Meir had just called Kissinger concerning the story in Friday's *Star* that we were squeezing her about withdrawal. President said she knows that is not true. Kissinger said he mentioned to [Assistant Secretary of State] Joe Sisco the president's conversation, using the president's hardware and software formula. That has been leaked to a newspaperman. President said who in god's name would do that!? Kissinger said there had been only three people who knew this. President said that is terrible. He told them not to put this on the diplomatic wire, so they tell some newspaperman! Kissinger said . . . they couldn't have picked it up anywhere else. He told the president an Israeli newspaperman knows it now. Kissinger said he had told Mrs. Meir the president would look at her request sympathetically, and he wanted her to look at his. President said he had said, in order to do better on hardware, they must do better on software.

Kissinger told president Mrs. Meir had said she knew it didn't come from him or Kissinger. But she was very upset. Kissinger said he had apologized to her on behalf of the president for any embarrassment such a leak might have caused her. President said he is convinced these State people are always around for this purpose. He said he didn't think we would tell them anymore. They have talked themselves out of the ballgame. They can't wait until they rush to a newsman. Kissinger agreed. Kissinger said his feeling now is the new Sisco formula isn't so bad, except that to spring it within 48 hours of the president's seeing her, and while she is still in the country, is not the time to do it. President asked Kissinger if there were any way he could tell Sisco all hell is breaking loose because they leaked it. Kissinger should tell him it is not a bad formula but not to do it while she is in the country—wait until she leaves. . . .

$$4$$

The Moratorium and Mobilization Protests, Nixon's November 1 Ultimatum to Hanoi, the My Lai Massacre, and Warsaw Talks with China

October–December 1969

In October and November 1969, huge Moratorium and Mobilization protests against the Vietnam War were held in Washington and other cities around the country. Nixon had earlier warned Hanoi that unless a significant breakthrough was made in the Paris peace talks by November 1, he would take steps of great consequence in the war, meaning massive escalation (the same threat Kissinger had made to Xuan Thuy in August); Kissinger told Nixon in October that if U.S. casualties increased significantly "we have an excuse for what we are planning to do." Nixon directed Kissinger to warn Soviet Ambassador Anatoly Dobrynin that he was "out of control" on Vietnam. In mid-November, the story of the horrendous 1968 My Lai massacre in Vietnam, when U.S. Army soldiers murdered over 350 South Vietnamese civilians, broke. Although it had taken place during the Johnson administration, it was a damaging revelation for the Nixon administration as it tried to maintain public support on Vietnam. Secretary of Defense Melvin Laird told Kissinger, who knew My Lai would be "a terrible mess," that he would "like to sweep the whole thing under the rug," but they knew that wasn't possible. In December, the Nixon administration's door to China opened a crack: at China's invitation, the U.S. ambassador to Poland met secretly at the Chinese embassy in Warsaw with the Chinese chargé d'affaires to discuss the resumption of ambassadorial meetings. It was the first time China had invited such a meeting since its revolution 20 years earlier.

President Nixon

October 8, 1969, 6:30 p.m.

Nixon and Kissinger mull over their "option to the right" on Vietnam—Nixon's November 1 ultimatum to North Vietnam and threat of major escalation. They also consider making a big announcement on November 1 to demonstrate their peace efforts instead. (The New Jersey elections they weigh produced the first Republican governor, William Cahill, there in 16 years.)

... Kissinger said that we are finally getting Laird [to come] around. President added that Rogers is now sold on what we are doing and couldn't figure out why. He didn't raise cease-fire or other things. Part of the fact could be that we have an option to the right. Kissinger said they are all terrified as to what you will do on November 1.... Kissinger said he was giving a lot of thought [to the possibility that] the president decided not to go right on November 1 due to the elections in New Jersey. Kissinger added that the president could do a number of things that would give him another month for decisions. The president said that he would like to do something on November 1 anyway. Kissinger thought maybe a report to the people. The president wanted to do more. Kissinger said he should make a move that would indicate to the American people a greater interest in peace. The president said rather than react to October 15 [the Moratorium protest], let it go and then announce that we will ask for time on November 1 for major announcement....

Kissinger said it might really worry them [the North Vietnamese] if you revealed, on November 1, every secret contact we have had. That would be very unusual and something we might consider doing if we have practically given up on them. ... It will take some of the steam out of November 15 [the Mobilization protest]. It will hurt [Democratic gubernatorial candidate Robert] Meyner in New Jersey. It would mean to Hanoi that you are ready to clobber them....

President Nixon

October 10, 1969, 7:30 p.m.

Nixon says he will end the war before the 1972 election, and they confer on his November 1 ultimatum and Operation Duck Hook, their plan for massive escalation ("it's got to be ready"). Nixon says the secret Cambodia bombing "is more important than anything else."

... The president said by '72 the war is going to be over, and he is going to be the man who ended it. ... There's a lot of rough stuff coming up. ...

President said it isn't just this issue, but the next one and the next one that comes up. What about Korea? What about Berlin? Kissinger said he is convinced that if we yield on this one, we're just inviting the Soviets into a confrontation....

President said in the Joint Chiefs meeting on Saturday he was going to let [Chairman Earle] Wheeler give a report. ... Kissinger said they should believe that president is serious about the November 1 plan; if not, they won't give him any planning cooperation. Must be careful about telling them [their plan for Duck Hook is] inadequate; they're terribly sensitive.

Kissinger said he thinks that really by November we ought to be in as good shape as possible. President said yes, it's got to be ready. President said whether the United States will be able to see this thing through at the present level is a question, but if they escalate, we have got to respond. Kissinger said if we can keep casualties down over the next four weeks it will be good. But if they go up dramatically, we have an excuse for what we are planning to do. . . .

President said the best news all day is the Cambodian strike. He said he is convinced—he knows Kissinger disagrees with him on this—but he is convinced that this is more important than anything else. . . . Here we are hitting them and hurting them and they don't get anything out of it. Kissinger said that they had found a new area, just north. Same rate of explosion, something like 70 secondaries. President said "suppose it blows in Cambodia." President said we could just say we were just hitting areas on the border. Kissinger said we can stop it at any time. President said should we? Kissinger said I don't think we should. President said it indicates a certain toughness to them. Kissinger said we might stop it as we get closer to the 1st. President said why not stand down everything? . . . Just stand down and don't say why. . . .

President Nixon
October 20, 1969, 8:25 p.m.
Nixon instructs Kissinger to be threatening about Vietnam in his meeting with Ambassador Dobrynin the next day and warn that he was "out of control."

President said in the meeting tomorrow . . . if the Vietnam thing is raised—try to get it raised—the president wants Kissinger to shake his head and say, "I am sorry, Mr. Ambassador, but he is out of control. Mr. Ambassador, as you know, I am very close to the president, but you don't know this man—he's been through more than any of the rest of us put together. He's made up his mind and unless there's some movement"—just shake your head and walk out. He's probably right now figuring out what was said [that afternoon]. Kissinger said he might type up everything the president said on a plain slip of paper. The president said that was fine, and Kissinger should put in whatever he wanted. Say since he gave us his notes he's entitled to my notes. The president said he'll say, "What does this mean? Are you threatening me?" And Kissinger should say, "Please now, Mr. Ambassador, the president isn't threatening you. He just wants a little movement." . . .

Melvin Laird
October 25, 1969, 10:40 a.m.
Former president Lyndon Johnson had taken loads of highly classified materials down to Texas for his memoirs and presidential library and wanted many of them declassified.

. . . Laird asked if Kissinger had sat in with President Johnson and President Nixon when they met in San Clemente [the so-called Western White House in California] on declassification. Kissinger said yes. Laird asked if the president had agreed to declassify papers one to five years old. Kissinger said no. . . . Laird said . . . they want to declassify a lot of stuff gotten through intelligence that would be dangerous. . . . We'll have to play the bad guys. Kissinger said Johnson was afraid that he wouldn't get release of anything for five years. Kissinger said he wanted any documents that will be declassified in the next five years to be declassified now so he can move them into his library. Kissinger said there is absolutely no agreement on one to five years. . . . Kissinger said we want to help him; Laird agreed. Laird said but he's got everything down there; he's got a lot of stuff. Kissinger said he's got 32,000 documents. Laird said he's got CIA, NSA, DIA stuff—Jesus Christ! Kissinger said the NSA stuff shouldn't go at all— it's absurd to say one to five years. Laird said . . . he took some very sensitive things down there. He's got a bunch of guys who are eager and who say that Johnson was told by the president that this could be done. Kissinger said no, that's not so. . . . Laird said these papers won't help the book, but they make his library more attractive—they've got Daily Intelligence Reports, DIA reports, summaries from code word stuff. Laird said he'd had no idea Johnson would bundle up everything—all the code word stuff! Kissinger said those things can't ever be declassified. . . .

Melvin Laird
October 28, 1969, 12:20 p.m.
Kissinger is outraged to learn that Gerard Smith, the head of the U.S. delegation at the upcoming SALT talks in Helsinki, was meeting with Ambassador Dobrynin.

Laird just wanted to check something out with Kissinger. Laird said as Kissinger knows, Gerry Smith is meeting with Dobrynin on Thursday on SALT. Kissinger: God damn it! No! I don't know it! Laird said he had just met with some others on this and they want some good solid instructions for him on what to talk about. Kissinger said he's got no business discussing anything. Laird said he didn't want to get Kissinger upset, just wants guidance for Smith. Laird asked if Kissinger followed. Kissinger said he not only followed, he is going to get instructions out on it right away. . . .

President Nixon
November 3, 1969, 11:33 p.m.
Nixon complains that Rogers and Laird were not enthusiastic about his speech that evening, in which he condemned the "vocal minority" of antiwar protesters for trying to "impose" their views on others and appealed for support from "the great silent majority."[1]

. . . The president said Rogers and Laird called. The president thought they were a little shaken. But the point is that they should have been ecstatic. But neither showed that—they haven't got the guts. I think they'll have to go. Kissinger said they didn't behave very loyally these last few days—they let the White House carry it. The president said they're not going to [his Florida compound in] Key Biscayne, that's for sure. . . . The president is going to write them a letter, cold turkey. He's going to dictate a memo on how they must handle the speech. Kissinger agreed.

Kissinger said he knew [CBS's Marvin] Kalb wouldn't like the speech. The president said, no, he's a communist. . . .

Daniel Davidson
November 5, 1969, 10:20 a.m.
Former NSC staffer Davidson, who had been wiretapped at Kissinger's behest and then forced out for a perceived security violation (Kissinger directed his military assistant, Alexander Haig, to fire him),[2] asks about Kissinger's discussion with Newsweek's Joel Blocker about his departure.

. . . Kissinger wanted to assure Davidson that Blocker had mentioned Davidson to Kissinger only briefly and asked whether there was an ideological reason for Davidson's departure from the NSC staff. Kissinger said he had the highest regard and warmest personal feeling for Davidson. There was nothing secret or complicated. . . . Blocker had mentioned the fact that so many people had left Kissinger's staff, but if he talked to the people there were perfectly natural reasons. Davidson said he left for ideological reasons. . . .

Kissinger said he still had the same feeling for Davidson but he wouldn't be able to go into the whole thing. When it is all over they would discuss it, and then Davidson would agree that it was in his best interest. Davidson said it didn't seem to be that way now. . . . Davidson said one day he got a call from Blocker asking about Dean Moor [also of the NSC staff] and Davidson said he was a pretty good man. Blocker said Kissinger told him Moor was a lightweight. . . .

William Rogers
November 11, 1969, 12:45 p.m.
Rogers wonders if Kissinger's notetaking on a flight was for a memoir.

. . . Rogers said he wanted to see the notes Kissinger took on the plane coming back from Key Biscayne. Kissinger said he never does anything with them—he doesn't show them to the president. Rogers said are you going to write a book? Kissinger said no, he was never going to write a book. Kissinger said he just takes the notes so if the president should ask about something, he could refer to them. Rogers said if he does ask, on the key points he'd like to have a chance to express his views to the president, if it's of any consequence. Kissinger said he doesn't quote what Rogers says at a meeting—it never comes up that way. . . .

Melvin Laird
November 21, 1969, 3:50 p.m.
A week before this conversation, Seymour Hersh had begun publishing stories on the My Lai massacre in March 1968 in South Vietnam. Army platoon leader William Calley Jr. was charged with the murder of 109 civilians. The Cleveland Plain Dealer *had just published eight photos of the massacre taken by army photographer Ronald Haeberle (which then ran on CBS).*[3]

Kissinger was calling about the atrocity case. The president wants to make sure Laird got on top of that—got a game plan. Kissinger said it was going to be a terrible mess. . . . Laird said he thinks the guy is going to plead insanity, and Laird thinks he'll get off. Laird asked if Kissinger had the pictures. Kissinger said no. Laird asked if Kissinger would like to look at them. Kissinger said should I? Laird said Kissinger might as well not. They're pretty terrible. . . . Laird said it didn't happen on our watch and we're going to make that clear before the Fulbright committee. Kissinger said Haldeman heard that the army is trying to impound the pictures—that can't be done. Laird said the pictures belong to the guy [Haeberle, who took photos on both an army camera and his own camera], so we can't do anything with them. . . . Laird said they're already published in the *Cleveland Plain Dealer*. Laird said some of the press wants us to give them out, but we're not going to. Kissinger said no, we don't want you to, that's right. Laird said the sergeant has already given them out.

Laird said about a game plan, he'd like to sweep the whole thing under the rug, but you can't do that. Kissinger said we just need some unified line. Laird said he's going to say that he discovered it in March; he was shocked; he ordered a full investigation. . . . Laird said he thought about how to sweep it under the rug. Kissinger said we can't do that. Laird said these are lousy-looking things [the photos]. Laird said those boys had been suffering terribly; one of their boys had been killed just 24 hours before. Laird said you can understand a little bit of this, but you shouldn't kill that many. Laird said there are so many kids just laying there; these pictures are authentic. Laird said he didn't know what to do; it bothers him, but he doesn't know what to do. . . .

Laird said he may send a game plan. Laird said we've got all kinds of problems with this atrocity thing, but we've got to be careful that we don't take on everybody on the Vietnam War thing. Laird said he thinks we can sell a lot of young people and other people if they know what our policy is. . . .

Melvin Laird
November 27, 1969, 10:40 a.m.
Laird, who wanted U.S. troops out of Vietnam much faster than did Kissinger and was always plotting ways to speed the process up, explains what he meant at a press

backgrounder about withdrawing troops and denies saying that he didn't care what Nixon was doing.

Kissinger told Laird that he had just heard from Haig about what these reporters have been saying. The reporters said that Laird had given a backgrounder and said that he didn't care what the president announced, he was going to continue withdrawing troops. . . . Laird said that wasn't true. Kissinger said he told them there was no such thing as a Defense withdrawal policy, only a national withdrawal policy, and there has never been a disagreement. There is the president's policy, which has been worked out together with everybody. . . . Laird said this whole thing came up because of the transcript being released by the Foreign Relations Committee. They have been leaking out bits of that at a time. . . . Laird said the impression he got was that there was no plan by the president. . . . Kissinger said that is totally wrong and Laird knew what Kissinger's view was on that. Laird said he only talked to three of them [reporters]. They were pressing and they called him at home. . . . Laird thought the impression was given that the president hadn't approved a plan. Kissinger said that impression wasn't given and they know it. . . . They said that Laird . . . in effect didn't care what the president was doing. Laird said he would like to hear somebody tell him that. Kissinger told them there is no Laird plan different from the president's plan. . . . Laird said they were just trying to bait this one. . . . Kissinger asked who the reporters were. Laird said they were people who were in backgrounder yesterday morning. Laird recommended that Kissinger not call them. They swore Laird to secrecy and Laird told them to call Kissinger. . . .

Melvin Laird
November 28, 1969, 5:40 p.m.
Three days earlier, Nixon had renounced first use of chemical weapons and use of biological weapons, and said he'd asked Defense to make recommendations on the disposal of biological weapons. Laird and Kissinger hotly debate the source of a leak that the Joint Chiefs and Pentagon had initially taken hard lines against reducing the U.S. biological warfare capability.[4]

. . . Laird said he didn't always want to complain, but he had a complaint about the NSC meeting. Laird said there was a leak . . . on biological research and chemical warfare, as if the Joint Chiefs had been uncooperative. Kissinger said who leaked it? Frankly I thought it came out of Defense. Laird said it did not come out of Defense! Laird said his people think it was ACDA or State. Laird said only Wheeler and himself could have leaked it, and he knew it wasn't Wheeler, and it wasn't himself. Kissinger said he went to the president and told him that the Joint Chiefs were cooperative. The president said maybe one of Laird's people did it, thought it would make him look good. Laird said it makes it more difficult. Laird said there were too many people in that room. There were many from

ACDA and State, only two from Defense in that room. . . . Laird said this will work if we trust each other, but we don't. . . .

Ernst van der Beugel
December 5, 1969, 4:20 p.m.
The former Dutch official van der Beugel and Kissinger mull over Harvard and Kissinger's former colleagues there, who neither find interesting. ("I'm not one of these little academics" was the tone Kissinger conveyed when he was at Harvard, one colleague said.)[5]

. . . Van der Beugel said he is telling Kissinger for his own good, Harvard isn't an interesting place anymore. It is a pedestrian place. Kissinger said that's his feeling; it is dull. . . . Kissinger said his ex-colleagues have nothing to say that is interesting. Van der Beugel said Harvard used to be a window on the world; now it is only a window on Harvard. Van der Beugel said people just spend their time wondering where the trouble [i.e., student protest] starts tomorrow. Van der Beugel said he finds New York thousands of times more interesting. Kissinger said oh, far. Kissinger said when he leaves here he intends to get a job there. . . . Kissinger said when he goes to see his children he gets a few of his friends together but they have nothing interesting to say. Kissinger said, how do they feel about me? Van der Beugel said there's great resentment about the policy, but nothing like the Rostow situation. [Former national security adviser Walt Rostow was not hired back by MIT after he left the government.] Van der Beugel said there's a complete break with the policy. Kissinger said but they have no policy of their own. Van der Beugel said they would welcome you with open arms after one or two or three years. Kissinger said I have no intention of going back. Van der Beugel said his advice would be against it; it is an uninteresting, rather violent, parochial place. . . .

President Nixon
December 13, 1969, 12:59 p.m.
Walter Stoessel, the U.S. ambassador to Poland, had met secretly at the Chinese embassy there with the Chinese chargé d'affaires to discuss the resumption of such ambassadorial meetings. (They'd last been held in early 1968.) Nixon and Kissinger wanted to keep the content of the discussion secret, but the State Department had given accounts to other countries.[6]

. . . Kissinger said the other problem he wanted to mention is that there's been an unbelievable amount of leaking from State on the Chinese meeting; they gave a full debriefing to the Japanese and the Japanese are leaking it now. . . . President said they debriefed the substance of the conversation? Kissinger said yes. President said what the hell for? . . . Kissinger said I don't know how the Chinese will react. President said this was deliberate on the part of State so that China will get mad and start talking. President said these talks with the Chinese, and with the Soviets, ought to be handled on a confidential basis—that's what they agreed to in the talks. Kissinger said we set it up so carefully, and over such a long period of time, and if they think we're only trying to get propaganda they'll have to hit us back. . . . President said this is an order: there is to be no debriefing to any Soviets, just as we are not to inform the Chinese of what the Soviets talked about. . . . To put on wires this monstrous stuff is ridiculous. . . . President said we'll kill this child before it's born. Kissinger said right; I don't care about these talks; we don't have anything to talk about anyway. President said we all know that, but the Russians aren't going to believe we didn't have anything, and the Chinese will believe we are playing them off against the Russians. Kissinger said they might think we are in cahoots to embarrass them with other communists. . . .

President Nixon

December 13, 1969, 2:07 p.m.

Secretary of State Rogers gave a speech on the Middle East several days earlier, which became known as the "Rogers Plan," in which he said "we do not support expansionism" and that Israel's forces should withdraw from territories it took in the Six Day War in 1967, as stipulated in UN Resolution 242. Nixon and Kissinger discuss the speech—they passed word to Israeli Prime Minister Golda Meir to "slam" Rogers and his plan—a third Moratorium antiwar protest, and youthful dissent.[7]

. . . President said some interest would be served by expressing some disappointment in Rogers's speech. Kissinger said yes. President said . . . say the president's private reassurances remain firm—no change. President said it's just a damn charade we're playing. . . . Tell her [Meir] I think it helpful to indicate disappointment with Rogers's speech. President said it gives us a bargaining position with the Arabs. Just be sure the private reassurances remain firm. Kissinger said they are all stirred up; [Jewish activist] Max Fisher called this morning and said we are undercutting the Jewish position. . . . President said there's no reason for us to take the heat off this; let them [at State] explain this. Kissinger said that's right. Kissinger said [Senator Jacob] Javits has been screaming too. President said let him scream at Rogers. . . .

President said you know this is the Moratorium day, and there were just 12 at American University. . . . President said those kids are not dumb; they can read the polls and they know their parents don't approve. Kissinger said and they respect success; they want something to succeed, something they can admire and emulate; they are looking for fathers, something to look up to. They are rootless; that is their basic problem. President said but they had an issue to bring to this Moratorium—My Lai. President said but they didn't do a damn thing. How do you explain that? . . . Kissinger said they want a leader who has a grasp of things; your press conference was successful because you can tie things together. Kissinger said one-sentence answers makes them feel you are on top of things, and the November 3 speech gave them the same feeling—you explained it. Kissinger said in a revolutionary period, the worst thing is to give in to every manifestation of dissatisfaction. . . .

Elliot Richardson
December 15, 1969, 11:50 a.m.
Kissinger asks Undersecretary of State Richardson to plug the leaks on the Warsaw meeting with the Chinese chargé.

> . . . KISSINGER: . . . Can we stop that infernal leaking on China? I thought, and the president thought more strongly, that the Warsaw thing was very poorly handled. We spend weeks painstakingly setting it up and then it was buck-shotted to all the embassies. . . . We'd like to do it mysteriously. The less we give them that they can reject, the less they can feel we are using them. There isn't all that much to negotiate about. We have to improve the atmosphere and give them the feeling we are talking. We must avoid propositions they have to turn down. . . .
>
> RICHARDSON: It rather worries the Russians, though.
>
> KISSINGER: And it should.
>
> RICHARDSON: Dobrynin has brought it up the last couple of times I've seen him.

Bill Moyers
December 30, 1969, 10:00 a.m.
Former Johnson press secretary Moyers erroneously believes that Kissinger is pushing disengagement from Vietnam and recommends that he set straight former defense secretary Clark Clifford and Harvard professor Stanley Hoffmann, who believe otherwise. Kissinger denies that Melvin Laird was advocating de-escalation.

> MOYERS: I want to report a couple of things just between us. . . . A friend of mine at dinner in Washington last week told me he had been at a dinner where Clark Clifford was also present. Sometimes Clark can act on misinformation. Clark got him in the corner and told him the real surprise in this administration is Mel Laird fighting hard for de-escalation, but can't penetrate Kissinger and Nixon. I think the way to handle Clark is have lunch with him some day and straighten him out.
>
> KISSINGER: That Laird is the champion rascal. Never once has Laird made a proposal in either of these directions to us. It seems he goes all over town saying he does, but never once in any sense at all, written, oral or by indirection, has he made such a proposal.
>
> MOYERS: . . . The second comes from a member of the faculty and a friend of mine at Harvard at dinner. He had dinner with Stanley Hoffmann and the

same kind of line was being taken by Stanley . . . that Kissinger is being taken over by Nixon's view of the world. He said, "The prolongation of disengagement by Henry surprises me. I think he is getting into the same trap that Walt Rostow got into." I think you can pull Stanley back. . . . To both of these people I said you are really wrong about that. Because I am sure that if there is any one man prudently pushing the disengagement processes it is Henry. . . .

5

French Plane Sales to Libya, B-52s over Laos, Japanese Textile Negotiations, Hitting SAM Sites in North Vietnam, Danielle Hunebelle, and Thai Troops in Laos

January–March 1970

In January 1970, the press revealed that France was selling jet fighters and other weapons to the new Muammar Gaddafi government in Libya (the numbers of which, by France's reluctant admission, kept going up). This disturbed Israel, which feared some could wind up in Egypt, and the Nixon administration. In February, the administration secretly began B-52 bombing in northern Laos using a false-reporting system, as with the secret Cambodia bombing. But the bombing was immediately picked up by the press and set off members of Congress, who were also troubled by other secret U.S. operations in Laos. The administration was also bombing surface-to-air missile sites and nearby locations in North Vietnam, claiming "protective reaction" against enemy fire.

Also in February, the French journalist Danielle Hunebelle began doing a profile of Kissinger for French television that would turn into a nightmare for him due to Hunebelle's romantic obsession with him. Meanwhile, Kissinger's negotiations with an emissary of Japan's prime minister to reach an agreement to limit Japanese textile exports to the United States were stalled by what Kissinger saw as Japan's broken promises and inflexibility. He was apoplectic when Nixon's friend Donald Kendall—PepsiCo's CEO—got involved in the negotiations.

In March, the administration found itself on the defensive over newspaper reports of two Thai battalions flown by the CIA into Laos to help stave off enemy advances.

John Ehrlichman
January 10, 1970, 5:30 p.m.
Ross Perot, the Texas billionaire and advocate for the release of American prisoners of war, said he would consider paying North Vietnam $100 million to release all of them.[1]

> EHRLICHMAN: Your friend Ross Perot is going to be on [the ABC talk show] *Issues and Answers* tomorrow and then after that he is going by to talk to Averell Harriman [an elder statesman].
> KISSINGER: Hasn't anybody got this guy under control?
> EHRLICHMAN: What he wanted to know was if you had anything he should diplomatically probe.
> KISSINGER: No, he should just please get back to making money. . . .
> EHRLICHMAN: Okay, so tell him to just go and play the dumb Texan.
> KISSINGER: What does he think he is up to?
> EHRLICHMAN: He is in the big time.
> KISSINGER: Well, can't we put him into the big time?
> EHRLICHMAN: We have tried, but it just wasn't big enough. . . .

William Rogers
January 15, 1970, 12:35 p.m.
French Ambassador to the United States Charles Lucet had informed Kissinger that France was selling military planes to the new military government in Libya. France had acknowledged several days earlier selling around 50 Mirage jet fighters to Libya; it would later admit selling 100, then "closer to 110," planes. Both the policy and the secretive way it was handled were controversial.[2]

 . . . Kissinger: It is awful. He was giving it to us in such a way—a personal message from [French President Georges] Pompidou to the president. Strictly personal. Nothing to be done about it. Their argument was that the Russians would supply these things if they did not. . . . They are not only Mirages; some are reconnaissance planes. You just know the Libyans have no conceivable use for them.

> ROGERS: Of course not. . . . They could never fly that many planes. They don't need anything like it.
> KISSINGER: . . . I think it is an irresponsible thing to do because the Israelis are going to get wind of this.
> ROGERS: It is impossible to keep it tight. What concerns me particularly is it's going to make our relations with them very strained. We were off to a pretty good start with the French and this is going to make it difficult. There is nothing we can do except show our displeasure.

KISSINGER: If they had sold 25 Mirages, it would have been understandable, but when you go to 100 it is a very thin veneer. You know it isn't for Libya. They say they will get a commitment these planes can't leave Libya. . . . They have to be flown by Egyptian pilots. They don't have enough.

ROGERS: That is going to make the Pompidou visit very cloudy.

KISSINGER: They are trying to keep it very tight. . . .

ROGERS: This makes our policy more difficult to support now because it confirms some of the suspicions that Israel had about France. . . . It makes it difficult for us not to proceed to get more aid to Israel in a military way.

KISSINGER: We will be in very tough shape now. . . . I did not argue with him at all. I said very coldly, "You are not consulting us; you are informing us." Then I made the sarcastic statement, "We will see whether it is pilots or equipment that will determine things." . . .

Melvin Laird

January 26, 1970, 9:25 a.m.

Faced with an impending enemy dry-season offensive in northern Laos, Laird and Kissinger consider B-52 strikes there, which would also send a message to Hanoi. Though Laird said he favored the bombing, he wanted his representatives in meetings to argue against it so the record would show Pentagon opposition in case of leaks. (Kissinger never could figure out where the wily Laird actually stood.) Laird and Kissinger both wanted the strikes handled secretly. The bombing would start in mid-February and last several months; a false-reporting system was employed.[3]

. . . LAIRD: I want you to understand what I am doing. We have a target for the B-52s in Laos. In the interagency group I am telling them to talk against it.

KISSINGER: Are you for it?

LAIRD: Yes, but not in that channel. We can hit it now.

KISSINGER: So I can tell the president you are for it?

LAIRD: I want a new assessment on the targeting. I am expecting one today and I will go over it carefully. I told the president that as soon as we got a target I will hit it. . . . In these meetings it is best to take an opposite position. . . . Just wanted you to know that my people are taking a position I don't agree with, and then we will hit that target without fanfare. . . .

Melvin Laird

January 26, 1970, 4:32 p.m.

Kissinger says a previously dubious Secretary of State Rogers now tends to favor the B-52 bombing in northern Laos but wants a letter from Laird supporting it.

KISSINGER: Have you been browbeaten by Bill? . . . He is leaning toward doing it. He wants a letter for his Eyes Only. . . . A piece of paper over here saying you are recommending it and why. . . . He wants to know how essential that is. . . .

LAIRD: You will have to talk to Bill. He is very upset. . . . I wish it hadn't gotten into that channel. . . .

Mr. Yoshida
January 26, 1970, 8:10 p.m.
Mr. Yoshida was the pseudonym of an emissary of Japanese Prime Minister Eisaku Sato who negotiated with Kissinger over U.S. imports of Japanese textiles. U.S. textile manufacturers wanted reductions and Nixon sought an agreement with Japan. In Yoshida's conversations with Kissinger, he employed the alias to foil any eavesdropping, and his "friend" was Sato and Kissinger's "friend" was Nixon.[4]

KISSINGER: I am calling you about the problem of last week. We are completely confused here. The conversation took place, and nothing of the sort you told me happened. Your man was very tough and uncompromising. . . . My friends say maybe that piece of paper we both worked on has no authority, and it completely ruins our channel. We would appreciate it if you could tell us honestly if this will be done. . . . There has never been a sign of intention of carrying it out. Our negotiator doesn't know what is happening. I tell him something is going to happen and nothing happens.

YOSHIDA: Your man met our new man, and our new man here didn't offer your man here anything at all?

KISSINGER: Not at all. . . . He took a step back. . . . It will destroy this channel because no one will believe us again. . . .

U. Alexis Johnson
January 27, 1970, 9:00 a.m.
Kissinger informs Undersecretary of State Johnson that they'd been betrayed by the Japanese.

KISSINGER: I read through all the papers on this damn thing. . . . All this proves is that we got double-crossed rather than snookered.

JOHNSON: I really hate to believe that. I can't understand it. It's really not in character, and it's not in their interest.

KISSINGER: I called him [Yoshida] last night, said I'm getting out. I said we cannot go any further on our side. . . .

Earle Wheeler
January 27, 1970, 10:00 a.m.
Kissinger asks JCS Chairman Wheeler if an enemy troop concentration in northern Laos could be attacked with tactical aircraft rather than B-52s, partly to lessen the public outcry if it became public.[5]

> KISSINGER: I was just talking to the president on this business, and one of his problems is that all the principals have taken great care to protect themselves in writing. . . . If you flew every tactical thing against this, can you do some damage?
>
> WHEELER: Oh, yes, and we are already, but B-52s are more suitable. . . . I understand State is taking a very negative view.
>
> KISSINGER: There was no positive view from your shop [Defense]. . . . If you were to fly every tactical airplane against this target, would that help?
>
> WHEELER: Yes, but . . . they are flying now. We will do that anyway.
>
> KISSINGER: . . . Will you send everything out against them?
>
> WHEELER: I will do that. . . .

Melvin Laird
January 27, 1970, 10:08 a.m.
While waiting for Nixon's authority to use B-52s, Laird thinks they better hit the enemy troop concentration with tactical aircraft before it breaks up.

> . . . KISSINGER: On that northern target. . . . Bill has come in with a scorcher. He let it fly. . . .
>
> LAIRD: We should have gone on that by 10:00 today. I better start flying tactical today. The target will disperse when we go in with heavy tactical air, but I'm afraid it will disperse anyway. . . . It's the best target we've had for 52s since I became secretary of defense—they should start hitting it now. Four thousand troops won't stay together that long. If I don't hear from you by 10:30, I'll tell them to use tactical air—not the best, but we'll have to do it. Put as many sorties in there as we can fly. . . . We've never had this many troops together. Bill Rogers was raising hell with me as if I were irresponsible.
>
> KISSINGER: No, the president is on your side.
>
> LAIRD: He's usually on my side, but I usually don't get anywhere. . . .

President Nixon
January 27, 1970, 5:15 p.m.
Nixon and Kissinger confer on bombing SAM sites in North Vietnam and their public rationale. They'd been striking periodically in the North since taking office, allegedly

in response to enemy fire at U.S. reconnaissance planes, and the day after this conversation U.S. fighter bombers struck a SAM base 90 miles north of the DMZ near the Laotian border.[6] Nixon and Kissinger are disturbed by Vietnam Commander Creighton Abrams's position that bombing in the South should take priority over bombing in the North. They also consider Earle Wheeler's possible replacement as chairman of the Joint Chiefs of Staff by Chief of Naval Operations Thomas Moorer. And they want to step up the bombing in the South, given growing enemy infiltration from the North. Nixon wants to "get this damn thing over with."

NIXON: Did you find those targets yet?

KISSINGER: They found at least two others in addition to the one.

NIXON: . . . Is that enough to give them a shock effect?

KISSINGER: Yes. . . . They will notice you are not doing just tit-for-tat.

NIXON: They will note it is something new?

KISSINGER: Up to now we have hit only at SAM sites from which they attacked. Now we are hitting all the SAM sites in the vicinity.

NIXON: We agree we will go on these three. . . . Don't you agree with my deal—no tit-for-tat?

KISSINGER: I agree completely. What I told Mel is to hit all the sites in that area. . . .

NIXON: They will know now they got hurt.

KISSINGER: We will just say we hit the SAM sites.

NIXON: It [a plane] was brought down by SAM, and therefore we hit the SAM sites in that area. We may not have to explain anything.

KISSINGER: No, because they will not give us a map of their SAM sites. . . . Laird said he isn't much in favor of hitting the North and we ought to do what Abrams recommends—just to hit more in the South. I am concerned about this metamorphosis of Abrams's views, and Abrams may think he is going to become the next chairman of the Joint Chiefs.

NIXON: I tell you right now it is going to be Moorer. . . . I can't believe Abrams is against hitting the North.

KISSINGER: He didn't ring true when he talked to you. I remember how upset he was on the flight to Bangkok and Saigon when you were talking troop withdrawals and how nonchalant he was when you talked a few months later. I would feel more comfortable if he still holds that view after the chairmanship is settled. He seemed to me to take troop withdrawals a little too easily in that conversation. When you said cross to Cambodia, he said no, I wouldn't want to do that. I don't know what has caused him to change. . . . It [becoming chairman of the JCS] may be in the back of his own mind. And I think the more quickly we settle it, the better off.

NIXON: I am convinced it should be the navy man. I think it is the navy's turn.

KISSINGER: After all, Wheeler hasn't shown anything in the last six months.

NIXON: Yes, he sort of pooped out, but he is tired. How about this navy fellow? Will he hit it hard?

KISSINGER: He is not a great brain, but he will hit it hard. . . .

NIXON: Prepare a note from me to Abrams. I am going to put it in writing that I want him to step up the attacks now in the South.

KISSINGER: I don't think you ought to put it in writing. That is the sort of order you ought to be able to put orally and get it carried out.

NIXON: Say in view of the infiltrations now above everything we ought to succeed. . . . I want to look down the road and see when we are going to get this damn thing over with. There is no answer to winning it.

KISSINGER: If they don't start negotiating in February then I think some jolt may be necessary. . . .

President Nixon
January 28, 1970, 3:55 p.m.
Nixon directs Kissinger to have the military bomb as many SAM sites as possible in their target area in North Vietnam, suggesting use of B-52s.

NIXON: I just wanted to be sure that you follow up on hitting as many SAM sites as they can find. Any in this area, not just one. Tell these fellows it's an opportunity. Maybe six or eight. If there are others a few miles away, get those. What do they use?

KISSINGER: [F-]105s.

NIXON: Not B-52s?

KISSINGER: We have never used B-52s in North Vietnam.

NIXON: Now would be the time.

KISSINGER: It is better to save those. B-52s are for area work and this is a pinpoint job. . . .

NIXON: No more of this tit-for-tat. . . . If there isn't one in the area tell them to find others. . . . Bring in the planes and run them out. . . .

Danielle Hunebelle
February 16, 1970, 9:15 p.m.
Hunebelle, a French journalist, wanted to do a profile of Kissinger for French television. She would soon develop a romantic interest in him, but Kissinger, while typically flirtatious, ultimately spurned her. Hunebelle later suggested they had some sort of relationship.[7]

. . . Kissinger asked Hunebelle what she wanted from him—Kissinger said she would get it anyway, so she should ask quickly. Hunebelle said she intended to do a profile of him for TV. Hunebelle asked if any networks had done a profile on him. Kissinger said he has never had a profile done by anyone. . . . Hunebelle said she knew Kissinger spoke French well. Kissinger said he was immune to her—it was all her tactic. . . . Hunebelle said the crew was arriving tomorrow night. Kissinger again said just tell him what she wanted and she would get it. Kissinger said once you find your master, you don't fight it. Hunebelle said the best thing would be to follow him for two days. . . . Kissinger asked if he could take out a girl in the interim or if they expected him to be a monk. Hunebelle said but of course. . . . Hunebelle said she would like to spend a week in Washington if she could, but she didn't know how the crew will work out. Hunebelle said the crew was Swiss because all the French TV crews were communists.

Hunebelle asked Kissinger if he would be free for dinner tomorrow. Kissinger said he did have a dinner date but he would check. Kissinger said she was ruining his love life. . . .

Hunebelle said they would go to Harvard and interview people who could speak French. Kissinger said wait a minute, he couldn't let her show this in America. . . .

Melvin Laird
February 23, 1970, 2:20 p.m.
Kissinger is outraged over a cable by U.S. Ambassador to Thailand Leonard Unger to JCS Chairman Earle Wheeler on the B-52 bombing of North Vietnamese and Pathet Lao troops in northern Laos. By now the bombing had been reported in the press.[8]

> KISSINGER: Did you see that cable by Unger? That crazy SOB.
>
> LAIRD: I'm going to cable him.
>
> KISSINGER: Tell him it was done on highest authority. This was unbelievable. He has no right to talk to the Joint Chiefs in such a way.
>
> LAIRD: He shouldn't wire Wheeler anyway.
>
> KISSINGER: I'm sending it to Elliot [Richardson] with a note that he is to be brought under control.
>
> LAIRD: I think we will have to let him know in the future.
>
> KISSINGER: How about the Menu [secret Cambodia bombing] series?
>
> LAIRD: . . . He knows nothing about that. . . .
>
> KISSINGER: You had better send him a message.
>
> LAIRD: I will let Wheeler send it and tell him that we will give him information through the back channel for his Eyes Only, and if he has to tell, then do it after the strikes. . . .

Robert McNamara
February 25, 1970, 9:15 a.m.
Former secretary of defense McNamara and Kissinger take up Danielle Hunebelle and her French television piece on Kissinger, for which she interviewed McNamara.

MCNAMARA: That woman is fascinating.

KISSINGER: Overwhelming!

MCNAMARA: I wanted you to know I have seen her.

KISSINGER: You get a kick out of her once, but when she's around constantly—

MCNAMARA: She's worried about the way things are coming out. She's smart and has talent. I think she will turn this into something favorable for you, but you should keep in mind that there is the chance it could be something quite less. It's really in her hands and I think she will do a good job. Relax and let the thing come through—your personality and mind.

KISSINGER: This woman has been living on my doorstep. Every time I have a few minutes, there she is. She's the only person I know who can make me lose my composure.

MCNAMARA: She thinks she hasn't caught you.

KISSINGER: Her idea of catching me is to catch me in my underwear. . . .

William Rogers
February 27, 1970, 2:40 p.m.
Kissinger and Rogers debate releasing information on U.S. operations in Laos in the face of congressional and press criticism. Rogers wants to let Senator Stuart Symington declassify and release his earlier closed testimony at Senate subcommittee hearings on Laos.

. . . ROGERS: I want to know what the president wants, and we should have someone running this thing.

KISSINGER: The Symington thing? He doesn't want to do it this time.

ROGERS: I want to do it this time.

KISSINGER: He wants to discuss the public statement on Laos.

ROGERS: That's the Symington problem.

KISSINGER: On one level. But he wants to discuss how to get through the immediate period. Do we declassify the Symington stuff or what? We will thrash it out at the meeting.

ROGERS: He should be there. . . . There has been so much said and he is not briefed on it. It's building up on the Hill. . . . What do we do about disclosure? The newspapers are all after us. When I was up on the Hill the House only asked about that. . . . It's building up to what Lyndon Johnson had [criticism of his lack of candor]. . . .

President Nixon
February 27, 1970, 6:45 p.m.

Nixon disagrees with Rogers's idea of releasing his closed Senate testimony and wants to "fuzz" the CIA's involvement in Laos. (He would claim falsely on March 6 that no Americans had ever been killed in ground combat in Laos.)[9]

> ... NIXON: ... I think we got Rogers around a bit.
>
> KISSINGER: It got him off Symington.
>
> NIXON: I'm going to ignore Symington. . . . We don't have to explain. Bill was wrong. That would escalate it. It's a Washington story—people in Oklahoma know nothing about Laos. . . . We want to make clear we have no combat forces in Laos. No one cares about [B-]52 strikes in Laos. But people worry about our boys there.
>
> KISSINGER: That's what's the problem with CIA.
>
> NIXON: We won't mention that. We will put out a silly figure and they are there—I'll have to fuzz their capacity. Noncombative and none killed. That's the only way you can show they are noncombat. . . .

President Nixon
March 19, 1970, 12:20 p.m.
Nixon demands a more urgent response to North Vietnamese and Pathet Lao advances in Laos.

> ... KISSINGER: ... I think it is safe to say, Mr. President, that the overwhelming majority of the bureaucracy is extremely gun-shy about doing anything. They are gambling that it's going to stop. . . .
>
> NIXON: Just say they have got to do something immediately. . . . Cancel what you are doing. Call them over immediately and tell them the president wants an action plan on his desk by 3:00. Cancel all their luncheon plans; cancel yours. Get the fellow out of your office who's there. Tell them I want some action, because I've made the decision.

Melvin Laird
March 19, 1970, 7:10 p.m.
Laird says he'll tell other departments that one air strike in North Vietnam was "protective reaction"—a response to North Vietnamese missiles launched from SAM sites—only to realize that won't wash.

> ... KISSINGER: And how would you handle the other departments?
>
> LAIRD: I wouldn't say anything to anybody. I will say it is protective reaction. . . .
>
> KISSINGER: It was discussed at WSAG as a possibility.
>
> LAIRD: Oh. Then they'll tie it up. I guess we'll have to tell them.

KISSINGER: Or can you just stone-face it?

LAIRD: I can't do that with Bill Rogers. That would undermine any chance for cooperation in the future. . . . They'll get the word at State that they haven't hit out of those sites in a month. . . . You have to keep a certain confidence with people who work together. . . .

H. R. Haldeman

March 20, 1970, 5:25 p.m.

Kissinger complains that Press Secretary Ronald Ziegler was running too often to Nixon with questions, the latest about two Thai battalions flown by the CIA to Laos to help defend a key army base in jeopardy.[10]

KISSINGER: Al Haig is enraged and ready to tear Ron Ziegler limb from limb. He constantly gets some trivial problem and asks the president what he should do. On some of the issues the president doesn't know the answers. The other day he had the president and me in the president's office for one and a half hours on something we already had the answers to and the president finally came up with the same answer. On this Thais in Laos, he came to Al, who was working on something else for the president and couldn't give him much time. Ron stormed out of here and went to the president. We nearly had the whole thing set up but he just got everything in a mess. To panic the president is just not right. If he wants to get the facts from us and our recommendation then he should get the president's views if he is not satisfied. If the president had told him something wrong, it would have been a problem. We had to work it out with two other governments. We are going to get him in and give him hell. I wanted you to know in case he comes running to you.

HALDEMAN: He won't come to me, but he is trying to do his job the same as the rest of us and we are all trying to accomplish the same thing.

KISSINGER: He should have the facts before he goes to the president.

HALDEMAN: He has a frustrating job trying to get the facts.

KISSINGER: He won't get them from the president. . . .

HALDEMAN: Don't blow your temper with him or everything will blow. . . .

President Nixon

March 20, 1970, 7:09 p.m.

Nixon grumbles that State put the public handling of the Thai troops in Laos in his lap, and Kissinger worries that Laos could fall without the B-52 bombing. They also discuss the Paris peace talks. "We are either going to do it at Paris or we will do it the other way—but we are going to do it," Nixon declares. Referring to the North Vietnamese, he says "we are going to kick the shit out of them—anything . . . short of nuclear weapons." Kissinger had told Nixon the day before that "there wasn't much we could do militarily" to force Hanoi to settle or surrender, which sent Nixon "through the roof."[11]

> ... NIXON: Why didn't State put that out instead of kicking it over here? They threw it to Ziegler and now Ziegler had to throw it to me. . . . The newspaper stories are wildly exaggerated—we had nothing to do with it [a Thai battalion].
>
> KISSINGER: Well, we paid for it.
>
> NIXON: But they don't know that. . . . They don't have to put out a press release.
>
> KISSINGER: I have given the strictest instructions not to say anything.
>
> NIXON: They say these things can't be done—for a year we hit Cambodia, but no one knew.
>
> KISSINGER: Dick Helms sent over a memorandum from the station chief in Laos that said without the B-52s the whole thing is going to fall apart. . . .
>
> NIXON: If anybody asks me about that I will say, yes, we will continue to do that. The thing to do is not to be a bit defensive about it. We have to say that the enemy is threatening our position in Laos.
>
> KISSINGER: I still hope this thing in Paris will work out—certainly after two more meetings something should.
>
> NIXON: I don't know if we can wait that long. . . . I think they may be diddling. . . . They know that we won't hit them if we are talking to them. The Laos thing should be some message to them.
>
> KISSINGER: Oh, they will notice that. I don't know what they are up to, but they can't just be diddling us along. . . .
>
> NIXON: We are either going to do it at Paris or we will do it the other way—but we are going to do it. I have been reading these figures over the last three months—if we killed one-third of what they say, there wouldn't be anyone left in North Vietnam.
>
> KISSINGER: . . . There is a breaking point. . . . They just aren't talking in these meetings as they were before. They aren't going to make it last for another three years. . . .
>
> NIXON: I would tell them to fish or cut bait.
>
> KISSINGER: When you read the transcript, you will see that they have given a hell of a lot more than we have. . . .
>
> NIXON: They have not given us anything. . . . What we have to do is create a provocation to hit them. We are not going to hit them the way Johnson did. If we provoke [them] we are going to kick the shit out of them—anything . . . short of nuclear weapons. That's why I approved the B-52 thing so fast. We are already being blamed for being in Laos, what difference does it make if we hit them with little planes or big ones? We may as well use the big ones.
>
> KISSINGER: I will give them an ultimatum that if they don't give us something I will break off. . . .

President Nixon
March 20, 1970, 7:55 p.m.
Nixon orders more bombing of SAM sites in North Vietnam, and they want to be sure that Laird continues the secret bombing of Cambodia.

> NIXON: What I was thinking about was that you should give Wheeler a call and make sure he knows what I said about this SAM decision. . . . We have the [B-]52s in here and they will go. SAMs we will hit and hit fast. I want it done Sunday. . . .
>
> KISSINGER: I was just talking to Laird to make sure he will keep the Menu thing going.
>
> NIXON: Put it in writing and I will sign it. . . . Never send anything to Laird in the future without sending it to Wheeler. Send them just a memo on Menu. Hit the SAM sites and send a memo signed by me. We will get this bureaucracy in shape.
>
> KISSINGER: I couldn't agree more.

U. Alexis Johnson
March 23, 1970, 8:35 a.m.
Kissinger is angry that Donald Kendall, CEO of PepsiCo, is involved in the negotiations with Japan over reducing U.S. imports of Japanese textiles.

> . . . KISSINGER: God damn it. Who the hell is he? . . . I told them Kendall has no standing. . . . That guy's a menace. . . . I can't stand him and I avoid him like the plague. . . .

Mr. Yoshida
March 24, 1970, 6:40 p.m.
Kissinger tells Japanese Prime Minister Sato's emissary that Kendall didn't speak for the administration.

> . . . YOSHIDA: . . . Kendall has made a concrete proposal.
>
> KISSINGER: But Kendall does not represent us.
>
> YOSHIDA: That's quite clear. When you told me I immediately told my friend [Sato]. . . .
>
> KISSINGER: What does your friend think Kendall represents? Why do we have to negotiate with Kendall when we can talk directly? . . . I am told Kendall's proposal is unacceptable to us.
>
> YOSHIDA: If that is unacceptable to you, we have to stop that progress. . . .

Mr. Yoshida
March 25, 1970, 6:40 p.m.

YOSHIDA: Kendall implied that he represents the thinking of your people.
KISSINGER: Nonsense! . . . My idea is the one we want. . . . We have canceled
    his trip—that should give you some idea of how much he represents us. . . .

William Leonard
March 26, 1970, 3:45 p.m.
*Danielle Hunebelle had asked CBS if it was interested in purchasing rights to her
French television profile of Kissinger. Leonard was a CBS News executive involved
with 60 Minutes.*

KISSINGER: I have Hunebelle chasing me and I want to know what you are
    negotiating.
LEONARD: We are not negotiating anything. We heard about and later she
    called attention to your film. . . . She asked if we were interested. . . .
KISSINGER: She made a sucker out of me. I would never have agreed to this if
    I had known what she was doing. . . .

President Nixon and Julie Nixon Eisenhower
March 26, 1970, 5:10 p.m.
*After Nixon asks about the bombing of the SAM sites in North Vietnam and one of
the Thai battalions in Laos, he puts his daughter Julie on the line.*

. . . NIXON: . . . We going to take out those SAM sites?
KISSINGER: That's done.
NIXON: Good. And take out those troops coming through the SAM sites?
KISSINGER: That's also done.
NIXON: What about the other six SAM sites?
KISSINGER: After the 4th we will hit them.
NIXON: And the Thai battalion, are we going to get them in there?
KISSINGER: That's also done.
NIXON: And there's going to be no announcement. We are just going to do it.
    We don't have to explain it. It's the Thais defending their own country. . . .
    Here's Julie. She's going to give you a little encouragement.
JULIE: Hi, Dr. Kissinger. . . . Daddy says you are supposed to bomb somebody.
    I don't know what he's talking about.
NIXON: That's a real American. . . .

6

Arms to General Lon Nol, Beecher Leaks, the Invasion of Cambodia and the Hunt for Supplies and COSVN, an Explosion of Protest, and the Heaviest Bombing of North Vietnam Since 1968

April–May 1970

In March 1970, Cambodian leader Prince Norodom Sihanouk was overthrown in a coup and the anticommunist prime minister General Lon Nol took control; Nixon ordered all-out covert support. Secretary of State William Rogers opposed the administration's move to secretly channel millions of dollars to Cambodia for buying weapons through Australia. "Sending money through black bags," he warned, would become known. In April, a leak to William Beecher of the *New York Times* revealed the administration's decision to supply several thousand automatic rifles captured from enemy forces in South Vietnam to the Lon Nol government, infuriating Nixon. "They'll leak us to death," CIA Director Richard Helms feared.

In late April, U.S. and South Vietnamese troops invaded enemy bases in Cambodia along the South Vietnamese border to demonstrate Nixon's toughness to North Vietnam, keep Lon Nol on his feet, destroy the bases, capture enemy weapons and supplies, and seize COSVN, the elusive, mobile enemy command headquarters for operations in South Vietnam. Rogers warned that the invasion would be "traumatic" for Nixon, and indeed protests convulsed the country. "This has to be done fast," Nixon said. "Get the goddamned thing over," he told Kissinger. David Rockefeller, the head of Chase Manhattan Bank, was quite disturbed by the invasion, and more specifically by the explosion of protest, and urged a speedy withdrawal.

The administration unleashed the heaviest air raids north of the DMZ in North Vietnam (and the furthest north) since the Johnson administration's bombing halt in November 1968; it falsely claimed they were "protective reaction" against enemy anti-aircraft fire. A leak to Beecher on the bombing, which the administration hoped would not attract much attention, prompted several more FBI wiretaps in which Kissinger, who was alarmed by the leak, was directly involved. He tried to kill the story. The administration stonewalled the press on the bombing.

Ronald Ziegler
April 15, 1970, 11:25 a.m.
Kissinger tells Press Secretary Ziegler not to reveal they were arming Lon Nol.

ZIEGLER: How should I handle the Cambodian arms situation?

KISSINGER: Say we haven't had a formal request yet. We are in favor of neutrality. Waffle it. I wouldn't indicate we are going to give any. The less visible we do it, the better it is. . . .

President Nixon
April 17, 1970, 11:32 a.m.
Nixon stresses that Lon Nol is his man in Cambodia, not ousted Prince Sihanouk; he wants the Japanese to support him, the CIA to help him, and the firing of officials who disagree.

NIXON: . . . The line of our enemies and many of our people here are playing that Lon Nol may not make it and Sihanouk is our best bet. . . . The Japanese think so. . . . Call in the ambassador and tell him that we consider Lon Nol's prospects excellent and we would find it difficult in our relations with them if they supported the other side. And convey to Sato that we would be upset if Japan doesn't support him. Get the CIA jerks working on Cambodia—I don't see this about two sides. . . .

KISSINGER: [CIA Director Richard] Helms said yesterday after my conversation with you that they would throw it into high gear.

NIXON: Lon Nol is it and I would urge widespread demonstrations against Sihanouk. . . . Get Helms's radio to broadcast in there that Sihanouk is coming in with North Vietnamese liberators. . . . I want everyone in this government to know we are supporting the government in power. . . . Anyone who does not follow this will be fired. . . . There is no possibility of our supporting Sihanouk and we are supporting Lon Nol. Tell Helms to have printed one million leaflets with North Vietnamese and a picture of Sihanouk saying "Liberate Cambodia." Get my point? . . . Get a program and have a report on my desk at 4:00 on how they carried it out.

William Rogers
April 21, 1970, 10:35 a.m.
Secretary of State Rogers is opposed to covertly channeling money to Cambodia for buying weapons through Australia. (Ten million dollars was channeled through Australia.)[1]

> KISSINGER: The president got up at 6:30 this morning, to everyone's dismay. When I came in he called in Helms and me and said to get that money through to the Cambodians through the Australians. . . .
>
> ROGERS: I think he is making decisions off the drop of a hat. We can make a good case for helping but we should do it openly. We can make a good case too that this might not be a good time—this government might not last.
>
> KISSINGER: He feels to put in a lot of aid is self-defeating. What he thinks is to do things to help their morale but not their huge requests. That's why he is doing this.
>
> ROGERS: We should think carefully [about] what we are doing while he is bucking up their morale. . . . If they go down the drain and it becomes known—and I think in this day and age it will be known . . . we are sending money through black bags—we have paid a high price. . . . Take Japan, for instance. They are not doing anything.
>
> KISSINGER: They don't want to expose themselves because they don't think it [the government] will last.
>
> ROGERS: Exactly. . . .
>
> KISSINGER: Do you think there's a prayer for Vietnamization if Cambodia is taken over?
>
> ROGERS: Yes. . . . That assumes that conquering a country is peaches and cream. . . . They would have trouble taking control of it. . . . On this Australian thing, how would it work?
>
> KISSINGER: The Australians would give it as their money.
>
> ROGERS: And we would re-pay it?
>
> KISSINGER: That's right. . . . We can say we didn't want to be publicly involved and it isn't our money. . . .
>
> ROGERS: What worries me is how little any other government wants to get involved. . . .

William Westmoreland
April 21, 1970, 12:05 p.m.
Fearful of an enemy takeover in Cambodia, the administration was considering attacks on enemy base areas there along the South Vietnamese border. Kissinger asks General Westmoreland, the U.S. Army chief of staff who had been commander of

U.S. forces in Vietnam under President Lyndon Johnson and who had recommended cleaning out the bases then, for his opinion.

> . . . KISSINGER: Do you think the Vietnamese can move in and handle it without us, except for artillery and air support?
>
> WESTMORELAND: Yes. . . . With our support on the borders and helicopter and tactical air they can be effective. But I don't think they can clear them out.
>
> KISSINGER: Can we?
>
> WESTMORELAND: We would be hard-pressed in the rainy season, but it could be done. If General Abrams wants to we could do it.
>
> KISSINGER: Would it be worth it?
>
> WESTMORELAND: If we could destroy the COSVN headquarters [the alleged headquarters of North Vietnamese operations in South Vietnam], this would indeed. We have an apparent idea where it is. . . . Troops would have to move into the area and stay there some time. It would be costly with respect to casualties. . . . But we could do it. . . . The Vietnamese would be less effective, but with the proper support they could be effective and would be desirable. . . .

William Westmoreland
April 22, 1970, 10:45 a.m.
Kissinger preps Westmoreland for a big NSC meeting on Cambodia that afternoon, and they discuss options for invading the enemy's bases ("sanctuaries") along the border.

> . . . KISSINGER: Can you see that whoever comes stands firm? . . . The president said to me he can understand the political people thinking of reasons why we shouldn't, but the military usually stands with its commander-in-chief, and he wants to do something.
>
> WESTMORELAND: If I am there I will assure you I will stand that way. . . . We have about a month before the rains will affect operations in that area. But it's important that we take advantage of the good weather remaining.
>
> KISSINGER: We will move next week. . . . I have three operations in mind . . . : (1) doing the thing we are doing at present [South Vietnamese cross-border operations], (2) some large thing, but not for investiture of the sanctuaries, (3) all-out investiture of the sanctuaries. . . .
>
> WESTMORELAND: Let's put it this way. It's essential to do what we want that we deal in division-size force, probably 10,000 men.
>
> KISSINGER: Right. If that case could be made this afternoon it would be a great help. . . . I hope you need a political analyst in the army. I'll never be able to go back to Harvard.
>
> WESTMORELAND: You're very tough. . . .

Richard Helms
April 23, 1970, 9:30 a.m.
Helms and Kissinger discuss the leak to New York Times *reporter William Beecher of a cable on the administration's clandestine provision of the captured enemy rifles to Cambodia.*[2]

> . . . HELMS: Who put out the Beecher story?
>
> KISSINGER: It must be somebody who's seen the cable.
>
> HELMS: It must be State.
>
> KISSINGER: It couldn't be Defense; they weren't opposed to it.
>
> HELMS: That's right. We're now in that situation I've been uncomfortable about all along. They'll leak us to death. The Congress will get ahold of it and kill it before we've had a chance.
>
> KISSINGER: There will be a bloodbath if it keeps up.
>
> HELMS: This is just awful.

William Rogers
April 23, 1970, 12:30 p.m.
Nixon had "exploded" at the Beecher leak and Rogers's people at State were suspects.[3]

> . . . ROGERS: I wish the president wouldn't jump to the conclusion that we leak every time.
>
> KISSINGER: He called people and someone said it had to come out of there.
>
> ROGERS: Who?
>
> KISSINGER: I don't want to say. But it wasn't one of your subordinates.
>
> ROGERS: Why Beecher [a Pentagon correspondent]?
>
> KISSINGER: They leak it in one department and give another guy the story to protect that department. . . .
>
> ROGERS: Laird thought it came from Saigon.
>
> KISSINGER: Except they don't have the cable.
>
> ROGERS: Yes, they did. . . .

President Nixon and John Stennis
April 24, 1970, 4:06 p.m.
The options under consideration in Cambodia included a U.S. attack on the Fishhook enemy base area along the South Vietnamese border (where COSVN was thought to be located) in combination with a South Vietnamese attack with U.S. air support on the Parrot's Beak base area, which Nixon had already authorized. Nixon was by now leaning toward doing both. Kissinger had Senator Stennis, the chairman of the Senate Armed Services Committee, in his office to explain the need for a move into Cambodia; Nixon phoned Kissinger by prearrangement.[4]

KISSINGER: I have talked to Senator Stennis—in fact, he is sitting here now. I would like to report to you his conclusions in his presence. . . . I explained the consequences of a collapse of Cambodia . . . your reluctance to get involved in a war in Cambodia, and your conviction that the aid program as such is not going to be effective for about a year or so. . . . I showed him the map of these base areas which are really part of the war in Vietnam. . . . He said of course his first preference is air action. Second, wherever possible, his preference is South Vietnamese ground forces. If necessary and if helpful to the war effort in South Vietnam, he could see the utility of a raid of several weeks' duration that included American ground forces, as long as it sped up the end of the war in South Vietnam. . . .

NIXON: [Speaking to Stennis] . . . I will sum up what my views are: (1) I don't want us to get into a quagmire of military aid to Cambodia. . . . A few rifles doesn't bother you, does it? . . . With regard to these areas: (1) as far as American activity is concerned, the first choice is air action, including the B-52s, which only you and Senator [Richard] Russell know about [the secret Cambodia bombing]. It's the best-kept secret of the war; (2) we will also consider the possibility of tactical air to follow. But that is all air action on the borders—not inside. . . . As far as any ground action, there will be no ground action with relation to Cambodia. . . . If ground action takes place, we will have the South Vietnamese do it. . . . (3) our other option we will not exercise unless we have to—that of having Americans helping South Vietnamese only if we consider that that will, in the long run, help reduce our casualties in Vietnam. How does that sound to you?

STENNIS: It sounds good—I will be with you on the nailhead.

NIXON: We are not going to get involved in a war in Cambodia. We are not going to occupy Cambodia. . . .

President Nixon
April 24, 1970, 5:06 p.m.
Kissinger was going over the planning for Cambodia with Earle Wheeler and Richard Helms, both advocates of the U.S. Fishhook invasion, when Nixon called. Nixon is gung-ho on the use of tactical air along the border, hitting all of the enemy bases. "If it isn't done, it's your ass," he tells Kissinger.

. . . NIXON: . . . How's the meeting going? Are the boys in good spirits?

KISSINGER: There's nothing like a spanking to make them behave.

NIXON: Do they see it's a big deal?

KISSINGER: Wheeler said he never thought he'd live to see the day he could do one of these operations.

NIXON: He's even pleased with COSVN! This one is a hell of a thing—this pincer thing. . . .

KISSINGER: . . . They have a proposal from Abrams along the lines of your thinking to start tac-air all along the Cambodian frontier, which would include COSVN headquarters, but not pay particular attention to it. It would hit every base area.

NIXON: He thought of it independently? Do it! Do it! And Laird is to follow this up. Tell Wheeler no crap now. I don't want to order tac-air unless it is done. Damn it, they don't do these things. You are in charge. If it isn't done, it's your ass. [Kissinger laughed] . . . Pass a message to Abrams back channel that I have ordered it. When will tac-air begin?

KISSINGER: We will leave it up to Abrams, but no later than when the operation in the Parrot's Beak occurs.

NIXON: The point is it will divert them—bombardment before invasion.

KISSINGER: And to keep them pinned down. . . .

William Rogers
April 28, 1970, 7:20 p.m.
Nixon had by now ordered both the Parrot's Beak and Fishhook attacks.

. . . ROGERS: I really think he should get over this feeling that people aren't behind him. A president, if he wants honest expressions of opinion, has to encourage them. He shouldn't distrust them if they do give honest opinions. . . . I think this will be a traumatic experience for him.

KISSINGER: We will take tremendous heat for a week. We have to stick together.

ROGERS: If it is a great success, there is no problem. If it is a flop, that is another ballgame.

KISSINGER: It isn't that they haven't fouled up things before.

Earle Wheeler
April 30, 1970, 10:37 p.m.
JCS Chairman Wheeler and Kissinger discuss the invasion and heavy air raids being conducted in North Vietnam just above the DMZ; B-52s were now openly bombing Cambodia.[5]

KISSINGER: They better find something in there.

WHEELER: I know they will—I don't think they can move those bunkers. When I talked to Mel, he asked about a certain operation. It is in the air right now.

KISSINGER: We just want them to pay attention.

WHEELER: It was "quite substantial," were the words I got.

KISSINGER: You have good targets up there?

WHEELER: Yes—we have pictures of them. Apparently the boys laid on a good effort.

KISSINGER: You have 48 hours to keep it up. . . . Is there anti-aircraft there? Have they been making it hard?

WHEELER: They have been making it difficult. Their instructions are protective reaction.

KISSINGER: . . . The only thing that breaks my heart is he could have gone three steps further with this speech [that evening announcing the invasion]. But that may come. . . .

WHEELER: I know you will never be welcome again at Harvard. . . .

William Rogers
May 1, 1970, 3:00 p.m.
Nixon's announcement of the invasion had sparked nationwide protests. Rogers mocks the early results of the invasion and urges an early exit.

. . . KISSINGER: Your prediction wasn't very wrong, was it?

ROGERS: No. We can turn it around if the military results are good. Hasn't turned up a lot yet.

KISSINGER: They claim to have turned up so much in the shallow operations.

ROGERS: I saw a film that just looked like they were turning up chicken coops. . . . I think it would be better to get out sooner than six to eight weeks.

KISSINGER: Right. We are hoping for three or four. . . . But if you say three weeks to the public, after 22 days they begin to scream.

President Nixon
May 2, 1970, 12:55 p.m.
Nixon wants Rogers to publicize on a CBS special report fruitful results of the move against COSVN and stresses that the invasion "has to be done fast" (mainly to quell the domestic uproar over it).

NIXON: . . . What have they found on COSVN?

KISSINGER: None of the equipment. They found 100 bunkers and an extensive tunnel complex.

NIXON: Make sure he has that. Let him put that out. . . . I wonder if they are being aggressive enough in the Parrot's Beak area.

KISSINGER: . . . I am told they are doing well for an ARVN production. Looking at their casualties—they have lost 60, which means they must be doing something. . . . The psychological blow to them [the North Vietnamese] is already very considerable.

NIXON: It's considerable only for the American people. This cannot drag on for three or four months. . . . This has to be done fast. The chiefs are not thinking fast enough. Does Abrams understand? They have to take risks and jump in. Bomb whatever is necessary. . . . Get for Rogers some facts on the bunker thing. If we can, get a new picture. . . . Elliot Richardson will be on the NBC special.

KISSINGER: He didn't do well at the congressional briefing. . . .

NIXON: Two days and they don't have much.

KISSINGER: Not in COSVN. But the first 2–10 days they were not going to look for things but to get the enemy out of there.

NIXON: Get that across to Rogers. . . .

Melvin Laird

May 2, 1970, 4:00 p.m.

William Beecher of the New York Times *would come out with a story the next morning that 128 U.S. fighter bombers had conducted a heavy bombing raid in North Vietnam, the largest since the November 1968 bombing halt. Hanoi charged the United States with violating the bombing halt. U.S. officials falsely claimed that the raid was "protective reaction" against anti-aircraft guns. That evening, Kissinger's deputy, Alexander Haig, transmitted a request to the FBI for wiretaps on Beecher and three officials, including Laird's military assistant Robert Pursley (the prime target being Laird). Haig testified later that Nixon directed him to make the request and that Kissinger (who was with him or had just left) "fully agreed with it." Kissinger tells Laird that Beecher and Max Frankel of the* Times *were onto the raid, which the administration had hoped wouldn't attract much notice.*[6]

KISSINGER: I just had a call from Beecher and Frankel. He has a full order on that 134 plane deal. . . .

LAIRD: You mean last night?

KISSINGER: And the night before. He talked to Haig. It's not protective reaction and was authorized at the same time as Fishhook.

LAIRD: I don't know how he picks that up. Did you talk to Bus [Earle Wheeler]?

KISSINGER: Just this minute. He said subject to my talking to you we should put a hold on the other three [raids].

LAIRD: . . . I had better let [Pentagon spokesman Daniel] Henkin handle this. . . . I cannot believe it came out of the General Staff. I have not told Henkin.

KISSINGER: That thought has crossed my mind. In my staff it's me, Haig, and one other person. Did you tell Bill about it?

LAIRD: By telephone but not the messages.

KISSINGER: This is frankly a military-type leak. Who else would give a damn about planes?

LAIRD: . . . We will have to handle it in Saigon about it being north and a plane shot down. Tell Frankel that we lost an aircraft and they fired at our aircraft along the DMZ.

KISSINGER: How about those other three things? Should we stick with them that were authorized yesterday?

LAIRD: I think we have got to. Don't you? I hate to back off right now. . . .

Melvin Laird
May 2, 1970, 4:03 p.m.
They decide to postpone two other raids.

LAIRD: That story is coming out of Hanoi.

KISSINGER: The first story came out of Hanoi. . . . Frankel called in and said he had hot poop from Beecher on 134 planes.

LAIRD: . . . Their reporter was in the strike zone. We are using the protective reaction story. . . . I think we should slip the other 24 hours.

KISSINGER: It's probably underway now.

LAIRD: One, but we have two more going. . . . One strike will go, but hold the other two.

Daniel Henkin
May 2, 1970, 4:12 p.m.
Kissinger tells Defense spokesman Henkin that he will have to lie if he calls Max Frankel, the Washington bureau chief of the New York Times.

. . . HENKIN: I told Beecher we conduct protective reaction strikes whenever there are crew casualties and plane losses. . . .

KISSINGER: Should I call Frankel? It's not normal for me not to return calls. I had better not because I will have to lie.

HENKIN: We never lie.

KISSINGER: We are not that moral, except for Ziegler.

HENKIN: We just don't say. . . .

Max Frankel
May 2, 1970, 4:45 p.m.
Kissinger tries to kill the story.

KISSINGER: . . . Do you have people listening in on this? . . . I simply want to say that in the light of a lot of things that if you blow up this story it will be strongly against our national interest. This is simply my personal judgment. . . .

Max Frankel
May 2, 1970, 4:55 p.m.

KISSINGER: Henkin is going to call you. He will give you as many of the facts as we can. The other comment I made to you is personal. I don't want to be written up in the history of the *New York Times*. . . . This is one of those things in which I am talking as Henry Kissinger. . . .

Earle Wheeler
May 2, 1970, 6:00 p.m.
Kissinger instructs Wheeler to continue the air raids.

KISSINGER: I just had my skin taken off on those flights. He [Nixon] says he will take the heat and it's none of my business on what heat he takes. The policy is that we have been fired at from these areas. . . . Hit those three targets. Get your planes up there. . . .

Melvin Laird
May 2, 1970, 6:10 p.m.
Kissinger informs Laird that Nixon wants to keep the bombs falling and to "just stonewall it."

KISSINGER: I just talked to the president at length. You were right in your attitude. We should just hang tough. He also ordered those three strikes to go forward. . . . Make sure they go today. He wants you—your instinct was right—just stonewall it. . . . Will you lay it on immediately?
LAIRD: . . . We might as well get this heat over with.

Spiro Agnew
May 2, 1970, 6:30 p.m.
Kissinger tells Vice President Agnew to stonewall it too.

KISSINGER: All hell is breaking loose on this exercise north of the DMZ. Someone leaked figures. The president figures since he is taking heat he might as well continue. He wants to be sure that if they ask you tomorrow you don't know the details . . . but our policy is protective [reaction].

Anything that shoots at us we will fire back. We stonewall it coldly. It won't give you too much pain.

AGNEW: Not a bit.

KISSINGER: The president feels he has crossed his Rubicon. . . .

H. R. Haldeman
May 4, 1970, 1:42 p.m.
Haldeman says the shooting of student protesters by National Guardsmen at Kent State, killing four, "doesn't hurt us." ("This makes it a lot worse," he wrote in his diaries.)[7]

. . . KISSINGER: I have good news for you. We are hitting another base area tonight and one a night this week.

HALDEMAN: I have news for you. Three killed at Kent State college. One student and two National Guard. They are using guns. That doesn't hurt us. . . .

President Nixon
May 4, 1970, 4:45 p.m.
Nixon and Kissinger agree that they'll get blamed for Kent State, and Nixon says a national student strike over Cambodia doesn't worry him "if it's peaceful."

. . . NIXON: At Kent State there were four or five killed today. But that place has been bad for quite some time—it has been rather violent.

KISSINGER: It was all the last week before this. But now they'll blame it on us.

NIXON: Oh, of course. . . . What about the student strike tomorrow? If it's peaceful, it doesn't bother me. . . . You don't know what will happen. If they're out of classes they'll be able to raise hell.

KISSINGER: They may hold teach-ins.

NIXON: That doesn't bother me. . . . We have to stand as hard as a rock. Everybody's been through this: de Gaulle, Marcos. . . . If countries begin to be run by the children, god help us.

KISSINGER: That's right. Of course, student disorders don't hurt us politically.

NIXON: They don't if it doesn't appear that we caused them. . . .

President Nixon
May 4, 1970, 8:20 p.m.
Kissinger reports that Soviet diplomats were quite friendly with him despite the invasion.

KISSINGER: I just got back a little while ago from the Soviet embassy and I think we have their attention. They were falling all over me. . . . The atmosphere was very, very cordial and they wouldn't do that unless they were under instructions. . . . If they had wanted to show dissatisfaction, I wouldn't have been invited and they wouldn't have fallen all over me. . . . They were worried. I was friendly and said everything we have said to you still goes. . . . May say a few things at the UN, and Dobrynin may come back with some sort of nasty message. . . . They wanted reassurance there wouldn't be toughening. . . . The mood there was one to keep relations. . . .

President Nixon
May 5, 1970, 7:40 p.m.
Nixon asks Kissinger to raise the morale of his top aides Haldeman and Ehrlichman, and he wants to get the invasion over with and the military to move more quickly. But they should "take a few casualties" to capture more impressive enemy caches of weapons and supplies. He and Kissinger expect big caches soon.

NIXON: I was just talking to Bob and he has, of course, got these enormous problems—meeting with John Ehrlichman on the student thing and all. . . . You constantly want to keep him bucked up. . . . The main thing is the military has to get off its fat butt.

KISSINGER: Abrams is starting three more operations tonight.

NIXON: Good. Get them done. You understand I have to start announcing next Tuesday that we are getting out. . . . How about Parrot's Beak?

KISSINGER: Parrot's Beak is mostly ARVN.

NIXON: That doesn't matter. I would like to get out. . . . The moment we can announce withdrawal we will be in good shape. . . . We have to get out of the area as soon as it is completed. I want to get out a day early. Get the goddamned thing over and get out of there.

KISSINGER: By next Thursday?

NIXON: We may have to say we will be able to do it sooner. . . . What about the caches?

KISSINGER: They are beginning to find a lot of stuff now. . . . The problem is they have to sweep the area to make sure there are no large hidden forces. As soon as they do that they will move in forces and start digging up earth. The other base areas are much smaller.

NIXON: The main thing now is to get out of COSVN more impressive caches. . . . Even take a few casualties in order to show [the caches] by the end of the week. I don't think they will stay in until the end of June. Don't let them think they will be in there. The whole thing is I know the army always takes longer than they need. They have to move faster.

KISSINGER: I am really driving them. I have asked Wheeler for a schedule of when they will be out of various places.

NIXON: The main thing is to get some big stuff fairly soon. I have a feeling we are going to get some real big stuff in the next few days. . . .

KISSINGER: I am convinced we are going to get large caches.

NIXON: I think it will have an enormous effect on the enemy. . . . Let me suggest when you talk to Bob, talk to John too. He is terribly concerned about the riots. Get to him the point that we can't cave to the radicals. . . .

David Rockefeller

May 6, 1970, 10:56 p.m.

The Chase Manhattan Bank chief executive is troubled by the invasion of Cambodia and the explosion of protest and advocates a quick withdrawal, "the sooner the better." Kissinger tells him the invasion is "a great success."

. . . ROCKEFELLER: I must say I think time is of the essence. I am terribly disturbed by what one hears on every hand. It is distressing.

KISSINGER: What people have to ask themselves is what is the cause and what is the symptom—and whether trying to take weapons away from them with which Americans are being killed, and to implement a policy of withdrawal, justifies wrecking universities and the very fabric of our society.

ROCKEFELLER: I met with 40 students from the Columbia international center and had a chance to tell them some of the things you and Bill Rogers said. . . . I think it was useful. But on the other hand, there is no question that the more moderate ones are terribly upset. I think myself if you can succeed quickly, all can be retrieved.

KISSINGER: Certainly, when I was young, I often felt intensely about something for which I felt ashamed of a few months later. The question is by yielding to them now, are we helping them?

ROCKEFELLER: If it drags on for a couple of months, it can be very difficult to—

KISSINGER: We are almost certain to conclude it by June 15.

ROCKEFELLER: The sooner the better. . . . How is it going?

KISSINGER: Militarily and diplomatically, it is a great success. . . . The cohesion of our society depends on the leaders sticking together no matter what their reservations are.

ROCKEFELLER: It's very serious indeed.

KISSINGER: The time for telling the students is after this immediate situation.

ROCKEFELLER: Deal with this as quickly as possible. . . .

Otis Chandler

May 6, 1970, 11:10 p.m.

Chandler, the publisher of the Los Angeles Times, *is also worried. Kissinger tells him, too, that the invasion was going well and says "the faculties are the problem" more than the students. He disparages Yale President Kingman Brewster.*

CHANDLER: What's going on in Indochina, may I ask? We are confused.

KISSINGER: All we want to do is clean the supplies out of these base areas. We have no intention of staying. We will be out by July 1 and probably well before then. We will be winding up some the end of next week. From the military and diplomatic points of view, it is going very well. . . . The military objective is being achieved, which is to disrupt their supply system. . . .

CHANDLER: These kids are not sophisticated. On the surface, the president's San Clemente speech said things are going well—150,000 [U.S. troops] are coming out, Vietnamization is working well—and since then there has been such an abrupt change. We are bombing north of the DMZ, and then there's this Cambodian thing. The kids interpret it as the president changing his whole policy. That is why the campuses are on fire. . . .

KISSINGER: . . . Our problem is the faculties and administrators. I had Stanford students in today. The kids were fine—they didn't like it, but they are understanding. The faculties are the problem. . . . The immediate problem is to get through this crisis without being driven off by a student rebellion. We have to go through with it now. Would there be any negotiations with the Soviets or the Chinese if our government was so weak and the leadership group so feeble that they can be driven off by universities on these issues? The second problem is how do we re-establish communications with these kids? I talked to the president tonight. We will make this a top priority as soon as the current operation is successfully concluded. . . .

CHANDLER: . . . We have been for you and the president all along the line. I have been counseling our editorial writers not to go overboard. . . . Is there any way of slowing Kingman Brewster down? He is hot at the moment. . . .

KISSINGER: He's a cheap grandstander. . . . These things Kingman Brewster is doing [against the war and his statements on a Black Panther trial in New Haven] are an abdication of his generation. They are looking for heroes, not buddies.

CHANDLER: I thought maybe somebody could talk to him.

KISSINGER: I tried to one night—he is extremely emotional. . . .

Milton Katz
May 7, 1970, 9:35 a.m.
Harvard professor Katz and Kissinger consider a possible meeting between Kissinger and Brewster.

… KISSINGER: I understand that Kingman Brewster is putting out a petition. The basic problem is that nothing these petitions can do is relevant to these operations, which will be over in a few weeks. It cannot be in anybody's interest for us to collapse in the face of this. It's an exalting feeling to be at one with your students, but that is what made Nazis in the '30s. A leader should put a brake on emotion. At least Kingman should come and talk to me. I don't want to call him, but I know he is a friend of yours.

KATZ: … My offhand reaction is that … you should call him. … He has an emotional problem and he has made a couple of remarks he will regret. … I wrote him a different kind of note—it was a tranquilizing note as a friend standing by him in a time of stress. … At a time like this he needed a friend who wouldn't knife him in the back. …

William Rogers
May 7, 1970, 9:03 p.m.
Rogers bemoans the campus protests and attacks by Agnew and Nixon on student protesters, and he and Kissinger are dismayed by a White House statement implying they'd found COSVN, the alleged enemy command headquarters, which the White House was under pressure to find.[8]

… ROGERS: These student protests are greater than any of us anticipated. One hundred thirty-six universities are now closed. If one could talk individually with them, we could change their minds. … The faculty have all the credentials of erudition and thoughtfulness, but they are more emotional than the youngsters. Most of it is psychological—it's all mixed up with what Agnew said, the president's unfortunate statement about bums, their worry that they will be drafted. … One word of caution I would like to make— on what we find in Cambodia, I hope we don't get so eager that we don't overstate what we have accomplished. … Didn't the White House put out a statement today that we found COSVN? …

KISSINGER: I saw it on the ticker. If the White House put it out, it was unauthorized. We haven't found it. … It's conceivable that one of these salesmen put it out.

ROGERS: We surely have a lot of salesmen … telling people what to say. …

Spiro Agnew

May 8, 1970, 11:15 a.m.

Nixon had reportedly assured university presidents in a meeting with them the day before that hostile comments about campus dissent would cease, specifically referring to Agnew. Kissinger tells Agnew that the report was inaccurate. Agnew did not think that he should shut up, as Nixon indeed wanted.[9]

KISSINGER: I wanted you to know I was at that meeting with the president yesterday. He did not say anything like the papers reported. These presidents made an impassioned speech about muzzling you, to which he said absolutely nothing. They said they hoped you weren't going to make an inflammatory speech in Georgia on Saturday night. . . . There was absolutely no discussion of muzzling you. . . .

AGNEW: The thing that bothers me is that yesterday [his aide C. Stanley] Blair got a call from Haldeman who indicated he had direct instructions from the president that I should stop making this kind of speech, to cool things down and whatnot, and I am out here in Los Angeles with the press over me like a tent, asking me, were you really muzzled? And the whole thing comes just as I am going on *The David Frost Show* for 90 minutes. Haldeman said I was to cool off this stuff and this was instructions from the president. I told him if the president wants this, I want him to call me, I don't want anything secondhand. I haven't heard anything from him, but it has put me in a box.

KISSINGER: . . . My own view is that you haven't said a tenth of what these bastards have said about us. I haven't called them names, and they are calling me a war criminal.

AGNEW: . . . It made the interview very difficult because I didn't know what to do. I felt like I had had my legs shot out from under me. . . . All of a sudden I had a bunch of vultures all over me. You can't imagine the glee with which the press descended on me. . . .

Robert McNamara

May 10, 1970, no time

The former defense secretary commiserates with Kissinger.

MCNAMARA: Time is a salve. Don't think America is going to fall apart.

KISSINGER: Members of the establishment have an obligation to keep our society together. . . . The kids are all right—the professors are appalling.

MCNAMARA: Talked with a professor the bank was considering hiring; he was an absolute nut—completely unreasonable. Wanted to organize a general strike. Would tear country apart. . . . Would never have done Cambodia, but have strong belief in correctness of action. . . . I strongly believe in your course. . . .

President Nixon

May 12, 1970, 6:45 p.m.

Nixon recounts his first meeting with his "special adviser" on campuses and youth, Vanderbilt Chancellor Alexander Heard.

> . . . NIXON: . . . One thing Heard said was he was horrified that the students on his campus were wearing armbands with American flags on them taking off after the demonstrators. What's wrong with that? I really worked him over.
>
> KISSINGER: He looked pretty shaken. I saw him in the hall.
>
> NIXON: . . . What really shook him was I said I don't think we should [bestow] blood money on university professors who don't believe in national defense. You should have heard him squeal. These people were just cowering when they heard that. Your friend [Harvard President Nathan] Pusey isn't going to get any more blood money. . . .

President Nixon

May 22, 1970, 6:20 p.m.

Nixon wants Secretary of Labor George Shultz and other staffers to quit moaning about the administration's credibility gap and to fire CIA Director Richard Helms.

> . . . NIXON: . . . Shultz and others were saying that there was a credibility gap. . . .
>
> KISSINGER: Shultz has been agonizing about it for a year. He's too sensitive. . . .
>
> NIXON: . . . I think you should shape up the staff and cabinet. They are all too shell-shocked. We should say, good god, we've done something good. . . . They shouldn't be apologetic about the credibility gap—there is none. . . . After hearing Helms today, after November he goes. He doesn't have any character. Why don't people stand up and say what they believe?
>
> KISSINGER: First they have to believe in something. . . .

President Nixon

May 26, 1970, 2:45 p.m.

Nixon is determined to get Indonesian military assistance to the Lon Nol government in Cambodia. President Suharto of Indonesia was in town. (Indonesia supplied thousands of AK-47 assault rifles.)[10]

> . . . NIXON: They should provide assistance and we will replace it. . . . Let's get going on that subject. I assume they are following up on getting some captured equipment over here.

KISSINGER: That is being done. . . . I didn't realize how intensely interested they were in Cambodia.

NIXON: Of course. This fellow is no Marxist. . . . It is vitally important to have other countries help them in some way. Now here is a country that is willing to help. We tried to get the Thais. But now this country wants to help. What in the hell happened here? . . . If Indonesia wants to send this ammunition, they should do it. . . . I ordered this three weeks ago. . . .

Brian McDonnell, Cambodia and the Press, U.S. Air Strikes and South Vietnamese in Cambodia, Frictions with State, and a Tenuous Middle East Cease-Fire and Clashes over Credit

June–August 1970

In June 1970, Kissinger struck up a friendship with a young pacifist, Brian McDonnell, who'd been fasting in Lafayette Park across the street from the White House in protest of the invasion of Cambodia. Against White House opposition, Kissinger met with McDonnell to try to keep him from "starving to death." The administration was still trying to get its story out on the success and rationale of the Cambodia invasion. It was also conducting air strikes in Cambodia in support of the South Vietnamese troops still there.

In July, Egypt's President Gamal Abdel Nasser accepted a State Department proposal for a cease-fire in the Suez Canal zone and renewed negotiations. Israel subsequently accepted it too, but not before receiving assurances of U.S. weapons shipments and threatening to take out Egyptian surface-to-air missiles on the west side of the Suez Canal. Secretary of State William Rogers had opposed giving Israel the weapons if it delayed the cease-fire and accused Kissinger of screwing up the negotiations with Israel through his separate channel to them (feeling it gave them "two ways to play it" and that he should "take the lead"). He and Kissinger fought over turf and who would get the credit for the cease-fire.

Leonard Garment
June 2, 1970, 10:07 a.m.
*Kissinger tells Nixon adviser Garment that he wants to meet with McDonnell, who'd
vowed to fast until the Cambodian invasion ended or he met with Nixon. The actress
Shirley MacLaine had asked Kissinger to try to persuade McDonnell to end his fast.*[1]

> KISSINGER: A good friend of mine asked me to see this fellow that is starving
> to death. While our public relations people are opposed, I am for it. I un-
> derstand you know him. . . . If it could be done without publicity, I would
> like to tell him that if he is fasting to get us out of Cambodia, it's a stupid
> sacrifice. . . .
>
> GARMENT: He wants to see the president.
>
> KISSINGER: Out of the question. Let me see him first. . . .
>
> GARMENT: A minister buddy of McDonnell said he would end the fast if he
> saw the president.
>
> KISSINGER: Maybe I can get him to stop his fast. . . . Invite him to lunch! . . .

Leonard Garment
June 2, 1970, 12:00 p.m.
*Garment arranged a meeting with McDonnell at the home of the Reverend John
Turnbull.*[2]

> GARMENT: Okay, Henry, we are all set. It can be any time tomorrow morn-
> ing. He and his co-faster, the ex–West Point fellow, have been staying with
> a bunch of other people. So this Reverend Turnbull—
>
> KISSINGER: Do you think they would make a public splash of it?
>
> GARMENT: No. Let's do it quietly and let them give it out later.
>
> KISSINGER: I am doing this on my own. I will tell Haldeman afterwards. I just
> don't see how we can let anyone fast to death on that issue. . . .
>
> GARMENT: The indication I had from Dr. Turnbull was that he might be
> persuaded to stop his fast if he sees you or the president. . . .
>
> KISSINGER: . . . I will tell them I have done it afterward. Then if it gets out, it
> gets out.
>
> GARMENT: Why don't you touch base with Haldeman first?
>
> KISSINGER: Because I mentioned it to him this morning and he had a sour sort
> of reaction. . . .

Alice McDonnell
June 8, 1970, 3:10 p.m.
*McDonnell's wife sternly presses Kissinger on her husband's request for a meeting with
Nixon.*

MCDONNELL: Brian wanted to know mainly whether you were able to see President Nixon regarding the possibility of a meeting.

KISSINGER: I have talked about our conversation with him.

MCDONNELL: What was his response?

KISSINGER: I told Brian . . . that I would do my best to arrange a meeting after he starts eating. . . .

MCDONNELL: We were under the impression that it was going on, the meeting, whether or not he will go off the fast. . . . You have not talked to President Nixon and asked him?

KISSINGER: I have, yes.

MCDONNELL: What did he say?

KISSINGER: It would destroy the whole thing if I told you and start a set of newspaper stories. . . . He was very impressed.

MCDONNELL: . . . An appointment would have to be made after he goes off the fast?

KISSINGER: Yes, and I would support it strongly. I would appreciate it if we could keep these to ourselves and not in the newspapers.

MCDONNELL: The conversation we are having now? Did that embarrass you, especially with the president?

KISSINGER: No, I did it on my own. . . .

David Packard

June 9, 1970, 8:25 a.m.

Kissinger tells Deputy Defense Secretary Packard that Nixon was enraged over a front-page story in the New York Times *that said U.S. military commanders and intelligence estimated that only 30–40 percent of the enemy's arms and supplies in its bases in Cambodia had been found.*[3]

KISSINGER: I've just talked to the president. He's almost beside himself over the *New York Times* story of only 40 percent being picked up.

PACKARD: I don't know what we can do.

KISSINGER: I'll tell you what he wants to do. He wants the name of the person who talked and he wants him fired by noon. . . .

PACKARD: I don't know how these reporters make these numbers out.

KISSINGER: They don't make them out. They are told these figures. They talk to people. . . . We've been through this twice before. . . .

President Nixon

June 9, 1970, 3:15 p.m.

Nixon and Kissinger denigrate an antiwar letter by Nobel Prize winners.

... NIXON: ... What in the name of god has this come to, Henry? Have you
ever heard such drivel as that? ... They all suck around. ... What do they
want us to do? They don't like it because they are not consulted. ... Tab A is
a list of Nobel winners and all have received funds from the government. ...
We are going to stop subsidizing people who don't support us. ...

KISSINGER: For two decades pure scientists were thought to be equally wise
outside their fields. They don't really understand what they are saying. They
are naive beyond expression. ...

David Packard
June 13, 1970, 2:05 p.m.
*Kissinger pushes Packard to carry out tactical air strikes in Cambodia that Nixon
ordered.*

... KISSINGER: The one thing that is maddening is to send over a presidential
order and have nothing happen.

PACKARD: There's not much that can be done now in Cambodia. ... We can't
use tactical air for attacks on towns unless we have ground control with it.
We can't run out there with tactical air and get the thing settled. It would
be helpful if he understood the problem. ... We can't tell much by reconnaissance. By the time the pictures are developed the people have moved.
You can't fire from the air without someone to tell you who's the enemy and
who isn't. It's a little more complex than it appears. ... It would be helpful
if he understood what can and can't be done.

KISSINGER: His present impression is that nothing is being done. ...

David Packard
June 16, 1970, 8:35 a.m.
A front-page New York Times *article that morning said South Vietnamese and Cam-
bodian troops had failed in three attempts to expel the outnumbered enemy from
Kompong Speu, which Nixon is hot to capture.*

KISSINGER: The president just read the newspaper and read that there are
1,500 troops in Kompong Speu and 5,000 on the outside. He said anyone
who says he can't find targets there now should look for another job.

PACKARD: Well, then maybe we should look for another job.

KISSINGER: He wants that road opened if it takes the whole Vietnamese army
and he wants a report in two hours, not of what can't be done, but what can
be done.

PACKARD: The problem is they're holed up inside the town. We've got it surrounded. But the trouble with air strikes—the enemy's in the middle of the
town—we could bomb it but it would destroy the town.

KISSINGER: No, don't do that. My job is to transmit orders, but also to make some sense of them. . . .

President Nixon
June 17, 1970, 9:12 a.m.
Nixon advises Kissinger how to handle Max Frankel and Hedrick Smith of the New York Times *for a story on the administration's decision-making on the Cambodian invasion, and he wants a report "every hour" on what is going on in Cambodia, fearing it might go down the tubes. He grouses that the South Vietnamese forces there are just "rambling around."*

. . . NIXON: One thing you have to watch for: I do not think that Frankel is interested in the process and he is using that as bait because he knows that you want to get that out. Rick Smith has been reporting from Vietnam and they are the most distorted stories of any. Smith is very clever. I met him in Israel in '67 and he will suck up to you and make it appear he is for you. I just want you to know what they are after. I think they are after something else. I don't mind you seeing him. Just be sure we give them what we want. He has been out there and his reporting has been very bad. You have not one but two enemies, and Smith is a very clever little boy. . . . Just remember that he is out to get you. . . . He is pro–Viet Cong. He is the worst of the major reporters. . . .

KISSINGER: [Frankel] said they have concluded that this whole thing was more carefully thought through than they thought. . . .

NIXON: . . . He is nice and pleasant . . . but as mean as a snake. . . . I would be quite cool about the fact that the *Times* has done a bad job of reporting. Be tough. . . . Some Cambodian brigadier general says there is five divisions ready to pounce on Phnom Penh. I doubt if they are, but that kind of talk is bad. It presents psychological problems. What is that general doing that we sent out? . . . They sit there in Phnom Penh and they are not really getting out. That general is supposed to get in there and see what's needed this week. . . . I want a report at 5:00. Intelligence, arms in, and what you have done to get Vietnamese in. . . . Let them [Packard and Moorer] know I want a report every hour. . . . I read there was another town retaken but the road is still closed. . . . They don't have the staying power. . . . They are rambling around. . . . They took this town and didn't get anybody. They weren't there to get people but to scare people. . . . More Vietnamese, flotilla up the Mekong, fly in weapons. It's a war of nerves now. . . . I want a report at 5:00 today of what they have done. I consider it of the highest urgency, and you cannot see me without it. . . . People will say that if Cambodia is lost it's what the whole thing was about. . . .

Ronald Ziegler
June 18, 1970, 10:02 a.m.
Washington Post gossip columnist Maxine Cheshire had reported that the actress Jill St. John had been Kissinger's dinner partner at a Hollywood party months earlier, had seen him since, and met Rogers in his company.[4]

ZIEGLER: How should I deal with these questions I am getting? May I say that I introduced you to Jill St. John?

KISSINGER: I have not been so mad since I came here. . . . Rogers came over to my table in a restaurant. What am I supposed to do, shoot him?

ZIEGLER: I know her very well.

KISSINGER: How should I handle it?

ZIEGLER: Laugh it off. Cool it. Don't show you are concerned.

KISSINGER: I don't know where the press agent gets that on Mexico City. [He said Kissinger had invited St. John to attend World Cup soccer matches with him there during an official visit] . . . I am beside myself. It's character assassination.

ZIEGLER: You are the envy of everyone in D.C. That's not character assassination! . . .

William Rogers
June 18, 1970, 10:55 a.m.
Kissinger says he did not talk to Max Frankel for the Times *article about the administration's decision-making on the Cambodia invasion, and they discuss lies by Melvin Laird.*

ROGERS: I have a request from the *New York Times.* They want to talk to me about Cambodia. They say they talked to Mel.

KISSINGER: They have not talked to me about it. Who is it? Frankel?

ROGERS: Yes.

KISSINGER: He called me and said he wanted to come in and review . . . the decision process. I had at first scheduled a tentative appointment for yesterday and then canceled it because I wanted to think about it.

ROGERS: I don't think we should do it. . . . What they did in the Cuban missile crisis—they got a whole team and wrote a story about everybody's views.

KISSINGER: I can tell you now I will not tell them anything about anybody's views. . . . The only reason I would talk is to get out the White House perspective. . . . It really doesn't do anybody any good.

ROGERS: What happens is in the case of Mel he has been saying a lot of things and he doesn't tell the truth.

KISSINGER: That is true. He has been putting out stories he did not know about the strikes [in Cambodia]. He was sitting there when the president ordered them. He knew about every one of them.

ROGERS: He also put out the story he was the architect of the final plan and it was his idea.

KISSINGER: He said he enlarged the WSAG. It has had the same members all the time except for three days. . . .

William Rogers
June 23, 1970, 9:10 a.m.
Rogers is irritated that Kissinger talked to Max Frankel and Hedrick Smith of the New York Times *for its piece on the Cambodia invasion after Nixon had said not to talk to them and Kissinger had suggested it was not in their interest.*

ROGERS: . . . Why did the president change his mind?

KISSINGER: He got a report that they were running it all over town. The only thing I gave them was what meetings took place, no substance. . . . He just wanted to get across that there was a regular procedure followed. The only thing they got is a calendar.

ROGERS: And the people who attended?

KISSINGER: Yes.

ROGERS: That puts me on the spot—I am the only one who hasn't seen them now.

KISSINGER: They have already seen lower-level people at State. . . .

ROGERS: I don't think so. . . . Did you tell them about the time I wasn't able to go on the *Sequoia* [the presidential yacht]?

KISSINGER: No, that I specifically did not tell them. . . .

ROGERS: . . . The president always says don't tell anybody a thing, and then we wind up telling them. . . .

William Rogers
June 23, 1970, 9:15 a.m.

ROGERS: When did you see them?

KISSINGER: Late last night, about 6:30.

ROGERS: The president is unfair to me on these things. If you and I have an agreement [not to see them] he shouldn't change it without giving us a chance to talk about it. . . . It puts me on the spot when I haven't seen them and then I have to go back and say I'll see them. . . . I really do get upset about the lack of coordination. I think it's a bad mistake. He starts saying let's not talk about this to anyone at all and we end up with everybody seeing them except me. . . . You should have told him about our agreement. . . .

Mr. Yoshida
June 24, 1970, 6:20 p.m.
Kissinger informs Yoshida, the emissary of Japanese Prime Minister Eisaku Sato on the negotiations to limit Japanese textile exports to the United States, that the talks have collapsed.

YOSHIDA: Is that Mr. Jones?

KISSINGER: Yes, it is.

YOSHIDA: This is Yoshida. I conveyed your message to my friend [Sato] soon after we talked together yesterday and he understood.

KISSINGER: I understand, but the talks have broken down today. . . . And the negotiations are finished.

YOSHIDA: I am very sorry. I was concerned. That is why I called you.

KISSINGER: Your people said that they couldn't deliver their industry and that was that. . . .

President Nixon
July 12, 1970, no time
Nixon and Kissinger disparage intellectuals, and Kissinger agrees with Nixon that AFL-CIO President George Meany merits more respect than Harvard President Nathan Pusey. Nixon says that all of the intelligentsia's predictions about the Cambodia invasion were wrong, and Kissinger points out other predictions intellectuals made that proved wrong; Nixon is eager to publicize them.

. . . NIXON: I was looking at the news magazines and I saw that *Life* had an article in their front cover . . . that Cambodia was . . . a disaster. . . . There really is a death wish, isn't it?

KISSINGER: The American intellectual community has an investment in defeat. . . . For a number of reasons. First of all, they predicted it. Second, because they are afraid that if this succeeds other things like it might be tried. Thirdly, because they so distrust this country. . . .

NIXON: Well, they only trust, what, themselves and their brilliance? Good god, you put them in charge of anything. . . . Look at this bastard [his campus adviser Alexander] Heard. Put him in charge of something, he comes up with nothing. Absolute drivel, drivel. I'll tell you about the intellectual community. I used to have great respect for the professors . . . but I have none now. Because they never come up with anything. They never have any damn guts. I have a hell of a lot more respect for George Meany than I do for the president of Harvard. . . . Don't you?

KISSINGER: Oh, no comparison. The labor people have had to learn that words alone do not achieve objectives and they have had a very hard school. . . .

NIXON: . . . I have an intuition that the Cambodian thing came out better than we could have dreamed. Look, the Chinese didn't intervene and we didn't put the Russians and Chinese together. I think you ought to have a backgrounder sometime and point that out. That these are the things that the intelligentsia wrote. . . . And another thing, that we would have huge casualties, that Cambodia would fall. . . . Every prediction has proved wrong. . . . Tell it to somebody who is really writing it and will get it out, and will say, you know, those who commented on Cambodia probably would like to go back and burn their columns. Use that phrase. They all proved wrong, didn't they?

KISSINGER: That is certainly true. But so has the intellectual community on almost every foreign policy prediction in the last 10 years. They predicted that the [1968] bombing halt would lead to fruitful negotiations, it hasn't happened; they predicted that the Soviets would help us, that hasn't happened . . . they predicted that if you went to ABM, it would hurt SALT, the opposite has happened. They said you couldn't get along with the Russians, that hasn't happened.

NIXON: We have gotten along better with the Russians better than anybody else.

KISSINGER: Certainly far better than Kennedy. So almost every prediction has turned out to be incorrect.

NIXON: . . . Sit down with an intelligent intellectual sometime and, I mean, get it printed. . . . Say, all right, I'll give you this as an exclusive if you will use it. Every prediction has proved to be wrong. And they better look to their problem a little rather than to ours. . . .

Ronald Ziegler
July 15, 1970, 9:35 a.m.
William Rogers had said at a press conference that the short-term prospects for the Vietnam peace negotiations after the setbacks the enemy suffered in Cambodia were "not too bright."[5]

ZIEGLER: What is this Rogers—

KISSINGER: The SOB is trying to prove that everything the White House has done since January 20, 1969, has been wrong and he is trying to save the country. This is hardly the thing to say.

ZIEGLER: There must be some unseen subtlety that my lack of foreign policy experience doesn't comprehend. Is it part of some grand strategy?

KISSINGER: There's no grand—it's a stupid statement because it will be used to prove we haven't tried in the negotiations. . . .

Joseph Kraft
July 15, 1970, 5:00 p.m.
Kissinger denies to syndicated columnist Kraft any differences between him and Rogers.

> KISSINGER: On the alleged conflict between Rogers and me, there may be something I am obtuse to, but I am not aware of it. . . . There's no tension that I am aware of. These policy disagreements appear in the papers but not in personal confrontations. . . .

Joseph Sisco
July 17, 1970, 9:30 a.m.
They take up a prospective visit by Israeli Prime Minister Golda Meir, which Sisco wants to discourage, suspecting she will ask for aid, but does not want to turn down for political reasons.

> KISSINGER: [Israeli Ambassador to the United States Yitzhak] Rabin was in yesterday and—
>
> SISCO: Yes.
>
> KISSINGER: Your voice falls immediately—and I told you a few weeks ago he wanted to know what I thought of Golda Meir coming over. . . . I told him I didn't think much of it. He said yesterday she is determined to come for a speech. Just a pretext. I said I would have to talk to the president.
>
> SISCO: . . . She probably thinks from an internal point of view it's essential. For us it would be better if she didn't come at all. I think we should discourage her. But if she does come she is not to come here with a shopping bag. If it's characterized as anything more than to give a speech at the UN and informal tour with the president of what's going on, but if she says anything about economic aid or military aid then she had better not come at all. . . . The president cannot put this on paper. Two months before elections he cannot turn it down, but from a domestic point of view [if] she comes here putting forth demands then it becomes another problem regarding elections and the Jewish community. And this is not lost on the Israelis that she has leverage here during the elections. . . .

Joseph Sisco
July 23, 1970, 9:45 a.m.
In a promising development, Egypt's President Gamal Abdel Nasser had accepted a U.S. proposal for a cease-fire in the Suez Canal zone and renewed negotiations in the Arab–Israeli conflict, a Rogers and Sisco initiative that Kissinger had opposed, believing he could manage the conflict better than State.[6]

SISCO: . . . Don't be too shocked if there is blood and thunder out of Nasser.
If they have accepted this proposal, they will have to cover their tracks, particularly with the Palestinians. So whatever comes out of their people will
not be too surprising if it is strong. We should watch our intelligence to see
whether the Russians primarily influenced the Egyptians or the Egyptians
influenced the Russians. . . . I have the feeling the Russians moved them
toward a more constructive reply. . . .

KISSINGER: That's what I think. . . .

Yitzhak Rabin

August 5, 1970, 11:10 a.m.

*Kissinger complains to Israeli Ambassador Rabin about not being forewarned of
Israeli military actions. Israel, which had earlier agreed in principle but with real
reservations to accept the cease-fire proposal, had continued daily air raids against
Egyptian positions along the Suez Canal, where the cease-fire was supposed to take
place, and struck in Jordan. Kissinger asks when Israel will adhere to and sign the
cease-fire. Rabin wants some weapons (including Shrike missiles and Phantom jet
fighters) from the United States first.*[7]

KISSINGER: . . . If you are planning to do something I think it would be in everyone's interests if the president did not read about it in the newspapers
first. If you could give us a few hours' warning. . . .

RABIN: It is my interpretation that it is activity prior to cease-fire. . . . Once we
agree to cease-fire we will commit ourselves to the terms of the cease-fire.

KISSINGER: But you have not agreed yet, have you?

RABIN: No, only in principle.

KISSINGER: Let me sum up my understanding—until you have agreed to the
cease-fire you have no restrictions.

RABIN: Exactly.

KISSINGER: You will implement the cease-fire whenever it will be agreed
upon?

RABIN: Whenever it will be agreed upon. . . . Cease-fire is something that has to
be reciprocal, mutually observed according to terms that have to be worked
out.

KISSINGER: . . . You will sign the cease-fire if you do not get the equipment?

RABIN: Well—

KISSINGER: I understand what you are saying. . . . I will look into the question
of deliveries tomorrow.

RABIN: The question is the sooner the delivery will be, it will be much easier for us to cope because this kind of equipment can help us only when it

comes to SAM sites. Our intention is to use this equipment against the SAM sites, with first priority to newly established ones near the Suez Canal. . . .

Joseph Sisco
August 5, 1970, 3:40 p.m.
Sisco tells Kissinger about a military package he hopes will help persuade Israel to formally accept the cease-fire, which Secretary of State Rogers doesn't want to provide if Israel drags its feet.

SISCO: I am trying to get the cease-fire proposal into effect, but it's very complicated. . . . I wanted to report to you where we stand on the question of the military assistance which Israel has requested. They want as a matter of priority four things: (1) helicopter standoff equipment to help jam SAM electrical equipment, (2) Shrikes, (3) CBUs [cluster bombs] to attack SAM sites, (4) pods—electrical equipment. I have had two good talks with Packard. He will, by tomorrow morning, see what is possible to present to the Israelis. But there needs to be a discussion with our secretary of state. . . . The secretary believes that the overriding objective should be to get the cease-fire working immediately. If there is any further delay there may be incidents and also a loss of momentum. . . . Let me give you the secretary's thinking on this: If the Israelis are the cause of any delay in the establishment of a cease-fire, we shouldn't provide the equipment. If, however, the Egyptians cause a delay and in a manner which would improve their situation, then we should study the whole thing further. In other words, the secretary wants to look at the existing situation before we go ahead. Rabin has informed the Pentagon . . . that unless they get the four items and get the opportunity to hit the SAM sites, there may be a delay on the cease-fire. This is a form of pressure that didn't go well with the secretary. We took the view that the compelling need is to get on with the cease-fire and that it is just as much in the interest of the Israelis to do so as the others involved, if not more so. But the problem is that if you have a cease-fire and then the Israelis make a dramatic attack, the other side will feel the need to restore the balance, and then you might as well not have a cease-fire.

KISSINGER: If there is a cease-fire will they get the equipment?

SISCO: Yes, the secretary feels that we should give them the equipment, and Dave Packard agrees, if there is a cease-fire. . . . The secretary and I agree that the overriding consideration is to get the cease-fire as quickly as possible. . . .

KISSINGER: How does the cease-fire look to you?

SISCO: There's a real hope. My only worry is that the Israelis will be insistent about getting the equipment and hitting the SAM sites before it [the cease-fire]. . . .

Joseph Sisco
August 5, 1970, 6:40 p.m.
Ambassador Rabin had apprised Kissinger of Egyptian and Soviet movement of surface-to-air missile sites closer to the west bank of the Suez Canal; Israel was threatening to take them out.[8]

> KISSINGER: I have just seen Rabin. . . . He painted a rather somber picture . . . about the creeping moving forward of the SAMs—they are now within 15 kilometers of the canal.
>
> SISCO: . . . The SAMs have been there for some time—there has been no change in the SAM sites in the 30-kilometer zone since we made the proposal. Where there has been a creeping process has been within the 30- and 50-kilometer zone.
>
> KISSINGER: But the point Rabin is making is that they will not accept a cease-fire unless these things are moved back. . . . Rabin says three things: (1) they won't implement the cease-fire, (2) they will take action to remove the SAMs with or without our weapons, (3) they will not feel restricted by the limitations up to now.
>
> SISCO: That is a new wrinkle.
>
> KISSINGER: I said I will transmit, word for word, this to the president. I said I cannot speak officially, but your actions are inconsistent with our peace initiative and will be taken amiss by our senior people. . . .

President Nixon
August 5, 1970, 10:18 p.m.
Kissinger updates Nixon on Israel's conditions for formally accepting the cease-fire (which it then withdrew) and threats to take out Soviet SAM sites near the canal, which he suspects they will carry out. He also reports that a boat piloted by right-wing Cubans from Miami was trying to sink a Soviet tanker.

> KISSINGER: Mr. President, I'm sorry to disturb you. There are two matters. First, Rabin came in late this afternoon in an agitated frame of mind about the cease-fire and made a tough statement about the whole trend of public discussions going against them, and the fact that while discussion of a cease-fire is going on, the Soviets have advanced SAM sites to a distance of roughly 30 miles and established a site within 10 miles of the canal, which gives them a shot into the Sinai and also the capability to protect artillery positions along the canal. He said there were two demands: (1) insist that the Soviets pull these back to where they were before, or (2) get them equipment to take them out—or failing that, they wouldn't accept a cease-fire and would take them out in their own way. I was tough with him. I said I would

transmit this to you and that you were deeply concerned. I said if they did this, we wouldn't think it was in the spirit of a peace move. Three hours later, he called back . . . saying they were withdrawing the conditions. He still said they would take out these sites by direct or indirect means but would accept a cease-fire. I personally conclude that they are going to take them out tonight. . . .

NIXON: Well, there is no cease-fire yet.

KISSINGER: Right, it is not our concern. . . . They are approaching again a state of extreme agitation and they could hit the sites and then accept a cease-fire. The second item is we have a report that a heavily armed boat has left Miami manned by Cubans to sink a Soviet tanker which is off the coast of Florida heading for Cuba. We have a Coast Guard ship trying to escort that Soviet tanker, just in case the Israelis hit tonight. This would look like we were slapping them [the Soviets] in the face. Subject to your approval, I think we should let that Coast Guard ship shepherd that Soviet tanker out of harm's way.

NIXON: Sure.

KISSINGER: We can try to intercept that other boat and stay with the Soviet tanker. . . . If one of their ships was sunk off Miami it would look like a kick in the teeth. I would guess that the Israelis, if they don't hit tonight, will strike within the next 48 hours. Rabin does not talk idly. I think they have decided to move.

NIXON: . . . See that that tanker is protected. . . .

William Rogers
August 7, 1970, 12:00 p.m.
Israel had officially accepted the cease-fire, which had gone into effect along the Suez Canal, and peace talks were to begin under the auspices of UN representative Gunnar Jarring. Rogers complains about a meeting Kissinger had with Rabin that "screwed up" their negotiations with the Israelis.

ROGERS: I just read the memcon [memorandum of conversation] of your meeting with Rabin last night. I think it was a mistake for him to do that.

KISSINGER: It went immediately to Sisco.

ROGERS: But for you to meet. He thinks that way he can get two shots. It's so screwed up at the moment. How did you leave it?

KISSINGER: That he would be hearing from Sisco. Every time I made a move I checked it with Sisco and reported back to him afterwards.

ROGERS: I think we should do it one way.

KISSINGER: My understanding is that I have followed exactly what Sisco told me. . . .

William Rogers
August 7, 1970, 12:30 p.m.

Rogers's displeasure over the White House's plan to announce the cease-fire rather than let State do it (ultimately Rogers did) and Kissinger's separate channel to the Israelis sets off a heated exchange. Rogers feels he should "take the lead."

... KISSINGER: ... What the president wants is to give the announcement here and give the backgrounding to you. ...

ROGERS: But if the thing falls through, which it might, and they had the statement from the president, he'd have egg on his face. ... If you announce it you are going to get a million questions that can't be answered. ... We may now have ruined the thing.

KISSINGER: Not me, because you haven't been talking to me.

ROGERS: These things are operational and I think I should take the lead. This meeting last night screwed it up so badly—

KISSINGER: Don't be ridiculous.

ROGERS: I'm not being ridiculous.

KISSINGER: You are being absurd. The thing was totally screwed up and everything I did was checked with Sisco. ...

ROGERS: You either have somebody running the operation or you don't.

KISSINGER: If you have a complaint, talk to the president. I am sick and tired of this. If he [Rabin] has a message for the president, he isn't going to give it to you. ...

ROGERS: He didn't have a message for the president; he wanted to talk with you. When you have an audience with him they think they have two ways to play it. I don't think it's a good procedure. ... You and I don't see alike on these things. ... If they have a feeling that there are two channels to the president they will use them differently.

KISSINGER: I didn't take it to the president. He doesn't even know about it yet.

ROGERS: But they think you did. It would be helpful to me if, when all it is is carrying out orders, you would not take part in the discussions. When they have a message, that's different, but when they have a complaint about something they did with us, you should refer them to me or Sisco. I don't think when you have such a critical matter they should have a feeling that they have got two ways to play it. ...

KISSINGER: There is no separate channel. Every conversation I have had I have sent you a memcon and I have checked every comment with Sisco, and I have been told the fact that I backed Sisco has helped.

ROGERS: Why do you think they go to you?

KISSINGER: To try to end-run and get the president to overrule you.

ROGERS: That's right.

KISSINGER: But that has never happened.

ROGERS: But why give them the impression that it might?

KISSINGER: I thought they were going to tell me that they had attacked the SAM sites across the canal.

ROGERS: I'm not making any headway. I think this is operational—I don't think you should see these people. . . .

Ronald Ziegler

August 8, 1970, 12:45 p.m.

Chalmers Roberts had written a piece in the Washington Post *that said Kissinger and Rogers were "eyeball to eyeball over who gets credit" for the peace initiative. Kissinger "just can't swallow the apparent early success of the Middle East plan because it is Rogers'," H. R. Haldeman wrote in his diary. "In fact, he's probably actually trying to make it fail for just this reason." Rogers was "ebullient" over the success of his initiative.*[9]

KISSINGER: I wanted your judgment on the Roberts column.

ZIEGLER: . . . I don't think you came off bad.

KISSINGER: . . . I did not say anything about Rogers but he is saying lots about me.

ZIEGLER: I know. I think it comes off even. . . . This is petty, bureaucratic feuding. . . . You are going to come off all right in this. . . .

KISSINGER: Four-fifths of the instances have been started by them [the State Department]. . . . You know, I don't give a damn about getting credit for me. I just want to get it for the president. It's an outrage that Rogers is saying the Cambodian decision was the president's and he was against it. Then he is taking full credit for the Middle East.

ZIEGLER: . . . Don't drop to the level they are on. You pull off the role of the aloof intellectual, close to the president. . . .

William Leonard

August 11, 1970, 4:33 p.m.

Kissinger goes over his conditions for appearing on 60 Minutes *with CBS News Vice President Leonard. Leonard agrees to let him veto use of a section or exchange, or to retape or rephrase his remarks, without giving up ultimate editorial control. "Completely off the record, we don't want to put in anything you don't want said," Leonard says.*

. . . KISSINGER: . . . It's easier for me to talk if I can look at what I have said and say what I don't want used . . . so you can't chop things out and use them out of context. . . .

LEONARD: As a practical matter it's not a problem. . . .

KISSINGER: . . . You might think something is more important than I intended it. Or you may take a sentence out and change the entire meaning.

LEONARD: That's possible. What I can say is that not only would we, as a practical matter, listen to what you said afterwards on what you said, and if you say a paragraph or section is wrong, please don't use it, or come down and do it again, that's all right. . . .

KISSINGER: . . . If you agree that if I say don't use that whole question and answer and you won't use it, that meets a concern, or let me do it again and rephrase it.

LEONARD: We can do that. . . . If you say "I said that badly" or "I don't want that," then we will heed that. I don't want a secret agreement that we can't live with in public—I can't do for you what we can't do for LBJ, or the president, for that matter, and that is give you the assurance that the final editing decision-making will not be in CBS News. . . . Completely off the record, we don't want to put in anything you don't want said.

KISSINGER: . . . If I can look at the transcript and if I say there are some parts I don't want in and I will take your word that you will edit it to see that what I want said is fairly done. . . . I might suggest to Mike [Wallace] that if you use A then you have to use B.

LEONARD: Done. I want to sit with you and watch that edition of *60 Minutes*. I will be right next to you when it goes on the air.

KISSINGER: This will be my first exposure of this kind. Hunebelle trapped me. . . .

LEONARD: You will not regret it. . . .

60 Minutes Debut, Subverting Allende in Chile, Jordan on the Brink and Intervention Planning with Israel, and a Trumped-Up Soviet Facility in Cuba

September–October 1970

In September 1970, Kissinger was immersed day and night in "the Jordan crisis," as Washington viewed it. Jordan's moderate King Hussein was under threat from the Palestinian insurgents, and the Nixon administration, worried about Syrian or Iraqi intervention in support of the Palestinians, debated U.S. versus Israeli bombing to save the king, which Kissinger and Nixon considered essential to prevent the radicalization of the Middle East. They believed the Soviets were stoking the Palestinian insurgency to expand their influence in the region. After murky moves of Syrian tanks and armored cars into Jordan, a desperate Hussein requested both air strikes and ground intervention, the latter being interpreted by U.S. officials as American. But U.S. ground intervention was a forbidding prospect in Washington and both politically and logistically untenable. Nixon and Kissinger agreed that they needed a plan for "punishment" of the Soviets, however, through "a merciless air strike on somebody," as Nixon said. Israeli Ambassador Yitzhak Rabin argued that air strikes might not be sufficient to save Jordan and that Israeli ground action was needed. Nixon, who had earlier favored U.S. over Israeli air strikes, preferred Israeli bombing but agreed to support Israeli ground intervention under certain conditions (e.g., that it be confined to Jordan and that Israeli forces withdraw when the Syrians withdrew). Israel had its own conditions. The Syrians later pulled out.

Meanwhile, U.S. intelligence had picked up what Kissinger saw as signs of the construction of a Soviet nuclear-submarine base in Cuba, ones he overdramatized: it turned out to be a support facility.

Mike Wallace
September 10, 1970, 10:15 a.m.
*Kissinger is angry with Mike Wallace for filming Nancy Maginnes (his future wife)
for the upcoming* 60 Minutes *program on him.*

KISSINGER: I will not cooperate with you if you don't remove that crew from outside Nancy Maginnes's room.

WALLACE: We weren't going to do a thing on that, but then the *Washington Post* has a big picture of the two of you at the showing of *Waterloo.* . . .

KISSINGER: Keep her out of it. Use someone else.

WALLACE: . . . We would just say this is someone of more consequence to Henry. I said we would stake you out. . . . She will have to be mentioned.

KISSINGER: The way you said it yesterday you were not going to mention her.

WALLACE: We were not going to talk to her. Then we see a big picture of you and her last night. *Time* has a picture of you dancing, and now in the *Post.* . . .

Margaret Osmer
September 10, 1970, a.m.
Kissinger takes up the matter with CBS producer Osmer, whom he dated.

OSMER: It's not my fault.

KISSINGER: I think it's an outrage. This isn't *Confidential* magazine. . . . You went to photograph her, staking out the hotel.

OSMER: . . . I had long talks with Mike about it. I did everything I could. He sees it in the paper, he reads *Newsweek* and the *Washington Post.* He's a newsman; he says, "If they can do it, why can't I?" I'm sorry. But on the other hand, you are a very important person.

KISSINGER: Yes, but what you don't think about is that in addition to her own feelings there is her situation at home. And the news coup you may score bears no relation to the anguish it causes.

OSMER: But he can't ignore it.

KISSINGER: Why can't he? This isn't a story about my sex life. My relationship to her has nothing to do with my job here. List me with all those movie stars. They love it and it doesn't harm me. . . .

OSMER: It's not going to be that bad.

KISSINGER: You know I like you very much, but with all due respect, you can't judge that. This means a great deal to her and she doesn't deserve it. . . . She's deeply upset. . . . If you would just lay off her now. . . . You've got the film.

OSMER: We've got virtually nothing. He said he just got her in the doorway. . . .

Richard Helms
September 12, 1970, 12:00 p.m.
The socialist Salvador Allende had been elected president of Chile on September 4, and the conservative Chilean media tycoon Agustin Edwards was coming to Washington to warn of the consequences.[1] *CIA Director Helms and Kissinger hope to prevent Allende's ratification by the Chilean Congress.*

> HELMS: We live in trying times. Have you heard from Don Kendall [CEO of PepsiCo]?
>
> KISSINGER: He has been trying to get me, and my moronic people turned him off.
>
> HELMS: He talked to me last night. He is getting Edwards up here from Argentina. Edwards has on his mind the state of morale in the embassy. There's a problem here.
>
> KISSINGER: Have you seen the cables in from Santiago? Have you seen the one that [U.S. Ambassador to Chile Edward] Korry disavowed in his other cable? He sent one cable that said there's no chance [to block Allende] is wrong and that he thinks there's a chance but he is the only one who thinks so in the embassy. . . . I am calling a 40 Committee [on covert operations] meeting for Monday. We will not let Chile go down the drain.
>
> HELMS: I am with you. . . .

Donald Kendall
September 14, 1970, 10:20 a.m.
Kendall and Kissinger plan a meeting the next morning with Edwards and Attorney General John Mitchell, where Edwards would sound the alarm about the threat Allende posed to businesses in Chile. That afternoon, Nixon would give Helms his marching orders: prevent Allende from taking office or unseat him, getting rid of him if needed.[2]

> . . . KISSINGER: I might get Mitchell to join us.
>
> KENDALL: That would be terrific. . . . I am taking my father to see the president today. . . . I will mention Edwards to him. I don't know what it will take to turn this around at State but I want him to get the flavor.
>
> KISSINGER: It's a disaster.
>
> KENDALL: It is and I don't understand the American people.
>
> KISSINGER: They don't know about Chile.
>
> KENDALL: I will tell the president he cannot stand for a Cuba in his administration.
>
> KISSINGER: Tell him that. . . .

President Nixon

September 17, 1970, 9:00 a.m.

A military government had taken over in Jordan amid fierce fighting with Palestinians, and King Hussein had declared martial law. Kissinger deemed it essential to preserve Hussein's rule, even by U.S. military intervention if necessary. Nixon, who was in Chicago, says that if the Iraqis or Syrians intervened in support of the Palestinians in Jordan (there were already 17,000 Iraqi troops in Jordan), "we should use American air and knock the bejesus out of them." But sending ground troops was another matter. Though they believed the Soviet Union was fueling the insurgency in Jordan, it would warn against outside interference.[3] Kissinger worries that if Hussein falls it will push Egyptian President Nasser and the Soviets "in a radical direction."

> KISSINGER: During the night Jordan blew. The king moved troops into Amman; he has taken the western and southern suburbs and is advancing into the city. He seems to be gaining the upper hand. . . . I talked to Bill, Sisco, Moorer, and Packard—everyone is aboard. They all recognize that it is a crisis.
>
> NIXON: A crisis that's good.
>
> KISSINGER: If the king wins, the peace offensive has a real chance.
>
> NIXON: We've got to help him. How about the fleet?
>
> KISSINGER: It's up there. One thing, everyone agreed you must not come back. It would create a crisis atmosphere. We moved the second carrier into the Mediterranean. We've got almost the entire Sixth Fleet near Cyprus now. There's another force with helicopter capability on the *Guam*. It was going to go to the Mediterranean anyway and we are moving it into that area.
>
> NIXON: But this becomes necessary only if the Iraqis or Syrians move?
>
> KISSINGER: Exactly.
>
> NIXON: If they move, my strong feeling at this time is that we should use American air and knock the bejesus out of them.
>
> KISSINGER: That's our feeling.
>
> NIXON: It would be a show of strength on our part. . . . I think a move on our part shows guts, having to do with these hijackers also. [Palestinians had earlier hijacked several airplanes and forced them to land in Jordan and Egypt, taking hostages.] I think the U.S. ought to do something if it's air. If it requires men, that's another thing. . . . The king's move is a result of our encouraging him, is it not? . . . He ought to be backed up.
>
> KISSINGER: We sent out a cable to that effect last night. We think the cable we put out Monday stiffened his back, the one saying we can't tolerate the taking of American hostages. . . . I have talked to the British—they are prepared to put out a five-power statement which is in effect the same thing as you

said on Monday, that we hold the guerrillas responsible for the safety of the hostages. . . . We also have a package of what we think the king needs.

NIXON: On this one I am sure you are going to find Sisco would be all aboard and Bill will be because it's the only chance for his peace offensive.

KISSINGER: Exactly. If it fails, the cease-fire and the peace offensive are dead.

NIXON: It would be worse than before we started; the fedayeen would have the upper hand.

KISSINGER: It would push Nasser in a radical direction and would push the Soviets that way and would make the Israelis unwilling to accept promises.

NIXON: I want you to push through the bureaucracy my feelings, having a landing team ready for evacuation. As far as their going in and fighting, that's another thing. This would get the Russians in. . . . This will show whether we have any stake at all left in the Mediterranean.

KISSINGER: . . . Bill is all on board on doing the maximum possible to strengthen the king. On the Israeli versus U.S. question, I haven't talked to him in detail. I will get a read on that.

NIXON: I think U.S. air has a lot to say for itself. . . . What this is is a civil war in Jordan with Iraq and Syria in on it. How about your calling [Soviet chargé d'affaires Yuli] Vorontsov and saying "Lay off, boys."

KISSINGER: I think we should be enigmatic and say nothing. They will pick this up.

NIXON: Okay, this will worry them. But we want the Sixth Fleet stuff in the open. . . . I want them to know we're moving. I want everything that can be done to be done in the open. The wear and tear on the nerves between the Syrians and Iraqis is very important. . . .

William Rogers
September 17, 1970, 9:20 a.m.
Secretary of State Rogers strongly favors Israeli over U.S. air attacks in Jordan if needed.

. . . KISSINGER: The only thing I wanted to check out was between U.S. and Israeli air intervention. What is your judgment as to which would be preferable?

ROGERS: I am in favor of the Israelis doing it. In fact, it's almost commanding, the reasons are so strong. It would be in line with their national interests; it would help in preventing the Iraqis from having a hand in the government of Jordan. The king can give as the reason the Israelis are on his soil is because of the acts of the fedayeen. Third, if we are going to have any peace, Jordan and Israel will have to work together anyway. . . . Also, what if we failed? For Israel to bail us out would be awful.

KISSINGER: Yes. . . . The president's instincts are the other way, but he's not adamant.

ROGERS: If we play it right, we may be able to pull out the whole thing.

KISSINGER: And if we pull it out the peace offensive has a real chance. It would be good for credibility with the Israelis and show the Arabs that moderation is the only course. . . .

Frank Shakespeare
September 17, 1970, 6:55 p.m.
U.S. Information Agency Director Shakespeare apprises Kissinger of hawkish off-the-record remarks Nixon made during a meeting with editors of the Chicago Sun-Times *that the paper was publishing.*

SHAKESPEARE: . . . They have alerted all the wire services that at 6:00 Chicago time they will be coming out with a big story. This is what the president said to the editors and broadcasters: "If the Syrians or Iraqis intervene in Jordan there are only two of us to stop them, the Israelis or us. It will be preferable for us to do it. The Russians are going to pay dearly for moving the missiles in [Egypt]. The Israelis are going to get five times as much as they would have if the missiles would not have moved. We are embarking on a tougher policy in the Middle East. The Sixth Fleet is going to be beefed up. I was having an argument with Kissinger, who thinks we blew it in Jordan. We will intervene if the situation is such that our intervention will make a difference." The *Chicago Sun-Times* is saying as a lead that "it was learned today from high sources that the U.S. will intervene in Jordan if the Syrians or Iraqis move." . . .

KISSINGER: What does he mean that I thought we blew it in Jordan? I have been raising hell with him along the lines that we have been behaving and that Jordan was about to blow. . . . I think the secretary of state is going to have a bloody heart attack. . . . Those fools at State think I am putting him up to it. It doesn't give me any pain.

Alexander Haig
September 20, 1970, no time (evening)
Syrian tanks and armored cars had entered Jordan (though the numbers were unclear), and Nixon and Kissinger thought the Soviets were behind the thrust, or at least urging the Syrians on—testing them again, as in Egypt and Cuba. But Soviet chargé Yuli Vorontsov said they were urging restraint on the Syrians.[4] Haig, Kissinger's deputy, says the situation in Amman with the Palestinian insurgents was precarious, and Kissinger declares that Rogers's peace initiative was a big mistake; he doesn't want any "pansy" language in a memo to Nixon. They discuss Soviet

intentions, and if a move against Syria was needed they favor Israeli over U.S. intervention.

> ... HAIG: ... I don't think things in town [Amman] are as good as they have been reported to be. . . . There has been heavy fighting all around the embassy. I'm just not sure things are going as rosy as everyone seems to think.
>
> KISSINGER: Jesus Christ. Of course, to start that peace offensive in June was the worst mistake we made. To reply to Soviet SA-3s [SAMs] by starting a peace offensive, directed at Israel, that was our disaster. . . . If we had given 50 Phantoms to Israel, would we have been as badly off as we are now? . . . On that memo to the president, that is another thing that concerns me. Make sure there isn't any of this pansy [NSC staffer Hal] Saunders language in it. It has got to be firm, strong, and definite. . . . I would have a concluding paragraph: "The possibility cannot be ruled out that as in Cuba, as previously with the missiles, when they offer us a cease-fire that we have got a pattern here of reassurance and at the same time a reassurance to cover an aggressive move." Don't you think?
>
> HAIG: ... On this one, you could make a good case that they have nothing to do with it.
>
> KISSINGER: I don't believe it.
>
> HAIG: Well, I don't either but we have no evidence of it. . . .
>
> KISSINGER: Look, they offered a cease-fire and put in SA-3s. They offered Cuban reassurance and put in a naval base. I just don't trust these sons of bitches. . . . They are thugs. . . . But actually . . . domestically it is better for us if the Israelis get involved.
>
> HAIG: Oh, I think so too. I just think the other is out of the question.
>
> KISSINGER: We need the others [options] in reserve for a Soviet move.
>
> HAIG: That's right. . . . You've got more flexibility this way. And on top of that you bring down the house of cards over the issue before it surfaces. . . .

President Nixon

September 20, 1970, no time

The president and Kissinger confer on a tough statement by Rogers on the crisis, Israeli versus U.S. air attacks, and potential intervention by Israeli ground troops. Nixon worries that Israeli intervention will inflame Arab countries, and he and Kissinger both know the Israelis "don't need any encouragement" to come in. But they could "clean them out." Kissinger favors U.S. bombing if it were of short duration. They agree that U.S. action would have to be quick and overwhelming.

KISSINGER: . . . Bill decided to put out the statement in his own name, which was very good—it made it tougher. . . . Said we have had information that Syrian tanks have invaded Jordan. . . . That the broadening of the conflict will have serious consequences—we demand immediate withdrawal of these forces. . . .

NIXON: Well, that is probably the right level for it to come from at this point. . . . It also gets State into the business, too.

KISSINGER: And it is the first time he has engaged his own prestige, which will affect his subsequent actions. . . . The king has appealed to us again for immediate help, but it is night there now. He has also asked us for reconnaissance, and we are feeding him [Israeli] intelligence which we are getting. . . . He doesn't know where that intelligence is coming from. . . . And I just wanted to warn you that if this thing keeps up, within the next 24 hours, I would guess by tomorrow morning, we may reach the decision point as between U.S. and Israeli action—that is, if the king loses the tank battle. . . .

NIXON: . . . We are prepared for our air action, is that right?

KISSINGER: We are prepared for our air action, Mr. President. We can run 200 sorties a day from the carriers. The land-based planes—we have had a full study made that looks pretty grim. The only fields we could use are in Turkey, and the Turks almost certainly won't give us permission. The only other fields would be in Greece or Crete, and for that we would have to use air refueling and it would take us eight days to get them ready. . . .

NIXON: What about the plan based on the carriers?

KISSINGER: . . . They could do a good job on them. Their handicap is that if that fails they can't follow it up with very much, unless we want to get ground forces fighting the Syrians, which is a rough decision to make.

NIXON: Which we don't want to do, but which the Israelis would be delighted to do.

KISSINGER: Right. The Israelis can fly 700 sorties a day, but we are in a position to do 200 sorties and we could do quite a job on them.

NIXON: Well, has the king indicated that he would like the Israelis to come in?

KISSINGER: The king at an earlier stage had asked the Israelis whether they would be willing to come in if he asked for it. That was a month ago. It was during the last crisis. Sisco thinks that he would if things got to that point.

NIXON: Well, the difficulty there, Henry, though, is that while that may cool the immediate situation . . . the other Arab countries . . . have to line up with Syria in that case, don't they?

KISSINGER: That's right. . . . There are two advantages to our coming in—the one you gave and the one that the Russians are less likely to take us on than the Israelis. . . . The advantage of the Israelis going in is that they can follow it up and they can escalate it more easily than we.

NIXON: Oh, yes, there is no question that the Israelis going in is good, due to the fact that they not only have the air but they have got a helluva good ground punch—they could just put them in there and clean them out.

KISSINGER: That's right. They have more air and more ground and therefore they might deter a purely Arab response more easily than we; and, secondly, hated as they are, they are at least recognized to have a local interest in the thing, while we, coming from thousands of miles away fighting the Syrians, have a serious problem and the Arabs might unite against us too. We would be the imperialists coming in.

NIXON: Well, they are more likely to reunite against the Israelis than us, though.

KISSINGER: The hatred of the Israelis is undoubtedly greater.

NIXON: That's what I mean. Of course, the point is that the Israelis start with an enormous disadvantage in that respect. That is the thing I am concerned about.

KISSINGER: That's true. . . . But they decouple us a little bit. . . . The problem we have is if we don't succeed and then the Israelis come in, that's the worst of everything.

NIXON: And of course the other side is if we succeed it has considerable impact—cooling the whole situation and acting forcibly in a critical area. . . . And the message to the Russians is a helluva lot more if we come in than if the Israelis [do].

KISSINGER: If we could do it with two or three strikes or two or three days' operations, I would favor our doing it. If it is a two-week sort of thing and if it is not decisive—

NIXON: What is Sisco's reaction at this moment on this point?

KISSINGER: Sisco prefers the Israelis. I am slightly more on your side on this than Sisco's.

NIXON: What does Bill say?

KISSINGER: The last time I talked to him he preferred the Israelis, but in the meantime you had talked to him.

NIXON: Well, I didn't get into anything except that we didn't want the Israelis. It is so easy to fall into that—to have them go in, and they don't need any encouragement. They'd love to go in for other reasons.

KISSINGER: You are absolutely right. And the Israelis would have the advantage that it is dammed hard to get them out once they are in.

NIXON: That's right. They would just occupy some more territory, wouldn't they?

KISSINGER: Well, whether they do it vis-à-vis Syria, I'm not so sure.

NIXON: Well, in any event, the Syrians would fear it.

KISSINGER: The Syrians would fear it. Of course, there's a third problem that we may not have any choice about—I don't think the Israelis would hold still for very long if the Syrians seem to be winning. They seem already to have mobilized a bit, which is a good deterrent. . . . Incidentally, we picked up an intelligence report this morning—not very reliable, but interesting— that the Russians gave the Syrians a carte blanche, which proves when you told me Friday night they may be playing us; your instinct about the Russians is usually remarkable.

NIXON: . . . Well, this note that they gave us over the weekend is—

KISSINGER: Just to keep us quiet.

NIXON: To keep us quiet and threaten us and so forth. In the meantime, they say, "Stir it up, boys; give them trouble; give them trouble. Face them down." That's what they are going to do. Well, we may have to come to the Israelis, but I just want to be sure that at this point—that's why I've been so strong on it—we don't leave any impression we might come to them or they'll come in precipitately. . . .

KISSINGER: No, it is absolutely right that we don't get anywhere near the situation where we seem to be egging on the Israelis, because they don't need any encouragement. . . . I don't know what the congressional reaction would be if we got involved. If we did it in a two- or three-day operation, I think we'll be all right—or even a week.

NIXON: How do we justify two or three days? Suppose we were to call the Congress in and say we are doing it for one purpose—to save Jordan.

KISSINGER: To save Jordan and to prevent a general Mideast war. But it's tougher if we do it. . . . And curiously enough, we might get more support if the Israelis do it. My major worry is if it doesn't work and another little country—it will work if we are determined enough, but these Syrians are the craziest of the lot.

NIXON: Yeah, they might fight a long time. Well, when we are quite confident it will work with the Israelis—

KISSINGER: Nobody has any question about that. . . . They've beat them to a pulp once before [in 1967] and they haven't improved that much. . . .

NIXON: . . . Either we have to do something—we cannot let the Syrians get away with this—or we've got to support the Israelis in doing something. We cannot make a public statement and not back it up. . . . Having taken the position, we must act one way or the other; either the Israelis or ourselves. . . . Our action would have to be quick and surgical.

KISSINGER: Well, our action would have to be overwhelming.

NIXON: Yes, that's right.

KISSINGER: We can't have another even three months' war. . . .

President Nixon
September 20, 1970, no time
Nixon and Kissinger consider unleashing U.S. bombers in Jordan and thereby punishing the Soviets.

… NIXON: I'm just thinking of a contingency as to what we could do with
   air. . . .

KISSINGER: Oh, we could wreck them.

NIXON: That's what I mean. . . . We have to be prepared for some punishment . . . because we have said we'd hold them responsible. And we've got
   to keep our pledge in that respect.

KISSINGER: Absolutely. . . . It will help in general to play a very fairly hard line
   also in respect to our other [problem in Cuba with the purported Soviet
   submarine base], too, because it will help our credibility with the other
   problem. . . . I will get a contingency plan worked out today. We have a plan
   on the tanks and so forth. We don't have a clear plan on what you just said
   on a punishment.

NIXON: Yeah; we should have one, though.

KISSINGER: Absolutely.

NIXON: We may be faced with that, and I want to have something we can do—
   not just make a big statement. We just go in with a merciless air strike on
   somebody—even the Syrians. . . .

Yitzhak Rabin and Joseph Sisco (Sisco was in the office with Kissinger)
September 20, 1970, 10:00 p.m.
*Kissinger informs Israeli Ambassador Rabin, who was in New York at a dinner in
honor of Prime Minister Golda Meir, about an appeal from Jordan for an Israeli air
strike on Syrian troops.*

KISSINGER: . . . We have just got a request from the Jordanians via the British
   which requests an Israeli air strike on Syrian troops which allegedly have
   taken Irbid and are heading south and massing.

RABIN: I understand what was requested. I understand against whom. I didn't
   understand which area.

KISSINGER: . . . We have no independent information of our own and we
   wanted to ask you whether it would be possible for you on an urgent basis to undertake some reconnaissance to confirm this and then just get in
   touch with us.

RABIN: Fine. . . . I just got a cable from our people talking about 200 Syrian tanks in the area of Irbid. . . . They were heading towards Irbid. . . . I
   understand exactly what you ask us.

KISSINGER: And could you do it on the most urgent basis?

RABIN: First I will go to the prime minister here. . . . Do you look favorably to this request? What is your position?

SISCO: I think we want to exchange views with you on this as soon as you are able to give us a picture of how serious you think the situation is there.

RABIN: It looks to be quite serious. . . .

William Rogers and Joseph Sisco (Sisco was still in the office with Kissinger) September 20, 1970, 10:10 p.m.

Sisco relays Jordan's request to Rogers. Kissinger and Sisco had since read a "desperate" message from King Hussein saying air strikes were "imperative to save his country."[5] What's more, he was now requesting ground troops too—which Kissinger read as U.S. troops. All three officials support Israeli air strikes to save the king. But U.S. troops "is different," Rogers says.

. . . SISCO: Here is what came in, Mr. Secretary, from the king at 3:00. "Situation deteriorating dangerously following Syrian massive invasion. Northern forces disbanded. [Irbid] occupied. Having disastrous effect. . . . I request immediate intervention, both air and land, to safeguard independence of Jordan. Immediate air strike from any quarter plus air cover are imperative." . . .

ROGERS: Intervention by us or Israel? By anybody?

SISCO: It obviously leaves both options open, in my judgment.

KISSINGER: The way I read it, air strikes from any quarter and the ground forces from us.

SISCO: And they would also like British intervention. In light of this my own feeling would be that we now amend what we were going to tell Rabin. . . . Give Israelis essence of the information in this message and go beyond merely a request for reconnaissance but to say to them that we would look favorably if they took this action. In fact, as we were talking and this message came in Rabin said there was no difficulty, but the first question the Israelis would ask is would the Americans agree we should do this? And we fenced, but this is an understandable question on their part.

ROGERS: My view is that we should favor it because if the king goes down the drain then the goddamn thing is a total mess. . . .

SISCO: One would hope that whatever the Israelis did is sufficient.

ROGERS: I think the question of whether we should land troops is different. As long as we are sure the king is requesting Israeli air support. . . .

KISSINGER: . . . The fact seems to me to be that if there isn't an air strike the whole thing may come apart. I don't think we have any choice.

ROGERS: No, I don't think we have any choice. What it amounts to is Israel is just doing it now at the right time.

SISCO: Bear in mind that the Russians are behind the Syrians. . . .

Yitzhak Rabin
September 20, 1970, 10:35 p.m.
Kissinger apprises Rabin of Hussein's request for immediate air strikes and ground forces and says the United States would "look favorably" on Israeli intervention. Rabin wants an assurance that if the Soviets intervened, "we can rely on you."

KISSINGER: We have had another message and another conversation with the president. . . . This is the message from our ambassador [in Jordan] who says he had a phone call from the king at 3:00 a.m. local time pointing out that the situation was deteriorating dangerously. A massive invasion. The northern forces were disbanded. Irbid occupied. . . . This was having a disastrous effect on the troops in the capital. He therefore requests immediate physical intervention, both air and land. Especially he wants immediate air strikes on invading forces from any quarters. In light of your information we have discussed [this] with the secretary of state and the president and we can now assure you under these circumstances we would look favorably on your actions, and the president has asked me to tell you if you undertake such action we would of course make good any materiel problems that might arise as a result of these actions, and we are cognizant of the fact we would have to hold the situation under control vis-à-vis the Soviets.

RABIN: I would like to make it clear that the president looks at it favorably.

KISSINGER: That is correct.

RABIN: Second, if there would be a question of materiel you would find ways to compensate what would be the outcome.

KISSINGER: We promise that.

RABIN: Third, if there would be certain problems with the Soviets we can rely on you.

KISSINGER: That is exactly correct and we are taking some immediate precautionary measures to put ourselves into this position.

RABIN: Give me two or three minutes and I will bring it to Prime Minister Meir and I will discuss it with her and be in a position to tell you. . . .

President Nixon
September 21, 1970, about 5:30 a.m.
After being awakened by Haig with another message from Rabin, who said vehemently that air strikes might not be sufficient and that Israeli ground action was

needed,[6] Kissinger reports to Nixon. The president is hesitant about Israeli ground intervention. Kissinger is also nervous.

> KISSINGER: . . . I just had a call from Rabin. . . . They've made reconnaissance. . . . It confirms our information. There is a massive Syrian force there, and it is in the town of Irbid. . . . They believe that air alone won't do it, and that if it's done, ground action will be necessary either at the beginning or shortly thereafter. And they wanted to know what our reaction to that would be. . . .
>
> NIXON: Well, the problem we have here is that the message requested only— and it's specific as far as they were concerned—air action.
>
> KISSINGER: Well, it is unambiguous about air action.
>
> NIXON: . . . He doesn't want to take the action unless they go in on the ground at this time now. . . . That's what he's really saying. . . . The concern I have is that—and I trust they're considering this adequately, too—ground action presents, in a maximum way, a much more difficult reaction point . . . invasion and all that sort of thing. . . . Rather than if you just hit in the air at the outset at least. That's one thing. But of course they wouldn't comprehend this, I suppose. But the idea of Israel invading Jordan—that's the point, see. That's the point I think they may be missing.
>
> KISSINGER: Right. Well, their view probably is that they want to be sure that if they move militarily at all, they better succeed. . . . It presents a massive problem . . . of the king. The king's position, I think it's safe to say, for his own survival will have to be to disassociate himself from any action, but more even from the ground action. . . .

President Nixon
September 21, 1970, about 5:50 a.m.
Nixon instructs Kissinger to convey to Rabin some stipulations on U.S. support for Israeli ground intervention. Bombing is preferrable, he stresses. But if Israeli ground troops are needed, they should be confined to Jordan and not go into Syria. But bombing in Syria is okay. With ground action, "they're going to have a hell of lot bigger problem," Nixon says.

> NIXON: . . . Tell him these are the principles that . . . I consider imperative: (1) first, the operation must succeed; (2) success diplomatically as well as militarily must be considered; (3) if it is militarily feasible, they must lean in the direction of accomplishing a true air action alone in the first instance, having in mind the fact that that might have a psychological impact, which is needed; (4) if, however, that proves to be militarily and overall inadequate, again what is necessary to achieve success would have our support;

(5) . . . the action on the ground as distinguished from the air must strictly be limited to Jordan. Invasion of Syria would be very difficult. Bombing in Syria is not difficult. . . . Air action alone is preferred from all standpoints, if it will work militarily. . . . They'd go to Damascus [in Syria]. For Christ's sake, if they start doing that, the Russians then have a real cause. . . . The Israelis have mixed motives, and also they have their military bureaucracy. . . . Their mixed motives are that they'd like to go in there, you know, and fuck a little of the ground, and second—

KISSINGER: They want to really tear up the Syrians for once, whom they've never had a crack at.

NIXON: I hope to Christ they do! But the other thing is their military bureaucracy, you know—these ground guys say, "God, we've got to go in and do this, too." The only thing is I have just a hunch—an intuition—that if they go in with massive air . . . it should be limited air action for the first 24 hours.

KISSINGER: I don't think they'll do that.

NIXON: . . . It could have a psychological effect and could turn this thing right around. . . . I would say if air action went to ground action . . . they're going to have a hell of lot bigger problem. . . .

Joseph Sisco
September 21, 1970, a little after 6:00 a.m.
Kissinger informs Sisco of Israel's view that ground troops were needed. "I think we have no alternative," Sisco says. But they needed to discuss the matter with Rogers.

. . . KISSINGER: We've had a call from Rabin. . . . Their judgment is that air action alone is not enough to be decisive and that ground action is necessary. . . . I talked to him also about getting out of there if they go in, and I stated our strong view on that. But I have to tell you in all candor he was not unambiguous in his reply. I then called the president and communicated this to him. His first reaction was that this is, of course, more difficult than air. . . . He wants me to pass the following information to Rabin. . . . Air action alone would be easier, but we would support ground action if they thought it necessary. . . . What do you think of this?

SISCO: . . . On substance, I think we have no alternative. . . .

KISSINGER: Should I call Bill and tell him the same thing?

SISCO: . . . I think you ought to put it to him. . . . And we'll see how we go.

KISSINGER: Well, wait a minute. You can't see how you go because, right now, I've got an order.

SISCO: Yeah, well, I know, but we've got to tell the secretary. . . . I don't think you'll find him a problem. We had a very good talk with him, and I think he would say to you put it very strongly to the Israelis in terms of our very strong preference. . . . I think he'll just have you put a little greater emphasis on the air. . . . I think you'll find that he will see also that there's no alternative. . . .

President Nixon
September 21, 1970, close to 6:30 a.m.
The president wants to make sure Israeli troops don't stay in Jordan long.

NIXON: It seems if they go in on the ground, I think they should announce that they will withdraw . . . when the Syrians withdraw from Jordan. . . . They shouldn't leave the implication, which again will make it politically more difficult for them then, to just go in and sit there. Don't you think so?

KISSINGER: Right. . . . They'll be tough as hell on all these things. . . .

NIXON: Therefore, it's also a position that we're going to have to take with them later. . . .

KISSINGER: I, incidentally, asked him [Rabin] that point, and he said, "Well, this depends on how things develop in Jordan; if the whole thing comes apart." . . .

NIXON: I mean, that's a different ballgame. . . .

Alexander Haig and William Rogers
September 21, 1970, about 6:30 a.m.
Kissinger and Haig discuss the Soviets' "game plan." After Rogers joins them, they consider a report that the Israelis were already in Syria; Rogers, like Nixon, worries about Arab reaction to Israeli intervention in Jordan. If the Soviets intervened, Kissinger says, "we would have to be prepared to be very tough in warning them off," which could be "handled." But Rogers isn't convinced.

. . . HAIG: . . . The situation in Amman, the Sit[uation] Room tells me, is getting worse. . . . I think they have sped some more people in there, too. . . . This is a typical Soviet exercise.

KISSINGER: . . . I now see the game plan. They were going to use the peace talks to overthrow the king and in the meantime strengthen the Egyptians. . . . And then really put the squeeze on the Israelis. . . . That's the only thing that makes sense.

HAIG: That's right. And, in the meantime, obviously they bilk the Syrians. They've just been active across the board. . . .

[Rogers joins the conversation.]

KISSINGER: . . . I talked to the president. . . . Our preference is for air in the first instance, but that if they believe ground forces are essential, we would support that also. . . .

ROGERS: We have here a cryptic message which just came in. It says ". . . the Syrian police communications indicate that the Israelis have landed forces from helicopters in Syria." What do you think of that?

KISSINGER: . . . For all we know, they may be running around there already. . . . That's not my impression, though. . . . Unless they are absolutely tricking us, and I don't see what advantage it is to them to trick us about asking for our support for a move that they say they'll make later and then make it ahead of time. . . .

ROGERS: . . . The chances of saving the king are probably pretty slim anyway— I can't imagine any Arab can survive very long if he has to call upon the Israelis to save him.

KISSINGER: Well, my guess would be that he would disassociate himself. . . . I don't think he can admit that he called them—that he asked for air strikes.

ROGERS: Yeah. . . . What if [Israeli Foreign Minister Abba] Eban says to the Arabs that the Israelis have, without a request from Jordan, invaded their land, which will probably mean an Arab–Israeli conflict. I don't see how Nasser can stand by and do nothing if it doesn't appear that this was done at the king's request. . . . Which means really that we'll be faced with the problem if he does that, if Israel doesn't succeed, that they'll call on us. . . .

KISSINGER: . . . There's no doubt that the action will succeed and there's no doubt, I think, that the Israelis can handle the Egyptians together with the Syrians. The question that arises is if the Soviets intervene, and there we would be obliged to help support them. . . . I think the realistic occasion for American intervention will arise . . . if the Soviets were to intervene one way or the other. And we would have to be prepared to be very tough in warning them off. . . . I think it can be handled—with a lot of excitement, but I think it can be handled.

ROGERS: Well, it's awfully damned difficult to make these judgments. . . . The trouble with that is, so was everybody confident that the king could handle the fedayeen, and apparently he can't. . . .

Yitzhak Rabin

September 21, 1970, 10:25 a.m.

Kissinger tells Rabin he will be getting the green light from Sisco on Israeli ground intervention but not to say much in reply, and Rabin, who reports that a large Israeli force will be required and that the move might incite Egypt, raises some pointed questions.

KISSINGER: We have asked Sisco to talk to you in a few minutes and you will be getting a call from him. He will give you a reply which in principle is yes, but I would like to make the following suggestion. The less you say in reply, the better. Just say you will communicate with your government and then come in and see me. It's terribly important that we know who says what to whom and I will give you guidelines on that.

RABIN: In the meantime I have instructions too. . . . The gist, after the decision that took place, estimates that our military activity to prevent Syrian and Iraqi taking over in Jordan would require activation and operation of a relatively large force on our part. Second, we have to assume that as a result there might be resumption of hostilities even along the Suez Canal. . . . I have been instructed to make clear certain points. The first, will the U.S. approach Israel formally in this matter? Second, will the king agree to request our assistance and undertake methods of communication and coordination? Third, a little more clarification—how will U.S. prevent Soviet participation? Fourth, is it understood that the U.S. will side with us in the international political arena, including UN veto on grounds that Syria threatens Israel and not only Jordan? We might find ourselves in and they will order our withdrawal immediately. The fifth question, is it clear that Israel will not be held responsible for the fate of the hostages? . . . I can get Sisco's answer and communicate it back and then wait.

KISSINGER: . . . Just get Sisco's answer and we will discuss—make the first point to him. That's been our great contention here and it's important they hear it from you. . . . Then call Haig and make an appointment here. You will have to assume what I tell you is in the interest of everybody. . . .

RABIN: I have a cable that says if we have positive answers the tendency of the cabinet is to respond positively. . . .

KISSINGER: That's what I want you to communicate. Just that much, no more. . . . Then come in and go back to him. I will decide how to handle it. . . .

Yitzhak Rabin
September 21, 1970, 7:05 p.m.
Sisco had raised with Rabin a possible Israeli diversionary operation in Syria, and Kissinger sternly tells Rabin that they needed to know if he still thought that a major Israeli military operation in Syria, as a possible alternative course, was feasible. With some exasperation, Rabin explains that Sisco had misinterpreted him.

KISSINGER: There is a point of clarification I want to raise with you. What did you tell Sisco this afternoon about the alternate plan we mentioned to you this afternoon, the alternate courses of operations?

RABIN: He raised the question. He said they estimated that Jordan didn't want ground operations in Jordan and he asked about the possibility of carrying out diversionary action in Syria. He asked my opinion. I made it very clear that diversionary operations cannot achieve anything unless the purpose is to eliminate the forces in Jordan.

KISSINGER: I want to get one thing clear. Did I understand you correctly when we talked this afternoon that if a major operation was carried out in Syria, from a military point of view this was a feasible operation? You and I have to be meticulous in our understandings, for this reason: what you tell me I report to the president. When another version is reported, my version must be the correct one. Otherwise there is no sense in my talking to you. I reported my understanding of the conversation this afternoon—from a purely military point of view you expressed the thought that this might be . . . the effective way of doing it.

RABIN: Exactly.

KISSINGER: We were told this evening that it was your judgment that from a military point of view it was not feasible.

RABIN: . . . He talked about diversionary tactics. I went into detail and explained to him. . . . He doesn't understand the difference between diversionary and military actions. . . . It's really unbelievable. . . . I don't believe in diversionary. . . .

U. Alexis Johnson
September 25, 1970, 8:00 p.m.
U-2 spy planes had recently detected signs of the construction of a Soviet naval base in Cienfuegos, Cuba. Kissinger had warned the Soviets at a background press briefing that afternoon that the administration would view the establishment of a strategic submarine base in Cuba "with the utmost seriousness."[7] He exclaims to Undersecretary of State Johnson that they shouldn't say anything else and condemns a Pentagon briefing about the alleged construction of the base.

. . . KISSINGER: . . . The president urgently instructs us that we keep our mouths shut! I think we should stand on what was said today.

JOHNSON: Boy! Boy! God! We had that so carefully worked out.

KISSINGER: The trouble is that after the Defense Department we had to say something here or be badgered.

JOHNSON: Dave Packard said he is just standing on his head over there. Everything went bad.

KISSINGER: I find out now that they gave pictures of the barges and showed them on TV.

JOHNSON: Oh, no! Oh, god!

KISSINGER: So they must have had a package ready. When we sent over guidance, they must have thought this is it—they could go. If we had anything beautifully set, this was it.

JOHNSON: There is nothing we worked on more carefully than this.

KISSINGER: What we said was nicely threatening to the Soviets and nicely reassuring to us. . . . I know from Secretary Rogers if anyone opens his mouth he will hang him! . . .

Mr. Yoshida
October 18, 1970, no time
Kissinger complains to Japan's emissary on the negotiations to limit Japanese textile exports to the United States that his promises had not been carried out.

. . . KISSINGER: . . . I must say that your side has not come up with anything that we can even consider. . . . Our people don't believe you are serious. . . . Because we are not seeing any concrete results out of our channel. Nothing has ever happened the way you and I talked. . . . We have to recognize how it looks to my colleagues. They don't even know you. All they know is that I tell them that I have reason to believe that the following things will happen. Then they never happen.

YOSHIDA: Yes, that is true. To a large extent I know that has been the case. . . .

KISSINGER: In fact, we are just not very eager to talk to you anymore because we frankly have been very disappointed. . . .

YOSHIDA: I personally feel terrible about this. . . . I am getting more and more pessimistic. . . . We have agreed that something will happen and which has not happened. . . .

KISSINGER: Nor has anything happened anywhere close to what we agreed. . . .

U. Alexis Johnson
October 19, 1970, 12:55 p.m.
Nixon is reluctant to have U.S. Ambassador to Chile Edward Korry visit Chile's incoming socialist president, Salvador Allende, out of concern for what he will say.

KISSINGER: . . . The big problem is that he's reluctant to let Korry run loose. He did not make a very good sale when he talked to the president. . . . So he disapproves the contact or negotiation with Allende prior to the inauguration. If we could convince him that Korry was only going to warn him, he might change his mind.

JOHNSON: I put it in those terms.

KISSINGER: I know, but he doesn't think he'll stick to it. . . .

JOHNSON: . . . You would not want Korry to even make a courtesy call?

KISSINGER: Let's be honest. Do you think Korry is tamable? There was another thing we all found striking. For the whole week he was selling one line on the deals he was going to get; then on Saturday he switched it to a warning.

JOHNSON: . . . With the absence of any message from the president it would be a hardline statement we would be making. The lack of a courtesy call would be a very powerful signal.

KISSINGER: That's my instinct too. . . . You feel he should make a courtesy call?

JOHNSON: Yes, and he should talk from the points we have made here. . . .

KISSINGER: He is absolutely not authorized to negotiate anything. . . .

President Nixon
October 23, 1970, 8:50 a.m.
A CIA-assisted plot to kidnap and remove Chilean commander-in-chief General René Schneider, who opposed military intervention in Chilean politics, to pave the way for a coup against Allende had ended in his shooting (he later died) but no coup.[8]

NIXON: What's happening in Chile?

KISSINGER: There's been a turn for the worse but it hasn't triggered anything else. The next move should have been a government takeover, but that hasn't happened.

NIXON: You mean if something happened the people would get so disturbed that they would take over the government?

KISSINGER: That was the theory, but they're a pretty incompetent bunch. . . . The election [in the Chilean Congress that would ratify Allende as president] is tomorrow and the inauguration is the third. What they could have done is prevent the Congress from meeting. But that hasn't been done. It's close, but it's probably too late. . . .

9

The Son Tay Prison Raid and Heavy Bombing of North Vietnam, Charles de Gaulle's Funeral, South Vietnamese Operations and U.S. Bombing in Cambodia, and Laos Planning

November–December 1970

In November 1970, U.S. forces conducted a bold raid on the Son Tay prison camp deep into North Vietnam west of Hanoi to rescue American prisoners of war. But the operation was an intelligence failure (and then a roll of the dice with late inauspicious intelligence), and there were no longer any Americans there. Simultaneous with the raid, the Nixon administration conducted heavy bombing in the Haiphong–Hanoi area. It portrayed the bombing as "protective reaction" against enemy fire on unarmed U.S. reconnaissance planes well south of Haiphong and Hanoi; it was thus lying about both the reason for and location of the bombing. (It was eventually forced to admit the truth.) Kissinger even lied to Secretary of State William Rogers about where the bombing was taking place.

The same month, former French president Charles de Gaulle suffered a fatal heart attack, and Nixon and Kissinger attended his memorial in Paris.

Also in November, enemy forces launched an offensive in Cambodia that Nixon placed great urgency on foiling. But after the domestic uproar over the earlier Cambodia invasion, he was adamant that American airlifting of South Vietnamese troops and supplies into Cambodia to counter the offensive be kept quiet and that no U.S. ground forces be deployed. But he fervidly ordered massive U.S. bombing of Cambodia. "I want them to hit everything," employing every conceivable type of aircraft, he directed Kissinger, who chuckled about

Nixon's order ("Anything that flies on anything that moves," as he described it) with his deputy, Alexander Haig.

Meanwhile, planning for a U.S.-supported, ill-fated South Vietnamese invasion of Laos had begun.

Ronald Ziegler
November 2, 1970, a.m.
Kissinger accuses Press Secretary Ziegler of revealing his presence at a restaurant frequented by the Hollywood set in Los Angeles.

KISSINGER: I appreciate the way you got my personal affairs all over the White House.

ZIEGLER: What do you mean?

KISSINGER: Telling Haldeman and Ehrlichman about me at Scandia last night.

ZIEGLER: I didn't mention it to a soul. And you may be leaking it yourself. . . .

KISSINGER: It was either Haig or you because you're the only ones who knew.

ZIEGLER: You draw your own conclusions. The press was trying to track you down all over town. They wanted your predictions of the outcome of the elections. The president wants you to make some statements on how you think the elections will come out. Will you do that?

KISSINGER: Certainly. Just tell them I hope all the traitors will be defeated.

President Nixon
November 9, 1970, 3:40 p.m.
Nixon asks about secret planning to rescue the POWs at the Son Tay prison camp, which would be combined with two days of massive bombing that was partly a diversion.[1]

. . . NIXON: . . . Is the Laird plan going forward? When does that come off?

KISSINGER: 21st–25th.

NIXON: I thought so. It's worth a try. I want to look at it again in terms of the Mickey Mouse way they were talking. It's like football, if you fake you have to have the bait. You have to bang them. . . . Unless you really make the fake look real, it won't work. . . .

Alexander Haig
November 10, 1970, no time (morning)
Former French president Charles de Gaulle had died and Kissinger and Haig scramble to get a statement together. (Both Kissinger and Nixon make racist remarks.)

... KISSINGER: Now do you think these great brains we've got could possibly get these four sentences of a public statement finished? ... After three hours of work?

HAIG: Well, this is this goddamn speechwriter exercise we go through; they all think they are going to make the history books by what they write.

KISSINGER: Yes, but the point that I'm making is I don't care about the feelings of other elements of the bureaucracy, I care about results. ... What would it do if we had a decent statement? Nothing. They would scream and yell. ... Hell, I can do it in five minutes if you would just send somebody out to the house with the stupid thing. ... Please let's have the goddamn statement ready and then let Ziegler be ready to go and say we are going, so that we don't follow every African state. ...

President Nixon
November 10, 1970, no time (morning)

... KISSINGER: And I think we ought to announce that [his attendance] fairly quickly because otherwise 50 African nations are going to get ahead of us and it will be announced.

NIXON: Yeah. Now, I don't want a delegation. ... I don't want a bunch of jerks going with me. ... In other words, I don't want any goddamn senators and congressmen that I'll have to talk to. ... About 100 African nations, all those jackasses will be there, and so I think we ought to go. ...

President Nixon
November 10, 1970, no time (morning)
Nixon is adamant that Secret Service agents not sit next to him at the memorial.

... NIXON: ... Now! I am just sitting here and I haven't told Haldeman yet, but I am not going to have the goddamned Secret Service sitting in that pew with me. Now, that's not done by any other government and I'm not going to. ... If they are, I am firing the Secret Service. Now, they have ruined every rally picture with that and they are not going to do it here. ... I am giving the orders right now, these son of a bitches are not going to be there. ... By god, in that French cathedral we are either going to be safe in it or they are going to blow it up—one of the two. That's all there is to it. ... Now, I assume everything can be done Thursday—the funeral, and if [French President Georges] Pompidou sees us it will be in the afternoon, right?

KISSINGER: That's right. He will see you for 15 minutes.

NIXON: And then that's all we want. I will put in my call on Pompidou and then out we'll go and go right to the airport and off we will go. ...

President Nixon

November 14, 1970, 2:20 p.m.

Nixon and Kissinger discuss North Vietnamese firing on U.S. reconnaissance planes and U.S. bombing in retaliation, and the planning for the rescue of American POWs at the Son Tay prison camp and simultaneous bombing of the North.

> . . . KISSINGER: They fired at planes again today and made a statement on Hanoi radio that there was no understanding [at the time of the 1968 U.S. bombing halt against shooting down U.S. reconnaissance planes].
>
> NIXON: There was! . . . I think it's time for a hell of a good bang. Whatever happens on the helicopter thing [Son Tay].
>
> KISSINGER: I am getting plans for the whole operation. . . . Maybe hit two or three places like the dumps where the fire came from, where there are a lot of supplies.
>
> NIXON: . . . Give them a big bang. We have good reason to do it. If they have a lot of supplies, knock the hell out of their supplies. We can't temporize.
>
> KISSINGER: We will do it in conjunction with the helicopter thing so they won't be in a high state of alert.
>
> NIXON: I agree. The whole thing should be done then. . . . They won't know where the next blow is coming from. But don't publicize it. . . . Nothing is to be announced from out there. We will merely say it was in reaction to [firing at U.S. planes]. . . . I would like to see the plan. I think it's a good one. Did you tell Bill?
>
> KISSINGER: I am planning to tell Bill Monday or Tuesday. . . .
>
> NIXON: Talk to him with Laird. . . . Tell him it is a protective reaction plot. Don't build that up too much. Say we are going to hit a couple of places because they have been firing on planes. . . .

President Nixon

November 16, 1970, 8:50 p.m.

They consult again on the Son Tay raid and the bombing.

> . . . NIXON: Saturday, the 21st.
>
> KISSINGER: Assuming there is a full moon, assuming there is good weather that night. The morning after they go on . . . that operation, go after the supply dumps.
>
> NIXON: They are hitting the supply dumps second rather than first?
>
> KISSINGER: Yes, they will go on a state of alert if the supply dumps are hit first. . . . If they get out with the number of prisoners they expect to get out with, they may get out as many as 90, but they are pretty confident to get around 50.

NIXON: Based on simply letters?

KISSINGER: Letters, photographs, and considering that we have only got nine prisoners out as long as the war has gone on.

NIXON: If we get nine, that would be a hell of a thing.

KISSINGER: If we get any we will get more than nine, assuming their intelligence is good. . . .

William Rogers
November 20, 1970, 3:45 p.m.
An early report on Son Tay is not good: there were apparently no prisoners there. Intelligence had recently determined there was a low chance they were still there, but reconnaissance flights had detected activity.[2]

KISSINGER: We just got a flash from [Pacific Commander John] McCain indicating it may be nothing. But my supposition is that he wouldn't have sent it if he didn't know. Either it was not there or they moved them. I think under these conditions we should say nothing. . . .

ROGERS: What a disappointment. All those people and that work.

KISSINGER: They went in and out so fast that it worked either as planned or was a dry hole. . . .

William Rogers
November 20, 1970, 5:32 p.m.

ROGERS: Is there any further word?

KISSINGER: No word since the garbled transmission. They should be on the ground, and we should be hearing shortly. I'm positive it was a dry hole. They wouldn't have transmitted that message unless they were pretty sure. Laird and Moorer seem to think so too. . . .

President Nixon
November 20, 1970, 6:25 p.m.
Kissinger conveys to Nixon the latest on the raid, which Nixon says "proves they could do another one," and they discuss the bombing of North Vietnam, which he wants portrayed as "protective reaction." Nixon is eager to do "something daring" again, even an "end-of-the-war plan" involving "quarantining Vietnam while we withdraw." (H. R. Haldeman wrote in his diary that day that Nixon wanted to give Hanoi a "last chance, then pull out" of peace talks, "mine Haiphong (or blockade), take offensive, and announce stepped-up withdrawals." Kissinger didn't think the plan would work.)[3] And Nixon wants heavier bombing of the North.

KISSINGER: Mr. President, we have confirmation now and the original report was right. Everyone got away—no one was hurt and there were no casualties. . . . This was a telephone report. We are getting a flash message—a full report in. I asked the same question—whether there was ever anything there or what it was. There wasn't a trap or they wouldn't have gotten away uninjured.

NIXON: It was a complete surprise—but a little late.

KISSINGER: It was bad luck.

NIXON: It was not bad luck at all. We haven't paid any price at all. It was just a little exercise, but it proved we could do it. It proves they could do another one.

KISSINGER: That's right. They could hit something else with that sort of thing. The other thing is going.

NIXON: Good. One or two [air strikes]?

KISSINGER: It depends on the weather. One, certainly.

NIXON: Get a message to that colonel congratulating him. . . . Say I am proud of him and his men—the daring, the execution.

KISSINGER: I have done that. It ran like planned. . . .

NIXON: Poor Johnson and even Kennedy. They stomped around and didn't do anything.

KISSINGER: If they had taken the initiative, we wouldn't be in the mess we are in now.

NIXON: I like the idea of something daring. You and Laird work quietly on it. This is the end-of-the-war plan. Do it on the basis that we are quarantining Vietnam while we withdraw. What South Vietnam does after that is their business. The only problem is what the Russians will do, but let them do it.

KISSINGER: They have played a very rough game with us.

NIXON: It will change. This strike today will hurt. . . . We are going to start, in effect, by re-bombing the North on the basis of protective reaction. We took this one—another next week. If they ask questions, Mel says it was protective reaction—he's good at that. We couldn't do it earlier because of the weather. For every one they give us, we give them more.

KISSINGER: They have told us now they will shoot any other planes.

NIXON: I want to see some of the plans. If they give us any provocation—

KISSINGER: It was a little pinprick before—they used 10 planes. It was nothing to talk about.

NIXON: Use 100 planes—knock the sons of bitches out. . . . It's amazing—20 miles from Hanoi [the Son Tay raid]. That proves something, too.

KISSINGER: I am sure they are shaken.

NIXON: We say nothing. Deny everything. It could have been a search-and-destroy operation, which we have going all the time. That really must screw up Hanoi.

KISSINGER: They are totally confused. They can't figure out what hit them.

NIXON: Tell Moorer to have the same colonel brought back for planning. He must have great imagination. He will find another one. I like guys like this. . . .

President Nixon
November 20, 1970, about 6:40 p.m.
Nixon asks for the latest on the raid.

NIXON: . . . Anything new?

KISSINGER: No final word, but I am pretty certain. . . .

NIXON: Oh, well, this is fine. . . . It was a brilliant move, brilliantly executed. We'll find something else to do. . . . There were no casualties, right?

KISSINGER: Yes, and our intercepts say the enemy is totally confused. They don't know what has happened. . . .

William Rogers
November 21, 1970, 1:45 a.m.
The bombing of North Vietnam, where "wave after wave" of U.S. planes were drop-ping their payloads, including on Haiphong and near Hanoi, killing many civilians, had begun. Melvin Laird would publicly describe it as "protective reaction" well south of Haiphong and Hanoi against enemy fire on unarmed U.S. reconnaissance planes, a lie. The U.S. command in Saigon imposed a blackout on the bombing.[4] Kissinger tells Rogers that the areas in North Vietnam that Hanoi radio reported were be-ing bombed were not being struck, and they debate what to say, if anything, about the failed Son Tay raid. Remarkably, not only was the administration lying about where it was bombing and why, but Kissinger was lying to the secretary of state about it.

KISSINGER: . . . The area that they are reporting is not where the air strikes are going on—they are reporting Haiphong and the province where that other operation [the Son Tay raid] went on. So, what Defense wants to do is to come out with the agreed statement on the protective reaction part, and then the question is should they say anything about the other operation? . . .

ROGERS: I am inclined to think not. . . .

KISSINGER: Well, my first reaction was exactly the same as yours. . . . On re-flection, the only other thing we could add to it so that we are not accused of creating a credibility gap is just a sentence saying in addition there was a commando raid on . . . what we had reason to believe was an American pris-oner of war camp north of that area and we found the camp vacated with no American prisoners there.

ROGERS: Did we get a full report on it? . . .

KISSINGER: We know that there were no Americans there and that it had been empty for several months. . . .

ROGERS: How is Hanoi reporting the prisoners business?

KISSINGER: . . . In effect they are reporting that waves of American planes have started attacking at 2:30 Hanoi time, which is, of course, the other operation. . . . The areas they mentioned we didn't bomb. Some of this may have been just complete confusion on their part as to what did go on. . . . We should say . . . we conducted a commando raid by a small team against a suspected prisoner of war camp for the purpose of saving American prisoners. . . . We found that the camp had been vacated several weeks previously. All members of the commando team returned safely and there were no casualties. . . .

ROGERS: Do we know it was vacated two or three months ago?

KISSINGER: That's what the report said that we got—that it looked as if it had been uninhabited for several months.

ROGERS: I thought they told us they had seen a lot of activity there from the air.

KISSINGER: Dammit, they told us—when I got the briefing they told us that they had been moving people in. Had gone from 60 to 90 [prisoners] and that's what they told you.

ROGERS: Yeah, they told us that there was some recent activity there. . . . It makes us look awful silly if we say we conducted a commando raid and the camp had been vacated two or three months ago.

KISSINGER: Well, we don't have to say anything. We can just say this didn't happen. I mean, we can just say nothing. No air attacks took place north of the 19th parallel. [Haiphong and Hanoi were well north of the 19th parallel.] . . . Our concern is that if any of these guys blab when they come back—after all, there are 60 people involved.

ROGERS: Yeah. Oh, it will be known in the camp—we can't avoid that. Can't we say that the camp had been vacated but there were no casualties?

KISSINGER: Certainly. We found that the camp had been vacated and there were no casualties. We don't have to say how long ago.

ROGERS: I think maybe that's the way to do it. I suppose we might as well say it first rather than have it dragged out of us tomorrow. . . .

William Rogers
November 21, 1970, 9:00 a.m.
Kissinger provides an update on the Son Tay raid and they decide to keep silent about it for now.

KISSINGER: . . . They apparently killed five guards. Went through the compound and felt that it had been used as a prison but not used for several months. There was no one else there. They killed two others, making it a total of seven altogether. Put some ordnance in near there to keep those troops from coming in—all according to the plan. It was a beautifully executed plan—it was just bad luck that there were no prisoners to extricate. Laird is going to make a brief protective reaction statement. . . . We should not go with this commando operation. . . . Next week if things cool down a bit. . . .

President Nixon
November 21, 1970, 11:45 a.m.
Kissinger confers with Nixon on their "protective reaction" public line on the bombing and denial that they were bombing in the Hanoi–Haiphong area. And they agree that they should say nothing about Son Tay. "Tell Laird to stonewall it right through," Nixon orders. He wants "more schemes of this sort." If the North Vietnamese do not release their POWs, Kissinger says, "We would go back to bombing the living daylights out of them."

KISSINGER: I just wanted to bring you up to date on a few things. Hanoi radio started reporting massive air attacks. Their radar probably picked up the commando raid and they are picking up diversionary strikes. Said we attacked one of our own POW camps. [This was not Son Tay.] Laird is issuing a short statement. I worked with Laird and I talked with Rogers, so we are all on board that we didn't hit anything north of the 19th parallel, and [the strikes] caused by fact that they were hitting some of our unarmed reconnaissance planes, and this was done in protection. Talking about saying something about the commando operation, but they would just say it was another Bay of Pigs and decided not to say anything about it.

NIXON: I don't want anyone to say anything. . . .

KISSINGER: At 11:30 this morning Laird put out a statement saying that the strikes were ending at 6 p.m. today, and second, no air attacks on POW camps and holding them solely accountable for American lives. The other operation went beautifully, except no one was there. They killed five guards.

NIXON: Guards were still there? Why would they have guards there if there were no prisoners? Do you suppose they could have hidden them underground?

KISSINGER: Guards or caretakers but they were military personnel. If they had hidden them they would have been expecting us and hit us with a buzz saw.

NIXON: Why do the military guard the place if no one is there?

KISSINGER: Just to keep the natives from moving in or perhaps just to move people through. It was damn bad luck. The whole operation worked exactly as they planned. The weather is so bad that we are not getting photo reconnaissance on the areas hit. But the visual reports say that we are doing a lot of damage.

NIXON: . . . On this other operation I want you to hold right to the line and do not discuss it at all. No comment whatsoever. . . . What do they want to talk about it for?

KISSINGER: They would like to crow about it a little bit. It was a beautifully executed operation deep into enemy territory and their office [Defense] had a lot to do with it. . . .

NIXON: We will recognize them and let them know we thought they did a good job. We won't talk about it now but later we will explain what happened. Get that colonel back here. Get in a group of them. Get Defense to work on similar actions. They must have some others but thought they would get turned down so didn't propose them. We are going to be out of there in a year so we can do some of these things. What do we care? . . . Proves that something can be done. We need more schemes of this sort. For the past five years no schemes because nobody approved them. Well, we will approve them. We only have one year left. . . . Why don't we put some of the South Vietnamese on this type of operation? They have a big army. Scare the hell out of these people.

KISSINGER: Certainly. Now that they have seen that we can do it they are probably doing a lot of thinking. To land 20 miles from their capital and get out does not reassure them.

NIXON: The failure will not be discussed . . . successful operation. We went in to see if there were any there and got rid of the guards. . . . Other operations being planned. . . . We would like to look for another one. How many POWs do they have?

KISSINGER: . . . Have 400 with several hundred missing.

NIXON: This is the only major initiative to negotiate. What will they do with them if we don't negotiate and just pull out? Kill them?

KISSINGER: Oh, no. We would go back to bombing the living daylights out of them.

NIXON: Seven-day strike so that we do not have to maintain the tension during all that time. As you recall, seven-day strike hitting complexes up there would give them a blow that would set them back several months. . . . What we need is more imagination in some of the things we can do now. . . . We do not talk about POW thing. . . . It was just one of our routine . . . search-and-rescue operations. Tell Laird to stonewall it right through. . . .

John Freeman

November 21, 1970, no time (evening)

Kissinger tells the British ambassador to the United States that all of the U.S. bombing of North Vietnam was "south of the 19th parallel," hence way south of Hanoi and Haiphong. The administration would later have to acknowledge that that wasn't true.[5]

> .. KISSINGER: We are right now conducting some pretty massive air attacks in North Vietnam . . . in the panhandle area which . . . are technically in response to the shootdown of American planes but for your information primarily designed to hit some of the supplies they have piled there for their very large, high infiltration that is going on at this moment. . . . Secondly, you should also know that for the prime minister's own information that this . . . was done at this particular time as a cover for a commando raid where we were trying to free some American prisoners in a camp that we had identified. . . . And that raid unfortunately failed. . . . Hanoi claims that Haiphong and the belt north . . . is being attacked. That is not true; all the bombing is south of the 19th parallel. . . . But there was air activity in that northern area in order to . . . deflect the radar from the commando raid. . . . But it did not drop any ordnance. . . .

Melvin Laird

November 23, 1970, 8:57 a.m.

Kissinger objects to Laird holding a briefing on the bombing, afraid of what he might say. Laird says he will declare that it was all "below the 19th parallel."

> . . . KISSINGER: . . . I had an anguished call from State about your briefing this morning and what the point of it is. . . .
>
> LAIRD: We are just giving a report that there were no planes lost.
>
> KISSINGER: But you won't give any details? . . .
>
> LAIRD: [We will] tell them we were after anti-aircraft missile sites. . . .
>
> KISSINGER: But you won't go into a long explanation of where we hit?
>
> LAIRD: We will say there were strikes authorized for 18 hours but terminated in 16 hours due to bad weather. . . . All strikes were below the 19th parallel. Period. . . .

President Nixon

November 23, 1970, 7:06 p.m.

Laird held a press conference that day with two commanders of the Son Tay raid, which drew both criticism and applause in Congress.[6] *With some fervor, Nixon directs Kissinger to help rally the supporters and bloody the critics.*

KISSINGER: Mr. President, I just wanted to tell you I talked to Senator [Robert] Dole who was locked in a tough debate with Kennedy and Fulbright.

NIXON: Kennedy in it too. Good, get him in it! . . . How about getting Laird to get those two guys down there and give them a briefing. . . . No excuses and no apologies of any kind. . . . At the staff meeting tomorrow morning, if one of those sons of bitches sticks his head up, knock it off! People have got to start being proud to be Americans! . . . Dole realize what a gutsy move it was? Was he in the debate? Laird probably didn't prepare him for the goddamn debate! . . . Tell Mel he has got to get [Senator Henry "Scoop"] Jackson and Dole briefed. Get [Senator Edmund] Muskie on the other side of this one. . . . Otherwise the press will play this up the wrong way. Do you comprehend me now?

KISSINGER: Right, Mr. President.

President Nixon

December 2, 1970, no time

Kissinger had attended an Army–Navy football game that featured a halftime ceremony honoring participants in the Son Tay raid and POWs.[7] Kissinger tells Nixon about it and conversations he had with some wives of POWs, and they castigate the "cheap little bastards" in Congress and the media who criticized the raid, some of whom were now showing their lack of principles by backing off their positions. Kissinger says head U.S. negotiator in Paris David Bruce should demand a list of American POWs, and Nixon wants him to threaten escalation.

. . . KISSINGER: . . . [Senator] Hugh Scott was on the train going up there with me, and—you know, he's an opportunist—but he said that Muskie and Kennedy are all on the wrong side of that issue, and they are pulling back like crazy. . . . And he's attacking, which is another sign that it must be pretty safe.

NIXON: Well, did the audience react? . . .

KISSINGER: A tremendous ovation. And I've talked to five of these wives. . . . I said to one of these girls . . . "What is really moving is that you don't bring any pressure on us to just end the war so that you get your husbands back." They said that would be denying everything he believes in, and we'd be betraying him if we did that.

NIXON: Boy, aren't they something!

KISSINGER: Then, when you see these cheap little bastards—

NIXON: Yeah, well, the cheap ones like the Muskies and the Teddy Kennedys.

KISSINGER: And the Fulbrights.

NIXON: And the silly little columnists. . . . Good god. . . . You know, Henry, it's no credit to them that they begin to sort of crawl off that position when public opinion—

KISSINGER: Not at all.

NIXON: The bastards—that shows they have no principle at all. That's not a good reason to crawl off it. If they believe it was a mistake and this and that, they should stick to it. . . . As far as the people are concerned, they would just as soon you'd bomb the whole damn place.

KISSINGER: Exactly, they don't care where.

NIXON: . . . The [*Washington*] *Post* is trying to make something of it, but they're just desperate as hell. . . .

KISSINGER: And the *Post* is just an organ of the Democratic community. . . . One thing that I thought Bruce ought to do at the meeting on Thursday . . . he should say that it is bad enough that you don't release the prisoners but there is no excuse whatever for not giving the list of prisoners, and I hereby call on you to at least put these wives out of their misery. . . . It's inhumane; this is behaving like the Nazis did in World War II.

NIXON: Good, use exactly that phrase.

KISSINGER: Because that's what the Nazis did with Soviet prisoners, they wouldn't release their names. . . .

NIXON: . . . I think we have got to get a hell of a lot rougher, you know. [Former chief negotiator Henry Cabot] Lodge used to make these pleading little noises about prisoners over there and that didn't do any good. . . . Of course we are in this position now too where we got the enemy just bamboozled as to what's going to happen, because on the one hand Rogers in court testifies that we don't plan to escalate and haven't, and Laird says we might. . . . I want Bruce to make no damn bones about it when he gets up there. . . . He's got to take the line that we've got other options. . . . Start laying the groundwork for a break-off of the negotiations if necessary. . . . Hellfire, if we're going to get out anyway, what the hell we got to negotiate about? . . .

President Nixon
December 9, 1970, 12:20 p.m.
Enemy forces had launched an offensive in Cambodia's northern front and Nixon places great urgency on thwarting it, though he doesn't want U.S. planes involved in an airlift of South Vietnamese troops.

. . . KISSINGER: . . . In Cambodia the communists have started an attack and have beaten up Cambodia. Perhaps we should have an airlift of the area. It's best to start our offensive or we will be in a rescue operation.

NIXON: . . . No question of going forward if we can get them to do it. . . . Any question about Moorer knowing about the urgency I put on this problem? . . . Any air needed, put it in there. On the infiltration, maybe you have to bang earlier.

KISSINGER: If the airlift is undertaken we may be [asked] to fly the planes for it.

NIXON: No. That should be avoided. See what they can do on their own for a change. That will open a whole can of worms.

KISSINGER: I favor the ground offensive over the airlift because we don't want a South Vietnamese unit trapped up there.

NIXON: Make sure they are going at breakneck speed. Hit them before they hit us. . . . How about another strike at the choke points? It's not fiddle-dee-dee as before. . . . We are not going to lose this at this point. I don't want Americans on the ground in the North but we will do anything else. . . .

President Nixon
December 9, 1970, 8:00 p.m.

NIXON: Moorer can prepare this operation in Cambodia in terms of airlifting. . . . If we airlift supplies that's not a problem and the men just happened to be in the plane. . . . They can put a piece of cotton candy on the plane if they want to. . . . I think we ought to take a chance provided it is an airlift of supplies. . . . And if there are a few forces on it, fuzz it up for a change.

President Nixon
December 9, 1970, 8:45 p.m.
A fired-up Nixon orders Kissinger to tell JCS Chairman Thomas Moorer to plan a massive U.S. bombing attack in Cambodia using "every goddamn thing that can fly" to "hit everything." Nixon condemns the air force's "goddamn milk runs" in Cambodia and its "disgraceful performance." It was time to "get off their ass and start doing something." "Right now there is a chance to win this goddamn war," he declares. Nixon also decides to order U.S. airlifting of both supplies and South Vietnamese troops into Cambodia to counter the enemy offensive but wants "absolute security" on it and no troop numbers released. Worried about losing supplemental aid to Cambodia, he is adamant that no U.S. ground troops be used. But Cambodia cannot go down the drain.

. . . NIXON: . . . I want you to get ahold of Moorer tonight and I want a plan where every goddamn thing that can fly goes into Cambodia and hits every target that is open. . . . That's to be done tomorrow. Tomorrow. Is that clear? . . . Now, that is one thing that can turn this around some. They are running these goddamn milk runs in order to get the air medal. . . . It's horrible what the air force is doing. They aren't doing anything at all worth a damn.

KISSINGER: They are not imaginative.

NIXON: Well, they're not only not imaginative but they are just running these things—bombing jungles. . . . I want everything that can fly to go in there and crack the hell out of them. There is no limitation on mileage and there is no limitation on budget. . . . Now, the second thing on this drill. . . . We're not going to do it on the basis of an open-ended commitment but on the basis that you are going to . . . airlift supplies to a place, and so you airlift a hell of a lot of troops with it too. Now, there must be absolute security on it. It should be supplies. . . . The troops have to unload them, don't they? . . . We are airlifting supplies, and, sure, there are some troops, but I don't want any numbers out. . . . I don't want the air force bragging about it, and I don't want a goddamn thing said. . . . Get 'em ready and do it. . . . We will take the heat on it. I'll do it, but it is on the basis of the airlift thing and that's all. And they have got to remember that there is absolute security on this, having in mind that we have a situation here which is political, which is going to be with us until about the 23rd. . . . Then we either have the damn supplemental [aid legislation] or we don't have it. . . . So we don't want them to screw that up. . . . I see no objection to it if it doesn't screw up the supplemental. . . . But there is absolutely—they are not even to submit to me any plan that requires the use of American ground forces. Under *any circumstances whatever*!!!! Is that clear? . . . And I am not going to keep it open at the press conference. . . . I am simply going to say that we don't have any such plans. . . . We can't play these Mickey Mouse games right now. We have got—

KISSINGER: No, no. I agree with it!

NIXON: We have got to get down to the real thing that matters, and the thing that matters is . . . if we don't get this supplemental through. . . . Unless we make an absolute commitment that no American ground forces are going to be used in Cambodia, you will never get the supplemental. . . . God damn it, Abrams can do more, and that damned air force can do more about hitting Cambodia with their bombing attacks. . . . The whole goddamn air force over there farting around doing nothing, and I have watched that stuff and they aren't doing a thing. I mean, they get one or two trucks a day and fly 800 sorties and get 1,500 air medals. You know, that's all it is. . . . It is a disgraceful performance and they are going to get off their ass and start doing something on it. I want gunships in there. That means armed helicopters, DC-3s, anything else that will destroy personnel that can fly. I want it done!! Get them off their ass and get them to work now.

KISSINGER: Well, we will get it done immediately, Mr. President.

NIXON: What is needed here is they need a little drive out there. I don't know what the hell is the matter with them. . . . I am not going to have another crisis on Cambodia hit us in the face like it did last year. That again was a case of them not being on top of things. . . .

KISSINGER: The problem is, Mr. President, the air force is designed to fight an air battle against the Soviet Union. They are not designed for this war. . . . In fact, they are not designed for any war we are likely to have to fight.

NIXON: That's right. There isn't going to be any air battle against the Soviet Union, as you well know. . . . The difficulty is that they need some TBFs [torpedo bombers] and a hell of a lot of SBDs [dive bombers] and things like that could go in and knock the hell out of them. Bazookas. . . . A World War II air force would definitely make the North Vietnamese—

KISSINGER: That is unfortunately true.

NIXON: And we do not have a World War II air force. . . . Now, god damn it, maybe they have some stuff over here than can do that. I want that examined tomorrow. . . . And get those goddamned jet pilots the hell over to Taiwan and get somebody else out there that can fight them. . . . Get some conventional prop airplanes over there fast. . . . We've got a lot of prop airplanes left. I have seen them on the runways. The National Guard's got them. . . . Every prop plane that could be made air worthy for the purpose of fighting the kind of battle we need to fight there. I want the goddamn planes over there. . . . Shake up this air force and tell them exactly that I have reached the conclusion that they are designed to fight only the Soviets and they are not doing worth a damn here and it's time we are going to start doing different.

KISSINGER: . . . I will get the bombing campaign laid on for tomorrow.

NIXON: I want them to hit everything. I want them to use the big planes, the small planes, everything they can that will help out here, and let's start giving them a little shock. . . . Right now there is a chance to win this goddamn war, and that's probably what we are going to have to do because we are not going to do anything at the conference table. But we aren't going to win it with . . . the kind of assholes who come in here like today saying, "Well, now there is a crisis in Cambodia." Hell, I have been asking about it for the last two weeks, you know, and you said no, there isn't one.

KISSINGER: . . . I asked them every day. I sent backchannels. For three months I have been bugging them about that column that is now being attacked. . . .

NIXON: . . . I want something done tonight. I don't want any screwing around, and I want that air force to make its study immediately of anything in conventional World War II–type craft that can be used over there. . . . I want a new plan. I want it fast and let's get going. Also, the program for the South Vietnamese to make the ground attack is laid on, it's approved as of today. . . . We worry about the Chilean elections and we worry about whether or not there is going to be a vote on Guinea and all that bull, and the only thing that really matters at this point is this, and I just want everybody to clear their minds of all this other crap. Let the State Department handle that. I don't give a god damn what happens in those other places now. . . . But this does matter and I just think that we have made a mistake here. We haven't put enough emphasis on it and let's start putting the emphasis in there where it matters. . . . For the next two months I don't want to see anything about Chile, I don't want to see anything about Biafra, I don't want to see anything about Guinea. I don't want to see anything about all the other crap. Doesn't make any difference right now. The Pakistan elections. . . . Right now, Henry, we have got to concentrate on what can make or break us. . . . Otherwise the whole thing will go down the drain. . . .

Alexander Haig
December 9, 1970, 8:50 p.m.
Kissinger amusedly apprises his deputy of Nixon's order for the all-out Cambodia bombing.

KISSINGER: I just had a call from our friend. . . . He wants a massive bombing campaign in Cambodia. He doesn't want to hear anything. It's an order, it's to be done. Anything that flies on anything that moves. You got that? [Haig sounded to the transcriber of the tape like he was laughing.]

KISSINGER: Thirdly, now hold onto your hat. . . . He wants an inventory of every prop plane that's suitable for operations out there. . . .

HAIG: For close air support.

KISSINGER: Yes. That's actually not a bad idea. . . . Can we at least get a massive bombing attack into this area?

HAIG: Yes.

KISSINGER: How about B-52s? . . . Let him lay some in there. . . .

President Nixon
December 19, 1970, 5:30 p.m.
The president and Kissinger hash out the forthcoming U.S.-supported South Vietnamese invasion of Laos, including their handling of Melvin Laird and getting him to sell it internally—"We'll let Laird be the mastermind," Nixon says.

. . . KISSINGER: . . . Laird is going out there [to South Vietnam] early January and I think you may have to tell him before he goes what we are thinking of because otherwise it will surface out there and he'll try to kill it.

NIXON: . . . Well, we'll just tell him about the operation and tell him to keep it quiet.

KISSINGER: He's pretty good once he knows it's irrevocable. That's not the sort of thing he usually leaks.... Haig discussed it with [G. McMurtrie] Godley, our ambassador in Laos.... He's enthusiastic.

NIXON: Well, now can Godley get Souvanna [Phouma, the Laotian prime minister] to ask for it and cooperate?

KISSINGER: He thinks he can get full cooperation from Souvanna.

NIXON: Well, that will make a tremendous difference.... We'll bring everybody along....

KISSINGER: I think a good way of handling it is to tell Laird what you want ... and then he can help sell it when he gets back on the basis of his trip.

NIXON: That's right, good. And then get him a little credit.... And we'll let Laird be the mastermind.... Providing that it works. All I want now is to have something work.

KISSINGER: Well, this ought to work. I've looked at this concept and it really looks good....

Laird's Vietnam Machinations; More Strains with State; Planning a Meeting with the Kidnapping Plotters; the Ill-Fated U.S.-Supported South Vietnamese Invasion of Laos, the News Blackout and PR; and Slowing and Toning Down State on the Middle East

January–February 1971

In January 1971, acting on his own volition, Secretary of Defense Melvin Laird publicly declared an end to U.S. combat involvement in Vietnam within months. "What is he doing? Telling me to go fly a kite?" an angry Kissinger responded. On January 12, six political activists were charged with plotting to kidnap Kissinger and commit acts of sabotage, and seven others were named unindicted co-conspirators. Through his antiwar friend Brian McDonnell, Kissinger agreed to meet with several of the alleged co-conspirators.

In February, South Vietnamese troops, supported by American bombing, artillery, and helicopters—use of U.S. ground troops was politically untenable—invaded Laos to sever the main arteries on the Ho Chi Minh Trail, capture the key enemy logistics hub of Tchepone, and destroy enemy bases to halt the movement of North Vietnamese troops and supplies into South Vietnam, Cambodia, and southern Laos. The administration hoped the invasion would disrupt the enemy's logistics buildup and cramp an expected enemy offensive. Both Nixon and Kissinger were nervous about it. And the operation, ill-conceived and badly carried out, was a disaster. It soon stalled, coming to an unforced stop, with inadequately trained South Vietnamese soldiers battered by North Vietnamese units in intense fighting and suffering major casualties; North Vietnamese strength had exceeded expectations and Hanoi had advance intelligence on the invasion. Reports that it was bogged down upset U.S. officials, who began publicly backing off their goal of capturing Tchepone.

Meanwhile, Kissinger was trying to slow down State Department and UN initiatives on the Middle East that, among other problems, asked Israel to return to the borders before its conquests in the 1967 Six Day War, which Kissinger knew didn't stand a chance in hell of gaining Israel's acceptance and would lead to a public confrontation with Israel.

Ronald Ziegler
January 6, 1971, 10:08 a.m.
Melvin Laird had said in Paris on his way to Southeast Asia that the United States would end its combat role in South Vietnam by midsummer.[1]

ZIEGLER: Laird has said in Paris—

KISSINGER: Oh, no.

ZIEGLER: It's not really that bad; I just wanted to get some guidance. . . . He says we are way ahead of schedule and American forces will be out of the combat . . . by the end of this year.

KISSINGER: Don't make any comment on that. . . . I will turn Laird off. . . . I will tell you one thing, Ron, this administration is going to make a great contribution to theology because if we succeed with this cabinet there must be a god.

ZIEGLER: That's great. Be sure and write that down, Julie [Pineau, Kissinger's secretary]. Write it down and tuck it away for the future. . . .

Ronald Ziegler
January 6, 1971, 12:45 p.m.
Ziegler says he was "fuzzy" in a press briefing about Laird's remarks and Kissinger wants him to say nothing more.

ZIEGLER: We run into this all the time. Whenever we come out here [to San Clemente] it seems that Laird or Rogers has gone on a trip and we get into all sorts of questions about do you concur with the secretary of defense or don't you? I did not concur. It was pretty fuzzy and I kept wobbling around.

KISSINGER: I talked to the president and he absolutely wants to hold this line.

ZIEGLER: I am not going to state when U.S. ground forces are complete. . . .

KISSINGER: Ron, don't let them drive you any further.

ZIEGLER: What can I do when it is a statement by the secretary of defense? I can't just ignore it.

KISSINGER: I would not give too much credence to their statements. . . . I would just say we have no more to say. . . .

David Packard

January 7, 1971, 8:40 a.m.

Laird's statements on the end of U.S. combat involvement had appeared on the front page of the New York Times *that morning.*

KISSINGER: What is he doing? Telling me to go fly a kite? . . . If he wants a presidential directive I'll get him one. . . . The president is going to be fit to be tied. . . . Every place he goes he is popping off about the end of the combat role. . . .

William Rogers

January 13, 1971, 3:15 p.m.

Secretary of State Rogers is angry that U.S. Chief of Protocol Emil Mosbacher was offered the ambassadorship to the Organization of American States behind his back. Kissinger, who'd tried to persuade Mosbacher to take the job,[2] claims he has "nothing to do with these appointments."

ROGERS: Henry, I was talking to Bob Haldeman a little while ago and found out that the president offered the OAS post to Mosbacher. He said that the president talked to Mosbacher and that you talked to him and [Nelson] Rockefeller talked to him. God damn it, Henry, I did not even know about it. What the hell is going on?

KISSINGER: I have nothing to do with these appointments. I assumed you were aware of it. . . . My understanding was that Haldeman was going to talk to you about a series of appointments. Mosbacher asked my opinion about the job.

ROGERS: Did you tell him to go to Rockefeller?

KISSINGER: . . . Point is that Rockefeller knows quite a lot about Latin America.

ROGERS: Point is that I did not know anything about it and if you want to have a hand in appointments then I will just stay out of it altogether. . . .

KISSINGER: . . . I stay out of these appointments.

ROGERS: You do not if you talk to people, Henry.

KISSINGER: Not out of my initiative. I assume all the clearances were completed when someone comes to me and asks my opinion. . . .

ROGERS: Simple goddamn thing. . . . If you are going to be involved then I am going to stay out of it. And you cannot be not involved if you are going to talk to people. . . . I think it is a miserable idea. He is the least qualified for this position. . . . He doesn't know anything about Latin America. . . .

George Shultz
January 13, 1971, 4:00 p.m.
Kissinger tells Budget Director Shultz that Nixon wants to increase the Defense budget, then immediately calls Laird about it and says he has not talked to Shultz.

. . . KISSINGER: . . . He would like to add the 500 million to the Defense budget on the grounds that the Russians are beginning to harass us more.

SHULTZ: I don't know where he'd put it. . . . It would drive us out of our minds to change the Defense budget now. It is literally now being printed. . . .

Melvin Laird
January 13, 1971, 4:10 p.m.

KISSINGER: I have just been talking to the president on the Defense budget and he would like to add $500 million to it and the damn thing is practically locked up. . . . I have not discussed this with George Shultz so don't call him. . . .

Brian McDonnell
January 20, 1971, 11:28 a.m.
On January 12, six people had been indicted on charges of plotting to kidnap Kissinger and blow up the heating systems of federal buildings in Washington. Seven others were named as co-conspirators but not defendants. Kissinger's antiwar friend McDonnell, who had fasted to protest the invasion of Cambodia, says he was investigated about the alleged kidnapping plot and asks Kissinger to meet with two of the people who'd been named as co-conspirators. Kissinger says he will if they won't talk about it publicly.

. . . MCDONNELL: They have already bothered all of my friends—where I was, when, etc. It's disheartening—bothering people with no relationship to me. They get people excited without any kind of information.

KISSINGER: You can be sure I am not talking to anyone.

MCDONNELL: The whole scene of the indictment is whacked out. While there might be evidence, there is some disproportionate kind of thinking. . . . What I suggested to some of the people named as co-conspirators—they called me and I know them very well—

KISSINGER: Should you discuss this on the telephone? . . . I would be delighted to hear it, but I don't want to get you into trouble. . . .

MCDONNELL: The meeting last night was very open to anyone who wanted to come. . . . One of the things that came up is they would like to sit down with you as a man who has been threatened.

KISSINGER: Of course, I will do it. The co-conspirators?

MCDONNELL: Yes. I think it would be very good.

KISSINGER: I am willing to do it. Let me check with the security service first. . . . Like who? The nuns? [Several nuns and the Reverends Philip and Daniel Berrigan were among the alleged plotters.]

MCDONNELL: Particularly two people: Tom Davidson, ex-religious; and Bill Davidon.

KISSINGER: In principle, I am happy to do it.

MCDONNELL: First, I would like you to do a check with security, and two, think about the ground rules you would like.

KISSINGER: The only ground rule is they cannot come out and say they talked to me. They are the same rules as I had with you. If it's a personal dialogue, I would be happy to do it. If it is a publicity platform, I won't do it. . . .

MCDONNELL: The only assurance I can give you will be that I will ascertain to the best I can that this will not happen.

KISSINGER: That's fair enough.

MCDONNELL: . . . As far as my own safety, I feel very safe and it has even brought my brother close to me.

KISSINGER: On this conspiracy? . . . But you couldn't be part of it, judging it on human grounds.

MCDONNELL: I can honestly say the things I know about in regard to talk about your being kidnapped—which I brought to you—was true. The people are so confused.

KISSINGER: I have never told anyone what you said. They got the information from other sources. . . . I remember you thought it was sufficiently realistic that I should take precautions at the UN meeting.

MCDONNELL: The fact that I thought it was reasonably real has nothing to do with the people in this particular indictment. You are a popular cat.

KISSINGER: That is reassuring to know. . . .

Brian McDonnell

January 21, 1971, 9:20 a.m.

McDonnell and Kissinger confer on the meeting with the alleged kidnap plotters.

MCDONNELL: Talked to them and they thought your schedule was the most taxed. But under these circumstances they accept it. . . .

KISSINGER: Are any of them indicted?

MCDONNELL: No.

KISSINGER: Okay. . . . You are coming with them?

MCDONNELL: They thought it best. . . . The subject of the discussion would be nonviolence. I mean, they are not going to be asking you to intervene [in the kidnapping case] or anything like that.

KISSINGER: I couldn't. I don't know enough about it to. But I want to do it and I think I can get it done.

MCDONNELL: Okay. But I have told them, and I give you my word, this is neither a plot to sit-in or a plot to get publicity.

KISSINGER: Okay. We'll get together.

William Rogers
January 26, 1971, 3:30 p.m.
The State Department had insisted on Laotian Prime Minister Souvanna Phouma's approval of the forthcoming U.S.-supported South Vietnamese invasion of Laos, and Rogers and Kissinger discuss a cable from U.S. Ambassador to Laos G. McMurtrie Godley to Souvanna.[3]

KISSINGER: I just wanted to touch base with you. Regarding that cable from Godley, we should make Godley tell Souvanna a little more so that he has no misconceptions of what is involved.

ROGERS: . . . I think he has to tell him exactly what we have in mind. If he has objections and claims duplicity, it would be a catastrophe. . . . We shouldn't say it's just a raid. . . .

KISSINGER: I think we have to give some feel for the length. That assessment the president had makes the specific point that if it is short, it will not be very effective. Therefore, I think if we go in there, we should go in with the determination to stay through the better part of the dry season.

ROGERS: There's no point in doing it unless you do.

KISSINGER: The heat won't get any less.

ROGERS: It will get greater.

Richard Helms
January 29, 1971, 9:15 a.m.
Kissinger asks CIA Director Helms his view of the invasion of Laos. The first phase, a U.S. blocking operation just south of the DMZ and U.S. occupation of the abandoned combat base at Khe Sanh in northern South Vietnam, was about to commence.[4]

. . . KISSINGER: I haven't had a chance to canvass you—having seen these things come and go, is it desirable?

HELMS: On the question of militarily, no contest, but with the statesmen we have to get a better feel of it out there. We could have a military victory and a political disaster. But it's important if we can bring if off because there's no doubt on the importance of the area. We could set this fellow back.

KISSINGER: . . . Are you as optimistic about '72 as some of our colleagues? Without it?

HELMS: I think that it's down the track that is our problem. We are pulling our troops out and propping the South Vietnamese up but the time of greatest danger is '72. The whole statistical base points in that direction. One other thing: I was not aware from the briefing we got on phase one that there was involved a question of taking over Khe Sanh and getting that airstrip taken up. There will be a rise in American casualties during that. . . . A lot of North Vietnamese troops up there. . . .

Melvin Laird

February 2, 1971, 2:57 p.m.

Laird predicts heavy fighting in Laos since the North Vietnamese had been fore-warned. (They were aware of the invasion plan, though not the timing nor the precise location, and prepared for it, including defending the approach to Tchepone, a key enemy transportation and logistics hub.)[5]

. . . LAIRD: . . . I am inclined to go along. It's going to be a hell of a battle because they have been forewarned. They will be ready for us and we will lose some helicopters but you have to take some risks. It's going to be a tough few weeks . . . and we will have a tough reaction around this town and the country. We will not have people supporting the Laos thing. . . .

KISSINGER We have taken the heat before.

LAIRD: . . . Vietnam will succeed without it but it's added insurance. . . . There will be a hell of a battle. . . . Surprise is important and there is no surprise. We won't lose too many Americans, but helicopters and pilots. South Vietnam will get a bloody nose. They will panic because they haven't had a bloody nose in 18 months. . . .

J. Edgar Hoover

February 4, 1971, 10:25 a.m.

FBI Director Hoover reports on a wiretap check that Kissinger had requested on himself.

HOOVER: I wanted to call you and tell you—I didn't want to put it in a letter—that that check you asked us to do on the possibility of wiretaps on your wires both at the office and at home was done and we found nothing.

KISSINGER: I am glad to hear that. . . .

HOOVER: If there is any time in the future that I can be of service to you, please call on me.

KISSINGER: Thank you very much. I appreciate everything that you have done. I would hate to see the government without you. . . .

Melvin Laird
February 4, 1971, 10:57 a.m.

Laird and Kissinger believe that Pentagon spokesman Jerry Friedheim should "stonewall" (one of Laird's favorite words) questions about U.S. reconnaissance teams in Laos.

. . . KISSINGER: On Friedheim yesterday, he was asked about recon troops in Laos and he refused it.

LAIRD: They shouldn't ask that. We have recon units in there but some are in combat.

KISSINGER: [Operation] Prairie Fire units. How should we handle it?

LAIRD: It's a problem. We have Americans in there. We have to be careful not to say they are not there. We [could] say they are there for recon but not for combat.

KISSINGER: Can we say that?

LAIRD: We can for interdiction but they are in there for other reasons.

KISSINGER: Can't we say for recon and keep it confused?

LAIRD: . . . We have to fudge that because they come back and talk about it and they have been fighting. It's better not to say anything sometimes. Our people really took the heat on "no comment" and some people in the town panicked. People in this town have to say "no comment." . . . Just stonewall it.

KISSINGER: Yes.

LAIRD: It will get hot and some boys want to be friends with these guys [reporters]. They will gut you when they can. . . .

President Nixon
February 4, 1971, afternoon

Nixon and Kissinger consult on Kissinger's briefing of Representative Gerald Ford, the House minority leader, on the impending invasion and agree that the Chinese are unlikely to intervene. Ford is all for it.

. . . NIXON: . . . After you have finished with Jerry, I will talk with you later this evening about the possible contingency of what is done in case of Chinese reaction.

KISSINGER: That's almost certainly not going to happen because they have made a public statement—

NIXON: . . . I agree it shouldn't happen but I noted something here that Souvanna said something about Laos being closest to China.

KISSINGER: He is concerned because the Chinese are building a road in northern Laos. They will not come this far south. We are making a contingency plan for an attack across the Plaine des Jarres.

NIXON: . . . I cannot see Chinese walking in there with the thought we might bang them.

KISSINGER: I cannot conceive that they will.

NIXON: Okay. Is Jerry getting the full picture?

KISSINGER: Yes. . . . I said, look, we are putting our chips on two South Vietnamese divisions; we don't know . . . how good they will be, they have never had a really rough opposition, although we think they are the best divisions they've got. . . . I said, now, the first thing before I ask you to do something is to find out what you think of it. And he said, are you insulting me? This is tremendous. . . . We can write the speech for him if we want to. Give him talking points. He'll line up others. . . .

Max Frankel
February 4, 1971, 7:00 p.m.
Kissinger claims to Frankel, the Washington bureau chief of the New York Times, *that he "raised unbelievable Cain" when he first heard of the news blackout that the U.S. military command in Saigon had imposed on the invasion of Laos. Actually, he'd agreed to it.*[6]

FRANKEL: I wondered if you were free to tell me the purpose and an explanation of the embargo that is giving everybody so much trouble. Was it strictly military or what?

KISSINGER: The truth really is that, first of all, it was put on by Abrams— strictly off the record, don't use that. I really was beside myself when I first heard of it. He felt it was necessary for military reasons. We then got an intelligence report which indicated that if we went down Route 9 [just below the DMZ] . . . this may lead to an increase in casualties. Once I got this intelligence report, I felt I could not in good conscience insist on getting it changed. Since then we have merely gone along with Abrams. This was not a Washington decision. . . . I can assure you—I don't want this to be used on Friday—when I heard about this I raised unbelievable Cain with our military people here, but then I finally yielded to our field commander. . . . That is really the explanation for the embargo. I am embarrassed now that they believe this was a magnificent ploy to cover [the invasion buildup]. . . . I can assure you this was not to hide anything. . . .

President Nixon
February 7, 1971, 10:35 a.m.
They confer on mistaken U.S. bombing of South Vietnamese troops.

KISSINGER: . . . That attack on the ARVN now looks like it was a U.S. plane rather than North Vietnamese. It looks like it was a navy plane doing an instrument check.

NIXON: We don't want to let it get out.

KISSINGER: I have not seen the paper but I imagine it did get out. It was on our side of the frontier. But this is better than if it was a North Vietnamese attack.

NIXON: Well, U.S. attacking ARVN has happened before, hasn't it?

KISSINGER: Yes, it has. . . .

President Nixon
February 7, 1971, no time
Nixon and Kissinger denigrate their critics, and then take up South Vietnamese operations in Cambodia and Saigon's military capability. They believe they may be ensuring South Vietnamese President Nguyen Van Thieu's reelection by the Laos invasion.

. . . NIXON: . . . Their interest is really that we do bad. That's all. They are more interested in that than the war go bad. . . .

KISSINGER: Absolutely no doubt about that.

NIXON: It is really an unbelievable attitude.

KISSINGER: Well, it is terrible. . . . They have no concern about the country. They are more afraid that you will do well than of anything else.

NIXON: . . . You know, if we had not done this they would have pilloried us. . . . The president got cold feet. . . . Strong man thing would have been out the window. . . . The State Department would have leaked it all over town that they stopped me.

KISSINGER: That's right. And that the peaceful State Department—

NIXON: And Laird would even do it. Oh yes, he would get his oar in. . . . Do the South Vietnamese or ARVN think that they are doing all right in Cambodia? They are not concerned about their casualties, are they?

KISSINGER: Oh, no. No, no. Their casualties aren't bad. . . . And at the same time, Mr. President, that hasn't hit the papers at all, there is an 8,000-man operation going on way in the south to clear out a small base area. Who would have thought last year that they could do three operations like this simultaneously?

NIXON: You know, they just may have grown up. After all, they have got a bigger army than North Vietnam now, haven't they?

KISSINGER: Oh, yes. . . . In another year or two the North may have to worry about what they will do in the sense of going north.

NIXON: Well, really? I should say they would because [doesn't] South Vietnam even now have a better air force than North Vietnam?

KISSINGER: Oh, no comparison. . . .

NIXON: They also have better trucks, haven't they?

KISSINGER: Much more mobile.

NIXON: . . . Better equipment. Now, for god sakes, I don't see North Vietnam knocking them over. . . .

KISSINGER: I think after this blow it's going to be, if it goes well, very, very tough for them. . . . We may be re-ensuring his election by this.

NIXON: Oh, well, there is no question about that. . . . Hell, he'll have heroes, giving Vietnamese medals. . . .

Melvin Laird
February 23, 1971, 8:10 a.m.
The media were now reporting that South Vietnamese forces in Laos were bogged down for the fifth straight day, with heavy losses.[7] Nixon was angry about the reports on television, which cited unhelpful statements out of Defense and State. Yet the invasion was stalled.

KISSINGER: The president is having conniptions about TV reports last night and this morning saying Defense and State are saying the operations are stalled, the roads aren't cut, and the White House is putting an optimistic gloss on it all. We shouldn't be in that position; we have got to make people shut up. The purpose of it is to cut roads.

LAIRD: It's to disrupt operations, and our statements are going along that line. . . . The problem is people are trying to give the idea we are going to Tchepone; they should keep that down. . . .

KISSINGER: . . . Most of these troubles occurred on a background basis.

LAIRD: We didn't give any on a background basis.

KISSINGER: And you'll give a confident one tomorrow?

LAIRD: Yes. . . . But I shouldn't be overconfident. . . .

President Nixon
February 25, 1971, evening

Kissinger, who knew the invasion was stalled, doubted that enemy movement on the Ho Chi Minh Trail had been disrupted, felt the military were not giving him the facts, and was now questioning the invasion's objective of seizing Tchepone, and Nixon look for silver lining.[8] They also take up Laird's opposition to a big air strike in North Vietnam.

. . . NIXON: Well, the thing that I think is encouraging is Moorer says don't worry, we're going to stay. They seem to be confident they can stick it out. I have a feeling the other side is having one heck of a time. They haven't got much left.

KISSINGER: They have exactly one division left in North Vietnam. If we could land an armored division there, we could drive to Hanoi. I mean, it's not something we ought to do, but they are stretched to the limit, and if one looks at it from their point of view, they haven't cracked the South Vietnamese 10 miles from their border in an area in which they have their munitions stockpiled.

NIXON: Well, I think one thing that is very important at this stage . . . is that aerial strike. . . .

KISSINGER: But Mel called this evening about it. . . .

NIXON: He doesn't want it.

KISSINGER: He doesn't want any; he thinks it is politically very dangerous right now. . . . He thinks it will look like an act of desperation.

NIXON: Could be, or do you think that's just something to say?

KISSINGER: Well, I'm sure if it weren't that argument, he'd find another one, because this fellow [Laird's military assistant Robert] Pursley is just dead set against it. But we are not in that much of a hurry, we can wait a few days.

NIXON: Yeah, we could do it next week. . . . I tell you, it can have a crucial effect. . . . This desperation argument is ridiculous. Mel opposed this thing, he opposed [the invasion of] Cambodia, let's face it.

KISSINGER: That's right. And he opposed every strike you've done before. . . . He then carries them out with great vigor.

NIXON: That's right. Well, nevertheless, we're going to take a look at it, and even suppose it is desperation, so be it. . . .

Joseph Sisco
February 27, 1971, 5:05 p.m.
Assistant Secretary of State Sisco and Kissinger disagree about a State Department cable on possible steps toward a Middle East peace agreement and terms. State and UN Special Representative Gunnar Jarring were proposing terms that included Israeli withdrawal to the pre-1967 borders (or at least interim withdrawals), which Kissinger knew wouldn't fly with Israel, and which it had just reiterated.[9]

SISCO: Henry, I just wanted to tell you I sent over . . . a cable and I sent it to the secretary with a chit that I thought it should be cleared with the White House.

KISSINGER: If I understand the meeting this morning, I thought everything should be cleared over here. To whom does it go and what does it say? . . .

SISCO: It is just a cable—what I am trying to avoid is what could happen on Monday. The Israelis go back to Jarring on Monday—

KISSINGER: They will not change their position.

SISCO: . . . In this cable I have laid down a little scenario and I think we should go to both Tel Aviv and Cairo and get their views over the weekend.

KISSINGER: I can give you what Cairo will say. I could write the response. . . .

SISCO: I have a paper on the overall program and where we go from here and the results, but I have been working 18 hours a day, Henry. . . . I didn't particularly want to spend 10 hours in the department today writing this cable. . . . It tells no one to do anything. . . . The secretary [Rogers] did not want to bulldoze the president. He just wanted to go over everything step by step so that he would have a complete understanding. The poor guy, I know he has a lot of things on his mind.

KISSINGER: . . . Secure frontiers and '67 frontiers, I don't know if he knew the difference between them.

SISCO: Not a hell of a lot. . . . We have a series of problems coming up with Israel. It is the beginning of the rocky road.

President Nixon
February 28, 1971, 11:30 a.m.
Kissinger believes that State's cable on a Middle East peace settlement will provoke "a brutal public confrontation with Israel" and wants to slow down State's peace initiatives. (He sought a stalemate until the Soviets urged compromise on Egypt.)[10] *He wants to get something from the Soviets in return for Israeli concessions.*

KISSINGER: State wants to send out a cable which I believe will be the first step in a confrontation with Israel.

NIXON: Did you discuss it with Sisco?

KISSINGER: Yes. . . . We gave him some word changes designed to soften it to the degree possible and they have accepted them, but the basic problem remains one of strategy. . . . If we had known it was developing this way earlier we could have perhaps worked bilaterally with the Soviets and gotten a great deal more for what we are going to have to do to Israel—perhaps even the summit. Now it appears we will have to go with the cable, but we should try to slow State down. . . .

NIXON: Stay on top of this, Henry. Determine where we are going and check with the Soviets. See what we can get from them.

KISSINGER: At this point I think we are bound to get a brutal public confrontation with Israel. If they cave we will pay a price for nothing. I only wish we had moved with the Soviets and gotten something for it. . . .

NIXON: Should we let the cable go?

KISSINGER: I am afraid our only alternative is to do that. But someone else should be put in charge. It's moving too fast this weekend. Laird and Rogers are locked together. Therefore, I think for now it is best to let the cable go with the changes I have suggested to State plus a bid to get something from the Egyptians. The important thing is to slow the process down for now.

NIXON: All right, Henry. Clear the cable but tell Sisco I don't wish this to move to a blow-up with Israel. Tell him to delay and filibuster to the extent possible. We must be in a position to see what we can get. We should not be polemical or abrasive. It cannot be helpful at this time to put pressure on Israel. . . .

The Laos Invasion—Tchepone, the Hasty South Vietnamese Retreat, Rout Stories and Bad Press, the PR Offensive, Upbeat Military Reports, and Whistling in the Dark; Kissinger's Meeting with the Kidnapping Plotters, Cover Stories, and Lies; and Another Round of Bombing of North Vietnam and "Protective Reaction" Claims

March 1971

On March 6, South Vietnamese troops finally captured the critical enemy logistics hub of Tchepone (what little remained of it) during the Laos invasion, but they retreated after holding it for only three days. Kissinger and Nixon wanted them to remain on the offensive. But they withdrew toward South Vietnam and abandoned bases under heavy enemy fire. JCS Chairman Thomas Moorer, Commander Creighton Abrams, and Ambassador to South Vietnam Ellsworth Bunker maintained that press reports of panicky South Vietnamese retreats were mistaken and that the withdrawal was not a rout, as the press described it. Kissinger conveyed their upbeat assessments to Nixon but knew the South Vietnamese were retreating just as fast as they could and "bugging out," which was a huge political problem at home. He callously threatened not to have them airlifted out. He denounced the military's conduct of the invasion and was furious that Washington wasn't forewarned of the quick South Vietnamese withdrawal from Tchepone. Nixon ordered a propaganda offensive to counter the bad press and wanted the invasion over and off television.

After maddening weather delays, Nixon and Kissinger unleashed heavy bombing of North Vietnam, far into the North, which the administration portrayed as "protective reaction" but which Nixon and Kissinger knew well was not; the raids involved more planes and more territory than any strikes in the North since the previous November's bombing of the Haiphong–Hanoi area. Waves of planes also hit Laos.

On March 6, Kissinger met with three of the activists who had been named as co-conspirators in the alleged plot to kidnap him. When word of the meeting got out, to Kissinger's displeasure, he lied to other officials about who he'd thought he was meeting with, claiming that he didn't know the co-conspirators would be there, that he went "into orbit" (as he told H. R. Haldeman) when he found out they were, telling Ronald Ziegler that he thought he was meeting with Swarthmore students, and claiming to Haldeman he thought they were Haverford students.

Henry Graff
March 1, 1971, 11:10 a.m.
Columbia University historian Graff and Kissinger share their contempt for other intellectuals.

... GRAFF: I am very troubled by what our fellow historians are doing. I think this is a period in which the social scientists have committed treason. The amazing lack of information. . . .

KISSINGER: The intellectual community is abdicating. The misrepresentation, the gloating in what they consider American defeats. The total inability to grant even the possibility of good faith.

GRAFF: This is what disturbs me. . . . It's the intellectuals—our colleagues— who behave as if the ideas they dream [up] over cocktails haven't been thought of before. And maybe that the attack on the university . . . is a commonsense response to the vacuity on the campus. . . .

President Nixon
March 6, 1971, 9:20 a.m.
Nixon and Kissinger discuss bullish reports on the invasion of Laos and the press. Kissinger thinks the invasion will turn out better than the invasion of Cambodia and that there's little chance it will fail. They also discuss Nixon's order to begin heavy bombing of Laos and Cambodia. (Over a thousand planes were sent into action the next day.)[1]

NIXON: I just got a brief report from Moorer. He said things are really jumping around there. . . .

KISSINGER: The radio reported they are already in Tchepone. If not, it's just a question of hours.

NIXON: He said it's an interesting thing, not a word about the war on the front page of the *Washington Post* this morning.

KISSINGER: It's gone to the back pages.

NIXON: Isn't that something? Our allies are doing well. That would be bannered in World War II. These bastards—isn't it terrible?

KISSINGER: . . . They have all the heights overlooking Tchepone. Made another landing at the outskirts of Tchepone. . . . Abrams has sent a backchannel to Moorer saying he would have all the roads around Tchepone cut in the next few days. . . . I think your Laos operation is going to turn out better than Cambodia. In the whole Cambodia operation we captured only 3,000 tons of ammunition. I talked to my briefer this morning. He is an army colonel in the Haig style—a tough combat type. He says he sees no way by which we can lose it. I think that is right. . . . Strategically this is more important than Cambodia. . . .

NIXON: Abrams seems to feel better now, does he?

KISSINGER: Yes, he is on top of it now. . . . Abrams is now going like the Abrams of Cambodia, and for a week there it looked like he was shell-shocked.

NIXON: Maybe it was that he ran into those 100 tanks. . . . I think Laird has held back on the air strikes for two weeks. Now that we have ordered it, they will give our people a shot in the arm.

KISSINGER: The Russians, I will have to tell you, are going to scream a bit. . . .

William Rogers
March 11, 1971, 12:35 p.m.
Kissinger and Rogers fear that if U.S. Ambassador to Chile Edward Korry is removed without finding another position for him, he will spill the beans on U.S. covert operations against President Salvador Allende. (Kissinger's deputy, Alexander Haig, had advised Kissinger to be "very cautious" with Korry since he could reveal "a great many secrets," and thus it was "essential" to offer him another job.)[2]

. . . KISSINGER: . . . About Korry in Chile, I am worried that he is dangerous.

ROGERS: I told them to go ahead with the nomination for his successor.

KISSINGER: We ought to find some job for him. I am terrified of his knowledge of some of these considerations in the 40 Committee [on covert operations] and what he will do when he has defected. I don't like him; he has been a disaster there. . . . He sat in on two 40 Committee meetings when we discussed parliamentary ratification [of Allende]. He sent a long backchannel of what to do. He is nutty enough to write a long exposé. He is broke, too.

ROGERS: I agree with you. He is nuts. He is now sounding off on how much he favored the visit of the *Enterprise*. [Allende had invited the visit by the aircraft carrier but Kissinger and Rogers opposed it and the invitation was turned down.][3] He had told us he was against it.

KISSINGER: He always has two cables in the works.

Brian McDonnell
March 11, 1971, 3:07 p.m.
Evening Star columnist Mary McGrory was writing about Kissinger's meeting several days earlier in the White House Situation Room with three of the activists who had purportedly conspired to kidnap him—William Davidon, Tom Davidson, and Beverly Bell. McDonnell, who knew some of the alleged conspirators, and Kissinger were unhappy that Davidson had spoken to her.

MCDONNELL: I have bad news. Tom Davidson talked with McGrory at the *Star* and she called me for a statement. I didn't give it. . . .

KISSINGER: Is he quoting me?

MCDONNELL: I don't think so.

KISSINGER: I wish the word of honor of some of these people would mean something. . . . Some of my colleagues will get restive.

MCDONNELL: . . . It was a personal meeting and it was agreed no press coverage.

KISSINGER: That's best. I will say nothing. . . . It's a personal meeting which you arranged and you are not at liberty to speak about it.

MCDONNELL: Okay.

Mary McGrory
March 11, 1971, 5:00 p.m.
Kissinger tries to persuade McGrory not to write about the meeting.

. . . MCGRORY: . . . I heard about your meeting with the co-conspirators. I wonder if you have anything to say.

KISSINGER: I don't really think so. It was arranged by Brian McDonnell, whom I like. I don't feel I want to talk about it. I much prefer that it not be written about.

MCGRORY: It won't hold in that group.

KISSINGER: . . . We made an agreement it would be on a human level without any publicity. . . .

MCGRORY: They have the impression you did not expect to discuss it, but they were free to after a couple of days or so. . . .

KISSINGER: . . . That was not my impression and not Brian's. . . . I'd just as soon not have anything written, but I leave it to your judgment.

Dan Rather
March 12, 1971, 5:14 p.m.
CBS News's White House correspondent asks about the meeting with the alleged conspirators. Tom Davidson had said that Kissinger "sees himself as the conscience of the administration."[4]

RATHER: I am sorry to bother you on such a trivial matter, but it's nailing down the McGrory article and whether it happened and the account is correct.

KISSINGER: The event happened but had nothing to do with the plot. . . . It was not intended for publicity. . . .

RATHER: The story didn't get out at your initiative?

KISSINGER: Absolutely not! . . . I didn't say I was the conscience of the administration. . . .

Ronald Ziegler
March 12, 1971, 5:50 p.m.
Kissinger briefs Press Secretary Ziegler on the meeting. "I thought I was seeing a group of seven Swarthmore students," he claims. He wrote later that he thought he was meeting simply with a group of Brian McDonnell's friends to discuss the war and social problems.[5]

KISSINGER: You've probably seen the ticker stories. . . . On the Saturday meeting.

ZIEGLER: Oh, yes. I've seen not only the ticker but the story in the *Star*. Why did you do that, Henry?

KISSINGER: If you knew how that came to pass you wouldn't believe it. I thought I was seeing a group of seven Swarthmore students. This guy brought these guys instead. This is strictly for you—we might as well make a plus of it. I decided, and Haig agreed, that I might as well talk to them. These people are not indicted; they are just part of the group. The position I've taken is that I see a lot of people opposed to the administration to listen to them and give them the sense that we are open to their concerns, even if we can't share their conclusions. I won't say what happened at the meeting. . . . Do you think this is damaging?

ZIEGLER: No. If we had sat down and planned it we wouldn't have done it, but this has happened and it's okay. So what? It gives us a little color. We're all too brittle; we should loosen up a little.

KISSINGER: I'd like to, but you people won't let me.

ZIEGLER: You're loose enough, Henry. I'm talking about the rest of us. . . .

Richard Kleindienst
March 12, 1971, 7:22 p.m.

Deputy Attorney General Kleindienst wants to know the details of the meeting because of the possible legal implications for the government's case against the indicted conspirators. "I didn't know they were coming in," Kissinger maintains.

KISSINGER: Listen, I tell you, I am mortified by this event.

KLEINDIENST: Don't worry about that, Henry. We just want a factual, objective account of what has occurred with respect to the case. It is for my eyes only. If any statement is going to be made, we will be talking to you about it. . . .

KISSINGER: What do you want?

KLEINDIENST: Where this was, and how it came about, what was said. No comment on it, just the actual facts. . . . Hereafter . . . I would be very careful.

KISSINGER: I didn't know they were coming in. They were already sitting in the Situation Room when I learned they were here. I thought it would do more damage to throw them out and have them say I refused to meet with them than to listen to the substance of what they had to say.

KLEINDIENST: Did the two people involved say anything about the Berrigan case?

KISSINGER: At the end, one of them said . . . they wanted to bring in a defendant the next time they came back.

KLEINDIENST: Well, send over what you have. Nothing to get upset about, and I don't want you to get upset. We are the lawyers in the case and want to look at what the implications are.

KISSINGER: . . . It will not be released?

KLEINDIENST: Not to be released, it is just for our people and the lawyers. . . .

H. R. Haldeman
March 13, 1971, 10:17 a.m.

Kissinger claims to White House Chief of Staff Haldeman that he thought he was meeting with some Haverford students "friendly to the Berrigans" and blames Brian McDonnell for bringing in the kidnap plotters instead. "They should be decapitated,"

Haldeman says, speaking figuratively, one has to presume. Kissinger worries about Nixon's reaction to the meeting.

KISSINGER: I wanted to give you the background on the fiasco on these Berrigan people.

HALDEMAN: You are calling on your enemies now.

KISSINGER: People get so uptight about it. I don't think it's hurting us.

HALDEMAN: I don't know whether it hurts or helps. I don't think it makes any difference one way or the other. The *Miami Herald* carried a story with a big smiling picture of Henry Kissinger on the front page.

KISSINGER: Though it wasn't deliberately planned, I have to take the credit for it. I have been in touch with Brian McDonnell, the fellow who fasted in the park, for a year. He called two months ago—in case the president asks—to ask whether I would be prepared to see some people friendly to the Berrigans. He then called a few weeks later saying he would like to bring in seven students from Haverford College, where he teaches. I said fine. . . . Instead of students, he brought in these people. I found out only minutes before the meeting and I went into orbit. They were already in the Situation Room. I talked to Haig and we agreed that to throw them out without hearing them at that late time would be worse than listening to them. At that time, I did not know they were co-conspirators. I just thought they were sympathetic to the Berrigans.

HALDEMAN: Were they interesting?

KISSINGER: Honor is not an outstanding attribute of doves. There was an understanding this was to be off the record.

HALDEMAN: I am sure it will go away. J. Edgar Hoover may be upset.

KISSINGER: I talked to him last night. He said fine; he is okay. Kleindienst is a little bit upset. . . . I don't know whether it hurts us to show humanity toward these people.

HALDEMAN: It doesn't do us any good. It dignifies them. They should be decapitated. People plotting kidnaps we shouldn't see. . . . You didn't intend to meet with those anyway.

KISSINGER: If I had known it two hours before, I would have turned it off.

HALDEMAN: It isn't going to make much difference one way or the other. The story has a little drama to it because of the kidnap thing, but I imagine we will survive that.

KISSINGER: Will you explain it to the president?

HALDEMAN: Sure.

KISSINGER: How it came to pass?

HALDEMAN: He may not even see it.

KISSINGER: He will see it all right. If he doesn't, Bebe [Rebozo, his friend in Florida] will call it to his attention. . . .

Brian McDonnell
March 13, 1971, 12:00 p.m.
Kissinger suggests that McDonnell write for the record that he thought he was just meeting with "friends of the Berrigans."

. . . MCDONNELL: I am not worried about them. I am worried about you. It was such an awful thing to have happen to you.

KISSINGER: I will have to take the heat for a few days. This will all blow over.

MCDONNELL: I am going to send you a letter giving the sequence of facts and what took place. And I would like to send a letter to your boss [Nixon] and apologize.

KISSINGER: No, that is not necessary. It might be good to have some confirmation on what took place for Mitchell and Hoover, though.

MCDONNELL: I will write who was to be invited, the sequence of facts, and what took place.

KISSINGER: I thought they were just friends of the Berrigans. . . .

William Rogers
March 17, 1971, 5:06 p.m.
The media were reporting the retreat of South Vietnamese troops toward their border and their abandonment of firebases under heavy enemy fire in Laos, with mounting casualties. Rogers, who had worried about the serious risks of the invasion and South Vietnamese capabilities, and Kissinger think things are not that dire, though "they may be lying to us all."[6]

ROGERS: I wanted to talk about the situation in Laos. From television and radio, it looks like we are getting clobbered.

KISSINGER: It's unbelievable.

ROGERS: I had a briefing from the Pentagon, and they said it was working all right.

KISSINGER: That is my impression. I get a briefing every day. The president has called Moorer, and I read the military reports. . . . They all claim things are going exactly as they want them to go. Haig is out there. He called this morning and said the same thing.

ROGERS: The fact that it appears we are getting clobbered at the moment doesn't hurt, just so we know the facts. If we are having a problem, it's a hell of a lot better to stay quiet than pretend everything is rosy.

KISSINGER: I couldn't agree more. The president called Moorer personally. A colonel briefs me position-by-position daily. But they may be lying to us all.

ROGERS: . . . I hope they are telling the truth.

KISSINGER: The only thing that gives me slight confidence that it is the truth is Moorer called Abrams a half hour ago. Abrams said this is poppycock. . . .

President Nixon
March 17, 1971, 7:43 p.m.
Kissinger tells Nixon there is no basis for a report of South Vietnamese fleeing a firebase in Laos. "I don't care about the losses," Nixon says. He wants a PR offensive against the bad press, grouses that the U.S. Air Force "has no guts," and orders an immediate air strike.

KISSINGER: I talked to Moorer and he had talked since my conversation with him at 3:00 to the chief of staff out there and says this is one of the weirdest things—there is absolutely nothing to it. . . . In intercepted messages the other side is saying to their headquarters that the South Vietnamese are retreating in good order. . . . He's talked to the 1st Corps commander . . . and to Abrams and they all say this was a planned operation. There were losses.

NIXON: I know that. I don't care about the losses.

KISSINGER: But it's the same as Hill 31, which was a debacle for the enemy; they also claimed that we were getting whipped. And there is no evidence to back it up. . . . Of course you can't guarantee they didn't see anybody running where they were.

NIXON: Of course.

KISSINGER: It's a battle.

NIXON: That's right. But these smart son-of-a-bitching reporters. I really think some of them are trying to serve Hanoi now.

KISSINGER: I believe they have a vested interest in our losing.

NIXON: Put them out on a limb. You briefing tomorrow?

KISSINGER: There's a group of Republican leaders. . . . I'm going to brief them and get Moorer over here.

NIXON: You get Moorer over here and pour it to them. Say this is the most distasteful reporting in history. . . . Has the weather cleared yet?

KISSINGER: No, but I think in two weeks it's a disgrace [if the air strike hasn't been carried out].

NIXON: There's going to be a new chief of staff of the air force, I can tell you that. They have no guts, no imagination, nothing. My suggestion about the B-26s—nothing!

KISSINGER: No. They've been doubling the number of gunships. But if it hadn't been for your pushing they wouldn't have done that.

NIXON: . . . I want you to call Moorer right now and get the strike laid on. . . .

Thomas Moorer
March 18, 1971, 9:10 a.m.
Kissinger complains that the South Vietnamese were heading in the wrong direction and "bugging out" and were not disrupting the movement of enemy personnel and supplies down the Ho Chi Minh Trail as planned. He threatens to leave them in Laos.

. . . KISSINGER: . . . They are not trying for our objectives. . . . I have been telling senators that we are moving out of Tchepone to hold [Route] 914. Now they are not moving near 914. I think they are bugging out.

MOORER: They are moving back faster than we expected.

KISSINGER: In a strategically unproductive direction. They are moving along Route 9 [back toward South Vietnam]. . . . The original idea was to stay in Tchepone for a month or two and block roads . . . but they are not in Tchepone or on 914 to do any defense. . . . They keep pulling off. To me it looks like they are doing what they said they were going to do last week and bugging out of Route 9.

MOORER: It's apparently Thieu alone who is doing this. . . . So we need to put some backbone back in them.

KISSINGER: What are we going to tell the senators today? At this rate they will be out by April 1. . . . Thieu is setting himself up for a massive bug-out on our part. . . . The thing is they will kill us domestically. If they had told us a week ago they were doing this we could have said we have our victory. . . . Of course we control the helicopters.

MOORER: We can't just leave them in there.

KISSINGER: Why not? . . . Send a backchannel to Bunker and have no illusions of what we will do here. . . .

Thomas Moorer
March 19, 1971, 11:15 a.m.
Kissinger condemns the military's conduct of the invasion and reports that Alexander Haig, who was in Southeast Asia, believes that the South Vietnamese army lost its will.

. . . MOORER: . . . Abrams thinks they have a solid plan.

KISSINGER: They have had solid plans for six weeks and not executed one. . . . If these guys had told us when they took Tchepone [they planned to leave soon] we could have planned it to protect the president in the best way. Instead they have us babbling the wrong things and now they have us on the defensive. Throughout this operation no plan has stuck for a week. . . . Haig feels the ARVN lost its stomach for Laos. Just wants to get out in an orderly fashion. . . .

MOORER: I think that's right.

KISSINGER: He recommends that the pressure from Washington to stay be terminated and try to get them out. . . .

John Vogt
March 19, 1971, 8:45 p.m.
Kissinger and General Vogt, the director of the Joint Staff, discuss bombing North Vietnam, where Nixon wanted to hit a major supply transshipment point, Quang Khe, but which had been delayed by bad weather. Vogt says when the weather lifts, they can "always gin up missile sites," thereby falsely claiming "protective reaction" against enemy fire.

. . . KISSINGER: What about the air strikes?

VOGT: It is still the old problem. Another alternative involves all-weather birds. . . . Quang Khe. Ships come in, pipelines and all that.

KISSINGER: . . . How much population?

VOGT: Nothing in that immediate area, it is wide open.

KISSINGER: Yeah, but we can't claim protective reaction.

VOGT: We can always gin up missile sites. . . .

KISSINGER: There has been 16 days of uninterrupted rain. . . . What is the ceiling?

VOGT: . . . Nine thousand feet for dive bombing with five miles visibility.

KISSINGER: Where in the world are you going to get that except the desert or Africa?

VOGT: . . . Something in the coastal areas could probably be created in the area in a day or so. . . . In any SAM area, they [the planes] need maneuverability room.

KISSINGER: Have they got that many missiles there?

VOGT: Yeah, they have moved a lot of them in. . . . They have been building up while the weather has been providing cover for them. . . .

KISSINGER: It is a great tragedy—it would have been a political plus for psychological reasons. . . . After taking all this from them and not doing anything. . . .

President Nixon

March 20, 1971, 10:30 a.m.

Nixon wants the South Vietnamese withdrawal from Laos over with and off American television screens. "I have no doubt that the enemy is on the verge of cracking," Kissinger says.

KISSINGER: . . . I talked with Moorer. The facts are as I suspected and I get my insight from a colonel who briefs me. They are getting out faster than they have told us.

NIXON: That doesn't bother me. When you came in last night you said if they are going to do it we might as well get it over with. Get the goddamn thing off TV. . . .

KISSINGER: . . . Over a period of months it will be vindicated. Morale is high and Thieu thinks it's a major political achievement for him. . . .

NIXON: The main thing is to get out without getting a major battalion knocked off. . . . Isn't it amusing that these critics have it both ways, because they squeal on the incursion into Laos and now they are squealing because they are getting out. . . . I don't believe the heli-pilots but that captain [who] said the ARVN are fighting damn well. They have to be killing a lot of people. Even the ones that lost in World War I, they inflicted twice as many casualties on the enemy.

KISSINGER: In this case it's five times. I have no doubt that the enemy is on the verge of cracking on Laos. He has thrown in everything. . . . They are running out of steam soon. . . .

President Nixon

March 20, 1971 10:50 a.m.

Nixon and Kissinger talk over their PR offensive against stories of panicky South Vietnamese withdrawals; Nixon wants to find out the truth.

NIXON: One thing I wanted to ask you about was on the news I saw last night; they had a film report on the low morale of the ARVN troops when they were coming out of combat and how they were panicking. Be sure that is hit hard. Some troops under fire were panicking. What is the general situation? . . .

KISSINGER: We depend on reports we get from Abrams and Bunker. They say that the units are not panicking. Of course, when they are being taken out under fire there may be some incidents.

NIXON: The enemy too.

KISSINGER: I would hate to be in a B-52 box when they start dropping.

NIXON: [White House speechwriter Patrick] Buchanan said it was another rough night on all three networks. . . . We will just knock it right out of the box. First Abrams will hit it, then Bunker and then I will hit it. . . .

KISSINGER: I will make sure this gets out. I am going to get a little group together next week and work out an assessment for you. . . . We have reports from Bunker and Abrams and they do not confirm this news report at all.

NIXON: I want you to ask specifically about these stories and what is the truth. . . . There was this CBS film and an AP dispatch saying that the ARVN were withdrawn because they refused to fight anymore. . . .

President Nixon

March 20, 1971, no time (late afternoon or evening)

Amid more news stories of South Vietnamese fleeing from bases in Laos under heavy enemy attacks, Kissinger says that JCS Chairman Moorer has had no reports of troops retreating in panic. He and Nixon also discuss downings of U.S. helicopters, which plagued the invasion. Nixon wants the rout described as "a withdrawal as planned." And they consider whether Commander Creighton Abrams should hold a press conference on the record in Saigon (the answer being a resounding no).

NIXON: I was just taking a look at the evening papers here. They are hitting pretty hard on this whole business . . . of the South Vietnamese in flight and so forth, and I think that under the circumstances Abrams should really hit that. . . .

KISSINGER: The thrust of the story is that these units are leaving in panic and that they are rushing to the helicopters.

NIXON: Of course they are.

KISSINGER: Moorer says it could of course happen that a platoon here and there is doing that. . . . But he does not believe that, he has had no reports. . . .

NIXON: . . . I don't care how they are coming out, but this has to be knocked down due to the fact that of course they are going to come out. When they are under attack, the poor bastards want to get out of there as hard and as fast as they can. . . . When you realize you are breaking off and you're going out, you're going to get home.

KISSINGER: Now this helicopter colonel whose units, after all, were all over the place says that his impression is that the South Vietnamese fought very well. . . .

NIXON: The other thing it says is that 15 helicopters are lost. Now, that cannot be in my opinion correct. . . .

KISSINGER: No, no, but what they said was destroyed or damaged.

NIXON: Well, now, for Christ's sake.

KISSINGER: And 96 percent of those that were damaged are flying again. . . .

NIXON: . . . I would not hesitate to be very, very categorical on this. The point is they are coming out and . . . there is no reason to let it appear that it is anything but a withdrawal as planned. Naturally they are taking some casualties as they come out but they are giving a hell of a lot. . . .

KISSINGER: Now, Moorer when he was talking to me said that Abrams has never had a briefing on the record yet and he was wondering whether . . . we couldn't let him do it on a background basis. . . . Because if he goes on the record and they ask him "Were you ordered to do it?" and he says yes—

NIXON: No, no, no. We must not say we have ordered him to do it. . . . He shouldn't answer it ever. . . . This should not be on the record. . . . Oh, no, no. Just like he's always done. . . .

[Phone ringing, blocking out Nixon's voice.]

KISSINGER: Look, I'm on the line with the president!!

NIXON: . . . He can be honest and candid and knock down this idea of fleeing. . . . The idea that they are fleeing and disarrayed and so forth, it's just got to be, if it isn't true, knocked down. If it's true, goddamn it, then he'd better handle it as well as he can. . . .

President Nixon

March 20, 1971, no time (about 8:00 p.m.)

Kissinger transmits confirmation from Ambassador Ellsworth Bunker in South Vietnam and Haig, who was returning from there, that there's nothing to stories of South Vietnam soldiers fleeing in panic. "It's a whole bunch of crap," Nixon scoffs. He wants to "hit" the press "right in the lower buttocks." And he wants the Pentagon, including Melvin Laird, and Abrams in Saigon to step up to the plate on PR. But he worries about the impact of the invasion on the South Vietnamese.

KISSINGER: Mr. President, I've covered every base I possibly could on all of these things. . . . I talked to Haig because Haig actually only left there 18 hours ago and he talked to Abrams. . . . He said there was nothing to it. . . . Bunker, with whom I just hung up, said that he had had no such report. . . . Now, Haig tells me one of the big problems was that for about four days the South Vietnamese were just shutting off with us and weren't telling us what was going on. . . . But Haig said as of 18 hours ago . . . the report was that it was at that point an orderly retreat. Ellsworth said the same thing.

NIXON: Not retreat, withdrawal. . . . The main thing now though is to knock down and destroy that rout [story]. . . . I'm perfectly prepared to do it, but by god, I want them to step up to it too. . . . There's some truth always in it, but I think what it is is the press out there is just . . . frantically trying to make this appear like a [rout]. Now, of course, Henry, that makes it all the more important for us to . . . hit them right in the lower buttocks; they will have a hell of a time recovering from that.

KISSINGER: No question about it.

NIXON: And they will squeal and squirm. . . . Abrams has just got to be told to do the right thing.

KISSINGER: Well, I've seen the cable that went out to him, Mr. President. I made sure this time that there wasn't going to be any slip, and we put in this cable nobody gives a damn about how many helicopter sorties they fly, we want to get an overall, confident appraisal. . . .

NIXON: The public information people, all of them who have the opportunity, should just stonewall it. . . . Ziegler should say nothing about the reports, about the retreat and all that sort of thing. . . . Let the Pentagon step up to this. . . . I just know when you get in a PR battle, by god, it doesn't make any difference what the facts are, you win the PR battle. . . .

KISSINGER: . . . There couldn't have been many wars where one's own press gloated over what they can represent as a defeat. . . .

NIXON: . . . A lot of these people are perfectly susceptible to the far left or infiltration, Henry. Let's face it. . . . You know those two [reporters], good god, they are under discipline.

KISSINGER: No question about it.

NIXON: . . . The public relations thing, we've got to step up to this thing. Abrams will do it, I'll do it on Monday night, and then what's going to happen the next week?

KISSINGER: I thought, Mr. President, I would brief the White House staff and some of our public relations people on Monday. . . . To get them positioned so that they don't go blabbing all over town and so that some of our people who talk around the press can have a common line. . . .

NIXON: . . . Let the Pentagon do it. And let Laird do his little deal. . . . You see, what I'm concerned about is . . . whether or not this kind of story . . . has an effect on the South Vietnamese population, on the South Vietnamese armed forces. . . . You see, this idea of retreating and panicking and the rest will now be—you can be sure that the American press will be damned sure this gets all over Saigon, you understand that.

KISSINGER: . . . I will get an assessment from Bunker on that tomorrow.

NIXON: I'm not interested in an assessment, I'm interested in counteracting it. . . . Feed the side of the story about the panic of the North Vietnamese side, the huge casualties—get out some of the stories about the problems they are having. Force the networks to carry some of that. . . . That it was a success, that the South Vietnamese fought bravely, that there was no rout, that it was a withdrawal as planned, period. . . .

Alexander Haig
March 20, 1971, no time
Kissinger's deputy phones from Hawaii on his way back from Vietnam. An upset Kissinger, who "willingly assumed a field marshal role when things went well, but . . . became irritable and upset when Lam Son 719 [the invasion] stalled," Lt. Gen. Bruce Palmer observed,[7] bewails the hasty South Vietnamese retreat from Laos and that they weren't forewarned that the South Vietnamese would be leaving Tchepone and heading home after only three days there. His assessment to Haig is the polar opposite of the administration's public line on the invasion.

... KISSINGER: . . . You know, this screwing around just is ridiculous because they are going out just about as fast as they can.

HAIG: Well, that's right, although he [President Thieu] allegedly put the brakes on that.

KISSINGER: Oh, that's bullshit. They will be out by Tuesday.

HAIG: . . . I just don't think it can be done that way, sir. It just won't go that fast, but it will be fast.

KISSINGER: Well, it's as fast as they can get them out, they're going. . . . Why in Christ's name weren't we told? . . . There wasn't a hint of it.

HAIG: No, and I don't think they knew, and that's one of the main problems you have. These people are getting mysterious on us. . . . If you have a serious fracture there, you've got a major problem. . . . I think it happened just out of the sheer wave of concern for their losses and what have you. I think it's in good shape right now.

KISSINGER: Well, they got a massive problem for themselves here. . . . You have to understand that until Thursday morning we were getting briefed every day exactly the opposite way.

HAIG: That three-day period was a lot tougher than people had thought.

KISSINGER: But they didn't even tell us there was a three-day period, Al. . . . How in Christ's name can they give air support if they don't know what's happening?

HAIG: I went through that very carefully. . . . Two of these units just never communicated, they never passed the word what kind of problems they were having. . . . Had this one outfit go straight to the pasture. . . .

KISSINGER: I mean, this is an unbelievable surprise to everybody. . . . And you know what it will do to us domestically. . . . Do you think these guys are leaving in a panic, or are they leaving in some sort of order?

HAIG: I think they are leaving in good shape so far. . . .

KISSINGER: Are they being badly chewed up?

HAIG: No.

KISSINGER: I mean, are they preserving their combat effectiveness?

HAIG: Yes, yes, all but the one. . . .

KISSINGER: Well, Al, you know who all is coming out of the woodwork here, so there is no sense kidding anybody. . . . If they had told us a week ago, we could have positioned it. . . . We are having a hell of a mess here. . . . The problem is how we are going to get through the next two weeks without everyone panicking. . . .

Thomas Moorer

March 21, 1971, morning

The weather-delayed bombing of North Vietnam had finally begun. U.S. planes flew far into the North in what the military command described as strikes in response to enemy anti-aircraft fire. The heavy raids involved more planes and covered more territory than any other attacks on the North since the previous November. Waves of planes were also sent into Laos.[8] *Moorer reports on the start of the bombing and Abrams's encouraging assessment of Laos.*

. . . KISSINGER: How does it look?

MOORER: It looks good, all the air force planes are out, no losses. . . . They seemed to have wiped out all those missile sites in good fashion. . . . I've just been talking to Abrams not less than five minutes ago about the next step. . . . I said we are really getting flailed around here by the papers and so on. I said do you get any indication that our boys are folding up? He said absolutely not, and he says some of the battalions have been hurt but . . . the other side has really been hurt, and he says he sees nothing whatever in the overall attitude to indicate any weakening of the heart. . . .

KISSINGER: But why are they getting out so fast then?

MOORER: Well, I tell you, once you start that kind of operation, they have had to move like that. . . . You got to do it fast. . . . Abrams says that they are . . . "badly hurt." . . .

KISSINGER: . . . The problem is how are we going to handle it in the next few weeks when the jackals start screaming. . . . I mean, the major thing now is to keep everybody cool enough so that they don't stampede this into a Dien Bien Phu [the French defeat in 1954]. . . . Look, I think we have set them back several months. . . . And these units that fought there would have fought later somewhere.

MOORER: . . . Not only that, it's our time to choose.

KISSINGER: Exactly.

MOORER: I think the South Vietnamese for the first time have the initiative. . . .

KISSINGER: That's right. Well, hell, you know my instinct tells me if we could have thrown in an American division at this point, we would have cracked the whole outfit on the other side. . . . I think we were within a division, of somebody's division, of ending this goddamn thing.

MOORER: Chewing up those people pretty heavily; what they would have done of course is recede into the hills.

KISSINGER: Yeah, but that would have . . . enabled us to sit on the loot. . . .

President Nixon

March 21, 1971, 10:00 a.m.

Kissinger advises Nixon that they are portraying the heavy bombing of the North solely as "protective reaction," and they agree that it had to have a serious effect. But they wish they'd announced the South Vietnamese withdrawal in advance. Nixon is gung-ho on a planned (later aborted) South Vietnamese raid in Muong Nong, a village and enemy base area by the Ho Chi Minh Trail in Laos. Kissinger conveys Abrams's upbeat assessment. "We are so goddamned honest . . . we have never lied," Nixon says.

. . . KISSINGER: Moorer says they did get the strike off last night and the preliminary results indicate that very large success. . . .

NIXON: Are there any reports of that on the radio on the strike?

KISSINGER: Not on the radio yet. There were some twitches in news bulletins. But we are putting it entirely on the basis of protective reaction.

NIXON: Just absolutely low-key, and don't have air force or navy say anything about how many planes or anything of that sort. . . . This is one where I'd just say it's routine.

KISSINGER: Exactly.

NIXON: And incidentally, I thought about it a lot last night after we talked. I'm convinced that it was exactly the right thing to do. You don't change your plan on a thing like this solely because of a twitch in a battle situation. If you do, you've forgotten your main goal. Our main goal really all along has been, well, not only the psychological but also the one of knocking out some of those supplies so that they won't get down there. It's going to make a hell of a difference. Those strikes . . . they had to do some good.

KISSINGER: Oh, no question about it. . . . At this stage in the dry season, if it takes them even two or three weeks to get stuff back down from Haiphong, that's that much closer to the rainy season. . . .

NIXON: This is the thing about the news stories. They indicate the South Vietnamese retreated from two more bases today. Well, for god's sakes, if we had said it two days ago, Henry, which is what we should have done, there wouldn't have been any problem. We would have said they are going to leave eight bases. All right, so you are going to leave eight bases. Period.

KISSINGER: Yeah, that's where we had the problem, in not knowing. . . . They are still planning that other operation [Muong Nong]. . . . And if they do that, then towards the end of the week there'll be some upbeat news again.

NIXON: . . . They must not go out on a retreat note. They've got to go back in and give them another whop. . . . Can you tell them how strongly I feel that they must do it? Put it not on the basis of the situation here, but on the basis of his [President Thieu's] own political situation, that the news here will eventually filter back there and that that will make his people think that they suffered defeat. So the thing you've got to do is to give them another whop.

KISSINGER: Right; it would totally confuse our critics here, and it would give the other side a shock, Mr. President.

NIXON: Hell, yes! They've moved a lot of stuff there.

KISSINGER: Oh, yes; that's where they should have gone to begin with. . . . Moorer's view is Abrams feels very confident. He asked him, is there any panic? Is there any defeatism? . . . He said none—that the morale is very high; they haven't the slightest sign of defeatism. . . .

NIXON: But he knows these stories are pouring back in here about running and panic?

KISSINGER: Oh, yeah. . . . Actually the news stories aren't running so badly.

NIXON: . . . Well, these news stories go up and down. . . . The thing that we always forget here is that we are so goddamned honest. Johnson, of course, just lied, deliberately lied about the whole thing. And McNamara lied at Johnson's direction. Now, we have never lied. I will never lie; I can't live with that. On the other hand, I know psychology, and, therefore, we've got to look ahead and point out this thing. And we've also got to knock down the lies of the other side. They are lying all the time about this.

KISSINGER: Absolutely. I think that Abrams believes, Moorer believes, that this operation in total was a considerable success for us, and I think we ought to stress that. Even that *New York Times* writer says it set the other side back by several months.

NIXON: That might be a good thing to quote. . . . Quoting the *New York Times* is a real slap in the face at the leftists. . . . As far as anything else is concerned, the main thing is I think the psychological—Thieu has a psychological victory to win. He's got to give them one more whop. . . . God almighty, if those planes are worth one damn. . . . I have no faith in the air force. Those little navy planes—those attack planes—they must be getting something, Henry. Those guys are really pinpointers.

KISSINGER: And when they know where the enemy is—this isn't a case of just guessing. When they are attacking a hill, you know where they've got to be, and every time they've entered these areas after a strike they found a lot of bodies. . . .

President Nixon
March 21, 1971, 11:30 a.m.
Kissinger relays an account of a U.S. military officer who airlifted South Vietnamese out of Laos and was "shocked" by news reports of fleeing troops. Nixon wants him to brief legislators.

. . . KISSINGER: I talked to the colonel who had charge of the helo squad who were doing the moving of the troops.

NIXON: What kind of a guy was he?

KISSINGER: He is the kind of a guy that makes you proud to be an American. . . . He said the morale was high and they improved as they flew more. . . .

NIXON: . . . Tell Laird to have him go up and talk to some of the people on the Hill.

KISSINGER: . . . He is not the most articulate guy in the world.

NIXON: Hell with that. He has seen it.

KISSINGER: He has seen it and been in there and could tell them the straight story. He said that the enemy must be taking fantastically heavy losses. . . . Said that coordinating was an initial problem. They had not worked without American observers in there before and it was hard to get used to. Said among ARVN units the 1st Division was outstanding. Air force was good, and rangers were not really used to that type of intense fighting, and when he got there he did see some panicking among the rangers who were under very heavy fire.

NIXON: What does he think of reports he sees in the paper here? I mean, the origin, Henry—who the hell is saying this kind of thing?

KISSINGER: He is shocked by it. He says that a 19- or 20-year-old from a helicopter crew comes back and says to his buddies they were running but we saved them in time and the newspapers just follow them around and eat it up.

NIXON: God damn it, I do not think we should have put the press in. I would not have done it. . . .

President Nixon
March 21, 1971, no time
Nixon and Kissinger acknowledge that the bombing of North Vietnam wasn't really "protective reaction" against enemy fire. "I think they are taking a fearful beating,"

Kissinger says. Nixon wants administration officials to talk confidently about the Laos invasion. "If they lose the whole 10,000 that are still in there it's still a damn good thing," he says coldly, speaking of South Vietnamese soldiers.

... NIXON: They're threatening our forces, so we let them have it.

KISSINGER: Well, we'll put it on the protective reaction basis.

NIXON: Oh, exactly, I know, but you and I know what the reason is.

KISSINGER: That's right.

NIXON: This is all protective reaction. That's what they're going to explain it as, aren't they?

KISSINGER: That's right. And their strict orders are to that effect and they did have a lot of SAM firings last week. . . . But one reason is to use up the supplies they've got stockpiled near these passes. That's really the most fundamental reason.

NIXON: Sure, sure.

KISSINGER: And to improve their [the South Vietnamese's] general situation.

NIXON: Yeah. You know, one thing Moorer pointed out. He said that . . . they've never had so many of their people concentrated in as limited an area in the whole war. And as I pointed out to him, I said, well, that's a hell of an opportunity for our air, isn't it? . . . We must be just punishing them like hell.

KISSINGER: Oh, they must be taking—

NIXON: Sixty B-52, or whatever it was, strikes yesterday and in the night. He said the tactical air, gunships, helos, and the rest. Jesus Christ, I mean these people have got to be taking a hell of a beating.

KISSINGER: Oh, we are using up the best part of those regiments they've got there. They're not going to do any fighting the rest of this year. . . . If we had American troops there the other side would be breaking now.

NIXON: Yeah, if we had American troops what you'd do is to whip the division in behind them and go in and knock the damn thing off.

KISSINGER: Exactly.

NIXON: This may be the opportunity of the war.

KISSINGER: Oh, exactly, but I think they are taking a fearful beating.

NIXON: My view is, though, I really think more and more on balance, even though getting out is going to be a problem, on balance we're better to get out and have the damn thing off television. . . . They can claim victory; certainly South Vietnam will claim victory. . . .

KISSINGER: That's right, Mr. President. One would wish that the withdrawal had been going over a longer period just to make it look good. . . .

NIXON: . . . We've just got to take those stories for a while and then we'll have our own going back. . . . Next week the main thing is for all of our people to talk confidently about it. . . . I don't want just because . . . you might lose a battalion or two on the way out that we say . . . oh, gee whiz, we've lost the world. That isn't the case. If they lose the whole 10,000 that are still in there it's still a damn good thing. . . .

President Nixon
March 21, 1971, no time
Nixon and Kissinger muse about using the big B-52 bombers the next time they bomb North Vietnam, and Kissinger provides an update on the bombing; scores of fighter bombers were hitting targets way above the DMZ over two days.[9] Kissinger says they'd hit enough SAM sites to make their "protective reaction" claim plausible while pummeling the North.

NIXON: Hi, Henry, any late reports?

KISSINGER: Yes, Mr. President, we got some more of the bomb damage assessment. . . .

NIXON: Did we use B-52s?

KISSINGER: No, no, they have never been used in North Vietnam.

NIXON: Is there any reason not to?

KISSINGER: Well, except that it would be something new. . . .

NIXON: Well, we're not too late now. We'll take a look at it next time. I see no reason not to.

KISSINGER: I see no particular reason not to.

NIXON: What the hell, I mean, just use them.

KISSINGER: And they have the advantage of all-weather capability.

NIXON: That's right. . . . 52s don't use any visual bombing at all, do they?

KISSINGER: Not at all, no, Mr. President.

NIXON: They just go right in there. They could have just clobbered this damned place, couldn't they?

KISSINGER: They could certainly have taken out all the supply areas no matter what the weather. . . .

NIXON: . . . I think it's going to have some effect on these people. It's got to affect them.

KISSINGER: It's got to affect them, and even if you halve the claims—I mean, when they say the smoke went up 14,000 feet, they must have seen something.

NIXON: . . . It shakes the hell out of you to see those planes come over there. . . . They on the news yet?

KISSINGER: It's been on the news ticker. . . . But the ticker handles it in an absolutely low-key manner and as a protective reaction strike. And they've gone after enough SAM sites to make this plausible and they seem to have taken out enough of the SAM sites to . . . have hurt the other guy. . . .

NIXON: I'll tell you, they're going all-out there, and that's why I hope the hell
we're just clobbering them there in the air, too. We are, aren't we?
KISSINGER: Oh, yes. . . .

Martha Mitchell
March 23, 1971, 12:45 p.m.
*Crying, Martha Mitchell, the wife of Attorney General John Mitchell, whose son from
an earlier marriage was in Vietnam, threatens to embarrass Nixon.*

MITCHELL: I have told everyone there to tell you to go to hell. . . . You have
sent my son to Vietnam in the worst position. The whole thing has been set
up. . . . It stinks to high heaven. . . . I think they are trying to get me—you
know. Did you see CBS this morning? . . . They showed a picture of me and
said something about "the outspoken Martha Mitchell." I am so sure it was
set up. And someone is trying to get me to say things. They are trying to get
me to embarrass the president.
KISSINGER: But you wouldn't.
MITCHELL: I could. . . . I am terribly upset.
KISSINGER: I will look into it myself.
MITCHELL: Oh, shut up! I—I could kiss you! . . .

President Nixon
March 28, 1971, no time
*Beginning on March 25, Pakistan, a military dictatorship Kissinger and Nixon sup-
ported, committed wholesale atrocities in Bangladesh (then East Pakistan), killing
hundreds of thousands of people, perhaps up to three million, in response to a Bengali
nationalist uprising that called for self-rule. It was a horrific slaughter and went on
for months. Kissinger tells Nixon about a cable from Archer Blood, the U.S. consul
general in East Pakistan, who was horrified by the genocide, urging that the United
States speak out against it, at least to Pakistan.*[10]

. . . KISSINGER: . . . We've had a bleeding cable from our consul in Dacca who
wants us to put out a statement condemning what the West Pakistanis are
doing. But, of course, we won't consider it.
NIXON: Oh, for Christ's sake.
KISSINGER: Well, he's just one of these pansies.
NIXON: And he says condemning them?
KISSINGER: Yeah, for genocide.
NIXON: Well, now, remove him. I want him out of the job. . . . That kind of a
fellow with that kind of lack of balance. . . . He's obviously in there joining
one side or the other. He's supposed to stay out of this goddamned war.

KISSINGER: That's right. If we do that we're going to have anti-American riots in West Pakistan.

NIXON: That's right. I don't want that kind of fellow there and I want his background checked immediately.... Then kick him the hell out of there.... Isn't that awful? Jesus Christ. I mean, I wouldn't put out a statement praising it, but we're not going to condemn it either.

KISSINGER: ... Even if we didn't have that relationship with Yahya [Khan, president of Pakistan] ... there's nothing we can say that isn't going to get us more trouble than it's worth, for either side. ... Everyone in Washington is postured correctly. They all understand that you don't want to say anything. ...

President Nixon

March 29, 1971, no time

Enemy sappers had attacked a U.S. firebase in northern South Vietnam, killing 33 and wounding around 80.[11] *Nixon wants the disaster "handled properly for a change" and to find out the identity of the U.S. military spokesman who "popped off" about it.*

NIXON: I wanted to be sure that in the handling of that firebase thing that ... people have the good sense not to have a bunch of goddamned press people come in there and ... take pictures. ... Who's handling it? Is that Abrams again? ...

KISSINGER: That's Abrams, and I will check immediately on how they're going to handle it and let you know.

NIXON: Well, I would think that it would be handled just as a routine matter. Hell, we've had other times we've lost 24 or 25, you know.... But Haig just attributes it to negligence, huh?

KISSINGER: To a considerable extent. He says a unit that does its job can't get into a position like this. Because there were only 12 enemy killed and that indicated to him that they sneaked in there.

NIXON: ... Now, for Christ's sakes, they don't get those figures out either.... You don't say ... they were surprised, overrun, etc. They'll build it into a hell of a story unless it's handled properly for a change. And they've screwed every story up so far. Find out who that major was who put out that statement? ... Somebody on Abrams's staff obviously.... They ought to be a little more careful of ... having junior officers go out and talking to the press. The services are getting like everybody else, State Department officials and the rest. ...

KISSINGER: Well, in Saigon they are just terribly bad. They have got the press running all over them and they have lost any sense of proportion.

NIXON: . . . I want the statements made by people who know the whole thing and not people just giving bits and pieces. . . . This fellow shouldn't have popped off like that. . . . You know, a major, for example, doesn't really know everything that's going on.

KISSINGER: Certainly not. . . . Majors shouldn't talk to the press at all.

NIXON: 'Cause they don't know how.

KISSINGER: Exactly.

NIXON: The press always sucks them into one statement they're going to use and then they think they're giving a balanced story and what happens is that the unbalanced part comes out.

KISSINGER: That's it, they give them a headline.

NIXON: That's right, that's right. It's really something the way our people seem to have a compulsion to talk to the press. I just think all through government you've just got to put a tighter rein on this exposure to the press. People who talk to the press have to be people on the highest levels who know every-thing, and nobody else. This press running around with junior people and they get them drunk or they talk to them—

KISSINGER: Flatter them. No one wants to admit he doesn't know anything, so they make it up. . . .

My Lai; More Troop Withdrawals; U.S. "Moral Bankruptcy" in Pakistan; the Opening and Invitation to China, the Soviet Game, and Picking an Envoy; Creighton Abrams's Indiscretion on Laos; Allen Ginsberg's Overture; and an Ambiguous SALT Announcement Negotiated in the Back Channel

April–May 1971

On March 31, 1971, William Calley was sentenced to life imprisonment for his role in the My Lai massacre in Vietnam. Secretary of Defense Melvin Laird acted to keep under wraps a year-old report on the massacre by a commission led by General William Peers that described the massacre in detail and documented the army's cover-up of it.

On April 7, Nixon announced the withdrawal of another 100,000 U.S. troops from Vietnam over the coming months. He felt his speech needed to "cheer up" Americans after the calamitous invasion of Laos by conveying that the war was coming to an end. If his call for negotiations to end it didn't elicit a favorable response from Hanoi, "we will bomb those bastards off the earth," he told Kissinger.

The day before his speech, diplomats at the U.S. consulate in Dacca, East Pakistan, issued a scathing telegram expressing strong opposition to U.S. policy in Pakistan and condemning the administration's failure to denounce the genocide in East Pakistan perpetrated by the Pakistan military dictatorship. The cable infuriated Kissinger; Secretary of State William Rogers also found it "outrageous."

On April 14, the White House announced the relaxation of a long trade embargo with China, and Premier Chou En-lai received the U.S. table tennis team in Peking. Kissinger told Nixon, "We have got to have a diversion from Vietnam in this country for a while." But Kissinger had to reassure Nixon that he would get the credit for the China opening.

On April 17, Commander Creighton Abrams ill-advisedly told reporters that another South Vietnamese move into Laos "could not be ruled out," raising the specter of a repeat just when the uproar over the earlier invasion was dying down. A few days later, the Beat poet Allen Ginsberg proposed to Kissinger a meeting with Kissinger, Nixon, left-wing political activists, and others, perhaps "naked on television."

In late April, Kissinger received a message from Chou En-lai that China was willing to receive a special emissary from the United States to arrange high-level discussions whose ultimate purpose was to fundamentally open relations. The following month, the United States and the Soviet Union announced that the SALT talks that year would focus on limiting both ABM defense systems and offensive weapons (though the wording was ambiguous about the sequence). The announcement required Nixon and Kissinger to conspire on how to inform titular head U.S. SALT negotiator Gerard Smith and Rogers of SALT negotiations conducted behind their backs.

Melvin Laird
April 3, 1971, no time
Laird says he is going to try to keep the Peers Commission's report on the My Lai massacre "bottled up for another 12 months."

> . . . LAIRD: There's one thing, Henry. I wonder if you or the president . . . shouldn't read the Peers Commission report, which I've put a clamp of secrecy on. . . . Because sooner or later, that thing will [get out]. . . . We are keeping it now classified on the basis that it . . . might prejudice the judicial process. Now, there are some people who have read it and I think you should know that . . . [Representative] Eddie Hébert . . . and [Senator John] Stennis has read parts of it. The parts on the sex offenses, sodomy and rape. I wouldn't let them use those in the prosecution, but they are in that report.
>
> KISSINGER: . . . I know somebody at the White House ought to read it.
>
> LAIRD: Somebody ought to read that goddamned report, Henry. But I don't want to get that thing so circulated—we've got to handle it very carefully,

because I'm going to try to keep that bottled up for another 12 months. There'll be a great demand to make that public. You know, [Robert] MacCrate, who is Rockefeller's counsel, is going to take the president on on this thing. . . . He was the counsel for the Peers Commission.

KISSINGER: Let me talk to Rockefeller and see whether I can get him [to] shut up a bit. . . .

LAIRD: I think he's been talking a little bit too much, I think to some of our friends on the *New York Times* and some other places. And I just hate to have this whole damn thing surfaced. . . . I just think we've got to be very careful.

KISSINGER: . . . I frankly don't want to do [read] it myself. I don't want to get into that review process.

LAIRD: I think it's better if you don't, but somebody ought to. I don't even think Bill should read it. . . .

KISSINGER: No, Bill ought to stay out of it, too. It's a loser.

LAIRD: But I think somebody should read it so that they know what [it says]. . . . You know, the press is after it. We will not give it to them. . . .

President Nixon
April 4, 1971, no time
Nixon and Kissinger confer on Nixon's upcoming speech on Southeast Asia, including the invasion of Laos, when he would announce the withdrawal of another 100,000 U.S. troops by December 1. Nixon says the speech must lift Americans out of their depression. Kissinger tells him it kills the press "that you are so serene." He and Nixon disparage the press and instruction at Harvard.

. . . NIXON: . . . It must have lift, and we've got to speak with confidence. . . . It should be more one of "Well, we are coming to the end." . . . They've just got to be reassured. The American people right now, you know, are in sort of a psychological depression, and the reason they are in that depression, Henry, is this goddamned television. . . . It's just been pounding them night after night. It is just shameful. Look what it does to people. No wonder it depresses them. So what we have to do is to cheer them up a little. . . . You know, the Calley thing, of course, got some of the hawks even saying let's get the hell out. . . .

KISSINGER: . . . But the play of the news is no longer quite as negative in a subtle way. . . . They're beginning now to report some of the achievements on Laos, and the hysterical gloating tone is out of it to a considerable extent.

NIXON: The gloating over the defeat. . . . Wouldn't it really kill them if they knew I don't read them?

KISSINGER: It already kills them that you are so serene. . . . About 80 percent come in and say, "Now tell me the truth. Is the president really so calm? Or is he nervous?" I said I've never seen him waver in any of these periods.

NIXON: That burns them up, doesn't it?

KISSINGER: You know, they are used to Johnson rooting around and beating his breast.

NIXON: I saw Kennedy the day after the Bay of Pigs and, boy, I tell you. If ever I had seen a guy who had lost his cool, that was one.

KISSINGER: Oh, god yes.

NIXON: And that was, of course, crap. Nothing to that.

KISSINGER: Well, that was a one-shot operation.

NIXON: Well, it was easy to handle, too.

KISSINGER: From which it was easy to recover.

NIXON: . . . Well, anyway, if the serenity bugs them, they'll get bugged with that because we've just got to plow right ahead on that score. . . . There isn't one student of a Harvard professor that could stand up to me for five minutes in a debate.

KISSINGER: That's what they don't like about you.

NIXON: There's not one of them that could stand up for one of those press conferences without a note. 'Cause they don't teach that anymore.

KISSINGER: Exactly. And also the way you have everything organized. You know, when you can say to Howard K. Smith [of *ABC Evening News*], "The following are the three points"—1, 2, 3 in grammatical sentences.

NIXON: That's right. There's not one of their students who could do that. . . .

KISSINGER: Well, none of them could because they don't teach them anymore, to be that disciplined in their thinking. . . .

President Nixon
April 5, 1971, 9:15 p.m.
Nixon says he's not interested in his staff's advice on his speech since they knew nothing about foreign affairs and were too focused on their critics, when "goddammit, we've told the truth about everything."

. . . NIXON: . . . They don't know a goddamn thing about this. . . .

KISSINGER: And they don't know what we will be hit with if this whole thing comes apart.

NIXON: They don't know a thing about foreign policy. . . . All they are concerned about is revenue sharing, the environment, and all that crap, which doesn't amount to anything.

KISSINGER: They want to take off the immediate pressure, this is their overriding concern. . . . And that I don't believe can be done. I mean, it can't be done their way because once you accept the premises of McGovern, you are fighting on his ground and it wouldn't be in character. . . .

NIXON: Oh, of course, these goddamn doves . . . I've determined to just see it through and the hell with them. . . . If it fails, it fails.

KISSINGER: Well, it's a heroic posture, Mr. President.

NIXON: Well, hell, believe it or not, there is no other course for the country. These people—I mean, that's why our domestic side, while I'm interested in their views, why they're irrelevant—they don't know what the hell they are talking about. . . . I must say that they are so terribly obsessed with listening to television, reading all of our critics. . . . But they read all that and they say, well now, just a minute, is this true? Have we overstated anything? . . . I constantly get back to the fact that I don't think our own people know enough how to defend us.

KISSINGER: That's right, that's right. They are astonished by some of these things or by what we have accomplished. I mean, we've kept our promises, we will have taken out several hundred thousand, two-thirds of our forces.

NIXON: . . . They read the critics and they get the impression that, dammit, we are lying, that we are covering up. . . . And goddammit, we've told the truth about everything. . . .

William Rogers

April 6, 1971, 9:35 a.m.

U.S. Consul General Archer Blood and most of the rest of his consulate in Dacca, East Pakistan, had dispatched a scorching telegram expressing their strong opposition to U.S. policy in Pakistan and its "moral bankruptcy," including the administration's failure to denounce the genocide in East Pakistan committed by the Pakistan government and protect its people while "bending over backwards to placate" the government. Rogers tells Kissinger, who grew furious about the cable, "It's inexcusable . . . it is outrageous."[1]

ROGERS: I wanted to talk about that goddamn message from our people in Dacca. Did you see it?

KISSINGER: No.

ROGERS: It's miserable. They bitched about our policy and have given it lots of distribution so it will probably leak. It's inexcusable.

KISSINGER: And it will probably get to Ted Kennedy. . . . Somebody gives him cables. . . .

ROGERS: It's a terrible telegram. Couldn't be worse. Says we failed to defend American lives and are morally bankrupt.

KISSINGER: Blood did that?

ROGERS: Quite a few of them signed it. You know, we are doing everything we can about it. Trying to get the telegrams back, as many as we can. We are going to get a message back to them.

KISSINGER: I am going in these two days to keep it from the president until he has given his speech.

ROGERS: If you can keep it from him I will appreciate it. . . . They talk about condemning atrocities. There are pictures of the East Pakistanis murdering people.

KISSINGER: Yes. There was one of an East Pakistani holding a head. Do you remember when they said there were 1,000 bodies and they had the graves, and then we couldn't find 20?

ROGERS: To me it is outrageous they would send this. . . .

President Nixon

April 7, 1971, 9:30 p.m.

Kissinger heaps praise on Nixon's speech that evening, which, besides announcing the U.S. troop withdrawals from Vietnam, had called on Hanoi to negotiate an end to the war and release all American POWs.[2] "If it doesn't work, we will bomb those bastards off the earth," Nixon says.

KISSINGER: Mr. President, this was the best speech you delivered since you have been in office.

NIXON: November 3rd [1969, when he appealed for the support of "the great silent majority" on the war] was better. But we will never have another like that again.

KISSINGER: November 3rd was not well delivered, if you remember, Mr. President. It was a powerful speech. I don't know if you saw the commentaries.

NIXON: No, I don't care what the bastards say!

KISSINGER: John Chancellor [of *NBC Nightly News*] was very favorable. Everyone was saying he is a strong man sticking to his guns. . . .

NIXON: This speech was a work of art. . . . How was the delivery?

KISSINGER: It was by far the best. It was dignified, strong. . . .

NIXON: . . . If it doesn't work, we will bomb those bastards off the earth. You agree, don't you?

KISSINGER: I think, Mr. President, we will have to make fundamental decisions in the next weeks.

NIXON: Assuming they don't negotiate then we will turn right hard, Henry!!

President Nixon

April 7, 1971, 11:45 p.m.

Nixon wants to know where his whining staff stand on his speech.

... NIXON: I talked to Haldeman and . . . said, you know, you haven't heard
from [Donald] Rumsfeld and you haven't heard from [Robert] Finch [both
counselors to the president] and you haven't heard from—well, [Nixon
counsel Clark] MacGregor was disappointed because we didn't announce
a bigger withdrawal. . . . You go to the staff meeting tomorrow and just
listen and find out where everybody stands. . . . They may not want to
see where they stand. If they have got the guts, we want to know now,
right?

KISSINGER: Exactly, Mr. President. . . .

NIXON: At the staff meeting you just watch; don't say much. . . . Just let it
come, smoke them out. They will be whining around; let them whimper
and whine and we'll find out who's who. . . .

President Nixon

April 8, 1971, 10:06 p.m.

*After agreeing that they should not declare an end date for U.S. involvement in Viet-
nam, Nixon tells Kissinger that Melvin Laird needs to "pipe down" on it. They also
take up William Calley and My Lai and the public debate over the massacre. The
explosion of public support for Calley was "the frustration of a people who are not
permitted to win the war," Kissinger says.*

... NIXON: I told Ziegler today that he should just . . . say, look, the president . . .
he's stated his position, I'm not going to go beyond it, gentlemen.

KISSINGER: Exactly, exactly.

NIXON: And any congressman or senator that thinks that we got a date in
mind, fine, but we're not going to say, because the point is we may have
a date in mind . . . but I'm keeping the option open of changing my mind in
November.

KISSINGER: Exactly. . . . If we say too much about the date, the next thing is
we're abandoning the prisoners. . . .

NIXON: Oh, hell yes. . . . Some way or other you've got to get Laird in so he'll
pipe down a little bit too about it.

KISSINGER: I've scheduled a lunch with him next week. I'm going to get Laird
quieted down. . . . I'm just going to tell him he'll get himself into such
unbelievable trouble. . . .

NIXON: He should also pipe down on the Calley thing. We got that in the
right position; we're not defending Calley, and we're going to let it run its
course. . . .

KISSINGER: I think that's right and I think the traditional process should
now take its normal course there. . . . That public furor had to be quieted
down.

NIXON: . . . Surprised us all, surprised the press and all the rest. It's probably a good thing that the country had that little spasm. . . . Give them a chance to just pop off steam. . . .

KISSINGER: . . . And no matter what they say now, no one can construe that outburst as a dove outburst, even if it took the form, perhaps, of wanting to get out of the war. It was the frustration of a people who are not permitted to win the war. . . . And that's quite a different thing.

NIXON: Exactly, and I think the liberals really know this. . . .

KISSINGER: Deep down the liberals know that.

NIXON: And they are in shock by it, because they were sort of hoping that the whole nation would sort of say, well, now we'll punish these—

KISSINGER: That's right. What they wanted was a feeling of revulsion against the deed. In fact, the deed itself didn't bother anybody.

NIXON: No, they, matter of fact, the people said, sure, he was guilty, but by god, why not? [Laughter.]

KISSINGER: Exactly. . . .

William Westmoreland
April 12, 1971, afternoon
Kissinger and Westmoreland, the U.S. Army chief of staff and Creighton Abrams's predecessor as U.S. commander in Vietnam, talk over the Laos invasion. Westmoreland had offered a "bleak" assessment of it to Kissinger in February.[3]

KISSINGER: I have thought with nostalgia and regret of our conversation here many weeks ago. You were right. . . . I was uneasy and didn't know what was wrong. I wish you had been wrong.

WESTMORELAND: So do I. Formidable undertaking. So much depended on communications and helicopters. . . . The operation was still successful. Our losses were heavier than might have been. Our materiel losses are shocking.

KISSINGER: In helicopters?

WESTMORELAND: That is public knowledge, but 94 artillery pieces and tanks and APCs. . . . Not revealed and shouldn't be. It gives you a better idea of what happened. . . .

KISSINGER: How did they think with these guys it could be done?

WESTMORELAND: They have come a long way and learned as time has gone on. . . . We would have been hard-pressed to run it ourselves and too much for these little fellows. . . . We should have pulled advisers before to shake them down so they would have self-confidence. We should have stockpiled airborne; they take terrible casualties. . . . Build up 120 percent overstrike. These things have to be anticipated. . . . Such a veil of secrecy Abe [Abrams] was afraid to take steps. . . . Too much secrecy in the plan.

KISSINGER: And not adjusting it to conditions when we hit them.

WESTMORELAND: . . . It puts a veil of caution on the whole thing. . . . Materiel losses . . . was most indicative thing on disorderliness and withdrawal. . . . Abe in the most difficult position you can hear of. Thieu took it over; Americans were taken out because Thieu talked to the field commanders. On one occasion we talked Thieu into a course of action and orders sent to [General Hoang Xuan Lam, the commander of South Vietnamese forces in Laos], who talks with Thieu and reverses it. It's awkward. You have to fully appreciate the position that Abe was in.

KISSINGER: . . . Your briefing at the end of February was very clairvoyant. . . .

President Nixon
April 14, 1971, no time

Nixon had announced a relaxation of trade and travel restrictions with China, and Chinese Premier Chou En-lai had welcomed the U.S. table tennis team in Peking, saying their visit had "opened a new chapter" in relations. Chairman Mao Tse-tung had ordered the invitation late one night after taking "his customary heavy dose of sleeping pills" but before falling asleep. Kissinger reports to Nixon that the easing of the long trade embargo with China was big news and says their China move will quiet intellectuals and journalists and that they have to be "cold" about Taiwan. The move was needed to divert public attention from Vietnam and "for our game with the Soviets." Kissinger and Nixon also hoped the Soviets and China would pressure Hanoi to end the war.[4]

NIXON: . . . Have you checked in to see how they played the Chinese thing today?

KISSINGER: Oh, yeah. It was tremendous . . . a tremendous thing on television . . . the lead item. . . .

NIXON: You mean rather than Vietnam for a change. . . . Now, on the China thing what we have to realize, Henry, is that in terms of the American public opinion, it is still against Communist China. . . . So we are not making any votes with this.

KISSINGER: No, but we are quieting the intellectuals and the newsmen.

NIXON: The intellectuals will worry. . . . They will think something else is up. . . . How about the Taiwan thing? That's sort of worrisome. . . .

KISSINGER: . . . It's a tragedy that it has to happen to Chiang [Kai-shek, Taiwan's president] at the end of his life, but we have to be cold about it.

NIXON: We have to do what's best for us.

KISSINGER: And in the long term it is essential for the values that he represents that there be continuity in our government here.

NIXON: Yes, and that he has here an administration that is not going to just stand by and let Taiwan go down the drain; we're trying to hold their position as best we can.

KISSINGER: Exactly. For every reason we have got to have a diversion from Vietnam in this country for a while.

NIXON: That's the point, isn't it? Yeah.

KISSINGER: And we need it for our game with the Soviets.

NIXON: Yeah, yeah.

KISSINGER: I mean . . . we would be doing the Soviets the greatest favor if we rejected this overture and we would get nothing for it; it would lead to tougher relations between us and the Soviets rather than easier.

NIXON: That's right, that's right. That's what they would like for us to do, they would like for us to sort of slap the Chinese in the face, but we're not going to. We're not going overboard but we're saying, well, if they open the door, we'll open the door.

KISSINGER: That's right. And actually now one would have to expect a hiatus of a few weeks.

NIXON: Oh, of course, nothing is going to happen for a while, but that's all right, just let this rest a while. You know, mutter around about it for a while.

KISSINGER: And of course with some luck we will get some nibble on the Soviet front now. . . . Well, it isn't even luck so much, it really logically ought to happen.

NIXON: . . . That's right. If they are at all logical, it damn well better, or they are a lot more rigid and stupid—

KISSINGER: I mean, there is nothing new they are going to learn about SALT; they are either going to move on that or not. And the other one, the summit, we have been kicking around for a year. . . .

President Nixon
April 16, 1971, 10:45 p.m.
Kissinger gushes over Nixon's interview at a meeting of the American Society of Newspaper Editors that was broadcast over the radio. Referring to his liberal critics, Nixon says his China policy "drives 'em nuts."

KISSINGER: I thought it was outstanding, and I was at dinner at, in fact I still am there, at Kay Graham's [owner and publisher of the *Washington Post*], but I'm where I can talk, and the Indian ambassador was there. . . . And [U.S. Senator] Adlai Stevenson is here, and the reaction is absolutely enthusiastic. . . . I thought you handled it with very, very great delicacy, the question of residual force, the question of withdrawal. . . . I thought you handled Vietnam with really enormous delicacy. I was just now assisted by the Indian ambassador, strangely enough, beating up Adlai Stevenson. . . .

NIXON: The poor bastard, he didn't know what to do, does he?

KISSINGER: Oh, no, the Indian ambassador is hitting him from one side and I'm hitting him from the other. . . . China was beautifully handled. I thought you were very wise and it was tremendously effective that you turned that first question into a little speech on peace. . . .

NIXON: That I sleep, that I dream about peace all night, yeah, I know, all that crap.

KISSINGER: . . . I must say I was tremendously impressed by the delicacy with which you handled the foreign policy questions, because this was a tough moment.

NIXON: . . . I didn't give a thing away on Vietnam, I didn't give a thing away on China. You know, on China I said, well, no, I'm not going to talk about that.

KISSINGER: That was beautiful. . . .

NIXON: But, you see, with the way the China thing now sits is that we haven't said a thing. . . .

KISSINGER: We haven't raised any expectations. . . .

NIXON: What I said . . . in effect, as far as we're concerned we're ready to trade, we're ready to exchange, but as far as recognition and all these technical problems, the other problems, we aren't going to talk about them right now. . . . Now, we're going to get a hell of a blast from the *Washington Post* and the *New York Times*. "Why don't we say we're going to recognize Red China?" Screw them. Don't you agree?

KISSINGER: They didn't get you to this point in your China policy; you did more in two years than they've—

NIXON: Oh, this drives 'em nuts, Henry, this drives 'em nuts. . . .

President Nixon
April 16, 1971, 11:22 p.m.
Kissinger reassures Nixon that he will get the credit for the China opening, which nobody else could have pulled off.

. . . NIXON: Because, you know, really, we make the breakthrough on China, this is the biggest thing that's ever happened in, you know, what, 20 years, Henry.

KISSINGER: It's a historic turning point, Mr. President.

NIXON: That's right. They all know it, don't they?

KISSINGER: Oh, no question, not a question.

NIXON: . . . We won't get any credit, but who knows.

KISSINGER: Oh, you'll get credit. On this you've gotten full credit, the first time.

NIXON: Do you think so?

KISSINGER: Oh, yes. . . . Well, they know it couldn't have come from anyone else, no one else had ever talked of it.

NIXON: All right. As a matter of fact, you and I know that without our leadership nothing would have happened here. Nobody else and no dove could have done this.

KISSINGER: Absolutely.

NIXON: Hubert [Humphrey, a U.S. senator and former vice president] couldn't have done it.

KISSINGER: No one could have done it politically, and no one could have done it within the bureaucracy because they didn't want to do it.

NIXON: That's right. . . .

President Nixon
April 18, 1971, 10:30 a.m.
Commander Creighton Abrams had told reporters that a new South Vietnamese move into Laos "could not be ruled out" and that it would involve U.S. support.[5]

. . . KISSINGER: . . . Abrams made an injudicious comment. . . . They said, "Is it possible that this drive [near the border] will go into Laos?" Well, actually, they are under strict orders, Mr. President, there will not be any of these horror stories coming out because we won't use many helicopters. And it has the advantage of tying down the North Vietnamese.

NIXON: . . . But the orders have got to go out there that I want Abrams and Bunker to pipe down. . . . The thing is that this is what the press is trying to do. They want a story. It doesn't make any difference what he does. I don't care if he goes in and bombs the hell out of them, but don't say it. The press wants to put Vietnam back on the front pages. This one little story, god damn it, is in two papers on the front page. Right?

KISSINGER: That's right. I talked to Laird about it. . . . He said he'd get right on the phone with Abrams. And, you know, when we wanted him to talk, he didn't. . . .

NIXON: He just got sucked into it. Some goddamned newspaper guy wanted to get a story to the effect we were going back into Laos, because the news guys out there are dying. Laos is over and the South Vietnamese hold the hill and now they are moving around and they are having their award ceremony. And I think they are just trying to suck poor old Abrams into—he just feels so compelled to be so goddamned honest all the time. Why doesn't he just shut up? . . . Jesus Christ, do what I say. Don't comment on that sort of thing, dodge it.

KISSINGER: . . . Instead of if he says, "I don't rule it out," and by the time they get through writing it, they're back in. Although, if one reads the actual stories, they are not written in a particularly inflammatory way.

NIXON: Yes, but Henry, most of them will see the little blip on television generally that says that we may go back into Laos. . . . When everybody was beginning to calm down about Laos they get all stirred up again. . . .

Gerald Warren
April 18, 1971, morning
Kissinger instructs Deputy Press Secretary Warren on how to handle Abrams's remarks.

KISSINGER: Hello, Jerry, the president is having conniptions about this goddamn Abrams quote. . . . How can you play it to keep it down?

WARREN: Well, wasn't he talking about their capability rather than what they were going to do? . . .

KISSINGER: Well, he said it isn't ruled out.

WARREN: . . . But he didn't say that we were planning such a thing.

KISSINGER: Well, but there may be raids in there, you see.

WARREN: Can we play it that what he was not ruling out . . . was the type of cross-border operations that we had prior to the Laos incursion?

KISSINGER: No, it's going to be larger than that. . . . Just say he was talking about capabilities. He was not projecting any specific plans. . . .

President Nixon
April 18, 1971, 10:45 a.m.
Nixon and Kissinger point out that neither the Democrats nor the State Department had recommended the opening with China, which Nixon had been talking about since day one. Yet they should not appear too eager with the Chinese. They ponder a possible summit.

. . . NIXON: . . . They try to say that this all happened because of their initiative and so forth. But it is really amusing to me, though, because while Mike [Mansfield, a Democratic senator] is honorable these other Democrats are not—the way they're all pandering around and trying to run over there to China and so forth.

KISSINGER: But the problem is they never recommended any of this, Mr. President. They can say whatever they want, this is yours.

NIXON: And neither did the State Department.

KISSINGER: That's right. The scope of it. The State Department was sort of crying around with recognition and that sort of thing.

NIXON: That's right. They were all talking about what was really what you call a tactical abstract thing which was really unfeasible.

KISSINGER: I showed [the *New Republic's* John] Osborne that little note you sent me on February 1st, '69, and his mouth really dropped way open. . . . It said I want you to explore on a highly confidential basis how we can improve our relations with Communist China, and above all how we can establish reliable private channels to them. . . . It couldn't be more explicit, Mr. President. You said I want no publicity whatsoever.

NIXON: That must have really killed him.

KISSINGER: Oh, god, his mouth really dropped about six inches. . . . They know damned well that on February 1, 1969, no State Department had gotten—

NIXON: February '69 no State Department had even talked to me.

KISSINGER: That's right. . . .

NIXON: Basically 10 days after I took office. . . .

KISSINGER: I think on this one, sure, the Democrats are going to start yelling now. They are going to come up with 50 hot gimmicks, but we are so far ahead—

NIXON: What they will come up with now is why don't we admit them to the UN? Why don't we recognize them and so forth? Well, that's all premature. . . .

KISSINGER: . . . My major worry is that if we get too eager that the Chinese will start going back into a shell. And that's why the way you have played it and that's where the Democrats could do damage.

NIXON: I sure as hell don't expect to get eager at all with the Chinese. Unless the Russian thing [summit] drops. Then the Chinese may want to be eager and we will too. . . . I think our Chinese game, Henry, should be played exactly as it is being played. Very cool and aloof, and yet the door is open now, you walk in, kids. It's your—

KISSINGER: Mr. President, I must tell you honestly I believe that we have a 30 percent chance, even if we played the Russian game, of having a high-level Chinese one [summit] next year. . . .

NIXON: We want to use it. We want it at the highest level too.

KISSINGER: That's what I mean. That's not at all excluded.

NIXON: Let me say that the more I think about the envoy thing [a U.S. diplomatic visit to China beforehand], if we are going to go I think we ought to go at the highest level.

KISSINGER: Well, I think the envoy could prepare for it.

NIXON: It might, but it might take a lot of the zip out of it too. You know what I mean, Henry. You just can't tell. I don't know if there is anybody we trust to send over there. That's—

KISSINGER: That's a bit down the road yet. First we need a reliable channel.

Allen Ginsberg
April 23, 1971, 7:50 p.m.
The poet Allen Ginsberg proposes a meeting with Kissinger, former senator Eugene McCarthy, CIA Director Richard Helms, Nixon, and several antiwar and civil rights leaders, perhaps even "naked on television."

GINSBERG: I am calling at the request partly of Senator McCarthy. Senator McCarthy told me to call you. My idea is to arrange a conversation between yourself, Helms, McCarthy, and maybe even Nixon with Rennie Davis, Dellinger, and Abernathy. [Davis and Dave Dellinger were antiwar leaders who had earlier been indicted over the 1968 Democratic Convention protests, and Ralph Abernathy was the president of the Southern Christian Leadership Conference.] It can be done at any time. . . . Perhaps you don't know how to get out of the war. . . .

KISSINGER: I have been meeting with many members representing peace groups, but what I find is that they have always then rushed right out and given the contents of the meeting to the press. But I like to do this, not just for the enlightenment of the people I talk to but to at least give me a feel of what concerned people think. I would be prepared to meet in principle on a private basis.

GINSBERG: . . . It is a question of personal delicacy. In dealing with human consciousness, it is difficult to set limits. . . . It would be even more funny to do it on television.

KISSINGER: What?

GINSBERG: It would be even more useful if we could do it naked on television.

KISSINGER: [Laughter.]

GINSBERG: . . . What shall I tell them that would be encouraging?

KISSINGER: That I would think about it very seriously.

GINSBERG: Good deal.

KISSINGER: I will call Senator McCarthy. I am leaving town . . . but I will be back on Monday. When did you intend to do this?

GINSBERG: During the May Day [protest] meetings in Washington. . . . May 2 or 3.

KISSINGER: May 2nd or 3rd. Damn it! I would like to do it in principle but . . . I may not be in town. If not, we can do it at some other reasonable date.

GINSBERG: I gather you don't know how to get out of the war.

KISSINGER: I thought we did but we are always interested in hearing other views.

GINSBERG: If you see Helms, ask him if he has begun meditating yet. . . . He promised to meditate one hour a day. I still have to teach him how to hold his back straight. . . .

KISSINGER: Where are you calling from?

GINSBERG: Sacramento, California—I just gave a talk on gay liberation. . . . I will try to arrange a private meeting. It would be good to talk to the army too—you know, the war people and the antiwar people.

KISSINGER: It is barely conceivable that there are people who like war.

GINSBERG: They might have some ideas. . . . You may have to subject yourself to prayer.

KISSINGER: That is a private matter that is permissible. . . .

President Nixon

April 27, 1971, 8:18 p.m.

Kissinger had received a message from Chinese Premier Chou En-lai that China was willing to receive a special envoy from the United States to arrange discussions between high-level officials to resolve disagreements over Taiwan. The ultimate purpose of the discussions was to fundamentally open relations between China and the United States. Kissinger and Nixon ponder who might fit the bill as the envoy, including Governor Nelson Rockefeller and Ambassador to the UN George H. W. Bush. (Nixon later decided on Kissinger, who told Nixon he was the only person who could really handle it, though Nixon worried Kissinger might get too much press that would detract from his own later visit to China.)[6]

NIXON: . . . How about Nelson?

KISSINGER: No. . . . Mr. President, he wouldn't be disciplined enough, although he is a possibility.

NIXON: It would engulf him in a big deal and he is outside of the government, you see.

KISSINGER: Let me think about it; I might be able to hold him in check.

NIXON: It is intriguing, don't you think? . . . How about Bush?

KISSINGER: Absolutely not, he is too soft and not sophisticated enough. . . . I thought about [HEW Secretary Elliot] Richardson but he wouldn't be the right thing.

NIXON: He is still too close to us and I don't think it would sit well with Rogers. Nelson—the Chinese would consider him important and he . . . could do a lot for us in terms of the domestic situation. No, Nelson is a wild hare running around.

KISSINGER: I think for one operation I could keep him under control. To them a Rockefeller is a tremendous thing. . . . Bush would be too weak.

NIXON: I thought so too but I was trying to think of somebody with a title.

KISSINGER: Nelson has possibilities.

NIXON: . . . Of course, that would drive State up the wall.

KISSINGER: He would take someone from State along, but he despises them so much he will take our direction. . . . On foreign policy, Nelson would take my advice. . . . He's tough.

NIXON: Particularly if you get him in right at the mountaintop and say, look, it will make or break you, boy. . . .

President Nixon
May 15, 1971, 11:00 a.m.
Soviet Ambassador Anatoly Dobrynin and Kissinger had agreed on joint U.S.–Soviet announcements on the upcoming SALT talks, stating that they would focus on limiting both ABM defense systems and offensive weapons (which Kissinger and Nixon advocated, though the wording would be ambiguous about the sequence; the Soviets advocated reaching an ABM agreement first). Nixon and Kissinger consult on how to inform head U.S. SALT negotiator Gerard Smith and Secretary of State William Rogers of SALT negotiations carried out behind their backs.[7]

NIXON: Well, you got everybody under control there?

KISSINGER: Yes. You know, it is tough going. I have a Verification Panel meeting now and Smith is dancing all over the place. He is so delighted with what he has that he wants to announce it. If we don't go on Thursday something may leak. . . . The proposal made to Smith was the one that we had talked about in February or March. . . . We have got more than Smith did but in a whole different concept.

NIXON: Smith is not to go out and State is not to go out and say that all because of Smith's brilliant negotiation we got this. . . . I have to see Rogers before him and I think I should see him alone. What should I tell him?

KISSINGER: Simply that we have this proposal. You should not be too modest about the agreement. The Soviets have accepted this and it is much beyond the agreement they offered Smith.

NIXON: Say in March they came back and this and that. I have no problem with Smith. I don't give a god damn about what he thinks. . . . I think I will start with Rogers simply by saying that we started in January and while you were away they came in with a response. . . .

President Nixon
May 17, 1971, 9:28 p.m.

They decide to delay speaking with Rogers and Smith about the SALT announcements until they're locked in.

NIXON: I was thinking that until we get the final word from Dobrynin that we really shouldn't go ahead with Rogers and Smith. . . . I can put the Rogers appointment off a day and you can tell Smith I want to see him a day later.

KISSINGER: . . . Say you have a cold or something.

NIXON: No, no; my schedule is too full. I have to see all these senators. . . . We may just be brewing trouble here if we start down the line with Rogers and Smith. We will wait and tell them when it's nailed down. . . . I can say I have gotten tied up myself, the railroad strike and so forth. . . .

Charles Mathias

May 19, 1971, 5:35 p.m.

Senator Mathias and Kissinger butt heads over Kissinger's failure to get back to Mathias, as promised, about a compromise that Mathias had put forward to a resolution by Senator Mike Mansfield that would halve U.S. forces in Western Europe. The Senate rejected Mansfield's and all compromise proposals for smaller reductions that day, including Mathias's pro-administration one. The White House opposed not only Mansfield but all compromise proposals.[8]

KISSINGER: Somebody said . . . that you might have been willing to withdraw your amendment if we had indicated an objection.

MATHIAS: I said I wanted to put in it what the president wanted. . . . I said I would have to have some guidance from you. You promised you would call me back in the late morning or early afternoon the next day. I canceled a college trustees meeting to be here to receive your call. . . . I said I would put words in or take words out, or kill the whole thing. . . . I would have been glad to withdraw it or anything else. But it's beyond that now.

KISSINGER: I indicated to enough people that I was opposed to it. I was certain the word had gotten to you.

MATHIAS: . . . I was reachable and canceled plans so I would be reachable. . . . These matters could have been solved simply. Without guidance, I want you to know I did the best I could to cooperate and offered you carte blanche. I said I would put words in, take words out, or withdraw it, but I needed to know from you. . . . I desperately wanted to do what the president wanted done here.

KISSINGER: I can't accept that. We are not that hard to reach.

MATHIAS: You said you were going to call back. . . .

KISSINGER: The word must have reached you I wasn't in favor of it. . . .

MATHIAS: When you didn't take it up, I assumed it was all right to use my own discretion and do the best I could with it. . . . I got the word that the White House was nervous—they didn't know what the final vote on Mansfield was and . . . that it would be useful for the president to have a fallback position which would be something that would be better than Mansfield. . . .

KISSINGER: One of us has been had. . . .

President Nixon

May 23, 1971, 2:30 p.m.

They denigrate Secretary of the Army Stanley Resor, who had resigned and voiced doubts about the Vietnam War shortly after announcing disciplinary action against two generals for their roles in the cover-up of the My Lai massacre.[9] They also disparage Army Chief of Staff William Westmoreland and Commander Creighton Abrams.

NIXON: Just as a thought—we got the *Post* right here and after seeing that story on Resor I thought, my god, I wonder if he may have been screwing up that thing out there. Did you see the story on him?

KISSINGER: Oh, yes indeed!

NIXON: Said he wasn't sure about the war and so forth. What in the name of god, you know? It shows you the problems of keeping these holdovers.

KISSINGER: That's the trouble we've had.

NIXON. Laird has got to really be taken to task. . . . He's got to shape those people up over there. If there are any more like this, get them out now. . . . Next year there'll be all these people coming out of the woodwork, and we don't want them in the government at that time.

KISSINGER: No question about it. . . . But here is a fellow who is still in office, and the day after [resigning] he already goes through this exercise. Anyone who knows him, I think, does not take him particularly seriously. . . .

NIXON: . . . But my god, for him to pull this kind of stuff is unbelievable. And you can see now how he screwed up My Lai and everything else. He is really bad news. . . . He is the same as that fellow they had in the UN—[former ambassador Charles] Yost.

KISSINGER: Who has had another article in there either today or yesterday on Vietnam again. . . . It's just the height of bad taste. . . .

NIXON: I thought Laird ought to tell Resor to pipe down. . . .

KISSINGER: And the hell of it is that you just recently have written him a particularly nice letter.

NIXON: And I said "special regret" or something like that—the son of a gun goes out and pulls a thing like this. . . .

KISSINGER: . . . Everyone in Washington knows already (a) that Resor is a lightweight and (b) what Resor thinks. So this is not going to come as any great surprise to anyone.

NIXON: . . . And of course Westmoreland hasn't proven to be any tower of strength either.

KISSINGER: Westmoreland is completely played out. All he remembers is what happened in Vietnam and how he nearly won the war at Tet [in 1968]. . . . And Abrams is finished.

NIXON: He sure is. Abrams had his great opportunity and muffed it [the invasion of Laos]. . . .

Anatoly Dobrynin
May 27, 1971, 5:46 p.m.
Four Soviet Jews were convicted that day of anti-Soviet activity and the State Department had denounced their convictions.

DOBRYNIN: . . . I have just seen UPI . . . to the effect that the U.S. today publicly condemned Russia for the conviction of the four Jews. The ticker said it was the strongest ever issued by the department.

KISSINGER: God damn them! . . . I gave them instructions at 1:00—

DOBRYNIN: It's on the ticker.

KISSINGER: Oh, god damn. You have to believe me—I did not know about this. . . . Tell them that I instructed the department—

DOBRYNIN: What kind of fools do they have? It is our law. Why should the department be involved in our condemning them? . . .

KISSINGER: Tell them that you brought it to my attention.

DOBRYNIN: And that from now on you will use much more control on this.

KISSINGER: From now on, I will take responsibility for matters of this kind. I will find out what happened.

DOBRYNIN: It definitely looks political.

KISSINGER: It may be something that was authorized three days ago. I will look into it and give you an informal opinion tomorrow.

DOBRYNIN: You don't have to give me an opinion. It's public—on the radio.

KISSINGER: You mention to them this was done prior to my discussion with you.

DOBRYNIN: Okay.

Lyndon Johnson
May 29, 1971, 3:25 p.m.
The former president is aggrieved that more documents from his administration haven't been declassified so that he can use them in his memoir.

. . . JOHNSON: One thing the president told me you are going to do is to see that they declassify everything that can be declassified as soon as possible. . . .

Under the archaic procedures they have at Defense and State they wouldn't release over 30 percent of the papers. They want to keep them another 20 to 30 years, and by that time anybody who knew anything about them has lost interest or is dead. Bobby Kennedy didn't hesitate to release the letters from [former Russian prime minister Nikita] Khrushchev. . . . They got a group to come down, and Rogers and Laird sent two or three men each. They spent about a month. What was concerning to them was to keep everything secret. What is compelling to us from my administration's standpoint and from your administration's standpoint, because they have almost the same foreign policy, is let the truth get out.

KISSINGER: We have the same enemies.

JOHNSON: . . . We are going to declassify everything unless you can prove that it will be harmful. . . . [Senator John] Williams changed the tax laws on me. . . . He came down here in 1969 and he wrote an amendment that took away any tax benefits you get from it [donating your official papers to the government, which Johnson had done with his pre-presidential papers, taking a large tax deduction].[10] So the situation is that today I haven't got a collection of papers. [Former secretary of state Dean] Rusk hasn't sent his. McNamara. You get no benefit from them. . . . The Library of Congress says there has not been one important gift of papers after that amendment has been adopted. . . . There are 500 people whose papers I should have. I have not received one set since this amendment was adopted. . . .

President Nixon

May 29, 1971, 4:00 p.m.

Nixon declares that if the North Vietnamese reject their "final offer" in Paris on May 31, he will unleash the bombers.

. . . NIXON: Okay, you are all set for your trip, huh?

KISSINGER: I am all set—we agreed on that speech exactly as you suggested. I am going to get right to the point.

NIXON: You will just lay it right in there, and as the other things come along, you sort of zing 'em in whenever you feel it is the right time, you know.

KISSINGER: You know, you are absolutely right. What we have to do is to convince the other side that this is indeed our final offer. And we can't do that by talking around the point.

NIXON: Talking around the point, and saying that, well, we are ready to be flexible again, and we have proved our good faith, etc. The hell with all that—they don't have any good faith—we don't either. Now we have got an offer—you can take it or leave it. This is it.

KISSINGER: In fact, I put in that there is no time left for philosophy and long expositions. . . . Here is our final offer.

NIXON: Great. And I think it will read well historically. It may work, who knows, it may shake them. But if they go back and turn it down, we know what our course is. But listen, if they turn it down, don't just think we're going back and make a peace offer. I am going to use whatever goddamn bombs we've got and we are going to bomb a hell of a lot in the North.

KISSINGER: They may in fact turn it down Monday, Mr. President. Because they must have a pretty good idea what it is going to be.

NIXON: If they turn it down Monday, then we are in a perfect condition to go forward and crack them. And crack them pretty damn good. . . .

Secret Senate Sessions on Laos; Retreat at Snuol; Pinning Laos on Kennedy; the Pentagon Papers—"This Is Treason," Kissinger's Distancing ("I Didn't Know the Thing Existed"), and Appealing to Lyndon Johnson; Kissinger's Secret Trip to China; Announcing Nixon's Visit to China and the New Public Mood; More Secret Vietnam Talks and the Impasse over Thieu; the Upcoming Rigged South Vietnamese Election; and Bypassing State on Berlin

June–August 1971

In June 1971, the U.S. Senate held closed sessions on the Nixon administration's clandestine war in Laos. A week earlier in Cambodia, badly beaten-up South Vietnamese forces fled Snuol, a key border town, with their hurried retreat under enemy fire drawing comparisons to the rout of the South Vietnamese in Laos in March.

On June 13, the *New York Times* began publishing the Top Secret Pentagon Papers, a history of U.S. decision-making in Vietnam, leading a livid Kissinger to rage about leaks that were destroying the government. He and Nixon considered this leak treason that was "actionable" (to use Kissinger's word). Yet his first reaction was that it helped them since it was a "gold mine" for showing how the Kennedy and Johnson administrations got them into the war, although it undermined negotiations with Hanoi. To distance himself from the leak and the leaker, Daniel Ellsberg, who had consulted for him, Kissinger claimed to William Rogers, Melvin Laird, and others that he never knew the Pentagon Papers study existed, at least in finished form, and never had a copy of it, although he knew about the study almost from the beginning, was sent a copy after it was completed, and had consulted on it. He lied repeatedly about it. He tried to get Johnson administration officials to condemn publication of the Papers, but, to Nixon's irritation, former president Lyndon Johnson did not want to "lobby" anyone or hold a press conference on the matter; Nixon wanted Johnson to take some of the heat that was on him. Kissinger advised that they "start hollering treason a little bit" at their Democratic critics.

In July, Kissinger took a secret trip to China to pave the way for the China summit. When Nixon dramatically announced Kissinger's trip and his acceptance of China's invitation for him to visit to pursue the normalization of relations, Kissinger was catapulted to worldwide fame. The same month, he had a secret meeting in Paris with the North Vietnamese, whose demand that the United States remove South Vietnam President Nguyen Van Thieu remained the main sticking point. Kissinger told Nixon he looked into it, but he and Nixon both concluded they couldn't do it because of the international ramifications and cost in U.S. credibility. They could not turn on Thieu. They reveled in public applause for their China move.

In August, Kissinger and U.S. Ambassador to West Germany Kenneth Rush circumvented hapless Secretary of State Rogers in forging a four-power agreement on Berlin that Kissinger told Nixon Rogers simply didn't understand.

Richard Helms
June 4, 1971, 8:05 p.m.
CIA Director Helms and Kissinger discuss secret Senate sessions on U.S. involvement in Laos requested by Senator Stuart Symington and whether to try to talk sense to him. (Symington was charging that the administration was spending far more for military activities there, including by Thai troops, Laotian tribesmen led by CIA personnel, and B-52 bombing, than it acknowledged.)[1]

> KISSINGER: The thing I hadn't realized is that on Monday they are going to surface this whole financing problem. . . . Is there any way we can keep Symington from doing this? . . .

HELMS: Who has paid for what?

KISSINGER: And out of whose hands.

HELMS: I don't know what we can do with Symington.

KISSINGER: Your calling him and telling him that this is going too far won't
work?

HELMS: . . . It is unfortunate, but so much damage has been done already,
I don't know if it would do any good. What does Mel [Laird] think?

KISSINGER: I don't know whose side Mel is on.

HELMS: That's what worries me too. . . .

President Nixon

June 4, 1971, 9:03 p.m.

*South Vietnamese forces, "badly battered," had retreated hastily several days earlier
from Snuol in Cambodia, with heavy casualties.[2] Kissinger observes that the many
casualties allegedly inflicted on the enemy were "out of proportion to the number of
weapons we captured," meaning civilians were killed. Kissinger thinks they should
consider firing Commander Creighton Abrams.*

. . . KISSINGER: . . . I've now gotten more reports from Cambodia and unfortunately the press was telling the truth and Abrams wasn't again.

NIXON: . . . We took a banging, huh?

KISSINGER: Yeah.

NIXON: How bad is it?

KISSINGER: Well, it's pretty bad; it was a lousy outfit, they obviously ran. . . .
We ought to look at this whole Abrams problem again.

NIXON: . . . What about this, the reports about casualties inflicted and so forth?
Did we inflict a lot or not?

KISSINGER: I don't know [laughter]. . . . Let me put it this way, they are out
of proportion to the number of weapons we captured. . . . They did inflict
some heavy casualties and the other side hadn't pursued, so this suggests
that they too took heavy losses.

NIXON: . . . The Abrams thing is a problem though, isn't it? . . .

KISSINGER: It's a problem.

NIXON: He and his staff too must be giving us a bunch of jazz.

KISSINGER: Yeah, they're pretty lousy. . . . Haig tells me he has a tendency
always to have second-raters around there.

NIXON: Well, I don't know how we can shake it up much now, can we? . . .
I don't know whether you can shake him up, that's the point.

KISSINGER: That's the thing that one might take a look at.

NIXON: I don't know, that'd be pretty drastic. . . . I mean, the psychological
effect of that . . . unless he did it for health reasons. . . .

Richard Helms
June 5, 1971, 10:00 a.m.
Helms and Kissinger agree that Helms should not give Nixon adviser John Scali and NSC staffer John Lehman briefings on U.S. activities in Laos, and Helms says he wasn't able to convince Symington not to hold closed-door Senate sessions on them.

HELMS: I had a call from John Scali at 11:00 last night and a call from John Lehman this morning wanting a briefing on Laos.

KISSINGER: Oh, for the love of Pete.

HELMS: I have not responded because I wanted to talk to you first. These things can become unmanageable.

KISSINGER: It's out of the question.

HELMS: Do you want to take them on or do you want me to call them back?

KISSINGER: Scali under no circumstances. He gets his information from me.

HELMS: That's what I thought. . . . In the conversation last night you would have thought he was a magician hired to take care of the public media. Since talking to you, I have talked to Symington. He is not to be deterred. He will go ahead and the general thrust—this is private between you and me and the president—the burden is that he wants to talk about B-52 bombing and the fact that the State Department fellows who talked before the committee have not leveled about the total amount of money being spent. He said it's time the Senate understood exactly what was going on in Laos. As far as the Agency is concerned, he says "you guys are doing a good job" and he will say it on the floor. This was the best I was able to do. . . .

Melvin Laird
June 5, 1971, 10:35 a.m.
Laird says Defense was stonewalling the secret Senate sessions on Laos.

. . . LAIRD: We are hardlining it to beat hell. But you know what they are going to do.

KISSINGER: Yes. . . . But I want as little cooperation as possible out of us.

LAIRD: There'll be no cooperation. . . .

Richard Helms, Melvin Laird, John Irwin, Charles Bray, and William H. Sullivan
June 7, 1971, 12:13 p.m.
Kissinger talks with Helms, Laird, Undersecretary of State Irwin, State Department spokesman Bray, and Sullivan of State about what Bray should say about U.S. involvement in Laos. They agree on limited disclosure and pinning it on President Kennedy. The mercenaries were Thai troops and CIA-organized Laotian tribesmen.

KISSINGER: Well, the question is . . . what is State going to say at its noon briefing?

IRWIN: . . . On the one hand we can stonewall. . . . But if we do that we fear that that will lead all the papers tomorrow to what comes out of the Senate debate this afternoon. . . .

BRAY: It seems to me that the questions will focus on the presence of "mercenaries" in Laos, on bombing, and on the general funding arrangements and the size of funds involved. . . .

KISSINGER: So we are agreed that the first point that we are going to make is this is a program that started in the Kennedy administration. Is this correct?

LAIRD: I think that's the only point I'd even make today myself.

HELMS: . . . I think if we try to get into too much detail before the debate has taken place we may find ourselves out ahead of the parade here and I don't see any necessity for that.

KISSINGER: And we give them an excuse for spilling everything.

SULLIVAN: . . . I think the only three points we wanted to make were (1) the fact that this began in the Kennedy administration; (2) that these people are volunteers at the request of Souvanna [the Laotian prime minister]; and (3) that we consider that what we are doing is within the legal precepts of all pertinent legislation.

KISSINGER: And that's all I would say.

HELMS: I think that's plenty. . . .

Melvin Laird
June 12, 1971, 2:20 p.m.
An adulatory magazine article about Laird had come out, one that discussed his push for faster troop withdrawals from Vietnam than Nixon wanted and that included the following line: "He seems to be far more successful than Secretary of State Rogers at containing Kissinger."[3]

KISSINGER: I have just read the *New York Times* article about you in the *New York Times Magazine,* in which some of your boys have really done quite a job. . . . Quite favorable to you, but it makes you the good guy and the president and me the bad guys. . . . The main thing I want to clear up is it claims you are the major spokesman for the withdrawal date in the administration and the president and I are blocking this. If it comes up we expect you to stick with the administration. . . . It says the president and I were skeptical about Vietnamization but you rammed it through and you prodded us to do a faster withdrawal. . . . It quotes you saying the White House announces all the good news and we give you all the bad news. . . . And basically that you keep pushing the White House. Somebody on your staff or in the Defense Department must have [talked], because there is a lot of detail there. . . .

President Nixon

June 13, 1971, 3:09 p.m.

They discuss the massive Pentagon Papers leak that would incite a furious Kissinger, a leading participant in White House discussions about how to respond to it, to fume about leaks that were "destroying" the administration's ability to conduct its foreign policy, stoking Nixon's own anger to "near hysteria."[4] That morning, the New York Times *had begun publishing portions of the Papers, a study commissioned by Kennedy and Johnson's secretary of defense Robert McNamara of U.S. decision-making in Vietnam. Kissinger and Nixon find the leak "unconscionable" and "treasonable," and Nixon wants the leaker put under oath.*

. . . NIXON: Unconscionable damn thing for them to do.

KISSINGER: Unconscionable.

NIXON: Of course it's unconscionable on the part of the people that leaked it. Fortunately it didn't come out in our administration. According to Haig it all relates to the two previous administrations. Is that correct?

KISSINGER: That is right. . . . In public opinion actually if anything it will help us a little bit, because this is a gold mine of showing how the previous administration got us in this.

NIXON: I didn't read the thing. Give me your view on that, in a word.

KISSINGER: It just shows massive mismanagement of how we got there, and it pins it all on Kennedy and Johnson. . . . So from that point of view it helps us. From the point of view of the relations with Hanoi it hurts a little because it just shows a further weakening of resolve.

NIXON: Yeah. . . . I suppose the *Times* ran it to try and affect the debate this week [on troop withdrawal amendments in Congress] or something.

KISSINGER: No question.

NIXON: Well, I don't think it's gonna have that kind of effect. . . . This is treasonable action on the part of the bastards that put it out.

KISSINGER: Exactly, Mr. President.

NIXON: Doesn't it involve secure information, a lot of other things? . . .

KISSINGER: . . . It has the highest classification. It's treasonable, there's no question, it's actionable. I'm absolutely certain that this violates all sorts of security laws.

NIXON: . . . I think you should talk to Mitchell and ask him about . . . getting this fellow in. . . . This was a security leak and we wanna know, what does he have? Did he do it? . . . And put him under oath. . . . Another thing to do would be to have a congressional committee call him in . . . and then he's guilty of perjury if he lies. . . . I would think it would infuriate Johnson, wouldn't you?

KISSINGER: Oh, god. Well, basically it doesn't hurt us domestically . . . no one reading this can then say that this president got us into trouble. I mean, this is an indictment of the previous administration. It hurts us with Hanoi because it just shows how far our demoralization has gone.

NIXON: Good god. . . . Listen, don't worry about this *Times* thing. I just think we gotta expect that kind of crap. . . . But, boy, you're right about one thing, if anything was needed to underline what we talked about . . . Saturday morning about really cleaning house when we have the opportunity, by god, this underlines it, and people have got to be put to the torch for this sort of thing. . . . My god, you know, can you imagine the *New York Times* doing a thing like this 10 years ago? Even 10 years ago?

KISSINGER: Mr. President, and then when [Senator Joseph] McCarthy accused them of treason [McCarthy had accused the Democratic Party and the Roosevelt and Truman administrations, among others, of treason for failing to root out communists] they were screaming bloody murder. This is treason.

NIXON: That's right. Well, whatever they may think of the policy it is treasonable to take this stuff out, it serves the enemy.

KISSINGER: Oh, it's one thing to [criticize], it's another thing to print 10 pages of Top Secret documents that are only about two or three years old. But they have nothing from our administration, so actually, I've read this stuff, we come out pretty well in it. . . .

William Rogers
June 14, 1971, 5:55 p.m.
Kissinger claims to a skeptical Rogers that he never knew the Pentagon Papers study existed and never had a copy, though he knew about the study almost from the start, was familiar with some of it, was sent a copy after it was finished, and had consulted on it.[5] Leslie Gelb, a Pentagon official at the time, was the chair of the study's task force.

ROGERS: I was getting ready for my press conference and finding out about the present list. I see on the original list on January 14, 1969, I don't know if you remember—

KISSINGER: I never had it.

ROGERS: The Gelb memo for the record says distribution of the task force study.

KISSINGER: I was a consultant for one limited [section]. . . .

ROGERS: I thought perhaps you might have forgotten it.

KISSINGER: I never had it.

ROGERS: Gelb lists . . . Henry Kissinger . . . as being approved [for receipt of it].

KISSINGER: I may have been approved but I never saw it.

ROGERS: Sometimes you get things like that and forget it.

KISSINGER: I knew they were doing a study in McNamara's period but the only time I had anything to do with it was when McNamara was secretary of defense. . . . They may have authorized to give it to me but I never got it. In fact, I didn't know it existed. . . . When I saw them there was a room full of documents, but I have never seen an integrating document. . . . I didn't know the thing existed. I am certain I have never seen it. . . .

President Nixon and John Mitchell
June 14, 1971, 7:19 p.m.
Nixon and Attorney General Mitchell decide to seek a court injunction ordering the New York Times *to stop publication of the Pentagon Papers. Mitchell says the "prime suspect" in the leak is Daniel Ellsberg, a former RAND analyst who had earlier consulted on Vietnam for Kissinger.*[6]

NIXON: What is your advice on that *Times* thing, John? You would like to do it?

MITCHELL: I would believe so, Mr. President; otherwise we will look a little foolish and not following through on our legal obligations. . . .

NIXON: Well, look, look, as far as the *Times* is concerned, hell, they're our enemies. I think we just oughta do it. And, anyway, Henry, tell him what you just heard from [President Johnson's national security adviser Walt] Rostow.

KISSINGER: Well, Rostow called on behalf of Johnson, and he said that it is Johnson's strong view that this is an attack on the whole integrity of government . . . that if whole file cabinets can be stolen and then made available to the press, you can't have orderly government anymore. And he said if the president defends the integrity, any action we take he will back publicly.

MITCHELL: Well, I think that we should take this. I'll do some undercover investigation and then open it up after your [Senator George] McGovern– [Senator Mark] Hatfield [antiwar resolution vote]. We've got some information we've developed as to where these copies are and who are likely to have leaked them, and the prime suspect, according to your friend Rostow you're quoting, is a gentleman by the name of Ellsberg, a left-winger that's now at the RAND Corporation, who also has a set of these documents. So—

NIXON: Subpoena them. Christ, get them.

MITCHELL: So I would . . . think that we should advise the *Times* we will start
our covert check, and after McGovern–Hatfield just open it up.

NIXON: Right. Go ahead. . . .

Melvin Laird
June 15, 1971, 8:15 a.m.
*Kissinger tells Laird, too, that he didn't know the Pentagon Papers study existed in
finished form. The previous weekend, Kissinger had called Laird to say Nixon was
quite upset with him for leaking the study, which Laird had heatedly denied.*[7]

. . . KISSINGER: I didn't know the study existed until—I knew McNamara was
working on it because I was helping him in 1967. But I didn't know they
had ever completed a document pulling it all together. . . .

LAIRD: Have you read the section on [negotiations]?

KISSINGER: No.

LAIRD: You ought to read it—it had to do with you. . . . The Johnson Library
copy was drawn out by Rostow and that's where it is. I hope it didn't leak
out of there.

KISSINGER: No, I think it leaked out of here. . . . I think it is geared to the
McGovern–Hatfield thing. . . . Don't you think the thing is an outrage?

LAIRD: Sure it is; this is a very serious security matter. . . .

KISSINGER: I haven't heard one word about you. In fact the president told me
he was very pleased with the way you have taken them on. . . .

Nelson Rockefeller
June 16, 1971, 10:10 a.m.
*Kissinger tells Governor Rockefeller they've narrowed down the list of possible leakers,
asks him to denounce publication of the Papers, and conveys Nixon's concern that he
might defend the* New York Times.

. . . ROCKEFELLER: Who put it out?

KISSINGER: Not in the government.

ROCKEFELLER: Did they steal these things?

KISSINGER: There were 45 volumes prepared in the previous administration
and taken out by the officials of the previous administration. We've got it
narrowed down to two or three. The man who did this won't be able to get
away with it. The president asked me to call you because . . . on the surface,
having the Democrats tear each other apart has certain attractions, but this
is an attack on the integrity of the government. It is like saying you can't
believe any president.

ROCKEFELLER: Did you know of the existence of this?

KISSINGER: No. This was prepared at the end of the Johnson administration. McNamara, with poor judgment, wanted an historical record. . . . I was down in 1967 for three days; I saw that the material was so massive I thought they could never put it together. At first I thought Laird leaked it, but this was not the case. There were 10 copies extant—one was sent to the White House but Johnson took it with him. I have never known it existed. . . . First of all it wrecks Johnson, which is unfair.

ROCKEFELLER: Typical of McNamara to get that put together.

KISSINGER: It makes him look like a tricky liar and it puts him out of context. . . . The president suffers from the illusion that you are close to the *New York Times* and you might rush to their defense if they asked for it.

ROCKEFELLER: You tell him that I take a worse beating from them than he does. . . .

Harry Rowen
June 16, 1971, 2:55 p.m.
RAND President Harry Rowen tells Kissinger that Daniel Ellsberg is probably the culprit and Kissinger agrees. Rowen was worried about being scapegoated for the leak partly because he had helped Ellsberg get access to the Pentagon Papers.[8]

KISSINGER: How are you?

ROWEN: Not very well given the subject I called you on on Monday. . . . It concerns a massive leak, and the upshot is a lot of evidence suggests that Dan Ellsberg is the guilty party.

KISSINGER: You believe he is?

ROWEN: His ex-wife is firmly convinced he is. He called on Monday to talk to his son to call his attention to the *Times* story [on the Papers], and in the course of the discussion he made remarks to the effect that he had done something at great risk, he was going to jail, etc. His ex-wife is concerned about his stability. . . . While I haven't seen him for the better part of a year, I have heard about his behavior. I think it is more than possible that he is the source.

KISSINGER: That is what I think, too. . . . No one is blaming RAND for it.

ROWEN: Good—I hope it stays that way. . . .

William Jorden
June 16, 1971, 3:04 p.m.
Former Johnson administration official Jorden conveys the latest from Lyndon Johnson's ranch in Texas.

JORDEN: I got the message you passed on this morning and talked to the boss about it. He said there's not much he can do with [Clark] Clifford or [Averell] Harriman, as you have probably concluded. He is willing to do anything he can to be helpful, but he is reluctant to launch lobbying from down here. He suggests (1) you may have already contacted McNamara—he thinks a thorough rundown from him on what he commissioned or who he commissioned might be good; (2) you contact people like [the journalists] Bill White, Dave Lawrence, and others who could be encouraged to try to put it in perspective and balance. He suggested getting someone there who knows and has influence with the heads of the networks to ask if this is what they want done to our country and try to modify their approach. Above all, he thinks it important to get a list of all the people involved in this study and get it published. . . . His strong inclination is to have a grand jury summoned to question people under oath individually. . . .

Henry Hubbard
June 17, 1971, 1 p.m.
Kissinger tells Hubbard of Newsweek *that he thought the study had been jettisoned.*

. . . KISSINGER: I conducted one study in 1967. . . . I came down twice, or maybe three times. I saw a mass of stuff they had on negotiations alone. I then thought, as a trained historian, and given the fact that these were very junior people, that it was an unmanageable task. I thought it had been abandoned. I knew they were working on it but I didn't know they had completed it. . . .

President Nixon
June 17, 1971, 7:40 p.m.
Nixon says he won't defend Lyndon Johnson unless Johnson speaks up about publication of the Pentagon Papers and takes some heat himself.

NIXON: I think it is important that you give Rostow a call. I will tell you the problem. He is telling Johnson—advising against doing the press thing. I am going to meet with 200 press tomorrow in Rochester and I am prepared and intend to defend Johnson on this whole thing, but I can't and won't do that unless Johnson will defend himself. He wants us to take the heat on this. . . . I don't care where he is, you call him and call me back. He is advising Johnson against this. He's got to have a press conference. . . .

KISSINGER: I don't believe he is going to have one but I don't think Rostow is advising him against it. I just don't think Johnson wants to have one. I didn't discuss a press conference but I did say there should be some statement from Johnson on this.

NIXON: Tell Rostow that unless he has a press conference, I am not prepared to defend him. Why should I?

KISSINGER: I don't think you should defend Johnson anyway. You should defend the presidency.

NIXON: It amounts to the same thing, a defense of Johnson. I don't think this is proper to put one side of the case out and not the other side. . . . Johnson should go to the mat on this, don't you think so?

KISSINGER: . . . It would get a brawl started between Johnson and the press.

NIXON: It would get it off us.

KISSINGER: But it also would drag it down to the level of whether Johnson was guilty or not.

NIXON: That's a hell of a lot better than whether we are guilty or not! . . .

President Nixon

June 22, 1971, 10:31 p.m.

Kissinger condemns a Mansfield troop withdrawal amendment on Vietnam that had passed the Senate, former defense secretary Clark Clifford's call for withdrawal, and other critics. "We have to start hollering treason a little bit," he advises. He takes satisfaction from the tarring of Kennedy administration officials with the Papers, including for complicity in the assassination of South Vietnamese President Ngo Dinh Diem in 1963.

. . . KISSINGER: I wouldn't be very conciliatory with Mansfield.

NIXON: I'm not going to be a goddamned bit conciliatory. . . .

KISSINGER: . . . Because what these people have done is unconscionable. When one looks at the combination of Clifford, the Papers. . . . It is unforgivable. Because everyone . . . had a chance to do it on McGovern–Hatfield [the antiwar resolution]; so they had their chance, and if they had stopped at that point we would have been in good shape. . . . We had them on their knees last October. . . . And then we let them off the hook. . . . But we have to start hollering treason a little bit.

NIXON: Oh, I think so. . . . I really can't do it.

KISSINGER: No, no, but Agnew could do it. . . . And some of our people could do it, and then they'd have to defend themselves.

NIXON: I wonder if Agnew shouldn't say something about that. . . .

KISSINGER: . . . I think he could give a ripsnorter of a speech. . . . They have a desire to lose. . . . They're not so worried about our getting out, they're worried about our getting out without Saigon going communist.

NIXON: . . . They want us to get out and have it go communist.

KISSINGER: Oh, yes. Absolutely. Because that means you have failed. And they can say they would have done it faster. . . . Each Kennedy is getting tarred now. I mean, these were the great Kennedy people who did all of this. And even back in the Johnson administration those were all Kennedy appointees. . . . [Congressman Pete] McCloskey is now saying that [former ambassador to South Vietnam Henry Cabot] Lodge contributed to the assassination. . . . So McCloskey is screaming that on the one hand the Americans pretended to be his friend and on the other they were killing him, which happens to be true. . . . If we said it they would accuse us of smears, but it's now coming out from the right people. . . .

NIXON: Play it hard. Play it hard.

KISSINGER: Mr. President, I'm absolutely cold about this. We'll play it hard. . . .

President Nixon

July 14, 1971, 12:50 p.m.

Kissinger had returned from his secret trip to China the day before, and the next evening Nixon would announce the trip and China's invitation for him to visit China before May 1972 to seek the normalization of relations. The announcement turned Kissinger into an international celebrity. Nixon was planning a celebratory dinner in Los Angeles with senior staff after his announcement. He praises Press Secretary Ron Ziegler's stonewalling on China and doesn't want Secretary of State William Rogers talking about it (partly to make sure he got the credit).[9] Kissinger says he'll fob off questions about whether he met with North Vietnamese negotiator Le Duc Tho in Paris during his trip. (He did.)

> NIXON: . . . I think this little idea of having our dinner tomorrow night, just the staff, is good for morale and everybody and a nice little gesture. We can do the inviting before they even know what we are going to say. . . . The boys have been great. Take Ziegler—he's been a real soldier. He stands up and takes the stuff and he knows something has been going on, but he's not like these guys who have to know everything. He'll now know why he's had to stonewall it. He's taken a hell of a beating from these bastards. We've just got 24 more hours to hold it. I don't think it will break now. You have got your people in solitary and Rogers won't talk. I think we were absolutely right in his not making a speech [on China] next week. . . .
>
> KISSINGER: And he ought to move his press conference, preferably to Friday, to let us ride as long as possible on this.
>
> NIXON: Maybe even over to the next week. . . . I told Haldeman they are not to say word one. Ziegler will say "I have nothing tonight but will have my briefing at 9:00 tomorrow morning," and you'll just be there. . . .
>
> KISSINGER: . . . And they'll be asking questions to which I'll refuse to answer, but will do so in a way that might be suggestive.

NIXON: They may ask, have you talked to Le Duc Tho?

KISSINGER: I will say "You saw my published schedule and I wouldn't presume to pretend that I could mislead so many newsmen." . . . I'll figure out something mysterious to say. . . .

President Nixon
July 15, 1971, 5:15 p.m.
Kissinger tells Nixon about a cryptic call he made to Senator Mike Mansfield about Nixon's China announcement that evening and that he kept Laird in the dark.

KISSINGER: I talked to Mansfield. I said the president wanted me to call you. He is giving a speech on a subject too sensitive to discuss on these phones. But he hopes you will agree with what he's saying. . . .

NIXON: He thinks it's Vietnam.

KISSINGER: Oh, certainly. . . .

NIXON: Has anything broken on it yet?

KISSINGER: No. Ziegler wouldn't even say whether it was domestic or foreign. And the departments are going crazy. . . . We just told them we've got something for you.

NIXON: That's good. I don't think it will break now. The news will be over at 7:30.

KISSINGER: . . . I called Laird. . . .

NIXON: But you didn't tell him what it was.

KISSINGER: No.

NIXON: Because he'd call the press right away. . . .

Anatoly Dobrynin
July 15, 1971, probably between 5:00 and 6:00 p.m.
Kissinger drops a bomb on the Soviet ambassador.

KISSINGER: The president asked me to call you personally. We have an oral note for your government when I am through. I will read the announcement the president is going to make and then I have a few comments to make. . . . "Premier Chou En-lai and Dr. Henry Kissinger . . . held talks in Peking from July 9 to 11, 1971. Knowing of President Nixon's expressed desire to visit the People's Republic of China, Premier Chou En-lai . . . has extended an invitation to President Nixon to visit China at an appropriate date before May 1972. President Nixon has accepted this invitation with pleasure. The meeting between the leaders of China and the United States is to seek the normalization of relations between the two countries." . . .

DOBRYNIN: Just a minute. The note which Colonel [Richard] Kennedy [a member of Kissinger's NSC staff] is going to give me is from the president to go to my government? . . .

KISSINGER: Colonel Kennedy is giving you an oral note. I am giving you some additional comments from the president. . . . "You know better than anyone the great efforts we have made over the past two years to make progress . . . and in particular the [high] priority of a meeting of our leaders. Your recent decision to delay [on a summit] has caused us to proceed." . . .

H. R. Haldeman

July 20, 1971, 11:22 a.m.

They weigh what to say to Time's *Hugh Sidey about Rogers's involvement in Kissinger's secret trip to China, which was zilch.*

KISSINGER: I had a call which I haven't taken yet, but they left a message from Sidey wanting to do a human interest story on the Nixon–Rogers–Kissinger planning sessions in the Lincoln Sitting Room. I think this is going too far.

HALDEMAN: Yes, you can only lie so far.

KISSINGER: I think we should say Rogers knew about it, but the planning was done by the president, with me doing the staff work. . . . We can't invent history. The guy didn't know anything. So far I've built him up.

HALDEMAN: But you shouldn't build him up any more, and you can't say he was in these Lincoln Sitting Room sessions. They start asking for dates and hours and you are going to have a real problem.

KISSINGER: There were some between the president and me there, when the messages [from China] first came.

HALDEMAN: When you came in with your hands trembling.

KISSINGER: I?!

HALDEMAN: Yes, the first message; he told me all about it.

KISSINGER: Oh, yes, and he was cool as a cucumber. . . .

Melvin Laird

July 21, 1971, 7:30 p.m.

Laird and an irritable Kissinger confer on an upcoming huge underground nuclear weapon test in Alaska and congressional funding for U.S. operations in Laos. Laird angrily denies putting out figures on U.S. spending on Laos.

LAIRD: . . . Evidently there is a report that has been sent to you by the undersecretaries group recommending against the Cannikin tests.

KISSINGER: I don't give a damn what they recommend.

LAIRD: We stood firm and got votes on the Senate floor . . . to go ahead with the tests. They have a bunch of smart, young guys—

KISSINGER: I know, I know! It [the report] will not be approved! Just relax.

LAIRD: I wanted to make sure. . . . Regardless of how many Safeguard sites [for ballistic missile defense] you have, you have to have this [missile].

KISSINGER: There is no question about that. You are going to hang tough on Laos? We are counting on it. Some people are saying you are putting out so many figures—

LAIRD: I didn't put that out! You know when that was first put out! Bill had a press conference and he was pinned down. I haven't put out any figures. . . . Every figure out has been put in the public record or put out by Dick Helms. . . . I don't go for this bullshit of people pointing fingers at me. This bullshit gripes me a little bit. . . .

President Nixon
July 26, 1971, 12:00 a.m.
Kissinger had just returned from a secret meeting in Paris with the North Vietnamese, whose demand that the United States remove South Vietnam President Nguyen Van Thieu remained the main obstacle to an agreement.[10] While Kissinger says he looked into it, he and Nixon conclude that they can't do it. Kissinger also discusses his meeting with Chinese Ambassador Huang Chen in Paris about his October trip to China to prepare the China summit; he thinks they shouldn't appear too eager to set a date but hopes for December. Kissinger says the North Vietnamese were tempered by his recent trip to China. And he and Nixon exult over public applause for their China initiative.

KISSINGER: Mr. President, I just this second got in.

NIXON: . . . You must have had quite a drill. You went to both places, huh?

KISSINGER: I went to both places, yes. First, at the Vietnamese—that took about five hours and they still can't make up their minds on the political issue. To all practical purposes, we have settled every other question. We went through every point in great detail, and they've substantially conceded us most of our points. . . . But on the political one, they are in a state of confusion. I mean, they are making so many different demands— sometimes they say we should just let [General Duong Van] Minh win or help Minh win [in an election in South Vietnam in October]. Other times, they say we should make a private deal with them to overthrow Thieu which wouldn't be published, and that would be enough. Then they say we have to replace the whole outfit. . . . I said several times, "You know, if you want us to overthrow him, it just isn't on and there is no sense in having another meeting." Le Duc Tho said, "No, no, we need one other meeting. . . . I want to come up with a new proposal." So I decided to give them one more meeting. . . .

NIXON: Of course, the political point is so fundamental, Henry, that I suppose the other things don't really matter, do they? In a sense—

KISSINGER: That's essentially true. . . . With these damn doves it doesn't help you much, but we have a superb public record because we've offered everything that could conceivably be offered except making a coup against Thieu. We've offered neutrality, we've offered limitations on military aid, we've offered a withdrawal deadline, we've offered hands off in the election—so there's really nothing that even McGovern would ask for that we haven't offered, and no one can say we ought to make a coup.

NIXON: No; I don't think so. . . . We can't offer to overthrow Thieu.

KISSINGER: I think it really would be too much, Mr. President.

NIXON: Not only would it really be too much, we couldn't do it because, good god, we've got enough on our plates. . . .

KISSINGER: Exactly. I've looked at it—

NIXON: Every friend we have in the world would just be petrified with that sort of a thing.

KISSINGER: Exactly, Mr. President.

NIXON: We're not going to do it.

KISSINGER: I've looked at it, you know, just to make sure that I would know what is involved, but I really—

NIXON: No, no, no. We just can't do it, and so that's that. So we'll just stand firmly for principle. But then it seems to me after the next meeting . . . we then have to really make a decision to go public and say what we have offered.

KISSINGER: Well, one thing they did offer firmly was they would settle prisoners for withdrawal. Now, that's no good to us before the election in Vietnam, but it might be something that come October you might want. . . . It's too high a price before the election because it might topple Thieu.

NIXON: Yeah. . . . Prisoners for withdrawal. That won't do. We've got to have cease-fire in it. . . . That looks like just a straight trade-off. . . .

KISSINGER: I talked to the others [the Chinese], who were extremely cordial. . . . They think that around October 15th is the earliest they can handle a visit by me. . . . I think it would be too early, Mr. President, to give them a date [for Nixon's visit]. We mustn't appear that eager. . . . What they had said was anytime in '72. So when I said, well, what if the president's schedule turns out to be more convenient earlier? They said, well, maybe as early as December 1. . . . I think towards the end of August we ought to propose December. . . .

NIXON: And, incidentally, we are not going to be eager, but they do want a public visit before the other visit?

KISSINGER: Yeah. . . . And I think we need it, Mr. President, so that we can work out the agenda so that you are not caught by surprise. . . . I did something which was a little devious. I said, well, we are under tremendous right-wing attack, and I said you have to remember the only man who can keep the right wing under control here is the president. I said you play too much with the left, the right will get even more inflamed, and that limits our abilities.

NIXON: Good. . . . I must say, though, you certainly got the impression that the fact that you walked in there from Peking shocked them [the North Vietnamese], huh?

KISSINGER: Oh, god, yes. Their whole tone towards me is completely different, Mr. President, in this series than it has been in any other series of meetings. And they are wavering. If they don't settle, it will be a very close decision. . . . I was absolutely brutal at the end. . . . I told them this is it. If that's all you've got to say, that's it. . . . There's no point in another meeting. . . .

NIXON: Well, one thing, Henry, I know, whatever the formulation is we cannot . . . because of the world repercussions and the repercussions every place from Indonesia to Korea and etc., Thailand—you just can't play any games on tossing Thieu over. That's how this whole miserable thing started. We ought to remember it was a coup [against Ngo Dinh Diem in 1963]. . . . And by god, we are not going to end it that way.

KISSINGER: Exactly, Mr. President. And also the impact we've already had with the Peking thing, we would just lose any credibility and moral standing if we now did this.

NIXON: That's right. . . . Frankly, let's face it, as we said, it just may be that if they don't settle, we just wind it down the way we have.

KISSINGER: And that's what they're afraid of.

NIXON: It would be long term, and we'll just continue to wind 'er down and get out in our own good time. . . . It's really an amazing thing . . . the way this thing [the China opening] has shocked . . . our usual critics. They just have a hell of a time knowing how to handle it, don't they?

KISSINGER: Absolutely; they haven't dared to pick on it yet.

NIXON: . . . [Nixon aide Charles] Colson got a report from the hardhats— [labor leader Peter] Brennan and his group in New York—[he expressed] his amazement that they were at their convention very strongly for what we were doing.

KISSINGER: Isn't that amazing?

NIXON: And [Frank] Fitzsimmons, the head of the Teamsters, called him. . . . You see, these hardhats and these sort of earthy fellows, they see what the real game is. They can see the Russian thing. Any sensible person does. And I also talked to Rockefeller today . . . he's just ecstatic.

KISSINGER: Oh, he's beside himself.

NIXON: . . . The mood really in the country has significantly changed. . . . There is a substantial right-wing thing but not nearly as much as you would normally expect. . . . But on the other hand, what has happened is that the left—the liberals, the peacenik types—they are just up a wall. They don't know what the hell to do with this.

KISSINGER: Exactly. And that in itself is a major diplomatic feat.

NIXON: Well, what it does, Henry, it buys us time gracefully and to bring Vietnam to some kind of an honorable conclusion. And I don't think we would have ever made it otherwise.

KISSINGER: We'd never have made it. Congress would have killed us.

NIXON: And it also may buy us some time on a few other things.

KISSINGER: Exactly.

NIXON: It'll be interesting to see what our Russian friends do now. . . .

President Nixon

August 5, 1971, no time

Nixon asks about a news report that the North Vietnamese were going to release 183 American POWs who a Swedish airline would fly to New York.[11] They also take up the great change in the public mood after Nixon's China announcement and the prospective Soviet summit.

NIXON: What is that story about the Swedes?

KISSINGER: There is absolutely nothing to it that I have been able to discover.

NIXON: . . . It seems to me they are not going to be foolish to do anything silly like that.

KISSINGER: Well, I don't exclude, Mr. President, that they may make a gesture on something. . . . But not of that magnitude. . . .

NIXON: Yeah. For what reason would they be doing it, then?

KISSINGER: Supposing they come back to us with an offer on Thieu that is not yet acceptable but is a small step in our direction. If they were to say that as a sign of their goodwill and their eagerness to get the thing settled they are letting these [prisoners] go and then even made it public, it would put us into a pretty tough spot. . . . The story came from a Swedish newspaper and we are trying to track that down.

NIXON: The minute I hear that I become suspicious.

KISSINGER: Exactly! . . . Of course, they also might have thought that this is the way to get themselves back on the front page.

NIXON: That's a pretty cheap way. . . . Of course, you have such a jackass government there that you don't know what they are up to.

KISSINGER: . . . Something is clearly going on, Mr. President. . . . You know, this Chinese move has knocked them off the front pages.

NIXON: It's just amazing. . . . Today, I got one question on Vietnam. . . .

KISSINGER: And I had dinner with Red Blount [the U.S. postmaster general] tonight, and of course he is ecstatic, but he said he has . . . a son . . . who had been a dedicated Democrat, worked his head off for Humphrey, and who has now written him a letter saying he is going to vote for you in the next election. . . . And he said that this just shows the complete change in attitude.

NIXON: Especially among the young. . . . And also really in the middle class— upper middle class.

KISSINGER: And also among the knowledgeable people, Mr. President. . . .

NIXON: . . . You know, I'm very curious, though, what our Russian friends will be up to. . . .

KISSINGER: . . . Actually from our point of view it's a little early for them to be coming through. . . . I think they will, Mr. President. They are really sucking around. Now, I have that letter for your signature tomorrow to [Soviet Communist Party General Secretary Leonid] Brezhnev. . . . And he is really panting for it. . . .

William Rogers

August 19, 1971, 1:12 p.m.

Rogers complains that U.S. Ambassador to West Germany Kenneth Rush was not following instructions in negotiating a four-power agreement on the long-contentious issue of Berlin (on Western access—it was in East Germany—political ties between West Germany and Berlin, and other issues). Rush was operating under Kissinger's instructions.[12]

ROGERS: I was going over this tentative agreement Rush made. It has a lot of what we think are failures to comply with the NSDM [National Security Decision Memorandum]. . . . I am now sending him a telegram telling him not to finalize it. . . . On access it's okay, but on rights and responsibilities we've taken a beating. In some places he directly violates the NSDM, uses words we expressly said not to. . . . I got the impression that Rush was disregarding all instructions. . . .

Anatoly Dobrynin

August 19, 1971, 1:50 p.m.

Kissinger tells Soviet Ambassador Dobrynin not to pay any mind to Rogers's objections.

KISSINGER: Rush went ahead and concluded the agreement. . . . State is going crazy because they don't know why it's working so fast, so he will come back for a week. He may not initial the agreement, but pay no attention. Everything will go on as it is. I can't refuse the secretary to call back the ambassador. If there's a disagreement between State and him, we will rule for him. . . .

President Nixon

August 19, 1971, early evening

They mull over the October presidential election in South Vietnam, through which Hanoi believed Nixon and Kissinger could get rid of President Thieu if they ensured a fair election. But to keep him in power, it was rigged by the United States, including through CIA operations approved by Nixon and Kissinger, and by Thieu himself mainly through legislation restricting who could run; Vice President Nguyen Cao Ky had been disqualified (then was later reinstated).[13] *Nixon and Kissinger agree that everyone should shut up about the election and that they will not turn on Thieu, though Kissinger worries about the fallout if Thieu runs unopposed. He also fills Nixon in on Berlin.*

KISSINGER: . . . We've just had a Reuters dispatch that Minh has withdrawn from the race in Vietnam [because of its rigging], and that will mean that some of our people are going to be anguishing all over the place. Now, I feel that . . . maybe Thieu was unwise in some of the things he did, but I think partly it's also rigged by the Buddhists and the communists. . . . And what we would like to do is to put a lid on comments on our side for a while—

NIXON: Total, total.

KISSINGER: —and see perhaps whether we could get Thieu to get a new election law, and, above all, I don't think we should turn on Thieu at this late moment.

NIXON: Turn on him? Never, never. . . . I hope never.

KISSINGER: Well, that's the trend in the State Department.

NIXON: Well, the hell with them.

KISSINGER: They see in this a god-sent opportunity to get rid of him.

NIXON: No, we must never do that. . . . They're to shut up. They're to say nothing without my approval. . . . The communists let Thieu win, so he wins.

KISSINGER: It's no crime to have an anti-communist win an election. . . . But we may be able to . . . get the election deferred, get a new electoral law or whatever. . . . If it's an unopposed election there's going to be all hell to pay. . . . Minh didn't even start campaigning. . . .

NIXON: Which proves he's under the control of the communists, huh?

KISSINGER: That's how it looks to me. . . . Or at least under the radical Buddhists who in turn are under the control of the communists. . . . We have one problem I wouldn't have bothered you with, with State on Berlin. . . .

They are now nitpicking away at it. . . . What I let them do is get Rush back next week. The agreement is done but I can't refuse to let the secretary of state talk to him. But if there is any disagreement we may have to invoke you to rule on behalf of Rush. . . .

NIXON: You mean State wants to delay it?

KISSINGER: State has a few legalistic nitpicks. . . . The basic fact is that we made . . . a proposal on February 6 and that the agreement we got is better in every respect than the proposal we ourselves made, which is almost incredible. . . .

NIXON: Well, why is State bitching then?

KISSINGER: State is bitching because it has moved so fast that Rush—it looks as if Rush did it all. . . . Then they found some legalistic things. Well, of course they must suspect that we did something from here. . . .

William Rogers
August 20, 1971, 10:35 a.m.
Rogers charges that Ambassador Kenneth Rush "openly violated the president's instructions" on the Berlin agreement and that Nixon will get pilloried over the deal.

. . . ROGERS: . . . I am worried the president is going to get a black eye.

KISSINGER: . . . Frankly, he would like an agreement, and fairly soon, for domestic reasons.

ROGERS: Well, if he and you are giving Rush the idea that it didn't matter—

KISSINGER: No one gave him that idea.

ROGERS: When we called him he said, "Have you checked with San Clemente?," which gave me that impression. . . . I think he will be accused of selling out Berlin. Rush has openly violated the president's instructions.

KISSINGER: He got no detailed instructions from me on any of the points you have in your telegram. The president did mention to him that he was eager to get an agreement and stated that fairly strongly. But it doesn't make any sense for him to say he wanted him to violate his instructions.

ROGERS: . . . He is acting as if this is his own baby. And I think the president will get clobbered. . . .

President Nixon
August 20, 1971, no time
Kissinger thinks they can avoid an impasse on the Berlin agreement because Rogers doesn't understand it.

. . . KISSINGER: Well, I talked to Bill this morning and . . . your instinct was absolutely right, he doesn't know what he's talking about. . . . I thought the best thing we can do is to low-key it to get Rush back. Let him fight for his draft, and if there's a deadlock we'll have to rule with Rush. I think I can avoid a deadlock, because frankly Bill doesn't understand it. . . . But what's basically getting these guys, Mr. President, is that they know damn well you've been in touch with Rush. . . . And they know you did it and it kills them. They were willing to settle for something infinitely less good. . . . They may have to give us a word or two someplace which doesn't mean anything, just to prove that Rogers has done something. . . .

William Ruckelshaus
August 23, 1971, 11:55 a.m.
Kissinger tangles with Ruckelshaus, the head of the Environmental Protection Agency, over Ruckelshaus's interest in hiring a member of Kissinger's staff.

RUCKELSHAUS: I'm calling about your employee Mr. Sansom. I understand you have been alerted to our interest.

KISSINGER: What does that mean, "alerted to our interest"?

RUCKELSHAUS: We made contact with him, specifically with the recommendation of George Shultz because we need that kind of—

KISSINGER: I don't give a damn what he recommends. He's got no right to recommend members of my staff.

RUCKELSHAUS: No, he recommended we fill this kind of position on our staff, not your man specifically.

KISSINGER: What are you trying to tell me?

RUCKELSHAUS: That we are very interested in him. . . . There is a very great need.

KISSINGER: There's a great need on my staff too. . . . If you think I'm going to approve it you're wrong. The thing to do is to come to me first, not after it is done. . . .

RUCKELSHAUS: I understood you were aware of it.

KISSINGER: I am not.

RUCKELSHAUS: You were not told by his immediate superior?

KISSINGER: No, I was not.

RUCKELSHAUS: I was told that you were.

KISSINGER: We can debate that for a while. . . .

14

Defense Leaks on U.S. Withdrawal from Vietnam and More Unguarded Remarks from Abrams, Another Round of Heavy Bombing in Southern North Vietnam (Nixon—"I Am Not So Goddamned Concerned About the Civilian Population"), Egyptian–Israeli Clashes and Retaliations, Upheaval in China and the China Summit, Kissinger's Second Trip to China, Reining in State on the Middle East, and SALT

September–October 1971

In September 1971, Pentagon sources told the press that all U.S. troops would be out of Vietnam by the following spring, and Commander Creighton Abrams assured Senator George McGovern that under the Vietnamization program of U.S. troop withdrawals, no U.S. ground forces or air power would ultimately remain in Vietnam—not even a residual force. Which did not go over well with Nixon and Kissinger.

That month they ordered an all-out, one-day air raid over southern North Vietnam that was disingenuously described (in now typical fashion) as "protective reaction." More strikes followed.

Israel and Egypt were then exchanging fire in and near the Suez Canal cease-fire zone, leaving the cease-fire at jeopardy of complete collapse.

In China, curious events—Mao's death? a leadership struggle over succession? preparations against a possible Soviet attack?—led Nixon and Kissinger to wonder how the 1972 China summit might be affected, or even if it would be canceled, and how these developments could affect their relations with China and their Soviet game. But the summit was on, and in October Kissinger took another trip to China to continue his preparations for it.

Also in October, an irate Kissinger complained that "that maniac" Rogers and the State Department were destroying the Middle East peace negotiations by, without consulting him, frivolously proposing talks between Israeli and Egyptian officials in the United States that he believed wouldn't get anywhere, would "kill the administration," and would even potentially lead to a war. He threatened a "showdown" in the Oval Office. And head U.S. SALT negotiator Gerard Smith was mad that he hadn't been told about the state of Kissinger's backchannel SALT negotiations nor about the upcoming Soviet summit.

John Scali
September 7, 1971, 9:54 a.m.
Kissinger tells Nixon PR adviser Scali that leaks out of State were part of a push against him.

> KISSINGER: I have noticed over the last week that State is mounting their annual campaign against me. . . . [Syndicated columnist] Tom Braden had an article and he said it was given by unimpeachable sources in State, and he is a friend and wouldn't shaft me. The *Wall Street Journal* had an article. . . . [UPI's Stewart] Hensley article today . . . I am sure it's the same source. The only way I can survive here is that they feel I am too dangerous to deal with. Either some people here help me or I will do it. . . . I will not play dead.
> SCALI: Don't jump to conclusions. . . . I am not sure it's State.
> KISSINGER: I am. . . .

Melvin Laird
September 14, 1971, 6:55 p.m.
Laird and Kissinger angrily butt heads over the report out of the Pentagon—which Kissinger thought was Laird's doing—that all U.S. forces would be out of Vietnam by the spring and Abrams's assurance to McGovern, who was in South Vietnam, that no U.S. ground forces or air power would ultimately remain in Vietnam.[1] Laird claims

that no one in the Pentagon was talking and that they shouldn't take McGovern's word. But Kissinger wants Laird to "scare your people."

KISSINGER: Mel, I was just talking to the president. We have been reading the *Star* story. We don't know what to do about the Pentagon.

LAIRD: That's just a cheap story!

KISSINGER: Pentagon sources.

LAIRD: Did you read my press conference about a week ago?

KISSINGER: No. Couldn't everybody just shut up! . . . Who the hell is Abrams to say there will be no residual forces!?

LAIRD: McGovern came out of the meeting with Abrams and said the Vietnamization program eventually would provide for the total withdrawal. . . . But no one is talking in the Pentagon. If you are going to take McGovern's—

KISSINGER: I don't give a damn about McGovern!

LAIRD: They are absolutely cheap stories. What they are doing is quoting military sources, but I guarantee there is no military—there might be some army officers—some are getting to the point where they think Vietnam has hurt the army.

KISSINGER: There will be no awards for getting out two months earlier. If we get out in a way that the communists are in power in Saigon, all this agony will have been in vain. . . . If you can just do the maximum to scare your people.

LAIRD: I have done that but you are going to get these cheap stories.

KISSINGER: Really, the president was extremely disturbed.

LAIRD: What did he say about [*Newsweek* columnist] Stew Alsop's story?

KISSINGER: He didn't say. But Stew is dying and he is no longer rational. . . .

LAIRD: I can't stop a cheap story like that. . . . There have been no questions answered on troop withdrawals.

KISSINGER: No conversations in the corridors?

LAIRD: I can guarantee you. . . . I said that there is *no*—absolutely nothing— goal other than the goal of the president. . . .

KISSINGER: Don't knock out [the] possibility of residual forces either. . . .

President Nixon
September 14, 1971, 8:25 p.m.
Nixon wants retaliation for enemy shootdowns of U.S. helicopters in South Vietnam and is irate over Abrams's assurance to McGovern. Nixon and Kissinger weigh firing Abrams. Nixon thinks Abrams is "drinking too much" (which he was).[2]

NIXON: I was wondering—I notice they got four helicopters—don't you think that is enough provocation to give them a couple of bangs?

KISSINGER: I have to look at the details of how they got them.

NIXON: I wouldn't be too ginger about that! What about McGovern and why is Abrams and everybody sucking around him?

KISSINGER: They are protecting their flanks. I raised hell with Moorer and Laird. They are going to send out additional orders to Abrams to keep his mouth shut.

NIXON: Do you think Abrams put out "getting out by spring"?

KISSINGER: No, I think that was by McGovern, but I think Abrams was protecting himself by saying there would not be a residual force.

NIXON: That's not his business! I think we have to consider withdrawing the son of a bitch.

KISSINGER: I think so, Mr. President. He is a meritorious person but he is no longer on top of this. . . . But it will look like the last days of the Johnson administration if we withdraw him.

NIXON: Get someone second in command that will keep him from drinking too much and talking too much.

KISSINGER: We can't get anyone that will keep him from drinking too much, but we can get someone to keep him from talking too much.

NIXON: They go together! . . .

Thomas Moorer
September 14, 1971, 8:35 p.m.
Kissinger conveys to JCS Chairman Moorer his and Nixon's outrage at the story out of the Pentagon and Abrams's comments to McGovern.

KISSINGER: We have been reading the Washington *Star*. The president and I are just beside ourselves. . . . The Pentagon story that all troops will be withdrawn . . . Abrams's comments as quoted by McGovern that there will be no residual forces left. . . . No military officer is to say one goddamn word about withdrawals!

MOORER: Right!

KISSINGER: We are not going to get an award in this administration for getting out three months early, only for being successful. . . . The other thing, tell the people in Saigon to shut up! . . . Just fire somebody. . . .

Melvin Laird
September 15, 1971, 8:40 a.m.
Laird vehemently objects to accepting McGovern's rendition of what Abrams said.

LAIRD: We've just been having a little meeting on this matter of Abrams's interview, and god damn it, Henry, last night you got in touch with Tom Moorer and didn't wait till the McGovern thing was in. If you're going to get screwed up about what McGovern says goes on, then I'm going to see the president. God damn it, I resent it.

KISSINGER: It wasn't just the Abrams thing. . . . What we said to Moorer was that no one should talk about troop withdrawals.

LAIRD: No one does, but to jump Abrams on this thing—

KISSINGER: No one was jumping Abrams; we just said that there should be no statements by anyone.

LAIRD: I'll handle that. . . . I just don't want Abrams jumped on something McGovern says. I want to know when these things are going on. . . . I'll defend Abrams any day in the week. . . . Abe has had to put up with more than any field commander ever has.

KISSINGER: That is true.

Thomas Moorer
September 17, 1971, 12:04 p.m.
Kissinger conveys Nixon's order for an all-out, one-day air attack in southern North Vietnam.

. . . KISSINGER: The second thing—about these strikes the president wants. . . . It has to be over in one day. . . . Dong Hoi, can you hit that without too many casualties? And you can put every plane into that area. . . . You do everything possible with as many planes as you want. We will call it a protective reaction, and do every violence you can do. . . . Put every plane you need into that. You can do whatever you want. . . .

Yitzhak Rabin
September 17, 1971, 12:35 p.m.
Egypt shot down an Israeli plane over the Israeli-occupied Sinai desert in retaliation for Israel's downing of an Egyptian fighter bomber over the east bank of the Suez Canal.[3]

. . . RABIN: . . . Did you know we lost a plane at 30 kilometers within our territory? They got it with SAM missiles, a big transport plane. It was, as a matter of fact, an electronic intelligence plane. . . . We lost seven people.

KISSINGER: Are you going to do something?

RABIN: . . . I wouldn't be surprised if something will happen. Not on a large scale, of course. . . .

Yitzhak Rabin
September 18, 1971, 9:45 a.m.

Israeli jet fighters had fired Shrike missiles at Egyptian positions in the Suez Canal cease-fire zone in response to Egypt's downing of Israel's plane, leading to rocket fire on both sides of the canal. Ambassador Rabin explains Israel's action and what transpired, and says that publicly Israel will state that it responded to missile fire on its planes (a statement an Egyptian spokesman called "ridiculous").[4] He also explains Israel's earlier downing of the Egyptian fighter bomber. Rabin accuses the Soviet Union of conspiring with Egypt.

KISSINGER: What the hell is going on?

RABIN: The whole idea is not to let them feel they can do whatever they want without any reaction on our part. . . . We look on our action as an act to restore the cease-fire rather than to break it. We don't think giving in will increase their interest in the cease-fire. . . . We used mainly Shrikes. . . . We publicly describe it as an encounter rather than as an initiative by us. Therefore publicly we will stick to the public statement that we were flying, they opened fire. We reacted. Second, we did not cross the Suez Canal because firing the Shrike there was no reason to cross the canal. . . . By the mere fact that we did not cross the canal we try to limit it to one incident, with the purpose that they learn that even though we are interested in maintaining the cease-fire we are not going to ignore something like they did yesterday.

KISSINGER: What happened when you shot down the Su-7 [Egyptian fighter bomber] earlier this week? Was that an accident?

RABIN: No. . . . The Egyptians declared there are no cease-fire anymore. . . . They started flying over the west bank of the Suez Canal. We did not want to allow them to fly this way. Therefore we instructed our units, a few months after they started, to have the right to shoot over every plane thus crossing the Suez Canal. . . . We opened fire on 14 occasions. . . . I am sure their action [shooting down the Israeli plane] was pre-planned. I am sure the decision to fire missiles is not taken in any low-echelon level. I know exactly the deployment that existed prior to the incident. The plane that was shot yesterday was at an extremely effective range of their normal deployment. I think they moved for the purpose of the retaliation that took place yesterday one or more [SAM] sites forward to the Suez Canal eastward to their normal disposition. This cannot be done without at least the Russian knowledge. . . . I have no doubt that the Soviets were consulted or were kept in the picture about the whole picture. I am sure what happened yesterday was pre-planned and certain moves had to be carried out to make it possible. Therefore it was a decision on the highest level with at least the knowledge of the Soviets. Therefore we had to react. . . .

Melvin Laird
September 20, 1971, 8:55 a.m.
Laird informs Kissinger that the bombing of southern North Vietnam was delayed by cloud cover.

> LAIRD: . . . It's the same problem we had last night. It doesn't look better for the next 24 hours either. . . .
>
> KISSINGER: . . . I don't know what sort of an air force we've got. This is the fifth time they have been unable to respond.
>
> LAIRD: They are capable of bombing—
>
> KISSINGER: They are capable of bombing only in the desert in July in clear weather if there's no sandstorm! . . .

President Nixon
September 21, 1971, 9:20 a.m.
The bombing had begun despite the clouds. Some 200 fighter bombers would strike up to 35 miles north of the DMZ in the heaviest raid since March.[5]

> NIXON: Did it get off? I didn't see it in the papers.
>
> KISSINGER: I heard it on the radio. It went off. Of course, with these incompetents it was worse weather than the day before. They did a good job on the oil [petroleum, oil, and lubricant] things. No place where they could see it visually. Some where it went through the cloud cover. . . . Two hundred sorties. . . . They said it's heaviest raid, which isn't true, since the bombing halt [in 1968].
>
> NIXON: We know that.
>
> KISSINGER: The psychological effect is considerable. Not all the damage we wanted, but what they did hit they did a good job on.

President Nixon
September 21, 1971, 5:30 p.m.
For several days in September, China's leaders had receded from view and all planes had been grounded; the annual National Day parade had been canceled. There were rumors that Mao was either seriously ill or dead and that a power struggle was taking place. It turned out that an alleged threat to Mao had died in a plane crash and several top Chinese leaders had been ousted.[6] Nixon and Kissinger ponder how the developments might affect the summit.

> NIXON: . . . We are bound to have, in my view, enormous speculation about this . . . and I don't think that hurts at all, in the sense that it just piques the interest again. Don't you agree?

KISSINGER: If this turns out to be a false alarm, I think it will only pique the interest.

NIXON: And if it is something else again we will have to play the game that way, but we have gotten our dividends in changing the game with our Russian friends.

KISSINGER: Fundamentally.

NIXON: . . . I think this is going to go forward no matter what happens now.

KISSINGER: Well, if they [the Chinese] were having a series of military alerts they would be preoccupied with those, and the other problem is that they don't know about the Russian summit. . . .

President Nixon
September 21, 1971, 6:45 p.m.

NIXON: I am just looking at the *Star*. They kind of placed it on the basis of Mao's death being rumored, but—

KISSINGER: Mr. President, nobody knows anything. It is pure speculation.

NIXON: I assume that. . . . I had the impression based on your conversation that Chou En-lai is running the show anyway.

KISSINGER: It is clear he is running the show. It is not clear that he does not need Mao [for] making it legitimate.

NIXON: But maybe they would get a pro-Russian in there.

KISSINGER: The counter-revolution would be violently anti-Russian and against us too. The Chou faction would continue the policy started by Mao. The Russians would have a very real problem. . . .

NIXON: We would still have the meeting, though.

KISSINGER: Yes, if Chou En-lai had effective control with Mao, he would continue it.

NIXON: The best thing to do would be do no damn speculation whatever, and in any event the world changes, and if he dies, we move in another direction. . . .

President Nixon
September 21, 1971, 11:00 p.m.
Kissinger thinks the events in China may reflect either preparations against a possible Soviet attack or a leadership struggle. If they are "jittery about the Russians," he speculates, "it actually means our game is succeeding." And if the Soviets "jumped" China, "we would have to go hard right" with the Soviets. Also, Nixon wants another air raid on North Vietnam—an even heavier one. "I am not so goddamned concerned about the civilian population," he says. The administration would bomb more targets in the North and the DMZ, as well as the Ho Chi Minh Trail in Laos, over several days.[7]

... KISSINGER: My instinct tells me, Mr. President, whatever it is it isn't the death of Mao. . . . Now, we know it was not us and we know it is not anyone we are watching, so it may have been the Soviets. So it may have a military significance. There could have been a clash, or they may genuinely think that the Soviets are getting ready to jump them. . . . When I was there, they told me that was one of their concerns, that after the announcement of your trip they thought that their neighbors might jump them, and we know from a particular source we have . . . that they went on full alert the day that they announced your visit. So it may be that. Of course, it may also be a leadership struggle. . . . I think there is the possibility Mao is dead, but there just isn't any reliable—there is no news at all to all practical purposes, except for these fragments. . . .

NIXON: . . . Of course, we should have a contingency in the event . . . that their announcement affects our operation. . . . It could well be that they are just jittery about the Russians.

KISSINGER: It could well be that. . . . Well, if they were jittery about the Russians and if that is all this is, then it actually means our game is succeeding. . . . And that will help the later evolution quite a lot. . . . I did, for example, get a report last week saying that all pictures of Mao were beginning to disappear, but that again, Mr. President, would not be consistent with his death. What interest would anyone have after he is dead to do anything with him except to build him up as a deity? . . . It may be just a war of nerves.

NIXON: My view is the Russians would never think of jumping, having in mind our trip.

KISSINGER: . . . They jump them, Mr. President, then we would have to go hard right.

NIXON: On the Russians? . . . Oh, hell yes. We are not going to have any damned condominium [possibly meaning treaty of cooperation or partnership] with the Russians, don't you agree?

KISSINGER: Absolutely. If they did that, we should rally our allies and knock off all détente and build up the defense budget and rally the American people and [escalate] the war in Vietnam brutally. . . . But I don't think that is going to happen.

NIXON: No. I am inclined to think it is going to work out in some way. . . . You may get a reply from them too [on the China summit]. However, I would say now that if you don't get a reply within a week then there is something screwed up. . . .

KISSINGER: Yes. If by the middle of next week if we have not had a reply then we are getting into a zone where it is going to be technically tough to arrange.

NIXON: As far as your trip is concerned?

KISSINGER: Yes. But something is clearly screwed up. That you can tell already because they have always been meticulous in their reply....

NIXON: You could have a group of younger officers that—you know, after all, the country is in a sort of miserable condition, let's face it, and it just may be that a group of younger officers came to their senses, hardliners, and said, well, the hell with them, we'll throw them out.... If they are hardliners, they are going to hardline on the Russians too.

KISSINGER: There is no question that a reconciliation with the Russians seems to me the least likely outcome.

NIXON: That, in my view, would be the greatest danger.

KISSINGER: ... Of course, one other possibility, Mr. President, on the more hopeful side, is that Chou En-lai is cleaning out the cultural revolutionists preparatory to your visit.... I mean, that would fit the evidence too—that Chou En-lai, knowing of my visit for which he wants to be ready, and of your visit, is consolidating his position....

NIXON: ... Having gotten away with this strike as apparently we have ... as soon as this weather clears, I would go back and clean out the rest of that stuff.

KISSINGER: I think that we should do, Mr. President.

NIXON: ... But god damn it, tell them I want some results.

KISSINGER: Well, they had pretty good results today, Mr. President, because we intercepted North Vietnamese communications in which they report themselves very extensive damage.... They reported heavy damage to POL [petroleum, oil, and lubricant storage facilities]....

NIXON: But as I understand it there are trucks and supply depots and other things, and I would just knock the bejesus out of them.

KISSINGER: But we didn't get the supply dumps other than POL near a port because we were afraid to hit the civilian population when we couldn't bomb visually. And that would be the most lucrative target when the weather clears.

NIXON: I am not so goddamned concerned about the civilian population. I am not so concerned about it.

KISSINGER: Well, it would give them a lot of pictures they could use.

NIXON: Maybe.... I think you ought to lay it on.... Above the DMZ we are just not going to tolerate this kind of buildup.

KISSINGER: Well, I think we can get away with one more, Mr. President. Then I would put a pause in of a few weeks.

NIXON: Let's make the one more damned good.... Both the Russians and the Chinese have got to know that we mean business.

KISSINGER: Absolutely. That's why this strike yesterday was so important.

NIXON: . . . If there is any psychological benefit left to what the hell we are doing to those people, this is going to do it. . . .

John Scali

September 29, 1971, 10:55 a.m.

Senator Edward Kennedy had told families of American POWs that their relatives were "rotting" in prison camps because the administration still had not responded to a North Vietnamese peace proposal for their release in exchange for U.S. withdrawal from Vietnam made several months earlier.[8]

SCALI: The president is anxious for Rogers to take on Teddy Kennedy.

KISSINGER: Rogers won't do it. . . . I have gone through this with him a thousand times. He will not do it.

SCALI: I am doing this at the instruction of the president.

KISSINGER: That's a beautiful statement. . . .

SCALI: Well, I hope you will reflect to the secretary of state the president's strong feeling that he should do it. I know what the president will say.

KISSINGER: No, you don't. The president will let him slide off. I will not talk against it, but I am not at all sure by the time he gets through he won't have made it worse. . . . If you can get the president to order it, it will be done. But it will be done in a half-assed way.

John Mitchell

October 8, 1971, 12:45 p.m.

Kissinger rails to Attorney General Mitchell that "that maniac" Rogers was ruining the Middle East peace negotiations. The State Department was proposing talks in the United States between Egyptian and Israeli officials, with Assistant Secretary of State Joseph Sisco as mediator and "catalyst." State was still pressuring Israel to give up some occupied territory.[9]

. . . KISSINGER: Do you know what that maniac did now? . . . The Egyptians are sending a secret emissary to New York and Sisco is to get the Israelis to do the same and Sisco will send messages back and forth like in 1948. Then they are going to come and ask us to squeeze the Israelis. The Russians will think we are screwing them. The Egyptians will think we are screwing them. There we are with this maniac with not one word to us. . . . I tell you, this will kill the administration. Everyone knows that State is not checking with us. The insolence, incompetence, and frivolity of this exercise is beyond belief. Leave aside the Russians, would you ask for a secret emissary to come and put your prestige on the line as an intermediate when there is nothing to believe that anything is going to happen?

MITCHELL: It's an exacerbation of the program he's been on all along with no
results.

KISSINGER: One doesn't move in such a situation without first knowing what
the parties are willing to give.... The insolence of treating the president this
way is beyond belief. It would be like you appointing a Supreme Court justice without consulting him.... I just don't know how to handle Rogers....
The Israelis will crack him in the teeth.

MITCHELL: They have before. They know the limb he's sitting out on....

Joseph Sisco

October 9, 1971, 12:50 p.m.

*Kissinger upbraids Sisco over State's independent moves on the Middle East, and
specifically its proposal for talks between Israeli and Egyptian officials in the United
States. He threatens to drag someone into the Oval Office the next time a cable goes
out uncleared by him and get them fired. Sisco says Kissinger needs to work it out with
Rogers, but Kissinger threatens "a showdown" instead.*

KISSINGER: ... I have been reading with mounting concern the cables ...
which we didn't have even the slightest courtesy of being informed of.

SISCO: We are doing what the Israelis have wanted for three years, bringing it
to direct negotiations.

KISSINGER: But if this fails, you will come to us and ask us to beat the Israelis
over the head.... The next time a cable goes out in violation of presidential
directives that they must be cleared, I will take the originator into his office
and one of us will come out without his job. I will insist that the originator
be fired or I will resign. I like you; I think you are the most creative assistant
secretary we've got. And I don't want you to be a victim.

SISCO: I'm afraid I will be. But I want you to know, I am no longer the principal
prime mover on this, Henry.... I have tried for weeks to create a dialogue
between you, the president, Secretary Rogers, and myself.... It is something
you and the secretary have got to resolve.

KISSINGER: We are not going to do it. He has got his directives. I am going to
create a showdown.

SISCO: I can't advise you on that, Henry. Frankly, I am no longer calling the
shots.

KISSINGER: If you try to run around between these two parties without knowing where the president will back you, you'll kill yourself.

SISCO: I know. There has been one basic rule in the problem: if you don't have
the backing of the president you don't have anyone. He insists that he has
his backing. I don't want to get between you and Rogers on this.... I have
done everything I can to create a dialogue between you.

KISSINGER: . . . I think what will happen is the president will start squeezing Rogers out of this like he has on everything else. . . . First, I want you to know what I am going to do, and I don't bluff. I would hate to have you end up as the fall guy.

SISCO: I am going to. I am going to be the fall guy.

KISSINGER: I will do my best to see that you don't. . . . And second, if we can get some advance information. . . .

SISCO: I don't imagine the secretary feels this is any new departure. He feels . . . he is trying to produce the kind of negotiation that the Israelis have wanted. He feels he has carte blanche to do this as he sees fit. He tells me he has an understanding with the president to do this. . . . I wrote a paper four weeks ago to try to create a dialogue. It never got beyond his desk. . . . I have never been comfortable in this job unless the president, the secretary, and you have all known what's being done. I have lost sleep over this.

KISSINGER: I think we are producing a war the way we are going. . . . You could let me have the reporting cable of the conversation between the secretary and [Egypt Foreign Minister Mahmoud] Riad.

SISCO: That was sent to you last night.

KISSINGER: I never saw it.

SISCO: It was sent last night; it goes automatically to you.

KISSINGER: No, it doesn't. . . .

H. R. Haldeman

October 9, 1971, 2:55 p.m.

Kissinger tells Haldeman that he thinks he can put a brake on State's Middle East initiatives but warns of "a first-class crisis with me" if State is not brought under control.

KISSINGER: I just wanted to tell you what I have done. I talked to Dobrynin. If I can get control of the cable, I think I can slow it down, until they see what the president wants. . . . I have told Sisco the next time a cable goes out that has not been cleared with us, someone will go into the president's office with me. He says Rogers has a backdoor into the president's office. He is troublesome, uneasy, and very worried. . . . I am telling you, you are going to get into a first-class crisis with me. I am not going to let this happen. Now Rogers is back here [from the UN] for three days. The next guy he will see is [Israel Foreign Minister Abba] Eban. The Israelis will be meeting for three weeks and then the meeting will deadlock. I haven't seen a cable. I don't know what Rogers said to Riad. . . . I am going to go into the president and tell him we have to play it this way or go without me. . . . I will have to keep on doing what I have been doing for over a year—keep things under control. . . .

What he doesn't know is that I have been saving him for a year and a half now. . . . If we had let things run their course there would have been three big blowups in the past year. Just like I have quieted it down now for two weeks. . . .

President Nixon

October 12, 1971, 8:30 a.m.

Nixon wants a public statement on Chile "knocking their brains out" on the Allende government's nationalization of American property. (Chile's controller general had ruled that two of three U.S. copper companies should not receive any compensation for their nationalization.)[10]

> . . . NIXON: . . . The only thing I see in the news is Chile, and I want to be tough with them. . . . Are you preparing something to say? I will say something but I want you to have your staff—get Haig to, the toughest son of a bitch you've got, to work something up. It's time to kick Chile in the ass. . . . I just want a strong statement knocking their brains out. What will we do?
>
> KISSINGER: We can cut off their credit.
>
> NIXON: I want a strong statement kicking Chile in the ass. Have [Treasury Secretary John] Connally make it. Really blast their butts. And don't bring State into it. What are they doing?
>
> KISSINGER: They are probably wringing their hands, but they should say something too. I will call Connally this minute.
>
> NIXON: I want to over-act on this one and I expect State to toe the mark. They have confiscated American property and we won't allow it. . . . I want the strongest action on it and I want it highly publicized and highly visible, and I want it on TV. . . .

Gerard Smith

October 12, 1971, 2:20 p.m.

Nixon had suggested at a news conference that day when he announced the May 1972 Soviet summit that he hoped to sign a SALT agreement there and that if the remaining issues were not settled by then, and he expressed hope that they would be, they would be discussed at the summit. Smith, the head of the U.S. delegation at the SALT talks, who felt Nixon's announcement put pressure on him to come to an agreement, though SALT was far from an accord, is also angry about not having been told about the summit.[11]

> SMITH: I read on the ticker that you and the president are going to negotiate SALT in Moscow.

KISSINGER: Oh, Jesus Christ, relax. For Christ's sake! Read what the president said.

SMITH: I am relaxed. I'm disgusted, but relaxed.

KISSINGER: They asked if SALT was going to be finished. . . . He said we are pushing ahead and we now expect that the SALT agreement we are working on will be finished. But if it's not, then maybe it will be discussed. . . .

SMITH: Henry, do you remember our discussion in December 1970 about whether we were planning for a summit? [Soviet SALT negotiator Vladimir] Semenov had been saying there would be one and so I asked you about it. You assured me that if there was one I would be advised. So we still took the position that in December of 1970 there was no discussion of a summit.

KISSINGER: In December of 1970, as it happens, there wasn't. . . . There was an earlier one which aborted, and that was it.

SMITH: I look like a fool with Semenov for not knowing about that. I will look like one this time. . . . What am I to say if I am asked if I knew about this by newsmen? Say, no, I knew nothing about it? . . . It would have been at least courteous to have the head of the agency [the Arms Control and Disarmament Agency, which Smith headed] directly responsible at least aware that the meeting had been discussed. When you have to read it on the ticker it makes you wonder. . . . I go into the secretary of state staff meeting and hear that there will be an announcement and don't know anything it's about. Then I am asked to talk about SALT. And a few hours later this comes out and I look like a fool. I don't know how you expect people to go playing along like this.

KISSINGER: I don't see how this affects you.

SMITH: That's the problem; no one sees how it affects anybody else. It makes me look like a fool with Semenov going around saying that I don't know about the discussions for a summit. . . .

President Nixon
October 12, 1971, 9:41 p.m.
Treasury Secretary John Connally had agreed to attend South Vietnamese President Thieu's inauguration following his victory in a one-man presidential election, after Secretary of Defense Melvin Laird and HEW Secretary Elliot Richardson had begged off.

KISSINGER: I've just talked to Connally, and he said if the president wants him to go, of course he'll go. . . . And I think it's a 10-strike. . . . He's a big man. . . . I said Laird couldn't change his program, even though he'll be there three days later, and Richardson says it hurts his domestic program. He said, "Hell, my domestic program can't be hurt, and I haven't got a schedule that the president can't change."

NIXON: . . . Well, he sees the big play.

KISSINGER: . . . He is the best man you could have sent.

NIXON: Former secretary of the navy, and he's known to be the second man in the government.

KISSINGER: Above all, he's the strongest man in the cabinet.

NIXON: That's right. He's a guy with guts. . . . And it'll really tear these other people to pieces. . . .

KISSINGER: That will really put it to them. . . . He said if the president wants me, I have no schedule problem. But that's what every cabinet member should say.

NIXON: They don't say that, though. They always determine what the hell is in their interest. . . .

Ben Bradlee
October 14, 1971, 9:55 a.m.
Washington Post executive editor Ben Bradlee and Kissinger discuss a forthcoming piece by the paper's gossip columnist, Maxine Cheshire, on Kissinger's dating of the actress Judy Brown, who'd done soft-porn films such as Women in Cages. *Kissinger told Cheshire he'd only seen Brown three times, but Brown said she'd been dating him steadily for over a year.*[12]

KISSINGER: I thought about this. You do what you want. The only thing I ask is you print it and I make no comment. I met this girl through Taft Schreiber [an entertainment industry executive and Nixon fundraiser]. . . . No one said she is playing in skin movies. I took her out twice more, and when she used me for publicity I dropped her.

BRADLEE: The trouble is it's in the trade papers and movie magazines. I killed it last night because it wasn't ready. I don't know what to do.

KISSINGER: . . . I didn't do anything wrong. That's my position and I refuse any comment. . . . I think it's a disgrace. . . . Three times in nine months is hardly an intimate relationship. The last time was when photographers were waiting and I walked out through the kitchen [of a restaurant] and dropped her.

BRADLEE: We may drop it. . . .

Robert Evans
October 26, 1971, 7:30 p.m.
The Paramount executive commiserates with Kissinger about the publicity on his love life.

... EVANS: My private life is coming along fine. The headlines have all been about you.

KISSINGER: I found out about these goddamn Hollywood stories.

EVANS: Disgusting, isn't it?

KISSINGER: It's the most humiliating thing that has happened to me.

EVANS: There is something to be learned from it.

KISSINGER: I barely know this girl!

EVANS: All you need is one bad apple. . . .

Fritz Kraemer

October 28, 1971, 4:30 p.m.

Kissinger's highly agitated mentor when Kissinger was in the army during World War II does not want to talk to a journalist writing an article about Kissinger for the New York Times Magazine, *and Kissinger blames Rogers and the U.S. mission at the UN for Taiwan's expulsion from the UN three days earlier. (He also felt Rogers had maneuvered the date for the UN vote so that the loss of Taiwan could be blamed on his trip to China, which had been admitted to the UN, from which he'd just returned.)*[13]

KRAEMER: Kraemer speaking. This damnable journalist—

KISSINGER: I have no objection to your talking to him.

KRAEMER: He phoned just 10 minutes ago and he said he had talked to you. . . . I want that in writing because—

KISSINGER: Oh, come now, Kraemer, I won't do that. . . .

KRAEMER: I am not an unfriendly man, but I will simply tell him that I have no written authorization, and I will not talk to him. You can tell him you have an impossible man on your hands. . . . I sit here in a highly nervous state. . . . I don't want to talk in such a situation.

KISSINGER: That's okay. On balance, I am not sure he would use this sympathetically. He might use it to show fascist sympathies and all that. . . .

KRAEMER: I am convinced that from what went on two days ago a new era will be counted.

KISSINGER: And you know why they voted? Because that son of a bitch at State [Rogers] wanted to take the headlines from my return. . . . The whole thing was geared to the publicity, not to what should be done. It was a fraud from the beginning to the end, because if you look at the votes against us, you can't tell me there were four or five that couldn't have been switched. . . . I told Haig months ago that they wanted to throw the vote, that they were deliberately miscounting and concentrating on the wrong countries. And then in the last two weeks they went into a buckshot approach which threw countries into domestic chaos. . . . There were a number of them that could have been gotten. . . .

KRAEMER: . . . Here, again! My secretary just put before me a note that [the journalist Barnard] Collier is calling. I don't want to see the man! . . . If you were to see me you would know something has happened to me in the last few days. I am not the man you left four weeks ago. Something has happened. I am not sleeping; I even take sleeping pills. . . . And I beg you to tell this man that you don't want me to. . . .

Robert Pursley
October 28, 1971, 6:40 p.m.
Kissinger laces into Laird's military assistant Pursley over the holdup on a paper about going to an all-volunteer army.

KISSINGER: I am calling you because I don't think Al [Haig] has managed to convey to you the urgency we are asking for the draft paper. Now we have got to have it. I am not going into the president's office again to be asked why I do not have it. Why is Defense stonewalling us? . . . Why don't you have it? . . . Why is it so hard to do? . . . I am telling you the president was so furious. . . . He thinks you are trying to avoid giving us a paper so you can play with us.
PURSLEY: That is not true. . . . We gave you three papers before.
KISSINGER: Yes, but they never amounted to much. . . .

The Pakistan–India Conflict—the United Nations, a "Soviet–Indian Naked Power Play," Border Clashes and Escalation, Cutting Off Aid to India, Disputes with State, Pakistan's Surprise Attack, Blaming India, Illegal Arms Shipments, Preventing "a Dismemberment of West Pakistan," Coordinating with China, Pakistan's Surrender and Gandhi's Cease-fire; a Cuban Attack on a Suspect Freighter; and Massive Bombing of North Vietnam

November–December 1971

In November 1971, after an Indian cross-border attack in East Pakistan, Pakistan retaliated by air and ground, and Pakistani troops entered India. Kissinger saw it as Indian aggression. In early December, Pakistan bombed Indian airfields in a surprise attack and shelled Indian forces along India's western border with Pakistan. A full-fledged war had begun. After the Pakistani military dictatorship's brutal crackdown in East Pakistan the previous March to stamp out the movement for autonomy there, India had covertly supported the Bengali insurgents demanding an independent Bangladesh, and it had planned to attack Pakistan before Pakistan attacked it.

Secretary of State William Rogers wanted to take the fighting to the UN, but Kissinger saw the UN as "a trap" and told him "that means Pakistan will get raped." (He also wanted to consult first with China, Pakistan's ally.) Kissinger believed the Soviets were colluding with India, which he claimed sought to "dismember" Pakistan. Nixon was red-hot to cut off aid to India. Rogers, who was not convinced by Kissinger's charge of Indian aggression and was worried about hurting relations with India, resisted it. But Nixon and Kissinger cut off most of India's military aid and suspended economic aid too. They still blamed India for the fighting after Pakistan's attack; the Indians were clearly the aggressors, Kissinger told Nixon. They worried that Rogers would not toe publicly their pro-Pakistan line. Nixon ordered a major PR campaign blaming India for the war. Nixon and Kissinger plotted on getting arms to Pakistan secretly— and illegally—through Iran and Jordan, and did. Nixon directed that India be squeezed to the max on aid, but ordered a discreet effort to get the administration's friends in Congress to spearhead it. Rogers thought Nixon was acting out of "petulance" and tilting too much toward China.

After Pakistan surrendered in East Pakistan and India ordered a unilateral cease-fire in West Pakistan, Nixon wanted the credit.

The same day, Nixon was enraged when a Cuban gunboat seized a freighter in the Bahamas operated by a Miami company owned by Cuban refugees and the bureaucracy took too long to respond; if Cuba tried it again, he wanted to "shoot them up."

Ten days later, the administration began among the heaviest bombing raids on North Vietnam since it took office.

Nelson Rockefeller
November 3, 1971, 7:00 p.m.
Governor Rockefeller tells Kissinger about a meeting he had with India Prime Minister Indira Gandhi, where they discussed the massive refugee crisis in India resulting from the savage Pakistani crackdown in East Pakistan.[1]

ROCKEFELLER: I am taking the liberty of calling you because Madame Gandhi is in New York and she asked me to come up. I have just spent an hour with her. She was telling me what is going on.

KISSINGER: I wouldn't believe half of it.

ROCKEFELLER: No, but, you know, you listen in this world. . . . She thinks it's beyond her control, and if it blows it's bigger than she is. . . . My impression is that she is damned scared about what she has got. . . . This is someone reaching out in desperation. . . .

KISSINGER: I have studied Indian foreign policy, and these characters have an enormous ability to get themselves into messes by letting events run away from them....

John McCloy
November 11, 1971, 6:30 p.m.
Kissinger asks McCloy, an outside foreign policy adviser and corporate lawyer, to serve as U.S. representative to NATO, laying it on thick.

... KISSINGER: So, as you know, the NATO ambassadorship is vacant at this moment. And the president asked me to explore with you whether, knowing it would be an enormous sacrifice, you would agree to serve there for a year. We need a towering figure there now. ... We have a lot of names, and it's a job that people are dying to get. But there's only one person who represents this great tradition of U.S.–European relationships, who has the stature in Europe . . . and who would have a voice in our councils that everyone would listen to.

MCCLOY: ... See, I represent all the oil companies. ... I have to make a living. ... I haven't got any reserve money. ...

KISSINGER: No, look, Jack, we know it'd be a sacrifice. ... And I must tell you honestly, we were thinking for a while along much more conventional lines, but as the president studied the problem . . . he thought that he should . . . send one of our towering figures over there. ... I really think the country needs you right now.

MCCLOY: ... I'll pick myself up off the floor and think about it. ...

President Nixon
November 13, 1971, 10:38 a.m.
Kissinger opposes taking the India–Pakistan dispute to the UN, given support for India there (though India had little confidence in the UN),[2] and wants to hear from China first.

... NIXON: What about the situation in India–Pakistan? ...

KISSINGER: If we go into the UN now, it is a trap. The Indians have more support there than we. And the State Department has no intention of supporting Pakistan in the UN.

NIXON: ... The Indians have most of the UN locked, of course.

KISSINGER: They have the Security Council votes locked. We don't want to be trapped into voting with the Soviet Union. ... We should ask both sides to stop their military operations.

NIXON: You think just let it wait? If they fight, they fight. India will roll over them pretty fast.

KISSINGER: . . . The Pakistan foreign secretary is arriving tomorrow—he claims to have a message from Peking. I think we should look at all this before we move. I don't think there will be a war next week. Sisco's great trick is to always say there is a speech. That is how he screwed up the Middle East. . . .

N. A. M. Raza
November 22, 1971, 3:23 p.m.
After an Indian cross-border attack in East Pakistan, Pakistan had launched air and ground assaults in response, and Pakistani troops had crossed into India. Kissinger advised Nixon that India attacked Pakistan in "a naked case of aggression."[3] Raza was Pakistan's ambassador to the United States.

. . . KISSINGER: If at all possible I would appreciate it if you would hold off going to the Security Council until Wednesday. I am meeting—but strictly for you—the Chinese secretly tomorrow. No one knows this. I would like to see what they intend to do. . . .

RAZA: Shall I inform my government?

KISSINGER: I will inform through my channel. But am counting on you. This is secret.

RAZA: No one will know. . . .

Joseph Sisco
November 22, 1971, 5:47 p.m.
Kissinger complains to Assistant Secretary of State Sisco that the State Department is not following Nixon's prescribed "tilt" toward Pakistan in the conflict, but Sisco says Kissinger's threatening manner with State is counterproductive.

. . . KISSINGER: The thing I find so hard to understand is why we don't get the basic tilt of the president straight. . . .

SISCO: We have that straight but these meetings we are having—you don't understand how intimidating you sound. You don't have to threaten us or intimidate us. We are trying to do the job. You will scare the hell out of so many people in this building that no one will give you the information you should hear. . . . You are a good professor and teacher but don't cut off your sources of information.

KISSINGER: My job is to get the president's wants.

SISCO: You are getting through. We have a responsibility also to say to you this is the way we read it. We know what the president wants. To make us feel that we are not doing what the president wants done—it's developing in that room. And you should be aware of it. . . .

William Rogers

November 23, 1971, 10:55 a.m.

Secretary of State Rogers wants to go to the UN, but Kissinger says "that means Pakistan will get raped." Rogers, who believed charges of an Indian invasion were inconclusive and whose frayed relations with Kissinger were fueling their disputes, is reticent to cut off military aid to India as Nixon directed. (The administration would subsequently cut off most of India's military aid and then freeze economic aid too.)[4]

... ROGERS: If it continues to build, and I think it will, then exhortations will not help and the UN is the only way out.

KISSINGER: Let's not kid ourselves—that means Pakistan will get raped.

ROGERS: They will if the fighting doesn't stop.

KISSINGER: India is outrageous. . . . I think we should cut off the military pipeline.

ROGERS: It's not substantial. . . . We will break ties with India. . . . On ammunition and such we should, but our radar equipment I think we should wait. . . . I think we should be sure to stay out of it. Get someone else to stop the fighting, and it's going on in three places now. . . .

KISSINGER: I think there's a shade of difference between State's and the president's views. He would like to tilt towards Pakistan and not India, and your people go the other way.

ROGERS: I don't see that. . . .

William Rogers

December 3, 1971, 10:15 a.m.

In a surprise attack, Pakistan had bombed Indian airfields; soon thereafter, it began shelling Indian forces along India's western border with Pakistan, a new theater of fighting. Rogers wants to delay or modify a noon statement on the India arms cutoff given Pakistan's attacks, but Kissinger disagrees; he and Nixon still blamed India for the fighting.[5]

ROGERS: Henry, I think in view of the developments in India and Pakistan, we ought to seriously consider delaying this thing until this afternoon, or, in any event, we've got to change the statement because it is out of date in view of what's happened. . . . It has deteriorated very quickly and it looks as if there is military activity in the West. The Paks say there is a good deal of ground fighting in the West.

KISSINGER: I think we have no choice. . . .

ROGERS: We can't talk about it in view of yesterday's news, it has to be done in view of today's news. It is getting to the point where none of these things have much significance because it is deteriorating so fast. . . . I think we

ought to take it to the UN simply because the Soviets don't want to. . . .
Let's do this. Hold up the announcement on the cutoff of the pipeline until
4:00.

KISSINGER: I don't know if I can agree with that. I don't see where one is
related to the other.

ROGERS: Well, if it is any source of embarrassment to you—

KISSINGER: I would go ahead with the cutoff and not make the long statement.

ROGERS: I think if we are going to the Security Council we shouldn't decide
the Indians are the guilty party, but that they have played a useful role.

KISSINGER: Okay, Bill. I'll be talking to you.

President Nixon
December 3, 1971, 10:45 a.m.
*Kissinger informs Nixon of Pakistan's attacks and that State doesn't want to cut off
arms to India. They agree to go to the UN, and Kissinger wants to "blast" the Russians
for both Vietnam and India. (He believed the Soviets were colluding with India and
sought to "give pause to potential Soviet adventures elsewhere.")[6] Nixon says Gandhi
and the Indians brought it all on.*

KISSINGER: Two matters I want to raise. It appears that West Pakistan has attacked because situation in East collapsing. State wants to use it as a pretext
not to put out statement at noon. I think it's more reason to cancel programs
[for India]. State believes and I agree that we should take it to the Security
Council once actions are confirmed. . . .

NIXON: Who will object?

KISSINGER: India and the Soviet Union.

NIXON: So we have to. . . . We have to cut off arms aid to India. We should have
done it earlier. . . .

KISSINGER: If they [Pakistan] lose half of their country without fighting they
will be destroyed. They may also be destroyed this way but they will go
down fighting. . . . I think I should give a brief note to the Russians. . . . A
strong blast at their Vietnam friends and behavior on India. We are moving
on our side but they are not doing enough on theirs.

NIXON: On India certainly, but on Vietnam I wonder if it sounds hollow. . . .
Pakistan thing makes your heart sick. For them to be done so by the Indians
and after we have warned the bitch. . . . They have brought it on. We have
to cut off arms. Why not? Because attacked by West Pakistan? Tell them
that when India talked about West Pakistan attacking them it's like Russia
claiming to be attacked by Finland. . . .

President Nixon

December 4, 1971, 10:50 a.m.

Nixon wants PR adviser John Scali unleashed on Indian aggression. He and Kissinger also plot on getting military aid to Pakistan secretly—and illegally—through Iran, which Pakistan President Yahya Khan had desperately requested and the shah of Iran agreed to do.[7]

... KISSINGER: It is getting clear the Indians are the attackers.

NIXON: Is that getting through on the press?

KISSINGER: I am getting with the intelligence people at 11:00 and then getting Scali to put it out.

NIXON: Turn Scali loose on this....

KISSINGER: We have had an urgent appeal from Yahya. Says his military supplies have been cut off—in very bad shape. Would we help through Iran? ... I think if we tell the Iranians we will make it up to them, we can do it.

NIXON: If it is leaked we can have it denied. Have it done one step away. Do you have to go through [U.S. Ambassador to Iran Douglas] MacArthur [II] to do it? ... That would not be safe. ... I like the idea. The main thing is to keep India from crumbling them up....

President Nixon

December 4, 1971, 12:15 p.m.

Nixon orders a stronger PR campaign blaming India for the fighting and Kissinger updates him on the situation at the UN. U.S. Ambassador to the UN George H. W. Bush introduced a resolution in the Security Council that day for a cease-fire and withdrawal of troops (meaning India's), which failed because of a veto by the Soviets.[8]

NIXON: Upon studying these reports on Pakistan—the main thing that needs to be done is the public relations side of it. As far as the White House, we are weaker than we should be. I want ... Scali turned loose on what we are doing ... and blame India. The libs can say we brought this on by the arms support to Pakistan. That will be their argument. India will be doing PR to make Pakistan look like it caused it....

KISSINGER: At the Security Council, the Indians and Soviets are going to delay long enough so a resolution cannot be passed. If it was, the Soviets would veto. UN will be impotent. So the Security Council is just a paper exercise—it will get the *Post* and *Times* off our backs. And the libs will be happy that we turned it over to the UN....

President Nixon

December 4, 1971, no time

Kissinger says the Indian occupation of East Pakistan will make Pakistan's atroci-
ties pale in comparison (a tall order), and Nixon orders that India be squeezed to
the fullest on aid. But he wants his allies in Congress to "take the lead" and engineer
it "discreetly." Kissinger points out that Treasury Secretary John Connally can turn
off the spigot to India "without the knife showing." They also mull over a prospective
backgrounder by Kissinger blaming India for the fighting. And Kissinger reports that
they'd sent a disavowable backchannel message to the shah of Iran about Iran's help
getting arms to Pakistan illegally. He also gives an update on the fighting.

> ... KISSINGER: And, Mr. President, actually in terms of the political situa-
> tion . . . in six months the liberals are going to look like jerks because the
> Indian occupation of East Pakistan is going to make the Pakistani one look
> like child's play.
>
> NIXON: Yes. Well, the main thing we're not going to do is be suckered by the
> Indians into a huge aid program. Now, that I want clearly understood. You
> know, after they have screwed this thing up, by god, I can't emphasize too
> strongly how I feel. We told Mrs. Gandhi we're going to cut off that aid and
> we're going to do it. Has the word gone out?
>
> KISSINGER: The word has gone out, Mr. President. . . . We've already told the
> banks to hold it. . . .
>
> NIXON: I see. And you're examining every other possibility of how we can
> squeeze India right now?
>
> KISSINGER: That is right, Mr. President.
>
> NIXON: It's to be done. Everything is to be held up. . . . The way I want that
> handled is for people like [Congressman Otto] Passman and some of our
> friends in the House and the Senate, even the more liberal types, to come
> out and say cut aid to India. . . . Let them take the lead rather than have us
> take the lead. . . . Can we put somebody to work on it so that it'll be discreetly
> done? . . . I think it's very important to put the burden on India on this. . . .
> We've got their enmity anyway. That's what she's shown in this goddamn
> thing, hasn't she?
>
> KISSINGER: I mean, it isn't that we are losing an ally. They were the ones that
> made a treaty with the Russians. . . . In fact, if we do it the right way, we
> can still get them to come back to us, to get back in our good graces. The
> Russians aren't going to give them $700 million in development money.
>
> NIXON: . . . But what do you think about your doing a backgrounder, or is that
> overkill?
>
> KISSINGER: I think it'd be overkill tomorrow, but what I might do . . . I worked
> out with Ziegler a procedure, which we've always wanted to try, where I step

into his briefing. I mean, he calls me in when questions start falling and says, "Why don't we get Henry on background on this?" And I just step into his briefing.

NIXON: Why don't you do that. . . . What you ought to do is look over the facts very, very carefully and then go out and give a hard-hitting briefing. . . . It would pit world opinion against these people. . . .

KISSINGER: That's exactly the way I feel about it. Because . . . then we have to have a basis for the actions in the economic field we are taking.

NIXON: Now insofar as those actions are concerned, we haven't had any squeals from the Indians, have we?

KISSINGER: No, no. See, that's again where State was wrong. The Indians have no interest in escalating this with us. Not a squeal. They will start squealing next week when the economic aid is cut off.

NIXON: . . . Anything that can be cut has got to be cut next week. *Anything.* . . . That's the only way the Indians are going to understand this. . . . Don't announce a thing. Just do it. . . . Connally understands it, of course.

KISSINGER: Connally has played beautiful ball. He knows how to do these things without the knife showing.

NIXON: Incidentally, tell him . . . if he has an opportunity to stick the knife in India in any public statement that he makes. . . . I think we should play a very tough game. I don't think the American people want to aid a country that is an aggressor.

KISSINGER: . . . When have these bastards ever supported us?

NIXON: Never.

KISSINGER: What can they do to us that they aren't doing now? I mean, if they want to be Russian stooges and have the Russians spend a billion dollars there a year, we can't prevent it. . . . Of course another thing we have done is to send a backchannel to the shah [of Iran] from you . . . trying to find out whether he wanted to give some support to Pakistan. . . .

NIXON: Are you sure that backchannel is safe?

KISSINGER: Yes.

NIXON: I wouldn't do it through MacArthur [the U.S. ambassador to Iran].

KISSINGER: No, no, that's why I didn't do it that way, and we didn't put it as a message. We put it as talking points so it can be disavowed.

NIXON: . . . God, you know what would really be poetic justice here is if some way the Paks could really give the Indians a bloody nose for a couple of days. The fighting—any report on that?

KISSINGER: . . . We got reports in East Pakistan that the Indians are surprised at the intensity of the Pakistan resistance. . . . In West Pakistan the Indians don't seem to have gotten very far. And there I think they're not going to be able to win except by wearing them down. . . . Of course, they've been playing a terrific game these last years. Every time one tank was shipped to Pakistan the Indians would carry on like maniacs, but they've been getting big shipments from . . . their own armaments industry.

NIXON: Well, we've got to get across the point that as far as our aid to Pakistan is concerned, that first, it was minimal. Second, that our mistake was, and I think that's the thing you want to make in your backgrounder, was that we didn't give more. . . . Let the Indians squeal. Let the liberals squeal. . . . I would be prepared to go out and say in view of this action that we regretfully cut off—until this action desists, all economic aid to India stops, period. They're in the business of being the aggressors. . . . Oh, I know all the arguments that, well, then we're choosing up sides, we're not neutral. Of course we're not neutral. Neither are the Indians. They're always neutral against us. . . .

Amir Aslan Afshar
December 4, 1971, no time
Kissinger speaks to the Iranian ambassador to the United States about establishing a backchannel to the shah for getting military equipment to Pakistan illegally. The next day the CIA station chief in Tehran met with the shah, who said he would be glad to help if the United States replaced the arms he sent. Nixon authorized the illegal arms transfers the following day.[9]

KISSINGER: I just tried to call you on behalf of the president. He would be interested on a personal basis to get the Iranian assessment of the Pakistan situation. Not through channels. . . . But maybe from the shah to you and then directly to me.

AFSHAR: All right, I will do that, Mr. Kissinger. Right away. And as you know, we are very much concerned about the whole thing. . . .

KISSINGER: Yes, but we want to keep—this is a personal message from the president. . . . And we don't want it in regular diplomatic channels. . . . Because we are sympathetic to anything you can do to give help there.

AFSHAR: . . . You mean the message is the oral message, yes, which I have just to deliver?

KISSINGER: Yes, and give it to me personally and to no one else. . . .

William Rogers
December 5, 1971, no time
Rogers cautions against hurting relations with India, taking "the exact Chinese position," and acting out of "petulance."

... ROGERS: Well, I think we have got a major decision if this thing continues to grow, and that is whether we want to burn our bridges behind us or not with India.

KISSINGER: Well, the other question is what do we gain by tacking towards them now?

ROGERS: Well, it isn't really tacking towards them now. It's just a question of how much do we want to get involved in the public mind with the war itself. . . . In the long run do we want to go all-out and take the exact Chinese position, or do we want to be somewhere in between? At the moment we are somewhere in between—between the Soviet Union and China.

KISSINGER: Well, our present position is to try to be, say, two-thirds of the way towards China but not all the way. But above all what we have here is a Soviet–Indian naked power play to dismember a country. . . .

ROGERS: I'm not challenging that. I'm just saying that I think the president should think through very carefully each step from now on. . . . I think we shouldn't act just in petulance. Christ, obviously it's annoying and obviously she's [Gandhi's] been a bitch. . . .

President Nixon
December 5, 1971, no time
Kissinger wants a meeting to knock down Rogers's view that they were tilting too much toward China and sacrificing relations with India. He notes that India had been bent on attacking Pakistan and says the Soviets had done nothing to restrain them. Nixon ridicules the notion that he'd acted petulantly and Kissinger warns of the consequences of a "dismemberment of Pakistan" (though India probably had no such designs).[10]

... KISSINGER: I think we ought to have a meeting of some of your key advisers tomorrow . . . because Rogers has been talking about how we are sacrificing—he's on this Chinese kick again. . . . I think if we don't, there will be leakages that we just acted impetuously. . . . The basic problem, Mr. President, is it's clear that we can't do anything directly to change the situation, but to set it up on the ground that we are sacrificing our friendship to India—there is no friendship left. . . . The Indians were determined, Mr. President, they attacked at the earliest possible moment they could. . . . All this talk about Russian restraint that we heard all summer was complete poppycock.

NIXON: . . . Everything we've done, everything we've said to the Russians and Indians had no effect, is that really what we're saying?

KISSINGER: . . . Maybe if we had been much tougher, but for that we had no domestic position. But certainly everything we have said has been without effect and they have geared it towards a humiliation—towards a dismemberment of Pakistan. . . . And the effect of that will be on all other countries watching it is that the friends of China and the United States have been clobbered by India and the Soviet Union. And I don't see how we escape that by tacking towards India now.

NIXON: Nope. . . . What is State suggesting that we do?

KISSINGER: They're not; they are refusing to make a suggestion. . . . And that we shouldn't act impetuously.

NIXON: What the Christ are we impetuous about? . . . Like what, cutting off the arms? A little prinking thing like that; why, what about the cutting off of arms to Pakistan, that was impetuous too, huh? You know, it's ridiculous; there's nothing impetuous about any of this stuff.

KISSINGER: . . . If we collapse now, the Soviets won't respect us for it, the Chinese will despise us, and the other countries will draw their conclusions. . . .

President Nixon
December 5, 1971, no time
Nixon says he will not let bygones be bygones with the Indians after the crisis.

. . . NIXON: . . . We are not going to roll over after they have done this horrible thing. They [the State Department] are not going to roll over and say, "Now, India, everything will be like it was and we'll come help you again." And I mean we will cut the gizzard out and let the Russians come help the Indians. . . . The arguments from the *New York Times* and others will be "We will buy ourselves a century or decades of hatred and suspicion from the Indian people." Bullshit! What has $10 billion of foreign aid bought us? . . . But hatred and suspicion from the Indian people.

KISSINGER: Exactly.

NIXON: Tell me one friend we've got in India, do you know any?

KISSINGER: Exactly.

NIXON: How about putting it that way? Just as cold as that. . . .

John Connally
December 5, 1971, no time
Nixon was convening an NSC meeting the next day to instill discipline in his troops and had ordered Kissinger to get Treasury Secretary Connally to follow the proper line on the crisis.[11] *Kissinger loads the dice in favor of it.*

KISSINGER: John, I wanted to call you because the president is going to assemble a group of the NSC tomorrow at 1:30 about the India–Pakistan situation. . . . Let me tell you what the issues are . . . and where the president tends to be leaning, but that's not in any way to prejudice your judgment. The basic problem is, now that the Indians have launched a full-scale attack into East Pakistan, how we should tilt. Now, the argument that State is making doesn't make any difference anyway, it's too late . . . [that] we will just drive the Indians into the Soviet arms if we get tough. . . . The thing that concerns the president and me is this: here we have Indian–Soviet collusion, raping a friend of ours. Secondly, we have a situation where one of the motives that the Chinese may have had in leaning towards us a little bit is the fear that something like this might happen to them. . . . So that some demonstration of our willingness to stand for some principles is important for that policy. Thirdly, if the Soviets get away with this in the subcontinent, we have seen the dress rehearsal for a Middle Eastern war. . . . What the president's tentative view is is to start throttling the economic aid program to India. . . . What do we get from them? . . .

CONNALLY: We don't get a goddamn thing.

KISSINGER: And when people say that we're driving them into Soviet arms, what does that mean operationally? . . . What more can they do than what they are doing? . . . And I think we have to show that it's too risky to kick us in the teeth. . . . So that is the way the issue may come up. . . .

N. A. M. Raza
December 8, 1971, 2:47 p.m.
Kissinger asks Pakistan's ambassador to stop sending cables on illegal arms shipments to Pakistan from Iran and Jordan.

. . . KISSINGER: Two things. One, tell your people to stop all cable traffic with respect to help on ammunition and so forth. We are doing what we can and we will send a coded message. It's getting too dangerous for you to send it. I will keep you informed. . . . We are here to support you. . . . I can give you news that we are getting something out of the shah for ammunition. You can send a cipher through me. . . .

Richard Helms
December 8, 1971, 6:10 p.m.
Kissinger and the CIA director discuss getting planes from Jordan or Iran, both of which supplied fighter planes, to Pakistan.[12]

KISSINGER: . . . Did you see the message from your [sanitized] station?
HELMS: Yes.
KISSINGER: We think we should go with this in the following way. We could never get the bureaucracy here to approve such a step.

[Series of sanitized exchanges.] . . .

> KISSINGER: I would go to a meeting tomorrow morning and browbeat them into acceptance but stop short of saying okay.
>
> HELMS: That's doable. The greatest problem with this thing is the leak problem, in my opinion. These foreigners will stand up to it but it will come out in this town. If this fellow goes ahead there will be suspicions at State and other places.
>
> KISSINGER: I will tell Alex Johnson to get State to keep their mouth shut. I have bullied them before. . . .
>
> HELMS: I think it will cause a hoo-ha and there will be a lot of cries against it, but it seems to be the only thing we can do. . . .
>
> KISSINGER: Is it the right thing to do or should we just stand down?
>
> HELMS: . . . On balance it's the right thing to do. It will make our problems [sanitized] increasingly difficult but I don't give a damn about that. . . . With Muslim helping Muslim, I would think we should try it.
>
> KISSINGER: If we do nothing we will surely lose. If we do something and do it daringly enough and do other simultaneous steps, we might get the Russians to call a halt to their games. . . . If Pakistan loses anyway we will be in a position to show our friends in the area a line that is not meaningless.
>
> HELMS: If not for that, I would advise against it. It's useful for the longer haul. . . .

N. A. M. Raza

December 8, 1971, 7:10 p.m.

Kissinger is adamant about maintaining secrecy on the illegal weapons shipments to Pakistan.

> KISSINGER: I just wanted to tell you for your own information and slight peace of mind that we are working very actively on getting military equipment to you—but for god's sake don't say anything to anybody! . . . I will explain to you about ammunition and airplanes. . . . Don't communicate that. . . .

N. A. M. Raza and Zulfikar Ali Bhutto

December 11, 1971, 7:28 p.m.

Pakistan Ambassador Raza and Foreign Minister Bhutto, who Kissinger had urged that morning to "work out a common position with the Chinese,"[13] convey their subsequent discussions with the Chinese in New York. Raza and Bhutto want to know if the United States will stand up to the Soviets. When they note that Ambassador Bush met with a Bangladeshi representative, Kissinger claims that Bush didn't know he was Bangladeshi.

RAZA: We have talked to the Chinese. They say, "We are trying to do something. So far the Americans have not come out with anything except behind the scenes. . . . If we do come in, we might be left high and dry." That is their main worry. . . . I have to convey something of your reaction—whether you will come out with something so the world and the Russians know you are serious. They say the Russians are the biggest bluffers, and also the biggest cowards. They want to make use of others to fight their war. If they are openly challenged then they will come down. . . .

BHUTTO: . . . They said something about your own position—"We don't know whether the U.S. has effectively and firmly told the other people."

KISSINGER: Tell the other people firmly what?

BHUTTO: You cannot intervene and you must stop intervening and if you intervene, then we have obligations to Pakistan.

KISSINGER: We have done that. . . .

RAZA: The point is that I should assure the Chinese as to exactly how you consider coming out with something strong instead of just writing a letter. They quoted the example of Cuba [the missile crisis]. The Russians tried to blast through; when they were faced down by the U.S., they backed off. The same thing in the Middle East. They also brought up the point—"You tell us these things but Bush is meeting with Bangladesh people, and the State Department is hobnobbing with the Bangladesh."

KISSINGER: But you know we are not talking to the Bangladesh. . . . He received somebody he didn't know was Bangladesh.

RAZA: This is not my view. . . .

Zulfikar Ali Bhutto
December 11, 1971, evening
Kissinger advises Bhutto that he and Nixon don't look kindly on Chinese accusations that they aren't acting strongly enough toward the Soviets.

KISSINGER: I have talked to the president and here is our view on the subject. First, in the light of all we have done, it is absolutely essential that we are not exposed to Chinese charges that we are not doing enough. Because if that is going to be the charge, why should we do anything? I mean, we are standing alone against our public opinion, against our whole bureaucracy, at the very edge of legality. . . . Now, secondly, if we do not hear from the Soviets . . . by tomorrow morning in reply to the presentations we have made to them, we will then go to the Security Council with a strong statement that a continuation of the war would be a naked case of [Indian] aggression. . . . So your Chinese friends and our new Chinese acquaintances will have no reason to question where we stand. . . . One way you can help us is to make clear to the Chinese that we have been strong supporters. . . .

President Nixon

December 16, 1971, 10:40 a.m.

With Indian troops threatening Dacca, the commander of Pakistan's forces in East Pakistan had proposed a cease-fire, after which he surrendered, and Gandhi offered a cease-fire in West Pakistan. Kissinger felt Gandhi's decision was a result of Soviet pressure, which "grew out of" U.S. pressure.[14]

KISSINGER: The Indians have just declared a unilateral cease-fire in the West. We have made it. . . .

NIXON: It's the Russians working for us. We have to get the story out.

KISSINGER: Already a call from State. Until this morning we were running the UN thing. Now they are. . . . You pulled it through and should take credit. I will give a backgrounder tomorrow afternoon. . . .

NIXON: The average person doesn't understand about this. Pick the real movers and shakers. . . . President made own decision. . . .

President Nixon

December 16, 1971, 12:40 p.m.

A Cuban gunboat had fired on and seized a freighter in the Bahamas operated by a company in Miami owned by Cuban refugees. Cuba said the ship was a "well-known agent" of the United States and that the owners had connections with the CIA.[15]

NIXON: I don't know whether with the other thing you are aware of it, but a big story down here [in Key Biscayne] is the shoot-out. . . .

KISSINGER: Yes, I was following it yesterday and we scrambled planes. . . .

NIXON: The wife of the captured captain is out here at the gate and I'm going to go out and express my sympathy on it. We cannot have this situation where the Cubans can pick up a boat in Bahamian waters and shoot it up. Are we protesting?

KISSINGER: Yes, we moved four F-4s to Guantanamo.

NIXON: Is there anything wrong with my expressing sympathy on this?

KISSINGER: I would like to know first what it was doing there.

NIXON: It was not in Cuban waters or attacking.

KISSINGER: It could have been on a raid.

NIXON: It wasn't. But if it was, I'm for that too. . . . I want to take a hard line when Americans are being shot up. . . .

Melvin Laird

December 16, 1971, 4:15 p.m.

Laird is upset that he was not told about the White House's dispatch of the Coast Guard after the Cuban attack on the freighter. Kissinger blames Secretary of State Rogers.

LAIRD: There has been some sort of communication fall-down over here. Yesterday in the early afternoon there was an approval over at the White House for the Coast Guard to go in—

KISSINGER: The president is fit to be tied.

LAIRD: He should be. I was never notified that the president gave approval on that.

KISSINGER: We gave approval and the next thing I know is State is bellyaching. . . .

LAIRD: . . . I want to protect the Coast Guard but they never told me. They called after the MiGs had been scrambled. . . . If the president authorized the Coast Guard we have to back the Coast Guard up. I am upset about this. We should have gotten F-4s into Guantanamo when the Coast Guard went out. . . .

KISSINGER: The president said do it and I say do it. An hour later Rogers calls and says it cannot be [done].

LAIRD: It wouldn't have happened if I was there. But I was bypassed. . . .

President Nixon

December 16, 1971, 5:15 p.m.

Nixon is incensed at his administration's weak response to the Cuban attack and says if Cuban President Fidel Castro tries something like this again, "I want a plan to go in and shoot them up." He's not worried about violating international law.

. . . NIXON: . . . You tell the State Department and the others I want a report. . . . That I am goddamned mad. . . . You are trying to get the British and Panamanians to protest, and we'll protest it to no one, I suppose. . . . I want a contingency plan for this sort of thing in the future. If Castro gives us anything like this in the future I want a plan to go in and shoot them up. We do nothing but make a timid protest. You say we will be on the edge of the law and all that; that doesn't bother me. Does it bother you?

KISSINGER: No. We were going to go into the British territorial waters. We were giving orders here; the bureaucracy was having heart attacks and then darkness fell. We would have done it.

NIXON: What is the objection from the bureaucracy on this?

KISSINGER: Complaining about international law; saying we would be getting into an argument with the Russians. . . .

NIXON: I am writing a memorandum on this and on Allende which is for your Eyes Only so you will know in the future how far I am willing to go. . . .

President Nixon
December 26, 1971, 11:45 a.m.
Kissinger tells Nixon about the start of massive unrelenting bombing of North Vietnam, stretching from the DMZ to some 70–80 miles south of Hanoi, that would last five days. It was among the heaviest attacks on the North since the 1968 bombing halt.[16] *They also discuss an enemy offensive in Laos, peace negotiations, and India's problems in Bangladesh (formerly East Pakistan).*

KISSINGER: They got the strike off last night, Mr. President. . . . They had good weather and they got everything into the air. . . . They think they can get at least 48 hours [of bombing] and maybe as high as 72. . . . We had to do it. . . . In the Plaine des Jarres, they are stepping up the infiltration.

NIXON: . . . They may be trying to get to a bargaining position. . . .

KISSINGER: And I don't think they'll let it get to the election without a negotiation.

NIXON: Well, we're gunning through. We're gonna be awful hard to negotiate with, though, at this point. . . . Just put out a new peace plan. Then it'll get a big play, and then they'll not answer it and that's that. . . . This [strike] is the one that hits mainly in the Mu Gia Pass area and that sort of place?

KISSINGER: . . . It hits all the storage areas along the coast too, and we're gonna wind up with hitting Vinh. They're gonna take out all the airfields and . . . we're hitting both of these transshipment points. And the major point is just to show them that there is still a sting left.

NIXON: Yeah. . . . I notice that, you know, our Indian friends are having trouble, aren't they? They're now admitting that they've got to stay in Bangladesh for a few months, right?

KISSINGER: . . . No one likes the Indians. . . . I'd think they're gonna look worse and worse as time goes on.

NIXON: Well, don't you think a little of the fact that they've been terribly cruel and deceitful is beginning to get through? . . . They're doing exactly what I certainly expected, they're occupying East Pakistan, and I don't think they're ever gonna get out, do you?

KISSINGER: Occupying East Pakistan. There are more verified cases of the tragedies under their rules than there were under the Pakistan rule. . . .

Relations with India and Bangladesh, the Radford Leaks and JCS Spying Operation, in Nixon's Doghouse and Under Attack in the Press, Bemoaning Rogers and Talk of Resigning, Haldeman's Incendiary *Today* Show Charge, Preparing for the Enemy Offensive and Intensified Bombing in the South, and the China Summit and Shanghai Communiqué

January–February 1972

As 1972 began, Kissinger's relationship with Nixon was under great strain, and had been for weeks. To Kissinger's ire, he'd recently learned that a young navy yeoman had passed mountains of NSC documents to JCS Chairman Thomas Moorer as well as to the columnist Jack Anderson (including ones showing the administration's support for Pakistan and hostility to India that it was trying to keep quiet while professing even-handedness). But Nixon had not prosecuted the yeoman nor fired Moorer, and he suspected Kissinger's NSC office of the leaks to Anderson. Kissinger's relationship with Nixon had deteriorated over these issues, Kissinger's handling of the India–Pakistan crisis, and other matters, and Kissinger believed that White House staff and the State Department were leaking against him. He was outraged at the White House's—and that included Nixon's—failure to defend him while he was under attack in the press for the administration's India–Pakistan policy, his secrecy, and other issues. His integrity was being questioned. His myriad frustrations with Secretary of State Rogers were reaching a boiling point, but Nixon was sick of hearing about them. Kissinger considered resigning. "I am not going to wind up as an Ehrlichman—an errand boy in the White House," he assured his friend Nelson Rockefeller.

In January, Nixon and Kissinger decided not to reciprocate an approach by India to open talks to improve relations until after the China summit in February (China being an ally of India's enemy Pakistan). Rather, they would "let them work their way back slowly."

In a *Today* show interview broadcast on February 7, White House Chief of Staff H. R. Haldeman told Barbara Walters that Nixon's Vietnam critics were "consciously aiding and abetting the enemy." That was "not what I had in mind," Kissinger told Haldeman afterward. The administration was then girding for an enemy offensive in South Vietnam and carrying out the heaviest bombing there in months after Nixon told Kissinger he wanted "to concentrate in a massive way everything we have got" in the Central Highlands.

Nixon and Kissinger were also preparing for the China summit. Upon their triumphant return on February 28, Kissinger had to reassure the right that they had not sold out Taiwan.

President Nixon
January 1, 1972, 10:57 a.m.
Nixon and Kissinger hash out India and its problems and whether to recognize Bangladesh.

    ... NIXON: I just noted Mrs. Gandhi made a speech to the parliament and she still takes her line that foreign aid has really never aided them, that they've paid back every bit that they'd ever gotten. . . . She's taking the public line that we don't understand her. . . .

    KISSINGER: Yeah, but the Indians are master psychologists. They've got to deal with us. Literally now they're in worse shape than ever. . . . They put themselves on the Soviet side. . . . They in '67 cold-bloodedly decided they needed the Russians to deal with the Pakistanis, and that we just weren't enough of a factor in that area; that's when they made their move. But now their problem is they cannot permit, for their own domestic reasons—if the Russians become too influential in India, the Communist Party becomes too strong . . . they can't have that. Secondly, this problem of East Bengal is gonna become harder and harder for them; now they have the problem that Pakistan used to have.

NIXON: It's how the hell to feed 'em and govern them.

KISSINGER: . . . They can't govern their own Bengalis. . . . They kept yakking about martial law in Dacca, but there's martial law in Calcutta also.

NIXON: Yep. With regard to the question of recognition of Bangladesh . . . it's premature to talk about that, isn't it, about what we say?

KISSINGER: Well, first, Mr. President, no one has recognized Bangladesh except Bhutan and India. . . . The fact of the matter is that at this point the Chinese would take violent objection because of their parallels to Tibet and Manchukuo. . . . I would just say up to now there are only two countries that have recognized it, that this is not an acute issue. . . . Of course, we have a consul in Dacca [Archer Blood] who's already put up a map calling it Bangladesh.

NIXON: Yeah, I know, the same bastard who was there before, isn't it?

KISSINGER: Yeah.

NIXON: He's really an all-out Indian lover, isn't he?

KISSINGER: That's right. . . .

Gerald Warren

January 6, 1972, 5:48 p.m.

Navy yeoman Charles Radford had passed loads of NSC documents to JCS Chairman Moorer in what was essentially a spying operation on Kissinger and fed papers to Jack Anderson. But Nixon, who needed Moorer to circumvent Melvin Laird and was reluctant to take on the JCS and harm relations, had not taken punitive measures, and Kissinger's relationship with Nixon had degenerated over these matters, his tirades against William Rogers, his handling of the India–Pakistan crisis, his mood swings, and thus wear on Nixon. Kissinger, who believed White House staff were undermining him in the press, angrily takes up the Radford leaks and lack of White House support with White House Deputy Press Secretary Warren.[1]

KISSINGER: How do you answer the question that . . . the White House who prosecuted the Pentagon Papers will not condemn that these papers are leaked?

WARREN: I can't.

KISSINGER: Neither can I.

WARREN: I want to help. But I don't know how. We are in a perilous situation.

KISSINGER: We are not if we have some guts.

WARREN: Let's sit down and talk about it.

KISSINGER: I will not. With anybody.

WARREN: That's the problem.

KISSINGER: I am used to associating with people who help each other, but here
when my name is mentioned everyone goes underground.

WARREN: I want to help.

KISSINGER: I know you do. I will protect myself from now on.

WARREN: I think you should.

KISSINGER: I tell you as a press officer, it's inconceivable. . . .

WARREN: Herb Klein [the White House communications director] wants to
talk about the Anderson papers with you.

KISSINGER: I will not discuss it. Tell him it's the duty of colleagues to protect me and I will not discuss it. Tell him to discuss it with Ehrlichman and
Haldeman. . . .

Gerald Warren

January 10, 1972, 1:20 p.m.

*Kissinger feels that Warren's denial that he had resigned was not a strong enough
statement of White House support for him amid rumors of his resignation.*[2]

WARREN: I just denied that you submitted your resignation.

KISSINGER: I am proud of the strong support that's being given.

WARREN: . . . I want you to know I did do that.

KISSINGER: Isn't that generous of you. Do you consider it a sign of support? . . .

WARREN: It wouldn't have been a sign of support if I weaseled on it.

KISSINGER: It's worth two or three more sentences. Such as it's an absurd
suggestion that's not worthy of comment. . . .

William Safire

January 12, 1972, 10:45 a.m.

*Kissinger had given background interviews with favored journalists in response to
White House leaks against him over his handling of the Pakistan–India crisis and
other issues, and in response to the White House's deflection of criticism of its
Pakistan–India policy onto him and failure to defend him. Kissinger claims to White
House speechwriter Safire that the journalists were calling him. He worries about
doubts about his integrity. His reputation for being candid with reporters had taken
a hit.*[3]

SAFIRE: You have been talking to a lot of people. . . . Every time I run into
anybody they say "I spoke to Henry about that."

KISSINGER: Like who?

SAFIRE: [Washington correspondent for the London *Sunday Times* Henry]
Brandon, [syndicated columnist Rowland] Evans.

KISSINGER: They called me.

SAFIRE: [Max] Frankel.

KISSINGER: I haven't said a word to that son of a bitch Frankel.

SAFIRE: You didn't call him on Sunday?

KISSINGER: No, I told him I wouldn't see him. Evans called me about another story.

SAFIRE: Joe Kraft is doing a good job for you in a friendly way.

KISSINGER: I must say the people doing anything for me are the Democrats, the Kennedys, and Rockefeller. . . . What would you think of my giving a press conference on Friday regarding the charges against the president, not me [on their Pakistan–India policy]?

SAFIRE: That is giving something that is dying new life. . . . The *Times* would just do an editorial diminishing it, and that just lathers up something that is dying a slow death.

KISSINGER: Yes, but I don't want the issue of my integrity dying a slow death. . . . Someone has been backgrounding that the whole thing was a disaster. . . . I consider the actions of the Nixon group an outrage. All of the Nixon people in Washington would say anything. Once the tide has turned, Colson and company will be thumping it [support for him] out like crazy— when I don't need it anymore. I am sure the tide will turn, but because of my Democratic friends, my Kennedy friends, and Rockefeller. . . . Everyone has called me. I haven't called a single person. . . .

SAFIRE: You mustn't be uptight about this. . . .

KISSINGER: You don't quite understand what I am after. I don't give a damn about my position. I left the Kennedy administration in the heat of things [he had been a part-time consultant and left frustrated with his outside role][4]. . . . So I am not concerned about that. I am concerned about my moral integrity, because if I lose that there is no point in my doing the job. You know as well as I know, Bill, the reason this attack is possible at all is because the State Department has backgrounded the press that we suffered a horrible disaster in India–Pakistan. . . . Look, all of this is handleable. What is not handleable is the loss of integrity. . . . I have been acting as a lion tamer and now they smell blood. . . .

Nelson Rockefeller

January 14, 1972, 1:00 p.m.

Kissinger, who had recently complained to Haldeman about attacks against him by the State Department, while Secretary of State William Rogers had said that he didn't trust Kissinger because of his lying to him,[5] talks with Rockefeller about his battle with Rogers. They discuss whether he should resign, White House pressure to negotiate a treaty with Rogers, a possible White House statement of support, and Nixon's failure to defend him.

ROCKEFELLER: . . . I have been praying night and day that steps are taken to keep your continuity there. I had a long conversation with John [Mitchell] and he has the full picture.

KISSINGER: . . . I have to decide—as long as I am dealing with this sort of person [Rogers]—whether to put the national interest above this dancing around. They [the White House and Mitchell] are now placating me. . . . They are trying to work out a treaty with Rogers as if he were an equal to the president. . . .

ROCKEFELLER: I took it on myself to make very clear what ought to be done. The way it was left was the idea [a statement of support] was thought to be very good and on the right occasion would be done. . . .

KISSINGER: . . . I am not going to ask for it. . . . I am certain it will not be done. . . . Or if it is done it will occur at a moment when I don't need it. . . .

ROCKEFELLER: But for the country and the future, the situation should be brought into focus. What is going to happen next year will depend on the capacity to preserve your leadership in this key role. Between you and me, there is a very eminent psychiatrist. . . . He said should you depart there would be a major drop in the stock market.

KISSINGER: I will not do anything to upset the national interest if I can possibly avoid it. I will think about this matter another 10 days to two weeks. If I decide to make a move, I will talk to you first. . . . John thinks he's settled it. I was disgusted. I can't negotiate a treaty with the president of the United States. As a man I have been working with for three years who doesn't know what he has to do to back up his chief advisers. . . . I don't think there is any point in talking with John Mitchell. He thinks he has handled it masterfully. He tells me I have to show Rogers more things . . . but that isn't the problem. . . .

ROCKEFELLER: I don't understand what the reluctance is.

KISSINGER: It is psychiatric. . . .

ROCKEFELLER: Would it be misunderstood if I talked to the leader?

KISSINGER: Yes. What galls him is he knows my personal feelings for you, which are not necessarily matched. There is respect and loyalty but not necessarily affection. If you talk to him, he will think I put you up to it. . . . If we continue with these petty things, I will be degraded to the level of so many of my associates. . . . I am not going to wind up as an Ehrlichman—an errand boy in the White House. . . .

President Nixon

January 16, 1972, 1:00 p.m.

Kissinger reports that India is interested in improving relations, and they decide to recall U.S. Ambassador to India Kenneth Keating to Washington to keep him from moving too quickly on smoothing relations before the China summit.

. . . KISSINGER: . . . The Indian foreign secretary has approached Keating and has said they are interested in an improvement of relations and they are prepared to open talks. So it's going just the way we thought it would.

NIXON: Keating's probably standing on his doorstep every morning waiting now.

KISSINGER: . . . My recommendation, Mr. President, is we cannot do much now before we go to China because the Chinese are psychopathic. We ought to get Keating back for consultation. It's a good excuse to do it. He's had this approach and we just want to have a good talk.

NIXON: Yes, in the final analysis, of course, as we get towards election time, we want to improve relations with the Indians for American consumption. . . . But don't do a damn thing now. . . .

KISSINGER: Well, I predicted that by this time next year we'll have better relations with them than we had before the crisis, and I still maintain it. They need it for their own reasons. By July there'll be visible progress, so I think immediately now the thing to do is get Keating back, which is a conciliatory move and it puts a lid on it until we get back from China. . . . We'll just tell Rogers you want to talk to Keating in the light of reviewing the whole India situation. . . . It has another advantage, that Keating is going to leak all over the place that the Indians made this approach to us. . . . Which will quiet the press down a bit because it will at least prove that we didn't drive them toward the Soviets. . . . But I completely agree with what you said. That it would be a great mistake if we rushed toward the Indians now. Let them work their way back slowly.

NIXON: That's the way that Keating would do it, though. He'll say, "Gee, isn't this great. Now I can go in and make an offer of $300 million worth of aid." No, sir. He just comes home for consultation. . . .

H. R. Haldeman

January 25, 1972, 8:55 p.m.

Nixon gave a televised address that evening in which he put forward a new Vietnam peace proposal and revealed Kissinger's secret meetings with the North Vietnamese in Paris and offers they rejected.[6] *Kissinger exults that CBS correspondent Marvin Kalb's comments, which he had fed him and other journalists at a background briefing, "couldn't be better."*

KISSINGER: How was CBS?

HALDEMAN: . . . Kalb and [Eric] Sevareid were both extremely good.

KISSINGER: Really? Well, those are the ones we briefed.

HALDEMAN: . . . Kalb especially has been very positive.

KISSINGER: Well, we're dangling that interview in front of him.

HALDEMAN: Okay, well, we'll just keep it dangling.... [Dan] Rather said, now don't you agree that the headline out of this will be that the president still has failed to set a specific date for withdrawal.... Kalb said ... it's a very fair approach, but it's very difficult because he's asking the communists to have faith in an electoral process, where they want a deal, not an election.

KISSINGER: That's exactly what our brief said. ...

HALDEMAN: He said in the first place the president's proceeding with Vietnamization, and he's taking troops out.

KISSINGER: Terrific.

HALDEMAN: But he's also said he's not gonna abandon an ally.

KISSINGER: That couldn't be better.

HALDEMAN: And he said the White House has emphasized the sense of the moral obligation here.

KISSINGER: Beautiful. ...

Barbara Walters
January 29, 1972, 8:33 a.m.
The day before, Walters had taped an interview with Haldeman for the Today *show, which was broadcast 10 days later. Haldeman's statement to Walters that Nixon's critics on Vietnam were "consciously aiding and abetting the enemy" would be the lead story on all three TV networks.*[7]

KISSINGER: How was the Haldeman interview?

WALTERS: ... He was terribly easy and answered everything. He's of course obviously very aware of everything he said. He said at one point anyone who disagrees with the president on this is consciously aiding and abetting the enemy. I said, but there are several people in the Democratic Party who are running for office who are still disagreeing; are you saying they are aiding and abetting the enemy? He said yes. I said do you mean George McGovern is doing this consciously? He said I won't name names, but yes.

KISSINGER: Are you going to use that?

WALTERS: Yes. It was very hot in his office, he wanted his fire going. I don't see how he works in there like that. ... He had his secretary bring in his home movie camera. Then after it was all over someone was in his outer office and he said, "Here she is," and it was the attorney general and we talked. It was that kind of atmosphere. I said it wasn't an interview that would make any headlines. He said, "I've given you some headlines." ...

H. R. Haldeman
February 1, 1972, 7:25 p.m.

Kissinger says a meeting that the "snake" William Rogers was having with Soviet Ambassador Anatoly Dobrynin the next day could jeopardize not only the Soviet summit but the Middle East and Vietnam.

KISSINGER: . . . I found out that Rogers is seeing Dobrynin. I know this sounds again like we are starting a constant fight, but this is going to blow up the summit. . . . Somebody has to be in charge. To let this snake maneuver between the two of us—

HALDEMAN: What do we do?

KISSINGER: No discussions until after the summit. First of all, it is an insolent note. It is useless. To say that he will cover the subjects covered at other levels of government, that's me. . . . The trouble is it gives Dobrynin the chance to maneuver between us. . . . And no telling what Rogers will give on the Middle East. Then Dobrynin can take whatever is the softer version and whipsaw us with it. . . . I sent him a Brezhnev letter, deleting the references to me. Now I have got to call Dobrynin and tell him what he knows and doesn't know. . . . He is all for surfacing the May 31[1971, Vietnam peace] proposal. No one has asked for it. It will only get us in trouble. . . . If he has this meeting you can't tell what he will do. What worries me is the Russian summit. Everything we give him he turns into a goddamn fight. . . .

Barbara Walters
February 4, 1972, 5:35 p.m.
Kissinger is concerned about Walters's use of Haldeman's provocative remark in his Today *show interview.*

WALTERS: I will be in the office for another half hour. Finishing up on Haldeman.

KISSINGER: Are you going to kill him with that quote?

WALTERS: He knew what he was saying. I am running it on Monday.

KISSINGER: So it will be obvious that it's spirit of the administration. . . . You don't think it will get a headline?

WALTERS: I know it will. When he said there are several kinds of interviews and I don't do headline interviews, he said I have given you some headlines. . . . He knew what he was doing. . . .

President Nixon
February 5, 1972, 11:30 a.m.
Nixon condemns the conventional use of air power and suggests a massive application of it in the Central Highlands in South Vietnam. (The administration had recently decided to increase its bombing there, believing that during an expected offensive by the

North Vietnamese and National Liberation Front, they would attack in the area.) Five days later, U.S. fighter bombers carried out in the Central Highlands their heaviest air strikes in six months.[8]

NIXON: Let me ask you one thing. This will be rejected by Haig and the military because it is inconsistent with the traditional way of things. And you may reject it on the ground that [Ellsworth] Bunker, etc. rules it out. The use of air power. When you study war—any war—the military are horribly conventional. They are basically interested in seeing that everything is timed and can't be responsible for anything that goes wrong. . . . What we are doing at the present time is extremely routine—we send out a number of planes . . . we routinely hit them and do it better than ever because of lasers and better intelligence, but on the other hand there might be something to be said for a stand-down. I am speaking about the period before we return from China, and then have a day or two, weather permitting, to concentrate in a massive way everything we have got in, say, the B-3 area [of enemy operations in the Central Highlands].

KISSINGER: I think it is a good idea.

NIXON: . . . For 48 hours we will hit everything in the B-3 area; everything that might cripple the North Vietnamese and hurt their morale.

KISSINGER: I agree.

NIXON: This was the Churchillian strategy. . . . We are not in a position to do it on the ground with Americans. And the South Vietnamese don't have the guts.

KISSINGER: They don't have the resources. Laird hasn't presented this to you adequately. . . .

NIXON: This stand-down has its points psychologically—they will think they have to defend every place. Drop 3,000 tons in 24 hours on the B-3 area. We want to get a division, not just a battalion. . . . Can you get Haig thinking on this?

KISSINGER: Haig is a very creative thinker. We will just tell the damn military to have their own schedule. This is no problem.

NIXON: Abrams doesn't think creatively.

KISSINGER: No, he is a shell.

NIXON: Give him this responsibility to see that carriers are moving and the [B-]52s are moving. I don't want any bullshit. . . . I want the air force and navy to follow this without compromise. I want them to hit everything in the B-3 area or northern part of the DMZ. . . .

KISSINGER: . . . I think it has great merit and I will start on it immediately.

NIXON: Knock the hell out of them. One of the problems before was that they never concentrated on anything.

H. R. Haldeman
February 7, 1972, 12:02 p.m.
Kissinger raises Haldeman's "consciously aiding and abetting the enemy" remark in his Today *show interview, which was broadcast that morning.*

KISSINGER: You got yourself some publicity. . . .

HALDEMAN: Ten days ago it was a point we were trying to get out. When you pounded on the president saying we need to take the attack.

KISSINGER: I was just pulling your leg.

HALDEMAN: Who told me to go on the show to begin with?

KISSINGER: That was not what I had in mind. . . .

H. R. Haldeman
February 16, 1972, 9:45 a.m.
Kissinger is aghast at a cable that Rogers sent to U.S. embassies in Europe.

KISSINGER: I just wanted to tell you our mad secretary of state sent over a cable which, in effect, recognizes East Germany.

HALDEMAN: What?

KISSINGER: That should never be put into a cable before it is discussed in the NSC. It's another attempt to bust the system. I propose to draft a note for the president saying he wants a full discussion on that after we return.

HALDEMAN: You should.

KISSINGER: He is unbelievable. . . . This is a major decision and it basically builds a confrontation between him and the president. If it is disapproved, he can say he is a great hero. We should sell it to the Russians if we are going to do it. . . .

HALDEMAN: You will stop it?

KISSINGER: Yes. . . .

President Nixon
February 16, 1972, 10:50 a.m.
They consider what Rogers and Assistant Secretary of State Marshall Green should do while they are meeting with Chinese Premier Chou En-lai and Mao Tse-tung at the China summit. They also take up analyses of China's leaders and Mao's writings.

. . . NIXON: . . . I'm concerned we may not have worked out with the Chinese the division here that will give Rogers and Green enough to talk about. . . . Rogers and Green will be totally out of tune with the long discussions Chou and I will get into.

KISSINGER: Then they'll leak it when they are back.

NIXON: I can't have that kind of conversation when I get back. Do I understand that Chou will be in the meetings with Mao and you will be there?

KISSINGER: Yes. . . . He insists on having Chou there, and there will be a notetaker and I will be there and we'll have [Kissinger aide Winston] Lord.

NIXON: What about the foreign minister?

KISSINGER: He won't be there.

NIXON: I know it's going to be difficult for Bill. He'll meet Chou, but that's the way it's got to be justified, that it's Mao's way of having a meeting.

KISSINGER: That's right. I think Mao will want to meet the whole party, so he will meet him. But as far as the division is concerned, I think they should start on exchanges, diplomatic relations, and trade. Then let them discuss Formosa. It won't hurt Bill to see how tough they are. And then if there's anything left, let them discuss Korea.

NIXON: Okay, just so he feels he is discussing everything.

KISSINGER: Just give him that as a first assignment. I will just tell Chou— within limits Chou will instruct him. . . .

NIXON: . . . I looked at the CIA analysis of Chou and Mao—I think they both were quite superficial.

KISSINGER: CIA is awful. . . . The best one we have in the [briefing] book is the last one. . . . It was done by a member of my staff from Michigan University. He did a book on Mao; he knows him well. It puts down most of his thought. . . . That I recommend that you read. . . .

NIXON: . . . You read Mao's stuff and he is all over the lot. He isn't consistent.

KISSINGER: Except in his revolutionary fervor.

NIXON: Yes, but not his tactics. He doesn't trust the intellectuals, and on the other hand he doesn't trust the peasants because they aren't educated enough.

KISSINGER: His great skill is to play every group in order to keep the maximum ferment.

NIXON: Because he doesn't believe in peace. He believes that out of conflict, pain, and suffering—

KISSINGER: That's why he tore his country apart in the Cultural Revolution.

NIXON: Because he believes that is the only hope to achieve something.

Barry Goldwater

February 28, 1972, 10:10 p.m.

Minutes after reaching his office upon returning from the China summit, Kissinger tries to assure conservative Senator Goldwater that the joint Shanghai Communiqué released at the end of the summit—which said the United States acknowledged that Taiwan was part of China and that its objective was the withdrawal of all U.S. forces there—did not mean U.S. abandonment of Taiwan.[9]

KISSINGER: I just briefly want to make a number of points about that communiqué. . . . The reduction of forces is merely a restatement of the Nixon Doctrine. . . . No condition of whether it would be this year or next.

GOLDWATER: Make it clear. . . .

KISSINGER: I said it on Chinese soil that the commitment was unimpaired and the president said it on his arrival tonight. . . . Taiwan is simply restated policy. . . .

GOLDWATER: Have him make it goddamn clear tomorrow. . . .

KISSINGER: The president will make it goddamn clear at the leaders meeting. . . .

GOLDWATER: . . . We will back him if he doesn't deviate from what he told us before he went over there. . . .

President Nixon

February 28, 1972, 10:55 p.m.

Nixon and Kissinger, who had phoned California Governor Ronald Reagan to mollify him on Taiwan after speaking to Goldwater, confer on the reactions of conservatives to the Shanghai Communiqué's pronouncements on Taiwan. Kissinger says they made a mistake including William F. Buckley among the journalists who'd accompanied them to China. (Though they'd hoped to win him over, he would condemn the communiqué.) They also discuss relations with the Soviets over the summit and Rogers's lack of enthusiasm for the communiqué. (He had been largely left out of the negotiations on it until the end and left out of the key negotiations generally at the summit.)[10]

. . . NIXON: The Taiwan thing—I think what has happened on Taiwan is the *Washington Post* coming out and saying Nixon agrees to withdraw from Taiwan.

KISSINGER: Reagan says there has been a little trouble with the evening papers there. . . . He never doubted you. He read the communiqué and knew this is our policy, the Nixon Doctrine. . . . The only other thing he would suggest is that we plant a question for Ziegler tomorrow asking, "What about our defense commitment?" and then we could answer, "As Dr. Kissinger said in Shanghai and as the president said last night, the defense commitment still stands."

NIXON: Think we should do that. Good.

KISSINGER: Barry Goldwater is a little more difficult. He wants to make sure you explain it properly tomorrow morning to the leaders. . . . Reagan congratulated you. He said this was one of your greatest weeks as president. Nancy [Reagan] was equally enthusiastic.

NIXON: She was? Reagan can see it in terms of political impact, in terms of television impact. . . . Bill [Buckley] has quite an influence.

KISSINGER: We made a mistake taking him. . . . There would have been a lot of columns he couldn't have written if he hadn't been along.

NIXON: I don't know how to handle him unless I just don't have anything else to do with him.

KISSINGER: Never take your opponents.

NIXON: Just never take your enemies; I've told Haldeman that a thousand times.

KISSINGER: . . . Last week the Russians sent us a message saying, "What's going on? You keep criticizing us."

NIXON: We aren't criticizing them.

KISSINGER: I sent them a message saying, "Quiet down; we are serious about pursuing a détente." Since then there have been no opposing articles, and TASS [the Soviet news agency] so far has communicated only in a very factual way.

NIXON: Get a meeting with Dobrynin, and it's probably worth it to bring him in to see me for a few minutes. . . .

KISSINGER: What worries me is these sons of bitches, they may get word to Peking that they met with the president as soon as he came back.

NIXON: You see him. . . . Tell him the president said he does want to see you prior to the trip. He wants to have a good off-the-record meeting with you to get your advice. Set it up for a little private dinner.

KISSINGER: My experience with the Russians is that you never lost by having a dinner.

NIXON: Hang that out there. Let him get the word to his government that he will be seeing the president. . . . Poor Rogers. I think you are right; he will be for this after the public reaction. We didn't stack that audience [a large crowd that greeted Nixon at the airport]. . . . They were with us; they started to clap when the plane drove up.

KISSINGER: And the cabinet was there. . . . They never have been out when things are tough. Elliot Richardson said this was a diplomatic master stroke.

NIXON: He sees it. Why didn't Bill see it?

KISSINGER: Because he doesn't have that sort of mind. . . .

John Scali
February 29, 1972, 5:50 p.m.
Nixon adviser Scali and Kissinger make fun of Rogers's performance at the summit.

. . . SCALI: You know, when he talked like that I wanted to slide under the table.

KISSINGER: You know, and when he talked about his meeting with the foreign minister—

SCALI: Yes, I sat through all of that, you know, and one of his assistants said, "Wasn't he great!," and I said, "I don't know. It seems like they're stalling for time while more important things are being done." You know, I could read the same things in the Peking newspaper. . . . Rogers, thinking he was really saying something great, said, "Mr. Foreign Minister, when you have a problem why don't you pick up the telephone and call me. Other foreign ministers do that all the time." I almost fell off the chair. Later, I was asked if he was serious when he said that. . . .

President Nixon
February 29, 1972, 9:00 p.m.
They ridicule Rogers's view that they had been "taken in" by China at the summit.

. . . NIXON: I talked to Haig. He said Rogers thought that you and I had been taken in by the communists. Hell, taken in!! Do you think that he thinks that you or I can be taken in?

KISSINGER: His mind is mixed up.

NIXON: For Christ's sake, Henry, could you ever be taken in? Could I ever be taken in? Will Bill never learn?

KISSINGER: This is a cold-blooded game; we need it for the Russians. If it serves the purpose, we will go against the Chinese. . . .

The Enemy Offensive in South Vietnam—U.S. Bombing and Shelling of the North, Weather Delays, Bombing in the South, Discord with Abrams and Laird, Expanding the Bombing Northward, Rolling Out the B-52s, and the Heavy Weekend Bombing of Haiphong and Hanoi; Kissinger's Secret Trip to Moscow; and Nixon's Threats to Cancel the Summit and Blockade the North

March–April 1972

On March 30, 1972, the anticipated enemy offensive in South Vietnam finally began. Thousands of North Vietnamese troops crossed the DMZ and with National Liberation Front troops forced South Vietnamese troops to retreat in disarray. Kissinger advised Nixon before the offensive that they "blast the bejesus out of" the North once it began, and while Nixon wasn't sure how much psychological impact bombing would have on Hanoi by this point, Kissinger said not hitting the North would look "psychologically weak," and Nixon knew they had to make it count. "The more we shock them, the better," Kissinger said.

While waiting for infuriating cloud cover to lift that was holding up all-out bombing in both North and South Vietnam, they authorized naval attacks above the DMZ—Nixon subsequently ordered them further and further north, and heavier, with mounting vehemence and frustration—partly for the psychological effect on Hanoi. He pressured Kissinger to get it done. Piqued by the holdup on unrestricted bombing (Nixon and Kissinger never knew if the military and the devious Melvin Laird were using weather as a pretext for keeping the planes on the ground), Kissinger lambasted the air force and wanted "a new secretary of defense" and a makeover of the military. Laird and Commander Creighton Abrams both wanted the bombing focused on the South, where the battle was, rather than the North. Nixon ordered JCS Chairman Thomas Moorer to unleash B-52 bombers for heavy strikes despite the cloud cover in both South and North Vietnam. "You'll hit something," he said breezily.

The administration undertook large-scale, intensive bombing in the North that ratcheted northward despite the poor weather. Still, Nixon complained that the military wasn't carrying out his orders, and he and Kissinger castigated its incompetence and lack of imagination. "Short of nuclear arms and getting too close to China, we have got to do what is necessary," Nixon declared. The administration reportedly first used B-52s in the North at this time; the point was "to show we are prepared to do massive escalation and warn the Soviets," Kissinger said. As Laird pointed out, the B-52 bombing of Vinh was not accurate; indeed, it was off a kilometer. Nixon and Kissinger questioned whether the Soviet summit could take place from a position of weakness in Vietnam, with Soviet arms killing Americans.

During the weekend of April 15–16, waves of fighter bombers and B-52s struck the Haiphong and Hanoi areas in a heavy attack. Abrams still wanted the bombing focused on the South and opposed it. Kissinger told Nixon that, despite the bombing, Soviet Ambassador Anatoly Dobrynin was "slobbering" to him over Vietnam and his secret trip to Moscow to prepare for the Soviet summit and discuss Vietnam, SALT, and other matters. Kissinger and Nixon both took pleasure in the intense bombing of Haiphong and Hanoi. "You see, they can't see the B-52s and they dropped a million pounds of bombs," Kissinger crowed. Nixon threatened to blockade the North and "starve them out if necessary." "I couldn't agree more," Kissinger replied.

Ronald Ziegler
March 9, 1972, about 4:00 p.m.
Kissinger tells Press Secretary Ziegler that under no circumstances should Kissinger's mother or father talk to a reporter about him.

ZIEGLER: AP doing a three-to-four-part series on you and want to talk with
your mother.

KISSINGER: No.

ZIEGLER: She said it would have to be checked with you.

KISSINGER: She is a menace. I have an 85-year-old child for a father. He is naive
on what they will write. He will tell everything about my youth. . . . I let them
[other journalists] photograph them and she gave them baby pictures of me
that made me look like a mongoloid idiot. I am very fond of them but they
are completely grounded. . . .

President Nixon

March 10, 1972, 5:30 p.m.

Nixon and Kissinger discuss the approaching enemy offensive in South Vietnam.

. . . KISSINGER: I think it is possible they will attack in the next 10 days. . . .

NIXON: We ought to start our preventive—

KISSINGER: I think we ought to wait until they attack, then blast the bejesus
out of them. Then surface these talks again.

NIXON: Yes, I agree.

KISSINGER: I think we should clobber them in the North.

NIXON: You understand the Chinese will take us on for that.

KISSINGER: Well, we don't owe them anything. . . .

President Nixon

March 11, 1972, 11:10 a.m.

*Kissinger reports that U.S. bombing in South Vietnam was going full-bore, but Nixon
wants him to "pound" JCS Chairman Thomas Moorer on it. Nixon questions whether
bombing the North will do much good, but Kissinger says not bombing would look soft.
If they do it, they "have got to make it worthwhile," Nixon says.*

. . . KISSINGER: In South Vietnam they are going full blast.

NIXON: Are we trying to concentrate in the B-3 [Central Highlands] area, or
just dallying around as usual? . . . I understand they can't hit everything, but
if they will just hit something instead of just sporadically.

KISSINGER: They are doing 50 percent more now than before the NSC meeting. I will give Moorer a call.

NIXON: Pound him in terms of hitting the South—that is where supplies and
personnel are. Get in there and do something about it.

KISSINGER: If they find military things in the DMZ north of the line, that is
technically North Vietnam but it is a violation of the DMZ.

NIXON: Yes. I think the North Vietnamese strikes can come. I don't think they are going to do a lot of good, but if they come have them come after the offensive breaks.

KISSINGER: I think so, because then we can put it on the basis that they tricked us. We made every effort to talk to them. We told them there would be no escalation and nevertheless they hit us. . . . We could just hit them. We told the Chinese and the Russians we would do it.

NIXON: That's right. The point of hitting them we have to weigh in terms of what good it does. As far as psychological good, I don't know at this point.

KISSINGER: I think not hitting them would be psychologically weak.

NIXON: In that case we do it, but if we do it we have got to make it worthwhile. Since they sent those MiGs up we should take out two or three airfields.

KISSINGER: . . . I think in the Dong Hoi area about 30 miles north of the DMZ. . . . We should do it not more than three days or a two-day package and let it sit for a while.

NIXON: It doesn't make any difference whether two or five, two is enough psychologically. . . . The psychological effect would be just hitting the North. But it is not going on for several days. . . . They don't have the weather problem, do they? Or do they always have the weather problem?

KISSINGER: We haven't had a month they didn't have the weather problem. . . .

William Rogers
March 16, 1972, 9:40 a.m.
Rogers and Kissinger discuss an announcement that day that the Soviet summit would begin on May 22. Rogers doesn't want to play second fiddle in Moscow as he did in China. They also take up a column by Jack Anderson reporting that U.S. Ambassador to France Arthur Watson got drunk on a flight to Washington, kept shouting for more Scotch, grabbed stewardesses, tried to stuff money down their blouses, and then finally passed out in the first-class section.[1]

ROGERS: On this business about the Qs and As today on the Soviet Union trip, I am perfectly prepared to be reasonable about how we state it, but I don't want it to appear that we in the State Department are only doing routine things. . . . They sent me something that said the State Department will handle diplomatic matters which will be okayed at the White House.

KISSINGER: What do you think we should say?

ROGERS: Well, first, this is a coordinated effort under the direction of the president, that the diplomatic and substantive matters will be handled the normal way by the State Department with full cooperation of Dr. Kissinger and his staff. . . . I think it gives us more of a chance to say this is a cooperative effort. The reason China was different was because we didn't have diplomatic relations with them. . . . I think this is important because there has been so much speculation. . . . I called Haig about the Watson thing. . . . We are going to try to turn off all comment. . . .

KISSINGER: That was a juvenile performance. It doesn't make one too confident, but the president really feels we ought to back him completely.

ROGERS: We don't have a choice at the moment.

KISSINGER: But if he does it again we have another situation.

ROGERS: It's wealthy men who are exposed to this sort of thing. It's only those like Nelson [Rockefeller] who keep their cool.

KISSINGER: And he flies in a private plane. . . .

President Nixon
March 16, 1972, 10:05 a.m.
They express skepticism about the Watson incident and Nixon talks of "fags" at State.

. . . NIXON: It's a hell of a lot better to get drunk than to take drugs. And chasing girls—that's the biggest bunch of [obscenity]. I believe somebody may have been mad enough to say something like that, but I don't believe it. My god, Anderson—any time he gets something like that he prints it. . . .

KISSINGER: That's why I didn't raise it with you, Mr. President. I don't believe it either.

NIXON: The State people are going to do something about it. They will do anything to get one of their people in and get ours out. They're all fags. They don't do anything about it if one of their guys is caught chasing another fellow down the street. . . .

Ronald Ziegler
March 31, 1972, 4:17 p.m.
Kissinger tells Press Secretary Ziegler he will not do an interview with CBS's Marvin Kalb because "it's been handled in the most tawdry, cheap fashion."

. . . KISSINGER: Listen, with the elections coming you people are not going to get me on television. What you want is for me to go up and praise the president on the China trip. The most useful thing we can do is that we show people that competent, first-class people are at the heart of affairs. . . .

ZIEGLER: I know that you were encouraged to do it.

KISSINGER: . . . It is a question of stupid, petty crap. Actually from my own point of view, it is good not to do it. I don't need it for my publicity. As a matter of fact it is a liability to me personally. This administration has always projected a cheap picture. . . . I am not going to get involved in the campaign in that direction. . . . I am not going to do it now because I think it's been handled in the most tawdry, cheap fashion.

President Nixon
April 3, 1972, 7:10 p.m.
The enemy offensive in South Vietnam had begun several days earlier, and North Vietnamese and National Liberation Front troops were forcing South Vietnamese troops to retreat in disorder. Nixon and Kissinger decide to authorize naval attacks in North Vietnam up to about 35–40 miles above the DMZ. Kissinger says if the cloud cover hampering bombing in both the South and North ever lifts, "they are going to pay a hell of a price. . . . I think we may get a settlement." Nixon wants to make sure Laird is on board with the bombing of the North, given that he and Commander Abrams wanted the bombing focused on South Vietnam, and raises leveling Haiphong. He feared a military defeat could cost him the presidential election and undermine his ability to negotiate with the Soviet Union and China.[2]

. . . NIXON: I was just wondering how they claimed to have gotten those tanks—just by accident?

KISSINGER: They got it partly with naval gunfire.

NIXON: Naval gunfire—that's safe enough for our boys.

KISSINGER: I think we ought to use naval gunfire in North Vietnam right up to the Dong Hoi area.

NIXON: Absolutely. Let's authorize it immediately. . . . Tell them to put naval gunfire along the whole road—it's by the sea. . . . Is the weather lifting? Is this a false report?

KISSINGER: I think if the ceiling gets up to 4,000 feet we can do a good job. No, no, the weather has been bad.

NIXON: . . . They claimed they knocked out 25 tanks.

KISSINGER: Twenty-seven tanks—cut it in half and we still have 15 tanks— and trucks.

NIXON: *Trucks.* Tanks are something!

KISSINGER: If the weather lifts early enough so that we can get in then they are going to pay a hell of a price.

NIXON: We will take out their tanks and artillery and they are going to have a hell of a time.

KISSINGER: We are going to have two weeks now that's going to be tough. In many ways this is a blessing.

NIXON: If the weather lifts it won't take two weeks.

KISSINGER: I think it will take a week or two. I think we may get a settlement out of this. . . . Laird has been crying all day. He wants to come over. I think we ought to let him come over tomorrow.

NIXON: Is he going to support this?

KISSINGER: Yes.

NIXON: He should come with Moorer. He should be worked over before he gets here. He has to be told we cannot lose here! I will do everything necessary, including taking out Haiphong.

KISSINGER: The more we shock them, the better.

NIXON: Is there anything we could do in the Haiphong area?

KISSINGER: I think it is still too early. I think the Russians will do something. They are not going to risk everything.

NIXON: They will risk summit, Berlin, German treaty—correct. . . .

President Nixon
April 3, 1972, 7:25 p.m.
Nixon orders that the navy be mobilized in force and to "bombard the hell out of that place."

NIXON: I wanted to be sure that you realize I think the idea of the navy is good—that means going in 40 miles. . . . Moorer will love the idea. Just tell him to get every damn ship out and bring that thing from the Indian Ocean. They can also send their carrier aircraft in and bomb that road.

KISSINGER: If they can get carriers and destroyers in there they can help Quang Tri [which was under siege in northern South Vietnam].

NIXON: Also, a huge naval movement would be noticed. Call Moorer right now. You don't have to send that through Laird.

KISSINGER: We will let him know.

NIXON: Okay, just let him know. Bombard the hell out of that place. . . .

KISSINGER: I think we can break their back now.

Nelson Rockefeller
April 4, 1972, 2:28 p.m.
Kissinger grouses that the holdup on the bombing of the North is "a disgrace."

. . . ROCKEFELLER: . . . Has the weather cleared up?

KISSINGER: Not yet. You know, we have a great air force. They can only fly over a desert in July. We tried to have them fly in November and they couldn't, in December and they couldn't, and now it's April and they can't do it. . . . I tell you, in the new term we need a new secretary of defense and redo our military establishment. This is a disgrace. I tell you, before the two weeks are up the North Vietnamese will know they had a war.

ROCKEFELLER: Good. I am waiting for Haiphong.

KISSINGER: Well, we are thinking along those lines. . . . We have got to bring our rebellious bureaucracy into line again. . . .

President Nixon

April 4, 1972, 8:45 p.m.

Kissinger is immensely frustrated about the holdup on the bombing, as they've "got this thing at the breaking point." "Mr. President, our major thing now is to get across to the Russians, to the Chinese, and to Hanoi that we are on the verge of going crazy," he told Nixon earlier that day.[3] Nixon again raises the possibility of hitting Haiphong and suggests focusing the bombing for now on South Vietnam.

NIXON: Wondered if you had had any reports on the weather.

KISSINGER: I was just calling Moorer. His report was it would be like today, with some holes opening up in the afternoon. It is heartbreaking. They have got the authorities, they've got the toughest president they are going to have, and the bastards can't go! They have started the shelling tonight.

NIXON: That will get a little shot across the bow, but that's about all. . . . They think it is going to break any time?

KISSINGER: Clear a little in the afternoon. Whenever it breaks, it's going to break!

NIXON: All hell will break loose. That's the time to give it to them. . . .

KISSINGER: Got this thing at the breaking point.

NIXON: I want you to go forward with the Haiphong thing. It intrigues me very much. Popping a couple in there would be useful. The weather up there is all right, isn't it?

KISSINGER: Yes. . . . I think it would be better if we waited. When other bombing—

NIXON: I agree, but if we are going to be stuck here too long—

KISSINGER: Not much more than 24 more hours. [Then] do something dramatic. . . . If we could just get these air force guys to fly. . . .

NIXON: Well, how about concentrating in the B-3 area?

KISSINGER: That they are doing.

NIXON: Since it is closed in, give a [big] strike to the B-3 area. . . .

Thomas Moorer

April 5, 1972, after 4:00 p.m.

Kissinger encourages Moorer to step up the bombing in both South and North Vietnam, particularly the latter, before the Provisional Revolutionary Government of the National Liberation Front makes another peace proposal.

KISSINGER: Two things—you noticed the PRG is holding a press conference tomorrow. If they come in now with a peace offer before we hit them we'll look awful.

MOORER: We are hitting all we can.

KISSINGER: The president asked, unless they have moved Route 1 [which traversed North and South Vietnam], we ought to know where it is.

MOORER: We know. They are shelling it.

KISSINGER: Why can't we bomb up and down it by instruments?

MOORER: We can.

KISSINGER: But we are not. . . . There's no law against going into North Vietnam along Route 1 either. . . . We have to start working them over. . . . We have to give the North Vietnamese a big clout. . . . John Vogt is going to be ready to go Friday? . . . If he doesn't know what's wanted we have got to get a civilian in there. . . .

President Nixon

April 5, 1972, 7:00 p.m.

Nixon wants to put some fire in the belly of incoming air war commander General John Vogt and is still raring to bomb Haiphong. He orders naval shelling expanded further up the coast of the North since the bombing was held back by the weather. "They haven't really shelled anywhere," Kissinger says. "You tell Moorer to get off his ass," Nixon commands. "Shell it now!" he bellows, referring to Dong Hoi, some 40 miles above the DMZ. He wants it "destroyed."

NIXON: When is Vogt going out there?

KISSINGER: Friday night. We could have him come down to Key Biscayne.

NIXON: . . . I would like to have him come down and I should talk with him before he goes. . . . I really want him worked over, dressed down. Tell him the whole future of his profession is involved here. . . . I think we are in the position where we could hit the Haiphong area. The public attitude may be such that we go now—they asked for it. I believe we could give it to them good.

KISSINGER: The first thing we should do is cripple this area so that we tie up the supplies into the battle zone. Then we should give one goddamn shot to Haiphong.

NIXON: Can I ask you to do one thing immediately? The restriction with regard to the 19th parallel doesn't include naval gunfire. Have naval gunfire take the road clear up to Haiphong. It is precise—it hits the road.

KISSINGER: Right now they don't have enough ships. . . . I think it is important to get the . . . area of the battle zones cleared up.

NIXON: So that they cannot reinforce. . . . You call Moorer. . . . Tell him to get his ass up to the . . . 21st parallel and shell the roads up there. . . . That isn't bombing the road, but it will be a signal. . . .

KISSINGER: They haven't really shelled anywhere north of the DMZ yet.

NIXON: Don't do it in a half-ass way like Johnson. If we are going to do it we are going to do it good. Get the goddamn ship above the DMZ and above the 18th parallel. Just so they fire shells on the road high up. Bombing is a problem—not naval shelling.

KISSINGER: We will pay the same price. My recommendation is to get something started that we can sustain.

NIXON: Yes, but right now there is a need for psychological [effect] too. We are waiting here and saying we want something we can sustain, wait until the weather clears, etc. In the meantime the psychological effect goes down. We need it tomorrow. You tell Moorer to get off his ass.

KISSINGER: I think we should shell Dong Hoi. That's about 40 miles up.

NIXON: They have not done it yet?

KISSINGER: They have not.

NIXON: I want a report. Naval ships can fire in the night—I know! Get up and shell Dong Hoi and I want them to report to me in the morning. Shell it now! . . . I know the psychological effect of this.

KISSINGER: I could not agree more. Dong Hoi I am strongly for. Because that's where they have POL and supply depots.

NIXON: Get the cruiser in. I want massive power and I want the place destroyed and do it now. . . .

Melvin Laird
April 5, 1972, 7:45 p.m.
Kissinger puts the heat on Laird and demands the naval bombardment of Dong Hoi—"you better get it done!" After Kissinger voices concern about hitting civilians, Laird says they will hit some but will go ahead. Laird, a devout Christian, says he'd been praying for the weather to clear up so they could expand the bombing in the North. It had been held up, he says, "because they have to watch out for civilian casualties—and massive."

KISSINGER: I just had a raging call from the president. He has talked to Reagan and Rockefeller and a number of others. No one can understand why we are not doing anything. . . . His view is that the military has been screaming that they have been hamstrung for a number of years. I don't want to hear from Abrams that he is field commander, because he [Nixon] is commander in chief. He is ordering tonight a naval bombardment of Dong Hoi and he wants it done by 10 o'clock tomorrow morning. . . . Somebody better get it into Abrams's head or he may not be field commander much longer.

LAIRD: We can get naval bombardment into seven miles there.

KISSINGER: We want storage areas and airfields bombarded. . . . Well, you better get it done! . . .

LAIRD: We will just tell them to do it regardless of what the consequences are.

KISSINGER: Just stay away from populated areas.

LAIRD: Bombing that way we will hit some population—but what the hell. We can do it. . . . If we had had 24 hours you would be proud of that air force.

KISSINGER: What do you mean 24 hours?

LAIRD: Clear weather. The A-6 is the only all-weather plane we have. It is a lousy way to operate. As far as Dong Hoi is concerned, we can hit the damn thing. The president has the idea that the naval—like bombing those islands in the Pacific during World War II—we can go some seven to 11 miles. But it is only every 10 rounds because it burns out the guns. But, what the hell, we can do it and we will do it.

KISSINGER: I would stay away from civilian casualties.

LAIRD: We will have some, but they can take the heat on that for a while. It will be forgotten in a couple of months. . . . The only way you can be sure is with air.

KISSINGER: We are talking about gunfire.

LAIRD: There will be some civilian casualties. I have all the statistics on that but I won't bother you with that. We can do it. Let's do it. . . .

KISSINGER: We want some effective action.

LAIRD: You will get all you want if you give me 12 hours—I have been praying. . . .

KISSINGER: But don't have civilian casualties.

LAIRD: I can't guarantee you that, Henry! . . . This is a great opportunity when they [enemy troops] are out in the open. . . . But according to my notes we must be sure it is massive. . . .

KISSINGER: I don't want to hear requests of authority when these guys aren't doing anything. They keep yakking about authority and are not using what they have.

LAIRD: But do you know why? . . . Because they have to watch out for civilian casualties—and massive.

KISSINGER: Okay, Mel.

Thomas Moorer and President Nixon
April 5, 1972, 9:27 p.m.
Nixon orders Moorer to unleash the B-52 bombers for heavy strikes, even "on the boondocks," despite the cloud cover, in both South and North Vietnam. The next day, hundreds of fighter bombers carried out heavy raids up to some 50–70 miles above the DMZ and below the DMZ.[4]

. . . NIXON: See, Tom, the thing I want you to do, now on the B-52s . . . for psychological reasons, now let's forget the cloud cover and all the rest and so forth, have them fly at 95,000 or 110,000 feet and drop their goddamn bombs on the boondocks, but get 'em. I want a hell of a lot of sorties flown by B-52s today, is that clear?

MOORER: Yes, sir.

NIXON: Get those 52s flying now at least, let 'em do it around the B-3 area. That's open, isn't it? . . . I don't wanna see another report with 16 sorties of B-52s. I want the enemy to know that we're really letting 'em have it. So, get 'em in there now. . . . We've got to have it for psychological reasons; we can't have this, what appears to be a pusillanimous effort. . . . We have to have some sort of massive strike in the next 12 hours, 24 hours. . . . And it doesn't have to be in that area of the battle even, put the damn thing down in the B-3 area, put the 52s in there and just knock the bejesus out of them. You'll hit something. . . .

President Nixon

April 8, 1972, 10:45 a.m.

After Kissinger gives Nixon results of the bombing in the South, Nixon says they need to send a "signal" to the North and wants 200 planes to strike there despite bad weather. They are both itching to use the B-52s. Nixon orders Kissinger to "take Vinh out," nearly 150 miles north of the DMZ—it was soon hit—to bomb North Viet-namese airfields and "do something to let them know we aren't screwing around." He and Kissinger castigate the military's incompetence.

 . . . KISSINGER: They are beginning to round up the bomb damage estimate. These massive air strikes are doing considerable good. . . . In the B-3 area 350 dead in one area just with air strikes. . . . Weather bad again over North Vietnam.

NIXON: So Moorer knocked off his strikes up there again? . . . We have got to have something that is a signal. . . . What became of the ones I told to go out there? I want 200 out there. Tell Moorer I am raising hell about this. Before we let ourselves in for any more double-talk, are they going to do [B-]52 strikes over some part of North Vietnam or not? . . . We haven't done one thing in the North that we shouldn't have done before. That is the trouble with these people.

KISSINGER: We need something to show that the old rules don't apply.

NIXON: What about the trucks? . . . If they are there let's hit that. . . . Have they come up with any goddamn idea or not?

KISSINGER: They have found one other point in North Vietnam suitable for [B-]52 attacks. . . . Another thing we can order is to give them the right to attack all planes in the air from the 20th parallel down. . . . And knock out some of the airfields there. But there is an argument to knocking out some of these MiGs because they are getting ready to deploy them into the South.

NIXON: Knock them out. But I don't think they have carried out any of the things I have ordered. . . . They have 200 here, 200 there, and farted around here and there. I am really getting damned disgusted with this thing.

KISSINGER: The fact is that the North Vietnamese are not advancing and I think we are going to break their backs.

NIXON: Now is the time to hit them. . . . I think we must right now do things there for American public opinion. It will be with us if we act strongly. . . .

KISSINGER: They are going to attack with the B-52s if I have to sit in the chiefs' office all day today myself. . . .

NIXON: What in the name of god have they done? . . . The truck parks would be worth it; in addition to that they could put a 52 in the battle area.

KISSINGER: We could have a 52 strike on Dong Hoi and that is the battle area.

NIXON: What about Vinh airfield? Is that still off-limits?

KISSINGER: We can extend the authority up there. It is right now off-limits.

NIXON: Take Vinh out. . . . Take it out immediately.

KISSINGER: In that case the best thing is to give them the authority to take out the airfields south of the 20th parallel.

NIXON: Let's go on that right away, Henry. Don't fool around. . . . Short of nuclear arms and getting too close to China, we have got to do what is necessary. Don't any of these people understand that?

KISSINGER: They don't understand the political elements. . . .

NIXON: That is my job. . . . They just carry out the orders. Give them the airfields. They don't have to have clear weather. . . . From the standpoint of American domestic psychology right now, they want us to do something we haven't done before. They want the enemy to be outraged. From the standpoint of the North Vietnamese we have got to do something to let them know we aren't screwing around.

KISSINGER: Absolutely. . . . We have to give them an absolute shock now. There are 43 more 52s they can now send out but they will have only half the bomb capacity of the present ones.

NIXON: That's great—are they saying we can't use them?

KISSINGER: They are wailing around, but I think we should use them.

NIXON: Isn't it frustrating to work with such—

KISSINGER: It is not to be believed. . . . They are all bureaucrats. Here they have a president who is begging them to do something and they have no ideas.

NIXON: With Moorer I would be very strong. . . . We can get Moorer on the phone and give him the authority to hit those airfields. He doesn't get the authority to hit those airfields unless they are going to hit them in bad weather.

KISSINGER: I think we should make it conditional on a 52 strike.

NIXON: We have got to make them fly some of the stuff in bad weather.... Can you think of anything else? You and Haig have been sitting there. I hope you have thought of something.

KISSINGER: We thought of the truck parks.... I think we are going to make somebody back off. If the South Vietnamese don't crack.

NIXON: If they don't crack this will be worth it, but they are not going to crack. Abrams couldn't have done that bad a job.... More wars have been lost by political leaders relying on commanders than I can possibly count.... After what they did to us in Laos, we are not going to rely on Abrams.

Melvin Laird
April 9, 1972, 10:40 a.m.
Laird advises against anyone talking on open phone lines about forthcoming B-52 strikes in the Vinh area of North Vietnam and points out that there will be civilian casualties. The administration reportedly first used B-52s in the North at this time.[5]

LAIRD: Henry, would you caution everybody not to use the White House board or open lines to talk about these B-52 strikes.... Just be sure they are not using the regular telephone.

KISSINGER: You know who is the worst villain.... The president.

LAIRD: But you have to make sure that these guys are protected. These strikes are going to work out all right.... But it is a big escalation. I don't want anything to happen to the planes and pilots unnecessarily.

KISSINGER: You think there will be a lot of screaming here?

LAIRD: Sure. But I don't want people to panic. This is a big symbol—like putting troops back in.... There will be civilian casualties.... You saw those pictures—there is civilian housing around there.

KISSINGER: Are you, on balance, against it?

LAIRD: No....

KISSINGER: What is your real view?

LAIRD: This will be the kind of plan the president wants as a major show of determination on his part. That is what he wants and he will get it.

KISSINGER: You think it's worth the heat?

LAIRD: We have taken heat before on things like this. You can't back away from that plan of showing strong determination....

KISSINGER: The president's judgment is this: if he keeps this thing going, you have to balance six weeks of agony against giving them a few shots.

LAIRD: You will have agony anyway....

President Nixon
April 9, 1972, 10:45 a.m.
They hash out plans for the B-52 bombing of the Vinh area and Abrams's opposition. Kissinger says the point of the bombing is to threaten "massive escalation and warn the Soviets." Nixon, who believes the more important thing is the bombing's effect on the North Vietnamese, thinks the enemy offensive is part of a Soviet conspiracy. Kissinger also reports that Max Frankel of the New York Times *ran a front-page article "pretty much as I gave it to him."*

KISSINGER: I wanted to review with you this large attack—Laird doesn't want us to use on the phone the name of the planes—which would come off this afternoon about 4:00.

NIXON: Does Abrams want to do it?

KISSINGER: Abrams's basic judgment is to use all assets in the military zones [in South Vietnam]. The argument for doing this is not purely military. It is to show we are prepared to do massive escalation and warn the Soviets.

NIXON: . . . Is that Vinh?

KISSINGER: In that area, yes. . . .

NIXON: What is Laird's problem?

KISSINGER: . . . He is not opposed. Abrams has been opposed on the ground that he wants everything in his area. . . .

NIXON: . . . The problem is Abrams doesn't want to divert six planes?

KISSINGER: Twelve planes. . . . I don't think Abrams's concern is a paramount one. . . . I am, on balance, in favor of doing it.

NIXON: . . . It seems to me that they could give a little shot. But don't put out 18 press releases.

KISSINGER: No—the press guidance is they just mention planes have been used, and in response to questions, they will say, "Yes, we have struck north."

NIXON: Say "We have struck in military areas [that are] in support of the invasion of the South."

KISSINGER: Exactly.

NIXON: What really inhibited Johnson throughout this thing was he was always worried more about the PR side. . . . Right now anything that can be done that might tip the balance is something we have to undertake. We have to put the chips in the pot. You believe the Russians will be more affected by this. I don't think that makes much difference. The main thing is what effect will it have on the North Vietnamese. Abrams thinks there would be more effect on the North Vietnamese in the battle zone?

KISSINGER: Twelve strikes in the battle zone will not make or break that operation. It will warn that restraints are coming off. . . .

NIXON: I think we have to go forward. . . . We all know what this is. It is a damn conspiracy. The Indian thing, the UAR [Egypt], and this is a massive attempt on the Soviets' part to put it to us. . . . Knocking off of the Soviet summit becomes more and more a possibility.

KISSINGER: I am afraid so. . . . I think our bargaining position in Moscow, if it came out of a position of total weakness, would be hopeless.

NIXON: I have been arguing for sending more carriers, planes, etc. and taking the heat on it because I realize everything rides on this. . . . With that much on the plate, we have to take whatever risks we can. I think we many times have done things like Menu [the secret Cambodia bombing] which didn't have a psychological effect.

KISSINGER: That had an effect but never decisive enough. And this won't be decisive.

NIXON: But it will have some effect. . . . Laird won't run out?

KISSINGER: I have him on tape. . . . He said if we want to get the message across, we do it. . . .

NIXON: Our planes must have hit something. . . .

KISSINGER: In the MR 3 front [a military region in South Vietnam], they found another 190 bodies from B-52 strikes. If they just dumped bombs out of the door, they would have to hit something. . . . Max Frankel with a little coaching from me has an article on the front page which is not bad at all.

NIXON: You keep that up.

KISSINGER: He printed it pretty much as I gave it to him. . . .

Melvin Laird

April 11, 1972, 8:18 p.m.

Laird and Kissinger debate bombing truck parks in the Hanoi area. Laird says the "most lucrative" targets are in the South, where the battle was, annoying Kissinger, who wants to show the Soviets that "we will come up North."

LAIRD: . . . Haven't been able to get a drone in on that Chinese truck park—

KISSINGER: No, what we want to get is those three around Hanoi. . . . That we were going to throw in as a bonus. We want the three they are yelling about around Hanoi. You were the one who was talking about that one.

LAIRD: I just . . . want to ensure there are trucks there. You understood that.

KISSINGER: I understood nothing.

LAIRD: . . . On the B-52s we have got that planned. It will be ready to go tomorrow afternoon. It will probably be that airfield. . . . As far as the number of planes, I think the priority should still be in the battlefield. And I wouldn't go over 18.

KISSINGER: Hit something more lucrative.

LAIRD: The most lucrative, according to Abrams and [Pacific Commander John] McCain, are in the battlefield area.

KISSINGER: They go through that all the time. They have lost us the war.

LAIRD: They have not lost us the war.

KISSINGER: For years they have been screaming about . . . restraint. Now we take the reins off and to get them to fly up North is like pulling teeth.

LAIRD: No, they will fly up North. We are doing these other strikes for political purposes, not for military purposes.

KISSINGER: And showing the Russians we will come up North. . . .

Melvin Laird
April 12, 1972, 9:40 a.m.
Laird reports that the B-52 bombing of Vinh was off a kilometer; thus, given the maps the military used, other B-52 strikes in the North will also be off a kilometer until a correction is made, with obvious ramifications for bombing civilians.

. . . KISSINGER: On the B-52 thing—that is going this afternoon?

LAIRD: Right. You know that strike on Vinh . . . the miscued radar show they hit on target. . . . This is doing it through the clouds. The maps must be off in calibration almost a mile—one kilometer.

KISSINGER: In other words, they didn't hit anything.

LAIRD: They hit but not that target. . . . They showed the charts were off one kilometer for bombing by B-52s. . . . In South Vietnam there is no problem, but in North Vietnam they will be off by as much as a kilometer. This is serious when it comes to hitting civilians with CBUs [cluster bombs], which they are doing. Last night at 1:00 a.m. I got a call. They were going to take the airfield, but the villages, I didn't think they should hit them before it's checked out.

KISSINGER: Well, I don't know if the airfield is worth it.

LAIRD: I think it is.

KISSINGER: How long is it going to take them to check it out? I don't know if we can fight a war with this military establishment. We are not interested in an airfield; we are interested in a bigger strike. I think we ought to call it off. We can't afford to horse around. It's got to be massive. . . . If the air force wants to fight their own war let them do it, but we want to bring this war to an end.

LAIRD: The weather is clearing up now, but Henry, you have to make sure your calibration on the chart is correct.

KISSINGER: Well, I'm going to the president on this. . . .

Melvin Laird

April 15, 1972, 11:50 a.m.

The weekend of April 15–16 waves of fighter bombers and B-52s struck the Haiphong and Hanoi areas. It was reportedly the first time that B-52s had been used on those two cities. B-52s also continued to pound southern North Vietnam. Creighton Abrams had sent a cable arguing for delaying the bombing in Haiphong and Hanoi, saying it would take assets away from critical fighting in the South; Kissinger had been upset by it.[6]

KISSINGER: I saw the cable from Abrams saying the risks were too great for this strike and under these conditions the president can't go through with it. . . . You said that by scaling down the effort you would have him aboard.

LAIRD: He is going to do it.

KISSINGER: I want two names to replace Abrams. Who should replace Abrams?

LAIRD: . . . It will be a mistake. . . .

KISSINGER: What is this? The field commander should do as the commander in chief says. . . . In every crisis, the president is left by his people.

LAIRD: Not by me, Henry. . . .

KISSINGER: Well, it is a heavy responsibility to overrule his commander.

LAIRD: . . . Abrams wants to use the assets in the battle and he thinks that going now doesn't affect the battle for six months.

KISSINGER: He will blame us for his failures. . . . You said by scaling down, everyone will be happy.

LAIRD: I didn't say that, Henry. . . .

Melvin Laird

April 15, 1972, 6:10 p.m.

Laird and Kissinger have a tense exchange about the bombing of Haiphong and Hanoi.

. . . LAIRD: A-6s started to attack and they are out. But, Henry, we have got to make plans and then stick with them. I am willing to send any kind of signals any place, but I think things get panicky.

KISSINGER: No, no one is panicky. Just having been through a lot of crises where everyone turns around afterward and says that wasn't what I wanted—

LAIRD: That's not the case as far as I am concerned, and I resent that. . . .

KISSINGER: No, not you, it was Abrams running around and saying things like that.

LAIRD: Abe doesn't run around and say things like that either and I resent that too.

KISSINGER: That's your privilege.

LAIRD: That is my privilege. . . . He [Nixon] knew how his field commander [felt] and Al [Haig] knew that too. And if the president didn't know it's because you weren't briefing him properly. . . .

President Nixon
April 15, 1972, 10:25 p.m.
Soviet Ambassador Dobrynin had come to Kissinger's home that evening to discuss Vietnam and Kissinger's upcoming secret trip to Moscow and other issues and prepare for the Soviet summit in May.[7] Kissinger tells Nixon that Dobrynin had an auspicious message from Hanoi and said Moscow was anxious for his visit. Nixon says they'll blockade North Vietnam if his meeting in Moscow is disappointing and flush the summit.

KISSINGER: I am sorry to bother you, but we got some pretty quick action out of our Soviet friends—Dobrynin was in slobbering over me. First of all, he had a message from the North Vietnamese for us which was a lot more conciliatory than the one that they gave us in Paris. . . . And it was the softest message that I have ever seen.

NIXON: . . . Does Dobrynin know that we hit them tonight?

KISSINGER: Oh, yes. . . . He said they are very anxious for me to come anyway, that Vietnam will be the first agenda item, that they recognize the urgency. . . .

NIXON: . . . I told you the Russians, if they decided not to have you come, then we blockade. You can't play the game any other way.

KISSINGER: Mr. President, you brought it to this point and no one else would have had the courage to do it.

NIXON: Well, we are ready to play it out too. Incidentally, if their meeting is disappointing, we'll blockade too, and throw the summit right down the sink too. I don't think they will let that happen.

KISSINGER: He was slobbering so much. Here we are bombing the capital and near the capital of one of their close allies. According to the peacenik textbook, he should be yelling and screaming. . . .

NIXON: You think your trip is on?

KISSINGER: The only question is whether we want them to send a special plane—I'm kidding—I mean, almost anything.

NIXON: They won't change their minds because of the bombing?

KISSINGER: Absolutely not. . . .

President Nixon

April 15, 1972, 11:30 p.m.

After exulting about all the dead bodies resulting from the B-52 bombing of Haiphong and the punishment they were inflicting, Kissinger and Nixon discuss Kissinger's secret meeting in Moscow (he would depart in five days), where Nixon says he either has to make progress toward a peace settlement or they will blockade the North; he wants him to threaten to cancel the summit if Russian weapons keep killing South Vietnamese and Americans. Nixon and Kissinger are both energized by the bombing. Kissinger says that what "brings the Russians in" on Vietnam is a perception that "the situation may get out of hand."

... NIXON: So certainly, Henry, they must be hitting something.

KISSINGER: Well, Mr. President, they claimed to have counted 10,000 bodies up to now, and if you cut it in half, there must be another 5,000 that they have killed that we don't find.

NIXON: Sure, sure.

KISSINGER: In B-52 attacks.

NIXON: Well, I'll tell you, they are being punished and they are taking heavy casualties. The bastards are—

KISSINGER: Mr. President, if they don't make it this time, they are not going to come back for two years.

NIXON: If they don't make it this time, we're out of the woods. But the point is that we have to realize, though, that our hole card is the blockade. However, that's why you've got to get it settled with the Russians now. . . . When you meet with them it's either got to be on the way to a settlement or we blockade. . . .

KISSINGER: And on the other hand, Mr. President, the major thing now is to beat down these North Vietnamese. I told them that you could not have a reasonable summit meeting if there were major action going on in Vietnam. . . .

NIXON: Good god, we can't go there with Russian tanks and Russian guns killing South Vietnamese and Americans. Hell, no, we're not going to go! . . . It means there ain't going to be no meeting, that's what he's got to understand. . . . Has it [the bombing] been carried in the news yet?

KISSINGER: Yeah. Heavily. . . . It's just the first wave there. It's wave after wave of planes. You see, they can't see the B-52s and they dropped a million pounds of bombs.

NIXON: What? A million pounds of bombs? . . . In the Haiphong area?

KISSINGER: In the Haiphong area. . . .

NIXON: You think they really hit something this time, don't you?

KISSINGER: Well, actually, we now have the photographs; they hit something last time too [in Vinh].

NIXON: Yeah. But this time they probably hit a hell of a lot, though, don't you think?

KISSINGER: Oh, god yes. And this time they did it visually, Mr. President. . . . They did it with radar visually.

NIXON: God damn, that must have been a good strike! . . . Of course, you want to remember Johnson bombed them for years and it didn't do any good.

KISSINGER: But, Mr. President, Johnson never had a strategy; he was sort of picking away at them. He would go in with 50 planes, 20 planes; I bet you we will have had more planes over there in one day than Johnson had in a month. . . .

NIXON: Well, that has more impact too. . . . That shock treatment of cracking them. The only thing I regret is that when we made this plan, we didn't take out the power plants. The power plants, that can really demoralize a person.

KISSINGER: Well, they have a power plant that they can hit south of the 20th parallel.

NIXON: I meant the ones in Hanoi—put out the lights.

KISSINGER: Well, it may be on there. . . . What they gave them was 10 targets, of which they were supposed to hit six.

NIXON: I see. Well, it's probably a pretty good strike, Henry, isn't it?

KISSINGER: Well, 196 airplanes, Mr. President, that's pretty serious. . . .

NIXON: Yeah. Well, anyway, we will hold on and see what happens. . . .

KISSINGER: Mr. President, if we had pursued the Laird strategy, we might have won in the South but the war would have dragged on and on and on, and winning in the South is no—doesn't bring the Russians in. What brings the Russians in—I mean, we wouldn't have won in the South, we could have held in the South—and what brings the Russians in is the fact that the situation may get out of hand. Pouring that fleet in there has made more of an impact on the Russians than the defense of An Loc [in the South], which they don't understand.

NIXON: Yeah. The fleet shakes them because they think it's a blockade. . . . And they're right. This time we aren't fooling. . . . I tell you, the thing to do is to pour it in there every place we can; just pour it down wherever the weather is and just bomb the hell out of them. I would think they'd be tearing the hell out of the I Corps [in northern South Vietnam] now, shouldn't they? The weather's pretty good.

KISSINGER: Oh, god—

NIXON: Are they hitting some things?

KISSINGER: Oh, yes. And they are tearing up the panhandle [in southern North Vietnam]. . . . And the cumulative effect of that is going to be quite a lot.

NIXON: Oh, Abrams has got the horses now. He can't blame it on anybody but himself. . . .

President Nixon

April 16, 1972, 3:30 p.m.

Nixon and Kissinger plot how to tell Secretary of State Rogers about Kissinger's secret trip to Moscow and how to conceal his departure.

. . . NIXON: . . . The other thing we've got to be thinking about is how to inform Rogers. . . . Well, is there any possibility that it could be handled in terms . . . of your going there for the purpose of a meeting with the North Vietnamese?

KISSINGER: Well, we will have to bring it into the Vietnamese context.

NIXON: . . . You would wait till you left before he was told?

KISSINGER: Yes, because he is going to drive you crazy if it is done before, and he will go to Dobrynin before. . . .

NIXON: We will simply handle it on the basis that we got this message from Brezhnev saying that he wanted to talk about Vietnam. . . . And that the North Vietnamese may be there. . . . It's really just a secret meeting like your Paris meetings. We don't have to be totally forthright. . . . Where do you want to leave from?

KISSINGER: . . . There is a dinner party here in town to which I thought I would go. . . . And I thought it would be good if they saw me. Then I will leave that dinner party, get dressed, and go to the airport about midnight.

NIXON: Good, good.

KISSINGER: Then people will have seen me Wednesday night. . . . If you could say you are going to Camp David Thursday night—

NIXON: To do some work.

KISSINGER: Then I would have the word put out that I am going there Thursday morning.

NIXON: . . . And there is no way they can check that. . . .

President Nixon

April 16, 1972, 4:25 p.m.

Nixon says they're going to blockade North Vietnam if the North Vietnamese don't agree to a private meeting in Paris soon (they wanted Nixon to stop the bombing and agree to resume the public talks first)[8] and will "starve them out if necessary."

. . NIXON: . . . Now that we've turned this screw, we've got to continue to turn it if they don't talk. In other words, the blockade has just got to go. In other words, we're going to crush these people now. They've asked for it and that's the way we're going to do it.

KISSINGER: That's absolutely right, Mr. President.
NIXON: Don't you feel that way?
KISSINGER: I couldn't agree more.
NIXON: And starve them out if necessary.
KISSINGER: I couldn't agree more. . . .

A Futile Meeting in Paris; Prodding the South Vietnamese; Soviet Summit in the Balance; Mining North Vietnam's Ports, Bombing Its Rail Lines, Resuming Heavy Bombing in the Hanoi–Haiphong Area, and Internal Dissent; a Supreme Commander in Vietnam?; the Battle and B-52s in South Vietnam; the SALT Agreements; and Danielle Hunebelle's *Dear Henry*

May–June 1972

On May 2, 1972, during the surging enemy offensive in South Vietnam, Kissinger had a fruitless secret meeting with senior North Vietnamese negotiator Le Duc Tho in Paris that left him resolved to a military confrontation. Nixon had wanted to strike again in the Hanoi–Haiphong heartland before or during his meeting to improve their poor bargaining position, and Kissinger believed they needed "a massive strike" that week (after his meeting). But they held off. In South Vietnam, their prospects were looking perilous, to say the least, with South Vietnamese troops fleeing under enemy attacks. Secretary of Defense Melvin Laird felt South Vietnamese troops needed "a kick in the ass" and command changes; his Vietnamization program at risk of collapse, he complained that the troops wouldn't take the offensive and that even commanders were fleeing. Nixon and Kissinger, who worried that the situation in the South could completely "come apart," wondered what might happen if they both canceled the Soviet summit rather than go with a weak hand and lost in Vietnam. They agreed that they had to "belt the hell out of them" in the North. Kissinger ordered contingency plans in case "the whole thing unravels."

Fed up with Commander Creighton Abrams, who he had determined to replace, and with Laird, Nixon directed that a new command structure, including a "supreme commander," someone with imagination who would follow his orders, be set up in Vietnam. But Laird thought the idea was ridiculous and threatened to resign, Kissinger was unexcited about it, and it was abandoned.

On May 4, to cut off North Vietnam's supplies, Nixon and Kissinger decided to blockade the North by mining its ports, including most importantly its main port of Haiphong, and to resume on a sustained basis heavy bombing of Hanoi and Haiphong and other targets in the northern half of North Vietnam; its rail lines to China were to be hit hard. Nixon declared that if the Soviets canceled the summit because of the mining and bombing (which looked increasingly unlikely), "we will turn on them hard." The administration was carrying out heavy bombing with B-52s in South Vietnam while continuing intensive bombing in southern North Vietnam.

In late May, Nixon and Kissinger traveled to Moscow for the Soviet summit, which yielded a SALT I arms control agreement. Kissinger worried that the administration's public relations hucksters would typically overdo the selling of it.

In June, *Dear Henry* came out, a book by the French journalist Danielle Hunebelle that told how she became love-struck by Kissinger while doing her earlier French television show on him. Kissinger sought the advice of Barbara Walters on how to deal with it. Walters recommended trashing Hunebelle as "pathetic," "this poor, sick lady," and offered to help.

President Nixon
May 1, 1972, 9:55 a.m.
The day before Kissinger's secret meeting with North Vietnamese negotiator Le Duc Tho in Paris, Nixon, who had received poll results showing his popularity rose with escalation in Vietnam,[1] wants him to go from a stronger position by conducting an air strike in the Hanoi–Haiphong area. Kissinger advises a massive strike that week.

NIXON: It seems to me extremely important that you not be involved in going over there at a time when they are so blatantly trying to have us in the position of weakness, without our doing something. I know your concern about hitting them before the meeting. . . . The longer we wait, the poorer our position is domestically. We don't need to be proving that we are seeking peace. We checked this out. As far as the people are concerned, the thing that will hurt domestically the most is to have them moving along with an invasion—having it appear hopeless—and then later on hitting. . . . It buys nothing with the doves, and the hawks don't need it. As long as the invasion has been proved, they say, damn it, hit it. There's no reason to try to appeal to these doves; you can't do it.

KISSINGER: I agree with that. Well, Mr. President, it takes at least 48 hours to get a major strike mounted against the North. At this point most of the planes have been needed in the South. I have nothing against hitting. I was in favor of a one-day strike this weekend and Admiral Moorer implored us not to do it.

NIXON: . . . What it looks like at present is that we are in a bomb shelter and they are hitting the hell out of us. . . . Something in that area while you are there or just before would be helpful.

KISSINGER: . . . That troop training area south of Hanoi that he [Moorer] said he wanted to hit—

NIXON: That would be good.

KISSINGER: . . . The only thing to consider is whether it is better for us to go totally savage. . . . Tonight whether we can divert some of the planes to the North, I will have to check with Moorer. . . . But we've got to make a massive strike this week.

NIXON: Don't want to wait till the weekend. In terms of domestic public opinion the most important thing is when they are kicking us we have got to be kicking them or we look bad. It doesn't appear that we are. . . . The only bombing that will have any effect on our opinion is the Hanoi–Haiphong area. . . .

President Nixon

May 1, 1972, 7:00 p.m.

In preparation for Kissinger's departure for Paris, Nixon says they may have to offer South Vietnamese President Nguyen Van Thieu's resignation (he had formally agreed to resign before a new presidential election as part of an earlier peace proposal), but before doing that they should "whack" Hanoi–Haiphong to instill fear of worse.

NIXON: The thing I think you should know—as you are quite aware, the bargaining position we have isn't very strong right at this moment. The fact of the matter is that both sides are now in the position of reaching the wire. It may be that going to the extreme of getting Thieu—taking him up on his offer to resign—is necessary. . . . When you are faced with a debacle your bargaining position changes. Before we go that far I believe we have to give them a whack on the Haiphong–Hanoi area. I think you would agree that would strengthen our bargaining position. They have no confidence in what we can do to save the South.

KISSINGER: I think it is premature to do what you suggest this week. If I make such an offer [for Thieu to resign] tomorrow they will think we are collapsing.

NIXON: . . . Set it up in such a way that we hit the Haiphong–Hanoi area before—the major reason for hitting that is the fear they have for what we can do to them. . . . I want you to know I am ready to fall on the sword and that means we will demolish them before we will allow ourselves to be defeated. . . . Just remember they are in for a hell of a shock if they turn us down. . . .

President Nixon
May 1, 1972, 7:10 p.m.
Nixon wants Kissinger to threaten Le Duc Tho with major escalation.

NIXON: One final point—I think you ought to do a little acting because these people—like the Russians—are liars and actors. I would simply say, look . . . as you know, I am deeply dedicated for peace and I have been able to influence the president in that direction, but I think I owe it to you to say I cannot control him.

KISSINGER: I think that will be very good.

NIXON: And that you heard what I said and you have never known him to understate what he will do. He has public support. . . . Put it that way!

Melvin Laird
May 2, 1972, 9:45 p.m.
Laird tells Kissinger, who had returned discouraged and probably angry from Paris after a short and unproductive meeting with Tho, leaving him resolved to "a showdown" (meaning massive bombing), that what the South Vietnamese need rather than better military equipment is "just a kick in the ass" and changes in commanders (which was soon done).[2] Laird considers Nixon's order to send out more B-52s rather than fighter bombers "nuts."

KISSINGER: What the president wants to do is send a mission out there leaving tomorrow night to look at the modernization needs and replacement needs of the South Vietnamese. . . . He wants to have a symbolic commitment to them . . . and to give them a shot in the arm. . . . And also to see whether they may need some heavier equipment.

LAIRD: Well, they don't need equipment, what they need right now is just a kick in the ass. . . . And they ought to change a few commanders right now . . . and move up some of those that have been performing well and kick those in the ass that haven't. . . . Of course, the problem that they have, and I think this has had an effect, is that they think that there is some deal going on . . . that they are going to be sold out. . . . But we have a lot more tanks up in Japan we can get down to them. . . .

KISSINGER: . . . Now, in addition he wants to send some more B-52s out.

LAIRD: Why, Henry, that is just crazy. . . . There is just no sense in sending any more B-52s. . . . Two F-4s carries as much of a load as a B-52 and they are much more effective than a B-52. . . . That is just nuts. . . . The old ones are all right, but these new ones that we've got out there—two F-4s does a better job as far as bombing is concerned and on this kind of bombing.

KISSINGER: Except they fly only when the ceilings are 5,000 feet and a few other things.

LAIRD: Yeah, but as long as you can't take out cities the targets are so limited. . . .

Melvin Laird
May 2, 1972, 10:10 p.m.
Amid worrisome South Vietnamese retreats and lack of initiative, Laird bemoans that the South Vietnamese aren't taking the offensive.

. . . LAIRD: . . . You gotta win this damn thing on the ground. You can't win the damn thing just with air power. . . . And those bastards, they keep their heads down and wait for the air power and they aren't doing any probing. . . . I think it's inexcusable the way they handled those tanks up there. They left them. . . . They got them over to a place where they couldn't get them back 'cause there was no bridge. . . . They were doing pretty damn well, and I think it's that artillery moving up and the fact that they stayed right under it and wouldn't move out against it, and they wouldn't give us any spotting as far as the aircraft. There were plenty of aircraft to use against it but they just stayed fixed. And then some of the leaders—the command left. . . . They've got the manpower . . . they're not short of ammunition, they're not short of guns. . . . I just don't see why the North Vietnamese should be able to fight better than they do. . . . You can't win that fight in the air. It's going to take those people on the ground to do some fighting. . . .

President Nixon
May 3, 1972, 6:25 p.m.

With South Vietnamese forces fleeing Quang Tri in panic and Hue and An Loc threatened, Nixon regrets not bombing Hanoi before Kissinger met with Le Duc Tho. He and Kissinger consider canceling or postponing the Soviet summit. Kissinger believes they should bomb Hanoi and Haiphong with as much time before the summit as possible if it's not postponed. They ponder what might happen if they cancel the summit and lose in Vietnam. Nixon raises again the possibility of offering President Thieu's resignation. They agree they've got to "belt the hell out of them" in the North for two days. And Kissinger says he'll get some plans together in case it all unravels.

... KISSINGER: The thing that worries me ... is not the loss of this or that town but the whole [thing] may come apart, where they lose enough units. That's the thing that worries me.

NIXON: In that respect, I think that my feeling that we probably should have hit them before you went was probably right. . . . You would have been in a little stronger position over there. . . .

KISSINGER: . . . I was in favor of it after the Quang Tri attack started. What stopped it over the weekend was that Abrams was screaming for the planes for himself.

NIXON: I know, I know. But we run into that every time, though, Henry.

KISSINGER: Well, at that time with everything coming apart—

NIXON: It would have been rather critical.

KISSINGER: Since that guy is dying to find an alibi. . . . The problem with Le Duc Tho yesterday was he wants to see how far this offensive goes and he wasn't going to settle in midstream and he wasn't going to give me something we were going to use domestically to give our people hope. . . . I'm having lunch with Dobrynin on Friday, I could say, "Now, look, Anatol, we're realists. There just can't be a summit with a president sitting in the Kremlin while Hue falls."

NIXON: That's right.

KISSINGER: "Why don't we agree now on postponing it for two months."

NIXON: Or one month. . . . But then on the other hand, of course, aren't you convinced that we do have to hit Hanoi–Haiphong once—

KISSINGER: . . . If you postpone, you'll also want to hit afterwards. . . . But I do not see how you can do nothing.

NIXON: Oh, Christ . . . I think that the [best option] might be hitting and running the risk of their postponing.

KISSINGER: That's right. . . . But then it is better to do it earlier than later. . . . If we are not going to postpone, we have to hit. If you are going to play the hitting game, it's better to do it with as much time between it and the summit as possible.

NIXON: . . . I just don't think the postponing is going to have that much effect on the situation in the South. . . .

KISSINGER: Mr. President, the point may be that nothing is going to have any effect on the situation in the South. . . . That's the tragedy of this situation.

NIXON: . . . But you had no idea that anybody would consider doing nothing. Good god, the only one that would do that would be Laird. . . . I'd like for you to run down in your own mind and sort of put it on paper what happens if we cancel the Russian summit. . . . We can't possibly be there in a position of weakness and I'm just not going to be there.

KISSINGER: . . . Supposing you're there while 10,000 Americans are captured in Binh Long? I mean, this thing could turn into a horrible de facto [defeat]. Under what conditions will you be there in general? After having made all these threats?

NIXON: No way, no way. No, we've got to start the hitting of the North. . . . We've got to do it in any event, so let's be strong in whatever position we have. . . . Maybe we have to make a big play. Maybe we have to go to Thieu and say, "Look here, boy." Get my point? You know, I don't believe in just letting what seems to be a disaster develop without going to the heart of the matter.

KISSINGER: Before we do that, I think we ought to go to the North Vietnamese. Well, even then you shouldn't do that in Moscow.

NIXON: Oh, hell no. No, we go to the North Vietnamese first by hitting them. Hitting them goddamn hard!

KISSINGER: Well, there's no sense in going to Thieu and asking him to resign unless you have a prior deal with the North Vietnamese.

NIXON: Yeah. But look, in any event . . . you've got to go first, Henry, with a . . . damn good strike in the North. That is absolutely indispensable to our policy. . . . And soon, huh? Unless we cancel. . . . And then you've got to look down the road to what is the Russian reaction. That's what I want to see if we cancel, what will they do. . . . You have the proposition where you cancel the summit . . . you lose in Vietnam . . . and . . . survive the election, who knows; things are very strange at the present time in this country. But then where are you?

KISSINGER: If you cancel the summit and survive the election? . . . Oh, then you are in a very strong position.

NIXON: That's a very, very big risk, but if you cancel the summit and lose in Vietnam, winning the election is going to be a hell of a tough thing to do, unless we are able to lose in Vietnam and do something about the POWs and so forth. . . . I have a gut reaction that we've got to give them one good belt.

KISSINGER: So do I.

NIXON: Come hell or high water, you know. . . . It's got to be for two good solid days; just belt the hell out of them.

KISSINGER: I agree.

NIXON: That's one thing we've got to do. . . . If we do everything we can and they still can't make it, then it's not our fault.

KISSINGER: And I'm going to have some contingency plans made here for that eventuality, Mr. President. . . . I'll just get Haig and one other person working on that.

NIXON: On what?

KISSINGER: On what happens if the whole thing unravels.

NIXON: Oh, hell yes, hell yes. . . .

President Nixon

May 6, 1972, 10:27 a.m.

Nixon orders a new military command structure in Vietnam, including a supreme commander, which Laird opposed. They also take up the forthcoming mining of North Vietnam's ports. Nixon and Kissinger had decided two days earlier to blockade North Vietnam and to bomb Hanoi and Haiphong and other targets in northern North Vietnam, including rail lines to China, on an ongoing basis. "I want that place . . . bombed to smithereens during the blockade," Nixon told Kissinger. Laird promised to carry out the mining, though he opposed it; Nixon doesn't want Laird to send him anything for the record to cover his ass.[3] And he trumpets blockades.

NIXON: Hi, how did you get along with Laird?

KISSINGER: . . . On the command changes he raised a lot of technical problems. . . . His major concern, Mr. President, is if you get a supreme commander . . . how the chain of command operates. They have got the communications running one way now and he doesn't want to get so much dislocation while this operation is going on. It is a reasonable point which at least we ought to look at.

NIXON: All right. But I have got to have the changes, Henry. Now, god damn it, I am just not going to screw around anymore out here. I am going to put everything in the pot. And then have the people around the bureaucrats tie my hands? . . . If I breathe I want them to breathe. And it has just got to be done. I want a more imaginative commander. . . . I do want the little son of a bitch from South Dakota [General William DePuy] out there, and I do want a new navy admiral, a four-star admiral out there. And I think . . . that fella that is about to retire, [Horacio] Rivero. . . . He has clout. He is awfully tough. And he will know it is his last hurrah, Henry, and he will do better than some young guy who is trying to pimp up and wants to be sure that he is promoted. . . .

KISSINGER: He [DePuy] is a good man. He is a mean, egotistical son of a bitch, but—

NIXON: He is mean, egotistical, and a son of a bitch, but he will take some action and that is what is needed. . . . Incidentally, when you mentioned the [mining] to Laird, what was his reaction? Did he gulp and say, well, the president is making a hell of a mistake, but I will go along—or how?

KISSINGER: No. He just said he would do it. He wasn't throwing his hat in the air either. Of course he has those two peacenik military assistants.

NIXON: . . . I don't want to see any papers from him on this. . . . He cannot write something for the record. . . . I am not going to have these people cover their flanks by writing something directly. He can write something for his files. But don't bother sending it to me for the record. The decision is made—it is irrevocable. . . . A blockade . . . if you keep it on, always wins. Have you ever known when it failed? . . . Put the Germans [on] their knees? In two wars, didn't they? But it ended the Civil War. I mean, the South would still be fighting if it hadn't been for the blockade. . . . And the mining—you study the plan. Now, I have deliberately, Henry, stayed out of this military stuff because I am not an expert. But I am counting on you and Haig to study these plans and really make them have the best plans you have possibly got. . . . How do you feel about the plans?

KISSINGER: Oh, these plans are perfect. . . .

President Nixon
May 6, 1972, about 12:20 p.m.
Nixon and Kissinger discuss an amphibious landing in North Vietnam and bombing near Hanoi. And Nixon reiterates his order for a supreme commander in Vietnam— even if it means Laird's resignation. Kissinger suggests Abrams (who he'd wanted to remove earlier).

. . . NIXON: . . . Now, do I clearly understand that we are going forward with the planning for the amphibious landing? . . .

KISSINGER: Yes, but that will take them a week.

NIXON: A week. Kick them in the ass. Tell them to get it done. . . . They are going forward with at least one strike by naval F-4s on the truck parks. Isn't that correct?

KISSINGER: Tomorrow night. . . . They have got a good target near Hanoi. . . .

NIXON: That will signal them. They will think that is it. . . . Have you thought more about Rivero, to get him over there? . . . I just like the idea, that tough, cocky little son of a bitch that has nothing else to do. . . . I am so tired of this business and we have got to shake up this command. I mean it—I don't think you really realize how strongly I mean this. . . . In fact, if it means Mel's resignation, that is fine.

KISSINGER: There is one thing I must say, Mr. President. I have been impressed the last two days by the way Abrams has thought of using the B-52s [in a concentrated manner where they would do the most good], and he is going after the artillery, etc. Maybe he has got his second wind, and maybe we ought to consider making him the supreme commander. And then putting that little son of a bitch DePuy under him.

NIXON: . . . Somebody tough has got to tell him that he reports to me and not Laird. . . . I want him to know that I am the commander in chief—not Laird—and by god, he is going to report to me directly. . . . If it is done that way I don't mind if Abrams does get off his fat ass and does something. Because he does know war. . . . If this doesn't pan out we will pin his ass. . . .

President Nixon
May 6, 1972, 12:28 p.m.
Nixon has second thoughts about Abrams.

NIXON: Henry, there is one potentially fatal flaw which probably hasn't occurred to you in Abrams as supreme commander. . . . Abrams, like Haig, and this is Haig's weakness, is basically an army man. Abrams as distinguished from Haig is not only an army man but he has a vested interest in having Vietnamization succeed. Abrams has always opposed the strikes on the North because it takes assets from the South. He does not understand the use of naval power. Now, that is why under no circumstances, and this is an order, will I take Abrams . . . unless we have Rivero there with him and unless there is a direct chain of command. . . . We have suffered with this son of a bitch on everything. We could have struck two weeks ago. We didn't because of Abrams. Don't you realize now the flaw of your argument? . . . I don't want him to short-change our efforts to destroy North Vietnam in order for a half-assed effort to do something in South Vietnam. . . . Now, the reason Rivero is important is that he then can say I need those carriers for the North to maintain the blockade. The blockade, Henry, is long term. Abrams is thinking short term.

KISSINGER: Exactly.

NIXON: Now we have got to get that blockade. Now, the blockade, the mining, and the strikes on the North . . . are at this point vitally important. We can't do the half-ass thing. . . . You may not realize how much we have crossed the Rubicon. . . . And, god damn it, you've got to win. . . .

Melvin Laird
May 6, 1972, 12:30 p.m.

Laird threatens to resign over Nixon's ordered command changes in Vietnam.

> . . . KISSINGER: What about the command thing? The president calls every five
> minutes.
>
> LAIRD: I can give you a paper on why it can't be done. . . . There are very few
> of our assets in Vietnam.
>
> KISSINGER: He wants to send Rivero to handle the navy part.
>
> LAIRD: That is crazy. I will leave and walk out the door. . . . He doesn't have any
> confidence in me. . . . To run something like that is fantastic. . . .

John Connally
May 6, 1972, between 12:30 and 1:00 p.m.
*Treasury Secretary Connally, a hawk who thought nuclear weapons were a real option
in Vietnam,[4] supports the mining of Haiphong and advises that Nixon fire dissenters.*

> . . . KISSINGER: . . . We have got a massive problem. Laird in his usual way is car-
> rying out the order, but he is on record now—he is opposed to it, he says
> it is a major political problem, domestically and internationally—it makes
> Vietnam the number one issue in the world. . . . In other words, he is totally
> opposed to it. I have talked to Dick Helms—he is opposed to it. I know god-
> damn well what Rogers is going to do. . . . I wonder just what your reaction
> to this situation is.
>
> CONNALLY: My reaction is that the action that he has taken is the absolutely
> correct action. . . . If he gets substantial dissension from those of authority
> who are supposed to be carrying out his orders, I think it leaves him no
> choice but to fire them. And I think he has to be prepared to go that far if
> their public utterances begin to destroy the SALT talks or the summit. . . .

President Nixon
May 6, 1972, 1:45 p.m.
*Nixon doesn't want any "asshole advice" from intelligence analysts or Laird on the
efficacy of blockading the North and says that they will bomb the rail lines to China
to keep Hanoi from circumventing the blockade and unleash "massive strikes." The
North Vietnamese will yield well before the six-month lifespan of the mines is over, he
thinks.*

> . . . KISSINGER: I have a meeting scheduled for 2:30 with some intelligence
> specialists, who don't know what this is about, just to review where the sup-
> plies are coming from and what the impact of various types of blockades
> are on the North Vietnamese and what has to be cut off where—to find the
> critical points.

NIXON: The main thing, though, is that I am not interested in Laird's or the intelligence community's asshole advice that it isn't worth doing. I have made the decision, Henry, and the purpose of your meeting is not to evaluate it—clear?

KISSINGER: Oh, no, Laird doesn't know this is going on, Mr. President.

NIXON: . . . How do the supplies move? They move on railroads, roads, or by sea. So we are cutting off the sea. . . . We are going to hit the railroads. . . . And also the massive strikes on all logistic things that they have, so that what is already there within the pipeline doesn't give them six or eight months to breathe. . . . I have confidence in so few of the military—but I think the navy must have enough clout left that they will do this well.

KISSINGER: Above all, Mr. President, these mines take care of themselves. It isn't a question of the navy doing anything—it is whether the ships are willing to challenge mines. And I doubt that seriously. . . . Give them a six-month lifespan which can be continued if still needed. Otherwise they will be there forever.

NIXON: It won't be six months, I can assure you. . . . The way we are pouring it to them now, it can't last long. . . .

President Nixon
May 6, 1972, 3:30 p.m.
Kissinger reports that Laird won't be a supporter of the mining inside the administration but will carry out his orders, thereby covering himself in both directions.

. . . KISSINGER: You won't get much support out of Laird now. . . . Feels that it makes Vietnam the number one issue, where for three years we put it on the back burner. I am just telling you what you are up against, but he will carry it out.

NIXON: What does he think the alternative is?

KISSINGER: To win in the South. If they fight it can be done, but if they don't fight it can't be won. . . . He is putting himself in the position of if it succeeds he carried out his job, his orders, and he won, but if it doesn't succeed, well, he said so.

NIXON: Where the hell does he think Vietnam is now but on the front burner? . . . Why in the world is Laird unable to see the critical situation in the South?

KISSINGER: He is trying to save Vietnamization and he basically feels the hell with it. . . .

Thomas Moorer
May 8, 1972, 6:18 p.m.

Several hours after giving Moorer the execute order for the mining, Kissinger directs him to give North Vietnam "massive jolts" in the Hanoi and Haiphong areas.

KISSINGER: Tom, follow on with the air campaign. . . . We want to make absolutely sure that we are not going to fritter our stuff away. . . . We want to stop them with . . . really massive jolts, so we are counting on a B-52 strike tomorrow night. . . . We want to hit the marshalling yards outside Hanoi; then we want to hit those Haiphong refineries again.

MOORER: I have been talking to John Vogt. He and Abrams want to hit the highway and bridges going into Hanoi. . . .

KISSINGER: We won't object to that.

MOORER: . . . You want a strike in Hanoi the next day?

KISSINGER: That is right, within 24 hours so that they don't even begin considering what to do about alternative routes, and then right after that POL again. . . .

Melvin Laird
May 10, 1972, 10:10 a.m.
Laird complains about news stories that he was opposed to the mining of North Vietnam's ports and that John Connally was primarily responsible for Nixon's decision.

. . . LAIRD: . . . These stories that they are putting out about how I raised all the negative aspects of this thing, and that it was Connally in his strong leadership who was the one—

KISSINGER: Oh, god damn it. . . . You mean the *New York Times* story?

LAIRD: Well, and there's another one that is in the *New York [Daily] News*, too, that says I was very negative and that—

KISSINGER: Oh, it's disgusting. It is revolting.

LAIRD: Because, you see, you've got to be in a position where you can raise questions.

KISSINGER: Mel, it's a disgrace. . . . Who the hell is Connally? I mean, what does he know?

LAIRD: . . . Those people over there, they must be talking. . . . Christ, that doesn't do any good to get that thing going like that.

KISSINGER: How can it be? If the word gets around that the secretary of defense was against and the secretary of treasury put it over, who the hell is going to be impressed by that? . . .

William Rogers
May 10, 1972, 10:40 a.m.

Rogers takes issue with the New York Times *story mentioned above, which portrayed Connally and Kissinger as the main influences on Nixon's decision, and about a call he received from a reporter who had been told he was opposed to it. Kissinger says he was beside himself over the* Times *piece, though he appeared from the piece to have talked to the reporter.*[5]

ROGERS: . . . Did you see the Bob Semple story?

KISSINGER: Oh, I was outraged. I was just going over to see the president and was raising holy Cain about it. . . .

ROGERS: *Newsday* called up yesterday and said that they had been advised by somebody in the White House that I was against what the president was doing—

KISSINGER: Well, it's that sort of shit, if you'll forgive me, that destroys us all. What good does it do? . . . I went over and I made the president call in Colson and Haldeman, and of course they all deny they did it.

ROGERS: Yes, well, you know it's goddamn infuriating because you break your ass working for him and then you read that kind of backstairs gossip. . . .

KISSINGER: And these nuts who put this out. . . .

ROGERS: . . . We had a series of meetings and I got the whole goddamn building behind this, and, you know, now the story comes out and they say, "Oh, for Christ's sake."

KISSINGER: . . . I was beside myself when I saw the Semple story. . . . It undermines the credibility of all those who now have to go out and defend it. They make us all look like whores. . . . It's outrageous. . . .

President Nixon
May 12, 1972, 8:40 a.m.
Kissinger reports the latest on the fighting and bombing in South Vietnam and assails the press for criticizing them for risking cancellation of the Soviet summit by the mining. He and Nixon believe the Soviets probably won't cancel, but a summit was "a mixed bag," and if the Soviets cancel, they will "turn on them hard."

. . . KISSINGER: Oh, on the military situation, the attack on An Loc is again very massive. . . . We put all our B-52 strikes in there. . . . The casualties have to be very heavy. . . . About 25 miles northwest of Kontum . . . the other side broke off the contact, so we went out and found over 300 bodies that had been killed by air strikes. At this rate of casualties it's just hard to see how they can keep it up. . . . What's so revolting is if the Soviets don't cancel the summit it won't be the fault of our commentators. . . . They're all drooling on, saying there is no proof yet that the summit will go on, that the Soviets are just in a holding pattern, and in effect almost challenging the Soviets to do something.

NIXON: Hoping that they will, aren't they?

KISSINGER: Of course.

NIXON: . . . If they don't they're going to look pretty bad, aren't they?

KISSINGER: Exactly. . . . I think it's slightly better than 50–50 now that they won't. . . . And in fact with every passing day it's more probable that they won't.

NIXON: Well, we have to remember that it poses awfully serious problems for them to cancel it at this point. . . . If they cancel this they're gambling on somebody else winning the election. And that's a helluva tough gamble right now because they know that we're going to put it to them. If they cancel, then they know we are then going to play it much harder militarily with the Vietnamese too. . . .

KISSINGER: You made this decision [the mining] with the high probability that it would be canceled.

NIXON: Eighty percent.

KISSINGER: That's right. I'd put it even higher—I thought it'd be 90.

NIXON: . . . I'm not all that hot for it because I really feel that if they go the other way our options aren't that bad either.

KISSINGER: I was going to say it's a mixed bag to go around with all these toasts to Soviet–American friendship.

NIXON: That's right. . . . You and I know there are reasons why it's the better bag in a sense, but on the other hand it's a mixed bag from the standpoint of what we've been doing here. And if the Soviets cancel we will turn on them hard too. Don't you agree?

KISSINGER: Absolutely. Totally.

NIXON: If we turn on them hard and then turn on them as the supporter-aggressors . . . use the goddamn tough language with them.

KISSINGER: Absolutely. . . . I don't think we'll have to do it, but we'll have to be careful when we're there, we'll have to be a little cooler in our toasts and so forth than we were in China.

NIXON: Oh, my god, yes. Words have got to be carefully—

KISSINGER: There's no telling what they'll do to us during the summit.

NIXON: That's right. We'll talk more about interests than about friendship.

KISSINGER: Exactly.

Melvin Laird
May 14, 1972, 9:40 a.m.

Laird objects to a forthcoming Time *magazine article that said Nixon was disappointed in him at a meeting on the mining of North Vietnam's ports and the bombing, and is completely fed up.*

… LAIRD: … One of my former colleagues up in New York called me last evening. He had been talking with some of the *Time* magazine people and they have a bad story that's going to appear. This guy told them he had talked to you about it … saying how disappointed the president was in me at the National Security Council meeting.

KISSINGER: Absolute crap. Total outrageous nonsense. I don't know where they get this from. …

LAIRD: I don't want to be built up anyway and if they think they're just tearing me down I'm not going to be around here anyway. I'm leaving. …

KISSINGER: I give you my word, Mel, not one of these things came out of the White House. … Who the hell does it make look good? If it makes Connally look good, who the hell is Connally as far as this operation is concerned? The secretary of the treasury doesn't matter.

LAIRD: Connally shouldn't be concerned about it anyway because I don't give a god damn about any job in this administration. …

Ken Clawson
June 2, 1972, 3:25 p.m.
The day after returning from the Soviet summit, which produced a SALT I agreement that included an ABM Treaty limiting each side to two ABM sites and an Interim Agreement limiting levels of strategic offensive weapons, Kissinger asks Deputy Director of Communications Clawson why they should prostitute themselves by overselling it.

… CLAWSON: … I am under some pressure from Haldeman and Colson—

KISSINGER: Let me tell you something as a friend. This operation suffers from one thing above all—compulsive huckstering. We are doing so well that we don't need to create stories. … Why should we turn ourselves into a bunch of whores?

CLAWSON: A good question.

KISSINGER: The worst thing for me, after I did all the briefing on the trip, is to step out and make another news story—I just think it would be nuts. … This story is selling itself. … I mean, for Christ sakes, how did we get to where we are? These experts were telling me only 8 percent of the people were for SALT and that no one understood it and I was putting too much energy in behind it. Now they are suddenly selling it as if it were soap. …

President Nixon
June 3, 1972, 10:00 a.m.
They debate whether to give the Joint Chiefs of Staff authority to bomb a hydroelectric plant next to a dam in North Vietnam.

KISSINGER: . . . They want to hit a hydroelectric plant which has 50 percent of the power supply. Unfortunately it's close to a big dam and if that dam bursts it's really going to be something. They claim they can avoid it.

NIXON: Well, I don't think we ought to do that right at this moment. . . . I think we should wait till—

KISSINGER: Till we hear what the [status of the peace talks is].

NIXON: Yeah. . . . If you do it just before then it's just too damn aggravating.

KISSINGER: Well, that's my instinct. . . . I mean, we ought to lift the restriction on Hanoi now. . . . We oughtn't to hit in the center of Hanoi, but we ought to hit in the outskirts, as we have.

NIXON: Yeah. . . . But as soon as we hear we'll knock that off too. . . . But on the dam I don't think I'd do that. . . . We should have no doubt about doing it if we strike out on the negotiating side, though.

KISSINGER: No question.

NIXON: Then we just go for broke. . . .

Melvin Laird
June 7, 1972, 6:50 p.m.
Laird wants to bomb the hydroelectric plant (which Nixon later decided to do).[6]

LAIRD: Say, Henry, back a few weeks ago before you went to Moscow I suggested that we hit that power plant up there that is built on that big new dam, and really this is more important than a lot of targets we hit. We don't want to knock out the dam but the transformers. There are only two in the country and it's a major part of their power supply.

KISSINGER: Do you want to send me a recommendation?

LAIRD: I want to just do it.

KISSINGER: Let me talk to the president about it. How many people would we kill?

LAIRD: . . . We are just after the transformers. . . .

KISSINGER: I am inclined to go along with it, but I want to run it by the president.

LAIRD: The assessment I have is it might weaken the dam but not have a serious effect. It would knock out the power. We would use the special planes that guide in on those particular transformers. We have been very successful with these new bombs. . . .

Barbara Walters
June 14, 1972, 1:55 p.m.
Kissinger asks Walters for advice on dealing with Danielle Hunebelle, the French journalist who became smitten by Kissinger while doing a film on him for French television. Hunebelle's book on Kissinger, Dear Henry, *was just coming out. Walters suggests that he say he feels "very sorry for . . . this poor, sick lady."*

. . . KISSINGER: . . . Barbara, I wanted your advice on something having to do with television. Don't know whether I ever told you about the nightmarish girl.

WALTERS: I hear the book goes on sale on Monday. I thought that's what you were calling about. I had her canceled. When I went off to California, Jean . . . gave me an advance paperback, and I thought it was just the worst piece of crap I've ever read.

KISSINGER: It is totally outrageous.

WALTERS: I read it and I thought, you didn't kiss her, you didn't touch her. You were as nice to her as you are to me or any reporter.

KISSINGER: I am a hell of a lot nicer—I like you.

WALTERS: If anyone reads the book, they will realize how absurd and ridiculous it is. What troubles me about it is that a lot of people are going to bother to read it and it will get all this kind of publicity. But we canceled out totally.

KISSINGER: I am wondering what you recommend I do. . . . You know, if you wrote a book like this, you would have 50 times the reasons than she did. You I genuinely like. Her, after the first meeting—you know, she is intelligent—she just turned into a nightmare.

WALTERS: Our show . . . I knew she was going to be on. So I called Stuart [Schulberg, the *Today* show's producer]. . . . I said, I can't interview her without saying that this is the worst piece of foolish trash. And it is obvious, even from her book, that after the first meeting you didn't answer her calls. You know, I'd either say this on the air or there is no reason to have her around. . . . But I am sure they will put her on Carson and Cavett and so forth.

KISSINGER: Can you imagine that I would have said to anybody, "I am your slave"? That I wouldn't do for somebody I liked.

WALTERS: . . . My first direction is always ignore it.

KISSINGER: That is what I have done up to now.

WALTERS: But I just wonder in some things like this whether you shouldn't make a short and rather humorous and sad statement . . . like she is kind of a nut. . . . I almost think the kind of thing you should say is "I feel very sorry for Ms. Hunebelle. I am sad that what was one of the many interviews should have produced such an emotional experience in her. I would be flattered if

I were not so disturbed for this poor, sick lady"—in that vein—making her pathetic rather than interesting. . . . One thing we could do if you wanted, when I was talking to Stuart this morning I said the only thing that I did feel that I would do on this book is a sort of byline piece. . . . I could do this kind of a thing and say that we—various reporters—have talked with you about her and your feeling is one mostly of pity for Ms. Hunebelle. . . . If anyone does call you about it who seems important, I would say "I hardly know her, and am sad that this lady seems to make so much of it. I've read the book and you can see that there's nothing to it. But I feel very sorry for her. . . . I am sad that she has blown it up to such an emotional experience, and I offer her my regrets." It is too bad you have to be plagued with it. It is a terrible piece of crap.

KISSINGER: I haven't read the English version yet.

WALTERS: All she talks about is what a wonderful person she is . . . and how you avoided her at every turn.

KISSINGER: You know, I am not exactly unattracted by women, but I found her physically repulsive. She was so persistent.

WALTERS: She looks sort of unattractive in the picture with you and Nixon.

KISSINGER: She is aggressive and I had to change my phone number.

WALTERS: I said to Stuart this morning that what she is so upset about is that you came to Paris and took out a very nice girl from CBS [Margaret Osmer], and for this she about committed suicide. It's just gossip, I said to Stuart, and I won't do the interview for the book.

KISSINGER: I have never taken her out.

WALTERS: That is also clear in the book—that you never took her out, that you never answered letters, that you never returned phone calls. However, if she goes on the shows like Carson and Cavett—they haven't read the book— my advice is not to say anything, and if asked treat her as you would a sick child.

KISSINGER: She will certainly go on Carson and Cavett.

WALTERS: I can find out for you. But also I am not terribly sure other shows won't turn her down as ours did. Realistically, she will probably be doing a lot of it—she came over here just to do it. You can also have one line. Of course, you can sympathize for her, because you know she is going to make a great deal of money. . . . Just treat it as though she is making a lot of money off you. . . .

Anatoly Dobrynin
June 24, 1972, 10:28 a.m.
Kissinger had just returned from a visit to China, where he had met with Premier Chou En-lai and other officials and told them about the Soviet summit and discussed

Vietnam. A newspaper column said he and Chou discussed how to deter the Soviets from attacking China. (He later offered Chou hotline communications that could be used to provide warning of a Soviet attack.)[7]

> ... KISSINGER: ... I don't know whether you read that Joe Alsop column yes-
> terday. . . . Well, it is pure, absolute, total mystery. . . . He said that I was going
> there to discuss military measures against a Soviet attack.
>
> DOBRYNIN: Why would he write something like this?
>
> KISSINGER: Anatol, I do not understand it. First of all, I do not believe there
> will be a Soviet attack. Secondly, I have said a thousand times that I have
> never discussed any military measures with him. . . .
>
> DOBRYNIN: . . . It is interesting why he would do it. . . . He has a good personal
> relationship—
>
> KISSINGER: He has an excellent relationship with me. I am so furious with him
> that I have ordered both Haig and of course myself to cut off all contact with
> him. . . . We wouldn't do it, it would be insane in the light of our present
> relationship. But it is an absolute outrage. . . .

President Nixon
June 24, 1972, 12:25 p.m.
*Kissinger raves to Nixon about all the B-52 bombers and air strikes in South Vietnam.
And he wants to set up George McGovern for an attack.*

> ... KISSINGER: Mr. President, Abrams has certainly learned one thing. He had
> 91 B-52 strikes around Hue yesterday. . . . That's three times as many as we
> used to do in all of Vietnam. . . .
>
> NIXON: I'll bet he's glad that we forced him to take those B-52s, don't you
> think?
>
> KISSINGER: Oh, god. That commander took me around that B-52 base. You
> cannot believe it. Those B-52s are stacked one on top of another. It is abso-
> lutely awe-inspiring. . . . They have a B-52 strike in Vietnam now every 41
> minutes.
>
> NIXON: Oh, boy. Listen, Henry, this is punishing these people, believe me.
>
> KISSINGER: I would say that if these 100 B-52s are dropping their bombs at
> random without even aiming at anything, they've got to hit something if
> it's in such a concentrated area.
>
> NIXON: Sure, sure, sure. . . . Well, look what's already happened. An Loc saved.
> Kontum saved. . . . At this point, the only thing keeping this war going is
> McGovern. . . .
>
> KISSINGER: . . . I'm wondering whether I shouldn't call McGovern and give
> him just enough of a feel for the negotiations so that we can say afterwards,

knowing what we're doing, the son of a bitch is coming at us anyway. . . .
And asking him to lay off for a while.

NIXON: If you could do it discreetly, I'd do it.

KISSINGER: Well, even if it leaks.

NIXON: All right, fine.

KISSINGER: I mean, I'd call him and say, look, I want you to know what's going on.

NIXON: I'd do it also with Humphrey and [Senator Edmund] Muskie. . . .
Cover Humphrey, cover Muskie. . . .

Ronald Ziegler
June 30, 1972, 2:17 p.m.

Press Secretary Ziegler asks for guidance on a story that recently departed treasury secretary John Connally, Kissinger's rival who would soon announce the formation of Democrats for Nixon, which he led, will probably head the U.S. negotiating team when the Paris peace talks resume.

ZIEGLER: There's a story out that the "former U.S. Treasury Secretary John Connally, a tough negotiator at world financial conferences, is likely to head the U.S. team when the Vietnam peace talks reopen next month."

KISSINGER: Total nonsense.

ZIEGLER: . . . "President Nixon said last night he had a very important government assignment in mind for Connally. . . ."

KISSINGER: Out of the question.

ZIEGLER: Now, you'll level with me—if you can't tell me—

KISSINGER: Look, it's never inconceivable to me that some of our associates are playing little games that no one else knows about.

ZIEGLER: Well, you would know about this, Henry.

KISSINGER: It is inconceivable to me that a thing like this would be planned without my knowing it. . . . I would violently oppose it if it were. . . .

The Disturbed Bobby Fischer; the Cockamamie Jimmy Hoffa Pardon and POW Scheme; George McGovern, Pro-Nixon Democrats, and the Thomas Eagleton Debacle; Bombing Dikes; the Nixon Campaign and Fundraising; Swifty Lazar's Pursuit of Kissinger's Memoirs; and the Jackson Amendment on SALT

July–August 1972

In July 1972, a Teamsters vice president came to Kissinger with a claim that North Vietnam said they'd release some American prisoners of war to ex–Teamsters President Jimmy Hoffa, who'd been imprisoned for several crimes before Nixon commuted his sentence. But, and here was the hitch, Hoffa was on parole and he needed a presidential pardon to travel to Hanoi. It was a "cynical, filthy" move by the North Vietnamese, Kissinger and Nixon thought. William Taub, Hoffa's shady representative, who professed falsely to be an attorney, was calling Kissinger. Nixon counsel Charles Colson advised Kissinger to tell Taub that a pardon for Hoffa was a matter for the Justice Department, not Colson or Kissinger. Colson said Taub was trying to extort money from Hoffa by freeing him of his legal restrictions on managing a union so that he could take over the Teamsters again ("Hoffa'd love to get his hands back on that billion-dollar pension fund"); Taub could then wring a big fee out of him. But Taub claimed to

Kissinger that senior North Vietnamese negotiator Le Duc Tho was delaying a trip from Hanoi to Paris so that he could see Hoffa in Hanoi.

In mid-July, Senator George McGovern was nominated as the Democratic Party's presidential candidate. The press reported that Kissinger had helped raise money for Nixon's reelection from Democrats who found McGovern too far left. Kissinger adamantly denied it, saying he didn't raise money and didn't attend meetings where money was raised, though "I cannot guarantee that people to whom I talk may not later be hit for money." After McGovern's running mate, Senator Thomas Eagleton, acknowledged getting electric shock therapy in the 1960s and McGovern began to back off him, Kissinger and Nixon disparaged McGovern's response to the crisis as waffling, weak, cruel, and tawdry.

That July the press was reporting that the United States had bombed dikes in North Vietnam, which risked catastrophic flooding. Kissinger told UN Secretary-General Kurt Waldheim, who had expressed concern about it and who Kissinger threatened to "smash" to his friend Nelson Rockefeller, that North Vietnam was waging a vicious propaganda campaign and that no dikes had been breached. Nixon told Kissinger "we may have to take them out."

The Hollywood agent Irving "Swifty" Lazar was then pursuing Kissinger to represent his memoirs, dangling a potential $3 million advance. ("It's a lot of money. It's never been done before.") Kissinger was all ears.

Kissinger was meanwhile finessing an amendment by Senator Henry Jackson, a critic of the SALT arms control agreement who believed it gave the Soviets a potential advantage; his amendment advocated a treaty that provided for parity in strategic weapons. Kissinger did not want the administration to promote it, partly because it would hurt relations with the Soviets, but told Jackson that they were "behind you 1,000 percent," at least with modifications, while telling Soviet Ambassador Anatoly Dobrynin that Jackson's amendment had been "totally emasculated."

David Frost
July 3, 1972, 10:45 a.m.
Television journalist Frost asks Kissinger to persuade the "mentally disturbed" chess master Bobby Fischer to get on a plane to Iceland for his World Chess Championship match with Boris Spassky.

> ... FROST: ... I've had three calls this morning about a hilarious diplomatic matter that I just wanted to ask you whether you thought it was worth anyone at the White House, from yourself down, as it were, doing anything about. ... It's about America's gift to the world of chess—Bobby Fischer.

He's a very, very mixed-up gentleman. I got to know him when he appeared on my show. . . . I lent him my lawyer . . . to sort out his various problems with the International Chess Federation. And he is in fact . . . mentally disturbed. . . . He thinks he's the victim of a conspiracy and goodness knows what else. And now, face to face with what he's worked for all his life, he's terrified to get on that plane to Iceland, and if he doesn't get on a plane to Iceland today he'll be disqualified. . . . My lawyer washed his hands of him because he got impossible two weeks ago. But now Bobby has asked him to get involved again. Now, Jim Slater, my business partner in London who is a chess fanatic . . . called me from London to say that . . . Bobby Fischer's latest claim was that he wanted 30 percent of the gate in addition to the prize money. . . . I think the Icelanders have now given in on the gate money. But Jim's point was that worldwide Bobby Fischer of America, the first American to be pitched against the Russians for the World Chess Championship, ain't looking too good in the world's press today. . . . And Bobby Fischer is greedy, but he's not greedy for money so much. . . . Paul Marshall, my attorney, thinks that's his way of revenging himself on the world that has mistreated him, by not turning up for his match. So of course what he is in fact destroying is himself. Anyway, Paul Marshall thought that one of the few things that would get him there, if it was thought worthwhile getting him there, and it will be awful public relations certainly if he doesn't, was a call from someone in authority like yourself, or whoever would make a call like this, saying, "Do it for America, Bobby, we're all rooting for you." . . .

KISSINGER: Yeah, I'll do it. I do all the nutty things around here. . . . I think if I call him I should just call him and tell him from a foreign policy point of view I hope the hell he gets over there.

FROST: Right. And I think he would be so thrilled. . . .

KISSINGER: I thought he was just plain chicken, but apparently he's really nuts.

FROST: Yes, it's deeper than just plain chicken. I just thought it was worth putting it before you because I think it is bad publicity for America. It may be unavoidable, but whereas if he wins—

KISSINGER: But is he in any shape to win?

FROST: I don't know. I mean, I guess those people have incredible nervous energy. You know, maybe this has put him in great condition, or maybe he'll be a basket case. . . .

KISSINGER: I'll give him a call. When does he have to get over there?

FROST: Well, that's the hell of it, Paul was saying. The only flight is an Icelandic Airlines flight through the night tonight. . . . It should have started Sunday and they gave him the maximum postponement, which is two days. And if he's not there tomorrow he's disqualified. . . .

Ken Clawson
July 3, 1972, 12:02 p.m.
Kissinger is loath to participate in the White House's "merchandising" of the Soviet summit.

... CLAWSON: Number one is the *Making of the Summit* special which we've agreed to with ABC.... It's part of the merchandising package that's coming out of the Russian trip....

KISSINGER: You wouldn't mind not using the word "merchandising" with me, will you? ... Has the president ever focused on this or is this one of these Colson hotshot ideas?

CLAWSON: No, sir, it is not a Colson hotshot. It was approved by Haldeman.

KISSINGER: You know, for six months they've been looking for a good television spot for me. I just can't believe that that is the one.... Hell, I'll do what people ask me to do, I don't give a damn....

President Nixon
July 5, 1972, 12:45 p.m.
Harold Gibbons, a Teamsters vice president and George McGovern supporter, claimed that North Vietnam said they'd release some POWs to Jimmy Hoffa if Nixon pardoned him so he could travel.

... KISSINGER: This fellow Gibbons is here with an odd proposition. The North Vietnamese have approached him and Hoffa's lawyer saying Hoffa should enter the negotiations and they'd receive them in Hanoi if we'd give him a pardon.

NIXON: Oh, my god.

KISSINGER: And they'd let him come back with some prisoners.... That's just a cynical, filthy—

NIXON: That is so cynical and filthy. I mean, give him a pardon? Good god. Also that screws us up. Hoffa's using them and they're using Hoffa in order to screw [Teamsters President Frank] Fitzsimmons, too.... Just say we can't negotiate in other channels.

KISSINGER: I've told them we can't negotiate in other channels and it can't be done.

NIXON: It's always their way too, you know, to say we'll give you three or four prisoners, and tokenism and so forth. These guys, though, are hurting, that's all.

KISSINGER: It's a pretty desperate move....

Anatoly Dobrynin
July 6, 1972, 12:30 p.m.

Kissinger complains to the Soviet ambassador about North Vietnam's alleged offer to release POWs to Hoffa, maintaining that North Vietnamese negotiator Le Duc Tho had talked to William Taub, Hoffa's purported lawyer. (Actually, Tho had refused to meet with him.)[1]

    ... KISSINGER: ... Really sometimes Hanoi is beyond my comprehension. Now what they have done, they've invited James Hoffa to Hanoi ... a man who was convicted, and they imply to him that he was a better negotiator than we. Le Duc Tho talked to his lawyer in Sophia and indicated they would give him some prisoners if he came. You know, it's stupid. ... What do you think would happen if I called the press together and said, "Look ... they are trying to get us involved with an ex-convict?" ... It's awfully hard to see how they can be serious if they keep doing idiotic things like this. ...

    DOBRYNIN: They have some ideas about some of your countrymen much different than what some other people have outside Hanoi. ...

    KISSINGER: Actually this particular move, if I wanted to be nasty, would play into our hands. ...

    DOBRYNIN: I don't really think it is connected with the negotiations. ... I don't know what they are doing this for. I never heard about it.

    KISSINGER: No, no, they got Le Duc Tho involved in it personally. ...

Charles Colson
July 10, 1972, 9:20 a.m.
Kissinger tells Nixon counsel Colson that he suggested to Harold Gibbons of the Teamsters that Gibbons rather than Jimmy Hoffa discuss the release of American POWs with the North Vietnamese when he's in Hanoi. Colson briefs Kissinger on the disreputable William Taub, who had been calling Kissinger after meeting with him. Colson advises him to tell Taub that a pardon for Hoffa is a Justice Department matter and to turn him off. Colson also reports that the prospects of Nixon's reelection look "frighteningly good."

    KISSINGER: Who gave me instructions to butter up Gibbons?

    COLSON: ... I didn't want you to butter him up, I wanted you to have him sent over to Hanoi. ...

    KISSINGER: That is what I am trying to do. ... He called me. ... The next thing I heard was at 9:45 that morning I got a message saying that Gibbons and Taub ... [were] on the way. ... Well, they got no comfort from me. I was extremely tough and told them it was out of the question that I would do anything. That we wouldn't tolerate having Hanoi determine our negotiator. The only thing is that I said to Gibbons that perhaps I would want him—if he wanted to go instead of Hoffa alone, without Hoffa, because he was going to go anyway. . . .

COLSON: Well, if he was going to be gone anytime I would love him gone starting this coming weekend. Because Monday the Teamsters will meet in California and Gibbons we know is a no vote. In other words, he will vote against the president, the endorsement of the president. . . .

KISSINGER: Well, now the immediate problem is Taub is calling me all the time. I haven't taken his call.

COLSON: Let me give you some background on Taub, because he called here some time ago and was very abusive to the gals in the office, and eventually I got him on the phone and . . . he was cursing me. Then I had a fellow here who knows Jimmy Hoffa call Hoffa, and Hoffa said he's trying to avoid the guy. He said he's an extortionist and he's trying to get him [Hoffa] loose and free of his restrictions so he can take over the Teamsters again, and then he wants to hold him up for a big fee. He said the guy is not speaking with his authority but I think the guy is speaking with Gibbons's authority. That's pretty clear.

KISSINGER: Gibbons was with him.

COLSON: Oh, sure, and you see . . . they are desperately trying to get Hoffa sprung loose of his restrictions [against management of a labor organization until 1980 as a condition of Nixon's earlier commutation of his prison sentence] so that he can take over the Teamsters. . . . They're trying to make it appear that we need Hoffa to get the endorsement, which is not true. And it would be selling out Fitz [Teamsters President Frank Fitzsimmons, Hoffa's nemesis]. I mean, it would be a terrible thing for us to do. Fitz is paranoid about it; any movement on the part of Gibbons or Taub into our circle and Fitz just goes up the wall because he gets very skittish. . . .

KISSINGER: . . . I expect a call from Taub. I've had several. I'll tell him we can't do anything for Hoffa, is that right?

COLSON: Yes. Well, I wouldn't put it that way; I'd say that the Hoffa issue [a pardon] has to be settled on its own and has nothing to do with this cockeyed proposal.

KISSINGER: Well, can I say it's under consideration?

COLSON: No, Jesus Christ, that would kill us. . . . What you say to Taub is that . . . the restrictions on Mr. Hoffa . . . is a matter that is the responsibility of the Department of Justice and that it's nothing that you . . . would have any interest in in terms of peace negotiations. . . .

KISSINGER: Okay, fine. I've already told him that. I'll just reaffirm what I've said.

COLSON: Yeah, what I said to Taub when he called here, I said, "Look, first of all, I resent your using this kind of a gimmick to try to indirectly get at a problem that you know the answer to directly. And secondly, you're asking us to rescind a very deliberate action of the president and the Department of Justice so that we can have Mr. Hoffa take part in some cockeyed peace scheme." I said, "That's just crazy and I don't like the technique you're using." It's a form of bribery, and I just shut him off very cold. And Taub is bad news. If you want to butter up—

KISSINGER: Yeah, no, no, listen, Colson, Chuck, don't repeat the same thing a hundred times. I didn't know who Taub was. I got a call from Gibbons, who said he had an initiative from Hanoi with respect to the release of prisoners. I had to see him. . . . I didn't know he was bringing Taub. I didn't know until he got here who the hell Taub was, and then I was pretty tough with him.

COLSON: I'm just saying now, from this point forward . . . it is in our interest to turn Taub off. Now, whatever can be done with Gibbons to butter him up or get him out of the country, all that's fine. . . . Let me assure you these guys are playing for very big stakes. You know, Hoffa'd love to get his hands back on that billion-dollar pension fund.

KISSINGER: Yeah, well, I'm not going to do any more than I've done, but on the other hand for me to refuse to see somebody who says he has information on prisoners would have been suicide. . . . I hate to send Gibbons to Hanoi before we've had our talks with the North Vietnamese, to tell you the truth. . . . The only other thing I may do is to call Gibbons later in the week and tell him that if he wants to return to Hanoi—I also told Gibbons he'd never go as our emissary, that if he went he would go on his own. I'd listen to whatever information he'd bring back, but I'd give him none to take there.

COLSON: That's good; that's excellent. Okay, I can handle this well with Fitzsimmons once we get their endorsement. . . .

KISSINGER: How does the political situation look to you as long as I got you on the phone?

COLSON: Frighteningly good, Henry.

KISSINGER: . . . I mean, we've got to get some enthusiasm on our side.

COLSON: Well, there's none at all because we're so far ahead. . . . If you look at any of the polls and you look at the incredible problems the Democrats have and the massive defections that will take place if McGovern is the nominee, you know, it's very difficult to get our troops all exercised because they figure the president is going to win all 50 states.

KISSINGER: Yeah, but . . . what we've got to do, don't you think, is to act as if we're going to lose all 50.

COLSON: No, not yet. At some point you want to scare people, yes, but right now what you want is the enormous winner psychology that LBJ had going in 1964 so that you get massive defections of Democrats, which is going to happen. In other words, make it a wise thing for Democrats to jump on our bandwagon. . . .

Ronald Ziegler
July 10, 1972, 10:10 a.m.
Kissinger is upset about a piece in the Washington Post *on the French journalist Danielle Hunebelle's book* Dear Henry, *in which she told how she fell in love with him.*[2]

> . . . KISSINGER: . . . Ron, did you see that interview that Sally Quinn did with that maniac Hunebelle? . . . They had a picture of me and a Hunebelle quote that unless you have a nuclear bomb you're of no interest to Kissinger. . . . I just wondered whether the time had come to slam her.
>
> ZIEGLER: Leave it alone, Henry. . . . The moment you slam her, you're going to have a whole series of other articles like that. Ignore her. . . . Henry, public figures are used. This is the case where she is trying to use you. . . . And the only thing you can do in this instance . . . is to ignore it. Because the moment—and you know you could write a book on this—the moment that a public figure responds to something like this, you don't benefit yourself—you simply escalate the person trying to take advantage of [you]. That would be the thing she would want more than anything else. . . .

William Taub
July 13, 1972, 8:37 a.m.
Jimmy Hoffa's representative claims that Le Duc Tho was delaying his departure from Hanoi to Paris to coincide with Hoffa's trip to Hanoi (an absurdity), and points out that Colson, who Kissinger says is one of the people reviewing Hoffa's request for a pardon that would allow him to travel, is friendly with Hoffa's rival, Teamsters President Frank Fitzsimmons.

> . . . TAUB: . . . Hoffa has decided that he very definitely would like to leave on the 27th . . . together with Gibbons and myself to Hanoi. . . . We have been getting communications from abroad within the last 30 minutes that would make his position far more important to this side in things that might occur over there that would be beneficial. . . . We hear from our people in Paris that Le Duc Tho was delaying his departure coming into Paris as to when Mr. Hoffa would arrive, and Hoffa said that it's necessary to confirm the date.
>
> KISSINGER: Yeah, but Le Duc Tho is already on the way, so this can't be right.
>
> TAUB: Well, I just talked to Paris. . . . Are we in a position to be able to know what will or won't be with respect to the dates—

KISSINGER: Well, I cannot tell you that. The people who are handling the legal question, as I told you, are the attorney general and John Dean in the White House. . . . John Dean and Chuck Colson. . . .

TAUB: Well, Colson of course you know is a nemesis to Hoffa. Colson is palsy-walsy with Fitzsimmons. . . . I have the same impression that Hoffa has, that if this comes down with Colson, because of an intimate relationship, that there would be a degree of prejudice that would be harmful to the effort of Hoffa. . . .

KISSINGER: Well, then deal with John Dean. . . . And the other person, of course, is the attorney general.

TAUB: Now Kleindienst is on vacation. . . .

Charles Colson
July 13, 1972, 9:22 a.m.
Kissinger reports to Colson that Taub and Hoffa planned to fly to Hanoi and asks who in the Justice Department he can pass Taub off to about a pardon. Colson suggests young Nixon counsel John Dean and brags that Teamsters President Fitzsimmons is "in my pocket" rather than the other way around. They also take up Nixon's reelection prospects again.

KISSINGER: Chuck, I had a call from Taub saying they have decided to go to Hanoi on the 27th. . . . Now, the thing is that he found out that Kleindienst is on vacation. Is there anyone in Justice he can talk to? I just want him off my back.

COLSON: Well, Kleindienst is not on vacation; he's probably ducking it. But I wouldn't take a call from Taub if his life depended on it. Yes, I would tell him to call John Dean here.

KISSINGER: I also told him to get in touch with John Dean and you, whereupon he blew his top and said you are in Fitzsimmons's pocket. . . .

COLSON: He's got the pockets a little reversed. Fitzsimmons is in my pocket. . . . He's a son of a bitch, a real extortionist. We'll take care of it. Why don't you just tell him to get in touch with John Dean.

KISSINGER: And you will program John Dean? . . . How does the political situation look to you?

COLSON: Great. . . . I'm just worried that it looks so good. It's very hard to keep momentum. . . .

KISSINGER: Well, I think we need a tough organization 'cause these guys [the Democrats] are going to be impossible.

COLSON: Yes, they are . . . very, very effective operators. They're shrewd.

KISSINGER: Yes, and unprincipled.

COLSON: Totally, totally. That just means we have to be a little unprincipled ourselves, Henry.

KISSINGER: Well, that doesn't come easy to you, I know.

COLSON: No, not to me. I have an overriding principle, which is I like to win. . . .

John Dean
July 13, 1972, 9:30 a.m.
Kissinger apprises Dean of Taub and Hoffa's scheme and suggests how to handle Hoffa's request for a pardon.

KISSINGER: . . . I've been bothered by this fellow Taub, who is Hoffa's lawyer, and they have a weird scheme by which Hoffa is supposed to go to Hanoi and get some prisoners. . . . And for that he needs a pardon, or something to make it possible for him to go. I have told him I absolutely do not tolerate other negotiators. . . . I was very brutal with him. I said if the North Vietnamese want to pick ex-convicts to release prisoners to, that's their problem. We will not play that game. But, on the other hand, I was certain that Hoffa's case would receive all the legal attention, you know, that these cases get, and that he would be neither helped nor prejudiced by this effort. . . . I think our strategy should be to be conciliatory and helpful but under no circumstances permit this negotiation to affect it. . . . So if, you know, without doing any more than another citizen gets, at least Taub can understand that you've been talked to.

DEAN: Well, we can give him a little stroke to make it look like we're very interested and concerned. . . .

Ray Caldero
July 13, 1972, 10:03 a.m.
A Nixon reelection campaign worker and Kissinger discuss how to deal with the actress Terry Moore, who Kissinger reportedly dated.

. . . CALDERO: I just got off the phone five minutes ago with Terry Moore.

KISSINGER: Well, that's why I'm calling you. She just called me and said she's got something set up with the Osmond Brothers. . . . I didn't know who the hell she was; she called up and said she was a friend of [Nixon's friend] Bebe Rebozo's, and she wanted to help out in the campaign. . . . She said, well, what do you do in the afternoons? I said I sit on the beach. She said, well, can I bring my kid and come by the beach? Well, she arrived with her kid and her mother, and drove us absolutely out of our heads. . . . I wasn't alone with her for 30 seconds.

CALDERO: Well, I know that. My only point is I recognize it as a potential problem because . . . she'll say to god knows who, gee, I was with Henry Kissinger on the beach yesterday. . . .

KISSINGER: Well, isn't she a little cracked?

CALDERO: It certainly seems like that to me. . . . I said, if you say something and you have a couple of drinks and you said you were with Henry Kissinger and a reporter is there, I said, this thing could be blown completely out of proportion. . . . And she said, I am now writing for 16 newspapers in a column. . . .

KISSINGER: Well, that's another thing. She spent about an hour at most with me. And now she's written a goddamn column about my kids. But, of course, the impression is that god knows what was going on if she's down here with her kids. . . . But can you get Terry Moore off my back? . . . She's written that article for the *Citizens News* about my kids, but, of course, she's building herself up as knowing me very well.

CALDERO: . . . Let me see if I can kill the column.

KISSINGER: . . . I thought I'd see her, get her lined up. . . .

Tom Braden
July 21, 1972, 5 p.m.
Columnist Braden asks Kissinger about reports that he helped raise funds for Nixon's reelection in California from Democrats who didn't care for Senator George McGovern, who had been nominated the Democratic Party's presidential candidate.

BRADEN: Listen, Henry, I heard a story I would like to check with you. When you were in California did you during the week of the Democratic convention meet with a number of people who were Democratic contributors?

KISSINGER: I want to be careful in my answer. . . . I do not raise money. I do not go to meetings at which money is raised. I do not participate in any way in that sort of fundraising or political activities. I cannot guarantee that people to whom I talk may not later be hit for money. If it is done, it is done without my knowledge, direct or indirect. When I was in California, Taft Schreiber asked me to have lunch with a group of businessmen and asked me to talk to them about the president's foreign policy. I did not know who they were, except senior people. I did not know whether they were Democrats or Republicans. . . . I did not discuss McGovern or the president as such. I could not tell if they were Democrats or Republicans, so you might say there were five Democrats—

BRADEN: They were all Democrats.

KISSINGER: I did not know. . . . I will not knowingly participate in anything of a partisan nature. . . . I will not attack McGovern and if you will talk to the people at the Bistro you will find I did not attack McGovern.

BRADEN: . . . Almost all of the people at the lunch were past contributors of the Democratic Party.

KISSINGER: I didn't ask them for money or support. . . . They maybe asked for money at some later time or with a phone call. . . .

Taft Schreiber
July 21, 1972, 6:03 p.m.
Kissinger wants some assurances from Nixon fundraiser Schreiber, who organized the lunch in California discussed above, about a dinner at which he will be speaking to Nixon supporters.

KISSINGER: . . . What I have to be sure of, though, is that this is a bipartisan meeting next week—they aren't all Democrats.

SCHREIBER: We were very careful—half and half at least.

KISSINGER: Secondly, there will be no fundraising at the dinner or afterwards right away. . . . In other words, when I leave the room, you won't immediately start badgering—

SCHREIBER: No, I'm going with you. . . . I'm not going to do anything like that because it would be very embarrassing. I have said to do it either before there is a dinner or a few days later drop in and see the people, but do not do it that way. . . .

KISSINGER: No, but they . . . cannot do it at that same meeting. . . . They cannot do it before I enter the room either.

SCHREIBER: This is not a fundraising affair. This is to have our friends meet you—and to really enunciate the president's policy. . . .

KISSINGER: Good. You didn't ask for money at that other meeting, did you? . . .

SCHREIBER: There was not one word said. . . .

Nelson Rockefeller
July 25, 1972, 3:00 p.m.
Kissinger asks Governor Rockefeller if he can persuade UN Secretary-General Kurt Waldheim, who'd expressed concern about U.S. bombing of dikes in North Vietnam and urged that it be stopped,[3] to pipe down.

. . . KISSINGER: Nelson, one thing I wanted to ask you is how well you get along with Waldheim.

ROCKEFELLER: Very well.

KISSINGER: I wondered whether on a personal basis you could warn him against getting himself involved in Vietnam, because we'll just have to smash him if he keeps this up. . . . He made a statement yesterday attacking our bombing. And we just can't have that. . . . And it's in his own interest, because we can kill him. We'll just get [Congressman Otto] Passman to withhold his appropriations next year. . . . If you could find a tactful way of saying that to him.

ROCKEFELLER: I can do that with no problem at all.

KISSINGER: Well, I think it would be a big help. . . . We can't have Waldheim throwing our domestic opposition into a worldwide communist movement. . . .

Kurt Waldheim
July 27, 1972, 10:23 a.m.
The UN secretary-general explains to Kissinger his remarks at a press conference on the bombing of the dikes. Kissinger says no dikes have been breached and asks why the North Vietnamese haven't filled the holes in them after earlier flooding. Waldheim is satisfied with his assurance that the administration was not intentionally bombing them. (Sweden's ambassador to North Vietnam and a French journalist had both said the dikes had been bombed intentionally.)[4]

WALDHEIM: I heard you were in New York yesterday but I couldn't reach you so I thought it best if I ring you up this morning. And I thought I should because of this incident with regard to the bombing of the dikes in North Vietnam. . . . I stressed that this information I got through private, unofficial channels . . . which our man got in Paris. . . . He was informed by the North Vietnamese delegation about the dikes. . . . Now, would you please tell the president for me the situation was very difficult because I didn't raise the question and they jumped on me. . . . But I do want to say that I have expressed my concern already, very early after the invasion started on some occasion.

KISSINGER: Yeah, I remember your conversation with the president very well. And our concern is just that this of course is going to become a major domestic issue. We believe that what Hanoi is doing is a really nasty propaganda campaign. If we wanted to breach the dikes North Vietnam would be under water now. I mean, there's no way of missing them. There's no rational explanation why we would have to hit a dike here and a dike there with little bombs that are not designed for it. Now, why is it that they don't fill those holes that they keep showing people? They haven't shown one single breaching of a dike and this is of course what concerns us.

WALDHEIM: I have seen some of the pictures which [U.S. Ambassador to the UN] George Bush showed me on the bombing of the dikes and I saw already in these pictures that apparently there are small craters caused by accidental bombing or by bombing targets, military targets, nearby.

KISSINGER: Exactly. I can assure you, Mr. Secretary-General, it is not our policy. . . . If we wanted to breach the dikes we could easily breach them. . . . And not even the North Vietnamese claim we have breached any dike. All they said is we've hit a few dikes. . . . I think they are in trouble because they didn't repair the dikes last summer after the floods adequately and they want to use us as an alibi. . . . This is an extremely sensitive issue with us.

WALDHEIM: Yes, I am fully aware now. . . . I didn't at all mean the allegations are correct. . . . I always conditioned it, if you read my answer, with "if the allegations are correct" I am concerned because this route would lead to human suffering and disaster. . . . Now you are telling me they are not correct and I think this satisfies the matter. . . .

Irving Lazar
July 28, 1972, 3:54 p.m.
The famous Hollywood agent Irving "Swifty" Lazar approaches Kissinger about selling the French-language rights to his books but really has in mind representing him on his memoirs, raising the possibility of a huge advance. Kissinger is interested.

LAZAR: Listen, I called you about something which is personal, but I was going to wait to see you, but then I thought I'd better tell you about it. When I was in Paris last, all of the publishers, the leading publishers . . . said to me, do you know Dr. Kissinger? I said yes, I do. They said, well, you know, we've never had a translation of any of his books in Paris. . . . These are the top publishers in Paris and as a matter of fact also in London who want to republish in French, and in other countries for that matter. . . . Is that of any interest to you?

KISSINGER: Yeah, in principle, yes.

LAZAR: Would you like me to do something about it? . . . They were especially interested in Bismarck and in Metternich [Kissinger's book *A World Restored: Metternich, Castlereagh and the Problems of Peace, 1812–1822* and an unfinished manuscript on Bismarck that was published in abbreviated form as "The White Revolutionary: Reflections on Bismarck" in *Daedalus*]. . . .

KISSINGER: Well, if you want to look into it. I think it's probably on a scale smaller than the one you usually operate.

LAZAR: My dear Henry, nothing would please me more. . . . It's not a question of commissions. . . . The fact of the matter is I was going to talk to you. . . . When I made an arrangement for at least two people—one was involving

Herman Wouk and the other was involving Truman Capote—in Truman Capote's case he was able to elicit three-quarters of a million dollars in stock in his contract for two novels . . . a considerable sum of money. It can be done, and as a matter of fact in Wouk's case it involved over a million dollars in stock of Time-Life, which owns Little, Brown. In your case, I can tell you now, I have been told by three major publishers with very conglomerate stock interests that at any time that you are ready to discuss a book of your own, and this not necessarily as a critique on your association with the president, nothing like that, just your own viewpoint of international politics we're talking about now—perhaps we have to discuss some other areas—but it would in no way be necessary or required or even expected that you would express a viewpoint of the president of the United States, both now or in the event that he were [re]elected and you did not choose to retain your position—we're now talking about three million dollars. I once told you in a rather jocular way at the Kirk Douglases that they were interested in two million; let me tell you, it's closer to three million. It's a lot of money. It's never been done before, but I can tell you that's what it would be worth. . . . I would like to come down to Washington and just spend a little time and discuss it with you.

KISSINGER: Well, I'd be delighted. . . .

LAZAR: I would be flattered beyond words. . . . At any rate what I will do for the moment is some of your books are out of print but I can get copies. If I find that I cannot, even from the publisher—

KISSINGER: I have some extra ones around.

LAZAR: . . . If you would be nice enough to send me a copy of each, I can tell you now that somewhere along the line . . . I'm talking about only a major publisher . . . we'll have an offer for you and then we'll see how interesting it is.

KISSINGER: Okay. . . . You know, I'll be on the West Coast, but you will be in Europe, the last week of August and first week in September.

LAZAR: I may delay my departure and wait for you. . . . If I could come to New York the second week in August I could come down to Washington then. . . .

KISSINGER: That might be a good idea.

LAZAR: I can see you before I go to Europe.

KISSINGER: Good, excellent. . . .

President Nixon

July 29, 1972, 10:10 a.m.

The administration had released a report stating that U.S. bombing had unintentionally damaged North Vietnam's dikes in 12 places but that the impact was minor.[5] Nixon says "we may have to take them out" after the November election, and Kissinger declares that "we must stop at nothing." They also discuss statements by George McGovern about his running mate, Senator Thomas Eagleton, who had acknowledged several days earlier receiving electric shock therapy for nervous exhaustion and depression in the 1960s. Kissinger disparages McGovern as a "tawdry guy."

... NIXON: Well, the dike story, I guess, got out all right.

KISSINGER: It got out all right, but of course the *Washington Post* put a dirty headline on it....

NIXON: ... I don't think the country gives one damn about these dikes. If they push it any further, I'll say, now look, if they put anti-aircraft on there and start shooting down American planes, of course we are not going to risk American pilots.

KISSINGER: And we have to consider the thing after November anyway; I wouldn't say that now.

NIXON: Right. I mean we may have to take them out.

KISSINGER: I think after November, we must do what it takes to end this war—we must stop at nothing.

NIXON: Damn right, and we are not going to hesitate about anything.

KISSINGER: We can't go through another two years. . . . McGovern is now shafting Eagleton. . . . McGovern has now, late last night, held a press conference in which he has really pulled the rug out from under Eagleton. . . . He says there are three questions: Eagleton's mental health, the impact on the Democratic ticket, and the question of whether Eagleton should have told him the full details to him before his nomination as VP. In terms of political impact, McGovern remarked, "A poll might show that 99 percent supported Eagleton, but 1 percent who opposed him would still lose the election for the Democrats in a close race." ...

NIXON: In other words, Eagleton's got to have 100 percent?

KISSINGER: Right. . . . I don't see how he can survive that.

NIXON: ... I think McGovern is very ill-advised to do this. He shouldn't have any press conference at this point. Wait until he has made a decision and until he has talked to him. Don't do that to a man—that's damn cruel.

KISSINGER: I think McGovern is showing himself a tawdry guy and weak. . . . Is this man fit to be president? . . . Either McGovern should have dropped him from the ticket right away, saying this is an absolutely clean, moral campaign and I can't have a man who lied, or he should have stood behind him and gotten Eagleton to resign—not to waffle around between first supporting him and then pulling the rug out from under him. . . . He hasn't done anything right yet....

David Abshire
August 4, 1972, 2:58 p.m.

Senator Henry Jackson, a critic of the SALT agreement with the Soviets limiting levels of offensive weapons, believing it gave them a potential advantage in missiles, had introduced an amendment urging that Nixon seek a treaty that would not limit the United States to levels of strategic weapons inferior to those of the Soviets. Kissinger tells Assistant Secretary of State Abshire they should not promote it.

> KISSINGER: Dave, I wanted to find out from you where that goddamn Jackson amendment stands. . . . Frankly, I don't give a damn if that thing dies. . . . I don't want us to be pushing it. . . . I told Jackson to go ahead and do what you want, but we are going to stay out of it, and then some of our eager beavers apparently were lining up support. . . . I would like to get back as close to the original position as possible, that we can tolerate it but not push it. . . . And I just don't want us to say we need it. . . .

Henry Jackson
August 6, 1972, 11:40 a.m.
Kissinger tells Jackson that they are fully behind him and will support a compromise to his amendment that deletes language objectionable to the Soviets. Kissinger says "the hell with" Gerard Smith, the head of the U.S. SALT delegation and the Arms Control and Disarmament Agency.

> KISSINGER: I want you to know we are behind you 1,000 percent. . . . Our problem is that we want to keep the Soviets quiet during this period that we are squeezing the North Vietnamese. . . . As long as you are willing to take out that paragraph that is invidious of the Soviets . . . I can go along with it. Now, you know Smith . . . wired again. But the hell with him.
> JACKSON: Poor Smith. He's been used by the people around him. . . . Those people are against the president. You know the story.
> KISSINGER: That's right. . . . They are against everything we have tried to do. . . . You know, these are the moralists who on the one hand bleed over every bomb dropped in Vietnam, but in strategic forces anything that doesn't kill 50 million they don't want. . . .

Anatoly Dobrynin
August 7, 1972, 10:55 a.m.
Kissinger advises Dobrynin that they were trying to get Jackson to agree to wording in his amendment that is meaningless and that it had been "totally emasculated."

> . . . KISSINGER: Now, Anatol, I wanted to talk to you about the Jackson amendment. . . . What we have done is to try to get his agreement to a formulation

which is essentially meaningless. . . . Now, we are taking out that paragraph in which he says if the Soviet Union does certain things . . . then it will have bad consequences. We don't mention the Soviet Union at all. . . . We will say it has no legal force. . . . And we are construing it only as a support of what has already been stated to the Soviet side by the administration. . . . Nothing is being said that is not already a matter of public record. . . . What we are saying—the Jackson amendment does not constitute a reservation or interpretation to the agreement in any legal sense. . . . It has been totally emasculated now. . . .

John Chancellor
August 21, 1972, 10:45 a.m.
NBC Nightly News *anchor Chancellor proposes doing a softball interview with Kissinger during the Republican Convention in Miami that "looks journalistic and credible."*

. . . CHANCELLOR: . . . You're going to be pursued by a whole pack of those floor people. . . . If you're in the first or second row there, there will be a lot of Secret Service people there in front of you but there will also be floor reporters shimmying down ropes and crawling under the chairs and there will be a big mob. . . . What if I were to come out to Key Biscayne on Wednesday morning and we would make a few minutes of film? . . . I think we can fashion something . . . that looks reasonable. In other words, it looks journalistic and credible, but doesn't end up with my hectoring you about negotiations that are underway. . . . Then you could get to the hall and say, "Look, I'm sorry, I'm saying absolutely nothing to anybody." And this gaggle of reporters would go away. Because everybody's editor is going to say if Kissinger walks in the hall, get him. . . . It's very easy for me either before or after sessions . . . to just get in a car very quietly and discreetly and turn up at Key Biscayne. No one would know and we could just simply do something on film that we could play that evening. And you could do it outside of all the tensions of the hall, which for you will be reasonably tense. I mean, there will be a lot of people shoving microphones at you. . . . And you can say, "No, I'm sorry, I'm here as an observer and I'm not going to say anything." . . .

Maligning and Attacking George McGovern; Nixon's Backing of the Jackson SALT Amendment; Connally and Resignation Rumors; *Kissinger: The Adventures of Super-Kraut*; the October Peace Agreement—Leaning on Thieu, His Rejection and "Suicide," Hanoi's Demand That It Be Upheld and Signed, "Peace Is at Hand," and Fear of a Blow-Up

September–October 1972

In September 1972, Kissinger was enraged to learn that a Nixon assistant had asked Nixon to phone Senator Henry Jackson in support of his amendment to the SALT arms control agreement. Worried about violating a promise he'd made to Soviet leader Leonid Brezhnev that they wouldn't support it, Kissinger by now just wanted the amendment passed and out of the way since it was holding up congressional approval of the SALT agreement.

In October, a book on Kissinger had his brother, Walter, a wealthy businessman, up in arms, as it reportedly alleged that Walter had benefited financially from nepotism as a result of Kissinger's position. Kissinger phoned *CBS Evening News* anchor Walter Cronkite to keep him from running with the story.

In mid-October, Kissinger reached a peace agreement at long last with the North Vietnamese. But South Vietnamese President Nguyen Van Thieu refused to sign it, believing his country had been sold out and betrayed by the United States. On October 26, after Hanoi put out the main points of the agreement, said it had been assured that the agreement was complete, and demanded that it be signed per the agreed timetable, Kissinger told Soviet Ambassador Dobrynin "your friends have gone crazy"; he held a press conference where he infamously declared, "We believe that peace is at hand." An overjoyed Charles Colson gushed to Kissinger afterward that his press conference, "one of the most brilliant performances I have ever seen in my life," had won Nixon's re-election and finished off Democratic presidential candidate George McGovern. But Nixon wondered whether Hanoi or Saigon might now "blow the whistle" on them by revealing that peace was not really at hand. Kissinger asked Dobrynin to take steps toward North Vietnam that would make it easier to convince South Vietnam to accept the agreement, and requested his help getting the North Vietnamese to delay the signing of the agreement so that he could work on Thieu. He not only had to persuade Thieu to get on board with the agreement but had to keep Hanoi from breaking off the peace talks.

Spiro Agnew
September 6, 1972, 11:50 a.m.
The vice president informs Kissinger that he'd received confidential word that George McGovern was sending a prominent emissary to Israel.

AGNEW: I had an interesting piece of information. I don't know whether it really is going to be of any assistance to you, but at the southern governors conference yesterday, in confidence from a source I can't reveal, except to say a very high source, word was passed to me that McGovern is getting ready to send a very visible emissary to Israel. . . .

KISSINGER: I think it's a ploy. That guy has done nothing that isn't tawdry.

AGNEW: Let me pass on to you the source. . . . It's Governor [Marvin] Mandel. . . . Mandel refused to go. . . .

KISSINGER: Is Mandel Jewish?

AGNEW: Yeah.

KISSINGER: What a tawdry maneuver. . . . If you said a hundredth of what this man is saying, you'd have the editorialists frothing at the mouth about this. . . . That campaign's deviousness. . . . I am seeing the Israeli ambassador . . . tomorrow and I'm going to raise hell—I won't mention this—I'll just tell him better not horse around with McGovern too much. . . . But I don't think they will because they count the aircraft carriers.

AGNEW: Yeah. But it just shows that he will go to any limits, any limits.

KISSINGER: You know, for a man to say he would padlock every base in Asia—

AGNEW: Isn't that ridiculous?

KISSINGER: Which means Korea, Japan—it would mean the end of our China policy because the only interest we have for the Chinese is our strength. It is unbelievable.

AGNEW: . . . He's making such an ass of himself.

KISSINGER: Oh, he's finished.

AGNEW: There's little that we need to say.

KISSINGER: You don't think that there's untapped resources there that we don't see?

AGNEW: No, I don't. . . . I think the reaction I've had as I've moved around from people—and Democrats, particularly these Democratic governors—they are desperately embarrassed by this man. . . .

Taft Schreiber

September 6, 1972, 12:35 p.m.

MCA executive and Nixon fundraiser Schreiber warns Kissinger that Irving Lazar, the Hollywood agent pursuing his memoirs, is "a total, absolute liar."

SCHREIBER: I'll tell you why I called you, Henry. A very close friend of mine is Dr. [Eliot] Corday. . . . And apparently he's talked to Irving Lazar, just shooting the breeze. I guess he knows Irving because Corday has some of Irving's clients. And Lazar said that you were probably not going to be in government much longer after the—

KISSINGER: Oh, he's out of his mind.

SCHREIBER: Oh, I know that. Much after the elections and that he's made a fabulous book deal for you. Now, I know Lazar very well and he's a very, very egotistical little maniac. . . .

KISSINGER: Lazar has no authority to make any deals for me.

SCHREIBER: I know that. . . . But I think Al Haig ought to call the guy and tell him that I had called you and made this report that Dr. Corday had heard this conversation, and if he's going to say anything to others . . . that he's embarrassing you . . . and that he's got to stop this. . . . Corday started to mention it to several people here at a dinner party, and I said no, wait a minute, please don't repeat this story, it is untrue. Irving Lazar is a total, absolute liar. I was incensed.

KISSINGER: Irving Lazar has been making propositions like this for two years to me.

SCHREIBER: I know that. But he's such a terrible man that he's liable—in other words, you can never tell, if [columnists Rowland] Evans and [Robert] Novak picked this up they can make a very nasty story out of it. . . .

Harold Gibbons

September 8, 1972, 11:40 a.m.

William Taub, Jimmy Hoffa's purported lawyer, had claimed in a front-page article in that morning's New York Times *that Kissinger had approved of a trip by Hoffa to Hanoi to obtain the release of American POWs. Kissinger asks Teamsters Vice President Gibbons to shut him up.*

KISSINGER: Do you think you can bring that lawyer under control? . . . You know what he's putting out is a lot of bullshit.

GIBBONS: I know it. . . .

KISSINGER: You know I never encouraged him to go there.

GIBBONS: That's exactly right; I was there.

KISSINGER: I don't want to take on Hoffa. . . . It won't do him any good. . . . He's saying he went around the government here saying he should get a passport because I wanted him to go. And he keeps putting out statement after statement. I won't lose from this—

GIBBONS: No, but Hoffa shouldn't be made the victim of it either, Henry.

KISSINGER: But I really believe Hoffa will be the victim of it because our Justice Department will start slamming restrictions on him. . . .

GIBBONS: . . . The son of a bitch [Taub], I don't know him—when I brought him in to you, Henry, it was only because . . . maybe it will work and I just wanted you to evaluate it.

KISSINGER: . . . You came to me before you went to Hanoi and we've had a perfectly decent relationship on it. . . . You reported to me before and after. . . . I told him he couldn't speak for us.

GIBBONS: You told him repeatedly, a dozen times. . . .

Avner Idan

September 16, 1972, 1:28 p.m.

Israeli forces had crossed into Lebanon to attack Palestinian guerrilla bases; a week earlier, Israel had bombed Palestinian bases in Syria and Lebanon (and at least one village, killing a mother and her seven children) in retaliation for the massacre of Israelis by Palestinian terrorists at the Summer Olympics in Munich.[1] Idan was a minister at the Israeli embassy in Washington.

. . . KISSINGER: . . . I must tell you, you are running an enormous risk in your relations with the president. You launched an action the day before I go to Moscow and you launch an action the day after I come back at a time when we are taking an all-out diplomatic position in your defense. . . . We cannot take this. Now, there is no president who has done more for you, and I can

tell you I have just come from the president and he asked me to call you. . . .
I don't know what the background for this particular action is. . . . But if you
prepared us a little bit for it. . . . You know, the president feels you totally
misled him last week. I know there was a Talmudic sentence that if I had
understood it properly I should have known, but I took it at face value and
reported it like that. It is a very dangerous game. . . . If you had said we will do
something but it will not upset the balance . . . we would have understood
it. We wouldn't have welcomed it, but we would have understood it. . . .
We are not children and we know what your needs are, but we also have a
very tough situation with the Soviets, and . . . we cannot have them totally
publicly humiliated. . . .

William Timmons
September 18, 1972, 4:23 p.m.
*Kissinger is outraged that Timmons, Nixon's assistant on legislative affairs, had Nixon
phone Senator Henry (Scoop) Jackson in support of the Jackson amendment urging
Nixon to seek an arms control treaty with the Soviets that would provide for parity in
strategic weapons; it had passed the Senate. Kissinger did not think the SALT agree-
ment needed any such amendment. But Nixon needed Jackson's vote on funding of the
Trident submarine.*[2]

KISSINGER: Bill, who programmed the president to call Jackson today? . . .
I hope you realize that this breaks a direct promise I made to Brezh-
nev . . . that we were not going to get ourselves officially behind the Jackson
amendment.
TIMMONS: Well, we're not out in front here. We've pulled off on it. . . .
KISSINGER: Didn't the president tell Jackson he was behind it and he was
going to do everything he could to pass it through the House?
TIMMONS: Well, I don't know what he said. . . .
KISSINGER: But you urged him to call him. . . .
TIMMONS: We put in a proposed request some time ago that after the damn
thing passed the Senate that the president might want to call him and thank
him for it.
KISSINGER: Well, you know, if you guys for little moves are going to jeop-
ardize things on which everything depends—we've got all of October
programmed with Soviet cooperative efforts with us.
TIMMONS: Well, we're not doing a thing on the Hill, Henry. We've just pulled
off completely. . . .
KISSINGER: Well, goddamn it, why didn't you tell me that he was going to call
Jackson?

TIMMONS: This had gone in a long time ago. You were gone!

KISSINGER: . . . I have now, within three days of leaving Moscow, violated a promise I made to Brezhnev on behalf of the president, and it's going to make us look like the worst triple-crossers ever.

TIMMONS: Has Scoop said anything?

KISSINGER: You know goddamn well he will. . . . If Jackson can say he had a call from the president congratulating him, we are in deep trouble. . . . I'm telling you we have something precariously worked out with the Soviets which is not in their interest but in ours, and if there's one thing we don't need it's a double-cross.

TIMMONS: Well, you know, when the president called me a half-hour ago or so and said he had talked to Scoop and he wanted me to know that, by god, we should do everything in our power to get the House to take the Senate version—

KISSINGER: Yeah, but the mistake was to let him call Scoop. Once he gets on the phone, there's no telling what he will say. . . . Look, five minutes after he talks to me, he will be on his goddamn knees begging you to call the House off, so that doesn't mean anything. . . . The president just doesn't know all the details. . . .

Anatoly Dobrynin
September 18, 1972, 5:00 p.m.
Kissinger apologizes to Ambassador Dobrynin about Nixon's "stupid" call to Jackson.

. . . KISSINGER: . . . I'm calling you about something else which is slightly embarrassing to me in the light of my discussions in Moscow. . . . Whenever they pass something through the Congress, our congressional liaison people just type up a note for the president and get him to make a phone call to the sponsor saying, you know, he's glad it passed. And I found out to my horror that the people did that with the Jackson amendment, and so he called Jackson today.

DOBRYNIN: Uh-oh!

KISSINGER: And I, you know, hope it won't come out, but if it does come out, I want you to know how it happened. . . . I'm raising unshirted hell here.

DOBRYNIN: Why don't you control them? I think you usually have very good control.

KISSINGER: I have a good control, Anatol, of anything that I can imagine happening. I do not have a good control over things I can't imagine. . . . I want to express my apologies. . . . It is so stupid that I don't know how to express it. . . .

Barbara Walters
September 18, 1972, 5:25 p.m.
Kissinger would like to have coffee with television journalist Walters after an interview,
but Walters points out a press report linking them that she did not like. (Walters was
separated from her husband, and a rumor was going around that she had left him for
Kissinger.)[3]

> . . . KISSINGER: When am I going to see you? . . . May I buy you a cup of coffee
> afterwards?
>
> WALTERS: Well, I don't know, that's awfully personal.
>
> KISSINGER: I know, I know, and you always try to keep your feelings out—
>
> WALTERS: I almost sent you a couple of clippings. . . . I'm so pure at heart
> that no matter what we do—there was a picture of us that was taken at Taft
> House. . . .
>
> KISSINGER: Is that where I had my arms around you? [Laughs.]
>
> WALTERS: No, I was standing next to the senator and you were standing next to
> his wife. . . . And the woman . . . said, "Although Dr. Kissinger and Barbara
> Walters came in together, it was absolutely and totally coincidental. They
> just happened to walk in together." . . . I was very disappointed by it. . . .

Dick Cook
September 19, 1972, 3:30 p.m.
Kissinger rails to Cook, who was on William Timmons's legislative affairs staff, about
the Jackson amendment, which was holding up congressional approval of the SALT
agreement.

> . . . KISSINGER: . . . I feel that we have just horsed around long enough. And I
> want this goddamn treaty to go through. I've heard now for six weeks that
> this Jackson amendment was under good control. . . . The whole thing has
> been a goddamn nightmare. . . .
>
> COOK: That goddamn [Congressman Gerald] Ford doesn't know his ass from
> a hole in the ground. . . . And if we get the [Senate–House] conference, the
> *Times* and all the wiseacre reporters will be there trying to generate a fight
> and try to get us in the middle of it.
>
> KISSINGER: Well, it is nothing like what is going to happen if that treaty is not
> being ratified because we want to add an amendment to a goddamn treaty
> which the president himself signed in Moscow. I mean, we don't have a leg
> to stand on with the Russians. . . . One thing we have just got to end now
> is this endless palaver on something I didn't want to begin with. . . . Every
> week I was told two more days and the thing would go away, and it's get-
> ting worse and worse. . . . But will you guys now get it passed? I really don't

give a damn—Jackson has had his run. It won't make any difference in the negotiations. . . .

Yitzhak Rabin
September 25, 1972, 9:47 a.m.
Ambassador Rabin asks about a report that Kissinger said he would resign if former treasury secretary and Democrats for Nixon leader John Connally were appointed secretary of state.

. . . RABIN: I saw today a cable written by the foreign minister that Rollie Evans told him that he had met you at a dinner and you said that Connally will be the secretary of state and you would resign. . . .

KISSINGER: Total nonsense. Now, Mr. Ambassador, do you believe that I would say anything so stupid to Rowland Evans?

RABIN: Yeah, this is what I was not happy about it because in this cable . . . it is a piece of information to the prime minister. . . .

KISSINGER: . . . Say this is typical Washington gossip and there is nothing to it whatsoever.

RABIN: . . . The cable went yesterday to Israel.

KISSINGER: Oh, that fool. . . . Believe me, you really should shoot that down. That's total nonsense.

RABIN: . . . Evans told the foreign minister that he had dinner on Saturday night with Kissinger and Kissinger said that the president is going to bring dramatic changes in the cabinet composition. Connally is the sole candidate to replace Rogers. If such a change will take place, Dr. Kissinger is going to resign from his job.

KISSINGER: Total nonsense. . . .

RABIN: You see, but I am sure that Evans said something of this kind.

KISSINGER: I don't doubt it, but Evans was trying to provoke him. . . . I mean, it's such a transparent maneuver that I'm amazed that he could fall for it. . . .

Joseph Alsop
October 2, 1972, 11:44 a.m.
Kissinger complains to columnist Alsop about a damaging article in Newsweek *by his brother Stewart.*

KISSINGER: Joe, I am concluding that the Alsops are my death. . . . Your brother Stewart has done an article. . . . I just can't see him socially anymore. . . . You know, every piece of crap that's been around—why I should be secretary of state, why Rogers should stay because . . . then at least there'll be an ineffectual guy there so that I can run it, why I will resign if Connally [gets appointed secretary of state], why it's in the national interest that I stay, as secretary of state, because (1) I can brutalize the Jews and (2) a Nixon without Kissinger is a scary prospect. Now, if he wants to get me out of here this month, he could have not written a better article. . . . I'm really beside myself about it. . . . It's the most damaging article to me that's been written in four years in the guise of being friendly. . . .

John Connally
October 2, 1972, 11:54 a.m.
Kissinger phones Connally about the article and denies that he would resign if Connally were appointed secretary of state.

KISSINGER: I keep reading in the papers how you and I are feuding and how I'm giving ultimatums if they give you a cabinet position. So I thought I better see whether you and I could have lunch sometime soon. . . . Stewart Alsop has a column this week in *Newsweek*. . . . It's the goddamnest column. You know, you're not the only victim; everybody is being torn apart. . . . He's not so much after you as after me. . . . It's an analysis of what's going to happen after the election and he says everyone expects Rogers to leave and me to leave. Then he says, well, the best solution is to let Rogers stay because then I can stay because it's helpful to have an ineffectual secretary of state.

CONNALLY: Jesus!

KISSINGER: Then he says if you came in as secretary of state I'd leave, and then he goes on from there. And, oh god, it's the goddamnest column.

CONNALLY: These bastards just have to speculate about something, don't they?

KISSINGER: Well, I just want you to know I have no such views. (A) I know that there isn't any job that you're after, but secondly, if there is—

CONNALLY: Secondly, I don't know of any job I'd take.

KISSINGER: All I can say is any job you can get would be a goddamned good thing for the country. . . . And I just want you to know, you know, there may be a lot of crap being written, but if you have no worse enemies than me, you're in great shape. . . .

Walter Kissinger
October 6, 1972, 3:40 p.m.
Kissinger's brother, a businessman, is upset about allegations of nepotism in a book by Charles Ashman titled Kissinger: The Adventures of Super-Kraut. *He wants to keep* CBS Evening News *anchor Walter Cronkite from disseminating the story and to possibly sue for libel.*

WALTER KISSINGER: Say Henry, I'm sorry to bother you, but something has come up that you probably already know about, but there is some nut . . . who has written a book about you. . . . *Henry, the Super-Kraut.*

HENRY KISSINGER: Somebody told me about a book by that name. Have you seen it?

WALTER KISSINGER: I haven't seen it, but I got a call this morning from someone in LA and found that this guy went on a station out there last night . . . and I gather he is going around promoting the book. But he said some real nasty things.

HENRY KISSINGER: About me or you?

WALTER KISSINGER: Basically more about you than me, because what he is suggesting is that I became chief executive officer and immediately—

HENRY KISSINGER: Don't answer—do not answer—it is the worst mistake you can make.

WALTER KISSINGER: Let me tell you what he said—may I? . . . He suggested that there has been a tremendous [increase in company value] here, and that's the result of government contracts, and, you know, also indicates nepotism, etc. In any event, we're getting the tape from the station this afternoon, and I believe that my communications director has talked to them, and I am also under the impression that this thing is going to be on the Cronkite show tonight. . . .

HENRY KISSINGER: . . . Are you sure it's going to be on Cronkite? . . . I don't think that Cronkite would run it. . . .

WALTER KISSINGER: I can have my communications director call Cronkite, you know, because—

HENRY KISSINGER: And ask him what?

WALTER KISSINGER: Simply this information came through the station manager. . . . I had three or four phone calls from various stations.

HENRY KISSINGER: You don't even know what the guy said, do you?

WALTER KISSINGER: I know the essence of what he said through a third party, but I'll have a tape here in about another half-hour. It is outrageous—it's more expensive to you than it is to me.

HENRY KISSINGER: On that basis I'd consider suing him for libel.

WALTER KISSINGER: Well, that's what I am thinking about. I've already brought our counsel in.

HENRY KISSINGER: Have you got any government contracts?

WALTER KISSINGER: To my knowledge, none. If we have any, it's maybe a tenth of 1 percent of this company.

HENRY KISSINGER: That's a perfect defense. . . . Hell, I don't even know what your goddamn company is making, much less what it is.

WALTER KISSINGER: If I'd explain it to you you'd probably still not understand it.

HENRY KISSINGER: That's right. So, well, on that one, I'd consider suing for libel.

WALTER KISSINGER: That's my thinking. . . . You want me to send the tape down to Washington if I get it this afternoon? I can put someone on the plane and get it down there.

HENRY KISSINGER: Ah, no, that isn't that important. Get it transcribed and send it to me. . . . I can find out about it.

WALTER KISSINGER: . . . The allegations that he has made—first of all, the facts are all wrong. He suggests that overnight after I came here the company went from $20 million to $120 million—it's all nepotism because government contracts were given—

HENRY KISSINGER: I get the point, Walter—I must run.

Ronald Ziegler
October 6, 1972, 5:35 p.m.
Kissinger asks Press Secretary Ziegler to phone Cronkite to find out if he is doing a segment on Ashman's book and to tell him they were thinking of suing for libel.

KISSINGER: I just had a call from my brother saying that there was a guy on a television station in LA . . . who is referencing a book that's being written called *Henry, the Super-Kraut,* who made a violent attack on my brother on the ground that his company went from a $20 million business to $120 million on the basis of my nepotism. . . . My brother thinks they are going to have it on the Cronkite show tonight. Now, my brother says that to the best of his knowledge he doesn't have any government contracts. He's head of a conglomerate and if they have any, it's one-tenth of 1 percent. Obviously I have never discussed business with him, I've never introduced him anywhere—I don't even know what his business is, to tell you the truth, except that he had some companies. Is there some way we can find out whether Cronkite is doing it? . . .

ZIEGLER: What do you want me to tell him?

KISSINGER: Tell him that I've told my brother to sue for libel if that's said. First, tell him it's totally untrue.

ZIEGLER: [Laughing.] Before we sue for libel, we'll tell him it's untrue.

KISSINGER: Do you want me to tell Cronkite?

ZIEGLER: No, let me find out and I'll tell him I had talked to you and you had talked to your brother about it, and your brother from his knowledge doesn't have any defense contracts—

KISSINGER: Government contracts. . . . He's got a conglomerate. . . . I don't know what it is. . . .

ZIEGLER: Is your brother that wealthy?

KISSINGER: Oh, yeah, he is, but hell, my brother is so square that it's not to be believed. My brother would turn down a government contract if it had the slightest thing to do with me. . . .

Walter Cronkite
October 6, 1972, 5:45 p.m.
Cronkite says the CBS Evening News *will not be running a piece on the book.*

KISSINGER: Walter, I had a hysterical phone call from my brother, who is not used to publicity like I am. He tells me on a CBS show on the West Coast yesterday there was somebody who accused him of having built up his business on the basis of his acquaintance with me. . . . He is under the impression you are going to use that.

CRONKITE: No, no. . . . I didn't know anything about that, to tell you the truth. But Ziegler called this afternoon . . . and said you were concerned about it.

KISSINGER: He never told me about it.

CRONKITE: I had never heard about it, so I checked up around here and they tell me that there was an interview based on some book apparently, and that it was offered to us—a network piece—and we ran it fast by a couple of people who said forget the whole damn thing. It is ridiculous.

KISSINGER: Well, my brother . . . first of all, I don't know what business he is in, to tell you the truth. . . . Secondly, he has no government contracts in any of his companies. And thirdly . . . he wouldn't get close to any government person as a question of principle. . . . If this is what was said it would be pretty rough and I would take violent objection to it, too. . . .

Anatoly Dobrynin
October 15, 1972, 9:55 a.m.
Kissinger requests from Ambassador Dobrynin a statement of Soviet intentions to reduce its military aid to the North Vietnamese that would give him leverage in upcoming talks with the South Vietnamese to convince them to accept the peace agreement he had reached several days earlier with Hanoi.

KISSINGER: I discussed yesterday the settlement with the president. . . . The two biggest problems are the units in the South . . . and most importantly the question of military supplies to them. And what the president wants to do is to write a letter to Brezhnev . . . and see whether it is possible for you to express in a strictly private way your general intentions in this respect. . . .

We have almost no incentive to settle it by November 7. . . . Because it can only make trouble and it cannot gain us a hell of a lot. But on the other hand, it's a war that's gone on for 10 years and if the conditions are right one shouldn't say just because there's an election one waits four more years. And Hanoi does seem ready to settle now. So if the conditions could be met we would settle quickly. Also, for your information I'm going to Saigon and I'll arrive there Tuesday. Now, if it were possible to get some answer from you by Wednesday, I wouldn't use it there but it would affect the confidence with which I act in insisting on a settlement, which, believe me, will not be easy for them to accept. . . . You see, if it leads to a blow-up in Saigon we will just have to delay. . . . We cannot have a public confrontation with Saigon during the election campaign. . . . We would certainly be prepared to reduce our military aid enormously. . . .

Anatoly Dobrynin
October 15, 1972, 8:35 p.m.
Kissinger also asks for Soviet pressure on the North Vietnamese to reduce their forces in South Vietnam, which will also help him get South Vietnamese President Thieu on board with the agreement.

> . . . KISSINGER: Now, the biggest problem I have concerns their own forces in the South, because the practical consequence of their proposal is that not only do they want to keep all of their forces in the South, they want Saigon to release 40,000 people whom they consider, you know, guerrillas, to then join those forces. And that is an almost impossible product to sell. . . . If they pull some of their units out, then I have a much better basis to talk. . . . I don't want to say exactly how many they should move.
>
> DOBRYNIN: It's a rather difficult thing for us to be involved in all this . . . how many, really.
>
> KISSINGER: But I don't even want to tell them how many they should move. . . . It should be a noticeable number. If we can get some assurances of that we are in a much better position to bring about the release of some of these prisoners. . . . I honestly do not believe that Thieu will release them if the North Vietnamese forces stay. . . . We have the massive problem of how to bring Saigon along with this. . . . Without any withdrawal on their side we are willing to make a big effort in Saigon, but I am not very optimistic. With some withdrawals on their side we can make a bigger effort and we can have bigger numbers released right away. . . . And tell Gromyko not to coach them.

They are tough enough without it.

DOBRYNIN: Well, we know this. This we know.

Anatoly Dobrynin

October 16, 1972, 10:40 a.m.

Kissinger was minutes from departing for Paris to meet with North Vietnamese ne-gotiator Xuan Thuy to work out the remaining issues in the peace agreement; then he would fly to Saigon to meet with Thieu to explain the agreement and persuade him to sign it. The plan was to then fly to Hanoi to initial it. Dobrynin asks about Kissinger's discussions with China on the agreement and the continued heavy bombing of North Vietnam. "I am a little worried," Dobrynin says, presciently.

DOBRYNIN: . . . Yesterday I checked with Haig about your approach to Chinese on this subject too. . . . You raise the whole spectrum of this issue?

KISSINGER: I raise the same with them as I raise with you.

DOBRYNIN: . . . And the same time on the military deliveries [to North Vietnam].

KISSINGER: That's correct. Especially the military delivery.

DOBRYNIN: . . . Because this is the main point, really.

KISSINGER: That's right. We don't have so confidential relations with them despite what your newspapers say occasionally, and therefore we haven't gone into quite that much detail about the forces. . . . But on the deliveries, we have mentioned it almost verbatim the same way. . . . I haven't got the means of talking to them as easily as to you.

DOBRYNIN: Yeah, I understand. I am sure you have in one way or another.

KISSINGER: Oh, no, I am in touch with them, but not as closely as with you.

DOBRYNIN: Today I heard you bomb North Vietnam now rather strongly. . . .

KISSINGER: No, no, that's under control. That's nonsensical baloney. I've got it now under good control.

DOBRYNIN: So it will be no surprise when you will be there. . . . Better not [chuckling].

KISSINGER: It's being cut in half. . . .

DOBRYNIN: What in general are your expectations?

KISSINGER: I think that if they show any understanding for our position on those issues, I think we will settle it in a couple of weeks. . . .

DOBRYNIN: Yeah, well, you see it's rather difficult now, because it looks so on the issue of the troops [North Vietnamese in the South]. . . . Now you have rather reopened this issue—this is why I am a little worried, quite frankly. . . .

KISSINGER: But they have to understand that I have an unbelievable problem in Saigon. . . .

Anatoly Dobrynin

October 23, 1972, 11:22 p.m.

Shortly after returning distraught from Saigon, where South Vietnamese President Thieu had refused to sign the peace agreement, believing his country had been sold out, and after receiving a message from North Vietnam accusing the United States of using a series of pretexts to prolong the negotiations and asking it to uphold the agreement,[4] Kissinger tells Dobrynin about his difficulties with Thieu and says he requested more meetings with Hanoi to discuss largely minor changes in the agreement, after which he will ask for no more changes.

... KISSINGER: We received a somewhat threatening message from Hanoi and the situation is this. They don't understand the American domestic situation at all. . . . If I had wanted to protract the negotiations, I could have easily protracted them. . . . Because I could have just haggled over every paragraph for weeks. . . . What we wanted to do is to settle it. . . . On the other hand, what we cannot do is to have a public confrontation with the South Vietnamese in the last two weeks of the elections and be accused by everyone of undermining the people for whom we've been fighting for four years. . . . Therefore if Hanoi forces us to choose between a confrontation with South Vietnam and a confrontation with North Vietnam, we will unhesitatingly choose a confrontation with North Vietnam. . . . Now, I have made a serious effort. And there have been certain difficulties. . . . We have proposed to them that they meet us again next week . . . to work out some of these issues. It is my judgment that most of them or all of them are a lot easier than the issues we've already settled. . . . They may think we are deliberately delaying it beyond November 7th so we can bomb them or do something. I give you the solemn assurance of the president that this is not the case. . . . Second, we have an obligation to our allies, however, and we cannot act in an unprincipled way. And we always told them we would have to discuss it with our allies. Now, they must have enough sources of information in Saigon to know what difficulties I have had. . . . Supposing Le Duc Tho and I met next week and supposing we could agree, then the only thing that has to be obtained is the agreement of our allies. There will not be another appeal for changes. . . . And we will make that as a flat commitment to you, not just to them. . . . And they have always known that I would have to go to Saigon. But now that I have all of Saigon's comments . . . if we can work out something, that will be then the final text as far as we are concerned. . . . You can guarantee that if we talk to them [the North Vietnamese], I will not ask them for any more changes.

DOBRYNIN: . . . What you are suggesting now is really to give a chance to meet once more and to discuss some maybe changes which you feel, as you put it, are rather cosmetic ones.

KISSINGER: That is correct.

DOBRYNIN: . . . And once you really come to agreement, then there will be no any more changes.

KISSINGER: I will make a commitment that we will not ask for any more changes. . . .

Ellsworth Bunker

October 24, 1972, 8:53 a.m.

Thieu had declared publicly that he would not accept the peace agreement and what was wrong with it, particularly that North Vietnamese troops would remain in the South and that he was being asked to participate in a coalition government with communists (which was not entirely true).[5] Kissinger tells Ambassador Bunker in Saigon that the South Vietnamese were committing suicide.

KISSINGER: Ellsworth, I'm getting in touch with you by cable on that one matter you sent me which I just received about the misinterpretation [of the agreement]. Now, if that stuff is put out it is total suicide. This is what we are fighting in the press here. Now if they say that's what it is, we're dead. . . . The reason I call you so urgently is just if there is any chance of getting to them tonight to calm them down.

BUNKER: I doubt it very much, Henry. . . . There are mass meetings being organized all around the country and people are getting stirred up against— all of the talk is against a coalition government and they are against a three-segment coalition government.

KISSINGER: Well, it's neither.

BUNKER: They are given the impression that this is what's trying to be forced on them.

KISSINGER: This could either be very clever or very insane. It depends on how they then represent the outcome. . . .

William F. Buckley

October 25, 1972, 11:30 a.m.

Kissinger tells his friend Buckley, who was also concerned that Kissinger had agreed to a coalition government in South Vietnam (it was an administrative body that would organize elections and implement the peace agreement but could well lead to a coalition government),[6] that Thieu was setting up "straw men" to knock over to claim victory and being "impossible." He worries about Hanoi backing off while he's trying to pacify Thieu.

KISSINGER: I can't of course go into great detail on the telephone, but what I can tell you is that we are now negotiating on much, much further, and not in the direction of coalition. . . .

BUCKLEY: Oh, that's the best news I've heard all week; that's wonderful.

KISSINGER: And I hope that our conservative friends don't panic on what is being put out by newsmen who have a vested interest in preserving coalition because they have been predicting it. . . . There will not be installed a caretaker government, a coalition government. In fact, I can assure you that the present personnel and government will remain intact. . . . But much of what's going on in Saigon is an Oriental sun dance in which he's trying to prove that he did it. And, he's setting up straw men so that he can claim later victory for what has been achieved.

BUCKLEY: I see. That's sort of unpleasant, isn't it?

KISSINGER: Oh, it's murderous. You know, what breaks my heart is if he had gone along with us we could have done it in one fell swoop; we could have killed the anti-Thieu agitation here once and for all and we could have destroyed all our opponents, because what we would have come out with would have been so shockingly different from what they expected. . . . I can see his point, but like all Vietnamese he's incapable of understanding the requirements of others. . . . We kept him in office, and, you know, it's really an amazing deal we are giving Thieu to develop. . . . But now by the time that three weeks of newspaper speculation [has taken place] it will look as if we dragged him kicking and screaming to his salvation. . . . We've gotten Hanoi to make concessions. . . . But now that we've gotten all of this out of them, and this other guy kicks it over, or seems to kick it over while he postures himself, they may pull back. This is my present nightmare. . . .

Anatoly Dobrynin

October 26, 1972, 10:40 a.m.

Kissinger had been awakened around 5:30 that morning to learn that Radio Hanoi had been putting out its version of the peace negotiations and summarizing the main points of the agreement. North Vietnam had been assured that "the agreement could be considered complete," it said. It demanded that it be signed by October 31 per the agreed timetable.[7]

DOBRYNIN: . . . I was sleeping and then at eight o'clock I hear on the radio. . . .

KISSINGER: Well, your friends have gone crazy. . . . I don't know what influence you have over them. We will give a rather moderate response to them. . . . If they go on an offensive for the next few weeks, you know, we'll take it for two weeks, but they'll pay for it afterwards. . . . It's very stupid because if they had followed what we told them there would certainly have been an agreement in three weeks.

DOBRYNIN: Well, you see, I think one of the reasons was that they really wanted you to come there. . . . And if you come and if you explain them . . .

they would be much more quiet. Because . . . they see that you refuse to go to Hanoi. . . .

KISSINGER: Because it would have led to an explosion in Saigon.

DOBRYNIN: . . . They have really high emotions . . . in Hanoi. This I can tell you quite frankly. . . . They really think of you as a man whom they respect but now they are angry with you. . . . I receive a report from Moscow how they react. . . .

Charles Colson

October 26, 1972, 7:26 p.m.

At a press conference that day, Kissinger had declared, "We believe that peace is at hand" and that "what remains to be done is the smallest part of what has already been accomplished." (For months Kissinger had tried to obtain something that at least looked like a peace settlement before the presidential election, while Nixon was prepared to wait until after the election to settle.)[8] *An elated Colson says Kissinger's press conference has won Nixon's reelection. Colson, who relates that the pollster Lou Harris is in their camp, tells Kissinger he "finished" Nixon's opponent, George McGovern, and gushes over his "master diplomacy."*

COLSON: Henry, I should have called you early in the day to congratulate you on what has to be one of the most brilliant performances I have ever seen in my life. . . . There aren't words to describe it. . . . Utterly spectacular!! . . . But more importantly, you put it across in such a way that no matter what happens now for the next 10 days, the election is settled. You've settled it. . . . It is a masterful performance. . . . I talked to Lou Harris this afternoon, who I was going to suggest you call at some point 'cause he's been awfully helpful to us. . . . The poll for this weekend, if it says any closing [between Nixon and McGovern] he will not print. That's not bad, to have him on our side like that. . . . I think what it will show is no closing because I think Lou will want to print a poll.

KISSINGER: . . . Has McGovern said anything about Vietnam now?

COLSON: He looks like a man who had four large turds for lunch. He came on the tube tonight and said, well, if this is really peace, fine. We could have gotten it four years ago, but this is what I've been trying to get accomplished and so therefore I'm very happy. . . .

KISSINGER: But there's no goddamn newsman who believes that we could have gotten it four years ago. . . .

COLSON: No, he's dead. He's gone, you finished him. . . . In all honesty I must say that I never thought that you would be able to negotiate a deal as good as this. . . .

KISSINGER: Well, I frankly, to tell you the truth, I wasn't sure we would come out that well, and now I'll improve it a little more in the next round. You know, just enough to let the South Vietnamese say they did something.

COLSON: . . . I feel privileged and honored to be serving with you in an administration that I think you have played a very, very large role in making it as historic as it will be.

KISSINGER: Well, Chuck, that means a lot to me. . . .

COLSON: I say that with all the sincerity in the world. I'm just very, very proud of you, I really am. Honest to god, I'm proud and I feel privileged to be part of it, because to me this is master diplomacy at its very ultimate best, and I feel kind of spine-tingly about it. . . .

President Nixon

October 26, 1972, 11:44 p.m.

Nixon, who thought Kissinger's "peace is at hand" declaration was "a disaster" (for hurting their bargaining position with Hanoi, disturbing Saigon, raising public hopes prematurely, and stealing Nixon's thunder),[9] is concerned that North Vietnam or Thieu could "blow the whistle" on them, meaning reveal that peace was not at hand.

. . . NIXON: . . . The North Vietnamese I suppose could blow it on us, couldn't they?

KISSINGER: But how? They've just put out the agreement and said it's fair. They want it—they're asking us to sign it! . . .

NIXON: Basically all you were doing was confirming their agreement.

KISSINGER: That's right. I began by saying their statement [on Radio Hanoi] is essentially correct, now let me just explain it in our language.

NIXON: Well, the way I said it, while there are some differences that have to be resolved . . . they're very small. . . .

KISSINGER: I wouldn't say they're very small. . . .

NIXON: And as far as Thieu is concerned, if he blows the whistle on us, then we're in perfect shape to twist his arm.

KISSINGER: Well, he won't blow the whistle because he's wily enough to see that we are protecting him, because at no point did I say . . . either that it was final or that we didn't take his view seriously. . . .

Barbara Walters

October 27, 1972, 7:20 p.m.

Walters brings up a column intimating that they were in a relationship, and Martha Mitchell, the hard-drinking wife of Nixon campaign director John Mitchell, who was embroiled in the Watergate scandal. Martha wanted Walters to have her on the To-day show. Walters also broaches a fake nude centerfold-style photo of Kissinger in the Harvard Lampoon.

KISSINGER: Well, I have a proposal for you. Why don't you say something nasty about me some morning and then come for lunch or dinner? Then no one will think that you are getting rewarded.

WALTERS: Yesterday—do you know who Earl Wilson is? . . . He's a syndicated columnist. . . . In yesterday's paper at the top of his gossip—"What's this between Henry Kissinger and Barbara Walters?"

KISSINGER: I'm flattered.

WALTERS: You are? That's why I can't come for lunch. . . . Martha Mitchell called me yesterday . . . wanting to come on the day after the election. She said, ". . . Will you put me on on the 8th and I'll tell everything I know?" I said, "We sure will." . . .

KISSINGER: I think she's nuts.

WALTERS: I think she's nuts too. . . . I don't think she's going to say any-thing. She said to me, "I've got a great deal to say; I've done a lot for this country." . . .

KISSINGER: Well, she needs publicity. She wants it. I mean, she's dying without it.

WALTERS: Well, you'd think that he'd [her husband would] shut her up. You know, at this birthday party that I gave that they came to—he was going to come on the program the next day and then he changed his mind. And I thought he was a darn fool to come on the program; I wouldn't have told him, but, you know, you leave yourself open for those questions. . . . How do you like your *Cosmopolitan* picture? . . . A producer showed it to me, and he said, "You know, I know you like him, but I really think he's gone too far." I got so upset. I thought, How could you do this? I mean, have you really gone this crazy since the last time I saw you? . . . Then I saw the appendix scar and everything. . . . Do you have an appendix scar?

KISSINGER: I do.

WALTERS: Then I'll take another look. For all I know, it may be the real picture. . . .

Charles Colson
October 30, 1972, 10:47 a.m.
Colson is adamant that Secretary of State William Rogers hold a press conference on the peace negotiations in order to attack George McGovern, who had said if elected he would reserve the right to renegotiate parts of the agreement and that he was "puzzled as to why the settlement comes in the closing hours of this campaign."[10] *Colson also*

advises Kissinger to listen to pollster Lou Harris's analysis, which was "scary" in the event the peace talks collapsed.

KISSINGER: Chuck, Rogers called in some anguish that he didn't want to have a press conference today, and there have been some developments that make it unwise, because we may be hearing something from the North Vietnamese today. . . . I don't think Rogers should be out on a limb without knowing what they're going to do.

COLSON: Well, I told him that he should go on his press conference just as we discussed at the 8:15 meeting and do nothing but kick McGovern for what he said yesterday.

KISSINGER: That's right. But he feels he can't do that and he has to answer other questions if he goes out there. . . . But can't we get Agnew to kick McGovern?

COLSON: No, no, no. Agnew doesn't know anything about this area. . . .

KISSINGER: I think that it is unwise to have Rogers go over the same ground as I did again.

COLSON: He's not going to go over the same ground you did.

KISSINGER: He says he can't avoid it. . . . He doesn't know the subject well enough; that's going to confuse the issue and he's softer than I am.

COLSON: . . . I called Haldeman and checked with him and he thought it was a damn good idea, the president did last night, you did at 8:15, so I really laid it on the rafters that this is one he had to do. And what he's doing now of course is his normal technique of divide and conquer.

KISSINGER: . . . You know, I'd like that one statement against McGovern but I don't want more.

COLSON: Well, why don't we just tell Bill Rogers to go down to the press room and make that statement and leave.

KISSINGER: Well, he claims he can't do that.

COLSON: Oh, that's plain bullshit! If he's told to do it, he can do it. Of course he can do it. Hell's bells, our guys are always hung up on this idea that they have to suck around with the press corps and answer their questions.

KISSINGER: Well, if you can handle it on that basis, that's fine with me.

COLSON: Well, it's going to be more than fine with you; it's going to be something you'd like him to do. . . . I see no reason that he can't go down there and read that. . . . Have you talked to Harris? . . . You know why you should? . . . Not just to thank him but to listen to his analysis. I just was talking to him and he said, boy, this thing [Kissinger's press conference] saved the day. He said, all of my poll data from last week shows that there was an enormous decay. However, he says, you fellows had better not build up the expectations and let them [the peace talks] now collapse. He said you will have a monumental problem on your hands. . . . You should listen to his analysis; it is goddamned (a) wholly impressive and (b) scary. . . .

H. R. Haldeman
October 30, 1972, 4:45 p.m.
They consider how to respond if Hanoi breaks off the negotiations.

. . . HALDEMAN: . . . We can deal with anything short of a total break-off without any real problem . . . but if we get the total break-off—

KISSINGER: I don't think we'll get a total break-off. . . . It would be a foolhardy thing to do. . . .

HALDEMAN: They are mad men enough that you've got to assume the possibility they will do the foolhardy thing.

KISSINGER: Well, if they do a total break-off, we must go on the offensive. Instead of defending ourselves, we must say we will publish everything we've offered them. . . . I'll say, why did we not meet that so-called [signing] commitment? For three reasons: one, because when we were in Saigon we got innumerable intelligence reports that they would receive a maximum of territory between the time of initialing and the time of signing, and that there might be a bloodbath, and that is now proven by events, that they are making that effort at just this time. Second . . . we had a clear understanding it was not a coalition government, so we had to get that straightened out. Third, we had never agreed to the fact that they could keep all their troops in the South, which happens to be true, and we wanted a unilateral withdrawal of some of their troops before the thing got signed. . . . And we can say these guys are obviously trying to stampede us in the last week of the national election campaign, but he [Nixon] will not let himself be stampeded.

HALDEMAN: I think that's exactly right. . . . The immediate concern here is that you apparently made the point strongly to him that we would be taking a murderous beating from the global press. . . .

KISSINGER: Well, but you see the liberal press in a way has made itself very vulnerable, because they are now moving to the right of us, the filthy sons of bitches. Sort of claiming we are letting poor old Thieu down. . . . So they can't very well blame us for trying to get additional safeguards. . . .

McGovern—"He's an Awful Man," Pressuring and Appeasing Thieu and Reneging on a Peace Agreement That Was "Good Enough," Moving Without and Threatening Thieu, the Connally Problem—"He's a Total Lightweight," Nixon's Distancing, Visit of a Thieu Emissary, Breakdown in Paris, and the Christmas Bombing

November–December 1972

On the eve of the November 1972 presidential election, Democratic candidate George McGovern charged that Kissinger's "peace is at hand" declaration on October 26 was a "cruel political deception" intended to falsely raise hopes. "He is a filthy son of a bitch," Kissinger told William Rogers. Kissinger had been backgrounding the press that the peace agreement was on track. Nixon trounced McGovern in a landslide.

John Connally was reported to be in line for a top post in Nixon's second administration, and Kissinger told Secretary of Commerce Peter Peterson that he would resign if Connally were appointed secretary of state (contrary to his previous denials, including to Connally); it would be "an incompatible relationship," he said. And he had been assured it would not take place, so if Connally were appointed, the "massive deception" alone would send him out the door.

South Vietnamese President Nguyen Van Thieu was then demanding scores of changes in the October peace agreement. Kissinger knew most of them would be rejected by Hanoi, particularly after he'd already accepted the agreement. Kissinger and Nixon considered going their own way without Thieu and making a bilateral agreement with North Vietnam, although they knew it would open them to heavy domestic criticism and both found the idea "repugnant." "It's a tragedy," Kissinger told Nixon, who was more inclined to go that route. They considered breaking relations with and turning on Thieu. They debated what to do if Hanoi was unyielding and they had to "cave." After Kissinger presented the North Vietnamese with 69 changes requested by Thieu and an angry Le Duc Tho made new demands too, an impasse resulted. Nixon told a Thieu envoy in Washington that Congress would cut off aid to South Vietnam if Thieu continued to reject the peace agreement.

In December, after lengthy negotiations failed to reach a new peace agreement and the peace talks collapsed, Nixon and Kissinger resumed heavy sustained bombing of North Vietnam, including B-52 bombing of Hanoi and Haiphong. Kissinger blamed Hanoi for the stalemate, though the blame lay with the United States for reneging on the October peace agreement. Kissinger told Soviet Ambassador Anatoly Dobrynin that his allies were lying to him about why the negotiations broke down. Kissinger acknowledged to Nixon that "we could have easily lived with" the October agreement, "but if we accept it now after all this arguing for changes it would make us look impotent."

On the eve of the bombing, Kissinger and Nixon anticipated with some relish the punishment and terror they were about to inflict on North Vietnam. When Kissinger pointed out that "the danger is that they may miss and hit a populated area, in which case it would be gory," Nixon was unfazed at the prospect. They unleashed the heaviest air raids of the war in the Hanoi–Haiphong area. Kissinger gave JCS Chairman Thomas Moorer carte blanche on targets. Nixon, too, thought the October agreement was "good enough," he told Kissinger; all they were getting now were little improvements in language: "Language doesn't mean anything—not a damn thing."

President Nixon
November 2, 1972, 8:50 p.m.
George McGovern had responded to a heckler by leaning over to him and saying softly, "I've got a secret for you—kiss my ass."[1]

> . . . KISSINGER: Did you hear what McGovern did tonight? . . . He got off an airplane and one of your supporters was standing there . . . and your supporter said—a young fellow—"You'll be beaten so badly on Tuesday that you'll wish you had never left South Dakota." So McGovern went up to him, put his arm around him, and said, "Kiss my ass."
>
> NIXON: Oh, my god. He's really getting—

KISSINGER: [Laughter.] And that's on the wires.

NIXON: Losing his cool. Like he told that woman … "You're a horse's ass," you know, when she wouldn't shake hands with him or something.

KISSINGER: He's an awful man.

NIXON: My god, I've been through much worse. [Laughter.] You just don't react that way. . . .

William Rogers
November 4, 1972, 10:00 a.m.
Secretary of State Rogers and Kissinger discuss McGovern's charges that Kissinger's "peace is at hand" statement was designed to falsely raise hopes before the election and that his own peace plan "embraced the same principles" that Kissinger had accepted in October but since rejected.[2]

… ROGERS: Did you hear McGovern last night?

KISSINGER: Oh, that son of a bitch. . . .

ROGERS: He was pretty effective actually. . . . I must say I thought it was one of his better ones in terms of sounding as if he meant it. . . . It was rough, too, you know, and dirty.

KISSINGER: He is a filthy son of a bitch. I mean, for him to say that this is his plan when he had—

ROGERS: Oh yeah, it is ridiculous, ridiculous. But it's tough. There has been so much said on Vietnam for the average person to follow. . . . People are really fed up to the gills on the goddamn subject. And when he says it, Christ, in order to negate it it takes you about two minutes to point out what he proposed and where we stand in the agreement. . . . But, you know, it is just absolutely false and the worst kind of deception on his part. . . . To pretend that what we have agreed to is what he proposed all along, it's absolutely false. You know, you've got to have a lot of guts to lie that much in public.

KISSINGER: I couldn't agree more. He will be all over the lot. You know, one minute he wants to overthrow Thieu and the next minute [his vice presidential running mate Sargent] Shriver bleeds about what we're doing to poor Thieu. . . .

Rowland Evans
November 6, 1972, 8:52 a.m.
Kissinger assures columnist Evans that the peace agreement is on track.

EVANS: For no attribution of any kind. Is this still on the track?

KISSINGER: Listen, it is absolutely on the track and exactly the way we described it. . . . You will see within the next two or three weeks that it is moving as I told you. But we had zero incentive for the sake of really public morality to stage a big spectacular on the last weekend of an election campaign. . . . I mean this is really filth, to suggest that the president of the United States in collusion with Hanoi would put on a tremendous hoax . . . just so he can keep the war going for four more years. . . .

Nelson Rockefeller
November 8, 1972, 9:45 a.m.
Kissinger brags to Governor Rockefeller about all the military equipment they were getting into South Vietnam before the Vietnam peace agreement was signed.

. . . ROCKEFELLER: Listen, Henry, who is making out best during this interim period? Which side?

KISSINGER: Oh, we are. . . . We're getting over a billion dollars' worth of equipment in there. We're sending in 280 jet planes, 400 helicopters.

ROCKEFELLER: Boy!

KISSINGER: We're sending in all the military equipment that was programmed into 1975 in one month.

ROCKEFELLER: No kidding.

KISSINGER: Two years' worth of military equipment.

ROCKEFELLER: How can you keep the North Vietnamese from blowing that up with rockets?

KISSINGER: We have put a provision in the agreement that any equipment that is destroyed, used up, or worn out can be replaced. . . . They actually would do us a favor to destroy some of it, we could put in more modern equipment.

ROCKEFELLER: I'll be damned. Well, you're fantastic, Henry.

KISSINGER: We're just going to park these planes wingtip to wingtip in Cam Ranh Bay, and the more they destroy, the better we like it. . . .

President Nixon
November 14, 1972, 9:35 a.m.
Kissinger recounts his dinner the previous evening in New York with the head of China's delegation to the UN General Assembly. He says the Chinese were delighted by Nixon's reelection, expressed "no particular support for the North Vietnamese," and were "violent on Russia." Nixon and Kissinger also take up a letter from South Vietnamese President Nguyen Van Thieu that demanded many changes in the peace agreement. To help appease him, Nixon suggests putting in some "fuzzy language" on the withdrawal of North Vietnamese troops from the South.[3]

. . . KISSINGER: And, well, first of all, personal felicitations from the prime minister to be conveyed to you, urgently again. And they are so delighted and you're the man who made the historic opening towards China and they'll never forget that. They were just burbling around.... And it's the softest I've ever heard them on Vietnam. No particular support for the North Vietnamese.... It couldn't have been that cordial unless they had a pretty good idea it was going to be settled.... They were violent on Russia, and I said, "Look... we have to make some tough decisions in resisting hegemony around the world in the next four years. And it cannot be in anybody's interest that the United States is put into a difficult position in Southeast Asia after the war ends."

NIXON: As a matter of fact sucked into a peripheral war anyplace, Henry.

KISSINGER: Things have to be kept quiet. They can't be immediately starting again.... He drank a toast to you and to your victory.... It was the warmest meeting I've ever had with them. And on Vietnam, it couldn't have been warmer....

NIXON: Now with regard to ... the letter that Thieu had sent to us.... I think that the tone is certainly conciliatory; the substance, of course, on the troop withdrawal is tough. Yet, of course, the way he puts it, it is a very cogent case... that they fight for 10 years and what happens is that... we get out and the North Vietnamese stay in.... He's concerned basically about the fact that after all these years, does he sign an agreement which says the North Vietnamese can occupy part of his country? That bothers him. Now, on that it seems to me that there could be some fuzzy language just in principle that at the conclusion of the juridical process ... that all the North Vietnamese troops go out or something like that.

KISSINGER: It can't be put quite that way, but the basic idea is correct.

NIXON: You've got to have something in there that says that the principle of the occupation of parts of South Vietnam by North Vietnamese troops is not recognized. That's his real problem.

KISSINGER: They will never—you see—

NIXON: They don't admit they have them, I know.

KISSINGER: You see, one thing that he doesn't recognize is it is actually an asset from the point of view of principle that they do not say they have troops there. They don't claim they have a right to have troops there. They claim they don't have troops there, which is a lie, but which from the point of view of principle is easier to handle....

President Nixon

November 15, 1972, 9:06 a.m.

U.S. Ambassador to South Vietnam Ellsworth Bunker had delivered a letter from Nixon to President Thieu in which Nixon said the United States would react strongly to any violations of the peace agreement by the North Vietnamese, but that South

Vietnam should not be an obstacle to peace. He had told Thieu a week earlier, "Your continuing distortions of the agreement and attacks upon it were unfair and self-defeating."[4] Nixon and Kissinger talk of going their own way without Thieu.

... KISSINGER: ... That goddamn Thieu—he's going through his stalling act. Thieu wouldn't receive Bunker for 24 hours and now he asks for another 24 hours to study the letter. He just won't meet. We have to go ahead on Monday, if we don't get his reply, without him.

NIXON: ... I don't see how he can continue to stall. What in the hell is he going to do? The way that letter is written—it's put in a context that we have to go another way if he doesn't go.

KISSINGER: I think we should get the best agreement we can next week, and if he doesn't accept it, go bilaterally with North Vietnam.

NIXON: We don't want to do that because . . . they will say, "Hell, you could have done that all along." Although we will do it! . . . We just don't have any real communication between him and Bunker. Bunker used to go and talk with him.

KISSINGER: Yes, as long as we did what he wanted.

NIXON: ... I was looking over his letter to us—it's just another song and dance.

KISSINGER: We have given him 15 changes which we are willing to press for and that's what they are now discussing. . . . We may have the North Vietnamese in a very tough frame of mind. We have no reason to believe that they will take all these changes. How many they take still remains to be seen. But I think at this moment they are less of a problem than Thieu. . . .

Peter Peterson
November 15, 1972, 12:47 p.m.
Kissinger tells Secretary of Commerce Peterson that he had been assured by H. R. Haldeman that there were no plans to appoint John Connally secretary of state or to any cabinet position, but that if Connally were appointed secretary of state he'd resign. Connally, he scoffs, is "a total lightweight."

PETERSON: ... Our friend Rollie [Rowland Evans, the columnist] called me about an hour ago to tell me that he had it on extremely high authority that your mutual friend and mine either has been or will be made a firm offer in the foreign policy arena, and that there was a report that he's going up to Maryland [Camp David] tomorrow. . . .

KISSINGER: I know he's going up. All I can say, I've been told exactly the opposite and other names have been mentioned to me. I would have to say that if this were to come to pass, the deception would have been so massive that, aside from the basic problem, I would no longer be able to stay. You know,

I would in any event not stay because in my judgment that is an incompatible relationship. . . . But if this were to be done, bad judgment would be compounded by massive deception. And in that case my decision would be made for me.

PETERSON: Yeah. Well, what does he say the reason is for the visit up there tomorrow?

KISSINGER: Oh, to discuss his political future. But I have been assured by him, by Haldeman, that they're not planning any cabinet thing for him. But, you know, it will strain them not to tell the truth, but I think they could manage it.

PETERSON: . . . I don't know who Rollie was talking to except the other day it sounded to me—

KISSINGER: It sounds like he was talking to the appointee. . . .

PETERSON: What is your best assessment of what they're going to do? Leave the current guy in or not? You don't think that's very likely?

KISSINGER: Well, they gave me a name; I don't want to discuss it on the telephone. And he won't set the world on fire, that's for sure. And that was given to me as the reason why they want him. . . . I know that during the campaign he [Connally] put out a lot of stuff that he would take this only if I left, and I traced two of them down and it came from George Christian, who was after all working as his press secretary. . . . But I frankly, Pete, I am really very relaxed. Not only am I relaxed, I'm not even sure that I'm not hoping for selfish reasons it comes out that way, because I just have no stomach for another four years of this.

PETERSON: . . . I find that prospect so unbelievable given all the effort that's gone into building bridges around the world.

KISSINGER: Oh, it's a disaster.

PETERSON: It's just unbelievable and I guess it's that problem that just absolutely baffles me given this other fellow's obvious hostility toward everybody.

KISSINGER: He's a total lightweight. . . . I mean, what the hell did he bring to the Treasury and what did he leave there? . . . Leaving aside also the fact that every personal relationship within the administration was exacerbated by him.

PETERSON: . . . I think this spot fills his political objectives pretty well. It would give him a dimension that he's seriously lacking. . . .

KISSINGER: All he needs is a foreign policy. . . .

PETERSON: Well, that's not the kind of thought that would occur to him. . . . From his vantage point he has a foreign policy and it's brilliant and it's bold and all the rest of us don't know what we're doing. . . .

H. R. Haldeman
November 15, 1972, 5:04 p.m.
Kissinger asks to be forewarned if Connally is appointed secretary of state.

... KISSINGER: ... I'm not going to be surprised with anything with respect to Connally without being told first?

HALDEMAN: No, sir. ... 'Cause that one is totally up in the air; the president is meeting with him tomorrow. ... The intention from here is nothing. ... There's the possibility of that changing.

KISSINGER: I beg your pardon!

HALDEMAN: There's the possibility, obviously, of that changing if he raises something. ...

KISSINGER: I should get the warning before it gets public.

HALDEMAN: Oh, sure. Good lord, yes.

KISSINGER: Because you know my view on this thing. ...

President Nixon
November 15, 1972, 5:46 p.m.
They discuss Nixon's recent letter to President Thieu urging acceptance of the peace agreement and ponder the upcoming negotiations with the North Vietnamese. Kissinger wants to "play it very tough." They decide that if they have to "cave," they'll do it later.

... NIXON: I must say the letter—as I reflect on it—while it had some grace notes is damn tough.

KISSINGER: Oh, it's extremely tough. ... It couldn't be anything else.

NIXON: Yeah, because, after all, we've been around the track on this. And damn it, they've just got to understand that we're backing up everything. ... You know, I've never been optimistic but I have a feeling that maybe it's going to work out this time. ... Mainly because he has no choice.

KISSINGER: He has no choice. It depends now how tough the North Vietnamese are going to play it.

NIXON: Well, so they play it tough. Then we settle on that basis and Thieu goes along. They'll have to make some changes, the North Vietnamese. ... We just say to them, "All right, we can't go back empty-handed," and then you get all that you can.

KISSINGER: Well, with your approval, Mr. President, I think I ought to play it very tough at the meeting—

NIXON: With the North Vietnamese? Oh, god yes.

KISSINGER: . . . And if we want to cave, we can always ask for another meeting and cave there. . . . I mean, supposing they absolutely refuse to yield. I think I should then say I'm going back to talk to you. . . . Rather than for me to yield at the end and accept the old draft.

NIXON: Oh, no, no, I agree with that. I meant they've got to make some concessions and that's to be expected. And as a matter of fact, I think that I should give you a letter which you can read to them at this thing where I say that we've got to have these and that's that. . . . I mean, that's a minimum that we've got to have—you know, something like that so—leave enough gobbledygook in. . . . But most of these idiots have got to be reasonable now, Henry, damn it. We're the only reasonable party and we're the ones that have got to bring this war to a responsible end.

KISSINGER: We've wound up in the curious position of mediating between the two Vietnamese parties. . . . Because they're both a little bit crazy. . . .

President Nixon
November 18, 1972, 12:02 p.m.
Kissinger tells Nixon of mounting problems with President Thieu. But "we can't tell Hanoi that we are having trouble," they agree. They decide to proceed without Thieu and get the best agreement they can, though they find making a bilateral agreement with Hanoi "repugnant."

. . . KISSINGER: . . . We had a phone call from Bunker . . . saying that now apparently the South Vietnamese are beginning to kick over the traces again.

NIXON: Oh, Christ.

KISSINGER: And I believe that we just have to continue now, and get the best agreement we can.

NIXON: Yeah.

KISSINGER: And then face them with it afterwards.

NIXON: How are they kicking it over?

KISSINGER: . . . He just said the news is not good, and their ambassador here has . . . some questions. . . . It's their old pattern; what they always do is they first read what you give them, then they raise a few technical objections, and then they just keep escalating it. . . .

NIXON: So Bunker says that they're . . . just being unreasonable as hell, is that it?

KISSINGER: That seems to be the case. But we can't delay the negotiation and we can't tell Hanoi that we are having trouble.

NIXON: No, sir.

KISSINGER: We're gonna play it like an accordion.

NIXON: All right. When you really come down to it, though, I just can't see how Thieu's got any other choice. God damn it, we've told him we're doing everything we can, and that's gonna be it. . . . But on the other hand, the idea of just making a bilateral thing, Henry, is—

KISSINGER: It's repugnant.

NIXON: Well, it's repugnant because we'd lose everything we've done. You know what I mean. People say that we coulda done that years ago.

KISSINGER: Well, if we can get a cease-fire in Laos and Cambodia, we can of course say we've put them in a position where they can defend themselves. . . . But it's going to be a miserable exercise. . . . But I just wanted to check with you whether it is in accord with your views that we proceed negotiating; we can't wait any longer for coordinating.

NIXON: Well, what would be the choice otherwise? I mean, you wouldn't go?

KISSINGER: That's right, and ask for another delay, but I think that's almost impossible.

NIXON: Well, you couldn't do that.

KISSINGER: I mean, not after we've announced it.

NIXON: No, no . . . I'd simply go. . . . Go right ahead on the same track, do the very best that you can. . . . Get the very best agreements you can. . . .

President Nixon
November 18, 1972, 12:18 p.m.
Nixon contemplates breaking relations with Thieu and rejects the idea of seeing his emissary and listening to more ultimatums. Kissinger fears that the latest South Vietnamese demands, on top of previous ones incorporated in the revised agreement they will propose to Hanoi, will kill it.

NIXON: Henry, you ought to inform Bunker that I have directed that we go ahead so that Bunker knows we are taking a hard line on this thing. . . . And inform him so that Thieu knows that there is no fooling around here and that this bargaining is—the time is over. The fellow has got to be out of his mind after the letter that I wrote. If after that we don't get anything, why, it may be one of those breaking of relations.

KISSINGER: He wants to send an emissary to see you personally too. . . .

NIXON: No, no, no. Not going to be any emissary. . . . We've had enough emissaries and that sort of thing. . . . I just think that Bunker has to get to him a message from me to the effect that we are going ahead, and as pointed out in my letter we're going to negotiate as hard as we can for the best position we can, and that we're on this course and that he must realize that we will not be subjected to harassment on this thing. . . . There are to be no ultimatums to come from them under any circumstances.

KISSINGER: . . . Again the trouble with them is every draft we give back to them already incorporates 70 percent of their changes. This has now been going on for three weeks. Now they sent us another batch of changes. I would say again we could accept 50 percent of them, but the trouble is if you accept all of these on top of all the others we have an entirely new document, and Le Duc Tho is going to walk out.

NIXON: No, no, no—just say that the document that we already have is the basic framework. And that's that. . . .

KISSINGER: . . . We already incorporated all the changes they made to me when I was there. Since then we have made two more revisions. . . . Now they have given us yet another 10 pages of comments. And the end result of that is to kill the agreement. . . . Because they are changing everything. . . .

Melvin Laird
November 27, 1972, 8:39 a.m.
Kissinger had returned two nights earlier from peace negotiations outside Paris, where he had presented 69 demands of President Thieu and Le Duc Tho had made new demands of his own, resulting in an impasse. He and Laird fume about a leak on secret plans to keep thousands of civilian personnel in South Vietnam—many in jobs previously performed by the military—after a cease-fire, who Tho had demanded be withdrawn.[5]

. . . KISSINGER: Well, all I can tell you is that if people do not shut up we'll lose everything we've ever achieved. . . . Every goddamn second-rater talks his stupid head off. . . . Every time a news story appears, the Vietnamese raise the ante.

LAIRD: Yeah, well, my problem is here that I think we gotta get people to shut up for a while, Henry, that's why I'm calling you. . . . You've read the *New York Times* this morning?

KISSINGER: Yes, and it's going to kill us. . . . We leak out all these things. . . . And it comes out of the Pentagon, it comes out of Saigon, and I don't doubt it comes out of the State Department.

LAIRD: Well, the situation is such that I think it's just got to be shut up all over, and this story, I'm sure that came out of the embassy. I think it's damaging.

KISSINGER: . . . I tell you, it's damaging from the point of view of the negotiations. . . . It isn't just damaging, it's absolutely killing us. . . . Now, these talks are going to blow up if this talking doesn't stop. Now they are demanding that all the civilians we had in the agreement the first time who maintain military equipment be removed. . . . Everything that we have nearly achieved is being destroyed because of a bunch of self-serving maniacs fighting inter-departmental battles. For what? We had it all set. We could have been at each other's throats for six months for all I care after it is signed, but now they're killing us with all these leaked stories over an agreement that will never be signed this way. . . . Can you get your people to shut up, and I will brutalize State.

LAIRD: I can get my people to shut up, I guarantee that. Now, this story is not from our people.

KISSINGER: Well, but there were a lot of other stories from the military people. . . .

LAIRD: Damn it, I'll—Jesus, I've ridden herd on that about as tough as you can. I'll do it again today. I'll personally crush the ass of everybody. . . .

Ronald Ziegler
November 28, 1972, 11:09 a.m.
Kissinger is upset about stories that he believed were put out by White House aides that Nixon had distanced himself from him and his positions in the peace negotiations; he thought the stories were intended to dissociate Nixon from their possible collapse.[6]

KISSINGER: Ron, I notice all these news stories about how the president has pulled away from me. I want to tell you two things: one, if these are put out by us we're going to look like horse's asses because the chances are nine out of 10 that it's going to work.

ZIEGLER: . . . Nothing's been put out along that line from here, Henry.

KISSINGER: And secondly, if we're going to have a repetition of the India–Pakistan situation [when he also felt White House staffers had scapegoated him and distanced Nixon from him through leaks] no one should think that I'm going to take it a second time. . . . And there should be no doubt about my attitude this time.

ZIEGLER: Henry, your South Vietnamese friends are doing this to you. . . .

KISSINGER: Yeah, but I think some of it is coming out of [Herb] Klein's shop. . . . For example, Jack Anderson called me this morning and . . . a White House staffer . . . gave him a rather good account of what had gone on, and then that the president slapped me down. . . .

H. R. Haldeman
November 28, 1972, 7:30 p.m.
Kissinger charges that State was putting out some of the stories that Nixon had dissociated from him and that Rogers wanted to "ride to the rescue" to pacify the South Vietnamese on the peace agreement.

. . . KISSINGER: I know for a certain fact that all last week, State was putting out stories that I had goofed terribly, that the president has disassociated from me, that Rogers had to step in to insist that the loopholes in the agreement would be closed. . . . You will see in *Time* they specifically refer to State Department stories that were being put out all last week. Now he's proposed that while I am in Paris, he go to Saigon and hold the fort there—

HALDEMAN: [Laughing.] That Rogers go to Saigon?

KISSINGER: That Rogers go to Saigon next week. . . .

HALDEMAN: Good god.

KISSINGER: I am not even saying that he is asking people to put out these stories, but I am saying he's creating an atmosphere where these stories then get put out, and for the last four months while he was on his knees you didn't get any stories like this, and starting last week he must have put out the word to build him up by any means. This is exactly what I predicted would happen. Now, you know for one thing it's personally maddening. But actually if Thieu reads stories like this that the president dissociated from me, that Rogers had to ride to the rescue—you read the *Boston Globe* today. . . . That explains also why Le Duc Tho asked me last week whether I was being asked to resign. . . . Why do we have to put up with it another four years?

HALDEMAN: We don't have to put up with it another four years. Jesus Christ, Henry, let's not be ridiculous. . . . Just say you'll raise it with the president— then tell him tomorrow the president said, for Christ sake, you're out of your mind. . . .

KISSINGER: I think it would be an absolute disaster to have Rogers in Saigon. And why does he want to go to Saigon? Not because he thinks we are in trouble but because we know we're going to settle it next week. . . .

President Nixon

December 1, 1972, 2:36 p.m.

Kissinger reports that President Thieu's envoy Nguyen Phu Duc and South Vietnamese Ambassador to the United States Tran Kim Phuong are concerned that the peace agreement doesn't require North Vietnamese forces to leave the South and had leaked an ultimatum Nixon had given them that congressional funding to South Vietnam would be cut off if Thieu continued to reject the peace agreement. But he thinks Saigon will sign it after it's concluded. Nixon wants Kissinger to threaten a cutoff of funding again and says if he meets with Thieu (who'd demanded a summit meeting), he will stress his interpretation of the agreement and all of its "trip wires."[7]

. . . KISSINGER: . . . They just say it's going to be impossible as long as there are North Vietnamese forces there. . . . They've leaked to the newspapers that you've given them an ultimatum. . . . I think the only other thing that can happen now is a meeting between you and Thieu . . . after the next round with the North Vietnamese, but before we conclude the agreement.

NIXON: Yeah, but you mean where he basically sits down and haggles about this whole thing. . . . You agree we can't do that.

KISSINGER: I agree completely. . . . What I think is going to happen, Mr. President, is that they are going to let us make the deal, they won't take any responsibility for it, and after it is concluded they'll join, saying they had no choice. . . .

NIXON: Well, you've got to tell them that this seriously jeopardize[s] my efforts to get these adequate aid programs. . . . To get the Congress to pass aid is always hard. But if they go along with this in a way that it appears that they are negative, they are just going to play into the hands of their congressional enemies.

KISSINGER: I've told them that it is absolutely essential that we end this in a way that Americans can be proud of it and feel that something worthwhile was accomplished. Then we have an interest in preserving it. But if they go along with it with this grudging attitude they are going to make it very tough for us to support them. Not because of intention, but because of the Congress.

NIXON: . . . As far as putting it out that I gave them an ultimatum . . . we denied that, but . . . we did give them an ultimatum. But my point is that as far as putting it out I don't think that hurts you . . . in dealing with Hanoi.

KISSINGER: No, that helps with Hanoi. . . .

NIXON: I wonder if Thieu can't be so foolish to think that . . . I don't mean what I say.

KISSINGER: Oh, no, I've made that again clear to them. . . .

NIXON: You should also make it clear this afternoon that it is very painful for me to have to take these positions. But I've never said anything that I don't mean. Never.

KISSINGER: Well, he's [Duc's] going back tomorrow and he'll be talking to Thieu personally. I believe that by the time we have this settlement worked out with the North Vietnamese next week, these fellows are going to come along.

NIXON: . . . For what purpose do we meet? For me to talk about the commitments?

KISSINGER: That's right, and to discuss the future of our relations there.

NIXON: . . . And also to discuss our interpretations of the agreement.

KISSINGER: That's right. That part, of course, couldn't be made public.

NIXON: Only after we sign it. . . . We cannot change it. We'll discuss how we are going to interpret it.

KISSINGER: Exactly.

NIXON: And that's very important. . . . Hell, that's all they need to know. Like they raise the point where the agreement doesn't provide for basically trip wires. God, it's full of trip wires. . . .

President Nixon

December 1, 1972, 6:02 p.m.

After another frustrating meeting with Nguyen Phu Duc, Kissinger advises Nixon that they should try to get the best deal they can bilaterally with the North Vietnamese. Nixon suggests sending Laird to Saigon to talk "cold turkey" to Thieu about a cutoff in aid if he doesn't sign the agreement and raises the possibility of turning on him. Kissinger thinks Thieu is worried that he won't win an election after the agreement is concluded.

. . . KISSINGER: It's tough going. . . . He gave me the same song and dance, that they can't support the settlement and they won't sign it. . . . I think, Mr. President, we have no choice but to do the very best we can in Paris next week. . . . You've done everything we can. I mean, it's a tragedy.

NIXON: . . . I wonder if we should [send] Laird there ostensibly to check the cease-fire . . . getting the message through to this fellow . . . the cold turkey message that politically we cannot wheel the deal unless they want to go along and that's it. Because if they are going to shit on it, we are going to have to turn on him. It's going to be unpleasant, but we'll just have to do it. I can't go down to that Congress and say, here they won't sign the agreement but we want $4 billion for aid. . . .

KISSINGER: Of course, I think also they are playing chicken with us, Mr. President. . . . I frankly don't see what Laird can add to what you've said, and it might give an impression of great insecurity. Nothing could be, I mean, more forceful or more ominous than you have said. . . .

NIXON: Well, don't get discouraged. . . . I think as far as the American people are concerned, most of them don't give one damn.

KISSINGER: Well, Mr. President, if you explain this agreement to the American people and say . . . we've done everything we can, we have to go it alone, I think you'll get very great support.

NIXON: Well, the support will be also to drop him [Thieu].

KISSINGER: Well, that's what I mean.

NIXON: That's the problem, isn't it?

KISSINGER: And it won't be that we have sold out, we have maintained our honor. It's a disaster.

NIXON: Well, I can't believe looking at the facts as they are that he can allow it to go to that point.

KISSINGER: No. . . . The real problem, I think, Mr. President, is that Thieu
has no confidence that he can win a political contest. . . . What he needs
is unconditional surrender. A smashing victory. It isn't a victory, it is a
compromise.

NIXON: It is a victory. We know that; it's a victory in terms of everything
they've insisted on before.

KISSINGER: Any energetic leader can play it into a victory. . . .

NIXON: Particularly when he was going to stay in power. . . .

Anatoly Dobrynin
December 15, 1972, 11:45 a.m.
*After returning from Paris, where Le Duc Tho began by angrily accusing Kissinger
of breaking his promises and by rejecting his proposed changes to the agreement, and
where each side then made concessions but failed to reach an agreement, Kissinger tells
Dobrynin that his allies in Hanoi are to blame for the deadlock. Nixon and Kissinger
had by now decided to resume heavy, sustained bombing of North Vietnam, including
B-52 bombing of Hanoi and Haiphong, to exert "leverage" on North Vietnam, convince both Hanoi and Saigon that they would retaliate to any enemy violations of the
agreement, and get Thieu on board.*[8]

... KISSINGER: I would not recommend to your clients to try to call on the
president. . . . I'll be glad to go over the issues with you. But as you could
have seen yesterday, it isn't the issues; they change issues so fast that we
can't solve them quickly enough. What we are trying to tell you is that
you are really not being told the truth. . . . For your own sake don't get
yourself locked into a position that they tell you. . . . They are lying to
you too. . . . The basic fact is we are ready to settle very quickly, and they
are not. . . . There is no doubt of it. Every day that we narrow it, the next
day they come in with four or five more issues. Now, the particular excuse they use at any given time is really unimportant. . . . You read the
transcript of the last day's meeting; you will see that it's irrelevant. . . . Le
Duc Tho thinks he's making a monkey out of me. Le Duc Tho thinks that
if he can just be nice to me that I'm so vain—and then puts me on television and he smiles. . . . I will also give you a copy of the text as it now
stands.

DOBRYNIN: This I think it will be a good idea. . . . What you are going to give
me is only for our own information. We won't argue with them. . . .

KISSINGER: I really don't know what we could ask you to do because—

DOBRYNIN: No, no . . . really it is difficult for us to do—to go and argue with
them. . . .

President Nixon

December 17, 1972, 10:45 a.m.

The day before beginning massive bombing in the Hanoi and Haiphong areas, Nixon talks of the advantage of conducting it when Congress is out of session and Kissinger acknowledges that "we could have easily lived with" the October peace agreement (thereby essentially rendering the bombing pointless). But the bombing would "make the agreement enforceable." Kissinger complains about a weather delay on hitting a power plant in the middle of Hanoi. But "I don't think there are going to be too many windows in Hanoi tomorrow." "Our strategy now has to be to turn on both of them," he advises, referring to Hanoi and Saigon. He thinks North Vietnam will probably capitulate quickly. "If you are willing to go six months, they're going to crack," Kissinger had told Nixon three days earlier.[9]

> . . . NIXON: . . . I really read the act to people around here. . . . Some of them said, oh, gee, it's too bad to have to do it before Christmas and have to do it before the inauguration. . . . You see, one of the beauties of doing it now, we don't have the problem of having to consult with the Congress. . . .
>
> KISSINGER: . . . These guys are just a bloody bunch of bastards. Dobrynin told me yesterday that they told the Russians that you would have to settle just before the inauguration. So you can see their strategy. . . . They were going to meet me again early in January—
>
> NIXON: And make us settle on bad terms.
>
> KISSINGER: Well, make us go back to the October 26 draft. . . . We could have easily lived with it in October, but if we accept it now after all this arguing for changes it would make us look impotent. With this blow they are going to get, they're going to scream for a few weeks, but . . . it's going to make the agreement enforceable, Mr. President; they are going to be very careful.
>
> NIXON: I think that point is . . . probably the most important point. With this blow, they are going to think twice before they break the agreement. . . . I don't do target lists usually, but I went over that goddamned thing with Moorer and Rush, and Moorer swears that this is everything they can get that's worth hitting, I mean without taking out too much civilian stuff.
>
> KISSINGER: . . . The whole bloody country is again covered with clouds, so they have to do it with B-52s. . . . You can't take out the power plant in the center of Hanoi, and, you know, if we had had 72 hours of good weather, we could have done the whole bloody thing in one blow.
>
> NIXON: Yeah. What happens then is the clouds are going to last forever. It

always seems that they do, although I don't believe our—

KISSINGER: The thing is going to last until the 20th now. We have had to cancel 65 percent of our strikes—

NIXON: . . . [Incoming Deputy Secretary of Defense William] Clements . . . says our air force is so goddamned impotent because we haven't got the right kind of planes. . . . Also they cost too much considering what their job is. He's so right.

KISSINGER: He's right on both counts. We have, Mr. President, to cancel over 50 percent of our targets during the dry season, and now they only have three or four days of what they consider flying weather in months. Now, that just means they've got the wrong airplane.

NIXON: By the way, at least the 52s will shake them, won't it?

KISSINGER: Yes. They are double-loaded. That's like a 4,000-plane raid in World War II. . . . Thirty planes are like a thousand and they are flying 127 double-loaded; that's like 250. So it's really between four and eight thousand planes, if they got them all over there. It's going to break every window in Hanoi.

NIXON: Just the reverberations?

KISSINGER: Yeah.

NIXON: Well, that should tend to shake them up a little bit. . . .

KISSINGER: Oh, yeah. . . . I don't know whether you've been in Saigon when they hit 30 or 40 miles away, how the ground shakes. . . . Well, this one is going to be two miles outside, and there are going to be about 50 of them. I don't think there are going to be too many windows in Hanoi tomorrow. But it would have been good if we could have taken all power plants simultaneously.

NIXON: But as it is, what are we going to get?

KISSINGER: Well, we are going to get the shipyards in Haiphong, we are going to get the marshalling yards, the railyards, Radio Hanoi, we'll get the transmitters at the outskirts of town.

NIXON: But we will miss the power plant.

KISSINGER: It's in the center of town.

NIXON: But it will still be there, and the day that it clears up they can go in and get it, can't they?

KISSINGER: Absolutely.

NIXON: That's a standing order to Moorer.

KISSINGER: . . . I think they are going to give them quite a shock tomorrow. We're going to have a little screaming here.

NIXON: Sure, they are going to scream. They always do. They would have screamed otherwise but for the fact that the talks were broken. Now we'll give them something else to scream about. . . . They'll scream now, well, the talks are broken and we have resumed bombing. . . . Ziegler said that handling it is going to be very, very good that way: we are continuing our activities to prevent another enemy offensive.

KISSINGER: That's right. They are building up.

NIXON: I know, but we are doing it for other reasons.

KISSINGER: Oh, no question about it.

NIXON: I mean, let them give their reasons. . . . And the fact that it has some truth in it helps.

KISSINGER: Well, Le Duc Tho asked that we send him a message as soon as he returns. He's returning tomorrow. . . .

NIXON: He will hear this message.

KISSINGER: That's what I mean.

NIXON: Yeah. If he will hear it, it won't have to be delivered by hand.

KISSINGER: . . . Our strategy now has to be to turn on both of them.

NIXON: As far as reassuring Thieu, no one could reassure Thieu more than I've reassured Thieu.

KISSINGER: Listen, you've made three solemn commitments to him.

NIXON: And I did it in two different meetings, and wasted a hell of a lot of time, and I also wrote him three letters.

KISSINGER: Of course, this insane son of a bitch, if he had gone along with us early in November, then all these fine points that people talk about now . . . would have been washed out in the victory. . . . I myself think that either the North Vietnamese are going to dig in, which I don't really believe, or they are going to cave quickly. And I think that's more likely.

NIXON: I don't see how they can dig in either 'cause they just can't figure they're gonna take this indefinitely. Now, the one thing that can encourage them some will be some of those statements, public outcry—

KISSINGER: Yeah, but they've seen that—

NIXON: They've seen that. . . . Let's face it, that's the beauty of the election. They saw all the public outcry was murderous during the election campaign and we won 61 to 38. . . .

Anatoly Dobrynin
December 18, 1972, 10:58 a.m.
Ambassador Dobrynin is disturbed by the bombing of Haiphong and Hanoi.

. . . KISSINGER: Well, I want you to know we've resumed bombing again to-day. . . .

DOBRYNIN: You mean a full scale?

KISSINGER: Oh, yes.

DOBRYNIN: Well, that's a pity.

KISSINGER: That's putting it mildly.

DOBRYNIN: Well, you put it mildly, but I'm not sure you understand what I say. . . .

KISSINGER: They've given us no choice. . . . What would they think would happen when there are 15 days of negotiations and they're dealing with the president? I mean, did they really think they could keep a presidential emissary [Kissinger] in Paris for nine days and play games with him? . . . We are still willing to settle on the basis that I described with you, and we are willing to do it quickly. But we are not willing to play games. . . .

President Nixon
December 18, 1972, 12:32 p.m.
Nixon asks about the bombing; when Kissinger points out that "the danger is that they may miss and hit a populated area," Nixon responds nonchalantly, "There will be some, sure."

. . . NIXON: . . . There are three waves?

KISSINGER: Yes, the third one will be at 5:00 tonight. . . . Then they go back to tac-air.

NIXON: Tac-air—you mean no B-52s at all?

KISSINGER: No, no, then at night they go in B-52s again. . . . It's going to be massive, it's going to be brutal.

NIXON: . . . You just don't want them to drop it on the boondocks. You want them to hit something.

KISSINGER: They are going to hit something. The danger is that they may miss and hit a populated area, in which case it would be gory.

NIXON: There will be some, sure. That always happens, doesn't it?

KISSINGER: Well, yes, but the targets should be far enough away so that they have some margin.

NIXON: We [don't] always know whether we are far enough away or not, Henry. We've been accused of [bombing] populated areas throughout this war and we've just got to take the heat. . . .

Ronald Ziegler
December 18, 1972, no time
Ziegler asks about a report out of the Soviet Union on the bombing.

. . . ZIEGLER: . . . TASS apparently dealt with a story that the repeated bombing of Hanoi now is occurring and there are large fires raging north of the city.

KISSINGER: That's probably true. . . . They were going after some railway yards and storage areas. . . . They hit something.

ZIEGLER: Hope it doesn't burn the city down.

KISSINGER: Oh, my boy, this is going to be brutal, believe me. . . .

Stewart Alsop

December 18, 1972, 5:58 p.m.

Kissinger claims falsely to columnist Alsop that his October "peace is at hand" statement had been discussed in advance with Nixon and that reports of a rift with Nixon are untrue.

> . . . ALSOP: . . . Let me ask you a question which you probably will not wish to answer, but when you said "We believe that peace is at hand," did that phrase come springingly to your brain or was it one that had been prepared in advance by the president?
>
> KISSINGER: No, actually, I'll answer it. It came from my brain but it had been discussed with the president, and all such speculations that the president pulls me back, and there was a disagreement between me and the president—total and absolute, demonstrable, outrageous nonsense. It isn't excluded that some of my heroic associates are putting them out; they're having a hell of a time knowing how to position themselves, you know, whether to the left or to the right of me. . . . I can only tell you that there was . . . nothing that was done inappropriately, was not previously cleared by the president, fully discussed with him, encouraged by him, or whatever other word you need. . . .

Thomas Moorer

December 19, 1972, 10:09 a.m.

JCS Chairman Moorer reports on the bombing. B-52s had pounded the outskirts of Hanoi nine miles from the city center and fighter bombers had conducted an unrelenting all-night raid on the city. U.S. bombers also unleashed hundreds of sorties against Haiphong and other areas in the North.[10] They were the heaviest raids of the war in the Hanoi–Haiphong area.

> KISSINGER: Tom, did the B-52s get out all right?
>
> MOORER: Yes. First wave, no problem.
>
> KISSINGER: And none shot down?
>
> MOORER: No. Now we got another group going about the middle of the day and another later on.
>
> KISSINGER: . . . You can go after the transportation targets whenever the weather clears.

MOORER: Yeah. Well, I'm sending a list of 50 more up there right now . . . which includes the transportation. And includes some, you know, up north that we were talking about. . . .

KISSINGER: We have to count on you that if you get any targets turned down [i.e., by Laird], that you let us know. . . . I mean, you can't just not do it without telling us. . . . As far as we are concerned, we have to keep up the pressure. . . .

Murrey Marder

December 19, 1972, 4:36 p.m.

North Vietnamese negotiator Xuan Thuy had placed responsibility for the failure to reach a peace agreement on the United States, saying Kissinger had asked in November for 126 changes in the agreement reached in October, the overwhelming majority of "fundamental importance." Kissinger tells Marder of the Washington Post *that is "a pack of lies." ("Exaggeration" would be closer to the mark, as he'd requested 69 major changes.)*[11]

. . . MARDER: What I wanted to say was we've had, as you know, the sayings of Xuan Thuy today.

KISSINGER: Which is a pack of lies. . . . He said we asked for 126 changes. . . .

MARDER: On the last day. . . . It was not consistent with anything else we've had here. . . .

KISSINGER: Well, I'm telling you that is a pack of lies. . . . We didn't ask for 126 changes any time. . . . You know, I don't know how the sons of bitches are counting. . . . There were never more than eight points seriously at issue at any time during these 15 days [which included the December negotiations]. . . . Just say administration officials made it clear that not a single change was asked for on the last day. . . . There were only four problems discussed the whole last week.

MARDER: . . . He says here no less than 126 changes in the accord drafted in October, and most of the 126 amendments that he's addressed were attempts to impose changes of substance which would have violated the fundamental rights of the people of Vietnam—

KISSINGER: But that's total unadulterated crap!!!! . . . Look, I can show you in the transcript that on Saturday night Le Duc Tho said to me, "There's only one issue left and all the rest is agreed on." . . . The major issue that was discussed occurred in one place and did not recur through the document. . . . But will you write this please by keeping the White House or anybody else out of it.

MARDER: All right, but I must use something—"Administration sources said the charge of 126 has no foundation whatsoever."

KISSINGER: That's right.

MARDER: That there was no such presentation on the last day and that at no time were there ever 126—

KISSINGER: Or anything remotely like it.

MARDER: . . . That is essentially what I needed, Henry. . . .

Melvin Laird
December 19, 1972, 5:35 p.m.
Kissinger stresses to Laird that the bombing of Haiphong and Hanoi was "indefinite."

LAIRD: Henry, on this three-day business I haven't really gotten any authority to continue going on this. I assume the plan is to continue strikes when they are authorized.

KISSINGER: Absolutely, there is no three-day thing. It is indefinite.

LAIRD: But the maximum B-52 effort was limited to three days.

KISSINGER: But what conclusion do you draw from that?

LAIRD: That in the memorandum I have on my desk the president doesn't give me authority to go beyond that.

KISSINGER: Absolutely not, this was supposed to be kept going. . . . Keep this going up until Christmas. . . .

Thomas Moorer
December 19, 1972, 5:44 p.m.
Kissinger gives JCS Chairman Moorer carte blanche on the bombing and wants a relentless attack.

. . . KISSINGER: I don't want to pick the targets for you but we want to make damn sure we don't get into the same syndrome we got into this summer. . . . Your mission is to have a maximum impact on the North. . . . Whatever your military judgment says we should do, that is fine.

MOORER: What I am putting up now is a heavy . . . continuous operation . . . rather than this three-day massive effort.

KISSINGER: After the three-day effort you will have a massive effort every day. . . .

MOORER: We will keep continuous pressure.

KISSINGER: You know what the president wants. . . . After tomorrow you go to 30 [strikes] with another massive effort. . . . We don't want them to feel we are letting up.

MOORER: We won't.

President Nixon

December 23, 1972, 12:50 p.m.

Nixon says it is a disgrace that they had to undertake the bombing to get Le Duc Tho's attention, and they complain about Laird's veto that summer of strikes Moorer requested; they want to implement a system whereby all of Moorer's requests go directly to them, but Kissinger worries that Laird could "blow." They plan for a "big strike" after a Christmas pause and "all-out" attacks until December 31 (when they'd offered to stop the bombing for the duration of peace talks).[12] Nixon also says the October agreement was "good enough" and that all they were getting now was "a little better language." Which didn't mean much.

NIXON: Anything new today?

KISSINGER: They flew 30 B-52s this morning and they all got back. . . . They went a little bit outside the Hanoi area this time—they went up into the buffer zone with China, where they had found 100 railway cars piled up. . . .

NIXON: You got his attention, huh?

KISSINGER: Ohhh, we got his attention, Mr. President, we have his attention.

NIXON: Isn't it a crime we have to do this, though? . . . How many times do you have to do it?

KISSINGER: Well, I gave him [Moorer] hell and he said during the summer he sent in at least 50 requests for new authorities which were disapproved.

NIXON: The point is, did we ever know it?

KISSINGER: No, and I think we ought to—

NIXON: That's the thing, Henry—I just can't understand why [he didn't] send them to me. You remember that I told him that he was to do that. Or he was just afraid of Laird, was that it?

KISSINGER: That's right. I think we ought to institute a system for [incoming Secretary of Defense Elliot] Richardson when he comes in that every request of the chairman automatically comes over here too.

NIXON: Absolutely. . . . I think we should institute it now.

KISSINGER: Well, we're having trouble with Laird as it is and we don't want him to blow before he leaves. . . . But we had a report, for example, from the Cuban ambassador in Hanoi, who is certainly not friendly to us, and he says they are in bad shape. There was a meeting of technical experts this morning again. . . . And they bled all over us again. . . . But again they didn't break off; they said we should set the next day, so we proposed the date to them. . . . I think their teeth are really rattling right now.

NIXON: They ought to be. . . . Moorer is preparing a big strike the day after [the Christmas pause].

KISSINGER: All-out.... I think, Mr. President, we ought to go all-out no matter what they reply until December 31.... I think if we can get some of these bridges if the weather clears, we will set them back two or three months again on the transportation, and their industrial capacity and their electrical system is being leveled right now—formerly we just went out after one of the buildings, the generator building—but now they are leveling all supporting facilities too.

NIXON: Good. We'll just continue on this course. . . . It's terrible that Thieu, Henry, as I reflected on our meeting with Haig, that Thieu—he has made a comprehensive settlement almost impossible, to be ever interpreted as a peace with honor. On the other hand, if we can get a comprehensive settlement . . . perhaps we can bring them around. But we should have had it October 8th.

KISSINGER: That's right.

NIXON: That deal was good enough. Language doesn't mean anything—not a damn thing.

KISSINGER: We would have had a great success and it isn't that much different anyway.

NIXON: You know the language doesn't mean much—you know it and I know it. Now we are stuck with getting a little better language.

KISSINGER: Exactly. . . . We just got a report that they are totally evacuating Hanoi.

NIXON: They think we are going to come at them with more stuff all over the city?

KISSINGER: That's right.

NIXON: That can't but affect their morale of their people, to evacuate that city.

KISSINGER: Oh, god yeah.

NIXON: Everyone talks about the ineffectiveness of bombing—it was not ineffective at all—I mean, it was damn effective—what the hell finished Germany? . . . The German armies were still fighting damn well but it was just tearing the hell out of their cities, the strategic bombing. We just haven't done it well enough, Henry, that's our problem.

KISSINGER: These guys—it's the tenth year of a war for them and just when they think they have it done, it starts again with increased ferocity—this must be a shocking thing to them.

NIXON: Right. . . . There's not a damn thing any of us can do, except to keep the heat on. I guess the heat is on Moorer enough, though.

KISSINGER: Oh, the heat is on Moorer enough now, Mr. President. I think frankly we ought to leave him alone for the next week or so.

NIXON: Fine, I'm all for it—he knows what he has to do and I think he's telling the truth—I think Laird is just—

KISSINGER: He's got a good plan now. . . . Their major emphasis now is going
to cut off Hanoi from the rest of the country. . . .

Melvin Laird
December 26, 1972, 9:20 a.m.
*The administration had resumed the bombing on a huge scale after the Christmas
pause.*

LAIRD: We got that targeting all on and there will be 120 of these birds up there
and all over targets within about 30 minutes. They will carry on their strike
within a 30-minute period. It will be a massive strike. We have them coming
in from all sides within that period. . . . Will be hitting Hanoi, Haiphong,
and Thai Nguyen. . . . They may miss some targets, but they will do the best
they can. There's a heavy cloud cover. . . . Will try and minimize our losses
rather than sending in at three times anyway. Coming in from north, east,
and west, all at different altitudes. . . .

President Nixon
December 26, 1972, 12:55 p.m.
*The North Vietnamese had agreed to resume negotiations as soon as the bomb-
ing stopped and proposed another meeting between Kissinger and Le Duc Tho on
January 8.*[13] *Nixon and Kissinger debate when to halt the bombing and agree that
they should resume it if Hanoi turns down "one last offer" of U.S. withdrawal for the
return of America's POWs. But they think the North Vietnamese are ready to settle.*

KISSINGER: Now we've had an answer from the North Vietnamese, and they
propose the meeting for the 8th. But that's a terrific cave. . . . They want us
to stop the bombing immediately. So what we are going to do is exchange a
few more messages with them to run it up to the 31st. . . .
NIXON: . . . The problem we have is that we've got to stay one jump ahead . . .
of the congressional people. When they come back I'll have to meet with
Mansfield and all those jackasses on the 2nd or 3rd. . . . I would like it announced, if possible, before the 1st. . . . We've got to keep the debate on our
grounds. Not ever let it move to their grounds. . . .
KISSINGER: I think we have now a good chance of winding it up at that
meeting, because we've gotten credibility with these guys again.
NIXON: . . . We either wind it up at that meeting or we go on option two. . . .
Before I go on [television], I want them to have an offer and a turndown on
that thing. . . . Because we have to have basically a rationale for bombing in
order to get the prisoners. . . .

KISSINGER: . . . Assuming the negotiations failed, then I come back, then you could go on television and say, "We can no longer pursue the October framework. I now make one last offer. Which is withdrawal for prisoners." Then if they turn it down, I'd resume bombing. . . . But I don't think it will come to that.

NIXON: Well, it would seem to me that in view of their reaction here the chances are they are ready to talk. I mean, they are ready to settle.

KISSINGER: That's my impression.

NIXON: But we have felt that before.

KISSINGER: But considering what we have done to them, this is a very soft reply.

NIXON: Yeah. Now the question is what do we do about the bombing between now and the 31st?

KISSINGER: I think we'd keep it up.

NIXON: That's my view too. . . .

PR on the Christmas Bombing; Agreement in Paris; Facing Down and "Turning the Screw" on Thieu, Threatening a Separate Peace and an Aid Cutoff, and Contingency Planning for a "Tragedy"; Initialing and Signing the Agreement; "Peace with Honor"; Memoirs and Interviews

January 1973

In January 1973, facing denunciations in the press of the December bombing of Hanoi and Haiphong, the administration moved to counter charges of barbaric terror bombing. Former secretary of defense and Vietnam War architect Robert McNamara phoned Kissinger to buck him up—"What you're doing is the right thing," he assured him.

In Paris, Kissinger and North Vietnam's Le Duc Tho settled the remaining issues in the peace agreement, with the final agreement bearing a strong resemblance to the October agreement that the administration had accepted and then gone back on. Nixon worried that they would be in "one hell of a spot" if South Vietnamese President Nguyen Van Thieu didn't accept the agreement by the time Kissinger initialed it in Paris; he directed that they be "uncompromising as hell" with Thieu, who, in an emotional state over the fate of his country, was still raising objections. They made plans to go forward without him, although Nixon was more worried than Kissinger that they would have to take that course;

he was also concerned that they wouldn't have "peace with honor" (meaning, particularly, honor) without Thieu's support of the agreement. "If he pulls back now, it's going to make us look so goddamn dumb," Nixon said. He thought they needed a "contingency plan" to "cut our losses but goddamned fast" if Thieu didn't go along, but still thought making a bilateral agreement with Hanoi would be a tragedy. Nixon and Kissinger decided to threaten Thieu again with a loss of U.S. aid.

But Thieu soon gave in and agreed to sign the agreement. Nixon announced that they had concluded an agreement "to end the war and bring peace with honor in Vietnam."

Neither took place.

Stewart Alsop
January 3, 1973, 9:12 a.m.
On December 29, Nixon had stopped the bombing in the Hanoi and Haiphong areas, with peace negotiations set to resume January 8. Kissinger tells columnist Alsop that all of the bombing's targets were military ones. (Only 12 percent of the attacks were against strictly military targets, and with inaccurate B-52s dropping 75 percent of the tonnage, hitting civilians was inevitable—over 2,000 were killed in Hanoi, despite evacuations.)[1]

... KISSINGER: You know, this bombing, with all the breast-beating that's going on—first of all, some day when this is over I'll show you pictures of the bomb damage. And while I don't doubt that some civilian targets were hit ... every target was a military target. ... Our objective was not to terrorize the population. Our objective was to do the greatest amount of damage in the shortest possible time. ... And I am certain that when one can get in there one will find that probably a few outlying districts were hit, but that there was no terror bombing. I'm not saying that they didn't miss occasionally. But I'm talking about the fact that every target that was approved was a clear, well-defined military target. ...

Melvin Laird
January 3, 1973, 4:00 p.m.
The Washington Post *had run a story that morning on the bombing of Bach Mai hospital in Hanoi.*

LAIRD: Henry, what I want to talk to you about is . . . all these goddamned stories on the bombing that are coming out are all negative. Now, I think we should let Saigon brief positively on our targeting. . . . All they are talking about is hospitals . . . and schools. Now, that isn't what our targets were,

and we've got a good story we can tell on military targets that were hit. . . .
I just hate to be on the defensive all the time about all these lousy stories. . . .
Down there and the press over here is just hitting us all the time. . . .

Spiro Agnew
January 3, 1973, 4:13 p.m.
In the Post's *story, Pentagon spokesman Jerry Friedheim had backed off earlier denials
and acknowledged that American bombs may have hit Bach Mai hospital, though he
repeated earlier dubious claims that the damage might have been caused by downed
U.S. planes or North Vietnamese air-defense missiles.*

>
> AGNEW: I wanted to express a very grave fear that Friedheim over at DOD is
> making a very serious mistake in the attitude he's taking about any acciden-
> tal or incidental bombing damage in Hanoi. . . . He was asked if action is
> being taken to punish the pilots for accidentally bombing the hospital and
> [a commercial] airfield. His response was no, no punitive action is being
> taken because we are not certain that the damage resulted from U.S. ac-
> tions. . . . That leads to a conclusion that if you were certain that the damage
> resulted from U.S. actions, we'd punish the pilots, which to me is a crummy,
> unconscionable chance to take in a war. . . . What the hell difference does it
> make? We're not going to punish any pilots, I hope, for bombing—if it did
> result, you know they didn't do it intentionally.
>
> KISSINGER: I will do something about it immediately.
>
> AGNEW: All right. I think it's a bad [issue] for us to get into, with all of the
> activity swirling around—the new committee that will build a new hospital
> over there and all that crap.
>
> KISSINGER: Revolting. I haven't seen anyone build a hospital when it was
> blown up in South Vietnam. . . .

Robert McNamara
January 3, 1973, 5:45 p.m.
*McNamara assures Kissinger that the Christmas bombing and his approach to the
negotiations were the right strategy.*

>
> MCNAMARA: I'm leaving for Africa in a few days before you return to Paris,
> or about when you do, and before I leave, Henry, I just wanted to call you
> and say don't worry about what's happening. . . . Christ, this is a time of
> trouble for you, I know that. And I am reminded of a remark you made to
> me about four years ago when you were beginning on this. I had been a year
> out of it. And I think you said that you thought that everyone that came
> close to Vietnam was in danger of being destroyed. Well, it isn't that bad,

Henry. It surely isn't going to be that way for you, and you are going to go down in history as the man who finally got us out of there. You will come through it all right.

KISSINGER: Bob, I really appreciate that.

MCNAMARA: I really mean this, Henry. I was in Aspen last week skiing, and we had a perfectly glorious time, but during the time three or four people called me about the bombing and all this stuff, and I get back into town and I read all this—I had my secretary clip all the columns while I was gone—and I read all that stuff and I hear all these rumors. I heard it before I left and I hear it now, Henry, and I know just exactly what must be on your mind and what's going on in that building over there. Just don't let it get you down, that's all. All this crap about the task being loose and ambiguous—look, Henry, you know and I know there is only one way to resolve this and that's to have a conscious ambiguity in the damn thing.

KISSINGER: Exactly.

MCNAMARA: And don't give up on that. That's the way to handle it.

KISSINGER: . . . A lot of this is put out by jealous bureaucrats.

MCNAMARA: I know it. . . . I don't have to tell you, you know where it's coming from as well as I do. It's coming from two different buildings in this city [State and Defense], and both of them are pretty damn close at hand. But anyhow, what you're doing is the right thing, Henry, and if it weren't for you I'd be deeply pessimistic about getting out of there. . . . And I think, Henry, this is not just my view, I should say also it's the view of some other of your friends, and, well, Mac [McGeorge] Bundy [national security adviser to Presidents Kennedy and Johnson], for example, and a lot of others that I know—so don't feel that everything's dark and bad. . . . Not everybody is as critical as some of these damn columnists and others. . . .

Thomas Moorer
January 15, 1973, 9:30 p.m.
Kissinger had returned from negotiations in Paris, where he had found a furious Le Duc Tho and claimed that the bombing was "not my responsibility." But they had settled the outstanding issues in the peace agreement, with the final agreement looking a good deal like the October one. Much of the NLF's 10-point program of 1969 was also in the agreement, suggesting that little was achieved during the four years of Nixon's war (though a provision that Thieu be replaced did not remain).[2]

KISSINGER: Tom, the president wanted to make sure that we are not cutting down sorties as a result of this. . . . The total number of sorties should be flown, they should just go to other places. . . . Now, we want to make a very major effort in Cambodia. That's the area which is least clearly defined in the agreement. . . . Could you start that immediately? . . . And would you do me a favor and hit that goddamned Chup [rubber] plantation [a North Vietnamese divisional headquarters that was also targeted to disrupt enemy supply routes]. You hit a lot of other things that haven't done any good. . . . But you don't have unlimited time. . . . Will you lay on a major effort in Cambodia to weaken the communists there as much as possible? . . .

President Nixon
January 16, 1973, 7:05 p.m.
Kissinger and Nixon agree that nobody should testify on the agreement until it's signed by Secretary of State Rogers in Paris. They also discuss Alexander Haig's talks with President Thieu about the agreement in Saigon. Nixon says there can be no further delay, that they will be "totally cruel" to Thieu if he doesn't finally go along with it, but that they will be in "one hell of a spot" if he doesn't. They also take up the enthusiasm at home for the widely expected agreement.

. . . NIXON: . . . How's it going with Rogers? Did you pin him down?

KISSINGER: Oh, yeah. I told him I wasn't going to come to the signing ceremony and that made him so happy that he forgot almost everything else. . . . He wanted to run right up to the Foreign Relations Committee and testify, and I said he shouldn't do that before the signing.

NIXON: Testify? Good god. . . . Never, never, never. We just play it very hard until this thing is signed. There isn't going to be any testimony. . . .

KISSINGER: And he won't know the agreements well enough by then anyway. . . .

NIXON: I have just been thinking that Thieu's tactic will probably be to ask for a delay of a week. Now I just want to be sure—I know Haig realizes that there can be no delay, no change. . . .

KISSINGER: Oh, Haig understands it. . . .

NIXON: Yeah. But don't you agree that that will be Thieu's tactic?

KISSINGER: Well, he will do two things. He'll ask for a delay and he'll start bitching about the protocols. . . .

NIXON: It's going to be, Henry, totally cruel, believe me. . . . You've never seen it if this son of a bitch doesn't go along. . . . If you don't have it before the 23rd [when Kissinger would return to Paris to complete and initial the agreement], we're in a hell of a spot. . . . So is he.

KISSINGER: That's right. In that case, we should just face him down and initial it anyway.

NIXON: I understand that. We initial it, but we're in one hell of a spot in terms of telling the people that this is the end.

KISSINGER: Of course. No question we need it.

NIXON: So he's got us by the balls too, hasn't he?

KISSINGER: . . . He has us by the balls if he wants to commit suicide.

NIXON: Incidentally, what do you hear from Timmons [Nixon's assistant for congressional affairs] . . . and the rest that are in contact with people as to how this damn thing is being—

KISSINGER: Oh, tremendous enthusiasm. . . . The congressional reaction, their only problem is to keep them from going hog wild. . . . And the press play is uniformly good. I have a list of press calls which is literally two sheets long now. . . . Oh, it's playing beautifully. And people like Taft Schreiber [the Republican fundraiser] are calling in. . . . He's just wildly enthusiastic.

NIXON: . . . You have kept in touch with Colson, have you?

KISSINGER: Oh, yes, I had a brief talk with him this morning. And he's extremely enthusiastic. . . . You know, in Key Biscayne you may not have a sense of this. There's a tremendous sense of excitement here. . . .

NIXON: Well, we'll see what Mr. Thieu does to it tomorrow. And if he doesn't do it, we may take him on before the inauguration. . . . And he cannot screw us again.

KISSINGER: Well, he isn't that insane. . . .

NIXON: Well, we'll see. You don't think he is?

KISSINGER: No. But I could be wrong.

NIXON: Yeah. We could all be wrong. . . .

President Nixon

January 17, 1973, 9:44 a.m.

President Thieu had raised many objections to the agreement with Haig in Saigon, and Nixon and Kissinger decide that if he doesn't get on board to tell him they will state publicly the reasons for the breakdown and will go forward without him and he will lose U.S. aid. But Kissinger doesn't think Thieu will refuse to sign the agreement. They also discuss Kissinger's upcoming meeting in Paris with Le Duc Tho to complete and initial the agreement, and what Nixon should say in his inaugural speech on the 20th—and what Kissinger should negotiate in Paris—if Thieu refuses to go along. Kissinger says Haig will reject Thieu's proposed changes in the agreement, and Nixon questions whether they'll have "peace with honor" if Thieu doesn't support it.

KISSINGER: I just talked to Haig on the secure phone and it has gone just about as we thought it would. He saw Thieu late today their time and Thieu handed him a letter listing all of his objections to the agreement. . . . But staying just short of rejecting it. . . . Haig's judgment is that we should now send him a very cool reply saying we've noted his objections, nothing can be done about them, we are proceeding to initial on the 23rd, that Haig will stop through there on the way back from Bangkok and receive his absolutely final reply. If that reply should be negative we will have no choice except to attack him publicly and that will lead to a cutoff of aid. . . . We would have to say we would have to state publicly the reason for the breakdown.

NIXON: Yeah, but that's what I meant. The letter should say that we would have to go forward. . . . You know, it's really a shocking thing, Henry, that at this point . . . he is still dug in, isn't it?

KISSINGER: No, I thought he would do it about this way, Mr. President. This son of a bitch is now building a record to prove that he was raped. So that when his own domestic opposition afterwards accuses him of having sold out, which they will, those irresponsible guys, he will then be able to say he fought until the last minute of the last day. . . . But when one reads their propaganda, Mr. President, they are definitely moving towards peace. . . .

NIXON: If he pulls back now it's going to make us look so goddamn dumb. . . .

KISSINGER: I don't think so, Mr. President. I think the record is now overwhelming. That we have made a massive effort to bring him along. That we have negotiated in good faith, that we have gone to the absolute limit of getting for him what could be gotten.

NIXON: Oh, we've done everything, I know that.

KISSINGER: But I think we can demonstrate this. But I don't think it is going to come to that point. . . .

NIXON: . . . I am just trying to get my own thinking for what I am going to be saying on the inaugural. . . . Suppose you have a flat turndown from him.

KISSINGER: I don't believe that, but if that were to happen then I think you should say we have today initialed an agreement which we think is fair. It is to be signed on the 27th and I would call on Thieu to sign it. I wouldn't yet say he has rejected it. I would give the impression that this is now before him—

NIXON: I get your point. Assuming that we hadn't had a public rejection, just make it appear as if that were the normal course of events. . . . On the other hand, then let's suppose that we put it to him and he doesn't sign. Do I raise the enormous expectation that peace is here?

KISSINGER: No, no, there will be peace then, Mr. President. . . . The way it will then work out is a cease-fire, withdrawal of our forces, and the cutoff of military aid to South Vietnam. They [North Vietnam] will settle for that.

NIXON: Oh, they'll give us that, of course, yeah. And that's what we will sign. That's what you will negotiate. Henry, I am trying to think what the hell you will negotiate with Le Duc Tho if you have a flat turndown from Thieu on Tuesday. . . .

KISSINGER: Well, what I think that I would first propose is that we would implement all the clauses of the agreement we can implement. . . . They will then come back and say, no, that's not right. There has to be some restrictions on military aid [to South Vietnam]. And I will get the minimum restrictions we can get away with. . . . The reason why I think they are going to accept it, Mr. President, is because the Saigon radio today, for example, put out that peace is near, or something like that. The official newspaper said—owned by that son of a bitch nephew [possibly Hoang Duc Nha, Thieu's adopted nephew, press secretary, and head of the National Commission for Information]—said we are not yet completely ready to sign the agreement. But he didn't say will never sign it. So, he is moving in his torturous, crooked, complicated, devious, petty way.

NIXON: The point is, Henry, he has no illusions that these objections he has will now be taken by Haig back and we are going to try to negotiate them.

KISSINGER: Oh, no. We'll reject them.

NIXON: I know. Haig has already rejected them, hasn't he?

KISSINGER: Oh, yes. Well, he gave them to him in this way: he gave them to him in a sealed envelope and said don't read them in my presence. So he obviously didn't want them rejected while he was there. . . . But they will be rejected, Mr. President. . . .

NIXON: . . . We have gone as far as we can. No more changes in the agreement can be made. We are going forward and initial it on Thursday, and . . . what is involved here is not simply the phrases of an agreement but what is really at stake here—far more than this phrase or that phrase of the agreement— is the continued support of the U.S. for the Republic of Vietnam and their efforts to defend themselves. We are going forward to sign the agreement. If your government does not . . . it will be necessary for me to stop aid.

KISSINGER: Exactly. . . . He [Haig] said his oral conversation indicated to him that he would sign it and that he is just posturing himself. . . . I think it is going just about as one could expect given the nature of that people.

NIXON: But I would make the letter this time very tough in substance, and I would smooth off the edges in its content. . . . It must have the veiled threat—one that can be clearly seen. We know what is beneath the veil . . . that the aid will be cut off. This is what is at stake. Therefore it is time for us both to recognize that we have fought a long time, that we can't get a perfect settlement. . . . And now whether we have peace—not only now but in the future—depends upon a continued close U.S. relationship. Your going along with the settlement and going along enthusiastically, as I will, would have an enormous effect on American public opinion and provide the continued support which we so desperately need in our Congress for military and economic aid to South Vietnam. . . . But just to get my thoughts very clear now, in the unlikely event . . . that Thieu says to go to hell—

KISSINGER: There will still be peace within two weeks, Mr. President.

NIXON: . . . It will not be peace with honor, right?

KISSINGER: No, I think we had peace with honor. I mean, we can't keep a man from committing suicide. . . .

NIXON: Now, what . . . position does this put Thieu in, though, when you stop to think of it, if we initial and he hasn't said anything?

KISSINGER: He's finished. He'll be overthrown. . . .

President Nixon

January 17, 1973, 4:50 p.m.

Nixon, who is more worried than Kissinger that Thieu will keep holding out, believes they need a "contingency plan" of making a separate agreement with Hanoi to "cut our losses but goddamned fast" if he doesn't go along and says goodbye to U.S. support.

. . . NIXON: The one thing . . . that has occurred to me that I think is very important to do is to have our alternate contingency plan fully worked out. . . . Haig, I assume, went through the drill that it was very important for him to win a few brownie points in my direction by the way he handled this. . . . It had no effect, though. That's the thing I'm concerned about a bit. . . . I think that talking absolutely fatalistically and in a way that is irrevocable is the only course. . . . Because that is the truth now, there isn't any fooling around at this point. . . . I do think the contingency plan should be well thought out so that we can put it into effect if necessary. . . . It would be a great tragedy if we had to put it into effect. . . . When I go on the 23rd [to announce the initialing of the agreement], the problem is that we then will have raised the expectations beyond belief, and then to have it shattered is going to be one hell of a thing.

KISSINGER: Well, that's why he cannot do it.

NIXON: I know. My point is, even though he cannot do it, if he does do it, we've got to . . . have a plan in effect to cut our losses but goddamned fast.

KISSINGER: Mr. President, the fact is that we are now doomed to settle.

NIXON: We're going to settle, I know, the point is, when I describe it . . . peace with honor and all that jazz, then the next day he says no, I won't go, see? Is that the time he would do it, in your opinion?

KISSINGER: If he does it, that's the time he'll do it. He won't do it. . . . If we know he's already turned it down, then we may have to go to another agreement.

NIXON: That's the point. . . . My feeling on that contingency is that if you know he's turned it down, you go right on over there, you complete the text of the agreement, you initial it, you come back and then we meet with the [congressional] leaders and say that you've initialed it and he's turned it down. Right?

KISSINGER: . . . And you go on television with a unanimous leadership behind you. . . . If he has, in fact, turned it down, then I think I should . . . go over and negotiate another agreement.

NIXON: Right. Then you come back and I announce that that's the agreement.

KISSINGER: That's right.

NIXON: And that we are going to make it on that basis . . . separate from him.

KISSINGER: That's right.

NIXON: Well, having thought through the contingency, and he's damned well got to think through it as well, I agree with you, he can't allow that to happen, can he?

KISSINGER: Whatever he thinks may happen under this agreement is certain to happen under any of the other courses.

NIXON: Oh, instantly too. Let's face it, the moment he—his people know and his army knows and all the rest knows—that the support of the United States is gone, for Christ sakes, Henry, they're down the tube.

KISSINGER: Absolutely.

NIXON: That's the point. They're down the tube. I mean, the psychological effect of that would be absolutely cataclysmic.

KISSINGER: That is absolutely correct.

NIXON: I think that's what he's looking at at the present time. . . . We won't worry about it, but we will prepare for it in case he does do some insane thing. . . .

President Nixon

January 18, 1973, 1:07 p.m.

Ambassador Ellsworth Bunker in Saigon had sent a cable about a letter he delivered from Nixon to Thieu that threatened to make a separate peace without him.

. . . KISSINGER: We have Bunker's cable now about his having brought the letter to Thieu. . . .

NIXON: Well, Bunker said he was shaking, but my goodness, Henry, we've shaken him before, you remember. . . . What the hell is new that shook him in this letter that wasn't in the other?

KISSINGER: Oh, you know, that you just didn't give an inch. . . .

NIXON: Did Bunker stay there while he read it?

KISSINGER: Yes, and he made a few nitpicking replies. But the nitpicks are diminishing too. . . . I think, Mr. President, this thing is done. We can't resume bombing now.

NIXON: Oh, I know, but god knows there's no way. . . .

KISSINGER: Therefore, we've got to get it wound up now. . . . He knows this week you've taken some irrevocable steps. . . . It was beautifully done. Calmly, deliberately, every day turning the screw a little more. . . .

President Nixon
January 20, 1973, 9:35 a.m.
Thieu had written Nixon a letter that said he was sending his foreign minister, Tran Van Lam, to Paris to handle the final negotiations and demanding a few more changes in the agreement.[3] Kissinger and Nixon discuss a reply stating that they would try to get one change that they agree should be made, threatening unilateral initialing if he didn't come along, and raising again the specter of an aid cutoff.

. . . NIXON: What is the word from Haig?

KISSINGER: Well, he's had a session and Thieu has written you another letter, but—

NIXON: Oh, god.

KISSINGER: But it's important I think that we are patient, because what the guy is doing, he's obviously posturing himself step by step. . . . In his last letter he made four conditions, now he's reduced them to two. And one we can't even consider, and one we can probably get him. He's also sending his foreign minister to Paris to meet with me.

NIXON: Oh, god.

KISSINGER: Well, Mr. President, it has an advantage. My first reaction was exactly like yours. . . . The problem with him is if we initial an agreement on Tuesday without physical participation by them, it's a great loss of face. If he has his foreign minister there, then he can claim he participated.

NIXON: Yeah. The foreign minister's his nephew?

KISSINGER: No. The nephew is that little bastard who is the minister of information. The foreign minister's an ass, and he won't be able to do anything. Now, what I thought, Mr. President, that we should do is this. We should send him a letter by you in reply. You are delighted his foreign minister will be there, and of course I'll talk to him and brief him fully, but you have instructed me to proceed with initialing. I will try to get that one change in the protocol that they want, and on this they are not wrong. . . . But what we should put in the letter from you is that you must have an answer from him by noon tomorrow whether . . . he will concur in . . . our initialing it. Because, if not, you will have to initial it unilaterally.

NIXON: Yeah.

KISSINGER: And you would then have to call the congressional leaders in Sunday night prior to my departure and inform them of that fact. . . . But once the congressional leaders are informed, aid will become difficult even if he then still finally comes along.

NIXON: Yeah. That the congressional leaders will, in my opinion, be adamant. Then we should go unilaterally and not seek further cooperation. . . . Why don't you say this, that before you leave for Paris on Sunday evening I have to meet with congressional leaders. . . . I will have to tell them yes or no whether or not he will concur in the initialing. . . . But if I tell the congressional leaders he will not concur, then it is my judgment, I am convinced after having talked to Senator Goldwater and Senator Stennis, who are his major supporters in the Senate, that they will throw up their hands, they will in effect inform me that the Congress will not go along with further aid unless he goes along on Tuesday. . . . If his answer is that he will not concur in the initialing of the agreement, that the congressional leaders without question will move to cut off assistance. . . .

KISSINGER: That's right, that's what we should do.

NIXON: And without question, I feel it is imperative that in confidence that I be able to tell the congressional leaders that he has objections, that we will do our best on them . . . but we are going to initial. But I must have a private assurance from him that I can pass on to them in total privacy, selected leaders, that he will concur. Otherwise, the aid which I very much want for Vietnam will be in very, very deadly jeopardy. . . .

Frank Sinatra

January 20, 1973, 4:30 p.m.

Kissinger asks Sinatra about an incident at a party the previous evening during the Nixon inauguration weekend with the Washington Post *gossip columnist Maxine Cheshire, who asked Sinatra afterward to apologize for the "unspeakable, unprintable" remarks he made to her. "You're nothing but a two-dollar cunt," he said. ". . . You've been laying down for two dollars all your life."[4]*

KISSINGER: Francis, is it true that you left a $2 bill in a wine glass for Maxine Cheshire?

SINATRA: I did.

KISSINGER: You're a great man.

SINATRA: [Laughter.] It was a scotch and soda.

KISSINGER: Well, whatever you put it in, you are a great man. You did what thousands have wanted to do here and—

SINATRA: I first identified her for her occupation in the world and then I gave her the $2. . . . That son of a bitch!! She's a bad dame, boy.

KISSINGER: Then you walked out of the party?

SINATRA: Yeah, I walked out. I didn't want to be molested by people like that. . . . I loved meeting your mom and pop the other night. They were so sweet.

KISSINGER: Oh, they were so thrilled!

SINATRA: You know, what I'd like you to do is to give me their telephone number in New York and when I go in, I'd like to call them from time to time.

KISSINGER: Aren't you sweet! . . . Well, they would be so touched.

SINATRA: All right. Now listen, I'm going to stay in tonight. I'm not going to go to any of those [inaugural] shindigs. . . . That's got to be a pain in the ass again.

KISSINGER: Well, that's what I think, but I've got to—

SINATRA: Your position is different.

KISSINGER: I've got to show myself. . . .

Ronald Ziegler

January 23, 1973, 7:30 p.m.

Nixon would announce that evening that they had concluded an agreement "to end the war and bring peace with honor in Vietnam," that it would be signed in four days, when a cease-fire would take effect, and that within 60 days all American POWs would be released and all U.S. forces withdrawn from South Vietnam.[5] But word had already reached the press about it, and H. R. Haldeman had assembled White House PR flacks.

KISSINGER: How's the news moving? What do the TV guys say?

ZIEGLER: They say that you initialed the agreement today and that it will be signed Saturday in Paris.

KISSINGER: Because that [obscenity] Rogers leaked it.

ZIEGLER: No, no, it's all out of Paris. . . . Now, Henry, let's you and I really sit down and program on how we put out the color. . . .

KISSINGER: Yeah. But Christ's sakes now, everyone take it easy till Saturday!

ZIEGLER: Absolutely. . . . But you've got to tell Bob that and move that to the president.

KISSINGER: Well, he's assembled all the flacks right now. . . .

ZIEGLER: Well, tell them nothing. Believe me, tell them nothing. . . . Everything you say in there will be said and those people in that room will broker it all over the goddamned—

KISSINGER: I will say nothing. . . .

President Nixon and Patricia Nixon

January 23, 1973, 10:20 p.m.

Nixon and Kissinger bask in Nixon's announcement, and Nixon's wife is on cloud nine.

KISSINGER: I thought it was magnificently done. . . . It was beautifully delivered and even [CBS's] Marvin Kalb is having a helluva time with it.

PRESIDENT NIXON: He doesn't know what to say, huh? . . . Well, that kills them, you know. The cease-fire kills them, the independent government for South Vietnam kills them, and they know that everything they said would not happen has been achieved. . . . We got all the conditions that we laid down.

KISSINGER: Well, I noticed the congressmen were just awestruck. . . . But Mansfield isn't out to be helpful.

PRESIDENT NIXON: None of them are. . . .

PATRICIA NIXON: Congratulations are to you! We've been betting on you for a long time now. Oh, it was just grand.

KISSINGER: Yeah, but it was the president's courage that carried us through this.

PATRICIA NIXON: Well, it took more than that. I tell you, it's just been so great and I think the whole country is relieved.

KISSINGER: Well, the press is dying.

PATRICIA NIXON: Oh, of course they're dying.

KISSINGER: All the things they said could never happen—you can't bomb them back to the table, you can't get them to make concessions.

PATRICIA NIXON: Exactly, now you just capitulate. . . .

Donald Marron
January 24, 1973, 2:17 p.m.
Kissinger tells a sympathetic Marron, the president of a Wall Street firm, that the Christmas bombing broke the impasse with Hanoi and that the civilian death toll was not particularly high.

. . . MARRON: Did the bombing work out as it was supposed to?

KISSINGER: Yeah. What do you think? There was a total deadlock in the middle of December. . . . And they settled within a week of resuming negotiations. . . . Now, you see, you've got all my colleagues at Harvard going into heart attacks about civilian people. Even the North Vietnamese claim that only 1,300 were killed.

MARRON: Yeah, that's right. And if you relate that to what's going on in the war, it's not a big number.

KISSINGER: That's a week's casualties. We've shortened the war by one week. . . . There would have been more people killed. . . . I mean, it's total hypocrisy for all these people talking of mass bombing. If we had wanted to kill people, there wouldn't have been a house standing in Hanoi.

MARRON: Well, that was my feeling. And I can tell you, I defended it vigorously at dinner parties. . . .

Robert Bernstein

January 25, 1973, 4:20 p.m.

Bernstein, the president of Random House, would like to publish Kissinger's memoirs, and even offers to serve as his representative on them.

BERNSTEIN: I've been thinking about all sorts of ways to get messages to you and I finally decided I really should call myself and tell you that if—there are all sorts of rumors around about the possibility—that doing a contract for—

KISSINGER: I will not do a contract for anything while I'm in this job.

BERNSTEIN: Well, I know that.

KISSINGER: I won't entertain an offer also while I'm in this job.

BERNSTEIN: Oh, all I really wanted to do was to tell you whenever the time comes that you are ready, I would like to say three things: (a) we are interested and would make a substantial offer, (b) I was talking to the Bradens [Tom, the columnist, and his wife, Joan] at one time and told them that I would offer my services if you wanted them, even if it wasn't going to be with us, to just talk to you about putting an offer together, and even if you decided not to give it to us, because I would hate to see you burned up with any professional agent, frankly, and thirdly, that I thought we could put together an offer that would be very interesting to you. So, all sorts of rumors about you in the *New York Times* which have come to me.

KISSINGER: Nothing to it.

BERNSTEIN: And all I really wanted to say is I think it would be worth your while whenever the time is right. We are in no rush and I certainly realize this is the wrong time, but I didn't want to be in a position of not having said to you that we are interested and think we have a few ideas that might be original and might be worth hearing at the time. Should I put that in a letter or—

KISSINGER: No. . . . I appreciate it very much but I think it would be highly improper for me to have any discussions on this subject . . . while I'm in this job. . . . And I don't even want to know what the offers might be. Now, every once in a while somebody gets to see me who I think is coming for some other reason who then manages to slip an offer in. That's happened only once. That is always the end of the conversation.

BERNSTEIN: I would not try that and—

KISSINGER: No, no, no, that's how that *New York Times* story got started. There is nothing to it, I will do nothing, but I do appreciate you are willing to talk to me.

BERNSTEIN: Should I just write and say that whenever the time is right we are interested? Or would you rather not even have that letter?

KISSINGER: Well, if you want to do that.... I'd be grateful in fact for your advice whenever the time is right, but that won't be until after I leave here....

James Reston

January 27, 1973, 1:04 p.m.

The venerable Reston of the New York Times *offers Kissinger carte blanche on an interview.*

... RESTON: ... What I would like to do about your sitting down and talking is for you and I to talk in a conversation recorded but within your control of it.... Put it on paper and then look at it and then tidy it up any way you would like, but get the main points. Then either at your disposal scrub the whole thing or publish it. But I would like for us to talk on that basis that you're entirely relaxed and philosophical about the whole thing, and then if you decide it doesn't work or it doesn't come off, well, then we'll forget it.

KISSINGER: Well, Scotty, I would really love to do it because I can't forget your decency in this really trying period in addition to my admiration for your work.... And let's discuss what the problems with it are when I see you.... You want me to come to your house?

RESTON: Yeah.... I just think it's better if we're not seen together in public.

KISSINGER: I think it's better....

Barbara Walters

January 31, 1973, 12:05 p.m.

Walters is angry that Kissinger went back on his word about doing an interview with her before one with CBS's Marvin Kalb. Kissinger grumbles about being turned into "a goddamned prostitute" by White House PR people.

KISSINGER: Barbara, how are you?

WALTERS: Well, I'm terrible.... You gave me your word.

KISSINGER: That is right. And the situation is as follows. Right now I'm disposed to cancel everything.

WALTERS: Well, I would prefer that.

KISSINGER: The situation is that I told Ron about our discussion and he pointed out that he ... had given his word to Marvin Kalb and CBS last

April, at a time that we had agreed to do it, scheduled a time, and then canceled it. Then he told me that he was going to get in touch with you and work something out that would be mutually satisfactory. That apparently hasn't been done.

WALTERS: Well, let me tell you what happened. NBC called me last night. . . . When we talked we were thinking about next week. And I was trying to do something so that we'd have not only the *Today* show but to have the prime time as well. . . . So they called me last night and said 10:30 to 11:00 either this Sunday or next Sunday, which is a good time. . . . Ron called and said, "Barbara, you were thinking of doing an interview with Henry?" And I said no, I wasn't *thinking* of doing an interview, he's given me his word. We've told our people. And then he said, "Well, we're committed to CBS." And I said, "You can't do that to me. . . . It isn't as if Henry said maybe I'll do an interview or we'll talk about an interview. He said, I will do it with you first, and if I don't do it with you I won't do it with anybody." And I said we waited and we were waiting this week to suit his time. I said this is not only embarrassing to me, this is insulting. . . . We've told our people, we've cleared the time, we deliberately waited to suit you. . . . You said to me, "Barbara, I will do the interview with you first," and then when there was some problem with Haldeman, you also said, "I'm in control of who I do interviews with and if they won't let me do it with you first, I won't do any." . . .

KISSINGER: . . . This is not something which is totally at my discretion.

WALTERS: But you told me it was. . . .

KISSINGER: Well, that's all right, look, I'm going to cancel them both. . . . I'm going to become a goddamned prostitute this way. . . .

WALTERS: You know, my feeling is this is an awful position to put me in. . . . If you cancel both, I'll live with it, but it's enormously insulting to me when I said to our people, look, he's going to do it. . . . I'm not just stuck with the *Today* show, we also do network things. . . . You told me you would do your first interview with me, it was that straight and simple, and you know it.

KISSINGER: That is right. . . . But I'm going to cancel them both. . . . I really want to get out of this job with a measure of dignity, and I don't want to turn into a goddamned prostitute. The only reason I'm doing anything at all is for the president. From my own point of view I should be off television for a month, and you know it. There's nothing I can do to add to what I've done last week and I should now just shut up. . . . I mean, I'm doing it because the president feels badly wounded and he hasn't been seen in the perspective of his overall foreign policy. . . .

Israel's Shootdown of a Civilian Libyan Airliner; Flacking Kissinger's Hanoi and China Visits; POW Releases, Peace Agreement Violations, and the Paris Conference; Diplomatic Killings in Sudan; Cambodia and Laos Bombing; and Aid to Pakistan

February–March 1973

On February 21, 1973, Israel shot down a civilian Libyan airliner that was off course over Israel-occupied territory in the Sinai Peninsula, killing over a hundred people. Kissinger opposed "popping off" about it ("planes get shot down around the world all the time without the United States saying something") and told Assistant Secretary of State Joseph Sisco, who found the shootdown "absolutely crazy," that they should not describe the Sinai as "occupied" or say "innocent lives" were taken. "I think it was really a blunder on our part," Israeli Ambassador Yitzhak Rabin confessed to Kissinger.

Kissinger had just returned from visits to North Vietnam and China; in Hanoi he had discussed with North Vietnamese leaders observance and violations of the Paris peace agreement and U.S. economic aid (meaning "reparations"). Both sides had accused the other of violations after the agreement was signed and the war had continued. After his trip, Kissinger, whose disgust with White House PR flackery knew no bounds, was furious when White House Communications Director Herb Klein, a "certified idiot," overdid the selling of it, showing pictures and film ("home movies") of Hanoi on national television.

Kissinger was also upset about the State Department's independent moves on the Middle East, which he saw as "a sure loser," pessimistic as he was about the prospects that peace talks would be fruitful, straining his relationship with Sisco, who threatened (not for the first time) to leave, urged Kissinger to sort out his differences with Secretary of State Rogers, and tried to convince him that he was his ally.

Hanoi was meanwhile placing conditions on the release of American POWs—such as U.S. adherence to the peace agreement—but Nixon threatened to ignore the agreement if Hanoi reneged on any element of it: "What the hell do we care about the agreement? What the Christ do we care? Nothing."

On March 1, when the U.S. ambassador to the Sudan, his number two man, and other people were taken hostage by Palestinian guerrillas, Nixon and Kissinger opted to take a hard line and not yield to the kidnappers: "It's too bad but that's part of the job of being an ambassador there, isn't it?" Nixon said.

Their stance was controversial: the two Americans were killed.

John Kenneth Galbraith
February 6, 1973, 11:05 a.m.
Harvard professor Galbraith offers advice on Kissinger's dealings with Harvard over his possible return.

GALBRAITH: . . . Now that you've finished with this relatively easy negotiation with Hanoi and come to the very difficult matter of negotiation with Harvard, I'd like to offer a word of expert advice to you. . . . Don't let them off the hook. Just say, you know, I would imagine that I might be more valuable sometime in the future than in the past. . . . Or, I can't see that anything that's happened these last years has really dulled my experience. Bear in mind that everybody up there will be suffering a little bit at the prospect of being in the same department—you know, having people say, "Are you in Dr. Kissinger's department?" You don't want to let them off the hook and make their life easier.

KISSINGER: Yeah. Well, actually, I know you're referring to that stupid press quote [that maybe he didn't want to return to Harvard]. . . . I didn't intend what they quoted. I just intended to say I am not going to apply to go back.

GALBRAITH: Don't even say that. . . . Say, "Someday I rather expect that I might be more valuable to a university than I was before." . . . Anybody coming back from outside is regarded as somewhat of a threat to the quiet, academic, and comfortable life of the inside men. . . . They have a dull life. Don't ease the situation for them. . . . It's the worst of all places except for the alternatives.

KISSINGER: . . . [Harvard President Derek] Bok left a message with me saying if I wanted his help, I should call him, but I won't do that. . . . That's a hell of a way of putting it to me. . . .

Joseph Sisco
February 21, 1973, 12:47 p.m.
Kissinger and Assistant Secretary of State Sisco debate a State Department statement on Israel's downing of the civilian Libyan airliner over Israel-occupied Egyptian territory in the Sinai. Kissinger doesn't want to condemn or judge the shootdown. Sisco says Israeli Ambassador Yitzhak Rabin was "just aghast" at it.

KISSINGER: Joe, do we have to pop off about that Israeli shootdown at all?

SISCO: Well, we are just developing a statement here. We haven't said anything.

KISSINGER: I mean, planes get shot down around the world all the time without the United States saying something.

SISCO: Yeah. Well, the secretary will probably get hit on this, and he will probably say this is a tragedy and express regret over some loss of life. . . . We suggest two simple messages from the president along the lines of the public statement of Golda Meir, which would limit it to an expression of condolences for the loss of life. . . . There were a lot of Egyptians on this plane.

KISSINGER: Why the hell did they do it?

SISCO: Well, Rabin off the record said to me, "Joe, it's absolutely incomprehensible". . . . I think it makes absolutely no sense whatsoever, even if the goddamn commercial plane was over Tel-Aviv. They shouldn't shoot it down. So, frankly, Rabin is just aghast and he has no better explanation than I have. I mean, it's crazy, absolutely crazy. A lot of planes have been shot down but never this kind of an incident in this way. But be that as it may, Henry, we're developing a statement. . . . We think it's a good idea to do this, and not tie it in, Henry, with calls for restraint, for this reason: a simple message of condolence which is completely depoliticized has the best kind of an impact.

KISSINGER: That I agree with. . . . I just don't think we should say it's incomprehensible and inexplicable. . . . We are concerned and we should just shut up and condolences are fine. . . .

Joseph Sisco
February 21, 1973, 1:47 p.m.
Kissinger doesn't want State to "blubber" about the shootdown, to describe the Sinai as "occupied," or even to say "innocent lives" were taken.

KISSINGER: Joe, if an Afghan shot down a Bangladesh airliner, would the secretary of state rush out with a statement?

SISCO: No, he wouldn't. This is actually, Henry, to—

KISSINGER: Do what?

SISCO: To keep the situation cool.

KISSINGER: Now wait a minute. That's one of these platitudes. Keep what situation cool? Where? I mean, who's going to do what?

SISCO: Well, I think the danger in this situation at the present time is that [Egyptian President Anwar] Sadat will feel himself under pressure from [Libyan leader Muammar] Gaddafi to take some counter military action. And I think the purpose of this statement really is basically to disassociate the United States from this action. And, I think myself, Henry, it's the minimum we can do.

KISSINGER: Do we have to blubber? . . . Do we have to say we were sad? . . . Can we drop the adjectives? . . . I'm going to subtract them. . . .

SISCO: . . . I think myself the dropping of the adjectives is fine. . . . But I think you really need to take this up with our seventh floor [Secretary of State Rogers's office was located there].

KISSINGER: I'm not going to take it up, I'm going to tell them. I just want to get a sane person's judgment. . . . Do we have to say "occupied Sinai"? . . . Do we have to say "unarmed"? . . . Do we have to say "innocent lives"?

SISCO: Well, I think Golda used something like this. We don't have to say any of these things, Henry, but I think this is, in the context of the situation, very minimal, very minimal.

KISSINGER: All I want to tell you fellows before you get to the last three days of the negotiations [on the Middle East], there are three and a half years to go through before the television cameras come in. . . .

SISCO: You're going to get a crack at this, fella. . . .

Thomas Moorer
February 21, 1973, 2:35 p.m.
Kissinger asks JCS Chairman Moorer to come up with a mine-sweeping plan in North Vietnam (the Paris peace agreement required the United States to remove, deactivate, or destroy its mines) that makes it appear that the operation is going at a faster pace without actually going much faster.

KISSINGER: Our little darlings in the North are bugging us on the mining, and said we are not going fast enough, which means you are doing what I've asked you to do. . . . Is there something we can do that looks like a speed-up that I could—but don't you get your eager beavers out there to do it, let me give it to them as a concession the president has ordered. . . . Now, for example, they want some trucks to help remove the inland mines. Let's get them those trucks; they want five or six trucks. . . . I don't want it really all that much faster, but those bastards, as long as you tell them you are doing something as an act of good will, they think they've gotten something out of my trip.

MOORER: Of course, the bastards only have about 25,000 trucks, you know. We'll give them six more.

KISSINGER: Tom, they are the world's biggest shits. . . .

Yitzhak Rabin
February 21, 1973, 3:40 p.m.
Kissinger speaks with the Israeli ambassador about Israel's downing of the civilian Libyan airliner. Israeli Defense Minister Moshe Dayan said the decision to fire on the plane had been made at the military level after it had ignored instructions to land and that he found no fault with it. An Egyptian government spokesman called the shootdown "an act of mass murder."[1]

KISSINGER: You've got our State Department in a state of advanced excitement. . . . What I've done is to tone down their public expressions to the minimum that I could. . . . What they put out, if you get outraged, just remember what it would have been. . . . I'm glad to hear that your military are just as stupid as ours.

RABIN: I don't want to talk about it on the phone. I doubt if I know the pilots; I don't believe that any Israeli pilots would have taken such a decision on himself. I'm quite sure that it was on instructions on a relatively [high] level. . . . I think it was really a blunder on our part.

KISSINGER: Yeah. Well, they were going to put out a statement about occupied Sinai and innocent civilians and outrage and so forth. . . . I took out every adjective, but I just want you to know we had no choice—well, it was perceived to be no choice.

RABIN: . . . I tried to have a meeting with some . . . American media people, because they said—

KISSINGER: Well, keep it cool.

RABIN: Oh, I kept it cool—

KISSINGER: The thing to do is to put it on the ground that idiocies happen everywhere.

RABIN: No, no. I put it this way. I said distinguish between issues that have been in headlines a few days and return to basic issues. Just keep out the speculative outlook.

KISSINGER: Exactly. . . .

President Nixon
February 21, 1973, 7:59 p.m.
Nixon finds Israel's downing of the Libyan plane "unbelievable."

> ... NIXON: ... You know, looking at this Israeli plane thing, that's a pretty rough deal, isn't it?
>
> KISSINGER: Yeah. I talked to Rabin this afternoon and said, "What the hell did you do this for?" He said frankly some high-ranking idiot goofed. He said no ordinary pilot would do this, and somebody must have given the order.
>
> NIXON: My god. ... I think they ought to really compensate them too, don't you think so?
>
> KISSINGER: Well, let me find out tomorrow when Rabin comes in what the situation was. There's no excuse for it whatever.
>
> NIXON: No, but you know a 707 is such an obvious commercial plane and they should have known what the hell it is. To knock down one of those is unbelievable.
>
> KISSINGER: No excuse for it, none at all. ...

Ronald Ziegler
February 22, 1973, afternoon
Kissinger is angry that White House Communications Director Herb Klein is over-selling his trip to Hanoi and China, and Ziegler erupts about his own problems.

> ... KISSINGER: But, you know, if Klein is going to be all over town, I am not in the same league with Klein. I'm not one of the goddamn hucksters here, which you guys have to get into your head. ...
>
> ZIEGLER: Henry, my friend, I do everything in the world I can to work out the thing in your interest.
>
> KISSINGER: I know, but I am absolutely outraged ... this goddamned Herb Klein ... certified idiot.
>
> ZIEGLER: Henry, I pick up the [phone] and I try and work out a time with you. You scream at me. I go into a goddamned morning meeting and I get eight people screaming at me. Herb Klein comes over whining on my goddamned desk. I'll tell you, I'm fed up with it. ... I'm getting goddamned tired—I dial Ehrlichman and talk to him about a problem, he's whining around about stuff. Good god in heaven, I can't—
>
> KISSINGER: All I'm saying, Ron, is foreign policy is the one area where we've maintained some integrity. ... And we've maintained integrity because I've kept the goddamned flacks out of it. ... And now this maniac who's gone around Hanoi taking pictures, which he wasn't authorized to do, is showing them on national television.

ZIEGLER: . . . If I call Klein, then I've got to waste two hours with him over in my office wanting to have Scotch and water and whining all over the place. I don't have time for that. . . .

Ronald Ziegler
February 22, 1973, 5:27 p.m.
Kissinger rails that the "idiot" Klein was going on a media circuit to plug Kissinger's trip to North Vietnam and China.

ZIEGLER: You got a problem?

KISSINGER: . . . Herb Klein is going on the *Today* show tomorrow about the trip. Ron, this cannot be turned into one of our goddamned circuses. . . .

ZIEGLER: Well, he wanted to use film, apparently, of Hanoi.

KISSINGER: He has no right to use film of Hanoi. . . . I thought he was coming with me to give him one last trip. I did not realize he was coming along for the usual flackery. I had no idea that he was going to go out on the circuits.

ZIEGLER: All right. I have not promoted it, I have not agreed to it, and I have told the people who have asked me that before one inch of the film from Hanoi or China is used that you must approve it.

KISSINGER: That's right. I totally disapprove of White House senior people going on the circuit with serious business. It wasn't a travelogue. . . . Frankly, I don't want him on any goddamned shows, he's an idiot. What good does he do us? Everyone up to now has thought this was a serious effort. . . . Somebody should have told me that this was even a conceivable possibility. . . . He would never have been on the trip. I've got to keep these people under control. The minute we start exploiting them [the North Vietnamese and Chinese] in this way they know we need them more than they need us.

ZIEGLER: Oh, I don't think Herb's going to do anything damaging.

KISSINGER: What do you know what's damaging? What does he know what's damaging? What do you think showing films from Hanoi, from a town where they don't let you buy picture postcards—

ZIEGLER: I'm not arguing, you know it's not my decision.

KISSINGER: But was Herb along to do this sort of thing?

ZIEGLER: Absolutely not.

KISSINGER: That was never explained to me. . . . Now it's turning into a huge promotion. Every time I look up the news summary, here is Klein popping off again. . . .

Herb Klein
February 22, 1973, 6:20 p.m.
Kissinger confronts Klein about his flacking of the trip.

KISSINGER: Herb, there must be a misunderstanding, because I have a violent view that my trip should not turn into flack operations. I don't care what good they may do in the short term. When I go on a trip, it's a business trip and I just don't want them on television. . . . My philosophy is that we have to have stature. We don't have to sell this like soap, and I have never after any trip had anybody on television—I haven't gone on TV unless I was pressured on it by Haldeman. And I am just very unhappy about this idea that we are going to show home movies now on television of a trip that I take. No country is going to have me on a secret trip again.

KLEIN: Henry, there certainly is not going to be any secret photo or anything of this kind. It isn't—

KISSINGER: It isn't a question of a secret photo—the question is that I am going on a trip to negotiate serious business. We bring you along so that you can get a flavor of it—the next thing we know we are on television three times a week or once a week or whatever pushing the trip. What purpose does it serve? Whom does it help? It helps maybe you, but it doesn't help anybody else.

KLEIN: I think it helps with the Congress in understanding what we are doing; maybe it will describe what kind of thing you do.

KISSINGER: Well, I don't want to describe what sort of thing I do. . . . I really feel I'll just have to go to the president if this thing keeps going.

KLEIN: You know me, that I'm not about to make a circus of anything.

KISSINGER: No, look, I like you, Herb, I have enormous respect for you. But . . . when I go on a trip and the president goes on a trip—he's a politician, he has to be exposed—I don't want exposure. I don't want the goddamn thing on television. When I move, the achievements have to stand and the countries I visit have to know that when I go there it's not a public relations exercise. This is even more important.

KLEIN: I don't think in the brief time that I am going to do this tomorrow morning he's going to find that it's going to sound like a public relations exercise.

KISSINGER: The point is, what are you doing? You are describing the atmosphere in Hanoi and Peking, right? What else can you do? That's not what I want. That's not what we go on these trips for. That was not my understanding of why you went along. . . . And when people negotiate with me they have to know everything I say publicly I cleared with Chou En-lai and with Pham Van Dong [North Vietnam's prime minister]. They were never told that any other member of our party was going to speak. And it is a totally different concept. I was told that you were coming along because you hadn't been on any other trip and that you deserved to absorb some of this atmosphere. I enthusiastically agreed to that, but it never occurred to me that after that it would lead to a lot of television things. . . . I don't see what this accomplishes. . . . I always conduct confidential negotiations. It was never that afterwards that we would then plug the trip. . . .

Joseph Sisco
February 22, 1973, 6:30 p.m.
Kissinger, who was reluctant to try to obtain a Middle East settlement without the promise that peace talks would be productive and he understood Egypt's views, rebukes Assistant Secretary of State Sisco for State's moves (it favored an interim settlement), which he sees as overly eager and independent and wanted to delay.[2] Sisco tells him to "get off my back," stresses he's on his side, and suggests he might resign. Sisco urges Kissinger to work out his differences with Secretary of State Rogers and to attend a lunchtime meeting the next day between Nixon and Egyptian President Sadat's national security adviser, Hafiz Ismail, and a Sadat political adviser.

KISSINGER: Joe, I have to tell you, I think you guys are going crazy again.

SISCO: What have we done now?

KISSINGER: I mean calling ambassadors, calling Ismail—I mean, goddamn it, it took us two years to get the Egyptians in the frame of mind where they were pleading with us to get into it, and now we are acting like puppy dogs.

SISCO: Oh, I don't think so, Henry.

KISSINGER: I will tell you something—I haven't lost one of these yet. And I'm not losing it—I will not tolerate it—and you remember this—I will not tolerate any area being segregated as the exclusive jurisdiction of anybody. . . . You ought to have enough experience, Joe, [to know] that it won't work—it didn't work—

SISCO: Henry, you ought to have experience to know that I am a goddamn lowly assistant secretary with practically no influence, and Henry, you can call me and bawl me out—I just don't have this kind of influence—I don't have this kind of power in the State Department. . . . You know, Henry, nine times out of 10 you call me and bawl the hell out of me I agree with you, and you are putting me in an absolutely impossible position. I don't know what to do—you've gotten me to the point—I'm saying to myself I might as well get the hell out of here.

KISSINGER: No, that I don't want you to do.

SISCO: I'm just not the secretary of state, Henry, and Henry, get off my back— because you're really criticizing me . . . when it's not justified. And Henry, I'm with you, I'm your friend, Henry. I keep telling you—

KISSINGER: What are guys planning to do tomorrow?

SISCO: . . . The secretary sent you a memo and I am certainly going to sit and listen.

KISSINGER: Are we going to make a proposal?

SISCO: We have no proposals to make—I mean, I haven't developed one purposely. . . . You and the secretary—I know what the problem is and I know what your problem is and I know what the secretary's problem is and I don't blame you for being angry, but Henry, I'm not trying to segregate anything. . . . You are really wasting your breath on me—you really are—frankly I am your friend—I keep telling you this. . . . As far as I am concerned you've got my support, you've got my loyalty. . . .

KISSINGER: How do you people visualize this thing is going to go from here? Tell me what you think the secretary thinks is going happen next.

SISCO: Frankly, I think he's quite adjusted to the notion that this is a listening month in terms of the Egyptians, a listening month in terms of Golda. . . .

KISSINGER: . . . We have the quarterback running in one direction and the halfback in the other direction and the other side wondering who's got the ball.

SISCO: Sure. The secretary, as you damn well know, was very anxious about making sure that there is no appearance of division between the White House and the State Department—who in the heck do you think told him this? . . . Henry, look, you've got to sort it out with him—and you're big enough to be able to sort it out. . . . What is the president going to do tomorrow?

KISSINGER: I don't know—there is great opposition from you people to have me sit in with the president.

SISCO: Oh, is that right? When did this happen?

KISSINGER: Today. So I can't absolutely guarantee it, but if he follows advice, he's just going to listen.

SISCO: For sure. What else is there to do? In the first place we are committed to check with the Israelis before we'd ever put anything together anyway, and if you do put something together, the first people you have to talk to, as that paper indicates that I gave you, is the Israelis—so you're not going to get anywhere.

KISSINGER: Oh, no, there's no danger about getting anywhere—I think if the British reported correctly, this thing is a sure loser now.

SISCO: Oh, it's a stiff arm, if that report that came in today—we're going to get stiff-armed. They're in a spot now where you are absolutely right—it has taken 18 months to get these people to crawl to us.

KISSINGER: Yeah, but that's one reason why we shouldn't blow it all by excessive eagerness.

SISCO: No, but you've got one other problem that you have to remember. Throughout the entire area the words that are being spoken by the U.S.

today [on Israel's downing of the civilian Libyan airliner] are being compared with the words spoken by the U.S. at the time of Munich [the Palestinian terrorist attack on the Israeli athletes at the Olympics], and this is a real political problem. . . . It doesn't bother me that we are being criticized in the Arab world today because we haven't condemned or used the kind of purple language that we used at the time of Munich, but you should be aware that the whole Arab press is saying, "Well, here we are—sweet words from the Americans, but we heard much more than sweet words at the time of Munich." . . .

KISSINGER: Joe, I know the position you are in—as much as you can control it, keep excessive energy from developing until we know where the hell we are going.

SISCO: . . . I just think, Henry, you have to take the lead and convene this session after the Golda visit and you have to approach it systematically and all possibilities have to be canvassed and directly with the president. . . .

KISSINGER: In five years this has never happened and it can't happen given the personalities involved. . . .

SISCO: Yeah. Well, it ought to be done somewhere and you're ingenious enough to know where it ought to be done. . . . Otherwise the danger you cited at the outset in terms of divisions and one person going in one direction and another in another is really very great, Henry. There is no point to it.

KISSINGER: Moreover, it's a sure loser. . . . Can you see how this negotiation can end in less than two years?

SISCO: Oh, no—long and drawn out. Henry, it's not necessarily a sure loser. . . .

William Rogers
February 27, 1973, 10:45 a.m.
Speaking from Paris, an irritated Rogers opposes canceling the international conference on Vietnam, which was part of the peace agreement and opened the previous day in Paris. But Nixon and Kissinger were angry that Hanoi was placing conditions on POW releases (like compliance with the agreement).[3]

KISSINGER: I've just been talking to Bill Sullivan [William H. Sullivan, a deputy assistant secretary of state]—

ROGERS: I know that. I'd appreciate it if you'd speak to me. . . . I have serious reservation about making any statement about canceling the conference.

KISSINGER: . . . There's no issue of canceling the conference. . . . He's asking you to demand clarification [on POW releases]. . . . And to conduct no other business until you've received that clarification.

ROGERS: . . . If we start saying things like that, we're going to have the other governments just say to go to hell. They're not too happy about it anyway. It seems to me I ought to be able to have the opportunity to talk to the other side. Honest. And then if it's unsatisfactory, then start making threats. But you'll find that some of the other parties are fed up anyway with the whole idea of the conference and they'll just say, well, you fellows have it, we're going home. . . .

KISSINGER: Well, I would doubt that, but still you—

ROGERS: I'm here, I can tell you that. . . .

President Nixon
February 27, 1973, 6:55 p.m.
Nixon and Kissinger discuss a North Vietnamese statement on POW releases and agree that if they bombed the North to get their POWs back, the American public would support it.

. . . KISSINGER: . . . One of the North Vietnamese said they have not suspended the prisoner release. . . . At the same time they haven't given us any prisoners. . . . I think they are not going to shake us down on this . . . because they know . . . the Chinese and Russians aren't going to jeopardize their relations with us. No one else is going to back them at that conference. And not only this, they know if you started clobbering them again, you'd have the American people with you on this. . . .

NIXON: . . . By god, the people would back you all the way.

KISSINGER: . . . But I don't think it's going to come anywhere close to that.

NIXON: I agree. But these things must be going through their minds.

KISSINGER: Exactly.

NIXON: They were certainly going through the mind of somebody as clever as Gromyko and people like that. . . . By Friday it either breaks or we are going to have to go to a very, very tough alternative.

KISSINGER: Exactly. By Friday if it hasn't broken, you'd have to do something pretty drastic. . . . I don't see how you could let Rogers sign a final act in Paris under those conditions.

NIXON: Never. . . . There can be no goddamned signing without the POW thing.

KISSINGER: Mr. President, he will swing along as he always has and by the end of the day tomorrow he'll realize that you've made him a strong man.

NIXON: Yeah, I saw in the paper tonight that he was threatening to leave.

KISSINGER: Kicking and screaming. We made him do it kicking and screaming. . . .

President Nixon

February 28, 1973, 11:30 p.m.

They take satisfaction in North Vietnam's decision to release the next contingent of POWs—their toughness had paid off. (North Vietnam had said that further releases were being suspended, pending a halt to U.S. and South Vietnamese cease-fire viola-tions. Kissinger and JCS Chairman Moorer had agreed five days earlier that South Vietnam was responsible for most of the violations of the peace agreement.)[4] Nixon says if the North Vietnamese renege on any part of the peace agreement, he won't pay any heed to the agreement.

KISSINGER: Just wanted you to know we've won.

NIXON: Oh, really!

KISSINGER: Yep. . . . They held the meeting and their spokesman said the way is now clear to continue the releases. . . . And if we had been anything other than—

NIXON: We wouldn't have had it.

KISSINGER: Never! They would have fiddled us along.

NIXON: Henry, you can be sure they were going to keep those people hostage. What have they done up to date? That's the thing that Bill [Rogers] and the rest have got to realize. They've been screwing us all the time. Now they're not going to do a thing and we'll continue to drag our feet on [clearing] those mines too.

KISSINGER: Mr. President . . . if we had accepted what they said this morning, that they would do it within the 60 days but in four stages, they would have had the four stages all in the last three days. Now, your statement . . . and your directing Rogers not to return [to the international conference], that did it.

NIXON: That's the point. . . . Believe me, we're not going to give them one thing if they renege on one part of this deal. . . . What the hell do we care about the agreement? What the Christ do we care? Nothing. . . .

KISSINGER: And they thought they could diddle us along and get a little public outcry started—focus it on Thieu.

NIXON: On Thieu. They were trying to do him in, Henry.

KISSINGER: That's right. . . . And we just reacted very toughly. We sailed the whole mine-sweeping fleet away. We didn't just have it inactive. . . . We moved it a hundred miles offshore.

NIXON: That's the stuff! And don't think they didn't notice that.

KISSINGER: Ohhh. They don't usually cave unless you kick them in the groin. . . . They tested you, you took charge and kept on course. . . .

President Nixon

March 1, 1973, 7:15 p.m.

U.S. Ambassador to the Sudan Cleo Noel, his deputy chief of mission, George Moore, and others had been taken hostage by Black September Palestinian guerrillas, who demanded the release of Palestinians held in Israel, Robert Kennedy's assassin, Sirhan Sirhan, and other prisoners.

NIXON: What's your report from Khartoum?

KISSINGER: Well, the report from Khartoum is that they are still being held. . . . And that our embassy is trying to start a negotiation with the Arabs. . . . I don't think we should give them directions on that. . . . I myself do not think it's a good idea for us to negotiate because that gets us into the middle of their demands.

NIXON: Yeah. You mean the Sudanese government should do it?

KISSINGER: That's right. Because if we negotiate, they are going to make demands on us.

NIXON: . . . The problem that I see here is that I suppose that we'll get a demand and I suppose the problem we have is the payment of blackmail in one form or another.

KISSINGER: Well, they've already demanded that we release Sirhan. . . . We won't do that.

NIXON: Yeah. Well, we can't do anything like that at all anyway. Don't you agree?

KISSINGER: Oh, absolutely. I don't think we can yield to anything.

NIXON: That's what I mean. You start that and, boy, you're going to invite it. It's too bad but that's part of the job of being an ambassador there, isn't it?

KISSINGER: That's right. . . .

President Nixon

March 2, 1973, 8:30 p.m.

Nixon and Kissinger believe that Noel and Moore are probably dead (they were killed by the guerrillas), as reported by a Sudanese major and the vice president of the Sudan, "who probably has an IQ of 25," Kissinger notes. "Well, in any event, we are doing exactly the right thing in taking the hard line on it, Henry," Nixon says.

KISSINGER: Information is just very fragmentary. . . . The Sudanese major who brought out the information now admits he didn't see any bodies. . . .

NIXON: But he says the Americans are dead?

KISSINGER: Well, that's what he says, but it is even possible, Mr. President, that nobody was killed.

NIXON: Hmmm, really?

KISSINGER: Well, I wouldn't want to hold that out, but I would have thought that if these Arabs wanted to establish their credibility—I mean, why would they kill the Americans in order to—

NIXON: That's why I wondered. Why they would kill us and not the Belgians? [The Palestinians had taken the hostages at the Saudi embassy in Khartoum during a reception there in honor of Moore and one Belgian diplomat was also taken and killed.]

KISSINGER: They would do it to increase their credibility towards the remaining hostages. To do that it would be better for them to exhibit a body.

NIXON: Yes, also to keep them alive in order to keep squeezing us.

KISSINGER: Well, if they keep them alive, people might think they wouldn't kill anybody. I can imagine that they'd kill somebody just to show they can do it, that they are determined. But then one would think it would be in their interest to produce a body. . . . Well, we were given official information from the Sudanese government.

NIXON: So we'll go ahead and lower the flags.

KISSINGER: We were told by the vice president of the Sudan, who probably has an IQ of 25, that this happened, and he, in turn, it now turns out, was told by a major, who had been negotiating with us.

NIXON: Well, I just pray it isn't true.

KISSINGER: I think the probability is that it's true. That they are dead. . . . But there is a slight glimmer, and we'll keep you informed of course.

NIXON: Well, in any event, we are doing exactly the right thing in taking the hard line on it, Henry. We can't give in on this.

KISSINGER: Absolutely not, Mr. President.

NIXON: We can't do it. . . . Nothing to do with their ransom demands.

KISSINGER: You wouldn't have yielded anyway, but this wasn't a case where you had any choice because—

NIXON: They didn't say give us a hundred thousand dollars; they said give us Sirhan, or whatever the hell his—

KISSINGER: Sirhan was just one of many requests. Their basic request is to get those terrorists out.

NIXON: That's right. And we had no control over that. . . . We're not going to give an inch on this business of paying something for them, no way. . . .

President Nixon

March 10, 1973, 11:45 a.m.

Nixon and Kissinger confer on Chinese, Iranian, and U.S. military aid to Pakistan.

... NIXON: I was thinking a little about our Pakistan thing. I just want to be sure that the Chinese are going to do everything they should here. . . .

KISSINGER: . . . The Chinese have given them equipment for two divisions. They've just given them 25 bombers. . . . I mean, if we won't give any arms at all, Mr. President, the Chinese will just despise us.

NIXON: I understand. I know why we're doing it but I want to be sure the Chinese play the game too.

KISSINGER: Oh, the Chinese are playing it. . . . The trouble is that they are short of equipment themselves. . . . In fact, the next problem will be to figure out a way to get some equipment to the Chinese. . . . I mean, we can't give them American equipment. I think that would be too provocative.

NIXON: To the Russians, yeah. . . .

KISSINGER: Maybe the Japanese.

NIXON: Hell, the British—let the British give them a few dollars. . . .

KISSINGER: . . . The Indian ambassador was in here as I was talking to you, and I gave him a general outline what we were thinking of. You know, I can't say he likes it but that he understands. What worries them is if we opened up the supply tap on a continuing basis.

NIXON: What did you tell him? That we weren't?

KISSINGER: I told him that this was not now contemplated.

NIXON: Not now contemplated. Good. You understand, that's exactly what we have to do.

KISSINGER: Well, we have to find a way of getting the Iranians to do it.

NIXON: Exactly. That's what I mean, the third-country tap that we're opening here.

KISSINGER: That's right. . . .

Alexander Haig

March 15, 1973, 9:33 a.m.

Kissinger and Haig agree that they should bomb Laos—despite a cease-fire agreement between the Laotian government and Pathet Lao (the leftist nationalist group fighting against the government) on February 21 that said foreign countries must cease all military intervention there.

... KISSINGER: Now, what is your view on the Laos bombing?

HAIG: Well, I think we're getting very close to where we're going to have to do something dramatic, Henry, with this thing.

KISSINGER: Now the question is, do we do it still while there are prisoners there or right after?

HAIG: I'd be inclined to do it before. . . . If you do it before you've really conveyed the impression that, god damn it, you mean business. . . .

KISSINGER: Well, that's my instinct. They might hold the prisoners but then we'll just have to bomb them in the North. . . .

Rowland Evans
March 27, 1973, 11:00 a.m.
Columnist Evans and Kissinger discuss H. R. Haldeman's possible resignation and the mounting Watergate scandal. Kissinger pleads ignorance about Watergate. (He had earlier warned Washington Post *publisher Katharine Graham against further reporting, saying it was overblown and to proceed carefully.)*[5]

. . . EVANS: I understand we're not going to have Bob to kick around anymore.

KISSINGER: I tell you, it'd be a disaster if he left. . . . Because I don't know who can hold this place together. . . .

EVANS: Oh, my god, this Watergate thing, Henry, has become an uncontrollable, dangerous mess. Really dangerous.

KISSINGER: Oh, yes, that I agree with.

EVANS: And nobody knows. Everybody suspects everybody else and nobody knows—that's the mystery of it.

KISSINGER: Neither do I.

EVANS: . . . Nobody knows the real story. Nobody even knows whether there is a real story to know. . . .

KISSINGER: I don't think there is. . . . I know probably less about it than you do. . . .

"Trouble-Making" Cables; Stepped-Up Bombing in Cambodia and Two Days of Air Raids in Laos; Watergate Explodes, Getting "Blood Flowing" and "Total Disassociation," Plotting with Garment and Shultz, and Pleading Ignorance of Watergate; the Wiretapping Breaks and Kissinger's Evasions and Lies; and Kalb Book Intrigues

April–May 1973

In late February 1973, Kissinger held secret talks in New York with Egyptian National Security Adviser Hafiz Ismail to understand Egypt's positions in Middle East peace talks and thus the prospects of an agreement. Joseph Greene, the U.S. representative in Egypt, who was mad that he was not told about Kissinger's talks, sent out cables in early April about them after a Saudi official apprised him of the talks. This did not go over well with Kissinger.

U.S. bombing in Cambodia had been continuously increasing since the January Vietnam peace agreement, despite an article in the agreement requiring foreign countries to end their military activities in Cambodia, Laos, and South Vietnam. In northern Laos, the administration carried out two days of bombing against an offensive by the North Vietnamese and Pathet Lao that the administration charged violated the February Laotian cease-fire agreement. Kissinger was outraged when a Pentagon spokesman revealed that the administration was considering bombing Laos before the bombing had begun, and about the "recalcitrant schoolboys" among his colleagues who were unenthusiastic about bombing against enemy infiltration on the Ho Chi Minh Trail in southern Laos and across the DMZ. He told Defense Secretary Elliot Richardson that the Laos bombing was to "give them a sense that we are just on the verge of going out of control and that they might be next," meaning North Vietnam.

That April, the Watergate scandal was snowballing, with daily revelations. Nixon counsel John Dean was cooperating with prosecutors to save himself, the cover-up of the Watergate break-in was continuing to collapse, and the break-in at Daniel Ellsberg's psychiatrist's office was revealed, among other developments. Kissinger advised Leonard Garment, who would replace the purged Dean as counsel to the president, that Nixon should get "blood flowing. . . . Blood and total dissociation. A frontal attack on these guys saying 'I was betrayed by my closest friends.' . . . But we'd need a guy who would be willing to set up them."

To distance himself from Watergate, Kissinger told journalists that his knowledge of it was hardly more than theirs and that he was only tangentially involved in internal discussions about it. But he consulted regularly with Garment and Treasury Secretary George Shultz about the scandal and told Shultz that daily morning meetings to deal with it were essential. He told the author Theodore White that Dean was just "a figure I saw sneaking around."

In May, after the administration's wiretaps of officials and journalists began to see the light of day, former NSC staffer Daniel Davidson, who had been wiretapped, phoned Kissinger to confront him about it. Kissinger insisted to journalists that he didn't request any wiretaps on anybody, that he had "nothing to do with" the wiretaps on reporters, and in fact had helped "protect the innocent." But he was pivotal to the initiation of the wiretapping, knew full well that the people whose names he or his assistant Alexander Haig submitted to the FBI would be wiretapped, and was a party to requests for a majority of the taps.

He also denied any knowledge of the operations of the White House Plumbers unit that investigated Ellsberg and broke into his psychiatrist's office, though Haig, his liaison to the Plumbers, conveyed some reports on their operations to him and Kissinger knew the Plumbers' purposes: investigating and plugging leaks. Indeed, he was a critical impetus to the unit's formation (though he probably didn't know it as the Plumbers).

In May, Kissinger asked Random House to consider publishing Marvin and Bernard Kalb's book on him that he claimed Norton was going to publish but wanted to delete all references that might be critical of him. Random House was keenly interested in Kissinger's future memoirs and thus wary of publishing anything that might "offend" him.

Joseph Sisco

April 7, 1973, 11:00 a.m.

Kissinger complains to Assistant Secretary of State Sisco about the cables from circumvented U.S. representative in Egypt Joseph Greene on Kissinger's secret talks with Egyptian National Security Adviser Hafiz Ismail.

KISSINGER: I've been reading some of Greene's cables. . . . What the hell does Greene think he is doing? . . . First of all, the things I allegedly said are so insane. . . . And secondly, is it conceivable to Greene that whatever I do I do on my own? . . . To me, these look like trouble-making cables.

SISCO: Well, I don't think so. . . .

KISSINGER: Well, I don't give much of a damn. He can keep on his merry way. . . . But on the face what was reported to him was so absurd. . . . You can rest assured that nothing I do is done without presidential approval.

SISCO: I've assumed that all the way along for four years. . . .

Kenneth Rush

April 9, 1973, 3:28 p.m.

Kissinger raises Greene's cables, which he thought painted him as a "villain," with Deputy Secretary of State Rush. Greene had reported in a cable the account of the Saudi official who told him about Kissinger's talks with Ismail.[1]

. . . KISSINGER: That idiot you have in Cairo keeps sending in cables that are bound to create nothing but trouble. . . . You know, his job isn't to be a detective and finding out what may be going on. His job is to find out and to see how it can be handled. . . . I'm counting on you to straighten him out. . . . But obviously something was going on, 'cause a lot of what he got [from the Saudi] was total garbage.

RUSH: I know it. But the bad thing was to put it in a cable. . . . Well, it's either naive or deliberately mischievous.

KISSINGER: Well, it's deliberately mischievous. There's no law that says he's got to be informed. . . . I don't believe that the Saudi just volunteered that information. . . . You know, ever since I said that there was a prior exchange, he's been sulking. . . .

Elliot Richardson

April 12, 1973, 4:40 p.m.

Kissinger complains to Defense Secretary Richardson that James Lowenstein and Richard Moose, staff members of a Senate Foreign Relations subcommittee, had been allowed to attend meetings in Cambodia on U.S. bombing there during a recent trip. The subcommittee's report found that the bombing, coordinated from the American embassy in Phnom Penh, had been steadily increasing since the Vietnam cease-fire in late January.[2]

KISSINGER: ... I've had a talk with Haig and he tells me that [U.S. Ambassador to Cambodia Emory] Swank, based on a joint State–Defense cable ... let Lowenstein and Moose sit in on all the targeting of operations in Cambodia, and I can hardly believe that.

RICHARDSON: I didn't know the cable provided for ... their sitting in on anything. I saw a cable which, in effect, instructed Swank to tell them what the process was and what the prior direction mechanisms were that were designed to minimize civilian casualties.

KISSINGER: Well, Haig tells me that Lowenstein and Moose sat in on the daily staff meetings at the embassy. ... I know that State has to testify before the Senate Foreign Relations Committee, but I don't think their interest and ours are identical. ...

RICHARDSON: It was in effect that we should tell them how the targets were determined, what in general they are, and so on.

KISSINGER: That's fine. ... Well, they better be prepared for the fact that they now know everything and that life is going to be unpleasant when they get back. ... It is a lousy practice to let hostile investigators from a committee sit in on embassy staff meetings. ...

William Clements
April 16, 1973, 1:56 p.m.
Kissinger vents his outrage to Deputy Defense Secretary Clements about a statement by Pentagon spokesman Jerry Friedheim on the impending bombing of Laos and about a lack of enthusiasm in the Washington Special Actions Group for striking in Laos, particularly on the Ho Chi Minh Trail, and against North Vietnamese movements across the DMZ, where Kissinger wanted the bombing concentrated.[3]

KISSINGER: Well, I've noticed that Friedheim has done exactly what we've told him not to do. ... "The U.S. is considering whether we will resume bombing in Laos." Now, god damn, it does us no good to start that debate before Hanoi's even protesting. That gives our opponent an eight-hour head start. I just am in despair over the way this government is running and I'm getting ready to tell the president that some really major surgery is needed. ... To me these WSAG meetings are like a bunch of recalcitrant schoolboys. ... There is no enthusiasm. I mean, when they don't want to do something, they lose us with proposals. We never get a proposal to do something. After all, the cease-fire is being violated every day. It isn't our job in the White House to drive you all. And here this is in total violation of what we told him to do and I would like to know one rational reason why we have to trigger Congress. We could have had another day of freedom from congressional screaming. . . . From now on, this stuff isn't free any more. I'm just going to drag department heads into the president and one of us is going to go. Because I'm just sick and tired of these performances at the WSAG and I'm sick and tired of my personally having to call every subordinate bloody officer in order to get presidential orders carried out. That's what department heads are there for.

CLEMENTS: Well now, Henry, do you feel that in any way we're dragging our feet over here on trying to support what you're trying to do?

KISSINGER: I don't know who is dragging their feet, but there is never any— never two people who just snap to and do it. . . . I know you are on our side.

CLEMENTS: Damn right.

KISSINGER: I'm not yelling at you. . . . Just trying to give you ammunition. . . . The only guy I feel I can call in Defense and get enthusiastic support is you. . . . Everybody else I call I have the sense that I am engaged in a battle with a bunch of fat lawyers who are trying to cut corners. . . . But here we are, the president is taking the heat, he's willing to do something. . . . Don't you think if you were in charge of a department you'd be out there on top of your ambassador to make sure this thing is going to run like clockwork? . . . It's the first time that the ambassador, who's been on our back all the time for bombing constantly, is canceling strikes. . . . Now your spokesman is getting us into the soup of the congressmen for nothing. . . . I think Friedheim must be told now that anyone who can't carry out White House orders ought to look for another job. . . .

Elliot Richardson
April 16, 1973, 2:03 p.m.
Kissinger also expresses his anger to Richardson over the dearth of enthusiasm in the WSAG about bombing in Laos and Friedheim's misstep.

. . . KISSINGER: . . . It's just getting impossible to do serious business this way. . . . We are now in the middle of a Laos bombing debate when we are not even bombing. . . . These WSAG meetings are getting intolerable. It's like a reform school. I sit there giving the president's views and the whole goddamn bureaucracy, they're shooting at it. . . . And I'm just going to force a showdown in front of the president and let him see whether he wants to run the government that way. . . . The North Vietnamese have given us a very insolent reply to a very conciliatory message by us. . . . They should have the feeling that when they get hit—that there are brutal reactions. . . .

All they understand is brutality or deviousness. . . . We are doing it to give them a shock. And give them a sense that we are just on the verge of going out of control and that they might be next. . . .

Leonard Garment
April 21, 1973, 9:35 a.m.
Nixon adviser Garment and Kissinger discuss the snowballing Watergate scandal. Garment had told Kissinger a week earlier that it was about to explode and required full disclosure and purging the administration—"cleaning house."[4] Kissinger wonders if Nixon aide John Ehrlichman was threatening to spill. He and Garment agree that the only thing that mattered now was saving Nixon. They believe the hush money paid to the Watergate burglars could not be justified as payment of legal defense fees. "One has to assume Watergate could not have been an isolated incident," Kissinger says, aware it was not. He advises that Nixon get "blood flowing. . . . Blood and total dissociation."

... KISSINGER: Well, everything you predicted is unfortunately coming true. . . . Mitchell is now threatening higher-ups. . . . And I've had another call from Ehrlichman . . . who's telling me that Haldeman and the president are like Siamese twins. If one goes, the other goes. . . . You don't suppose he's trying to threaten?

GARMENT: Well, Ehrlichman already tried to say . . . that he would like to be helpful in prying them loose. . . . Well, that's crazy. . . . Siamese twins can be separated. . . .

KISSINGER: I'm really getting worried. . . . If this goes much further we won't have a foreign policy left. . . . And it's got absolutely nothing to do anymore with who is liable criminally. . . . There are a lot of guys who aren't criminally liable whom you don't want in the White House.

GARMENT: I had a very funny conversation yesterday with . . . Bob Semple [of the *New York Times*]. . . . And the essence of what he said was no matter what happens here the president said the chips should fall where they may. For heaven's sake, make sure that happens and that the president is saved. . . .

KISSINGER: It's the only issue that is left. . . . You know, none of them has an explanation. Supposing these were legal funds. That won't stand up either.

GARMENT: That doesn't make any difference.

KISSINGER: . . . Why do you pay the legal fees of somebody who did something against—

GARMENT: Oh, lord, Henry, you can't. All of these funds were demanded by these men and by their wives and by their lawyers. . . .

KISSINGER: Well, this is without a doubt the most depressing period that I know in our history. . . . Look, when you told me last week about this time [about the extent of Watergate] I had to accept some of it intellectually but it was almost beyond my belief. It was beyond my emotional belief. Because another thing that is bound to come out now—one has to assume Watergate could not have been an isolated incident.

GARMENT: It was not.

KISSINGER: Because you don't throw that much machinery into motion if it was even one isolated—even if you assume it was an authorized incident.

GARMENT: It was part of a long, wide range of events.

KISSINGER: But that's going to come out too, isn't it?

GARMENT: Well, I think, as I said to you last week, that point [full disclosure] can be reached if action is taken where a variety of human institutional constitutional bargains can be struck.

KISSINGER: Yeah, but not much longer.

GARMENT: Not much longer. This is the weekend of the crucifixion and the resurrection. It's the time for action.

KISSINGER: I mean, if your advice had been taken last week . . . we would have been spared a week of testimony.

GARMENT: That's right.

KISSINGER: I had every impression that [Nixon counsel John] Dean and company are going to—

GARMENT: Talk, talk, talk.

KISSINGER: Spill their guts from now on.

GARMENT: It's not a question of impressions—it's a fact. Although it isn't clear to me what they think they are accomplishing. . . .

KISSINGER: Well, if these stories are right that Dean knew about the bugging [at the Democratic National Committee headquarters] and then was put in charge of the investigation—in addition to the unbelievable immorality, the incredible stupidity—

GARMENT: Correct. Well, we're past the point of diagnoses and analyses. The question is whether anything can be done that will cause some action to be taken.

KISSINGER: Blood flowing. Blood up to the neck.

GARMENT: Well, how can that be done?

KISSINGER: Don't you think?

GARMENT: Of course. . . . I told you last week, Henry.

KISSINGER: Blood and total dissociation. A frontal attack on these guys saying "I was betrayed by my closest friends. It was a horrible tragedy." But we'd need a guy who would be willing to set up them. What if these guys say no, it was all done in the Oval Office?

GARMENT: I don't know whether it was. I'm just wondering if they would say that. God knows what they would say. But I think people would set on them like a lynch mob to tear their tongues out. . . . I don't think people will listen to them or believe that. . . .

KISSINGER: I think the best thing is to leave the president alone. I don't think he needs advice.

GARMENT: A very strong memorandum was put in Haldeman's hands yesterday explaining as logically as possible why he should take action. But it won't help.

KISSINGER: Not even remotely. He [Haldeman] doesn't even understand what the issue is. . . . He puts it entirely into whether he can defend himself against criminal charges. . . . Well, supposing he could survive all this. Which is inconceivable. But—

GARMENT: I can't conceive of this government continuing with him in.

KISSINGER: But . . . suppose he survives and then becomes fair game again for the usual attacks. . . . There even isn't any question of surviving it criminally.

GARMENT: Christ almighty. Ten days ago, if he [Nixon] had acted then, we'd have all that time. Look what has happened in this period of time.

KISSINGER: On television now, they are playing tapes of what was said last year. I saw on the news summary . . . they played everything that Mitchell said last year and what he said yesterday.

GARMENT: And this will go on to the next stage and then the next stage. . . .

Joseph Alsop
April 21, 1973, 10:15 a.m.
Kissinger bemoans Watergate to columnist Alsop and declares that "my knowledge is barely more than yours." Alsop says Nixon "won't suffer."

. . . KISSINGER: Oh, Joe, this is a nightmare. . . . At the moment we were at the margins of our existence in the best of circumstances, our credit is being squandered with a frivolity that cannot be believed. . . . Without an enormous moral margin.

ALSOP: . . . I think the president has lanced the ulcer.

KISSINGER: Not yet. . . . Just pricked it.

ALSOP: . . . Well, I have the feeling it will be lanced. I want to talk to you very privately about that.

KISSINGER: Well, my knowledge is barely more than yours of the actual facts, but it'll be the damnedest war of all against all.

ALSOP: Well, I can see because most of the people involved are perfect shits.

KISSINGER: It's unbelievable. Using the government as their private possession, that is—

ALSOP: Deceit is the only weapon they understand and it is really rather a nightmare, but my thought about it is it won't last long . . . as the country doesn't basically want its president to be destroyed, and he won't suffer, but the thing is to get it over with and be surgical about it.

KISSINGER: Well, it will lead to a lancing. . . .

President Nixon
April 21, 1973, 11:40 a.m.
Nixon asks Kissinger to mollify Haldeman and Ehrlichman, who were in legal peril and could turn on him.

. . . NIXON: . . . I think that Easter you ought to call up to Camp David and just extend good luck to Bob and John. They are going through hell trying to figure out what to do.

KISSINGER: No question. I talked to them last night, just on the human basis. I mean, I didn't discuss this—

NIXON: I know. . . . We want to make it clear that we're trying to do the right thing. . . . How is their temperature? Is it all right?

KISSINGER: Yeah, but they are looking at it largely from the view of a criminal case. I no longer believe it is.

NIXON: No, I know that. It's a question of how it appears. . . . It isn't the court of law anymore, it's the court of public opinion. . . . When you're around up there now and Garment and some of the others come in and wring their hands, you tell them to calm down now. . . . You know, when we move, we'll move decisively, but I've got to do it my own way. . . .

Leonard Garment
April 22, 1973, 11:35 a.m.
Kissinger worries that it may not be possible to wall Nixon off from Watergate, and he and Garment are dumbfounded that Ehrlichman and Haldeman hired the same lawyer.

. . . GARMENT: . . . The president has a lot of problems—but that's self-evident.

KISSINGER: The newspapers are getting worse and worse. . . . There may not be the possibility of keeping the president out of it.

GARMENT: No, I don't think that is true, but I don't know how much longer. . . .

KISSINGER: I talked to Ehrlichman last night but they are still totally focused on the criminal aspect. . . . I think there is nothing to do now except to wait. And for us to stay in touch.

GARMENT: Yes. . . . One thing that really baffles me is that John and Bob Haldeman would have the same lawyer. It's as if it was a joint venture. . . .

KISSINGER: Another stupidity, isn't it?

GARMENT: Have you looked at the papers today?

KISSINGER: Awful.

GARMENT: . . . It's in his hands to do something. . . . Notify them [that they had to resign] tonight and should act tomorrow morning.

KISSINGER: Never.

GARMENT: Won't do it. . . . He has to strike everybody out. . . . He has to do a number of very dramatic things. . . .

Alexander Haig
April 23, 1973, 9:52 a.m.

Kissinger laments to his former deputy Haig, now the vice chief of staff of the army, that Watergate was inhibiting U.S. bombing in Southeast Asia and "looking almost worse than I feared," and Haig predicts that liberals were going to turn on Daniel Ellsberg, who was on trial over releasing the Pentagon Papers.

. . . KISSINGER: My problem is I don't see how we can get anything done in this climate. I mean, supposing we start bombing. This will crystalize all the congressional opposition. . . . And the whole credibility problem will be raised in connection with whatever we say we're doing it for. . . .

HAIG: I agree with that. . . . They have now shifted from pragmatism to principle so that they screw the president on this Watergate thing. The liberals are going to turn on that poor bastard Ellsberg. . . . I'm going out there tomorrow . . . to LA to this trial [to testify]. . . . I'm just going to do it very cryptically and say that you had him in San Clemente in August of '69.

KISSINGER: . . . And say he wasn't working on classified material [when consulting for him earlier].

HAIG: . . . Will you have said anything to him that will enable him to say that he was an official NSC consultant? He never got paid for it, you know.

KISSINGER: No, that's what he always wanted to be. . . . What I said, in fact, I can't guarantee.

HAIG: Well, I'll stay fuzzy on the thing. . . .

KISSINGER: To me this is looking almost worse than I feared.

HAIG: Yeah. . . . I just don't know what the hell he [Nixon] can do under these circumstances. The whole goddamned thing is up for grabs.

KISSINGER: Yeah. Unless he just acts with total brutality and daring. . . .

Robert Toth
April 25, 1973, 1:02 p.m.

Kissinger tells Toth of the Los Angeles Times *that he was not much involved in internal discussions about Watergate and not at all on remedies.*

. . . KISSINGER: I'd go very easy. My role in all of these discussions has been at the very, very periphery. Occasionally I'm asked one question without knowing all the facts. And occasionally people who are worried about how things are going are coming to me. But I have no systematic connection with any of the discussions. . . . And I would much prefer not to be mentioned at all in connection with these discussions, because it's highly misleading. . . . On my discussions on Watergate it would be totally, utterly incorrect to assume that I am involved or have been involved in any discussions on what to do. . . . But, you know, occasionally a question may be thrown at me. Having to do with general attitude. . . .

George Shultz
April 25, 1973, 6:20 p.m.
Treasury Secretary Shultz advises Kissinger that he is organizing regular morning meetings to deal with Watergate, which Kissinger considers "essential."

SHULTZ: The other day we talked about having a meeting at 8:30 to pull people together. I've started that now. . . . I had somebody call down and see if you could come. . . . We will have [one] every morning at 8:30 for however long in my office there in the White House. . . .

KISSINGER: Does Haldeman know about that? . . . I think you better tell him.

SHULTZ: Ehrlichman knows about it; he suggested it.

KISSINGER: Well, good. . . . I'll come Friday. . . . It's essential; it's essential. The demoralization is progressing rapidly.

SHULTZ: Well, I have had a hard time getting a phone call to Ehrlichman answered in the last few days and I don't imagine I'd have much success with Haldeman.

KISSINGER: Yeah. You haven't talked to the president?

SHULTZ: No. Have you?

KISSINGER: Very briefly, but he's not undertaking, at least with me, a systematic examination. . . .

George Shultz
April 27, 1973, 8:58 a.m.
Kissinger and Shultz consult again on Watergate.

KISSINGER: What do you make of this affair this morning?

SHULTZ: Oh, the course laid out is a disaster. And I think we should at least stop that.

KISSINGER: But I don't think there's a clue to what's going on.

SHULTZ: I don't either.

KISSINGER: I saw the president. We went over a list of things and at the end
   he said he's going to replace Haldeman and then Ehrlichman and business
   will go on as usual. That will not work. . . .
SHULTZ: Suppose I come to your office about 12:15 for a little while.
KISSINGER: . . . Let's do that. . . .

Howard Stein
April 27, 1973, 10:16 a.m.
*Stein, head of the Dreyfus Corporation (a money management company), conveys an
offer of assistance from former senator Eugene McCarthy, to which Kissinger responds
sarcastically, and they take up Watergate.*

STEIN: . . . I just wanted to mention to you that Gene McCarthy mentioned
   that . . . if there were anything that he might be able to do at this point—
KISSINGER: Isn't that nice. Isn't that big of him. . . . That is really big of him.
STEIN: So if there is anything that would be of any help in any way.
KISSINGER: Well, I have no idea what will be decided yet. But something—it
   can't be small. Well, I'll talk to Gene myself, but you tell him that I'm not
   surprised that he's a big man. . . . I want to wait here until the smoke clears
   a bit before I know what people can do.
STEIN: . . .Things have to go on.
KISSINGER: That's what some of the liberals don't seem to realize—when they
   scream for blood. Blood aplenty is bound to flow. . . . The problem is how
   to go on and what the economic program should be. . . . It's just how you
   instill the psychological feeling that it is all right. It is affecting the economy
   now, isn't it?
STEIN: Yeah. . . .
KISSINGER: Well, Howard, my judgment is that this situation will—must have
   a denouement within the next two weeks. . . .

Melvin Laird
April 30, 1973, 9:10 a.m.
*Former defense secretary Laird, who would soon be appointed Nixon's special counsel
on Watergate, gives a worrisome assessment of the political damage around the country. (Nixon had forced Haldeman and Ehrlichman out the day before, and fired Dean
and Attorney General Richard Kleindienst as well.)*

. . . KISSINGER: What do you think of where we are right now?
LAIRD: Well, you mean the administration? . . . It's in pretty bad shape. . . .
   I really think it's in worse shape out in the country than it is here in
   Washington.

KISSINGER: In worse shape?

LAIRD: In Washington I think people kind of shrug it off a little bit, but out there—you get out of Washington and I think that they think it's something rather criminal. They've got it confused—you know, these dirty trick things. . . . I was really kind of disappointed to be out around—I was glad to get the hell out of there, to tell you the truth, because I couldn't go anyplace without having kind of bad problems with a lot of my old friends in Wisconsin. It's really kind of bad. . . . It's better to be around Washington right now than it is out in the boondocks, I'll tell you that. You'll find these congressmen when they get back, who have been out home, are going to be coming back steaming. . . .

Elliot Richardson
April 30, 1973, 11:23 a.m.
Nixon had appointed Richardson to replace Kleindienst as attorney general. Richardson, who had tried to beg off,[5] is apprehensive about taking the job since he was considered "a team player."

RICHARDSON: You should have blocked it. . . . If I can help, I will do it. I kind of hate to—

KISSINGER: It is a horrible tragedy. . . .

RICHARDSON: I hope I turn out to be the right guy for this. The principal thing that concerns me was I am already titled as a team player.

KISSINGER: Everyone knows you are a man of integrity. . . . I happen to believe that this is . . . a time for justice, and I don't think anyone has as much of a feel for the real thing as you. . . . It was just impossible to even think of anyone who had enough of a sense for the complexity, humanly and every other way.

RICHARDSON: Well, I came to see that certainly when I saw the president.

KISSINGER: He is in very bad shape now.

RICHARDSON: I don't blame him. It is a very tough thing.

KISSINGER: And you know the nightmare about this is, god knows what they thought they were doing when they were doing it, but it was a series of inconsequentials. . . . I think if we now get it behind us and begin governing and begin asserting the national interest and avoid this terrible self-righteous [talk] . . . we can come up strong as a country.

RICHARDSON: I think the president could himself. It was that side of it I saw in that meeting yesterday.

KISSINGER: I think he can. . . . You are in a very decisive position, Elliot.

RICHARDSON: Well, I hope so. . . .

Alexander Haig

May 1, 1973, 8:20 a.m.

A distraught and evasive Nixon gave a televised address the night before on Watergate in which he announced the resignations of Haldeman, Ehrlichman, Kleindienst, and Dean, admitted no personal culpability while accepting "responsibility," and said, "There can be no whitewash."[6] Haig had replaced Haldeman as White House chief of staff.

HAIG: I just wanted to touch base with you this morning. What did you think of that last night?

KISSINGER: Well, it wasn't very strong.

HAIG: It was too long and crusty. Although I think—

KISSINGER: But at least it lanced the boil.

HAIG: Yeah, I think it's going to solve the problem.

KISSINGER: No, solve it it won't, but it'll be a big first step.

HAIG: Yeah. Yeah. I talked to him after you did last night. . . . And, you know, I think he really needs a little bolstering on this thing. He talked about that at some length.

KISSINGER: About me?

HAIG: Yeah.

KISSINGER: Why?

HAIG: How much he counted on you. He went on and on about it. He said you've been the one source of his strength and comfort and this and that and the other thing. Sort of surprised me the way he did it. . . .

George Shultz

May 1, 1973, 6:00 p.m.

Shultz and Kissinger disparage a cabinet meeting that discussed Watergate, and Kissinger complains about the FBI's presence in Haldeman's former office at the White House. (Agents had secured Haldeman's and Ehrlichman's offices that morning.)[7]

SHULTZ: . . . Were you aware of what was going to be said at that meeting?

KISSINGER: No, I thought it was appalling. I thought the whole tone was appalling. What did you think?

SHULTZ: I had exactly the same feeling.

KISSINGER: He [Nixon] isn't talking to me. I don't know what he's trying to do.

SHULTZ: Well, apparently we're to have a system [probably on government organization and personnel] with [Kenneth] Cole or [Roy] Ash more or less in charge.

KISSINGER: Well, that's unacceptable.

SHULTZ: That's what I would get out of that.

KISSINGER: Well, that's totally unacceptable.

SHULTZ: It seems to me you and I are sort of here on the basis that we have something to say about the substance, but that isn't regarded as very important right now. . . . I was very discouraged by the meeting.

KISSINGER: I thought it was awful. I thought it was ungenerous, irrelevant. In fact, even these FBI fellows—let's be honest, if there was an ethical problem, it was having FBI fellows in the office of your closest associate; whether they stood out in the hall or sat in his office is a presentational question.

SHULTZ: Well, yeah, there is a matter of decorum there. And also what was the FBI trying to prove? . . .

KISSINGER: . . . There shouldn't be FBI men in the halls of the White House. But . . . that's a cosmetic question. The ethical question is whether you have lost so much confidence in your closest associates that you feel that they must have their files secured by the FBI. . . . The aspect that bothered me was the Ken Cole–Roy Ash aspect. And the otherwise business as usual aspect. And keep things away from me.

SHULTZ: Well, we had the same reaction as before. Well, let us talk about it tomorrow morning. . . .

George Sherman
May 11, 1973, 5:40 p.m.
The Justice Department had sent a memo to the judge in Daniel Ellsberg's trial disclosing that Ellsberg had earlier been overheard speaking to former NSC staffer Morton Halperin through a wiretap on Halperin's phone. And the New York Times *had run a story that morning on the administration's wiretaps. Sherman of the* Evening Star *asks about the Halperin tap.*

. . . SHERMAN: . . . The memorandum that the FBI sent out to the Ellsberg trial—are you aware that they say the surveillance of Halperin occurred between the spring of 1969 and June of 1971? . . . That would mean that they were tapping the telephones of members of your staff.

KISSINGER: Look, I just don't want to talk about this subject.

SHERMAN: Well, at some point, you know, this gets close to the bone here. . . . But you won't even say that you didn't know that Halperin's phone was being tapped?

KISSINGER: First I want to see this [memorandum]. . . .

Phyllis Cerf

May 13, 1973, 1:00 p.m.

Kissinger asks Cerf, the widow of Random House co-founder Bennett Cerf, for help with Marvin and Bernard Kalb's book on him. Marvin Kalb had phoned Kissinger two hours earlier urgently asking to meet with him on an important matter and then come to his office.[8]

> . . . KISSINGER: Now, Phyllis, do you still have something to do with Random House? . . . There is a newspaperman here who has written a book about me . . . and which Norton was going to publish. And Norton in an excess of zeal is trying to get him to cut out all references that might be critical of me, and he thinks that this will destroy the symmetry of his book. . . . I just want to get him in touch with Random House. . . . I want to make clear I haven't seen the book and for all I know it may rake me over the coals. . . . [It was admiring.]

Donald Klopfer

May 14, 1973, 9:37 a.m.

Random House chairman and co-founder Klopfer phones Kissinger, who backpedals on his claim to Cerf that Norton wanted to cut all critical references to him. Klopfer says they are "vitally interested" in his memoir and thus "didn't want to do anything that would offend you," that is, publish the Kalbs' book if it was overly critical.

> KLOPFER: Mr. Kissinger, this is Donald Klopfer at Random House. I just wanted to have one word with you. I did talk to Mr. Kalb yesterday at your suggestion. . . . Now, from what Phyllis told me, evidently there's some derogatory things in there that Norton wanted to take out, or am I wrong?
>
> KISSINGER: That I have no reason to know either. Apparently what they wanted him to do was to compress the Vietnam chapter and to take out all references to the president. . . . On the theory that the less they tie me with Vietnam, the better off I am. If I understand it correctly.
>
> KLOPFER: How do you feel about it? Of course I can't talk intelligently without seeing the manuscript obviously, but—
>
> KISSINGER: I feel about it that a respectful author ought to be able to say anything he wants. I don't judge publishers. . . . If a respectable person does a serious book that's not totally flattering in every chapter I don't—
>
> KLOPFER: I think that's fine. I think that young fellow [David Landau] from Houghton Mifflin published a rather fascinating book about you [*Kissinger: The Uses of Power*].

KISSINGER: . . . I don't hold that against the publisher but that I thought had major errors in almost every other page. . . .

KLOPFER: It was an interesting book, though.

KISSINGER: I never read it from cover to cover. That book I found somewhat annoying but not enough to hold against the publisher.

KLOPFER: Right. Well, that's the main reason, since I know that Bob Bernstein has been talking to you and since we are vitally interested, I didn't want to do anything that would offend you in any way. . . . The whole thing is that we use our own judgment about that.

KISSINGER: . . . Unless the book was a deliberate hatchet job that a serious publisher should have seen through, I would not see any way a book could offend me.

KLOPFER: Good. . . . But I did want to check it directly with you, frankly, before even looking at the manuscript.

KISSINGER: No, I think you should go ahead and deal with it on its merits.

KLOPFER: On the merits only. Thank you very much.

Marvin Kalb
May 14, 1973, 9:42 a.m.
Kissinger reports back to Kalb.

KISSINGER: I just talked to the Random House people. . . . They wanted to know whether I would be offended if they published something that was in part critical and I said no, unless it were a hatchet job that the publisher should have known.

KALB: Well, that isn't the case. . . .

KISSINGER: So I said they should take this entirely on its merits and there was no possible way it could offend me. And I told him I had cooperated with it because of my high regard for you.

KALB: That's wonderful. That's stupendous!

KISSINGER: So I think they're extremely interested. . . . Have you told Norton yet?

KALB: I am sitting here, Henry, my stomach is turning over and I was just thinking how to quite say it, but I think that this call from you has given me new heart and I'm just going to do it. . . .

Robert Bernstein
May 14, 1973, 12:32 p.m.
Random House President Bernstein returns Kissinger's call about the Kalbs' book on him.

KISSINGER: . . . There were two newsmen here that are doing a book on me that they were going to give to Norton. . . . And then it turned out that Norton, probably in order to protect me, wanted them to condense the Vietnam chapter to a point that they considered unreasonable. And also to disassociate me totally from the president. Which they correctly didn't want to do. . . . I said the position I would take is if a publisher does a deliberate hatchet job on me . . . that would affect my attitude towards the publisher. But if they published a book that has critical passages, that is up to the author. And since they wanted to leave Norton, I thought I'd call you to see whether you were interested. . . . I haven't read the book, so I don't know whether it's favorable or hostile. . . . Don't publish it to please me. But don't fail to publish it if it's got critical passages.

BERNSTEIN: I think what you are saying is, publish it if you would normally publish it, and don't publish it if you wouldn't normally publish it.

KISSINGER: That's right. And anything that I might do later on [regarding his memoir] isn't going to be in the slightest affected by it.

BERNSTEIN: By whether it's good or bad.

KISSINGER: By whether its publisher has brought out books that . . . didn't share my high estimate of myself.

BERNSTEIN: I understand completely. . . .

Daniel Davidson
May 14, 1973, 12:45 p.m.
Former NSC staffer Davidson, who was among the officials wiretapped by the Nixon administration and was then forced out,[9] confronts Kissinger about the tap on him. He worries that his name will be mentioned in a statement by Acting FBI Director William Ruckelshaus on his investigation into the wiretaps.

DAVIDSON: I was driving out to Silver Spring just now, I looked at the *Star.* It said Ruckelshaus is scheduled to release at 2:00 the names of the NSC people whose phones were tapped. From what I was told last week it includes me. . . . His releasing any information is itself a crime.

KISSINGER: I don't think he's going to release any names.

DAVIDSON: That's what the *Star* said. If he doesn't, it's another matter.

KISSINGER: . . . First of all, I don't know if your name would be part—

DAVIDSON: An ex-member of your staff told me that last week—there were a number of them and indeed that my name was one that doesn't show any adverse information [i.e., a security leak] and that Halperin's name did, including some contact with a foreign embassy before Halperin's name came up. So I assume that this person knew what he was talking about. . . . Can

I see you in the next day or two? I think it is time we discuss what happened. . . . In the meantime, just assuming something comes out and I'm
asked . . . why I left, what is my answer?

KISSINGER: Because, ah, ah—

DAVIDSON: Personal reasons.

KISSINGER: Personal reasons. I mean, I can assure you, Dan, nothing will be
said from me that will cast any reflections on any member of my staff. . . .
You can count on the fact, Dan, that there is no sense of destroying any more
lives or causing any more anguish than has already been caused, and as far
as anybody knows, as far as any record shows, you left for personal reasons.

DAVIDSON: Let's talk next week, because I'd like to re-establish some record.
Because I think particularly now that I've been informed what I've always
thought was true, that . . . it did not show that I ever said anything that I
should not have said to a reporter. Which is a fact.

KISSINGER: I frankly cannot even affirm that that is true—I mean, I am sure it
is true, but I would have to check if it is.

DAVIDSON: I wish you would. . . .

Theodore White
May 15, 1973, 9:23 a.m.
*Author White condemns the "bloodlust" of those out to "get" Nixon. To distance him-
self from Watergate, Kissinger claims that John Dean was just "a figure I saw sneaking
around." He denies any knowledge of the operations of the Plumbers led by John
Ehrlichman, Egil Krogh, and David Young that investigated Ellsberg and conducted
the break-in at his psychiatrist's office. But not only was Kissinger furious over Ellsberg's release of the Pentagon Papers and urging that he be thoroughly investigated,
Ehrlichman had told him about the Plumbers' functions. Kissinger's deputy Alexander Haig had received reports on the Plumbers' activities in mid-1971 and reported
on them to Kissinger; Haig was Kissinger's liaison to the Plumbers. Plus David Young,
his former personal aide, had probably filled him in. Nixon believed Kissinger was
"up to his ankles" in knowledge of the Plumbers' activities. And "without any question, Kissinger's great alarm over the Pentagon Papers was the primary motivating
influence in the formation of the Plumbers," Charles Colson recalled.*[10]

. . . KISSINGER: . . . I mean, this country is in a suicidal mood.

WHITE: I don't think you know how bad it is. . . . People who telephone me,
important people, who say, "Get him, get him, get him." As if they were
gladiators that wanted to kill.

KISSINGER: And as if it weren't their president.

WHITE: It's unbelievable. I've never lived through anything like this. Bloodlust, that's what it is. . . . The only thing that could possibly go well is that

they finally get bored with it. I don't think there could be much more to write about.

KISSINGER: That's what I think every day and then some other horror emerges.

WHITE: . . . You know, this man Nixon is not a villain, period. I think he's got a great foreign policy, what the hell.

KISSINGER: And even these transgressions are gonna be seen in a—you know, they are not going to be excused but it takes a much more complex analogy of what really happened. You know, there's a Walter Mitty quality, because . . . I mean, who would burgle a psychiatrist's office? A psychiatric record is what the defense uses, not the prosecution. I mean, supposing you find that Ellsberg is crazier than a loon. What the hell can you do with it? . . . From the point of view of the government it was better to have him sane. . . . People forget what it was like here. . . . There were leaks of NSC discussions, who said what, throughout the administration. . . . Now they are going after what the FBI did to protect leaks. Which is totally different. It was always done in a legal framework. . . .

WHITE: What's the situation there at the White House? . . .

KISSINGER: Well, you have a group of people who believed in administrative loyalty but not in substantive loyalty. You know, they are not devoted to a cause but to a structure, and that structure has now disintegrated. So they are unguided bullets. . . .

WHITE: Did you ever know Dean yourself?

KISSINGER: He was a figure I saw sneaking around, you know, walking around the halls. And so I knew him, but I didn't know his name, and you know I never put his name with his face. I'd occasionally get a legal paper from Dean, signed Dean, but I never associated the young kid I saw running around with that name. I never was at a meeting with him. . . . I never heard him recite on any subject. . . . You see, the weird thing is, I know Krogh. I happen to know him because he was in the Bahamas once when I was there. Now, what is so amazing is he is a god-fearing, decent, middle American. This is not a nut. And he's dull, boring, and if you had told me six months ago that he would burgle an office, I would have told you that you had lost your mind.

WHITE: Were you aware of a Plumbers operation going on?

KISSINGER: No.

WHITE: You were unaware of it?

KISSINGER: I was unaware of the operation. A member of my staff [David Young] left me, when I was on my secret trip to China, and joined Ehrlichman's staff. Physically moved in there. And I thought for the first three months he was working on classifications. And he did; there was a study on classifications generated by the Ellsberg papers. After that, I didn't know what the hell he did. But I had never heard the word "Plumber," the content of their operation. And the first thing I heard about it was in April . . . when it came out in the newspapers. Nor did Haig ever hear of it. . . .

Joseph Kraft
May 15, 1973, 10:00 a.m.

Kissinger has a testy exchange with Kraft, who had published a column that morning saying that Kissinger had been "compromised" by Watergate and criticizing his evasiveness on the wiretapping of Morton Halperin at an earlier press briefing.[11] *Kissinger claims to Kraft, who had been wiretapped (outside FBI channels), that he had not been involved in the decision to conduct wiretapping and had not requested the tap on Halperin; both claims were untrue.*

> KISSINGER: Joe, I want you to know that I consider this article today the most skunky thing that I have seen anybody do. . . . Has it ever occurred to you that in the case of Halperin . . . that I was the one who kept him in the government? Why would I put a wiretap on somebody who had a security file . . . and whom I, personally in my own name, put on the staff? Whom, if I wanted to do anything to, I just had to withdraw my clearance from him. . . .
>
> KRAFT: Henry, what I wrote was not easy. You might think it was skunky. . . . Are you now saying that you did not participate in the decision to bug?
>
> KISSINGER: I am saying that I received the summaries; that the decision to do bugging, to do the bugging was not mine. That is correct.
>
> KRAFT: You did not participate?
>
> KISSINGER: I did not participate in the decision, but I was aware of it.
>
> KRAFT: . . . I think I want to stand on that story.
>
> KISSINGER: . . . Someday I'm certain the full complexity of these things will be apparent, but I will stand on the fact that I—well, never mind, I don't need to testify myself to you.
>
> KRAFT: That's right, you don't, but I don't need to testify myself to—
>
> KISSINGER: No one has asked you to.
>
> KRAFT: All right.

Seymour Hersh
May 15, 1973, 5:45 p.m.

New York Times *reporter Hersh plays up to Kissinger for a story he is writing on the wiretaps, telling him he is "a national asset," that "very clearly this was a decision made above you," sympathizes with the wiretapping, says no innocent people were hurt, points out "you had a terrific problem," and even advises the White House on*

PR. Hersh's story the next day emphasized that Nixon "personally authorized the wiretapping," and one the following day stressed that Kissinger "personally provided" the FBI the names of aides he wanted wiretapped. (Nixon later said that Kissinger "really wanted the wiretaps," "loved the wiretaps," and read the wiretap summaries "all the time," in the words of a Watergate prosecutor. "Henry ordered the whole goddamn thing," Nixon shouted in a taped conversation the day before this conversation. "... He read every one of those taps ... he reveled in it ... he wallowed in it.")[12]

HERSH: Hi, Dr. Kissinger. I know we're driving you half crazy. All of your friends are telling us if we don't stop, you're going to leave, and you're a national asset, and I think we all agree. ... I know most of the people who were tapped, but three of them I'm absolutely positive about. ... I'm just telling you this advance warning. It's going to be painful. It's Tony Lake and Dan Davidson ... and, of course, Winston Lord [all three were members of Kissinger's NSC staff]. ... Very clearly this was a decision made above you. ... I have now satisfied myself that you are absolutely right. This is a decision made specifically, of course, by the attorney general and the director of the FBI and also by Mr. Nixon himself. ... I must say, I don't understand why those people who handle press for the White House don't get up and say there are a lot of reasons and ... that you've discovered some very damaging things about three or four people. ... There was information that these did prove to be somewhat valuable in terms of who was talking about what.

KISSINGER: Because we don't want to hurt people.

HERSH: That's right. But nonetheless, if you don't say that, it seems to me you're all going to get trampled here. Particularly the president. The president, for god's sake, authorized these.

KISSINGER: That is correct.

HERSH: Of course, that's correct.

KISSINGER: But, Mr. Hersh, if you look at it from the point of view of results ... if I had wanted to get Mort Halperin, I didn't need to have a wiretap on him. ... Because you know how many people in this town were gunning for him.

HERSH: That's right.

KISSINGER: Particularly in this administration.

HERSH: And particularly since he [did] a stupid thing on his security clearance, I'm told by my FBI people.

KISSINGER: Exactly.

HERSH: He forgot to mention a trip to Russia.

KISSINGER: Exactly. ... If I wanted to get him, all I had to do was let them follow normal procedures. I kept him in the government and I kept him on as a consultant after he left to make him eligible for future employment. And, now, you know how devoted I was to Tony Lake. . . . And Dan Davidson is a friend of mine. And I'm sorry you have to mention their names.

HERSH: . . . I will say that most of these taps proved to justify, clear people who were suspected of things. But you had a terrific problem, you were moving into a very hostile bureaucracy. I mean, the funny thing is this all could have been—it's just like the Watergate—it all could have been handled with such great ease. I don't have to tell you that. Your instinct about press relations is much better than 98 percent of them. It's, one, tell the truth, and if you have to take a lump, take a lump. And if it comes out that there was a tap because of something, you stand up and say the president—well, let me read you a quote from a friend of yours. He said, "Damn right, we would have been irresponsible in 1969. It would have been the highest order of irresponsibility if we hadn't gone and put these taps on." But instead of saying that, we get the weaseling. Well, I'm writing this tomorrow, and that's at least going to do one thing, it's going to get it in focus that we had between you and any decision, we had the president and we had Mr. Mitchell and Mr. Hoover. And I have no idea whether you were swept along reluctantly or eagerly, but the fact is that I think this will put the record correct.

KISSINGER: But the question is, what were the motives here? And was any innocent person hurt?

HERSH: No, the answer is no.

KISSINGER: I think the motives were honorable and [the wiretapping] had to be conducted in the interests of the country. It turned out to be a protection for innocent people the way it was handled. . . .

HERSH: Look, get that goddamn Russian [Brezhnev] in here and get this off page one, that's all I can say.

KISSINGER: Well, let me say to you . . . that I appreciate the spirit with which you are handling this.

HERSH: Well, it's not going to be a nice story. I mean, it's going to be an honorable story and it's going to say very clearly that responsible people are convinced they had a serious problem and in the long run they discovered enough information to make them feel that it was justified. Which are very serious things to say. But, look, the other thing—the only spirit is truth, as you know, Dr. Kissinger, and I assume that's the one we all work on.

KISSINGER: Look, at this point, the only thing that needs to concern us all, whatever our different views may be, is to preserve some integrity and dignity for this country

HERSH: That's right.

KISSINGER: And to get us back to some things that we can be proud of. That is in everybody's interests at the moment.

HERSH: Agreed. . . . Well, look, I'm alarmed about one thing. As somebody who has been a neutralist—a neutral critic—I hate to see you do anything rash. I'll call up Matt Meselson [a Harvard professor] and tell him to give you a pep talk. Don't do anything rash, please don't. . . . You know, on the basis of conversation, somebody is going to float a story saying Kissinger is distressed and personally upset and ready to leave. . . . Your friends are talking that you're very upset, and I want you to know that in this office, anyway, as you know from your dealings with Bernie [Gwertzman], Scotty [Reston], and everybody—

KISSINGER: Look, you've been more than fair to me.

HERSH: Well, you know that. . . . As I understand it from someone who was close to the president, his motives were simply of a great concern of ensuring, you know, what he considered to be incredibly dangerous leaks were stopped, period. . . . By the way, it wasn't Mort Halperin, I'm sure you know that by now, who leaked it [the secret Cambodia bombing to William Beecher]. . . .

KISSINGER: I don't know who it was, but I never thought Halperin was a leaker. . . .

John Osborne
May 28, 1973, 6:30 p.m.
Osborne of The New Republic *asks Kissinger about a column by Joe Kraft applauding his achievements as a foreign policy "virtuoso" but condemning his "evasions and then outright lies" about the wiretaps.*[13]

. . . KISSINGER: . . . Look, the situation, despite what Joe Kraft said . . . I did not order these things, I did not request these things. I fulfilled criteria that was set up without me or by giving the names of people who had had access to the information under investigation. . . . I did my share in protecting the innocent. . . . He's called me a liar. . . . I have searched my files, my phone conversations, and all the records I could find, and he will not be able to sustain this. Now, what unnamed Justice Department sources say, that is a sign of the lynch atmosphere at this time. . . . If it should turn out that there is some evidence, I would like to see it. . . . I did not request the taps. . . . It turns out that my office—it supplied names in one or two or maybe more cases of people who had handled particular documents. . . . Now, the key point I want to repeat about these taps was that they were ordered by procedures that were then legal and in the belief that this was the precise procedure followed in previous administrations for these same purposes. . . . That part of it that I had any knowledge of, namely, who had handled what documents, may have been supplied by General Haig to his liaison officer at the FBI. I say *may* have been because I just can't find any record one way or other on that subject. . . . He probably did. . . .

OSBORNE: . . . Were you responsible, Dr. Kissinger, directly or indirectly, for any taps placed on the newspapermen and correspondents' phones?

Kissinger: No. No. I had nothing to do with that. . . .

Watergate, the Wiretaps, and the Plumbers; the Brezhnev Summit; Another Grain Deal; the Looming Cambodia Bombing Cutoff; Morton Halperin's Wiretapping Lawsuit; Memoirs; Nixon's Pneumonia; Dan Rather's Report on Kissinger's Move to State; the Butterfield Taping Revelation; and the Uncovering of the Secret Cambodia Bombing

June–July 1973

In June 1973, the Watergate revelations continued to pour out. Former Nixon counsel John Dean testified for five days on television before the Senate Select Committee on Presidential Campaign Activities, implicating Nixon in the cover-up. Other former officials also testified on the administration's illegalities and abuses of power. Kissinger felt the FBI, which he correctly believed was leaking like crazy, "must be brought under brutal control."

He continued to deny requesting any wiretaps on anybody, or that he knew about the existence of the Plumbers, or that he was aware that his former personal assistant David Young worked for them, or that he'd ever talked to Dean. All being untrue. He denounced Nixon's critics as "bastard traitors." He considered astonishingly stupid a counterattack on Dean by Nixon's Watergate legal counsel Fred Buzhardt when Dean was testifying to the Senate Select Committee.

On June 14, former NSC staffer Morton Halperin filed a lawsuit against Kissinger and others for wiretapping his phone. (Kissinger claimed to William F. Buckley, in quite a prevarication, that the wiretap "was done on his own by J. Edgar Hoover," who was in fact quite wary of the whole secret wiretapping program ordered by the White House.) Two days later, Soviet Communist Party General Secretary Leonid Brezhnev arrived in the United States for a summit that was eclipsed by Watergate.

In late June, with Congress moving to cut off funding for U.S. bombing of Cambodia, the Nixon administration agreed to a compromise cutoff date of August 15.

On July 16, Alexander Butterfield, a former aide to H. R. Haldeman, publicly revealed the existence of Nixon's tape-recording system to the Senate Select Committee. It was a bombshell. "There's no need to volunteer anything," Kissinger grumbled. The same day, in response to a report by Dan Rather that he would replace William Rogers as secretary of state in September, Kissinger told a journalist he was not seeking the job nor particularly wanted it.

In July, when the secret bombing of Cambodia in 1969–1970 and the false-reporting system to conceal it were revealed in Senate hearings and the press, Kissinger professed ignorance of the system, said he was never involved in any discussions about how the reporting should be handled, and that his office never ordered any false reporting. But he and his military assistant at the time, Alexander Haig, had worked with an air force colonel on the false-reporting system and approved it (though Haig was involved at a more detailed level than Kissinger). Kissinger said the idea that his office ordered the air force to come up with a false-reporting system was "total nonsense" and that he never dealt directly with the air force.

Jack Anderson
June 1, 1973, 4:29 p.m.
The investigative columnist tells Kissinger that former attorney general and Nixon re-election campaign director John Mitchell told Senate Select Committee investigators that Kissinger attended a regular morning White House staff meeting where Watergate and strategy toward it were discussed. Kissinger angrily denies it, calling it an "outrageous" lie.

ANDERSON: . . . I got a memo from inside the Senate committee investigating the Watergate, and it was a summary of John Mitchell's testimony. . . . He said . . . he had attended, right after the Watergate arrests, a regular 8:30 a.m. staff meeting that discussed Watergate and what the strategy should be, and . . . he listed those attending as Haldeman, Ehrlichman, [former Nixon assistant and Nixon reelection committee deputy director Jeb] Magruder, Colson, Henry Petersen [an assistant attorney general in charge of prosecutions, who would not have been present], and yourself.

KISSINGER: Henry Petersen? Oh, he's a goddamned liar. . . . I've never attended any such meeting.

ANDERSON: Is that so? Well, maybe it was Pete Peterson.

KISSINGER: Well, Pete Peterson is even less likely. . . . I have never attended a meeting at which Watergate was discussed. Never. . . . And it's a flat, outrageous, deliberate [lie]. . . . And about this there can be no ambiguity whatsoever.

ANDERSON: . . . Did you attend any 8:30 meetings?

KISSINGER: There was a regular big White House staff meeting. . . . And it was so boring that I almost never went. Never was I at a meeting in which Watergate was discussed. . . . This is not a case of the slightest ambiguity. I never attended any meeting where Watergate was discussed. Indeed, I was told that Watergate had nothing to do with the White House so that there was nothing to discuss. I believed until April the official version. . . .

President Nixon
June 1, 1973, 7:00 p.m.
Nixon says he's going to release the names of all the people wiretapped by Bobby Kennedy when he was attorney general and asks Kissinger to plant a story on it.

NIXON: You had told me that McGeorge Bundy had the effrontery to tell you that Bobby Kennedy in that period didn't have any taps. . . . Have you heard the figures? . . . Let's get away from the bullshit. Bobby Kennedy was the greatest tapper. Three hundred in 1963—almost 300—250 in the rest. And I'm getting the names and I'm going to publish the names next Thursday. . . . And let their assholes know that they're going to get this, Henry.

KISSINGER: I think you should, absolutely.

NIXON: Because they have done us in on this thing. Now, the biggest tapper was Bobby Kennedy. Now, Johnson doesn't appear to be so big but he had the Secret Service do it. And I've ordered [Secret Service Director James] Rowley to give me the names of the Secret Service taps and I'm going to put those on it too. . . . They started it. They want to have a gut fight, they're going to get one. . . . They think they know how to fight but they've never fought anybody before. . . . Now, this is not going to go out till Monday, but leak it to somebody. Talk to one of your liberal friends and say we've got a blockbuster coming out. Now, will you do that?

KISSINGER: Certainly I can.

NIXON: You can say, look, this whole business of tapping, they have really opened it up. . . . I don't want this goddamn hypocrisy.

KISSINGER: Well, if we can get the names, Mr. President, we ought to put some of them out.

NIXON: Not some, all of them! . . . I'm going to put the whole damn list out.

KISSINGER: Well, then they'll force us to put all of ours out.

NIXON: Oh, I don't give a damn about that. Let's put ours out. We're going to force them right now if they're going to play this game. Ours will get out anyway, Henry. You understand?

KISSINGER: But what we should do, in any event, is to get this list out.

NIXON: That's what I mean, yeah. Well, we're going to do that Monday, but just let one of your liberal friends know that there's a real blockbuster coming, that the most tapping was done in the Kennedy administration, the study has shown, and the facts are going to come out. You see, Eisenhower's figures averaged about 110. . . . Bobby Kennedy's averaged 240.

KISSINGER: Humph.

NIXON: Good god! . . . Johnson was very high his first year, in '67. Then in '68 it dropped to 80. But that year, everybody knows, he had the Secret Service do the tapping because Ramsey Clark was attorney general. . . . But don't let McGeorge Bundy give you any of that bullshit anymore. . . . It just gets beyond belief.

KISSINGER: Beyond belief.

NIXON: Double standards. . . . It's going to catch some of your friends incidentally. Because I know some of the names.

KISSINGER: Well, I wouldn't be a bit unhappy.

NIXON: . . . Boy, if they want a brutal fight, they're going to get one and they're going to get it goddamn soon.

KISSINGER: Well, they've been asking for it a hell of a long time. . . .

NIXON: Be sure McGeorge Bundy knows that this is coming out. That would be a very good one. . . .

Henry Brandon
June 2, 1973, 4:25 p.m.
Brandon of the London Sunday Times *and Kissinger discuss the administration's wiretaps. Brandon, who had been wiretapped (FBI Director J. Edgar Hoover may have suggested this one—he suspected Brandon of being a British intelligence agent— though the FBI would later strongly deny that Hoover "ever originated a single one of the 17 wiretaps" and Kissinger received reports on Brandon's), advises Kissinger to "clear the air." Kissinger, who had earlier assured Brandon that he was not responsible for the tap on him (he'd also once told Brandon that he lied to every reporter*

in Washington except him), claims that he also had "nothing to do with" the wiretap on Hedrick Smith of the New York Times, *though he'd personally requested it.*[1]

KISSINGER: Luckily I have now found all my records of this period, so I can no longer be accused of the things that I was. . . . Now I know what happened on May 9th [1969] . . . when the FBI said that I instigated it. . . .

BRANDON: Yeah. Well, I would put it on the record.

KISSINGER: No, it's not worth it. Later on, when it's somewhat blown over.

BRANDON: Well, I don't know. These things sort of snowball. . . .

KISSINGER: What I said was essentially true; whether I put out documents to support it or not doesn't make any difference. . . . It just starts a whole new round of controversy. . . .

BRANDON: I think it would still a lot of uneasiness. . . . I think if you can clear the air, all the better. I mean, you've done it with me, but—yesterday on the plane, for instance, [UPI's] Helen Thomas said to me, "Would Henry Kissinger apologize to you for tapping your telephone?" I get this all the time.

KISSINGER: I know. But I've said a hundred times I didn't tap anybody's telephone. I didn't give the order, and I didn't request it.

BRANDON: Well, it's still around that you requested it. In fact, gave the names.

KISSINGER: I gave the names, as I said the other day, of some people who had worked on the documents. I can completely prove who originated what names except this newsman [Smith], which I had nothing to do with.

BRANDON: But, you see, the newsman is lumped into the same bag. . . . The case of the newsman is the one that's most objected to. . . .

KISSINGER: That I had nothing to do with at all. . . .

Stewart Alsop
June 2, 1973, 6:00 p.m.
Kissinger and columnist Alsop condemn the FBI's and prosecutors' leaks on Watergate.

. . . ALSOP: . . . One thing is perfectly clear, and that is the FBI has been leaking like mad for several months. . . . And the prosecutors in particular and the Justice Department in general has also been leaking like crazy.

KISSINGER: That's right. . . . I think it is murderously dangerous and I think the FBI must be brought under brutal control. . . . What they do with their files is unbelievable. . . . Supposing this had been done during the McCarthy period. Who could have survived? . . . And the relish with which Murrey Marder writes—it didn't turn out to be true—the NSC staff has now cracked wide open—and we can expect similar revelations out of the NSC after the wiretapping. . . . Well, my staff didn't crack wide open. . . . They can't reveal anything reflecting I think on me. On Watergate they know nothing. That was totally out of my area. . . .

Jack Anderson
June 5, 1973, 9:08 a.m.
Anderson asks about Kissinger's impetus in the formation of the White House Plumbers who went after Daniel Ellsberg and his reported desire to take control of them (which is highly unlikely). Kissinger denies knowing that the Plumbers even existed or that he was concerned that Ellsberg would release other documents (both assertions were false), or that he was overwrought over publication of the Pentagon Papers. And he claims that he thought his former assistant David Young was doing a study of declassification of government documents when he was working as a Plumber, which according to Seymour Hersh was Young's "cover story"—Kissinger knew Young was investigating leaks and still saw him sometimes during this period. (H. R. Haldeman thought John Ehrlichman's selection of Young for the Plumbers unit was "bureaucratic genius" since he knew Kissinger was prone to denying knowledge of things he helped ignite.)[2]

ANDERSON: . . . But something more serious has reached us and I wanted to catch you before you left for Paris on this, because I understand there is going to be grand jury testimony on this on Friday. One of our sources in the prosecutor's office says one of the key witnesses . . . this is one of the key figures in this Watergate—one of the names that has been in the headlines. He has told prosecutors and they are going to take his testimony on Friday . . . about your role. And what he has told them . . . is that . . . after the Pentagon Papers appeared that you had become almost hysterical and had gone to the president and had said that this could destroy our foreign policy, and that it was you who had gotten the president all fired up about this, and that it was as a result of your entreaties to the president and your expressions of grave alarm that the president went to Ehrlichman and asked him to take charge of the Plumbers, and even thereafter both you and [Assistant Attorney General Robert] Mardian sought to take control of the Plumbers—you through Young and Mardian through others, and that Ehrlichman was put in charge nevertheless. . . .

KISSINGER: First, very shortly after the Pentagon Papers were published I left on my secret trip for China and I was of course concerned that the publication of the Pentagon Papers—this massive leaking—could have disastrous consequences on the conduct of our foreign policy. . . . Secondly, I never knew about the existence of the Plumbers. . . . I didn't know, I repeat, that the Plumbers existed. Young joined Ehrlichman's staff while I was on my secret trip to China. I didn't send him there. He made this arrangement with Ehrlichman himself. The only thing that I knew that Young was doing was a classification study on which I occasionally received memoranda signed by [Tom] Latimer who is on my staff and Young and [Egil] Krogh that had to do with the declassification of government documents. I knew nothing of any of the other activities. I have searched my logs—I never talked to Young on the telephone. I never had an appointment with him. . . . Young was an Ehrlichman staff member who happened to be paid out of our funds, and I had nothing whatsoever directly or indirectly to do with his operations.

ANDERSON: Good. This business about your expressing your great alarm to the president—hysterically, it said—I can't imagine your—

KISSINGER: . . . I doubt that anyone has seen me hysterical. . . .

ANDERSON: Had Ellsberg once worked for you years ago?

KISSINGER: Yes, Ellsberg was a student of mine and in the very early stage of the administration he participated in a review of Vietnam policy with me.

ANDERSON: Did that have anything to do with your concern?

KISSINGER: No.

ANDERSON: Did you feel that he might be giving out things?

KISSINGER: No. He didn't have any access to any inside information. This was an analytical study. I had no vendetta against Ellsberg. . . . It is a malicious lie to say that I tried to take control of the Plumbers through Young when I didn't know a bloody thing about the Plumbers. . . . See, you have two problems. You have the problem, was there a serious situation? About that there is no question. But does that justify extracurricular measures? . . . Or extralegal methods. . . . I believe one should operate within the legal framework. . . .

President Nixon
June 10, 1973, 11:05 a.m.
Uncertain of Nixon's political situation and authority amid Watergate, the Soviets had been wavering about Leonid Brezhnev's schedule and stops during the forthcoming summit in the United States.[3] Kissinger reassures Nixon that the summit was in good shape and disparages his critics as "bastard traitors."

KISSINGER: I just got off the phone with Dobrynin, and he said that this is one of these Moscow things. . . .

NIXON: Well, he didn't say that it was the lack of confidence in him or anything like that, did he?

KISSINGER: Mr. President, there is no lack of confidence in you whatsoever. . . . He's got seven agreements ready to be signed.

NIXON: Well, how does Dobrynin sound about the meeting? Is he still for it?

KISSINGER: Totally. We have the SALT principles all agreed.

NIXON: Is Brezhnev looking forward to it?

KISSINGER: Enormously, Mr. President. The problem is . . . these bastard traitors we have in this country. . . .

NIXON: Don't let this harping discourage you, Henry. . . .

KISSINGER: Mr. President, you and I have been through a lot of things together. It's always the same things and these bastards are now trying to deprive you of any success. . . .

NIXON: The real problem is this. They're trying to fight over all the things we beat them on. We beat them on China, we beat them on Russia, we beat them on the war, and they said that none of those things would work, Henry, and they all worked and now they are dying.

KISSINGER: It has not a thing to do with Watergate. Watergate just enables them to do those things they would have done anyway.

NIXON: . . . They've tried to knock everything we've done, but we've had an enormously successful policy.

KISSINGER: Mr. President, it will be a success. We have all the agreements done. . . .

NIXON: What I was concerned about in view of your earlier statement [is] that maybe the Russians were thinking about not coming at all.

KISSINGER: Oh, no. That's 1,000 percent. . . . There is nothing to be concerned about. Every document that needs to be signed is agreed to word for word. . . .

NIXON: These people—it is traitorous, isn't it? You've said that often before in that Oval Office. . . . Well, I'm not considering resignation, but taking their arguments at its best: Nixon and Agnew should resign and the Congress should name a president. It's unbelievable.

KISSINGER: Mr. President, a resignation will be a national catastrophe.

NIXON: It's never going to come.

KISSINGER: It would take a new president 20 months to get the feel of things and other countries to feel him, and by that time there'd be an election. It is out of the question.

NIXON: Oh, absolutely. It's a catastrophe—not only internationally, but domestically. It has such a shocking impact on the people. . . . Oh, for crying out loud, when Harry Truman was 20 percent to 23 percent in the polls, he was still pulling off Marshall Plans, and that's what we're in for.

KISSINGER: Mr. President, you can go down in history as a man who brought about the greatest revolution in American foreign policy ever.

NIXON: We have already. . . .

Robert Evans
June 11, 1973, late afternoon
Kissinger asks his friend Robert Evans of Paramount Pictures to get some western movies for Brezhnev to entertain himself during the summit.

KISSINGER: . . . Brezhnev likes cowboy movies—you follow me?

EVANS: Right. You need a good cowboy movie?

KISSINGER: We need some cowboy movies, but are there any with Russian subtitles? . . . Or can they be subtitled in a week—one or two movies? . . . We've got him there for two days next weekend. And the guy's crazy about cowboy movies. . . .

Frank Yablans
June 11, 1973, 5:15 p.m.
Paramount's president phones to work out the options.

KISSINGER: . . . We have Brezhnev in Camp David over the weekend and he's a nut on cowboy movies and I've got some cowboy movies but now I've found out he doesn't speak a word of English.

YABLANS: How about Hebrew?

KISSINGER: Hebrew I think he would love, particularly given the Russian fondness with Jews.

YABLANS: It has to be western? I have some—first of all, we don't subtitle Russian, we dub them.

KISSINGER: That's even better. What do you have?

YABLANS: I have *Romeo and Juliet.* . . . I have *Roman Holiday* with Audrey Hepburn. . . .

KISSINGER: Why don't you let me have those.

YABLANS: I'll tell you what, I think I have four films in Russian. . . . They are pictures that the Russians bought for distribution, so apparently it appeals to their taste. . . . And I'll have those sent up to you. . . . Also I'm going to try to subtitle *True Grit,* which is the John Wayne western. . . .

Alexander Haig
June 11, 1973, 7:35 p.m.
White House Chief of Staff Haig suggests appointing the nuclear physicist Edward Teller, one of the fathers of the H-bomb, "energy czar."

HAIG: Henry, we were just talking about, you know, Edward Teller would like very much to come in and join the administration in some function. . . . What do you think about making him energy czar?

KISSINGER: That's a goddamned interesting idea. . . . He'd tear up the pea patch, which is good.

HAIG: Damn right.

KISSINGER: You know, you'd get unbelievable flak for a while, but so what?

HAIG: Hell, you know, in energy, it's all peaceful use.

KISSINGER: Oh, yeah, I think it's a spectacular idea. He'd be imaginative. . . . I mean, he'd do the research, the programs—

HAIG: Strong on research development and—

KISSINGER: I think it's damned imaginative. . . .

Earl Butz

June 24, 1973, 11:32 a.m.

Kissinger speaks with Secretary of Agriculture Butz about a possible grain deal with the Soviet Union. He wants it kept secret, probably because a huge, heavily subsidized grain deal with the Soviets in 1972 led to a spike in U.S. and global prices for grain that hurt American consumers and was widely panned (the Soviets got the grain at bargain prices and a few big U.S. grain companies reaped windfall profits), and because word of the deal could itself send prices upward.[4] Butz questions the deal.

KISSINGER: Look, the Soviets yesterday, when they were talking to us, offered to conclude a five-year deal starting when this present one is finished, for the purchase of five million tons annually of grain. . . . Now, could you let me know soonest, one, what you think of this. Second, what this will do to our ability to sell grain to other countries in that period. Like the Chinese. Thirdly . . . how vulnerable it makes us domestically. . . . I need this to be kept secret.

BUTZ: That's right. . . . But I don't see what they give us in return for our guarantee to make this available. . . . If we guarantee to make a minimum of five million tons annually to them, they must have some concession they are making to us. . . . I know one of the things we'd like to get, of course, is more information out of the Soviet Union on their crop condition. . . . And I should think that if we are going to supply them a minimum like this we ought to be able to know if they will exceed it or not. This is one of our worries now, Henry, is that we are overcommitting ourselves for sales in the next 12 months beyond the physical quantities we will have available. . . . I wrote you a memo just the other day . . . about a conference we had with Huang Chen, the Chinese ambassador here. . . . And he was very frank about their need for grain.

KISSINGER: Yeah, but that is one of the things I would like to know. What is the impact of this on other countries? . . . And then we will probably opt for not doing it now. But since Brezhnev appealed to the president directly and personally asked for a decision, we can't just flick it off. . . . And will you make sure there is absolute secrecy?

BUTZ: I certainly will. . . .

President Nixon
June 24, 1973, 5:20 p.m.
Kissinger tells Nixon that both Butz and Treasury Secretary George Shultz (who'd warned about the "great stress on our food supply" from the grain deal) now think it is a great deal. And they believe the Soviet summit was a success despite being stuck with Brezhnev for an eternity. (It was basically "a bust.")[5]

KISSINGER: On the grain thing, Mr. President, I have talked to Shultz and Butz. Both of them think it is an extremely good deal; they have a few nitpicks on the letter that they would like to change; their only recommendation is not to announce it now. . . . Butz, who at first when I told him orally was making all the noises that covered himself with the *Washington Post*—you know, what are we getting for it?—is now enthusiastic for it—you know, they are paying cash, there is no credit—

NIXON: . . . The effort, for crying out loud, of the *Post* and others pissing on the other grain deal was ridiculous. That was a good deal.

KISSINGER: Of course it was a good deal. . . . And they are paying market prices for it [the grain this time]. . . . It's a first-rate deal all the way around. . . . I think it was an outstanding week, Mr. President.

NIXON: Ahhhh, it better be. For what we put into it—I mean, six meals with this guy was about enough to break anybody.

KISSINGER: [Laughs.] Yeah, that is the truth.

NIXON: Every night for six nights.

KISSINGER: That is true, Mr. President, and the sort of unrelenting pressure he puts on you. . . . But I think it was worth it, Mr. President.

NIXON: Of course. . . . Not only in terms of what the agreements were, but worth it in terms of what we found out with regard to their motives.

KISSINGER: Exactly.

NIXON: They were very frank talks.

KISSINGER: Which we could have found out in no other way.

NIXON: No way. . . .

Melvin Laird
June 26, 1973, 1:32 p.m.
The Senate had voted on June 14 in favor of cutting off funding for the bombing of Cambodia, and the House had now voted to extend a proposed cutoff of funding.[6]

LAIRD: . . . This is all going to be tied up in the context of Watergate. That's the problem with this damn thing the way it's going. . . .

KISSINGER: I just don't see how we can handle it. Everything is just going to come apart in Cambodia if we stop bombing. . . .

LAIRD: . . . It'll be a tough four weeks. . . . I mean, you're going to have Mitchell and Haldeman and Ehrlichman [testifying before the Senate Select Committee]. These guys aren't going to be a standup as a lot of people think they are, you know.

KISSINGER: Certainly not Mitchell and Ehrlichman. . . .

LAIRD: Yeah. You know, when they're facing the penitentiary. . . .

KISSINGER: Yeah, although they're not helping themselves. It doesn't do them any good to dump it on the president. It doesn't make them any less culpable.

LAIRD: No. . . . The problem that we have now, Henry, is that if it's absolutely essential for Cambodia, I think the best you can get is from 30 to 45 days [of more bombing].

KISSINGER: Thirty is almost useless; 45 could help. . . . We really have to think about whether we are not better off saying these sons of bitches just are responsible for the defeat. . . .

Carlyle Maw
June 27, 1973, 9:15 a.m.
Kissinger claims he never met or spoke with John Dean to legal adviser Maw.

. . . KISSINGER: Just been watching Mr. Dean on television. I don't think you'd hire him for your law firm, would you?

MAW: I should say not. . . . There is something awful funny.

KISSINGER: I never knew him, thank god.

MAW: Did you ever meet him at all?

KISSINGER: The amazing thing is I would get memos—legal memos from his office—and then I'd see this young guy run around the halls and I never put the name and the face together. I always thought that the counsel to the president had to be a senior guy. So I never thought that this young guy could be the John Dean who was sending me memos. . . . So I don't recall any meeting I have had with him. He may have sat in large meetings where he didn't say anything. But if I had to testify I would have to say I never talked to him. I have no recollection to any conversation with him.

MAW: That's good. He is not one to have dealings with. . . .

Taft Schreiber
June 28, 1973, 11:35 a.m.

MCA executive Schreiber and Kissinger discuss a potential position for Kissinger with MCA, an entertainment conglomerate, that its head, Lew Wasserman, was keen about.

> . . . SCHREIBER: Number two, Wasserman called and said . . . "You talk to Henry again? . . . Any more been said?" And I said, "I think we are on a time schedule and he would get back to us." So he said to me then, "I hear he is making a deal with an oil group." And I said, "I don't know—I don't think there is any glamour in that." Just wanted to tell you he bugs me all the time.
>
> KISSINGER: No, no, I'm not talking to anybody else; because of this Watergate thing I didn't think I could resign right now. . . . I thought that I should wait until this thing has quieted down before I go back to my original scheme.
>
> SCHREIBER: All right. Let me just say again that (a) that it should quiet down in due course and (b) the appetite is greater. . . .

Melvin Laird
June 28, 1973, evening

Kissinger complains to Nixon counsel Laird about the move in Congress to cut off the bombing of Cambodia; Laird was recommending a compromise whereby Nixon would agree to a cutoff by August 15 (which was done). They also bemoan a counterattack on John Dean by Nixon's Watergate counsel Fred Buzhardt, who'd sent a memo to the Senate Select Committee that placed much of the blame for Watergate on Mitchell and called Dean "the principal actor in the Watergate cover-up."[7]

> . . . KISSINGER: You know, it's almost beyond my comprehension, Mel, they're going to throw everything down the drain for nothing. . . . This is one of the most vindictive, cheap actions that I've seen the Congress take. And it's not just in Cambodia, it's going to hurt us murderously with the Chinese, because if they think that the Congress can do these things to us in Cambodia, what are they going to do to us elsewhere?
>
> LAIRD: The only problem is now, Henry, right now we've got no authority. We've got to get some authority.
>
> KISSINGER: That's right. . . . A few more memos out of the White House and we won't have any left.
>
> LAIRD: God, I wish people would keep cool on that thing for a while.
>
> KISSINGER: Well, did you know that they were sending out that memo?
>
> LAIRD: I knew that they were told to start attacking.
>
> KISSINGER: Oh, it's just too goddamn stupid. You don't attack when Dean is on the stand.

LAIRD: I understand that, Henry. Christ, I told that to Al [Haig]. I said, Al, you're making a mistake. Keep cool.

KISSINGER: That's right. I would have left this week to him. We shouldn't attack until all this testimony is out.

LAIRD: Right, and then you can have a press conference and do something, but wait till you're through with this thing.

KISSINGER: That's what I think. That just gives some ammunition to hit us.

LAIRD: Boy, I tell you . . . we've got to get together once in a while, Henry. This gets to be kind of a weird operation as far as I'm concerned.

KISSINGER: Look, Mel, you and Al and I when we're in the same town must get together. This is absurd. . . . If we let them play this game again we're going to have the same bloody nightmares as before. As I understand it, Haig refused it and then he [Buzhardt] went through Ziegler—that cannot be. . . . And as soon as other countries recognize how little authority there is left here we are just going to be in murderous difficulty. And we can't afford these stupid mistakes anymore.

LAIRD: I called Haig, you know, about this. I guess I should have called the president. But I understood that he was the one that was very much concerned and wanted something done. . . .

KISSINGER: The president always wants something done and we got into this mess because people reacted.

LAIRD: You can't overreact all the time, though. . . .

William F. Buckley
June 29, 1973, 9:10 a.m.
Kissinger and the conservative commentator bewail Watergate, and Kissinger takes issue with a mention in Buckley's National Review *of the lawsuit former NSC staffer Morton Halperin filed against Kissinger and others for wiretapping his phone. Kissinger claims that not only was the wiretapping legal but that he didn't order the tap on Halperin (which he had requested), and that it was "done on his own by J. Edgar Hoover" (an absurd assertion).*[8]

. . . KISSINGER: But I think the reaction of the opponents is even more revolting than the tawdry behavior of my ex-colleagues. . . . You know, to dismantle the country . . . because of what was a collection of petty crimes, unworthy and everything else, but still this is a dramatic dismantling of our foreign policy. . . . They know damn well we are in the process of negotiating the end of Cambodia.

BUCKLEY: That to me is truly shameful. And the remarkable thing is the total collapse of the Senate. It is absolutely corrupt. . . .

KISSINGER: And if this thing comes apart now we're going to have the Chinese move far left. . . . We'll have a bellicose Soviet policy and no public opinion to deal with it.

BUCKLEY: Yeah. . . . I wish the guy in charge had a better means of communicating this kind of thing to the American people, but unfortunately there is in our recent history a self-serving communication. . . .

KISSINGER: I know. But you know history is going to have a hell of a time explaining how it all happened. . . . And, for what? What I called you about yesterday was a relatively minor thing, which just shows you how attentively I read the *National Review*. Mentioning Halperin, it said that he is suing me for illegally wiretapping him and that he can stand to gain 75,000 dollars. . . . First of all, the wiretapping was perfectly legal when it was done, and it was authorized by the attorney general, recommended by the director of the FBI, and approved by the president. And in the fourth month in a law-and-order administration it wouldn't occur to anyone that this could be illegal.

BUCKLEY: Well, did your lawyers tell you that you can get the case thrown out of court?

KISSINGER: Yes. . . . But they printed it as if the illegality was a fact, that he is suing me for illegally wiretapping him. . . . But the process was declared illegal only in 1972—

BUCKLEY: After the fact.

KISSINGER: Yeah. Even then it wasn't applied to national security things. . . . Secondly, I can prove . . . that I didn't order the wiretapping of Halperin— that this was done on his own by J. Edgar Hoover because he had evidence that the man was a security risk.

BUCKLEY: Well, have you answered yet?

KISSINGER: No, I will not answer. . . .

BUCKLEY: I'll get that straightened out, Doc. . . .

Leonard Garment
June 29, 1973, 9:18 a.m.
Kissinger asks Nixon counsel Garment why the White House put out Fred Buzhardt's memo pinning the Watergate cover-up mainly on John Dean.

. . . KISSINGER: Well, why did we put out that statement the other day?

GARMENT: It's a long and complicated story. One of those things that happen when there is not good working morale and no real line of command.

KISSINGER: . . . To put it out while the guy is on the stand is nuts.

GARMENT: It wasn't put out. It was delivered in a rather haphazard fashion by Fred Buzhardt without appropriate [oversight]. . . . This has become an exercise in super-secrecy and it is very complicated. . . . People who are being secretive when they don't need to be. And so there are bungles. . . . And we're having more of the Colson [attack] madness so that the atmosphere is getting rancid once again. . . .

KISSINGER: You think we're going to make it?

GARMENT: Well, I think we could if there were better communication among ourselves. It's going to be a very difficult time. . . .

Taft Schreiber
June 29, 1973, 3:17 p.m.
Schreiber, a big Nixon fundraiser, and Kissinger object to testimony at the Senate Select Committee hearings on Watergate and to calls for impeachment.

. . . SCHREIBER: . . . One thing I am concerned about—I heard more testimony today and I feel so badly for the president for the things—the hearsay—the kind of things that they're saying and—

KISSINGER: It's unbelievable!

SCHREIBER: It's unbelievable and . . . I hope he keeps his courage up because the Democrats are having a field day. They're setting the stage for an attempt to impeach.

KISSINGER: That's one of the filthiest things that I've ever seen.

SCHREIBER: Yeah, it's immoral. . . .

Irving Lazar
July 2, 1973, 12:48 p.m.
Kissinger asks Hollywood agent Lazar, who Schreiber had earlier warned Kissinger was a "terrible" person, what kind of advance he might get for his memoir, given that he might be resigning. Lazar had earlier dangled $3 million.

KISSINGER: I just wanted to ask you one question. Since after these hearings are over I'll want to make some decisions.

LAZAR: You want to make a decision?

KISSINGER: I have to consider my situation. And I wondered from your knowledge of the situation, do you think that the sort of thing we were talking about is still feasible in the same range?

LAZAR: Just a little better, that's all. . . . I was conservative from the beginning as I usually am in order not to be in a position of embarrassment. I can only tell you it's the same, if not better—your position is the same if not better than it ever was. No question about it. I have never told you as much as I could have because you didn't want to hear it, which is fine. But I can only tell you that from my analysis and also from my rather conservative and most delicate inquiry, in just listening and not talking, it is my conviction that everything I told you is absolutely the case, if not better.

KISSINGER: Despite Watergate?

LAZAR: Oh, Watergate has nothing to do with it. If anything it enhances the potential of the enterprise many-fold because of reasons I'll discuss with you when I see you. . . . I assure you—this is not off the top of my head, I've thought about it many times—I can only tell you that, in the first place, if it does anything it enhances the project. And everything I've told you I've never pursued in accordance precisely with your directions to do no more than listen, and in my listening I've come to the conclusion that it [his estimate of the advance] was always conservative and fair and [I] will not be embarrassed when the chips are down. Which means a lot to me.

KISSINGER: Well, that I won't hold you to. I just wanted to get a rough estimate.

LAZAR: You haven't got a rough one. You've got a clear-cut—

KISSINGER: Right. Because some basic decisions of mine will be somewhat—

LAZAR: It is a clear-cut response to what you've asked me. . . . And the only reason I never talk to you about anything—

KISSINGER: No, I don't want you to. . . . And the only reason I asked you this was because I'll have to do some thinking when these hearings are over.

LAZAR: Okay, that's marvelous. . . .

President Nixon
July 4, 1973, 11:00 a.m.
On June 29, rogue elements of the Chilean army made a failed coup attempt against President Salvador Allende, which Kissinger had reported to Nixon was "an isolated and poorly coordinated effort." But Allende still had "massive problems," he says, and Nixon thinks the army may try again. They also take up the ITT scandal. (It had collaborated with the CIA to undermine Allende.)[9] They agree that then–CIA Director Richard Helms and Ambassador Edward Korry "screwed up" their efforts to prevent Allende from taking office.

NIXON: . . . I think that Chilean guy may have some problems.

KISSINGER: Oh, he has massive problems. . . .

NIXON: If only the army could get a few people behind them.

KISSINGER: And that coup last week—we had nothing to do with it but still it came off apparently prematurely.

NIXON: That's right, and the fact that he just set up a cabinet without any military in it is, I think, very significant.

KISSINGER: It's very significant.

NIXON: Very significant because those military guys are very proud down there, and they just may—right?

KISSINGER: Yes, I think he's definitely in difficulties.

NIXON: Well, we won't have to send the ITT down to help, will we?

KISSINGER: [Laughs.] That's another one of these absurdities. Because whenever the ITT came to us we turned them off. I mean, we never did anything for them. . . . I listened to them and said thank you very much and that was that.

NIXON: Frankly, you know, we left it to Helms, and he and the ambassador and so forth, they screwed it up.

KISSINGER: Exactly. It's the ambassador who screwed it up. . . . In '64 they put $2 million behind [Eduardo] Frei. In that [1970] election they had altogether $400,000 which they split evenly among the opposing parties.

NIXON: That's a disaster.

KISSINGER: So it didn't do any good. . . .

President Nixon
July 13, 1973, 12:39 p.m.
Nixon, calling from the hospital, says he heard that Kissinger's liberal friends applauded when they learned he had viral pneumonia.

. . . NIXON: Well, I had a rough night last night, but today, due to very heavy sedation and other things, I am feeling much better. . . . I will have to stay here at least five days, maybe six; if complications set in it could be worse. . . . Al told me your Georgetown crowd clapped when you told them the news last night.

KISSINGER: No, they were really quite concerned. . . . They have been hacking away at the president for months and now anyone who has talked to me has expressed deep concern in the last days. . . . And the decent people in this country need something. . . .

Dan Rather
July 13, 1973, 5:57 p.m.
The CBS News *correspondent asks about a report that Kissinger would replace William Rogers as secretary of state in September.*

RATHER: I am told by someone who has been very good to me over the years, which is to say who has seldom if ever been wrong, that in September you would become secretary of state and Secretary Rogers would go on to do other things. The question is whether that is true.

KISSINGER: If that is true, I have never heard of it. . . . Since I respect you greatly, I don't want to mislead you. It is not inconceivable to me that the president will make changes in the administration when he judges Watergate has reached a certain point. . . . All I can say is that the president has not discussed that with me. . . . You have to judge your other source.

RATHER: Right, but that is helpful. Frankly, the other source is such that I have every confidence that it is not something that he dreamed up, that much I know. It is entirely possible that he may have even talked to the president about it, although I doubt that. But it is conceivable that what he saw were tentative plans.

KISSINGER: That could be and it wouldn't be uncharacteristic for the president not to discuss matters like this until he has made his final decision. If anybody other than you called me, quite seriously, Dan, I would flatly deny it. . . .

President Nixon
July 14, 1973, 1:05 p.m.
Nixon, who was still in the hospital with pneumonia, complains about Senate Select Committee chairman Sam Ervin, and they consider his condition.

NIXON: Actually, look, Ervin and his bunch . . . are now becoming so violently partisan. . . . I can hit them harder, and I will, and I'm not going to lay back and take this. The second point is this silly letter of his suggesting that we meet. Of course, coming to the hospital was only coincidental, but that drives them right up the wall because they know very well I can't meet them for a week. . . . Apparently it was very acute, more acute than I had realized. . . . There is a very heavy fatigue factor which sets in; you are just very, very weak. . . . I have no reading—I just haven't got interest in it, so I'm just doing the minimum—laying around, which is hard to do, but as a matter of fact it may be a blessing in a way just to get the mind turned off for the week. I haven't had my mind turned off for a week for years. . . .

KISSINGER: You have been under this unbelievable tortuous pressure for the last few months. . . . It forces you to rest, and I really think we can get so much momentum in August and September that when these hearings resume it will be in a totally different climate. . . .

John Osborne
July 16, 1973, 2:45 p.m.
Osborne of The New Republic *asks about Dan Rather's report that Kissinger would become secretary of state in September. "I don't want the job particularly," Kissinger says.*

OSBORNE: Doctor, the State Department business. . . .

KISSINGER: . . . Look, you've been around long enough to know that this is not a thought that in this present situation he could not have considered. . . . I can tell you my own personal view is it is not a position which in itself I would have wanted. It is not a position that in itself I would even have considered accepting three months ago. . . . What I find so astonishing is that in this town the business of power is so all-consuming, and status— why would anyone want it right now? What the hell difference does it make what title anyone has? Up to now I've been able to get the things done that needed to get done from my present position. . . . It's not a position I'm seeking, that I can tell you now. . . . I don't want the job particularly. . . .

Peter Flanigan
July 16, 1973, 2:55 p.m.
Former Haldeman aide Alexander Butterfield had just revealed the existence of Nixon's tape-recording system in testimony before the Senate Select Committee, shocking Nixon. Kissinger, who advocated destroying the tapes, apprises Nixon assistant Flanigan.[10]

. . . KISSINGER: Alex Butterfield has just gone on national television saying that the president had every office he owned bugged. . . . All these sons of bitches who were counting how many times you mention the president in a press conference . . . are now volunteering information. There's no need to volunteer anything.

FLANIGAN: Unbelievable. I must say I thought Maurice Stans [former finance chairman of Nixon's reelection committee] and John Mitchell at least stood up.

KISSINGER: They were men. . . . Maurice Stans and Mitchell may have done wrong things, but they were at least true to themselves. But those bastards. Those guys when I gave a press conference would call me afterwards and say you mentioned the president only eight times, and in our judgment in a half an hour you should mention him 23 times.

FLANIGAN: . . . But Alex—I would have thought as an old military man he would have had a different approach to life. . . .

Dan Rather
July 16, 1973, 4:07 p.m.
Kissinger asks Rather about his source for his story that he would be appointed secretary of state.

KISSINGER: Dan, could I ask you something which I know you are very reluctant to do? . . . That story which you launched on Friday night—let me tell you quite candidly, I'm being accused of having launched this myself. . . . Can by any plausible stretch the source that gave it to you be called a friend of mine? I mean, somebody who would have an interest in promoting me?

RATHER: On the contrary. . . . Quite frankly, it's only my respect for you that leads me to go that far.

KISSINGER: Dan, I don't want you to tell me any more. . . .

Anatoly Dobrynin
July 16, 1973, 6:05 p.m.
Kissinger suggests that reports on his appointment to secretary of state have been put out by Rogers.

. . . KISSINGER: Well, you think I have an interest in putting out these stories?

DOBRYNIN: No, why should you? I think on the contrary, really.

KISSINGER: The opposite. . . . I think these stories are not put out by my friends.

DOBRYNIN: But why really is there such a sudden interest at this particular junction?

KISSINGER: Because it is conceivable that people who are in danger of being moved might put it out in order to avoid its happening. . . .

Seymour Hersh
July 17, 1973, 12:22 p.m.
Hersh of the New York Times *calls for a story on the administration's secret bombing of Cambodia, including the falsification of records on it. He says sympathetically that the bombing was justifiable, that even if Kissinger's military assistant at the time, Alexander Haig, conceived the instructions for falsifying the records, "that doesn't mean you had to know about it," and "there is a time for false reporting. . . . Nobody's suggesting anything wrong." Kissinger pleads ignorance of the falsification of the records. In fact, the false-reporting system, which violated federal military law, had been devised because of his and Nixon's repeated insistence on conducting the bombing secretly, and he and Haig (particularly Haig) worked with an air force colonel, Ray Sitton, on it and approved it.*[11]

HERSH: . . . There's no question that there was enough justification to bomb Cambodia, given [Cambodian leader Norodom] Sihanouk's cooperation [with the bombing] and the [enemy] buildup and also the fact that all the bombing was kept in to a very rigorously centered area. The only issue it seems to me in the whole issue of the Cambodian bombing in '69 and '70 is the falsification of records. . . . Well, listen, this person I talked with last night was in the government over in the JCS then . . . and the way he described the situation is . . . that the operation was conceived or the falsification of the operations were conceived in the National Security Council. He mentioned specifically Mr. Haig, and he says the reasons for it were quite good. . . . But the point is there was some means to set up a special reporting procedure just simply to prevent any and all leaks that could be embarrassing internationally. . . . It seems to me . . . if the air force was ordered to falsify documents as he alleges . . . it was done across the river over in the White House over in the National Security Council, at least the impetus for the program came [from] there. . . .

KISSINGER: Look, I made the mistake when these FBI wiretaps surfaced of talking on the basis of my recollection, and you know all these things happened four years ago. . . . So let me talk on an off-the-record basis. . . . One, if we're speaking about myself I don't know anything about the goddamned reporting system. So I wouldn't even know how to give an order to falsify it if I wanted to. . . . I never heard a discussion about how the reporting should be handled. I know we put great pressure on them to keep the thing secret for diplomatic reasons, but it seems to me almost out of the question that we told them how to report this thing. Our concern was not to have false reports; our concern was to keep the secrecy, and therefore it seems to me that this information you have is almost certainly wrong. . . .

HERSH: Now let me tell you exactly what the information is. It's a very emphatic that . . . the instructions for setting up the procedure were not conceived by any military officer. They were conceived by a civilian officer. . . .

KISSINGER: Yeah, but look, that's inconceivable to me. . . . If my life depended on it, I couldn't tell you how the reporting is done. . . . As I recall it, our pressures were to keep the thing secret but not to specify how that was to be achieved. . . . Incidentally, let me say one other thing. . . . There is no such thing as Haig doing it on his own.

HERSH: Of course not, but that doesn't mean you had to know about it. . . . The problem of course is the obvious one that, you know, in talking to military men there are ethical questions raised. You know, there is a time for false reporting; obviously it has a role.

KISSINGER: The first time I heard of false reporting was in a Monday newspaper. . . .

HERSH: Okay, I accept that.

KISSINGER: How they kept the information secured, that I just didn't look into, but that didn't in my mind presuppose false reporting. In my mind, it presupposes that only a tiny number of people knew about it. . . . That is my conception of how you keep things secret.

HERSH: . . . You know, nobody's suggesting anything wrong, but there should be some action taken to find out just who did.

KISSINGER: . . . That's right, I am looking into this. I have not been aware previously of any false reporting. . . . I just don't believe there was any order to [engage in] falsification out of the White House. . . .

Alexander Haig
July 17, 1973, 4:12 p.m.
Kissinger tells Haig about Hersh's call in order to get their story in order.

KISSINGER: This is not your biggest problem, but Seymour Hersh called and said he has received a call from the JCS who said the call [on devising the false-reporting system] came from civilian authorities, and they thought it was from you. I said, first, we were responsible for everything in this office, then that we didn't know ourselves, thirdly, that we didn't tell them what to report. Did we ever tell them how they should do their report?

HAIG: Hell, no.

KISSINGER: That is what I said.

HAIG: That is utter bullshit. Why should we even talk to them about that? Why should we even tell Seymour Hersh anything?

KISSINGER: Well, you can take that attitude, but I can't. I knew about the operation. Well, anyway, if he calls you, at least you know what he wants.

HAIG: Well, from the Department of Defense down we didn't know anything.

KISSINGER: I didn't say that, only that we [didn't know] the reporting procedure. . . .

Jess Cook
July 19, 1973, 12:50 p.m.
Time magazine correspondent Jess Cook asks about the secret Cambodia bombing. Kissinger says the notion that his office ordered the air force to come up with a false-reporting system is "total nonsense" and denies his and Haig's dealings on it with Colonel Ray Sitton.

COOK: I'm given to understand by some sources that the orders or instructions for the changing of the reports on the Cambodian bombing and falsifying and secrecy and so forth came from you.

KISSINGER: Total nonsense.

COOK: Well, the way this story goes, Laird and Wheeler—their denials are accurate and that it was the White House dealing directly with the air force.

KISSINGER: That is total nonsense. What do you mean?

COOK: Well, I mean that the instructions went directly to the air force.

KISSINGER: That is simply not true. . . . First of all, we don't know anything about the reporting system here. We wouldn't know how the air force does any reporting. Our instructions to Laird were to keep the information to as restricted channels as necessary—as possible. How they reported, I to this day don't know. . . . How the hell would we know enough about the reporting system in the air force to order anything like this? . . .

COOK: Well, didn't you on some occasions deal directly with the services?

KISSINGER: I cannot think of a single occasion when I did it. I've dealt with General Wheeler, but I've never gone below General Wheeler.

COOK: Well, how about Haig for you?

KISSINGER: You'd have to check with him, but to my almost certain knowledge he neither. . . . I've asked him the question whether we gave any instructions to anybody on the how to report, and to that the answer is no.

COOK: So you think it was a purely air force operation?

KISSINGER: I will not speculate on how it was done. I am saying that we did not issue orders from here, that we dealt with Laird and Wheeler on that operation, and that our participation consisted of approving the operation and asking that the operation, for diplomatic reasons, that the knowledge be confined to the minimum number of people. The nature of the reporting was not ascribed from us, nor did we even know how the reporting was handled. . . . We have never talked to the air force about this, and in any case, the chain of command didn't go through the air force, unless I am totally mistaken. I think the chain of command went from Wheeler to Abrams. The B-52s were under Abrams. . . . You know, we're dealing here with a situation where anybody can say anything. . . .

Seymour Hersh
July 19, 1973, 4:42 p.m.
Hersh asks Kissinger if he wants to go on the record with his previous denial of involvement in the false-reporting system.

HERSH: . . . What I wanted to do was to be able to if I could put your off-the-record disavowal of any falsification, which the Pentagon now says came out of the Strategic Air Command, on the record. . . .

KISSINGER: You can say that the White House neither ordered nor was it aware of any falsification of records. . . .

HERSH: And do you have any opinion . . . in general on falsification of documents?

KISSINGER: I think it is intolerable.

HERSH: Why is it intolerable? There are arguments that it is justifiable. . . .

KISSINGER: Look, I don't want to get into that. . . . I haven't the foggiest idea
of how they report these things. . . .

HERSH: Al Haig said it the best—he said, "Are you trying to tell me . . . that I
know what some major in Bien Hoa is doing or Henry knows what some
major in Bien Hoa is doing?"

KISSINGER: No, that is right. What we did was to tell Wheeler and Laird the
president wants this kept as secret as possible and as tightly as possible and
let's be confined to the minimum necessary number of people. What Laird
and Wheeler did to effect this, we don't know. . . .

Leonard Garment
July 20, 1973, 6:15 p.m.
*Kissinger objects to Senator Lowell Weicker's repeated use of the term "the Kissinger
tapes" to describe the administration's wiretaps in Senate Select Committee hearings.*

KISSINGER: Len, I've got here the transcript of the Mardian cross-examination
by Weicker and . . . Weicker keeps referring to the Kissinger tapes.

GARMENT: Yeah, that's the one thing I heard is that reference to Kissinger
tapes.

KISSINGER: And, you know, in itself there's nothing incriminating about it.

GARMENT: So what do you want me to do about it?

KISSINGER: But can one protest?

GARMENT: No, worst thing to do.

KISSINGER: But how can that son of a bitch call it the Kissinger tapes?

GARMENT: Because he's a son of a bitch.

KISSINGER: But why?

GARMENT: Because it's dramatic. . . . You know, he's coined a phrase. . . . Now
they'll be called the Kissinger tapes. . . .

KISSINGER: But why should one let him get away with it?

GARMENT: Well, what are your choices? One can let it ride or one can inflame
it into a major national issue by saying it's unfair and unjust and improper. . . .
I rather think it's pointless. It's a little bit like suing a newspaper for a libel
when the damage is really not that significant. You blow it up enormously. . . .
I really don't think there's much to be gained. . . .

KISSINGER: Except to shoot across their bow. Well, I'll wait. . . . He's bound to
come back to it.

GARMENT: Yeah, he'll come back to it, and I think at a certain point in calm-
ness and coolness rather than in anger something can be said that will be
effective, and probably by belittling—he's such a self-righteous prick. . . .

Lloyd Norman
July 26, 1973, 7:20 p.m.
Kissinger loses his patience with a Newsweek *reporter who asks him about the "cover-up" of the secret Cambodia bombing.*

NORMAN: . . . In talking to the people at the Pentagon . . . the cover-up of the B-52 raids on Cambodia was ordered by Dr. Kissinger.

KISSINGER: Cover-up? What do you mean, it wasn't a cover-up. Oh, well, I have given up on *Newsweek*. . . . The president ordered it and I acquiesced and it was decided by the National Security Council to do this. . . . You can write what you want—I don't give a damn. If *Newsweek* wants to turn everything into a conspiracy, they can do it. . . . That a cover-up was ordered by Kissinger is bullshit. . . . This will sound like Watergate. . . .

The Safire Wiretap and Safire's Angry Crusade; Nixon's Watergate Speech and Statement; Senate Hearings and Pentagon Releases on the Secret Cambodia Bombing; Legal Pleadings on the Halperin Wiretap; Nixon's Press Conference on Kissinger's Nomination as Secretary of State; Kissinger's Confirmation Hearings and the Wiretap Problem; Kissinger as Wiretap Victim?; the Coup Against Allende; and the Joe Kraft Wiretap

August–September 1973

In August 1973, William Safire, a former Nixon speechwriter who had been wiretapped and was now a columnist at the *New York Times*, arranged for a *Times* reporter to confront Kissinger about the wiretap, with Safire on another phone line. Kissinger maintained that he had no knowledge of it. Kissinger told Safire, who was mad about the tap, seeing it as "unconstitutional blackmail," and who believed Kissinger had requested it, that "this country is going to be destroyed by people who are thinking of their own purity." Kissinger thought Safire was now trying to blackmail *him* by demanding information on his wiretapping if Kissinger wanted to clear his name before a column Safire was writing on the administration's wiretapping came out. Safire's crusade against the wiretaps was supremely unwelcome to Kissinger. ("He's got a meal ticket that's a month's exercise," Kissinger told Ronald Ziegler. "Is he off his rocker?" Nixon asked.)

In mid-August, in preparation for a long-awaited Nixon speech to the country and white paper on Watergate, which Kissinger gave substantial advice on, Kissinger advised Nixon to say what he knew without "mentioning 20 other people, any one of whom can then start contradicting you. . . . And since most people at this point don't give a damn about the details, they might just feel that you've been totally candid."

To Kissinger's outrage and former secretary of defense Melvin Laird's own displeasure, the Defense Department had meanwhile released documents on the secret bombing of Cambodia, including on a cover story for the press and the falsification of the bombing records, to the Senate Armed Services Committee, which was holding hearings. Kissinger thought Secretary of Defense James Schlesinger, whom he berated over Defense's release of the documents, was "a disaster." He also angrily rebuked Deputy Defense Secretary William Clements: "Are you guys over there working for the same government, or are you working for yourselves?"

Kissinger was also incensed that the Justice Department, in a response to Morton Halperin's lawsuit against him and others for wiretapping his phone, wrote that Kissinger had requested the tap, which Kissinger continued to falsely deny. ("Technically, I didn't even give his name [to be tapped]," he claimed to a legal adviser.)

Shortly before his confirmation hearings to become secretary of state in September, Kissinger, who sorely wanted the job, learned that Defense was sending a paper on the secret bombing of Cambodia and the false-reporting system to the Senate Armed Services Committee. That news produced a loud obscenity. Kissinger prepped with Nixon aide Bryce Harlow on how to handle the even thornier issue of the wiretapping at the hearings.

Kissinger told Nelson Rockefeller that he too was wiretapped, through a method that allowed H. R. Haldeman to listen to his phone conversations, and he told Safire and a *Times* reporter that he suspected he was wiretapped by White House undercover operatives (through another method). He refused to meet with the columnist Joe Kraft and his attorney about Kraft's own wiretapping, which he was not involved in.

During Kissinger's confirmation hearings on September 11, democratically elected Chilean President Salvador Allende was overthrown in a U.S.-backed coup. Kissinger advised Deputy Secretary of State Kenneth Rush that "we didn't support it" and also denied helping to Mexico's foreign minister. Getting more to the point, Nixon observed to Kissinger that "our hand doesn't show on this one."

Joseph Kane

August 1, 1973, 2:30 p.m.

Kissinger tells a Time *reporter that the falsification of the secret Cambodia bombing records was for the military's own internal purposes.*

> . . . KISSINGER: . . . The military set up a reporting channel, a special reporting channel; that special reporting channel put in the correct information. . . . But then we get to the problem that the military, having reported this in a special channel, and correctly, they had an internal accounting problem, so that the falsification was to their own auditors and not the public. . . .
>
> KANE: So their need then was to balance their books.
>
> KISSINGER: That's my impression. . . .

William Safire and John Crewdson

August 3, 1973, 12:35 p.m.

Safire arranges for New York Times *reporter Crewdson to confront Kissinger about his wiretapping. Kissinger professes no knowledge of it, though Alexander Haig, his military assistant then, had requested the tap from the FBI. "The suggestion that Haig asked for this wiretap without the knowledge of Henry Kissinger is patently ridiculous," Safire observed later. Kissinger contends that it is impossible that Safire, who believed Kissinger requested the tap through Haig, was one of the 13 government officials wiretapped by the FBI. Crewdson, in his article on the Safire wiretap two days later, quoted a federal law-enforcement official as saying it was "inconceivable" that Kissinger did not know of the wiretap, noting that logs of wiretapped conversations were routinely sent to his office. And indeed Kissinger had requested its termination. Safire may have been wiretapped mainly because he was overheard on the wiretap on the British journalist Henry Brandon, though Safire believed it was "because I was talking to the press," period.*[1]

> SAFIRE: Henry, I'm sitting here with John Crewdson, a reporter for the *New York Times*. There is an important question I'd like you to answer for him. . . .
>
> CREWDSON: Dr. Kissinger, I have some information on excellent authority that among the 17 wiretaps that you requested was one on Mr. Safire's phone.
>
> KISSINGER: One, I did not request any wiretaps at all. . . . I knew about them and I gave the names of some people in specific categories. . . . Secondly, to the best of my knowledge, in this group there were no wiretaps on Bill Safire. And I can say the only slight disclaim I have to make is the newsmen's wiretaps were in no way brought to the attention of

my office. So I can say certainly Bill Safire's telephone was not tapped as part of that particular operation. Now, whether the [Anthony] Ulasewicz's and [Jack] Caulfield's—therefore the Plumbers—about whose existence I didn't know—did it, that I cannot judge.

CREWDSON: You say you suggested some 17 names, is that right?

KISSINGER: As I explained to the press, there were three categories among the government officials. Those who had unfavorable information in their security files; those who were discovered by investigation; and those who had access to the documents that were leaked, where we supplied the names of the people who had access to the documents.

CREWDSON: And Mr. Safire did not fall into the third category?

KISSINGER: Mr. Safire did not fall into the third category, and to my certain knowledge he was not part of the national security wiretaps that were initiated in 1969, which are the only wiretaps of which I have any knowledge. . . . It is inconceivable to me that Safire was part of it. If he was I would have no knowledge of it. It is possible that there were people being tapped that I didn't know about. . . . If Safire was tapped it was as part of a totally different thing, not connected with that original batch. You have to understand that after the original batch my office had no connection with any internal security operation, so it would have had to be in another group if it happened, which I don't know. But I can say that emphatically.

CREWDSON: Well, we have a contradiction. I'm not sure how it's going to be resolved.

KISSINGER: The only thing I can say is if there's a contradiction it must have been done in channels through other orders.

CREWDSON: My source claims that Safire was in the group of 17.

KISSINGER: If he is then somebody put people into that group that I didn't know about. . . .

SAFIRE: . . . Let's take the 13 in the government. . . . You can go down in your mind of those that you know were among those 13?

KISSINGER: That's right. There was no conceivable way you could have been in that category. . . .

SAFIRE: What you're suggesting now is that . . . of the ones that you do not know, I could have been one.

KISSINGER: It is possible that orders were given, since the authority was from Mitchell. I think if the authority came from Mitchell it is possible that somebody could have requested Mitchell to authorize a wiretap that I did not know about. Or it is possible that some of these extracurricular activities were conducted—that you were a part of those, like Caulfield or the Plumbers. . . . I have had occasion to review the records in my office . . . confined to the 1969 authorization and I know that you're not part of those.

SAFIRE: How can you know that, Henry? . . . Is it possible that I'm one of those 13?

KISSINGER: That I think is impossible.

SAFIRE: You can't know that because you don't know all 13.

KISSINGER: The reason I don't think it's possible is because at that time the only discussion concerned newspaper leaks of classified documents to which you didn't have access. In that original group there was no way you could have figured. Now, it is possible that some other enterprise was started, and that I couldn't judge, and it is even possible that they may have added names directly just between Haldeman and Mitchell. . . . It was not done as part of the national security operation of which I was familiar. I have to repeat, I cannot know what else may have been done. I just cannot believe it. But a lot of things happened that I couldn't believe. . . . I would consider it totally impossible and preposterous. . . . The only reason I'm not saying it flatly is because I've seen so many things happen that I would have thought impossible. . . .

William Safire

August 7, 1973, 6:15 p.m.

Safire and Kissinger have another go-around on the wiretap on Safire, with Safire wanting to get the tapes or transcripts. "I tell you, this country is going to be destroyed by people who are thinking of their own purity," Kissinger lectures him. Safire was trying to assemble a list of all the people wiretapped.

. . . KISSINGER: . . . I've told you I've searched my files and there is absolutely nothing in mine about it. I do not want to go to the FBI myself because this will leak.

SAFIRE: Well, my column is on Thursday. Which means I have to file it around 1:00 tomorrow.

KISSINGER: Well, I didn't say I wanted to see you before your next column. . . . To me this a human problem. I don't care what you write in your column.

SAFIRE: Well, I'm not worried about my feelings so much as I am about getting this thing out and in the open. I've got a couple more names of people who were tapped. I don't have all 17 but we are getting close. We'll get down to about three or four who haven't been named yet. I have a hunch—a strong hunch—and a good lead that they are White House non-NSC types. I told Haig today that I thought it was a terrible mistake . . . to keep them dripping out like Chinese water torture. The smart thing is to simply say these were the people. . . . He disagrees. So we'll have to flush it out. I want to get those tapes and transcripts and stuff back. I view it as unconstitutional blackmail. I was not tapped for a national security purpose. . . .

KISSINGER: Well, Bill, you know, I tell you, this country is going to be destroyed by people who are thinking of their own purity. . . .

SAFIRE: I'm also concerned that the FBI, which is a notorious leaking agency, has some conversations and taps and stuff of the president with his aides. I think that is reprehensible. 'Cause if it was a tap on me it includes conversations I had with the president in 1969. . . . Henry, if you think that all I am thinking about is my purity or vengeance or something like that, I am very sorry.

KISSINGER: You see, what is conceivable to me is that in some other tap you showed up as having been indiscreet and that then somebody, on what they defined as national security [grounds], ordered the tap. But it is not conceivable to me that a middle-level bureaucrat did that.

SAFIRE: Then it would have to be Bob Haldeman.

KISSINGER: I am not the only judge here of what constitutes national security. After all, all the taps that were done since 1970 that have been declared as national security were not done . . . through my office, or indeed with my knowledge.

SAFIRE: . . . Bob Haldeman . . . looks kind of hard at you and Haig.

KISSINGER: Well, we'll just have to find, first of all, the time when it happened. If we can find that then at least we can know who did it. But as far as I am concerned, Bill, by no conceivable stretch of the imagination could my office have had an interest in it, since the easy way to take care of any leaking of yours was to keep classified information out of your hands. . . .

SAFIRE: I've gotten a list of the NSC people who were tapped. Some who have been named and some who have not. What I'm trying to do is to make up the full list. . . . The three basic points are who ordered it, when did it cover, and the third point of home or at the office.

KISSINGER: I am sure it was not the office because I don't recall anyone who was done in the office, but I may be wrong on that too. . . .

SAFIRE: Well, I'm trying to find out, one, who ordered it and when. This stuff is lying there and it's not going to help the country to have it lie there, particularly the president with his aides.

KISSINGER: That is between you and Haig or whoever. . . .

Leonard Garment

August 7, 1973, 6:31 p.m.

Kissinger suggests to Nixon counsel Garment that Safire was trying to "blackmail" him by saying that if he wanted to "clear" himself, he fork over information on the wiretap on Safire. They both worry about Safire's inquiry into the taps.

KISSINGER: I just had a call from Bill Safire, which, were he not a valued former colleague, I would consider blackmail. He says he's doing a column on his thing for Thursday's paper, on which, if I want to clear myself, I have to give him some information by one o'clock tomorrow, which I said I wouldn't do. Now, have you been able to find out what period it was when it occurred in his case, if it indeed occurred?

GARMENT: No, not yet. And we're going to run into a problem because we'll have to get that from the FBI. . . .

KISSINGER: Now wait a minute. He also claims he's got the names of some of the other people and he won't rest now until they're all out.

GARMENT: Oh, boy.

KISSINGER: Now, I don't know whether it's possible to appeal to his—whether the word patriotism still means anything.

GARMENT: Yeah, but that might be a little risky with him at this point. I don't quite know what he's up to except that I think he sees himself being portrayed in a very favorable light among his colleagues. . . . Well, let me see if I can get the information on when. But even then you say he won't rest until he knows the names of the others?

KISSINGER: Yeah. Well, it's up to you how you want to handle it.

GARMENT: The specific information he wants from us is who knew about this, who authorized it, and when did this take place. If it was late in the game, then presumably you were out of it because you would have handed off the whole operation [to Haldeman].

KISSINGER: Yeah, but if it was early that still doesn't mean that I was in it.

GARMENT: But then it's a question of then he just has to believe you.

KISSINGER: Well, but I'm not so much concerned about myself. . . . I'm interested in [not] having, on top of everything else, that door reopened.

GARMENT: Well, I have the feeling from the chat I had with Bill that it's dangerous to fuss that much with him. He was laying down some specific demand. . . . Did he tell you that he spoke to Haldeman?

KISSINGER: Yeah. Haldeman, who said he had nothing to do with it, which is an outrageous lie. Because Haldeman knew about every last one of them. . . . He was the absolutely essential figure.

GARMENT: Yeah. This is complicated because I think what Bill is doing is laying the foundation to the extensive use of very private material and very private quotes in his book. . . . In other words, if he is victimized by this whole thing . . . he's going to say, "Well, no more rules of the game. I cannot write an honest book in spite of all of this without just laying it all out, just as I have in my notes." Be a hell of a book. So my guess is that nothing that is said will satisfy him.

KISSINGER: . . . I don't propose to talk to him again.

GARMENT: Let me see what information is available . . . without being too compromising and embarrassing. . . .

KISSINGER: Well, I would just be interested for my own information to know when this goddamn thing happened. Because on the face of it, what conceivable motive could my office have? He never handled any classified information. . . .

Alexander Haig
August 9, 1973, 6:37 p.m.
White House Chief of Staff Haig asks Kissinger to help rescue Nixon's forthcoming speech on Watergate, drafted by Ray Price.

. . . HAIG: . . . I wanted him to get you up here to help with this speech. . . . Ray's first draft, which I just left him . . . he had a total tantrum. It is a disaster. . . .

KISSINGER: What he really has to do, Al, is to get into his head what his basic strategy ought to be. And I really feel very strongly. It isn't just that he has to make a conciliatory speech and then go all-out. . . . He has to be the father of his country now. Not a raving maniac . . . not attacking the investigators. I think what he should say is we've just had some hearings that uncovered some bad things. But we have a national duty to make a distinction between those things that were in the national interest and those that were not. Now, let me tell you about Cambodia [the secret bombing], of which I am proud—which we would do again. . . . Let's let him say what we did and say I am proud we did it. There are many people who opposed us who are now using that as an excuse and let's keep our sense of proportion. . . .

HAIG: Exactly. Well, this is what I'm trying to get in this speech. The trouble is Ray came in with the goddamnest softest, bemoaning, breast-beating, groveling—

KISSINGER: He shouldn't be groveling. . . . It should be the speech of a strong man who is strong enough to admit that some things were wrong but who says now we must save this country and govern this country.

HAIG: Well, this is what I've just given Ray, exactly along those lines. To start out he takes care of his own personal culpability as based on the hearings, but that ain't enough. Something went wrong. What was it that was wrong and what were the reasons?

KISSINGER: Exactly. . . . And he can say . . . that I was trying to end the war. I did not want the U.S. to lose the war or to have all these people die in vain. . . . In the process we made these mistakes. . . .

Ronald Ziegler
August 9, 1973, 7:11 p.m.
Kissinger and Ziegler discuss William Safire's crusade against the wiretaps.

KISSINGER: Ron, what did old Safire have to say?

ZIEGLER: He was not hung up on the tapes at all.

KISSINGER: No, he's got a meal ticket that's a month's exercise.

ZIEGLER: No, I don't think he's going to be dwelling on it. . . . He feels what we should do is to meet the FBI just to give these goddamn wiretap files back to the 17 who have been taped.

KISSINGER: Oh, he's ridiculous. That would make it look as if we had done something illegal. . . . He's wrapped up in his own little ego.

ZIEGLER: Yeah, but he wasn't too emotional about it. Of course, everyone claims that you did it.

KISSINGER: . . . Why would I do it? I barely knew him.

ZIEGLER: I'm just kidding. . . . But he didn't seem to be all that stewed up about it. I mean, he's stewed up personally about it but I don't think he's going to be vindictive about it, Henry.

KISSINGER: I think he is. . . .

Melvin Laird
August 10, 1973, 9:38 a.m.
Nixon counselor Laird and Kissinger complain about the release of documents by James Schlesinger's Defense Department on the secret Cambodia bombing to the Senate Armed Services Committee, which was holding hearings on the falsification of records of the bombing. Kissinger claims he didn't know about conversations on the false-reporting system between Haig and a colonel, probably Ray Sitton, who devised the system at Kissinger and Haig's direction and worked with them on it. (Sitton would remember many trips to the west basement of the White House to discuss bombing targets and the reporting system with Haig and Kissinger.) Laird was then "ratting out" Kissinger on background to the press about the falsification.[2]

KISSINGER: I just wanted to check base with you before the newspapers start picking at everyone on the hearings yesterday on Cambodia.

LAIRD: Well, they're dumping everything, you know. They've even got those memos between Al and a colonel . . . which [said] we would start on using some bombing in South Vietnam and then carry it over into the sanctuaries. . . . And that cover story was worked out between your staff and the Joint Staff. There were several discussions on it and I approved it. I don't deny that.

KISSINGER: Well, Schlesinger claims they gave nothing except one look at an execute order.

LAIRD: No, they gave them the memorandum, too, and the execute order. The execute order doesn't have my initials on it, the memorandum does . . . explaining the 42 strikes [and outlining a cover story and calling for false reporting]. They gave them a memorandum from Wheeler to me asking me to go to the president and get approval of 42 strikes in Cambodia in a two-day period. . . . And then a day later on the bottom of the memorandum I say, "Approved, MRL." Because the last paragraph said we want you to take this immediately to the president.

KISSINGER: But why did they do that?

LAIRD: I don't understand it, Henry. . . . I think they think they are a new team and because they are a new team they want to start clean. . . . You can't be a completely new team, you know.

KISSINGER: I couldn't agree more with you, Mel. I'm shocked at this thing. I called Schlesinger yesterday and I said, "I do not think it is a good idea to turn over military orders to these committees."

LAIRD: Well, once you start you will have to give them all. . . . I understand they have two of the memorandums now of conversations between Al and some colonel over there. Now, they came before the memorandum came up to me. . . .

KISSINGER: Well, I don't know about these conversations.

LAIRD: Well, those things shouldn't be released anyway, Henry.

KISSINGER: And in any event you know these staff conversations go on all the time. I bet you didn't know what the colonel said necessarily and I didn't know necessarily. You know, we see the final product.

LAIRD: . . . Even the final product shouldn't be sent over in verbatim. You know what I used to do when they wanted those things? I'd have Fred Buzhardt go through them and paraphrase certain parts. . . . But now they're giving them the raw material. . . . And this was given to them openly.

KISSINGER: Well, that's nuts. Don't you think that's nuts?

LAIRD: Why, sure. I don't know what they are trying to prove. . . .

KISSINGER: . . . I mean, we didn't do anything wrong, for the love of Pete.

LAIRD: Well, you're never going to be able to do anything anymore around here, Henry. . . . If you're going to start giving out orders, execute orders, operating orders, all the confidential memoranda and everything else, we might as well close the Department of Defense down, there is no use having any deterrent.

KISSINGER: I couldn't agree more. . . . Well, let me raise hell with Schlesinger. . . . He is a disaster. . . . But are you going to defend the original decision [to secretly bomb Cambodia], or how are we going to do it?

LAIRD: Of course I am. I did it on the *Today* show. I thought I had it quieted
down. I'm going to do it again today in Chicago, but—

KISSINGER: I mean, we saved American life. There were North Vietnamese
troops there. The government of the country we were bombing were asking
us to do it. What the hell—one sometimes thinks we are in a madhouse....

James Schlesinger
August 10, 1973, 9:50 a.m.
*Kissinger expresses his anger to Schlesinger about Defense's release of documents to
the Senate committee on the secret Cambodia bombing, including a memorandum on
a conversation between Haig and the colonel that dealt with the false reporting.*

KISSINGER: Jim, I just had a call from Laird.... What the hell is going on? Why
do we have to put out execute orders?... What is possessing you people over
there?

SCHLESINGER: I don't know, I read about it this morning.

KISSINGER: You gave me your word yesterday morning.

SCHLESINGER: Wait a minute, Henry, you asked about White House orders.

KISSINGER: Right. Well, give me the rationale for putting out military orders.

SCHLESINGER: I don't know the rationale for putting that paper out.

KISSINGER: It does us no good. . . . We were in good shape at these hearings.
We had them quieted down. Mel thinks they were given a memcon of a
conversation between Haig and a colonel setting up some procedure.

SCHLESINGER: I don't know about that and I doubt that. Now I think we are
in good shape.

KISSINGER: I don't see the point.

SCHLESINGER: Wait. Let's stick to the shape we're in.... Damn it, we had [Sen-
ators Stuart] Symington and [Harold] Hughes on the ropes yesterday. It
doesn't come out that way in the press, but look at the TV excerpts from last
night. Bill Clements and Tom Moorer did a helluva good job yesterday....

William Clements
August 10, 1973, 12:38 p.m.
*Kissinger also vents his ire to Deputy Defense Secretary Clements about Defense's
provision of documents to the Senate committee. Clements says the matter was discussed with Schlesinger and defends the release of the documents. But Kissinger fears
more news stories on the falsification of the Cambodia bombing records. The execute
order of November 20, 1969, that they discuss was accompanied by an Eyes Only
cover memorandum providing for 41 B-52s to hit targets in Cambodia while other
B-52s struck targets in South Vietnam and Laos; the latter would provide "a credible
story for replies to press inquiries," it said. The memo, which is the same one Laird*

lamented above, called for the Cambodian strikes to be officially recorded as in South Vietnam.[3]

> KISSINGER: Are you guys over there working for the same government or are you working for yourselves?
>
> CLEMENTS: You must be joking.
>
> KISSINGER: We are getting deluged now with, did we approve that execute order on the 20th November 1969? . . . Well, first of all, why was it put out? What was the need for it?
>
> CLEMENTS: We felt like it was absolutely the thing to do, and this was thoroughly discussed with Secretary Schlesinger in this building in every respect.
>
> KISSINGER: Well, we are going to insist now that the things that affect the whole administration we get a chance to discuss it. . . . How do I answer the question whether we approved over here . . . that order of 20th of November?
>
> CLEMENTS: No, you did not and there is nothing on that piece of paper that indicates he [Nixon] did, and it was an ordinary run of business that Mel Laird as the secretary approved.
>
> KISSINGER: . . . I fail to understand the reasoning that went into—
>
> CLEMENTS: The reasoning was, Henry, that Senator Symington and Senator Hughes were not going to turn loose of this until they had some understanding of how these things were handled internally and who authorized these kinds of procedures.
>
> KISSINGER: Well, why couldn't that be said orally?
>
> CLEMENTS: Well, the effectiveness of it orally would not be near as good as the piece of paper.
>
> KISSINGER: The piece of paper was certainly effective. It made the front page again every place and it destroyed the superb testimony you gave on the merits of it.
>
> CLEMENTS: I don't think it did at all. I differ with you. And on top of that—
>
> KISSINGER: . . . I mean, it raises the whole issue now, who authorized what, all over again, which we had laid to rest once before.
>
> CLEMENTS: Well, the point of the whole thing and the whole exercise was in the piece of paper. . . . This is an execute and this is the cover stories; this is the way it should be handled and this will suffice for the press.
>
> KISSINGER: Listen . . . Seymour Hersh called and said he has been told in Defense that the memo released yesterday by Mr. Clements on bombing dated 20 November '69 was approved by you [Kissinger] and the president. . . . Now I suppose I should cover my ass and take it and say the president did it all.

CLEMENTS: Oh, don't be ridiculous, Henry. That was an ordinary piece of business....

KISSINGER: All I am saying to you, Bill, is by putting this stuff out we are now again in one of these intermittent fights within the administration. I know for a fact that in November '69 there was no longer any reason to get White House approval for individual raids.

CLEMENTS: Why, certainly not. And in the testimony yesterday, Admiral Moorer and I tried to make the point, and we did make the point and it was accepted, that this was completely routine and that Mel Laird signed out on many of these kinds of things....

KISSINGER: Well, for somebody who has been around here, Bill, we are now in another document fight. Now the *New York Times* could print a document. They could never print oral testimony to that.... I suppose somebody in this goddamn government has to assume responsibility, so the president will assume responsibility.... Our problem is that we are now again in an awful discussion.... Did the president authorize, order, or did I order or authorize this? I frankly don't think I knew about a November 20th raid on an individual basis.... The original procedure we knew about.... What do you want to bet that by Sunday at the latest, if not by tomorrow, the *New York Times* is going to have a major story claiming the president and I did all of this.... Before the week is up it will be the president ordering a cover-up and lying on Cambodia, and I ordering it.... We're going to be in one of these revolting exercises . . . which alone makes us unfit to govern because no one ever assumes responsibility. Everyone is covering his own ass.... We had the goddamn thing in its right focus when these documents showed up, which are now going to be another goddamn cause—

CLEMENTS: I just can't accept that....

KISSINGER: No, but the question is whether the administration should be constantly getting each guy like a bunch of piranha fish going after each other. . . . I'll either say nothing or I'll say, yes, we authorized the procedures. . . . Everyone dumps on everyone else and the buck finally has to come here. Then they all dump it in here. It's just a sort of a revolting spectacle....

Alexander Haig

August 10, 1973, 2:48 p.m.

Kissinger tells Haig about the release of the damaging November 20, 1969, cover memorandum on an execute order stipulating a cover story and false reporting on the secret Cambodia bombing.

KISSINGER: Those maniacs in Defense, you know, put out an execute order of November 20, 1969. . . . You know, it had details in there about how to mislead the press. . . . Why they put it out is beyond me. Now they've shifted the discussion away from the double-bookkeeping [reporting system], on which we were on good ground, to falsification for the press. And now inevitably it will get to the White House. If we can put out an execute for November 20, why can't we put it for the whole series?

HAIG: Why did they do this? . . .

KISSINGER: Because they are a selfish bunch of sons of bitches. They thought they could prove it was a routine matter and that it was comparable to something they had put out in the Johnson administration. But of course having done one, how can they stop the others? . . . I would like to get an order sent out by the president that none of these things can be done unilaterally by departments.

HAIG: Yes. It's inconceivable that they would have put that out. I thought yesterday you called Schlesinger and he said no.

KISSINGER: That's right. . . . Well, his argument was he thought I was talking only about White House documents and they are talking about Defense execute orders. . . . It's on the front page of every paper.

HAIG: I still don't give a god damn, Henry. They had cover-up for [Operation] Overlord [in World War II], they had the same thing done. They had phony briefings. They had phony plans circulating. . . .

KISSINGER: . . . There was no need for it. If it came out we can excuse it, but why volunteer it? What purpose does it serve? . . . I mean, it forces us into a two-week additional explanation. . . .

Alexander Haig
August 12, 1973, 12:30 p.m.
Kissinger confers with Haig on Nixon's forthcoming Watergate speech and a written statement he would release at the same time.

KISSINGER: . . . Len Garment showed me the new statement he did, which is in the first person. . . . I think it's damn good. . . . While this thing yesterday was "True Confession" crap. . . . I think you should cut out all sideswipes at Kennedy and Johnson. . . . And I think he's got to say a little more clearly—in fact a little bit of the stuff that's now in the white paper ought to be in the speech—he ought to say very clearly, you know, just say, "I did not do this." . . . And he's got to assume clearer responsibility, not just because it happened in his administration. . . . And then I think you ought to cut the tape section in the speech considerably. . . . Because it's not a good thing. . . .

President Nixon

August 12, 1973, 2:30 p.m.

Kissinger advises Nixon not to be overly defensive in his written statement and speech on Watergate. Nixon should "very calmly" state what he knew without "mentioning 20 other people, any one of whom can then start contradicting you," Kissinger counsels. He agrees with Nixon that most people were sick of Watergate and says things were "on the upgrade."

... KISSINGER: On that basis I think you're not so defensive.... And I think there's a certain advantage in the first person, if it isn't done like one of these "True Confession" ones, in which you are not mentioning 20 other people, any one of whom can then start contradicting you and drag you into a debate with your aides, which isn't worthy of a president.

NIXON: That's the whole point.

KISSINGER: But this one I have read and it simply very objectively states what you knew without any editorializing. It doesn't say "I was bewildered, confused"—

NIXON: Oh, crap.

KISSINGER: It just very calmly states what you know, and it makes a very impressive document.... And in fact, if you want to be totally offbeat, you might even consider reading it as a speech. It would be totally different from anything you've ever done. And since most people at this point don't give a damn about the details, they might just feel that you've been totally candid and put it all out.... I think the white paper yesterday when I saw it, I saw no way it could be rescued. But this one needs some work yet, and I talked to Charlie Wright [a Nixon Watergate defense counsel]. I had a few suggestions....

NIXON: The point is, if we could just get something I can put out. The damn thing could be a piece of toilet paper, and just say I put a paper out. As you say, the unwashed really don't care. They just want a—well, he put out a paper. Right?

KISSINGER: And also this has the advantage, Mr. President, that at press conferences you can stay within the confines of this paper, and you can't be drawn into these endless debates of what you said to—

NIXON: On such and such a day.

KISSINGER: On this date.

NIXON: If I can remember. And I'm not gonna get into that. I mean, I'm not a witness. I'm not a defendant. That's the thing, you see, about the other thing that concerned me. It put the president into the position of being a witness and/or defendant in this whole damned mess. Well, the hell with it. I'm not a witness or a defendant.... I'm basically a prosecutor trying to get the facts.

KISSINGER: Exactly.

NIXON: And I'm not gonna be in that position. . . . Well, anyway, it's sort of the dog days of August, and except for the *Washington Post* and *New York Times* most of the country doesn't give one god damn about what the hell happens in Watergate. They are sick of it, tired of it, you know. They want to get on with other things, Henry, believe me.

KISSINGER: I am sure of that.

NIXON: That's just what I sense from talking to a group of people. You know, it's finally gotten to that point. The postmortems go on among the Krafts and the jackasses like that, but most people don't give one damn.

KISSINGER: I think that is right.

NIXON: You know, they get sick and . . . very tired of something. They get tired of political campaigns, ice cream; they get tired of the energy crisis, or the environment crisis. Now it's the Watergate crisis.

KISSINGER: Well, I think also they want to have their government governed instead of—

NIXON: They may not understand that, but nevertheless, we do. [Laughs.] . . . Well, we've survived it, and we're gonna survive.

KISSINGER: Well, I think it's on the upgrade now. I think there's no question about this being on the upgrade, Mr. President. . . .

Bryce Harlow
August 15, 1973, 10:07 a.m.

Nixon aide Harlow and Kissinger mull over the perplexing process of writing Nixon's speech, which he would give that evening, and his statement. Harlow puzzles that he hasn't met with Nixon alone since returning to the White House staff and worries about what Nixon's isolation portends. They also take up a forthcoming Nixon press conference at which he would announce his nomination of Kissinger as secretary of state. Kissinger is sure it will not be done "with an excess of zeal." ("I did not really want to make Henry secretary of state," Nixon said later. But "with the Watergate problem, I didn't have any choices.")[4] Kissinger dismisses Ron Ziegler, who they worry is still talking to fired Nixon aides H. R. Haldeman and John Ehrlichman, as "sort of a court jester."

. . . KISSINGER: It's an interesting process, isn't it?

HARLOW: Well, you know, I really am quite surprised at what the boss is doing. I don't understand it. Has he consulted you further?

KISSINGER: No. . . . After I said what they didn't want to hear, that took care of that little exercise.

HARLOW: Apparently it's the damnedest thing. . . . Mel has had no input whatever. I had none whatever, and you had a slight impact on it that was really more on what he ought to do next than what he was then doing. And that's it. . . .

KISSINGER: The thing that bothers me, between you and me, is that there isn't anybody there who knows how to shape an intellectual product. . . . I mean, there's only one professional—that's Wright—and he doesn't know anything about politics.

HARLOW: Well, I'm in an odd situation here. I came in at his insistence to help him personally. . . . Six weeks now I've been here, at a cost of x thousands of dollars a month . . . in order to be helpful to this guy. He said three times to me I had to do that. And do you know what I've done for him personally since I've been here? I've talked to him twice on the phone. Once for three minutes about, and once for about 10 minutes.

KISSINGER: Do you mean you haven't seen him alone?

HARLOW: No, not since I've been here. In six weeks. . . .

KISSINGER: That's weird.

HARLOW: It is weird. I don't think that Mel has been alone with him either. . . .

KISSINGER: I've been alone with him, but as I told you the other day, if I said Attila the Hun has just crossed the Vistula and we'd better cut him off at the Urals by dropping a 10-megatoner, he'd say, "By god, that's the best idea I've heard all day. Order it."

HARLOW: . . . I don't understand what's happening or why. . . . I'm deeply worried about it for the country.

KISSINGER: So am I. . . . Listen, Bryce, the last thing you have to worry about is that that other thing will be done with an excess of zeal. . . . I haven't had any further discussion on it.

HARLOW: It has to happen this week, I understand.

KISSINGER: Bryce, between you and me, I don't think it's going to happen this week. . . . I would just as soon keep it on ice for a few weeks to see what happens.

HARLOW: Well, that press conference, of course, is much more important than what's happening today. That's the watershed on this . . . if he can bring himself to do it.

KISSINGER: Well, he's got to. He's got no choice. . . . He can delay it a week or two or three, but there's got to be a press conference.

HARLOW: Each day he delays it, of course, there's attrition.

KISSINGER: And it's got to be well before Congress comes back. . . . The president would at least lance that one boil.

HARLOW: Well, I think that will move him out of the danger zone, and back towards the high land.

KISSINGER: He's got to get these Gallup polls going up a little bit, don't you think?

HARLOW: Yeah, because these professional politicians move right in. . . .

KISSINGER: I haven't seen the speech. . . . The last draft I saw was the one after the one you saw, and it was worse than the one you saw. When I said that I've been excluded since then—I saw one draft in which he said he is against the deprivation of liberty to anybody, whether it's done by Haldeman or whether it's done by the Joint Chiefs of Staff when they have the draft, and that's why he abolished the draft. . . . A half-hour of screaming got it removed. It also got me excluded from any further discussions. . . .

HARLOW: Didn't you tell me that starting with your recommendation on Bob [Haldeman] and John [Ehrlichman] that this chill set in?

KISSINGER: On everything except my field.

HARLOW: . . . I really am deeply concerned . . . over what this portends for the country. . . . Because, you know, a lot of people are not going to take this kind of thing—they're gonna leave. George Shultz was not far away from that when I came in here. . . . But if this goes on these people will say what the hell, and then this whole operation will collapse, and then first thing you know he can get run out of office just on the ground that he can't run the government. . . . And that's what I'm worrying about. I mean, you can't run the government through Ron and Al.

KISSINGER: . . . Without Al, we'd be totally lost. I think Ron is just a sort of a court jester.

HARLOW: And he's a security blanket.

KISSINGER: He's the link to Haldeman.

HARLOW: Well, I think he's probably still talking to them [Haldeman and Ehrlichman].

KISSINGER: That would be an even worse disaster.

HARLOW: I'll bet he is, though. I'll bet he's leaning still on Bob and John in some ways.

KISSINGER: Yeah, but that would be a screaming disaster. And then we'd be better off bringing them back here where they can do day-to-day work. Their judgment wasn't any good when they saw all the papers. How the hell can their judgment be any good when they're sitting 3,000 miles away stewing in their own juice?

HARLOW: I'll bet you he's doing it, though.

KISSINGER: I'll bet you any amount.

HARLOW: I'll just bet you he's on the phone with Bob right along and Bob's guiding him, and that must gall the hell out of Al. . . .

Fred Buzhardt
August 16, 1973, 9:45 a.m.
A Washington Post *story reported that the Justice Department, in papers filed in response to Morton Halperin's lawsuit against Kissinger and other officials for the*

wiretapping of his phone, indicated that Kissinger had requested the tap. Kissinger claims to Nixon's Watergate counsel Buzhardt that he didn't and doesn't think he even requested an investigation of the leak on the secret bombing of Cambodia in May 1969 and other recent leaks (particularly one on SALT) that prompted the wiretap. Actually, he had spoken to FBI Director J. Edgar Hoover four times the day the Cambodia bombing story appeared, requested a "major" investigation, and said they would "destroy whoever did this." He was "livid," Nixon recalled. "This coverage was first instituted at the specific request of Dr. Henry Kissinger," the FBI recorded.[5]

KISSINGER: Fred, I see in the *Washington Post* that it is said that we admitted that I requested the taps on Halperin. . . . I will not hold still for this.

BUZHARDT: Henry, read the pleading [by Justice].

KISSINGER: I requested an investigation. I don't even think I did that, to tell you the truth. My recollection is not at all that. My recollection is that the president, Hoover, Haldeman, Mitchell, and I were sitting in the office, and Hoover said that Halperin had been a bad actor all along and that he would make him the number one suspect in his investigation. And after that he wrote me the letter. And his letter supports that version a hell of a lot better than that I requested anything.

BUZHARDT: Yeah, well, Henry, read the pleading. We changed the pleading as we agreed on yesterday. . . . It's got the president's direction in there. . . . I said and based on . . . other information in the hands of the bureau they installed taps. . . .

KISSINGER: Because, you know, the Justice Department is interested in covering for the FBI. What is the proof, incidentally—I mean, they've been putting that out constantly—that I requested anything on May 9th?

BUZHARDT: Well, you had a conversation with Hoover.

KISSINGER: Yeah, but in his letter to me all he said is that I requested him to look into leaks. . . .

Carlyle Maw
August 16, 1973, 10:17 a.m.
Kissinger complains to legal adviser Maw about the government's pleading in response to Halperin's lawsuit and claims that "my role in the Halperin tap was really nothing."

KISSINGER: Carl, I've now got that plea they made and I would feel a lot better if you had a chance to look it over. . . . I think that the trouble is that the counsel to the White House [Buzhardt] has an interest in protecting the president. . . . And the Justice Department has an interest in protecting the FBI. And he's [a Justice Department attorney] already got a story in the *Washington Post* today saying that I requested the tap to be put on Halperin. Now, I've shown you that letter which makes it clear that I didn't.

MAW: Oh, I don't think I would comment, Henry.

KISSINGER: No, I won't comment, but I wonder whether I should submit a separate plea.... You see, the facts are that this was ordered by the president in a meeting in his office which Hoover and Mitchell attended, and my role in the Halperin tap was really nothing. Now, I don't have to go as far as that. Technically, I didn't even give his name. . . . Didn't even give his name for investigation.

MAW: How did they get his name?

KISSINGER: Because Halperin was on their list to begin with. They had refused to clear him.

MAW: How did they get the others? Did you give any names?

KISSINGER: I gave the names of others who had access to classified information. But I never requested formally a tap....

Rowland Evans
August 17, 1973, 10:27 a.m.
Kissinger takes issue with a Washington Post *editorial on Watergate.*

. . . KISSINGER: Well, I tell you, I had great sympathy but I think the people are now getting demented. You read the *Washington Post* editorial—what the hell do they want? Full disclosure. What do they want him [Nixon] to do? They won't accept anything as full disclosure that doesn't lead to impeachment.... When your position is that you don't know anything, how can you make full disclosure?

EVANS: The tapes.

KISSINGER: Oh, come on. . . . The tapes are going to be inconclusive. I've not heard one of them and I bet you they'll be inconclusive....

Alexander Haig
August 18, 1973, 2:36 p.m.
Haig and Kissinger want a resistant Nixon to hold his press conference where he would announce his appointment of Kissinger as secretary of state but undoubtedly be grilled about Watergate.

. . . KISSINGER: Oh, well, he has been suffering from pleurisy—and he isn't going to do any work for a while. . . . Does that mean no press conference?

HAIG: I hope not—that would be a disaster.

KISSINGER: That's what I think. . . .

HAIG: I have gotten some material that indicates we are doing real well. But the press has remained very cynical through it all. And that is our problem.

KISSINGER: I think if he does a press conference in which he is very confident, just keeps that other thing that you discussed [Kissinger's appointment], they'll have something totally new to write about. . . . Well, he's got to do it sooner or later. . . .

HAIG: It's not easy. . . .

KISSINGER: Do you think that is his hesitation?

HAIG: Yeah. Among others.

KISSINGER: But do you think it will improve in a week?

HAIG: Never. It'll get worse. We've really got to push him to do this. . . .

Melvin Laird
August 27, 1973, 3:02 p.m.
Kissinger is furious that Defense was sending a report on the secret bombing of Cambodia and the false-reporting system to the Senate Armed Services Committee the week of his confirmation hearings to become secretary of state.

LAIRD: Say, Henry, I just wanted to alert you. . . . I think that you ought to read over that white paper on Cambodia here that they're going to send to the Senate Armed Services Committee.

KISSINGER: They're not going to send any goddamn paper if I have anything to do with it.

LAIRD: I just didn't want it to arrive up there about the time you were up for confirmation hearings. . . .

KISSINGER: Well, when are they wanting to do it?

LAIRD: Well, they promised to [Senator Stuart] Symington that the week as soon as Congress gets back.

KISSINGER: [Obscenity]!!!

LAIRD: You know, I don't want to get you upset, Henry, but I just think you ought to read it and somebody ought to look at it. I personally would like Al Haig and Bob [probably his former military assistant Robert Pursley] personally to go over it.

KISSINGER: I want *you* to go over it.

LAIRD: Yeah. If they go over it I'm satisfied. . . . And certainly if we are here and there is time I will read it over. But I don't want them to think that I'm first, because they might think that I'm concerned, because they might get all upset if I'm—

KISSINGER: Look, the SOBs have no business promising it.

LAIRD: . . . I just think that we ought to watch for it a little bit, because we had the thing quieted down once and they—it keeps opening up all the time. . . .

Bryce Harlow

September 4, 1973, 10:04 a.m.

Kissinger and Harlow prep on how Kissinger should handle the wiretapping at his confirmation hearings. Kissinger claims that his involvement was only consequential to "at most" three of the 17 FBI wiretaps, and that he could probably demonstrate that his overall contribution to the 17 taps was "minimal." (The FBI's records would list Kissinger or his assistant Alexander Haig as the person who requested the overwhelming majority of the 17 wiretaps. Haig, who made the bulk of the requests in his name, was generally presumed to be speaking for Kissinger; he acted as Kissinger's liaison with the FBI official William C. Sullivan, who coordinated the wiretapping, and always checked with Kissinger on them. "I never would have submitted a name that I did not get from Dr. Kissinger, or from the president with Dr. Kissinger's knowledge, and that only happened once," on May 2, 1970, Haig later testified. And he never went to see Sullivan about the wiretaps without getting Kissinger's authorization and then reporting back to Kissinger on his discussion with Sullivan.)[6]

KISSINGER: Well, if it's on substance, I'm all right. If they're gonna spend all their time on wiretapping we'll have a little problem.

HARLOW: Well, they'll spend some time on that, of course. Are you satisfied with your proposed response on that?

. . . KISSINGER: Well, I haven't gotten Buzhardt to produce it yet. . . . If I went through this list name by name, I could prove that at most I could supply the names of three people where my [involvement], it made a difference. . . .

HARLOW: Well, your story on this, I have found, is extremely—

KISSINGER: You know, I could make it even more compelling, but I can't do that. I could probably prove that of those 17 my contribution was minimal. . . . The only wrinkle in my case is that they made me supply a few of the names.

HARLOW: But you gave them the names of those with access.

KISSINGER: That's right.

HARLOW: You did not tell them to accept them, did you?

KISSINGER: That is right.

HARLOW: That was your participation.

KISSINGER: Of course I have no way of knowing what Haldeman may have told the FBI. . . .

HARLOW: Well, what they'll want to quiz you on is the check-off position you had.

KISSINGER: . . . I supplied the names of the people with access to information on my staff.

HARLOW: Realizing that they might well be tapped.

KISSINGER: That is right. The tapping was now an accepted investigative method.

HARLOW: So that you really had anticipation that they would be.

KISSINGER: That they *could* be. Not all of those I supplied were tapped, it turned out.

HARLOW: Yes. That some or all of them might be.

KISSINGER: That's right.

HARLOW: And the reason you agreed to this was that there were absolutely impossible and intolerable leaks taking place that had to be located.

KISSINGER: That's right. And that I was told that this had been done in previous administrations. . . .

Nelson Rockefeller

September 4, 1973, 12:05 p.m.

Kissinger tells Rockefeller that he (Kissinger) too was wiretapped and that he appeared to be "the chief target." (Haig had led him to believe that Haldeman or his assistant Larry Higby could listen in on his phone conversations. Both Haldeman and Higby denied it.)[7]

. . . KISSINGER: I'm spending all my time reading wiretap files to find out just what the hell went on. As far as I can figure out, I was the chief target.

ROCKEFELLER: Yeah, of course. I'm waiting to hear them, somebody, about the fact that you were wiretapped.

KISSINGER: We've developed that. . . .

ROCKEFELLER: So they were?

KISSINGER: Yeah, but they had a different system for me. They had the wires go straight into Haldeman's office. That's why we didn't show up on any tap.

ROCKEFELLER: You mean the actual phone so he could pick it up and listen? So he could listen in on yours anytime he wanted?

KISSINGER: Or his assistant.

ROCKEFELLER: Rather than a recorded. You going to bring that out?

KISSINGER: No, [but] it gives me some moral insurance.

ROCKEFELLER: I must say, it's unbelievable.

KISSINGER: Ridiculous.

ROCKEFELLER: . . . More intimate than we realized. Oh, brother, Henry, what a life. I figured they had to be doing something.

KISSINGER: That's how they did it. . . . Haig found it out. He picked up a phone and heard me on it.

ROCKEFELLER: You're kidding? It was still going then?

KISSINGER: Well, yeah. He didn't know it was there.

ROCKEFELLER: I'll be god damned. Did they do your home too?

KISSINGER: That I haven't figured out yet. I'm checking on it. This is strictly
for you. . . .

Elliot Richardson
September 5, 1973, 8:37 p.m.
*Attorney General Richardson gives Kissinger some unwelcome news on interest in
the wiretaps in the Senate Foreign Relations Committee holding his confirmation
hearings.*

RICHARDSON: Henry, I just got word a few minutes ago that the Senate Foreign Relations Committee has transmitted to us a demand for the FBI
report on those 17 taps. . . . It was a request apparently that went previously to Harlow and was turned down by him, and we'll turn it down also.
It's disturbing to know that they are aware of its existence. This is the summary report that you now have a copy of. . . . I think the situation does
warrant my getting together with you personally to talk about the tactics
of handling that problem. . . . I'm concerned about the overall line that
you take and how it relates to the [Halperin] lawsuit and how to minimize
problems.

KISSINGER: Well, it's obvious to me now that there's somebody either in
Justice or the FBI who is deliberately after me on this. . . .

Bryce Harlow
September 8, 1973, 1:35 p.m.
*Kissinger argues against being too unyielding with the Foreign Relations Committee
about turning over material on the wiretaps but wants to take a tough line on his
role in them if needed. He maintains that the wiretapped* New York Times *reporters
William Beecher and Hedrick Smith "put themselves" on the list of wiretap victims
"by what they wrote."*

. . . KISSINGER: . . . I think our tactics in the executive session should be much
less intransigent than Al recommends. I see nothing to be gained from it
from turning this into a tape issue. . . . But my impression is that now that
these guys have all made a record, if they're given something that they can
say they extorted from us or exacted from us, they'll subside. . . . But if that
is not true, then we can still have a confrontation. . . . If they start going after
me on the wiretapping, I will be much tougher this time. . . . What the hell is
it that I did wrong? . . . There were four reporters bugged. . . . One was put on
by the president personally for reasons I don't understand [Marvin Kalb].
The other was put on by J. Edgar Hoover personally [Henry Brandon]. So

that leaves two, William Beecher and Hedrick Smith. They put themselves on by what they wrote. You see, they didn't have to be requested. . . .

Kenneth Rush
September 13, 1973, 9:03 a.m.
Chilean President Salvador Allende had been overthrown in a U.S.-backed coup two days earlier, and then committed suicide rather than surrender. Assistant Secretary of State Jack Kubisch had told a Senate subcommittee that U.S. officials had received advance warnings of the coup, and that the last one, that the coup would take place on September 11, was conveyed to the highest levels the day before. Kissinger denies being told to Deputy Secretary of State Rush.[8]

> KISSINGER: I'm told over here, I don't know how true it is, that Kubisch went up to the committee to brief them yesterday. . . . We didn't have any idea of what the hell he was going to say, and it has the tendency of pushing everything into the White House again. . . . Now, this may or may not be true. . . . It certainly didn't penetrate to me. . . .
>
> RUSH: I haven't seen the newspapers but what Kubisch told me was that we knew nothing about it, that we had not been told about it and it came as a complete surprise to us. . . .
>
> KISSINGER: We didn't support it. Now, I am also told that people are raising the issue of [U.S. Ambassador to Chile Nathaniel] Davis coming back here. . . . I think the answer is that I asked for him three weeks ago when I was appointed and we left it up to him to pick the time. . . . And that's another good proof that we didn't know anything about it. . . . Of course it's an absurd situation where we have to apologize for the overthrow of a hostile government. . . . I didn't know that a coup was coming at any particular date. . . .

President Nixon
September 16, 1973, 11:50 a.m.
Nixon and Kissinger discuss the coup in Chile. "Our hand doesn't show on this one," Nixon observes, and Kissinger derides the "filthy hypocrisy" of critics of the coup.

> KISSINGER: . . . The Chilean thing is getting consolidated, and of course the newspapers are bleeding because a pro-communist government has been overthrown.
>
> NIXON: Isn't that something. Isn't that something.
>
> KISSINGER: I mean, instead of celebrating—in the Eisenhower period we would be heroes.

NIXON: Well, we didn't—as you know—our hand doesn't show on this one, though.

KISSINGER: We didn't do it. I mean, we helped them. [We] created the conditions as great as possible.

NIXON: That is right. And that is the way it is going to be played. But listen, as far as people are concerned, let me say they aren't going to buy this crap from the liberals on this one.

KISSINGER: Absolutely not.

NIXON: They know it is a pro-communist government and that is the way it is.

KISSINGER: Exactly. And pro-Castro.

NIXON: Well, the main thing was—let's forget the pro-communist. It was an anti-American government all the way.

KISSINGER: Oh, wildly.

NIXON: And you're expropriating [American property]. . . . No, don't let the columns and the bleeding on that—

KISSINGER: Oh, no, it doesn't bother me. . . .

NIXON: . . . It is just typical of the crap we are up against.

KISSINGER: And the unbelievable filthy hypocrisy . . . of these people. When it is South Africa, if we don't overthrow them there they are raising hell. . . .

Bryce Harlow

September 17, 1973, 6:15 p.m.

Senator George McGovern had just informed Kissinger that he would be voting against his confirmation as secretary of state as a stance against the administration's Indochina policy.[9]

KISSINGER: . . . McGovern just called and said he'd vote against me. . . . He said it is the hardest decision he had to make in a long time—it's giving him enormous pain . . . and it's a heart-wrenching thing for him and I know how much he likes me and admires me, but he has to make a stand against the administration. . . . Ted Kennedy called and said he wanted to get together with me later this week. From that I assume he's not voting against me. The son of a bitch can't be planning to vote against me and to see me.

HARLOW: Sure he can. . . . I can see Kennedy voting against you and then eagerly coming down to get your picture taken with him at your office. . . .

President Nixon

September 17, 1973, 7:13 p.m.

They discuss the day's confirmation hearings and a trenchant column by William Safire in the New York Times *that said the Foreign Relations Committee had feigned a confrontation with the Nixon administration over the illegal wiretapping, pretended to be a tough guardian of the right to privacy, and essentially conducted a charade. Which it did.*[10] *They also discuss the wiretap on Safire and McGovern's call.*

NIXON: How did you get along today?

KISSINGER: Well, they kept me up there for six hours. Largely because of Safire's article blasting them last week for being too gentle with me. . . .

NIXON: Why in the hell did he do that?

KISSINGER: Well, he said they should ask me more searching questions about the wiretaps.

NIXON: What a jackass. Is he off his rocker?

KISSINGER: Well, he's on that wiretap kick.

NIXON: Yeah, but for god's sake, Safire knows very well. You know how that [the wiretap on him] happened, you know. He was talking to Henry Brandon. Hoover picked it up. We didn't have a thing to do with it. The first thing you and I ever heard of it, Henry, was when it came out now.

KISSINGER: Well, Mr. President, as it turns out he was put on a tap when we were in Romania.

NIXON: Is that right? And neither of us ever knew about it and we would have discontinued it immediately. Anyway, so what a silly thing to have a next secretary of state screwing around with a peasant getting tapped like William Safire who knows damn well he's not suspected of a thing.

KISSINGER: Well, they didn't go into much of him. . . . McGovern called and said, "You know how much I like you, Henry, you know how much I admire you and I want to work with you, but my conscience forces me, to protest against the policies, to vote against you."

NIXON: That gets you the word on McGovern, doesn't it?

KISSINGER: Well, I said to him, "Senator, this does not affect my estimate of you." An ambiguous statement.

NIXON: You know, it's the best thing that could ever happen with our conservative friends to have McGovern vote against you. We need it.

KISSINGER: Exactly. That doesn't disturb me. . . .

NIXON: Remember on McGovern, though, never let the SOB in again now. . . . Not socially or otherwise. Never forget this sort of thing. He can't give you that kind of crap. That's what he's trying to do, vote against you and then be for you. . . . Doesn't that prove the total hypocrisy of the liberals, though, Henry? . . . All of the friends of yours that have—the Bradens and the rest— what's this all about?

KISSINGER: Absolutely. They're cowards. That's the worst thing. Total cowards. . . .

Emilio Rabasa

September 18, 1973, 1:47 p.m.

Mexican Foreign Minister Rabasa is concerned about claims in Latin America of U.S. involvement in the coup in Chile and urges against identifying too openly with the Augusto Pinochet dictatorship.

...RABASA: ... They are saying that, well, you know, you helped things that happened. ...

KISSINGER: No, that isn't true. Believe me, it isn't.

RABASA: Henry, you're telling me—I know it. But play it very cool at this moment.

KISSINGER: Well, we are playing it very cool.

RABASA: Because now they're saying that money is going to overflow over there.

KISSINGER: Oh, no, we're going to go slowly.

RABASA: And that the biggest national is going to go back again ... ITT.

KISSINGER: No, no, no.

RABASA: ... Any association of you, or the government, or the president would be terrible at this moment.

KISSINGER: No, no, we are moving very deliberately. ...

President Nixon
September 18, 1973, 11:15 p.m.
Pakistani Prime Minister Zulfikar Ali Bhutto was in Washington, partly to ask for arms, and Nixon and Kissinger discuss getting him weapons from Iran, given that an embargo on U.S. arms to Pakistan was still largely in place. They decide to play hard to get with India.

... KISSINGER: And what he's particularly interested in, which you might mention to him, is the possibility of getting some arms into his hands through Iran.

NIXON: Well, of course.

KISSINGER: And you might tell him that we will do our very best and that we are going to send [U.S. Ambassador to Iran Richard] Helms there to see what can be done. ... He had some doubt whether we are actually going to see what we can do about getting the arms into his hands.

NIXON: We sure as hell are going to do it. ... Mrs. Gandhi is now making sweet noises, but she doesn't mean it, and you know she doesn't mean it. And we are just going to play a little hard to get.

KISSINGER: Absolutely!

NIXON: ... I told him that I thought it was a mistake how [former ambassador to India Kenneth] Keating had advised us to treat her well. He said if we had treated her rough then, the war might never have happened.

KISSINGER: I think we made a mistake. Everyone told us—all our advisers told us that she was the leader of the peace party and therefore we had to strengthen her.

NIXON: I know, I know. But you remember, I had great doubts. . . . And then you remember that terrible toast that she made. . . . I was treating her as a leader rather than a woman and all that. As a leader in her own right rather than the daughter of a leader, and then she just came on with that moralistic lecture. It was unbelievable. . . . But my point is, they talk about tilting to Pakistan—we're going to do more of it. We're going to do it in order . . . to keep the Indians in line and let the Russians know that they aren't to screw around down there. . . .

William Safire
September 21, 1973, 3:02 p.m.
Kissinger tells the Times *columnist that he suspects he (Kissinger) was wiretapped by the Plumbers.*

SAFIRE: . . . Secondly, on a specific thing that one of the *Times* reporters got hold of, to find out if you can say anything about the wiretapping of Henry Kissinger. The story he's got is that you were the target of a Plumbers operation.

KISSINGER: I wouldn't be surprised, but that's not for attribution. . . .

SAFIRE: You can't give me a hint either way, off the record?

KISSINGER: Off the record, I expect it to be true.

SAFIRE: [Obscenity.]

KISSINGER: Well, that may explain some of the other things in a better—

SAFIRE: When? Back in '69?

KISSINGER: Well, I don't really want to go into it. . . . It makes it clear that the Plumbers were certainly not working for me. . . .

John Crewdson
September 22, 1973, 6:15 p.m.
Crewdson of the New York Times, *the reporter Safire was referring to, asks Kissinger about his source's claim that he was wiretapped by the Plumbers, conceived in a broad sense to also include other undercover operatives employed by the White House.*

CREWDSON: The story is somebody tapped your telephone. . . . I have been told by a source who is not in the executive branch that the "Plumbers," in his words, put a tap on some telephone used by you at some point in the last four and a half years. When he says "Plumbers," I don't know who he's referring to. I don't think he means the generic Plumbers in the sense of Krogh and Young. I think he probably means the Caulfield people. It was not done by the FBI, I know that. . . . But he further told me that you had been told that this had been done. . . .

KISSINGER: There is a limit to masochism. . . . Mr. Crewdson, in all honesty, I really don't know anything about it. . . . I've had ideas, but I really don't know anything authoritative. . . .

CREWDSON: You've got suspicions, but not—

KISSINGER: Not fact. . . .

CREWDSON: Would you object to this sort of a story appearing?

KISSINGER: I don't think it does anybody any good. . . . I'd just as soon not have any more wiretap stories. . . . I really basically believe that that period ought to be put behind us at some point fairly soon. . . .

Joseph Kraft
September 23, 1973, 9:58 a.m.
Kissinger tells columnist Kraft that he won't meet with him and his lawyer, Lloyd Cutler, about Kraft's wiretapping. It had been ordered by Nixon, through John Ehrlichman (it was not one of the 17 wiretaps conducted through normal FBI channels), and it was partly directed at Kissinger, who Nixon knew was leaking to Kraft. (Nixon was also disturbed that Kraft was in contact with the North Vietnamese.)[11]

KRAFT: I wanted to see you at some point in the near future if I could. . . .

KISSINGER: The one thing I can't do, if I understood you correctly, I can't meet you with your lawyer. . . . What I told you at breakfast is the total absolute truth as far as I'm concerned. I knew nothing about this at any point and therefore there is nothing I can contribute to it.

KRAFT: The point is I believed you. . . . The other 17 get off scot-free and have a clean bill of health. I didn't do anything; I didn't take any retributive actions with the Senate.

KISSINGER: But you weren't part of this program, so it never got out. You know, so it never could be discussed.

KRAFT: Oh, it could easily have been discussed, believe me. . . . The reason it wasn't discussed was because I did not push it the way your friend Safire did. It wasn't discussed because I was looking toward future guidelines, not toward doing anything. But when they come out with a report that clears them and leaves me hanging up there—

KISSINGER: . . . My difficulty with respect to it is that I know no more about it than you do. . . .

KRAFT: No, I assume it was Ehrlichman. . . . I come out with a bad name. . . . Could you meet informally with Lloyd and me for five minutes?

KISSINGER: I just cannot do it in my position. . . . What is it that I could contribute?

KRAFT: I guess what you could contribute is a statement that so far as you knew there was no national security interests involved. . . .

The Yom Kippur War—Egypt's and Syria's Surprise Attacks, Restraining Israel and Egypt, the Soviets and the UN, Regaining the Prewar Lines, Warplanes, Tanks, and Ammo to Israel, Israel's Counterattacks, the Cease-Fire and Its Collapse, Israel's Strangulation of Egypt's Third Army, and Brezhnev's Threat of Unilateral Action; the Watergate Tapes; and Elliot Richardson's Resignation

October 1973

On October 6, 1973, Yom Kippur, the holiest day of the year in the Jewish faith, Egypt and Syria launched coordinated surprise attacks in the Sinai Peninsula and the Golan Heights to recover territory lost to Israel in the 1967 Six Day War. In the U.S. government, it was unclear who had struck first; many suspected Israel had. Kissinger sought to restrain both Israel and Egypt. He hoped to get the Soviets to join the United States in calling for a return to the prewar lines, those established in 1967, in the UN Security Council. If the Soviets refused, he thought it would show they were colluding with Egypt and Syria, in which case the United States would have to tilt toward Israel (already of course an ally).

Kissinger warned Soviet Ambassador Anatoly Dobrynin against all-out support for Egypt and Syria, threatening additional U.S. military aid to Israel. But he and Nixon opposed further territorial acquisitions by Israel. Nixon worried that after Israel inevitably vanquished Egypt and Syria, Israel "will be even more impossible to deal with than before," and felt they had to rein Israel in. They had to "squeeze the Israelis . . . goddamn hard" when the war was over, Nixon told Kissinger.

Washington supplied Israel with weapons it urgently requested as covertly as possible to avoid antagonizing moderate Arab states; massive open support for Israel would also lead the Soviets to do the same for Egypt and Syria (though the administration ultimately undertook a huge military airlift directly into Israel, partly in response to a Soviet airlift and problems with its more discreet methods). Kissinger accused Secretary of Defense James Schlesinger's Pentagon of sabotaging the delivery of ammunition to Israel. "How can he fuck everything up for a week?" Kissinger complained to White House Chief of Staff Alexander Haig. But Schlesinger, who was not eager to help Israel maintain its 1967 conquests and was attuned to preserving Arab relations, said the Israelis had not mentioned any ammunition problems to him. Kissinger acknowledged that they were "blaming us for their own failures."

Well after a cease-fire was reached, one that swiftly fell apart, Israel completed an entrapment of the Egyptian Third Army on the east bank of the Suez Canal and attacked it. Kissinger was outraged: they could not make Soviet leader Leonid Brezhnev, who had pushed for the cease-fire and negotiated it with him, "look like a goddamn fool," he lectured Israeli Ambassador Simcha Dinitz. Brezhnev threatened to unilaterally send troops to enforce the cease-fire that he charged Israel with violating if the United States didn't act jointly with the Soviets. The United States went on a controversial heightened worldwide military alert in response to Brezhnev's threat. When the Soviets agreed to a UN resolution for an international peacekeeping force that excluded the major powers, Kissinger felt they'd won. Nixon suggested at a press conference that he'd forced Brezhnev to back down, angering Kissinger: "The crazy bastard really made a mess with the Russians," he told Haig.

Israel's encirclement and slow starvation of Egypt's Third Army risked another serious confrontation with the Soviets. Kissinger told Dinitz Israel would not be permitted to destroy it.

Also in October, after Nixon finally agreed to turn over Watergate tapes to Judge John Sirica under threat of impeachment by the House, Kissinger worried that "next they'll demand the papers." "I wouldn't have turned the tapes over," he told Ron Ziegler. After Attorney General Elliot Richardson resigned rather than fire Watergate special prosecutor Archibald Cox at Nixon's order, Kissinger told

Richardson he was "one of the guarantees of virtue in this administration," only to tell Nixon hours later that Richardson "stabbed you in the back."

Anatoly Dobrynin
October 6, 1973, 6:40 a.m.
The White House had received a cable from the U.S. embassy in Tel Aviv: Israel was reporting that Egypt and Syria planned a coordinated attack later that day in the Sinai Peninsula and Golan Heights. Israeli Prime Minister Golda Meir had conveyed that Israel did not plan to launch a preemptive strike (she worried it would hurt the chances of getting U.S. assistance and make Israel look like the aggressor) and asked the administration to try to prevent war. But if Egypt and Syria attacked, Israel said it would react "violently," Kissinger informs Soviet Ambassador Dobrynin.[1]

> ... KISSINGER: We have information from the Israelis that the Arabs and Syrians are planning an attack within the next six hours and that your people are evacuating civilians from Damascus and Cairo. . . . If there is an attack they will react very strongly and violently. . . . They have no plans whatever to attack. . . . But if the Egyptians and Syrians do attack, the Israeli response will be extremely strong. . . . The president believes that you and we have a special responsibility to restrain our respective friends. . . . Until an hour ago I did not take it seriously but we have now received an urgent phone call from Jerusalem saying the Israelis believe it will happen within six hours and they are mobilizing.
>
> DOBRYNIN: . . . Don't you think the Israelis are trying to do something on their own?
>
> KISSINGER: . . . We are telling them not to do it. I cannot judge it. . . . You can assure Moscow we are taking the most urgent messages with Israel. . . .

Mohamed El-Zayyat
October 6, 1973, 7:00 a.m.
Kissinger calls Egypt's foreign minister.

> KISSINGER: Mr. Foreign Minister, sorry to disturb you. We have had a report, which does seem very reliable, and an appeal from the Israelis, to the effect that your forces and the Syrian forces are planning attacks within the next several hours. . . . The Israelis have asked us to tell you of the seriousness, and that they have no intention of attacking, so that if your preparations are caused by fear of an Israeli attack, they are groundless. . . . And on the other hand, if you are going to attack, they will take extremely strong measures. . . . I want to tell you I have just called the Israeli minister and I have told him that if Israel attacks first we would take a very serious view of the situation,

and have told him on behalf of the United States that Israel must not attack, no matter what they think the provocation is. Now, I would like to ask you, Mr. Foreign Minister, to communicate this to your government. . . . Urgently. And to ask them on our behalf to show restraint at a time when we are at least beginning to—

ZAYYAT: I will do this immediately, although I am very apprehensive that this is a pretext on the Israeli part.

KISSINGER: If it is a pretext we will take a strong measure against them. . . .

Mohamed El-Zayyat
October 6, 1973, 8:15 a.m.
Zayyat reports alleged Israeli military attacks in the Gulf of Suez. Kissinger found the report "preposterous." Yet it was unclear who had fired the first shots in the war and many officials suspected Israel had.[2]

ZAYYAT: . . . Israelis took some provocation on the Egyptian borders. We have actually tried to repel them and are doing so.

KISSINGER: Did they try to cross the canal?

ZAYYAT: In the Gulf of Suez, a maritime action supported by planes. This is in our territory. . . . Apparently this military contact is happening in Egyptian waters. . . .

KISSINGER: As I told you we will oppose any Israeli offensive action. . . . I will work on this immediately. I would urge in the meantime to show restraint as much as possible and to confine any action to the place where it has started.

ZAYYAT: Inside Egypt is a bit difficult.

KISSINGER: If inside Egypt of course you will want to repel, and we are not urging not to defend your territory, but to try to confine [the fighting] and we will get to the Israelis immediately. . . .

Mordechai Shalev
October 6, 1973, 8:29 a.m.
Israeli Chargé d'affaires Shalev transmits a report of Egyptian and Syrian air attacks.

SHALEV: Just had a call from Jerusalem . . . hostilities were opened by the Egyptians and by the Syrians. Apparently mainly by aerial bombardment along the borders.

KISSINGER: I have had a call from the Egyptians saying you were undertaking naval actions on the Gulf of Suez on the Egyptian side.

SHALEV: Well, I don't know about that.

KISSINGER: It has not in the past been your preferred method of operations. . . . Again I would like to urge the greatest possible restraint.

SHALEV: I think you have assurances from us that we are not going to open [hostilities], but it looks that they have already opened. . . .

Alexander Haig
October 6, 1973, 8:35 a.m.
Kissinger calls Haig, who was in Key Biscayne with Nixon, to relate that war had started. They conjecture on the Soviets' role. "I think our domestic situation has invited this," Kissinger says, referring to Watergate. He wants Nixon, who was trying to get a defiant Vice President Spiro Agnew to resign while also dealing with Watergate, portrayed as on top of the situation.

KISSINGER: We may have a Middle East war going on today. . . . We got a report at 6:00 this morning that the Israelis were expecting Syrian and Egyptian attacks. . . . First I thought it was an Israeli trick for them to be able to launch an attack, although this is the holiest day. I called the Israelis and warned them to restrain. I called the Egyptian foreign minister urging restraint. I called Dobrynin. . . . I got a return call from the Israelis giving us assurances that no preemptive Israeli [action] would be taken. The Egyptian called me back to say Israelis were launching a naval attack in the Gulf of Suez, and 15 minutes later a call came from the Israelis saying that the Egyptians and Syrians were bombarding all along the fronts and launching air attacks. . . . All I want you to know is that we are on top of it here. You should say that the president was kept informed from 6:00 a.m. on and I will let you know what is going on.

HAIG: Have there been any border crossings?

KISSINGER: As of this moment I just know of a report from Jerusalem relayed to me by the Israeli minister—air attacks all along the Egyptian and Syrian fronts. I don't know what Israeli counteraction is. I have a report from the Egyptian that Israeli naval units are shelling them in the Gulf of Suez and they will be driving them off.

HAIG: What is your view of the Soviet attitude?

KISSINGER: My view is that they are trying to keep it quiet and they are surprised. . . . I think it is too insane for them to have started it.

HAIG: You never know. A lot of difficulties here.

KISSINGER: That is the one factor. I think our domestic situation has invited this. I think what may have happened is the Soviets told the Egyptians . . . that there will not be any progress unless there is stirring in the Middle East, and those maniacs have stirred a little too much. It looks to me now that the Israelis are certainly going to hit back hard. . . . Your position is that the president is on top of the situation and getting regular reports. . . .

Anatoly Dobrynin

October 6, 1973, 9:20 a.m.

Kissinger informs Dobrynin that Egypt and Syria had launched coordinated attacks. (Moscow had urged Egypt and Syria to avoid war and pursue negotiations to regain their territory captured by Israel in 1967 and predicted their swift defeat, as did Washington. Both Moscow and Washington would seek to preserve détente during the conflict while extending their influence in the region.)[3]

> KISSINGER: Our information is that the Egyptians and Syrians have attacked all along their fronts. . . . Zayyat is claiming the Israelis launched a naval attack on some isolated spot in the Gulf of Suez and that triggered the whole thing. . . . You and I know that is baloney: if they are going to attack they will not launch an attack in the Gulf of Suez. . . . We are using our maximum influence with the Israelis to show restraint. So far they tell me they have kept their response to their side of the line and that they have not made any deep penetration of Arab territory. But you know them as well as I do and it will not last much longer.
>
> DOBRYNIN: . . . Really madness.
>
> KISSINGER: Total madness. . . .

President Nixon

October 6, 1973, 9:25 a.m.

Kissinger tells Nixon that the Soviets apparently knew of the Egyptian and Syrian attacks in advance and that the war was almost certainly started by Egypt and Syria. Nixon, who shared Kissinger's view of Soviet foreknowledge, if not encouragement, thinks they should go to the UN Security Council. Kissinger wants the Soviets to join them in "a neutral approach." His strategy was to get the Soviets to collaborate in calling for a return to the prewar lines, and if the Soviets refused, as was likely, the United States would gain time for Israel to restore those lines, at which point it could accept a cease-fire. He sought to delay going to the UN.[4]

> NIXON: I wanted you to know I am keeping on top of reports here. The Russians claim to be surprised.
>
> KISSINGER: The Russians claim to be surprised and my impression is that they were supposed to be surprised because apparently there has been an airlift of dependents out of the area going on for the last two or three days.
>
> NIXON: I agree.
>
> KISSINGER: And so our impression is that they knew about it or knew it was possible. They did not warn us.
>
> NIXON: What is happening now? What is the status?

KISSINGER: Fighting has broken out on the Golan Heights and along the Sinai. The Egyptians claim that the Israelis had launched a naval attack in the Gulf of Suez which triggered the whole thing. That I just can't believe. Why a naval attack? The Israelis claim that so far the fighting is still mostly in Israeli territory and that they have confined themselves to defensive action. My own impression is that this one almost certainly was started by the Arabs. It is almost inconceivable that the Israelis would start on the holiest holiday for the Jews when there is no need to, and there is no evidence that the Israelis launched air attacks, and they gave us an assurance which we passed on this morning that they would not launch a preemptive attack. And we told the Arabs that if the Israelis launch a preemptive attack that we would oppose them, and they should exercise restraint. My view is that the primary problem is to get the fighting stopped and then use the opportunity to see whether a settlement could be enforced.

NIXON: You mean a diplomatic settlement of the bigger problem?

KISSINGER: That is right. There is going to be a Security Council meeting almost certainly today and we are still debating whether we should call it or the Israelis should. . . .

NIXON: I think we should. . . . I think we ought to take the initiative and you ought to indicate you talked to me.

KISSINGER: Let me call Dobrynin right away on that. In the debate there are going to be a lot of wild charges all over the place.

NIXON: Don't take sides. Nobody ever knows who starts the wars out there.

KISSINGER: . . . On the immediate thing we have to get the Soviets drawn in on the side of the Arab group—then it would be involved. If they join us in a neutral approach in which both of us say we don't know who started it but that we want to stop it, that would be best. . . .

Alexander Haig

October 6, 1973, 10:35 a.m.

Kissinger says if the Soviets don't join them in in petitioning the UN Security Council for a return to the status quo ante, it will show they are colluding with Egypt and Syria, in which case the administration would have to lean toward Israel. He advises that Nixon not return to Washington from Key Biscayne unless the Soviets refuse to cooperate.

KISSINGER: I wanted to bring you up to date on where we stand and to tell you my strategy. You may have to calm some people down.

HAIG: Good. I am sitting with the president.

KISSINGER: Okay. The Egyptians have crossed the canal at five places and the Syrians have penetrated in two places into the Golan Heights. . . . We have to assume an Arab attack. . . . The open question is, is it with Soviet collusion or against Soviet opposition? On that we have no answer yet. I have called, first, as far as our public position, the [UN] secretary-general, who leaks like a sieve, to tell him about all of the efforts we have made, and I have told him that I have been in touch with the Soviets. I have been in touch with Dobrynin and said we should jointly call a Security Council . . . and we jointly offer a resolution calling for an end of the fighting and a return to the cease-fire lines established in 1967. . . . This is designed in part to smoke them out. If they want the fighting stopped this will stop it fast. If they refuse to do this then we have to assume some collusion. Now if they refuse to do it we have two problems. The first is to get the fighting stopped and the second is the long-term policy. In order to get the fighting stopped we cannot give the Soviets and the Arabs the impression that we are separating too far from the Israelis. . . . If the Soviets could cooperate with us we will take a neutral position. . . . If the Soviets do not cooperate with us and wholeheartedly back the Arabs on the immediate issue of the fighting, we, in my judgment, have to lean toward the Israelis. . . . My estimate is that starting tomorrow evening the Arabs will have to give up territory. My view is if the Israelis make territorial acquisitions we have to come down hard on them to force them to give them up. . . . I think the worst thing we could do is to now take a sort of neutral position while the fighting is going on unless the Soviets take a neutral position with us. . . . If they don't join us and go to the other side we have to tilt. . . . If the Soviets are all-out on the other side we have a mischievous case of collusion . . . and we had better then be tough as nails.

HAIG: The president is seriously considering going back to Washington.

KISSINGER: I think that a grave mistake. There is nothing we can do right now. You should wait to see how it develops. . . . If the Soviets refuse to cooperate with us, we will know we are in a confrontation and he should then take leadership. . . . If the Soviets do not face us, then I think he should stay down there. . . .

Anatoly Dobrynin
October 6, 1973, 11:25 a.m.
Kissinger warns Dobrynin against all-out support for Egypt and Syria and says if the situation "gets out of hand" the United States will furnish Israel with the military supplies it requested.

. . . KISSINGER: I have talked to the president again and he wanted me to call you and to underline again his very grave concern that this not be used to destroy everything that it has taken us three years to build up.

DOBRYNIN: By whom?

KISSINGER: By any of us.

DOBRYNIN: Who, really?

KISSINGER: If you take the position of support all-out for the Arabs that would
be in effect encouraging what seems clearly to us an Arab attack. . . . Today
the Arabs are on Israeli territory but we don't believe this will last 72 hours,
and after that the problem will be to get the Israelis back to the cease-fire
line. . . . We have not responded to an urgent Israeli request for additional
military supplies. If it gets out of hand we will be forced to do that. For all of
these reasons it will be important to our own relationship that it be handled
as much jointly as we can. . . .

Anatoly Dobrynin

October 6, 1973, 7:20 p.m.

*Kissinger would like from Dobrynin some indication of what the Soviets are telling
the Egyptians and Syrians, but Dobrynin says he is not sure what Kissinger wants
from the Soviet Union, given its long position in favor of Israel giving up the occupied
territories. It would be "ridiculous" to tell Egypt and Syria that they cannot regain
their land, he says.*

. . . KISSINGER: If you can give us some indication what you are doing privately. . . . It will be kept confidential. . . . Our reading of the situation is
that the Arab attack has been totally contained, that now they are going to
be pushed back. . . . The Arabs have proved their point. They have attacked
across the canal. They can withdraw on their own and return to the status
quo. . . .

DOBRYNIN: . . . What do you want from our point of view, our position, which
is a principle from the beginning of '67? . . . For us to tell the Arabs is very
difficult. . . . The difficulties we are now facing is that the Arabs are trying
to regain the lands occupied by Israel. They have been using that argument
to us, and for us to tell them you cannot free your land, it is ridiculous. . . .
What course of action do you propose besides SC [UN Security Council]?

KISSINGER: A de facto return to the status quo ante. . . . The Arabs have now
proved their point.

DOBRYNIN: Henry, how could they? . . . Asking them to return somewhere if
they have nothing? . . . They [will] say you invite us to give back territory
that belongs to us. . . . They will say you are in collusion with the U.S. and Israel. . . . We their friends are saying go back from your own land. . . . It would
look like we are trying to sell them out. . . .

Mohamed El-Zayyat

October 6, 1973, 8:48 p.m.

Kissinger proposes to the Egyptian foreign minister a return to the status quo ante, hence the borders after the 1967 Six Day War, which Zayyat considers "completely unreasonable."

KISSINGER: . . . Our evaluation is that if the fighting goes on the Israelis will probably gain the upper hand. . . . We suggest that we would prefer a cease-fire plus a restoration of the status quo ante. . . .

ZAYYAT: Of course the question of, you know, when you think about 5,000 Egyptians killed and then going back to where we were is something out of the question in Cairo. If I were in Cairo I would think madness. . . . I don't know how many killed but could be thousands killed. . . . How can you advise anyone after doing this to go back where he was? I mean, this is completely unreasonable. . . .

President Nixon

October 8, 1973, 7:08 p.m.

Nixon says they need a settlement to prevent the Israelis from being too obstinate and aggressive after their military victory, though he recognizes they can't get Israel to return to the pre-1967 borders. Kissinger had suspected since the war started that Israel would try to go beyond the prewar lines and take new positions further into Arab territory, which he and Nixon oppose.[5]

. . . NIXON: The one thing we have to be concerned about, which you and I know looking down the road, is that the Israelis, when they finish clobbering the Egyptians and the Syrians, which they will do, will be even more impossible to deal with than before, and . . . we must have a diplomatic settlement there. . . . We must not tell them that now, but we have got to do it. You see, they could feel so strong as a result of this they'd say, "Well, why do we have to settle?" . . . We must not under any circumstances allow them because of the victory that they're going to win—and they'll win it, thank god, they should—but we must not get away with just having this thing hang over for another four years and have us at odds with the Arab world. We're not going to do it anymore. . . . You and I both know they can't go back to the other borders. But we must not, on the other hand, say that because the Israelis win this war as they won the '67 war that we just go on with status quo. It can't be done.

KISSINGER: I couldn't agree more. . . .

NIXON: They'll cut the Egyptians off. Poor dumb Egyptians getting across the canal and all the bridges will be blown up. They'll cut them all off—30 or 40 thousand of them. Go over and destroy the SAM sites. . . . Just so the Israelis don't get to the point where they say to us, "We will not settle except on the basis of everything we got." They can't do that, Henry. They can't do that to us again. They've done it to us for four years, but no more. . . .

Simcha Dinitz
October 11, 1973, 4:30 p.m.
Israeli Ambassador Dinitz suggests that Secretary of Defense James Schlesinger was holding up fighter bombers and tanks that Israel had requested.

. . . DINITZ: . . . Do you have any reply from your talk on the heavy stuff from Schlesinger?

KISSINGER: I mentioned it to him and he said he would look at the schedule again.

DINITZ: For your information about 12 senators called me. . . . All are on the committee for appropriations. Schlesinger said to them there were no problems. To some he said the White House is being difficult. To others he said there were logistic problems with transportation. Senator Jackson said to him perhaps we can move equipment from Europe or other places. Schlesinger said that they had not been asked to look into that.

KISSINGER: That is a lie. . . .

Simcha Dinitz
October 11, 1973, 8:10 p.m.
Jordan's King Hussein was under pressure to enter the war on the side of Egypt and Syria.

KISSINGER: . . . The British have approached us on two matters. They have been approached, as we have, by the king of Jordan, who is under enormous pressure. He wants to move a brigade into Syria out of harm's way. . . . They don't care what you do but they want to make sure you don't attack them. . . .

DINITZ: Will they fight us or will they just stand there?

KISSINGER: They will just stand there.

DINITZ: I will have to pass it on to my government. . . . This is called, Dr. Kissinger, to fight war with all of the conveniences. . . .

President Nixon
October 12, 1973, 8:38 a.m.

Kissinger and Nixon discuss the Israeli counteroffensive in Syria and military aid to Israel. They agree that U.S. intervention or "massive open support for Israel" was out of the question.

KISSINGER: . . . The Israelis are still advancing into Syria, although they are now getting heavy counterattacks and the Iraqi armor division is beginning to fight them.

NIXON: The thing we have here from CIA indicates that it was pretty tough up there in the Golan Heights. . . .

KISSINGER: That's right. But they claim to be advancing and they claim to be reaching their objective. . . .

NIXON: Now, what about our own activities with regard to resupply, etc.? Has anything gone forward in that respect?

KISSINGER: Well, last night we finally told Schlesinger just to charter some of these civilian airlines, airplanes from civilian airlines for the Defense Department, and then turn them over to the Israelis. . . . We've tried everything else and these civilian airlines just wouldn't charter to the Israelis directly. . . .

NIXON: But they have not yet actually run short of equipment?

KISSINGER: No. And of course the most important assurance you gave them was that you'd replace the equipment.

NIXON: The planes and tanks. . . . In terms of intervention, that's out of the question.

KISSINGER: Impossible.

NIXON: In terms of massive open support for Israel, that will just bring massive open support by the Russians.

KISSINGER: And it wouldn't change the situation in the next two or three days, which is what we're talking about.

NIXON: . . . The Israelis are not looking at two or three days. That's our problem, isn't it? They may be looking at two or three weeks before they can really start clobbering these people.

KISSINGER: In two or three weeks the international presses will become unmanageable.

NIXON: I see. Well, then, if it's two or three days then the Israelis have just got to win something on the Syrian front. . . .

KISSINGER: That's exactly it. . . .

James Schlesinger

October 12, 1973, 11:45 p.m.

Kissinger presses Schlesinger, a bitter rival who worried that meeting Israel's weapons requests might harm U.S. relations with the Arabs and lead to an oil embargo (a concern other officials shared) and was not disposed to help Israel maintain its 1967 conquests, to expedite delivery of ammunition to Israel and accuses the Pentagon of sabotaging it. (Kissinger complained repeatedly to Alexander Haig of Schlesinger's alleged sabotage.)[6] Kissinger wants Defense to lean on air charter companies.

KISSINGER: I've just been meeting on an urgent basis with Dinitz, who says they are running out substantially of ammunition. They based their strategy on the assumption that they would get the ammunition replaced this week, as the president had promised them on Tuesday, and that they are stopping their offensive in Syria because they can't move because of lack of supplies. . . . I know that you are serious, but I frankly have no confidence that [Deputy Secretary of Defense William] Clements and [Assistant Secretary of Defense Robert] Hill and company aren't sabotaging this every step of the way. . . . I just don't find the initiative. If they wanted something to happen, then it would happen. . . . Except for you I don't know anyone over there who has any intention of making this happen. You know that Clements would just as soon move them the other way.

SCHLESINGER: Well, he will do what the president wants.

KISSINGER: Yeah, but the way he interprets what the president wants is not necessarily what the president wants. . . . I just find it hard to believe that every company would refuse to charter unless somebody sort of told them in a half-assed way.

SCHLESINGER: . . . When are they going to start running out of reserves?

KISSINGER: They are out now. They have stopped their offensive. And they are now in deep trouble in the Sinai. . . .

SCHLESINGER: Well, if we started now and really turned the screws on these guys, I suspect that we can collect a few aircraft for tomorrow. But I think if you want to do something about it, you better let a U.S. aircraft fly all the way in. . . .

KISSINGER: But can't we turn the screws on these charter companies? I am just convinced that if the screws were turned, they would have produced.

SCHLESINGER: I think that that may be right. We never went back at them again because of the decision to go with the Military Airlift Command. . . .

KISSINGER: Well, if the charters picked it up here and the Israelis picked up what is already in the Azores, that would at least put some steam behind it. . . .

SCHLESINGER: Okay, let me see what I can do. One thing we could do, we could take these 10 or 12 C-130s that we are planning to give them and load them up and let them go all the way.

KISSINGER: Well, let's do that. . . . From our point of view we needed the Israeli offensive moving. . . .

SCHLESINGER: Well, Henry, it would have been desirable for them to tell us that they were going to run out of ammunition.

KISSINGER: Well, on the other hand I must tell you we told them every day that this stuff was coming. There wasn't a day that we didn't tell them that they would have 20 aircraft in the morning and then they didn't have them in the evening. . . .

Alexander Haig
October 12, 1973, 11:54 p.m.
Kissinger tells Haig about the Pentagon's foot-dragging on the ammunition delivery and asks him to threaten William Clements and Schlesinger.

KISSINGER: Al, you know, having a massive problem with the Israelis because the sons of bitches in Defense have been stalling for four days and not one airplane has moved. . . . After the decision on Tuesday not one goddamn shipload. . . . And they are now out of ammunition. They are stopping their Syrian offensive. The Egyptians have transferred artillery to the other side of the canal. . . . And may start an offensive tomorrow. So now the question is whether they are going to collapse in the Sinai, and you know what this does to the diplomatic scenario I described to you. . . . Which absolutely required an Israeli offensive. . . . And they told us they were running out of ammunition. They conducted the operation on the assumption that it would be replenished by the end of this week. . . . Now my orders apparently just aren't carried out over there. . . . Will you call Clements and throw the fear of god into him? . . . And also throw the fear of god into Schlesinger. . . . I do not believe for one minute that they can't get charters if they tell these charter companies that the next time they need a rate change they won't get it. . . .

Alexander Haig
October 13, 1973, 12:45 a.m.
Kissinger is fed up with Schlesinger's delays.

KISSINGER: He has no excuse—I explained the strategy to him in great detail. But he's afraid of Clements. . . . How can he fuck everything up for a week? He can't now recoup it the day the diplomacy is supposed to start. . . . Do you believe that the Defense Department couldn't get civilian charters—that Clements couldn't get on the phone and say, "Listen you sons of bitches, if you ever want to get Defense Department business again, you better charter." . . . You know goddamn well they didn't try.

HAIG: I don't think it's good for me to call Clements—I've had a piece of Jim's ass for about as heavy as it can be. I told him to get on the phone and call you right now. To have his man call the Israeli man. . . . And get the goddamn facts military to military. Keep the civilians out of it, find out what the hell they need. . . . He said the stuff is there in the Azores, he felt that's what was to be done.

KISSINGER: But Al, you know we've been through a lot of this stuff before. . . . They always do the one thing that doesn't get to Israel. You know, they'll dump it in the Azores, they'll take it to the North Pole, they'll get it to Greenland, Antarctica, any place. . . . And of course the whole goddamn strategy will now be out of whack because what will now happen is that the stuff will arrive just in time when you want them to stop. . . .

James Schlesinger

October 13, 1973, 12:49 a.m.

Kissinger accuses Schlesinger's Pentagon of "massive sabotage," but Schlesinger says the Israelis have been "perfectly relaxed" about their ammunition supply and didn't mention any problems to him. And indeed Israel was not short of ammunition. Kissinger thinks the Israelis are blaming them for their own failures—"you have the goddamn Israelis screwing up everything they are doing." (Their logistical command had lost track of ammunition in the pipeline.)[7]

. . . KISSINGER: . . . I just think there was massive sabotage.

SCHLESINGER: It's just not true, Henry. . . . We've been asking them what their daily supply is, they have exhibited no uneasiness about it at all.

KISSINGER: Because they don't trust the people in the room.

SCHLESINGER: You mean to say that when General [Mordechai] Gur is alone with General [Gordon] Sumner that he doesn't trust him? . . . Sumner has been trying to get it out of Gur for five days and Gur has been perfectly relaxed about the day's supply.

KISSINGER: . . . Dinitz claims that was because every day we told them, which is true, that they were going to get 20 planes moving. And every day it didn't happen. . . .

SCHLESINGER: Well, they simply cannot be that short of ammo, Henry. It is impossible that they didn't know what their supply was—and suddenly they've run out of it.

KISSINGER: Look, they have obviously screwed up every offensive they've conducted. And they are not about to take the responsibility themselves.

I have no doubt whatever that they are blaming us for their own failures. . . .
But the only way it is going to work out is if we are going to get a quick end
of the war. Of which we nearly have all pieces in place, but we need an Israeli
offensive. . . .

SCHLESINGER: Are they out of ammo or aren't they?

KISSINGER: How the hell would I know? They said they were stopping their
offensive. . . .

SCHLESINGER: It's amazing to me—I sat with them from 5:30 to 6:30 and they
simply did not mention ammunition problems. . . . All they talked about was
the re-equipment and to get it in within two days.

KISSINGER: They are so terrified now—or claim to be terrified—of . . . an
Egyptian thrust.

SCHLESINGER: That's incredible planning on their part.

KISSINGER: Look, they fucked it up.

SCHLESINGER: Okay, let me try to find out what the hell their status of supplies
situation is. We had the impression that they had 15 days of supply.

KISSINGER: I bet you they counted their supply on the experience of the Six
Day War. . . . I bet you they didn't expend as much in the whole Six Day War
as they do in one day of this offensive. . . . I must say in their defense . . .
we told them time and again that they were getting all the consumables and
they should fight as if they were coming.

SCHLESINGER: Right. But they never told us they were running short.

KISSINGER: Because you know what happened as well as I do. These guys got
the whole thing screwed up—every time. They are living in 1967. All day
long yesterday they were telling me they were heading for Damascus and
they were going to stop on the outskirts. . . . Now they obviously can't make
it. . . . No question in my mind that 80 percent of the blame is theirs. . . .
[Also] you have a few people down the line who were put there to sabotage
that stuff. Not by you. . . . I think on the other hand you have the goddamn
Israelis screwing up everything they are doing.

SCHLESINGER: If only they had said they had a problem. . . . Three days
ago they were telling us how happy they were about the consumable
situation. . . .

President Nixon
October 14, 1973, 9:04 a.m.
Nixon wants to offer the Soviets a carrot by "squeezing" Israel when the war is over.

. . . NIXON: . . . Look, we've got to face this—that as far as the Russians are concerned, they have a pretty good beef in so far as everything we have offered
on the Mideast . . . we were stringing them along and they know it. We've
got to come off with something on the diplomatic front, because . . . they'll

figure that we get the cease-fire and then the Israelis will dig in and we'll back them, as we always have. That's putting it quite bluntly, but it's quite true Henry, isn't it?

KISSINGER: There's a lot in that.

NIXON: They can't be in that position, so we have got to be in a position to offer something. . . . Because we've got to squeeze the Israelis when this is over and the Russians have got to know it. We've got to squeeze them goddamn hard. . . .

President Nixon
October 14, 1973, 11:10 a.m.
Washington was undertaking a massive U.S. military airlift directly to Israel (it had decided to forgo charters for a straight military operation despite previous reluctance for its military planes to be seen flying into Tel Aviv), partly in response to a Soviet airlift to Egypt and Syria, and speeding up delivery of Phantoms.[8]

. . . NIXON: And I am glad to hear that we are going all-out on this.

KISSINGER: Oh, it is a massive airlift, Mr. President. The planes are going to land every 50 minutes.

NIXON: . . . Get them in there. . . . I told them to check the European theater to see if there were some of those smaller planes that they need. . . . And the other thing is that these big planes, you can put some of those good tanks, those M-60 tanks on if necessary. . . . If we are going to do it, don't spare the horses just yet.

KISSINGER: Actually with the big planes, Mr. President, we have also flexibility. We can fly the Skyhawks in.

NIXON: Put them on the plane, you mean.

KISSINGER: Yes. . . . No country will let them overfly.

NIXON: All right. . . . If we are going to take heat for this, well, let's go. . . .

Alexander Haig
October 19, 1973, 3:20 p.m.
Kissinger vehemently opposes Nixon's plan to combine an announcement of Kissinger's trip to the Soviet Union the next day for negotiations on the Middle East with a Watergate statement by Nixon (when he would refuse a court order to relinquish his tapes and propose providing a summary instead).

HAIG: On this thing we are working on. The president wants to go out tonight and announce your trip.

KISSINGER: Impossible. . . . First of all, we have now told the Soviets we would do it at 2:00 in the morning. . . . He is going to make them both at the same time?

HAIG: Yes.

KISSINGER: A disaster. . . . My honest opinion is that it is a cheap stunt. It looks as if he is using foreign policy to cover a domestic thing.

HAIG: The domestic thing is not controversial. . . . A very good settlement. It would also look very weird for him to make a major announcement on Watergate and ignore the fact you are going to Moscow when everyone wants to know what is going on in the Middle East. I don't see it as a contrived phony. I think you have two very important things happening.

KISSINGER: He is not firing [Watergate special prosecutor Archibald] Cox?

HAIG: As of now, no. Just giving him a desist order which will probably result in his resignation.

KISSINGER: I would not link foreign policy with Watergate. You will regret it for the rest of your life. . . . It will forever after be said he did this to cover Watergate. . . .

Melvin Laird
October 23, 1973, 2:55 p.m.
Faced with possible impeachment by the House and a contempt citation, Nixon had reversed course and agreed to turn over Watergate tapes to Judge John Sirica.

KISSINGER: I know what you are going to tell me. You are a politician. Will you tell me the political significance. . . .

LAIRD: . . . It hasn't been handled well.

KISSINGER: It is a goddamn disaster. Everything was quiet and now this. . . . Is this going to quiet things any?

LAIRD: No. . . .

KISSINGER: Next they'll demand the papers.

LAIRD: Oh, Christ yes. . . .

President Nixon
October 23, 1973, 6:50 p.m.
Kissinger tells Nixon he cannot "do more without impairing the presidency."

. . . KISSINGER: Ted Kennedy called . . . and said you had settled it all this afternoon.

NIXON: You mean about Sirica? They will want it all for the [Senate Watergate] committee.

KISSINGER: They will want everything.

NIXON: No more!

KISSINGER: . . . You cannot possibly do more without impairing the presidency.

NIXON: . . . It is not possible. The next thing they will go into India, Pakistan, Cambodia, everything we have done. The Foreign Relations Committee will want everything. We are going to stand firm. This is a hell of a concession. There is stuff in there that is embarrassing. . . .

Ronald Ziegler
October 23, 1973, 7:30 p.m.
Nixon had fired Watergate special prosecutor Archibald Cox three nights earlier.

. . . KISSINGER: . . . Listen, we had Cox all set up by Saturday. If you had followed my tactics I would have left him right where he was for three weeks. At that point no one knew who Cox was. I would have then maneuvered him into a—
ZIEGLER: Even after turning the tapes over?
KISSINGER: I wouldn't have turned the tapes over. . . . I would have taken them into the Supreme Court. . . .

Alexander Haig
October 23, 1973, 8:00 p.m.
Kissinger and Haig ponder the ramifications of Nixon's decision to turn over the tapes to Judge Sirica.

. . . KISSINGER: . . . How are we going to resist giving up other documents now?
HAIG: We will just take them case by case and see what they do.
KISSINGER: That is the thing that worries me most.
HAIG: We will handle it. Muck through as we do all the time. . . .
KISSINGER: How is his frame of mind?
HAIG: Very down, very down. . . .
KISSINGER: . . . Where do you think it leaves him?
HAIG: It could be a disaster, but I don't think so. . . . In the short run we are in fine shape.
KISSINGER: My immediate worry is where it will lead to.
HAIG: That is the problem. . . .

Simcha Dinitz
October 23, 1973, 8:30 p.m.
In Moscow, Kissinger and Leonid Brezhnev had agreed on a cease-fire in the Yom Kippur War, and the UN Security Council had passed a U.S.-Soviet cease-fire proposal. But the cease-fire quickly fell apart.[9] Kissinger worries about Israeli forces cutting off supplies to the town of Suez and to Egypt's Third Army on the east bank of the Suez Canal.

DINITZ: I just talked to the prime minister and have the authority to pass on to Moscow that you can pass to Sadat our solemn pledge. If the Egyptians stop shooting we will not shoot either. . . . It was absolutely the decision of the Egyptians to break the cease-fire. . . . We are honestly and sincerely willing to accept the cease-fire, and right now. The Egyptians resumed the war, and as a result of this new territory was claimed. . . .

KISSINGER: . . . As you are in Suez city, some people will be starving in the next day or two.

DINITZ: We have not entered the city proper. We have gone around it.

KISSINGER: You have cut the road. Some people on the east bank will not have any water.

DINITZ: They had no business being there anyway. . . .

Simcha Dinitz
October 24, 1973, 9:22 a.m.
Kissinger complains that Israel was attacking Egypt's trapped Third Army, but Ambassador Dinitz maintains they were simply "returning the fight" after the army tried to break the siege.

KISSINGER: Mr. Ambassador, now we have got another message that you are attacking the Third Army.

DINITZ: No. . . . The cease-fire went into effect and then the Third Army has tried to make efforts to break out of the siege. And started attacking and even advancing. . . . It is a big power. When they returned fighting they have brought 30 Egyptian planes over to support the action and 15 of them were shot down by us. A big battle has developed over which we are just blocking the Third Army from getting out of the siege. We are not advancing. We are returning the fight. And the whole thing that has happened now is their attack to try to break out of the siege. Both northward, westward, and eastward at the same time. . . .

KISSINGER: Well, now, wait a minute—westward means they are going across the canal. Are they drowning themselves?

DINITZ: No, they are trying to break through the north of Suez, the bridgehead that we have closed.

KISSINGER: Look, Mr. Ambassador, we have been a strong support for you. . . . But we cannot make Brezhnev look like a goddamn fool in front of his own colleagues. . . .

Simcha Dinitz
October 24, 1973, 9:32 a.m.
Egyptian President Anwar Sadat had asked the United States to intervene to uphold the cease-fire.

KISSINGER: Mr. Ambassador, the message of Sadat to us asked us to intervene with forces on the ground. . . . Now, if he asks the same thing of the Soviets and if the Soviets put some divisions in there, then you will have outsmarted yourselves. . . . You had a tremendous victory—

DINITZ: . . . I have the solemn word, we are now only reacting, trying to block them from advancing, and we are prepared to stop the fight any minute. . . .

KISSINGER: You know, there's a limit beyond which we can't go, and one of them is we cannot make Brezhnev look like an idiot. . . . Last night I already had a call from Dobrynin in which they are accusing me of having gone from Moscow to Tel Aviv to plot with them [the Israelis] the overthrow of the whole arrangement we've made.

DINITZ: Well, that's ridiculous.

KISSINGER: Well, it may be ridiculous, but that's how war starts. . . . Don't tell me you're taking Cairo in order to prevent the breakout of the Third Army. . . .

President Nixon

October 24, 1973, 7:10 p.m.

After telling Elliot Richardson, who had earlier resigned as attorney general rather than fire Watergate special prosecutor Archibald Cox at Nixon's order, that afternoon that he considered him "one of the guarantees of virtue in this administration,"[10] *Kissinger tells Nixon that Richardson betrayed him. Nixon says he may die, and Kissinger observes that Gerald Ford, whom Nixon had nominated as vice president to replace Spiro Agnew, "just doesn't have it."*

. . . KISSINGER: Your attorney general stabbed you in the back. . . . The worst you can say is the firing of Cox was a tactical mistake by being too early.

NIXON: The point is that Cox was given an order and he defied it. If you defied an order when you were negotiating with the Russians, you would go down too. . . . We have cooled the issue somewhat by the Sirica thing. They are not going to get another special prosecutor.

KISSINGER: We can live with one other than Cox.

NIXON: Not with the authority to investigate the president. That is what Richardson sold out on.

KISSINGER: He picked the wrong man [as special prosecutor]. Then we gave him [Cox] a charter which gave your most violent opponent his [opportunity] to go after everything even if he couldn't get an indictment. . . .

NIXON: They are doing it because of their desire to kill the president. And they may succeed. I may physically die. . . . I'm frankly just very disgusted. It isn't just the press. . . . What it is is the leadership in the ivory towers in New York and the *Times* and the *Post*. They are destroying the country. They were all

McGovern supporters.... It brings me sometimes to feel like saying the hell with it. I would like to see them run this country and see what they do.

KISSINGER: Can you see [Speaker of the House] Carl Albert in this crisis? He would be running it from Walter Reed [Hospital]. And Jerry Ford, fond as I am of him, just doesn't have it....

George Rowland Stanley Baring, 3rd Earl of Cromer
October 25, 1973, 1:03 a.m.
Brezhnev had threatened to act unilaterally if the United States didn't act jointly with the Soviets in sending troops to enforce the cease-fire in the Middle East that he said Israel was violating (though he probably had no intention of intervening and urged collaboration). Kissinger, who was intent on preventing the introduction of Soviet troops, informs the British ambassador to Washington that the United States was going on a heightened global military alert.[11]

KISSINGER: Okay. We have had some disturbing information from the Soviets in a letter from Brezhnev to the president in which he asked us to dispatch Soviet and American military contingents to the Middle East, and that if we don't agree—"I will say it straight that if you find it impossible to act jointly with us in this matter, we should be faced with the necessity urgently to consider the question of taking appropriate steps unilaterally. We cannot allow arbitrariness on the part of Israel."

CROMER: Oh, no.

KISSINGER: ... I just wanted to tell you what our policy is and I hope in this grave situation we will get your support. We feel that the only chance we now have ... is defense readiness around the world....

CROMER: Sure.

KISSINGER: We are going to what they call our DEFCON 3 alert—cancel leave, alert planes, and so forth....

Alexander Haig
October 25, 1973, 2:35 p.m.
Egypt and the Soviet Union had agreed to an international UN peacekeeping force that excluded permanent members of the UN Security Council, hence the Soviet Union and the United States.

... KISSINGER: We have won. They have accepted the SC resolution without permanent members and we have just had a message from Brezhnev saying they are sending 70 observers to Cairo and they will be glad if we send 70 observers too.

HAIG: Well, well, well. Another stare down, Henry.

KISSINGER: And one move less and we would have had it. . . . And you and I
were the only ones for it. These other guys were wailing all over the place
this morning.

HAIG: You're telling me. Last night it seemed like someone had taken their
[balls] away from them. . . .

KISSINGER: We would have had a Soviet paratroop division in there this
morning. . . .

President Nixon

October 25, 1973, 3:05 p.m.

*Kissinger congratulates Nixon on his victory and complains about press speculation
that they had created the crisis, including the dramatic worldwide military alert, for
domestic reasons. He notes that Nixon had been prepared to go nuclear during the
earlier Pakistan–India conflict.*

KISSINGER: Mr. President, you have won again. . . . The Soviets have joined
our resolution at the UN barring permanent members after screaming like
banshees and we have had a reply from Brezhnev. . . . It accepts your proposal and says he is sending 70 observers and we should send 70 observers
also. . . . The [obscenity] are saying we did all of this for political purposes. . . .

NIXON: In other words, we set this up.

KISSINGER: At 4:00 in the morning.

NIXON: And that we created a crisis. I hope you told him strongly—

KISSINGER: I treated Kalb contemptibly at the press conference.

NIXON: What about Scotty [Reston]?

KISSINGER: I gave him a few facts. I said, "What would you do if seven . . .
airborne divisions were put on alert?" . . .

NIXON: Why does he think the president is up until 3:00 this morning?

KISSINGER: I said, "You think we staged all of this?" . . . I would treat the bastards with contempt. . . . Mr. President, you were prepared to put forces in as
you were prepared to go to nuclear war in Pakistan, and that was way before
you knew what was going to happen. . . .

Simcha Dinitz

October 26, 1973, 4:15 p.m.

*Kissinger objects strongly to Israel's entrapment of Egypt's Third Army on the east
bank of the Suez Canal, which risked another crisis with the Soviets (though he had
discussed with Dinitz the possibility of Israel destroying it if there were a showdown
with the Soviets). Israel sought to destroy it. But Kissinger wanted to preserve it and
Sadat, to avoid a humiliating Egyptian defeat, and to expand U.S. influence with
Arabs, not least of all Sadat.*[12]

KISSINGER: The Egyptians have asked for a SC meeting tonight. They have now made another appeal to us from Sadat and from New York . . . in which they say the Third Army will never surrender no matter what you do and that they will take drastic measures if you continue blockading them. . . . I have kept this from the president, who is preparing for a press conference. I don't want him to say something you will regret. I have no doubt what he will do. . . . Why don't you let them break out and get out of there?

DINITZ: We would be willing to let them break out and go home but they are not trying to break out and run. They are shooting at our forces and—

KISSINGER: Why can you not let them take the tanks with them? The Russians will replace them anyway.

DINITZ: We will not open up the pocket and release an army that came to destroy us. It has never happened in a history of war.

KISSINGER: Also it has never happened that a small country is producing a world war in this manner. There is a limit beyond which you cannot push the president. . . . You play your game and you will see what happens. . . . What will happen is another maximum Soviet demand, and you cannot put the president in a confrontation day after day. . . . I guarantee if you want me to take it to the president you will get a much worse answer. . . .

Alexander Haig
October 26, 1973, 7:55 p.m.
Kissinger hits the roof over Nixon's press conference that evening, where he suggested that he had stood Brezhnev down.[13]

KISSINGER: The crazy bastard really made a mess with the Russians. . . . First, we had information of massive movement of Soviet forces. That is a lie. Second, this was the worst crisis since the Cuban missile crisis. True, but why rub their faces in it? Third, Brezhnev and I exchanged brutal messages. That has never been acknowledged before. Four, Brezhnev respects me because I was the man who bombed Vietnam on December 18 and mined the harbors on May 8 [1972].

HAIG: I don't think that is a third of the problem. He just let fly. . . .

KISSINGER: Compare it with my press conference when I said there was no confrontation with the Russians. . . . He has turned it into a massive Soviet backdown. Brezhnev is known to his Politburo as a man with a special relationship with Nixon and he is being publicly humiliated.

HAIG: How about the rest of it? Disaster.

KISSINGER: Yes, a disaster of something that is already a disaster. We are getting a hotline message tonight. Would you call Dobrynin? . . . You better call in the name of the president and say he wanted to stress his close personal relationship with [Brezhnev]. In a replay on television it may look like he

is taunting Brezhnev. He wants him to know he places the greatest stress
on the personal relationship. This is inadvertent and will be corrected. This
guy will not take this. This guy over there is a maniac also. . . . He [Nixon]
just looked awful.

HAIG: He took on the press like I have never heard.

KISSINGER: They treated him in an unbelievable way.

HAIG: I will get to Dobrynin right away. If you talk to him tonight, take it easy.
He is right on the verge. . . .

Brent Scowcroft
October 26, 1973, 9:14 p.m.
*Brezhnev had sent a somewhat threatening message calling on the United States
to stop Israeli aggression and help get nonmilitary supplies to the encircled Egyp-
tian Third Army, and charging that the U.S. global military alert was unprovoked.*[14]
Scowcroft was deputy national security adviser.

. . . KISSINGER: That is going to be a lollapalooza.

SCOWCROFT: It's a dandy.

KISSINGER: The stupid SOBs have brought it on themselves. They are mad
heroes. If they had let us communicate to them. It is just enough to be
sick. . . . I don't know how we could have forced them [the Israelis] to do it
[provide relief to the Third Army].

SCOWCROFT: We can't really. . . .

Simcha Dinitz
October 26, 1973, 10:58 p.m.
*Kissinger impresses upon Dinitz that Israel must let nonmilitary supplies reach the
Egyptian Third Army.*

. . . KISSINGER: Let me give you the president's reaction in separate parts. First,
he wanted me to make it absolutely clear that we cannot permit the destruction of the Egyptian army under conditions achieved after a cease-fire was
reached in part by negotiations in which we participated. . . . Secondly, he
would like from you no later than 8:00 a.m. tomorrow an answer to the
question of nonmilitary supplies permitted to reach the army. . . . I have
to say again your course is suicidal. You will not be permitted to destroy
this army. You are destroying the possibility for negotiations which you
want. . . . It is inconceivable that the Soviets will permit the destruction of
the Egyptian army and that the Egyptians will withdraw their army. It will
bring down Sadat. It is not something he will agree to.

DINITZ: . . . Israel offers to let this army go intact with all sidearms but cannot have 200 tanks go with these people so they can go back on us.

KISSINGER: The agreement was cease-fire in place. Now they won't accept losing all that equipment and giving it to you.

DINITZ: They can blow it up. . . .

Golda Meir
October 27, 1973, 12:40 p.m.
Egypt and Israel had agreed to talks between senior military commanders over implementing the cease-fire, Egypt's Third Army, and other issues. But there was a snafu.

MEIR: I just want to say to you that there is one thing you just cannot accept and that is that this was something deliberate. . . . Our man went to the point of destination, waited, and when the group from Cairo did not arrive he went to the UN headquarters 10 kilometers away. . . . Our man was on the spot from 3:00 to 5:30. It is true that someone from here should have gotten in touch, but it was our assumption that from the Cairo side something went astray.

KISSINGER: With all due respect, we passed the message to Egypt and to request all conditions be accepted and you would be in touch with Zayyat to work out details. If that did not happen, Egypt did not have any way of knowing. . . . The fact is that your people did not make contact—they [the Egyptians] were waiting. You told us what to pass on to them—we did that. One person should have gotten in touch with the general. . . . Zayyat has just telephoned that the Egyptian convoy [with nonmilitary supplies for the Third Army] was ready.

MEIR: But Mr. Secretary . . . we don't see any convoy. What can be done now? An hour for early in the morning must be set, and where is the convoy? . . .

Golda Meir's Visit, Middle East Negotiations, the Arab Oil Embargo, and Wiretapping of Kissinger Revisited

November–December 1973

In early November 1973, Israeli Prime Minister Golda Meir met with Kissinger and Nixon in Washington; her visit was preceded by one from Egyptian Foreign Minister Ismail Fahmy. Meir's visit did not go well. Kissinger was demanding that Israel allow more nonmilitary supplies to reach the Egyptian Third Army trapped on the east bank of the Suez Canal and end its strangulation, and urging that Israel accept a withdrawal of its forces to October 22 cease-fire lines established before the encirclement. But Meir deeply resented the United States dictating Israel's negotiating positions and self-interest, and was suspicious of its motives and moves with Egypt and the Soviets. She made critical remarks about U.S. policy to senators. She and Kissinger were stale-mated. Kissinger threatened to act unilaterally if Israel didn't exhibit more flexibility.

In October, Saudi Arabia and other Arab oil-producing states had imposed an embargo on oil shipments to the United States in retaliation for U.S. support for Israel in the Yom Kippur War and for leverage. Nixon badly wanted to get the embargo lifted and gain a desperately needed triumph that would help re-new public confidence in him amid Watergate, but Kissinger wanted to show immunity to the Arabs' use of the embargo as a means of pressuring the United States to obtain Israeli withdrawals from occupied territories. "If he makes lift-ing of oil conditional on progress in the Middle East, we are dead," Kissinger told Alexander Haig.

On November 25, John Crewdson of the *New York Times* published a story (one he'd earlier discussed with Kissinger but held back) that Kissinger's phone might have been wiretapped, or at least that Kissinger had told a close associate that he was sure it had been tapped. Kissinger denied through a spokesman that he ever said that, and told Deputy White House Press Secretary Gerald Warren, "Today, no one is sure and I don't think it was."

Simcha Dinitz
November 2, 1973, 7:00 p.m.
Kissinger was pressuring Meir to make concessions that would end Israel's encirclement of the Egyptian Third Army and expedite movement toward a peace settlement, but Meir said continued resupply of the army was dependent on the fate of Israeli prisoners of war in Egypt and other issues, and demanded to know about Kissinger's discussions with the Soviets and Egypt behind her back. Israeli Ambassador Dinitz denies that she cast aspersions on U.S. policy to U.S. senators, as Kissinger had heard (she'd taken "potshots at Kissinger"), but Kissinger is not eager to meet with her again. They'd had a "frosty" dinner the evening before.[1]

> ... KISSINGER: ... Senator Stennis came to the White House—and he is not a troublemaker—to tell me he felt there was a whole series of charges in the prime minister's statements. . . .
>
> DINITZ: It was just a matter of a misunderstanding. . . . I frankly think the two of you should meet alone.
>
> KISSINGER: I don't think there is a basis for it. I think there are two possible ways. Either work out something we can do together, or if not, we will do the best we can do alone, after which we will work unilaterally. . . . After we sat together last evening, it didn't lead to anything.
>
> DINITZ: So I understand from your people. It didn't work.
>
> KISSINGER: That is an understatement.
>
> DINITZ: . . . I think there is a tremendous amount of misunderstandings. It is not true she has said half the things that were said. I was present—
>
> KISSINGER: A lot of things happened yesterday before anyone reported anything, starting with the breakfast. . . . I think we both know what is happening. We can see it in the press and elsewhere. . . .

Simcha Dinitz
November 2, 1973, 7:34 p.m.
Kissinger agrees to see Meir again but complains about a campaign in Israel against him and about Israel's intransigence in the peace negotiations.

> KISSINGER: Mr. Ambassador, I will be glad, if it is convenient, to call on her about 10:00 tonight. . . . But we have to get it down in some manageable form.
>
> DINITZ: She has asked me to call Stennis and some of the others. . . . The record of Stennis is incorrect. . . . She simply did not say it.

KISSINGER: He had the same impression as somebody else who was at the meeting. . . . That needles were being stuck into us. That the tone was not friendly. . . . A friend of mine from Jerusalem said a campaign was starting in Israel against me.

DINITZ: No.

KISSINGER: Why would he call? I don't care about campaigns. We have very specific problems. We have to do various things, if not by me, by somebody else. They will be done in opposition to Israel or together with Israel. If you think it is easier from postures of hostility, then they will have to be done that way. . . . I didn't make the toast at the dinner last night.

DINITZ: She felt that was a closed meeting.

KISSINGER: Those of my colleagues that were at the meetings I chaired for three weeks could not believe what they heard. It was astonishing. . . . I didn't want a collision course. . . . If you can get rid of some of your principals in this election we can do better. You have that choice. . . . We haven't made one single proposal on a long-term settlement and no agreements with anyone on a long-term settlement. I have told you a hundred times that there was not going to be an American plan. . . . My impression is you are so concerned about the long-term settlement you will not take the short-term settlement. When we meet we will tell her exactly what I believe must be done and we will see if you can do it or not do it. If you will not and you believe it is impossible, we will have to see what the president will decide at that point. . . .

President Nixon
November 3, 1973, 11:40 a.m.
Kissinger tells Nixon about his problems with Meir.

NIXON: How are you getting along today?

KISSINGER: I think these various maniacs are going to work me into a nervous breakdown. I sat up with Mrs. Meir last night until 2:00. I think we are making some progress with her but whether enough to satisfy the Arabs I don't know. . . . It was brutal; she called yesterday and I refused to meet with her—told her to send her representative. That shook her up a bit. . . .

Anatoly Dobrynin
November 3, 1973, 12:20 p.m.
Kissinger also tells Ambassador Dobrynin about his difficulties.

. . . KISSINGER: As of now we are having a monumental problem with Israel. You can get that from the newspapers. You can see how they are beginning to attack me. . . . I sat up with Mrs. Meir until 1:30 last night. And I can imagine prettier girls to sit up with.

DOBRYNIN: Well, sometimes you have to sacrifice. . . .

Alexander Haig
November 17, 1973, 8:50 a.m.
Nixon had said he hoped the Middle East peace negotiations would lead to an end of the Arab oil embargo.[2] Kissinger complains to White House Chief of Staff Haig that it undercut his negotiations.

KISSINGER: . . . [What] he said about that oil thing, it is totally contrary to my strategy and just about kills us. And he cannot repeat it; if he makes lifting of oil conditional on progress in the Middle East we are dead. . . . My strategy has been, and it has worked at least somewhat, to tell the Arabs if they want progress, they better lift the oil. . . . The other one is exactly what the Arabs are saying to us. . . . And it is exactly what I told [Saudi King] Faisal we wouldn't do. Be blackmailed. And that is really terribly serious, Al. . . . Because we can't deliver fast enough. . . . He should say . . . we will not be blackmailed. That the Arabs will pay attention to. And if we are blackmailed it will hurt our capacity to make progress. . . .

Simcha Dinitz
November 17, 1973, 11:12 a.m.
Egypt had earlier imposed a naval blockade on the Bab el-Mandeb Strait at the southern entrance to the Red Sea that was preventing Israeli shipping and was using it as a bargaining chip, but President Anwar Sadat had agreed to ease it.[3] Kissinger urges Dinitz not to ruin this overture.

. . . KISSINGER: I have been informed by the Egyptians that they will let those ships through and that orders have already been issued to that effect. . . . But they pleaded with me to avoid Israeli publicity. . . . I would ask you now, for Christ sake, you have achieved more than you had any right to given your behavior. . . . Really, now don't ruin this thing now because I think you've got every demand now that you came here with. . . . My judgment is that the Egyptians are looking for a face-saving way by which they cannot be accused of lifting the blockade. It's like you putting six roadblocks on the Cairo–Suez road and then remove them again. Now they must be given the same privilege as to be as obnoxious as you. . . . But what I'm really anxious for is the Egyptians have flatly told us they would let the ships through—that they will or have issued instructions that they may ask the ships to identify themselves. . . . On the identification my view is that this is something that cannot be maintained for any length of time. . . . I hope you realize the thin ice you are skating on, for Christ sake, and every time we make a proposal to you, you can't just say no. . . .

William Timmons
November 19, 1973, 10:10 a.m.
Kissinger grouses to Nixon's assistant for congressional affairs about all the meetings with congressional committees that Nixon wanted him to hold to restore confidence in him.

. . . KISSINGER: Now, secondly, your various notes about the committees I have to meet. Let me say this. Everybody knows that the president is very grandiose about signing me up. Every one of these meetings takes a morning. I've got to run a department, do the NSC job, and conduct all the negotiations and keep running around the world. It's just humanly impossible to do all these things. . . . I can't be just thrown around. The curse of this administration is that they drive everything into the goddamn ground.

TIMMONS: . . . He hits me on that every damn time I see him.

KISSINGER: But you know he is only thinking two days ahead. . . . I fail to understand what he is doing with all these sessions with congressmen except building a trap for himself.

TIMMONS: Well, he's trying to restore the confidence in his office. . . .

William Colby
November 21, 1973, 2:00 p.m.
Kissinger accuses CIA Director Colby of leaking intelligence on the probable Soviet shipment of nuclear weapons to Egypt during the Yom Kippur War (later confirmed) and information about the decision to go on the worldwide U.S. military alert during the war.[4]

KISSINGER: I keep reading your intelligence reports in the *Washington Post*.

COLBY: So do I, and I am getting very unhappy about it.

KISSINGER: Do we believe there are Soviet nuclear weapons in Egypt? I thought we had changed our minds.

COLBY: There certainly could be, and if so they would be under their [Soviet] control. We don't go down hard they are there. They brought something down there and they took something back. We cannot tell how much went down and how much went back.

KISSINGER: It is conceivable that all that went down went back.

COLBY: Quite conceivable.

KISSINGER: We don't have any sure evidence that they are there as this says.

COLBY: I will be damned if I know where this is coming from.

KISSINGER: I am figuring you put this in the *New York Times* too because it lets you off free.

COLBY: I am delighted to say I have not talked to . . . either of those two writers.

KISSINGER: It mentions that you were brought in late [on decision-making on the alert].

COLBY: I did not know whether that was complimentary or not.

KISSINGER: . . . At this stage noninvolvement in anything seems to be the best course. . . .

COLBY: I went through that with a red pencil. It is obviously a compilation. There are about a half-dozen sources there.

KISSINGER: Some of it is wrong. . . .

Gerald Warren
November 24, 1973, 3:35 p.m.
John Crewdson of the New York Times *was writing a story on the possible wiretapping of Kissinger's phone, perhaps by the Plumbers. He would report that Kissinger recently told a former White House associate that he was "virtually certain" his phone had been tapped.*[5] *Kissinger takes up the matter with Deputy White House Press Secretary Warren.*

KISSINGER: On that story. My worry is if I call him . . . well, first, I never said anything.

WARREN: Let me tell you what I said: "We have no evidence that Secretary Kissinger's phone has ever been tapped." . . . But your associate stands by it. . . . You are quoted as saying that you were virtually certain your phone was tapped in early 1969.

KISSINGER: I have no way of knowing. . . . Today, no one is sure and I don't think it was. . . . I just hate for the secretary of state to call that son of a bitch.

WARREN: I hate to see this get out with no challenge.

KISSINGER: I have had my press office deny it. What should I do?

WARREN: I think you should call the son of a bitch, excuse me, and tell him you never said that.

KISSINGER: I am not 100 percent sure I never said it to someone, but it would have to have been a goddamn close associate. That's my problem. . . .

Alexander Haig
November 24, 1973, no time
Kissinger is concerned that he might have said he was sure his phone was tapped and doesn't want to hand Crewdson a story. But he denies saying Nixon was approaching a nervous breakdown.

KISSINGER: Sorry to bother you but John Crewdson of the *New York Times* has a story that I told an associate that I thought my phone had been tapped and Jerry Warren thinks I ought to call him up and get it turned off. First thing, that gives him an interview with the secretary of state, and I maybe said that at one time. I have had my press office deny it and Jerry Warren has denied it. . . . I maybe said it.

HAIG: I don't doubt it. You and I have joked about it privately and publicly.

KISSINGER: And then he has his story, don't you agree?

HAIG: I agree. There is another rumor around, that you are quoted as saying the president, if he keeps it up, in a few weeks will suffer from a nervous breakdown.

KISSINGER: Absolutely not.

HAIG: Bullshit. . . . That's the newest one. That they are trying to push that he has a mental problem.

KISSINGER: About the mental condition of the president I have never said a word. . . .

Brent Scowcroft

November 25, 1973, 12:50 p.m.

Kissinger informs Scowcroft, his deputy at the NSC, that Nixon wanted to send an envoy to Saudi Arabia to persuade them to end the oil embargo, which undermined Kissinger's strategy to show imperviousness to Arab pressure to obtain Israeli withdrawals from occupied territories.[6]

. . . KISSINGER: He called me and he wants to send a special emissary to Saudi Arabia to get them to turn the oil on. . . . He does that and he is in deep trouble with me. We cannot have this now.

SCOWCROFT: Oh, no. That would be the worst possible thing to do.

KISSINGER: Besides, it will be refused. It will put us in the position of the supplicant.

SCOWCROFT: . . . Where do you think he got that idea?

KISSINGER: Probably from some of his oil friends. . . .

Joseph Sisco

December 3, 1973, 8:17 a.m.

Leslie Gelb had reported in the New York Times *that a consensus had been reached in the administration that it needed to put pressure on Israel to make significant concessions in the Middle East peace talks.*[7] *Assistant Secretary of State Sisco suggests that somebody else was talking and says he's decided to resign. (Kissinger would shortly promote him to undersecretary of state for political affairs, as he'd wanted.)*

... KISSINGER: Joe, have you seen the Gelb article in the *New York Times?* ... There is too much palavering in the department, and I am not Rogers.

SISCO: Yeah. What does he have to say? I don't know Les Gelb.

KISSINGER: That we are going to lean on Israel. That the settlement we made in Cairo had previously been worked out with Mrs. Meir. . . . That it had been done between the president and Mrs. Meir, which is totally—total crap to begin with.

SISCO: Of course it is.

KISSINGER: Yeah, but you know what that is going to do for us in Cairo. That I then went through a charade of pretending the Israelis might not accept. . . . I am going to hold bureau chiefs responsible from now on for leaks out of their shops. I cannot operate this way. . . .

SISCO: Well, look, Henry, I was about to call you on my personal situation. And Jean [Sisco's wife] is right here because we have been up, frankly, all night. And we have concluded, Henry, that while I am very grateful for the offer but we can't accept it. . . . We've thought it all over and there are just some very, very strong considerations that aren't reversible at the present time. . . .

James Schlesinger
December 29, 1973, 8:58 a.m.
Marilyn Berger had reported in the Washington Post *that a senior Defense Department official said the Arabs were eager to end the oil embargo and were looking for a way to do it without appearing to back down, and presented "a far more optimistic assessment" than Kissinger did that day.*[8] *Secretary of Defense Schlesinger acknowledges that he was the anonymous official.*

KISSINGER: Jim, I didn't talk to you yesterday about who gave that background on the oil thing to Marilyn Berger.

SCHLESINGER: That was me. They should not have given it out. . . . That was Kay Graham. She should not have used that material if she wants to speculate. . . . I detected some undercurrent towards you among those *Washington Post* reporters.

KISSINGER: I have too.

SCHLESINGER: They spend a lot of time trying to separate me from you. . . . You're so damn high at the moment that they want to tear you down.

KISSINGER: It's a combination. First, it's Dinitz, taking out insurance because most of those [reporters] are Jews. . . . They must get me if they get the president. . . .

Kissinger's Shuttle Diplomacy and Israeli–Egyptian Disengagement, More Resignation Threats, the JCS Spying Operation Breaks, and the Oil Embargo in Limbo

January–February 1974

In January 1974, shuttling back and forth between Egypt and Israel in a murderous diplomatic exercise, Kissinger negotiated an agreement for the separation and disengagement of their forces along the Suez Canal. Nixon, who was preoccupied with Watergate and the threat of impeachment and jealous of acclaim for Kissinger, had delayed green-lighting Kissinger's trip, to the resentment of Kissinger, who spoke again of resigning. Nixon still wanted badly to end the Arab oil embargo to show his leadership and reverse his fortunes.

Also in January, the earlier spying operation on Kissinger by the Joint Chiefs of Staff under Chairman Thomas Moorer, in which a navy yeoman purloined classified documents from Kissinger's NSC, hit the press. Kissinger denounced the "unbelievable SOBs" like former Nixon adviser John Ehrlichman who were apparently leaking the story, and told Senator John Stennis, whose Senate Armed Services Committee held hearings on this "tawdry subject" (as Kissinger called it), that the idea that Moorer was spying on him was "absurd," that he didn't know much about the whole affair—"I have no information," he claimed to Congressman Edward Hébert; his knowledge was "extremely limited," he told Stennis—and defended Moorer. (Kissinger knew critics would say the spying was undertaken because of his secrecy, which in part it was. He was also reluctant to criticize the military, the episode may have been somewhat embarrassing to him, and he may have been disinclined to add to the public catalog of sordid acts of the Nixon administration.) The revelation of the JCS's spying operation led to questions about Kissinger's knowledge of the activities of the Plumbers, the White House's extralegal investigations unit, since the Plumber David Young, Kissinger's former personal aide, was a key participant in the White House's investigation of the spying (another reason not to air it in public). Kissinger continued to dissociate himself from Young and his activities.

In January and February, Kissinger was also trying to negotiate an agreement between Israel and Syria on the disengagement of their forces on the Golan Heights—no easy task between bitter enemies—which Arab states were linking to the end of the oil embargo.

James Schlesinger
January 4, 1974, 2:50 p.m.
Kissinger had been meeting with Israeli Defense Minister Moshe Dayan, who had brought a plan to Washington for the disengagement of Israeli and Egyptian forces along the Suez Canal.[1] Dayan would meet with Defense Secretary Schlesinger afterward on Israel's weapons requests. Kissinger encourages Schlesinger to arrange a long-term supply in exchange for Israeli concessions on disengagement.

> KISSINGER: I am going to send Dayan off in a few minutes. . . . They are psycho-pathic. . . . They want some assurances of longer-term supplies. . . . I think you could tell them it's no problem and be willing to discuss a long-term supply proposal with them.
>
> SCHLESINGER: This is what the administration wants? . . . The P?
>
> KISSINGER: The president wants to do this if they are helpful in the political thing. . . . I think we will have less trouble from the Arabs if we do it clearly related to getting them to make concessions. . . . If they could see some positive tone. . . .
>
> SCHLESINGER: We will give them a positive tone. The things we will not be too positive about are . . . certain advanced items we just don't have in our inventory . . . still in R&D. This sophisticated stuff just isn't available. . . . They seem to have gotten their requests from the manufacturer's dream board. . . .

Alexander Haig
January 4, 1974, 3:35 p.m.
Kissinger expresses apprehension to White House Chief of Staff Haig about Nixon's reaction to his proposed trip to Egypt and Israel for peace talks, given that most everybody knew Kissinger was running the administration's policy and Nixon's jealousy over his preeminence.

KISSINGER: I wanted to check one thing to get your personal judgment. I have had a very good talk with Dayan. They have basically bought our concept. It is a tremendous advance. Really incredible. But there are enough wrinkles in it for them so it is hard to handle through diplomatic channels. If I talk to Sadat I could get the [disengagement] accomplished. But I know what our leader would think if I was to go out there. . . . This thing is now for the first time within manageable range but still not acceptable to the Egyptians. . . . I don't want to present it to him because he will go into orbit.

HAIG: I think we ought to do what will get this thing settled.

KISSINGER: I got him good publicity yesterday.

HAIG: Excellent, excellent. That problem is manageable. . . . [But] I would hate to think if you should go and get caught in a stalemate, I mean you are included in it.

KISSINGER: He would like it and then he could get rid of me. . . . I left San Clemente very depressed. I am beginning to wonder how long this [Watergate scandal] is manageable. . . .

Alexander Haig

January 8, 1974, 10:05 a.m.

Kissinger takes up his trip again and says he'd be happy to resign after a peace agreement is signed. He objects to Nixon's contacts with Sudan's President Jaafar Nimeiry behind his back.

. . . KISSINGER: So now we've got a message saying Sadat wants me to come. . . . Which means he is willing to settle fast. . . . I do believe that with all this fancy footwork going on if we don't wrap this thing up fast it will never happen. . . . But you can tell him, Al, that I'm perfectly willing to give him a terminal date for my tenure, and that I'm off his back then, but let's get this thing done—I'd be perfectly happy to resign as soon as this agreement is signed. . . . And tell him . . . that he will announce the settlement, not I, and that the [oil] embargo lifting will be done by him. Anyway, he can have my resignation. After last night, I don't think there is a basis for my continuing anyway.

HAIG: Yeah, I don't know what the hell that's all about.

KISSINGER: Whatever it is all about, Al, it means he's been in separate communications with a foreign government in the middle of a crisis.

HAIG: . . . Some first-class jerk called him in the night. . . .

KISSINGER: No, it's been going on for a week, Al, and Rose [Mary Woods, Nixon's secretary] told Scowcroft two weeks ago they were in touch with Nimeiry and to keep me out of it—or a month ago—Scowcroft told me about it at the time, and I just thought it was some first-class jerk carrying things back and forth and I never thought anyone could take Nimeiry seriously. . . .

Brent Scowcroft
January 8, 1974, 2:25 p.m.
Kissinger complains to his deputy about Nixon's foot-dragging on approving his trip and again threatens to resign.

. . . KISSINGER: Have you heard from Haig about this trip?

SCOWCROFT: No. . . .

KISSINGER: You know, here we are on the verge of breaking this thing. The secretary of state is invited to Aswan and instead of throwing our hats in the air, we're dancing around.

SCOWCROFT: What they're seized with is whether or not to release the milk and the ITT papers [on two scandals].

KISSINGER: Of course, those are matters of great importance.

SCOWCROFT: Well, that's where our priorities have gone.

KISSINGER: You know very well if there were national-interest concentration we would be in touch with [Egyptian Foreign Minister Ismail] Fahmy. There is no earthly reason to hesitate. . . . If he refuses it I will certainly leave. . . .

Donald Kendall
January 10, 1974, 11:10 a.m.
PepsiCo CEO Kendall tells Kissinger about the kidnapping of an executive of a PepsiCo subsidiary and declares that he will not pay any more ransoms "even if they kill someone," which Kissinger supports.

KENDALL: I don't know whether you have heard but they have kidnapped another one of our people in Argentina. . . . I talked to [John Kenneth] Jamieson of Exxon. They took one of their people also. I told him I thought it was about time the U.S. companies called a halt to this. We are not going to pay any more ransom. . . . They contacted us this morning and told us to name a figure of how valuable he was. Our people are anxious to offer some nominal fee. . . . If I do this, I am planning then to take a full-page ad in an Argentina paper and will say we are announcing we are not paying any more ransom money for people. We have advised our people and if they are worried to pull out of the country. Regardless of what they do we are not going to pay any more—even if they kill someone.

KISSINGER: I am in favor of that. . . .

Brent Scowcroft
January 10, 1974, 6:48 p.m.
Scowcroft reports that a story was coming out in the Washington Post *on the earlier spying operation against Kissinger by the Joint Chiefs of Staff under Chairman Thomas Moorer.*[2]

... SCOWCROFT: The story is going to break tomorrow. Any guidance for me?

KISSINGER: I haven't read the story. Keep me informed of what it says. My view is that I should say on the trip that I'm not going to make any comment while I'm in these negotiations. If forced into it, I'll say that the investigation [of the operation] was being conducted by Ehrlichman. Ehrlichman told me some of these allegations, which happens to be true.

SCOWCROFT: Apparently that's where the story comes from. . . .

KISSINGER: Those unbelievable SOBs. I don't know what twist they're going to give the story. I guess it's that we didn't tell them enough and therefore they had to spy on us. Is that the twist?

SCOWCROFT: That's what I understand—"Moorer spies on White House."

KISSINGER: . . . My tendency would be to play it down. To say the usual bureaucratic stuff. I would not take on the military.

SCOWCROFT: No. . . . And that part probably could be denied, couldn't it? . . .

John Stennis
January 10, 1974, 8:12 p.m.
Kissinger claims to Senator Stennis, the chairman of the Senate Armed Services Committee, that the allegation that there was a JCS spying operation against him is "absurd" and that he had no "independent knowledge" of it. He says that John Ehrlichman, who investigated the operation, may now be giving it the wrong "twist."

KISSINGER: Mr. Chairman, I'm going off tonight to the Middle East, and I know the story about Admiral Moorer allegedly spying on me is going to hit the newspapers tomorrow. . . . It's an absurd charge because Admiral Moorer was a close collaborator of mine. It was this yeoman who was leaking documents, as it turned out, to the newspapers. I have complete confidence in the chairman [Moorer]. I have no independent knowledge of the allegations. On the face of it, they seem absurd to me. . . . I think the chairman deserves your support, Mr. Chairman. They've attacked so many institutions that I don't know what's going to happen.

STENNIS: I don't either. . . . I might just announce rather early that I was going to go into it, take jurisdiction of it. Otherwise some other committee might. . . .

KISSINGER: On a personal basis, I think that would be a statesmanlike thing to do. I would rather for your committee than some of these that are out for publicity. You know the military. You understand what various things mean. In executive session I would be delighted to tell you everything I know, which isn't a great deal. Just for your information, [Moorer] handled some of the most sensitive things for us—on the China thing, for instance. Why he would want to steal documents is beyond my comprehension.

STENNIS: And it's contrary to the pattern of the man. . . .

KISSINGER: Speaking as friends, some of these people at the White House, like Ehrlichman, were very often doing these investigations to build up their own importance. . . . And he may have given it a twist that any knowledgeable man would never put on it. . . . To protect the integrity of the military would be a national service. I have no question about the chairman.

STENNIS: . . . If they call me in the morning, I'll say I don't believe a word of it.

KISSINGER: You know, there's undoubtedly something to it, but not what they're saying. I wouldn't necessarily assume that no documents were taken, but I don't think the chairman—

STENNIS: No party to it at all concerning you.

KISSINGER: Exactly. . . .

Edward Hébert
January 10, 1974, 8:22 p.m.
Kissinger also tells Representative Hébert, the chairman of the House Armed Services Committee, that the report of a spying operation against him is absurd.

KISSINGER: The reason I called—I've just been told there's a story breaking in the newspapers about alleged spying by the Joint Chiefs. . . . I just wanted to say I have no information. . . . It's absurd, since the chairman had access to all relevant information. And it's totally inconsistent with his basic pattern as a man anyway. . . . I'm not going to be making public statements on such a tawdry subject. . . . I just don't think we ought to get the military dragged into this mess.

HEBERT: I'm not going to do it. . . .

Robert Toth
January 21, 1974, 3:00 p.m.
Kissinger falsely denies to Toth of the Los Angeles Times *that he knew that his former personal aide David Young was involved in the investigation of the navy yeoman, Charles Radford, who stole NSC documents and turned them over to Moorer and columnist Jack Anderson.*[3]

... KISSINGER: Look, Bob. You know, I hardly have to tell you how outraged I
am about this thing. . . . It is 180 degrees off center. I did not know Young had
a report. I did not know Young was conducting an investigation. . . . I knew
John Ehrlichman was conducting an investigation but I was told to stay the
hell out of it. . . . This is a total outrage. . . . I was called by Ehrlichman . . . and
I was to stay the hell out and I would not be told the conclusions. I thought
they were out to get me. . . .

John Stennis
January 28, 1974, 2:45 p.m.

Senator Stennis asks for Kissinger's advice on whether to hold hearings on the JCS spy-
ing operation against him. Kissinger, who acknowledges that documents were stolen,
is dubious and distances himself from former Plumber Young. (At the hearings in
February, Kissinger and Moorer testified in secret, with Kissinger portraying himself
as "completely in the dark" about the operation.)[4]

STENNIS: I just want to take one minute of your time to see what you feel on
the Kissinger–Moorer matter.

KISSINGER: Fine, but I hate to have it called the Kissinger–Moorer matter. . . .
It was a lousy thing to have done but I don't think it warrants undermining
the confidence in the military. . . . It shouldn't have been done, it shouldn't
have been tolerated, but I don't believe it was a *Seven Days in May* thing.
I think it was sort of a cheap move to make a few points. I believe Moorer
when he says he didn't focus on it. He had a lot of other things to do,
and given my relations with Moorer, he didn't need to do it. . . . I have
never seen the report David Young wrote. I don't know what the allegations
are. . . .

STENNIS: Well, I don't want to get into this Plumbers group on this. I don't
have any confidence in them.

KISSINGER: . . . Young was on my staff and he did not inspire me. . . . He did
not inspire me with confidence that what he did do would be very serious
or balanced. I would never have imagined he would be given a responsible
assignment like investigating the military. As I have said publicly, I don't
know about his investigations. . . . I mean, here was a kid who was not doing
very well working for me thrown into the Ehrlichman atmosphere. He may
just have tried to prove how good he was.

STENNIS: I don't know if we have to go through all of that. . . . What do you
think of this? I would ask you and Admiral Moorer to each, separately, write
me a letter undertaking to tell how you feel about this matter. . . . Or, two,
we might be able to settle it by asking the two of you to come before the
committee and subject yourselves to questions.

KISSINGER: Yes, the only problem, Mr. Chairman, is that my own direct knowledge of this matter is extremely limited. It really is confined to listening to 12–15 minutes of a taped interrogation of Admiral [Robert] Welander. I would be glad to say that and what I know. . . .

STENNIS: It might just be that our committee would be convinced that you and Moorer worked together, had no grievance against one another officially or personally, and he was getting information anyway. Then so far as you and Moorer were concerned it might satisfy the committee. . . .

KISSINGER: . . . I have never felt any purpose would be served by digging up the matter now in a period when every other national institution is being questioned. . . . I will be glad to write you a letter stating what I know, and stating whatever it was could not be based on personal animosity, that we worked closely together, it strikes me as a bureaucratic gamesmanship, and it would not affect the confidential relations between Moorer and me. . . .

STENNIS: I think that would be splendid. . . .

David Rockefeller
February 8, 1974, 10:32 a.m.
They confer on whether Rockefeller should accept an offer to be treasury secretary in a sinking administration. (He didn't.)

. . . KISSINGER: David, you know my affection for the family and for you. It is a somewhat precarious position, if I can be honest with you. From the national point of view, you would of course be a tremendous asset, but you'd be out on your own.

ROCKEFELLER: No doubt about that.

KISSINGER: I wouldn't pay the slightest attention to what promises you are given; when the shooting starts, you are going to be there all by yourself. . . . You and I would work closely together anyway. . . . My basic view I think would be that the country is in such bad shape, and you can't really be diminished by stepping into a crisis; if it doesn't work it can't be a reflection on you, and so much needs to be done that can only be done by senior cabinet officers that on balance I think you'd be performing a service by doing it. . . .

ROCKEFELLER: The things one has to do at this time are not going to be popular.

KISSINGER: But David, I think the man who has the guts to walk alone and do what is right is going to sweep the country. I think the worst mistake any politician can make right now is to try to do what is popular. Look at [Senator Henry] Jackson, whom I don't even particularly respect, but whatever position he had [in the 1972 presidential race] is due to the fact that he stood for things that turned out to be plausible at least, if not right, and I think that what the country [needs] is a man who is willing to look at the future and willing to take it there. They are going to be so sick and tired of all these machinations after four years of Vietnam and what will certainly now be four years of Watergate that they will want integrity and direction. . . .

ROCKEFELLER: I think I certainly will get attacked.

KISSINGER: Of course you'd be attacked—but I think that will even make you visible. . . . We could have a partnership between Treasury and State. . . .

President Nixon
February 18, 1974, 10:00 a.m.

Kissinger apprises Nixon of his meetings in Washington with the foreign ministers of Saudi Arabia and Egypt, who would present him with an Arab proposal for disengagement of Israeli and Syrian forces along the Golan Heights. Kissinger doesn't think they should offer anything or accept any conditions for the lifting of the oil embargo. But Nixon, who Kissinger didn't want to "salivate" with the ministers, is impatient about getting it lifted.[5]

KISSINGER: Mr. President, I just wanted to bring you up to date on where the matter stands with these foreign ministers. . . . I followed the strategy which you and I discussed the other day, which amazed them because they had come here to haggle to see what we would pay for the embargo. Now I have the strong impression that they are going to lift it anyway and therefore I think you should see them. . . . But I think you should be very aloof and not offer anything to them. We've offered them everything there is to offer now. . . . I've told them that we can't accept any conditions. They were going to link it to Syrian disengagement. I said that under those conditions you can't meet them, so they are now going to take that linkage out and they are just going to state it as a series of three unlinked propositions: that they have agreed to the principle of lifting the embargo, that they want progress on Syrian disengagement, they want me to come to the Middle East. . . . I thought if you wanted to you could step out with them and say you are sending me back out to the Middle East. . . . It is just one way of emerging with something and then if they do lift the embargo it would be linked back to this meeting. . . . They are going to try to have a meeting of the oil ministers within two weeks.

NIXON: That is two weeks later than they are supposed to already. . . . You know, we have been around that track before, Henry, and it hasn't helped on the embargo. You see, my only interest is the embargo. That's the only thing the country is interested in. They don't give a damn what happens to Syria. . . . I think we should see them but I don't know that we want to build up the fact that you are going out there if it cannot be in any way linked to the embargo. . . .

KISSINGER: Well, it can't be linked to the embargo, Mr. President, and I think the more we build up the embargo the less we are going to get. . . . The most effective thing I have found with them is when I told them Saturday night that we don't want to discuss it anymore. . . . If it happens within two weeks . . . even though you can't announce it tomorrow it will be linked back to that meeting.

NIXON: At least it will show some action. . . .

The Lifting of the Oil Embargo, Israeli–Syrian Disengagement, Tensions with Schlesinger, Israeli Raids in Lebanon, and More Wiretap Questioning

March–June 1974

On March 18, 1974, Arab oil states finally announced an end to the oil embargo. Kissinger was then fighting an arduous battle to broker an agreement on Israeli–Syrian disengagement along the Golan Heights. Israel demanded that Egyptian heavy artillery that it said Egypt moved to the eastern bank of the Suez Canal in violation of its January disengagement agreement with Egypt be removed before the talks on Israeli–Syrian disengagement continued. An angry Kissinger threatened to pull out of the negotiations. He found Israel's behavior "outrageous," accused it of vastly overplaying the alleged violation and ginning up a crisis, objected to Israel linking Egypt to Syria, and warned that Israel was committing a "grave mistake." But he moved to get tanks and other weapons to Israel to improve its attitude in the negotiations. He told Defense Secretary James Schlesinger the more that Israeli Defense Minister Moshe Dayan was "strengthened, the better it will be." (The press was then reporting discord between Schlesinger and Kissinger, which they denied, and the two adversaries clashed over whose department was leaking.) But Kissinger wanted progress on the Israeli–Syrian disengagement talks before giving Israel all of the aid for arms purchases it was requesting—it was a matter of timing. "We also have the Arabs to consider," he told Nixon counsel Leonard Garment. And he didn't want the aid that Israel was getting to be perceived as a reaction to "screaming" in Congress in support of Israel.

In May, shuttling back and forth between Israel and Syria, and visiting a handful of other countries, in a grueling and often infuriating diplomatic exercise, an exhausted Kissinger finally obtained an agreement between Israel and Syria on the disengagement of their forces on the Golan Heights.

That June, the House Judiciary Committee was investigating the administration's wiretaps of officials and journalists as part of its impeachment proceedings, which led to more scrutiny of Kissinger's role in them. On June 6, at a press conference where he was repeatedly questioned about the wiretaps and even asked about a possible perjury indictment, a perturbed and flustered Kissinger claimed that he had not "directly" recommended any wiretaps. "These SOBs turn it into as if I'd been engaged in a criminal activity," he groused to Nixon afterward. He worried about being turned into "a Watergate figure."

James Schlesinger
March 14, 1974, 9:10 a.m.
Schlesinger, who had spoken in February with Kissinger about leaks from the State Department that they were "on a collision course," brings up the matter again.[1]

> SCHLESINGER: Now, there does seem to be some complaint of a division between you and me coming out of State still.
>
> KISSINGER: Impossible.
>
> SCHLESINGER: There was some coming out of the Pentagon—I did what I could to turn it off.
>
> KISSINGER: A lot is coming out. I met yesterday with the editorial board of the *Post*.
>
> SCHLESINGER: I met yesterday with the editorial board of the *New York Times*.
>
> KISSINGER: And I made a passionate defense of our relationship which happens to be true.
>
> SCHLESINGER: Yeah. Scotty Reston indicated he was getting some of this stuff and I think most of his sources come from State. . . .
>
> KISSINGER: It is total nonsense.
>
> SCHLESINGER: I told him, "Bullshit—you ask Henry." . . . Don't know where exactly he is getting this stuff, but it is obviously in the interest not only to the press but to some of the people of the bureaucracy to cause this kind of division.
>
> KISSINGER: Well, first of all it isn't true; secondly, the country can't afford it.
>
> SCHLESINGER: You bet, you bet. . . .

Alexander Haig
March 16, 1974, 3:25 p.m.
Kissinger voices concern to White House Chief of Staff Haig about a statement by Nixon that he was going to "lay into" Israel, and Haig reports that Nixon asked him

to get the black nuclear bag (which contained nuclear launch options and enabled a president to order an attack).

> . . . KISSINGER: . . . I am calling you about something the president said this morning which rather disturbed me. He was in a rather sour mood again. . . . He said after he is through with the Europeans he is now going to go after the Israelis, and he has been just waiting for an opportunity to lay into them. You know, he asked me how things were going and I said, well, they are going on schedule but it will take some weeks to get the Israelis ready to do this [an Israeli–Syrian disengagement agreement]. Now, I tell you, if he goes publicly after the Israelis, we might as well start a war.
>
> HAIG: Henry, don't be concerned about that. He is just unwinding.
>
> KISSINGER: . . . Our strength consists in the fact that we are moving the Israelis.
>
> HAIG: Listen, I was told to get the football at 2:30. . . . His black nuclear bag.
>
> KISSINGER: For what?
>
> HAIG: He is going to drop it [a bomb] on the Hill. What I am saying is don't take him too seriously.
>
> KISSINGER: Yes, but make sure he doesn't do it [go after Israel] in Houston.
>
> HAIG: Oh, god no. No way.
>
> KISSINGER: I tell you, it would be a disaster. . . .

President Nixon
March 18, 1974, 6:28 p.m.
Kissinger informs Nixon of the Arab states' formal announcement of the end of the oil embargo and says they need Israeli–Syrian disengagement along the Golan Heights to make sure it sticks. (The Arabs had tied progress on the disengagement to ending the embargo.)[2] *Nixon wants a permanent peace settlement.*

> KISSINGER: We finally got the official text. What happened is basically it is lifted unconditionally by the majority. With the proviso that they would discuss it again on June 1. . . . I got a message from Sadat and he said he will help me get the thing concluded by the end of April, which is also my plan, the Syrian disengagement, so then there won't be any problem anyway. . . . The major thing we need now is the disengagement. If we talk too much about permanent settlement—when I was there the last time I talked to Sadat, he isn't ready to discuss that. . . .
>
> NIXON: This is one thing we're going to do, though, Henry. . . . There is going to be a permanent settlement.
>
> KISSINGER: Of course, Mr. President, if we get into a forum where all of these issues get discussed together, we'll get killed.

NIXON: I agree, but we don't want to leave any illusions here with our friends here that this is it, you know, and the Israelis think that they can just dig in. . . .

Alexander Haig
March 20, 1974, 6:10 p.m.
Haig tells Kissinger about a reporter for the New York Post *(probably Michael Berlin) who was doing a story on Kissinger.*

. . . HAIG: Listen, I had some long-haired guy come in here today. He was the creepiest looking fellow I've even seen. . . . My god, the questions he asked.

KISSINGER: Like what?

HAIG: I don't know whether he's out to screw you or not.

KISSINGER: I'm sure he is. He's *New York Post.* Like what?

HAIG: You were using devious methods in the bureaucracy. You were para-noiac. . . . He just went on and on. . . . I told him you once told me acute paranoia in Washington would be diagnosed as excess[ive] compla-cency. . . . He wanted me to say you are an organizational disaster. . . . I said I don't know anybody who does it any better.

KISSINGER: After all, you know, we've kept the foreign policy and defense pol-icy going for five years in a disastrous situation. . . . He's trying to get to see me. Maybe I ought to see him.

HAIG: I think you should. He's not dumb. . . .

Simcha Dinitz
March 23, 1974, 1:00 p.m.
Kissinger angrily tells Israeli Ambassador Dinitz that he will pull out of negotiations on Israeli–Syrian disengagement if Israeli Defense Minister Moshe Dayan doesn't attend upcoming disengagement talks in Washington, and castigates Israel for de-manding that Egyptian tanks and heavy artillery that Israel claimed Egypt moved to the eastern bank of the Suez Canal in violation of the earlier Egyptian–Israeli dis-engagement agreement (the reason for Dayan's threat to cancel his visit) be removed before the talks continued.[3]

. . . KISSINGER: Thirdly, if Dayan doesn't come, I'll withdraw from the negoti-ation and state publicly what has happened and you do what you want. And then we will put somebody else in charge here. We have now communicated to other governments that Dayan is coming. Your behavior is outrageous and frivolous, and you know damn well we have told Sadat they should be removed by the time we fly our next [reconnaissance] plane. You know very well that he has told us the tanks would be removed and has not refused to withdraw the artillery. I have communicated with [Egyptian Foreign Minister Ismail] Fahmy yesterday, so it is entirely up to you if you want to play domestic politics. . . . We are talking about 72 lousy artillery pieces which we have told you we would get removed. . . .

DINITZ: Can I say something, Mr. Secretary?

KISSINGER: You can say something but I don't want to debate it.

DINITZ: . . . I think your reply to me now is based on the wrong assumption. It is assumed that we won't come or that we are looking for a reason not to come. The fact of the matter is both the prime minister and the minister of defense are very anxious . . . for Dayan to come. The point is that we are asking your help in moving—

KISSINGER: You have my help. . . . I've told you for months not to link Syria and Egypt together.

DINITZ: We are not linking Syria and Egypt together, but you will have to understand, Mr. Secretary, the situation in Israel; there is now questioning these violations and a question of credibility of the government.

KISSINGER: If by the time you get ready to settle it there is still violations, then you have a point. If at a time when you have been assured by the U.S. government, one, that the tanks would be withdrawn; two, that we are in active discussion with the Egyptians about the artillery being withdrawn; three . . . when we are pleading with you not to make an issue of it with the Egyptians, who are under attack from the Soviets already—

DINITZ: . . . We are really appealing to you to help us.

KISSINGER: That we are doing. I have already done it last night and if after the next flight they are still there, then we have a real problem. I have in any case told them to remove it as quickly as possible. . . . I have no question that they will do it. Why should they want to cheat with 72 artillery pieces? . . . It cannot be in your interest to have a public confrontation with Sadat. . . . Secondly, you cannot want to emphasize violations while I am in Moscow, for god's sakes. . . . You can tell them that we have personally intervened with the Egyptians. However, it isn't helpful to have all of this in your goddamn Knesset. Well, then it will be on every Moscow radio station to the Middle East. . . . I am holding this thing together against all probability here. If he doesn't come, I'm going on vacation. If the Middle East explodes in a nuclear war, I've canceled too many visits. I have asked the Syrians to come here on April 11. If this whole scenario, which has been designed in order to give you the maximum amount of time, falls apart . . . I can't do any more. . . . I can't go to Sadat every other day. I now have to go to Fahmy. Fahmy is much tougher on these things than Sadat. . . . What

I asked Sadat was, thinking that we were dealing with rational people, that by the next time our plane would fly, six or seven days, I expected that they would not find these things there. I didn't ask him to reply to it, because I wanted to do it in a face-saving way so that the next time we could report they weren't there. I have attempted precisely to avoid him having to back down. . . . We are not talking about anything but a technical violation which I am sure will be rectified if you do it in our way. And if you put Israel on a war footing over there, then keep the defense minister there and fake a great crisis . . . when you have Syria to worry about, then you can go right ahead and do it. . . . It is a grave mistake you are forcing us into. . . . It is a mistake because I am certain the next time we fly the goddamn things won't be there. I know Sadat; he isn't going to risk his relations with us for 72 artillery pieces. . . .

Alexander Haig

March 30, 1974, 10:05 a.m.

Kissinger says getting the tanks to Israel that Moshe Dayan requested would help improve Israel's attitude in the Israel–Syria disengagement talks.

> KISSINGER: Al, I'm meeting with Dayan today and you know on that Syrian thing what needs to be done. But one of their problems is that we've been dragging our feet on the arms supply. . . . One of his problems is the Soviets have put about 800 tanks into Syria since the war. We've only replaced 225 out of the 600 they lost. He feels he must have tanks. . . . I would like Dayan when he sees Schlesinger on Monday afternoon to be told he's getting this. So that he can go back to Israel as the man who produced it. That will then help us in the subsequent talks. . . .

James Schlesinger

March 30, 1974, 10:42 a.m.

Kissinger encourages Schlesinger to "strengthen" Dayan.

> . . . KISSINGER: We are going over with him the various disengagement schemes. He's really been the man who on the Egyptian disengagement and on the Syrian one has been the one who has carried the intellectual ball. It would be very useful if he could come back with some positive news on some of his concerns. . . . Frankly, we are counting very much on Dayan's support in this process. . . . The more he can be strengthened, the better it will be. . . .

James Schlesinger
April 12, 1974, 10:20 a.m.
A recent article by Murrey Marder of the Washington Post *said Schlesinger's Defense Department favored a tougher position in the SALT II arms control talks than did State.*[4]

> . . . KISSINGER: . . . what your guys are doing to me on SALT.
>
> SCHLESINGER: Now stop that. What are my guys doing to you on SALT?
>
> KISSINGER: All this stuff that they put out that I am for a softer position and Defense is just as happy that it isn't working so and so forth.
>
> SCHLESINGER: Are you referring to an article by Marder last weekend? I thought that came out of State.
>
> KISSINGER: Absolutely not. It couldn't come from State.
>
> SCHLESINGER: The tone, as I read that article, was that the reason that the thing fell apart [during Kissinger's March trip to Moscow to prepare for a Soviet summit] was that the president listened to the Pentagon rather than to you.
>
> KISSINGER: But that isn't true either.
>
> SCHLESINGER: I know it's not true.
>
> KISSINGER: Because the proposal is exactly what I recommended.
>
> SCHLESINGER: Look, there are fellows up there on the Hill that are continually attempting to inveigle me into saying something unfavorable about SALT I. In trying to get us into a dust-up. . . .

Joseph Sisco
April 14, 1974, 2:10 p.m.
Undersecretary of State Sisco and Kissinger ridicule a proposal of Soviet Foreign Minister Andrei Gromyko that he meet with Kissinger in Syria.

> . . . KISSINGER: Gromyko, the shit, excuse me, as soon as I said to him that I would meet him in Geneva, that of course he lapped up. Now he wants to meet me in Damascus if I go to Damascus.
>
> SISCO: [Laughter.] It is becoming positively shameful on his part the way he is doing this.
>
> KISSINGER: It is one of the dumbest performances I've ever seen.
>
> SISCO: He really said this to you very directly?
>
> KISSINGER: Yes, so I said I would have to think about it. . . .

President Nixon
April 16, 1974, 3:00 p.m.
Nixon and Kissinger think China wants warmer relations, which they believe is fed by their moves with the Soviets. They also feel public support of Nixon is "ready to break loose."

... NIXON: ... I had a little call from [Senator Mike] Mansfield reporting on his dinner with the Chinese. He says the Chinese are very supportive and friendly about the president and about you, etc.

KISSINGER: Oh, they are all-out.

NIXON: And they asked about his coming there. ... I think it is an indication that they want to warm things up a bit.

KISSINGER: No question.

NIXON: Another thing that is probably true too is that every time we sort of start to make a move towards our Soviet friends, they sort of move a little towards us.

KISSINGER: Exactly. That's what these idiots can't understand. ... What our critics don't understand, our China policy absolutely depends on our Russian policy. The reverse would also be true. ...

NIXON: Well, we are coming along, and just remember if we have been able to take the heat of this last year and accomplish what we have, we sure as the dickens are going to be able to take it a little while longer.

KISSINGER: Mr. President, I believe that the public opinion is on the verge of turning ... if there were just one unambiguous event like a House vote in your favor or something like this.

NIXON: ... There is an undercurrent of support there that is just ready to break loose. ...

KISSINGER: That is my absolute conviction—that is my firm conviction. ...

Leonard Garment
April 17, 1974, 11:23 a.m.
Kissinger tells Nixon counsel Garment there must be progress on negotiations on Israeli–Syrian disengagement along the Golan Heights before giving Israel all of the aid it wanted for arms purchases.

GARMENT: ... I have a fairly strong feeling that it will be helpful to go for the bundle on the aid to—

KISSINGER: Oh, come on. Look, tell the Israelis to lay off. ... They're again going through one of their suicidal periods. ... There's no chance of our giving them the whole thing now before Syrian disengagement. I mean, we also have the Arabs to consider. What should we give them $1.5 billion for? I have worked something out with Dinitz which we're going to do this week, and then we'll do the rest afterwards. We've got our Arab position, too, to worry about. ... If you want to do something, you tell the Israelis to be helpful on Syria because I'm going to withdraw from the negotiations if they're not going to do it. And then let them see how they can stand [before] the whole world in international forums. ... Here we are with a war going on on the Golan Heights with no progress whatever on disengagement. You

want the president to announce he's giving a $1.5 billion credit to Israel?
Do you think the president will approve this? He hasn't even approved
$500 million yet.

GARMENT: Well, I think he should. . . . I think it would be a message of con-
sistency in strength. . . . And I think that the Israelis do have some intuition
of a tragic destiny that may be multiplied by their congenital hysteria, and
I think at this time that kind of resolution of this particular problem would
have a great meaning.

KISSINGER: Well, he will get what I worked out with Dinitz. . . . Look, they
have gotten everything from us all along and that isn't going to change. It's
simply a question of timing. But even that isn't a major problem because he
will get the major part. . . . What you should tell him is that it is important
that we make some progress on the Syrian disengagement. . . .

Joseph Sisco
April 19, 1974, 9:12 a.m.
*Kissinger angrily presses Sisco on getting Israel $1 billion of the aid it sought, but which
he doesn't want to be seen as a response to Congress "screaming its head off" in support
of Israel.*

KISSINGER: Joe, why does it take five days to get a memo over here on assistance to Israel? . . . Now, it was important to me to get this determination
made before the Congress came back and all hell broke loose. And that was
worth more to me than whether every goddamn [bureaucrat] could sign off
on something on which the decision was never going to be made at any level
other than the president. . . . What we worked out was what I ordered, which
was 1 billion now and 1.2 later. Now, this I did in part so that I could sell it to
the Arabs. . . . That then we would give them the other 500 million in grant
in effect after the Syrian disengagement when the Arabs could understand
it. . . . But we are now in the situation, Joe, due to the goddamn bureaucracy
of the State Department—these memos always get written in some three-
hour period. It's a very brief memo. Had that memo been done Tuesday
when I requested it, we would have flushed out this problem on Tuesday.
I want this done before the Congress comes back and all hell breaks loose
in Congress. So that we are not reacting to the Congress. . . . If I had done it
in the White House I guarantee it would have been done in two hours. . . .
I would like to get the people who did this called on the carpet and told to
straighten it out.

SISCO: In any event . . . this has got to be revised somewhat to reflect what
you've just said here.

KISSINGER: But by that time it will happen just before I go to the Middle East.
It will look like blackmail. It will happen just when the Congress is coming

back and screaming its head off. In other words, the department has again brought about the exactly the opposite of what I wanted. . . .

William Colby
April 23, 1974, 7:45 p.m.
Kissinger asks CIA Director Colby for figures on foreign communist aid to North Vietnam for use in appeals to Congress for U.S. aid to South Vietnam, and wants figures showing the former is greater, even though Colby says it is less.

KISSINGER: Look, I have to meet with the congressional leaders tomorrow. . . . I need the figures, now, no matter how inaccurate they are, on what foreign assistance North Vietnam is getting. . . . Now, I know your figures are mushy, but the figures are going to be better than anything I can invent, and I think the most persuasive argument we can make in this town is to prove how world communism is uniting. . . . And if you can give me some idea how it compares to what we put into South Vietnam. Well, hopefully it will prove that more is going into North Vietnam.

COLBY: No, it won't.

KISSINGER: No sense having an intelligence system if it comes up with such confusion.

COLBY: No, you know—

KISSINGER: Go back to the drawing board.

COLBY: Okay, I'll see what I can do on that. . . .

Ronald Ziegler
June 4, 1974, 3:40 p.m.
Kissinger is furious that the State Department put out a statement saying the United States was restoring diplomatic relations with Syria.

. . . ZIEGLER: . . . Poor Jerry Warren [the deputy press secretary] is almost in tears. We followed the guidance that we got from NSC and the State Department on restoration of relations with Syria today, which was basically a "no comment and we have nothing to add to what Dr. Kissinger said in that regard as he left Syria." . . . Well, 45 minutes later the State Department issued a written statement saying that we were going to renew relations with Syria. . . .

KISSINGER: . . . But they couldn't have put out a written statement.

ZIEGLER: Yeah. Following the news conference in Damascus by the Syrian foreign minister saying that diplomatic relations will be restored. . . .

KISSINGER: Inexcusable! Absolutely inexcusable! I told them in answer to questions that they could say that in principle there has been agreement on it but there has been no decision whatsoever.

ZIEGLER: Well, it makes Jerry look like a fool and it makes the White House look like [one], because what we have said is we have nothing to add to the comments that the secretary of state made as he left Syria. And when you left Syria, you said, yes, there is progress in our relationship that could mature into—you know.

KISSINGER: I didn't know they put out a written statement. I'm going to raise hell! . . . Well, you tell Jerry it's unbelievable! . . . They shouldn't put out written statements without my concurrence and they shouldn't say things different from the White House. . . .

Harold Saunders
June 5, 1974, 8:53 p.m.
Kissinger lays into NSC staffer Saunders for the poor quality of a briefing book prepared for Nixon's forthcoming trip to the Middle East.

KISSINGER: . . . These talking points are an outrage and you'd better get these people in, and if they have to work through all night, they're going to work all night. . . . Economic Aid—that's BS. . . . It's got to be much more constructive. . . . And the same in Syria. How the hell can he go through four hours of meetings with these guys and not know a goddamn thing about it? . . . Where it says points to make and points to avoid—it just isn't worthy of him. You know, when I went to China with him with a lousy goddamn NSC staff, we gave him four whole books. Here I've been negotiating with the goddamn Middle East leaders for weeks, and we give him, what, 40 pages? . . . You know what papers the president reads and what he doesn't read. . . . What he god damn well doesn't read is something that says "Memorandum for the president, your talk in Saudi Arabia," and then my signature 20 pages later. Because unless he sees my signature on top, he won't know who the hell wrote it. I mean, since the days of Adam it's been done this way in the department.

SAUNDERS: Okay. That's State Department format.

KISSINGER: I don't give a damn. It is no longer State Department format; it has now been changed. . . .

President Nixon
June 6, 1974, 4:40 p.m.
During pointed questioning at a news conference that day, an irritated and rattled Kissinger denied that he played a "direct" role in the 1969 wiretapping of his NSC aides. Afterward, he was "shaken and disillusioned," Nixon wrote.[5]

NIXON: . . . Ron told me he thought your news conference played very well. He said the only thing he was mad about was the way they asked you all these questions about wiretapping. Let me say, don't ever be worried about that, and frankly if they ever hit me with wiretapping I'm going to say you're god damned [right we did] and some of you are going to be wiretapped—you ought to be. You know? It's disgusting.

KISSINGER: The disgusting thing is . . . the whole world applauds what is being done [in the Middle East], these SOBs turn it into as if I'd been engaged in a criminal activity.

NIXON: But wiretapping, Henry, all the wiretapping we did was totally legal, you would understand that. Every damn one was approved either by Mitchell or Hoover. . . . Some of them turned up some very important evidence, as you well know.

KISSINGER: That is right.

NIXON: And also there was three times as much under Bobby Kennedy as there was from us. . . . We don't need to be apologetic about it. . . .

Robert McCloskey
June 6, 1974, 6:40 p.m.
Kissinger asks State Department spokesman McCloskey about reactions to his news conference.

KISSINGER: Bob, I just wondered whether you had any reactions from the press?

MCCLOSKEY: I've only taken one call so far. . . . The conversation went like this: "Was he pissed?" I said, well, look, he was obviously very disappointed, coming back from another successful peace negotiation to have to face that kind of thing. . . . The guy who asked the question about a lawyer [whether Kissinger had consulted one in preparation for a possible perjury indictment] is apparently some new youngster from . . . the underground press. We're getting his name. . . .

Ronald Ziegler
June 7, 1974, 1:30 p.m.
Kissinger fears that he will be made "a Watergate figure."

ZIEGLER: . . . I thought you were very gutsy yesterday. . . . Very proud of you. You know what it's like to have the SOBs screaming in the room. . . . Of course, for heaven's sake, the secretary of state who has just returned from the Middle East, you know, following movement of historic proportions . . .

to hold his first press conference, to have maniacs like that screaming stuff like that, just is not tolerated by people. . . .

KISSINGER: But they won't rest now until they have made me a Watergate figure.

ZIEGLER: Well, no, they won't. You watch. You could tell how it was played today. I wouldn't concern yourself with that. . . .

Brent Scowcroft
June 21, 1974, 9:15 a.m.
Kissinger wants his deputy to convey to Israel Nixon's intense displeasure with Israeli air strikes on suspected Arab guerrilla bases in Lebanon right after he left Israel during his Middle East trip.[6]

. . . KISSINGER: Finally, would you call [Israeli chargé d'affaires Mordechai] Shalev and say you are calling at the request of the president, who is disturbed beyond expression that the Israelis started retaliatory raids on Lebanon the day he left there and the day he agreed to a statement on terrorism. And have kept it up now for a week. And that if they expect political support from us they cannot keep doing these things, and that we have now had the most violent protest from every Arab leader we visited. . . . And you just tell them to knock it off in no uncertain terms. . . . You know those guys are primitive.

SCOWCROFT: I find it unbelievable. If anything is calculated to drive our friend here up the wall—and it will look to him like an attempt to undercut his trip.

KISSINGER: That's right, and you tell him in the sharpest possible terms. . . .

Alexander Haig
June 21, 1974, 11:36 a.m.
Attorneys for former Nixon adviser John Ehrlichman had said that Nixon had ordered some bombing raids in North Vietnam directly through JCS Chairman Thomas Moorer outside of the normal chain of command, bypassing Secretary of Defense Melvin Laird (which Nixon and Kissinger had indeed done, though Laird was often later told or learned about it).[7]

KISSINGER: Al, what is this stuff of Ehrlichman's of giving orders to the chiefs out of channels?

HAIG: I saw that this morning. I don't know what the hell he's talking about, unless he's talking about—you remember the president would have those tantrums on the bombing stuff.

KISSINGER: But all of that went through Laird.

HAIG: Sure it did. But you remember he would go through the [roof] occasionally and saying "I'll deal just directly with the chiefs."

KISSINGER: No order was ever issued that didn't go through Defense.

HAIG: No, we'd never do it. Well, I can see why Ehrlichman might have the delusion.

KISSINGER: Well, that's a goddamn irresponsible thing to say. . . . I think the White House should say something about this. . . . Because we can't have a statement around that orders were given on bombing out of channels.

HAIG: No, that's crazy. . . . There were never any orders given to the chiefs that didn't go through there. . . . And where it happened it was a mistake and corrected at the time. You know, it may have been an oversight.

KISSINGER: Well, the fact is nothing ever happened that Laird didn't know about. . . .

Brent Scowcroft
June 21, 1974, 7:40 p.m.
They agree that Defense Secretary James Schlesinger should probably not meet with new Israeli Defense Minister Shimon Peres, given Schlesinger's troubled mood after his "outrageous" performance at an NSC meeting that displeased Nixon.

KISSINGER: Brent, when we were in Israel there was a tentative agreement that Peres would come here on Monday for a preliminary talk with Schlesinger and me. What is your judgment of Schlesinger's frame of mind?

SCOWCROFT: Not very good.

KISSINGER: Should he wait until we get back from Russia?

SCOWCROFT: I think so. . . . I would just be leery right now.

KISSINGER: That's what worries me.

SCOWCROFT: I think he's shaken up. I don't know what his frame of mind is, but I think it's not good.

KISSINGER: He's shaken up by what?

SCOWCROFT: Well, by, you know, his meeting with the president. . . . I think he understands that the president was not happy with him yesterday.

KISSINGER: Yes. It was one of the most outrageous performances I've ever seen.

SCOWCROFT: It really was. As a matter of fact, when the president called . . . he said something about, what did you think of your Defense colleague yesterday? And I told him I thought it was disgraceful. . . . I just think he's uneasy. I mean, in a period of instability, and I just don't know what he'd do. . . .

KISSINGER: Don't you think we ought to reestablish some contact?

SCOWCROFT: I think it would be helpful if we can.

KISSINGER: Okay, let's see whether he's free for breakfast. . . . If it's good for his ego, I'll come to him. . . .

The Greek Coup in Cyprus—the Ousting of Makarios, Consulting and Excluding the Soviets, the Unsavory Nikos Sampson, Collaboration and Conflict with Britain, Sisco's Missions, and Keeping U.S. Options Open; the Turkish Invasion of Cyprus—the Clerides Solution, Preventing War with Greece, Frustrations with Sisco and Underlings at State, Schlesinger's Arms Cutoff and Dissociation from Greece, and Threatening a Turkey Arms Cutoff; and More Wiretap Testimony

July 1974

On July 15, 1974, Cyprus President Archbishop Makarios was overthrown in a coup instigated by the right-wing Greek military dictatorship—the infamous colonels—a U.S. ally. Kissinger had foreknowledge of Greece's plan to overthrow Makarios, a nationalist and part of the nonaligned movement, and did not try to prevent it (possibly tacitly supporting it, or simply choosing to look the other way). The disreputable Nikos Sampson, a rightist who'd led an assassination team when fighting in a guerrilla movement against British colonial rule in Cyprus and for Cyprus's union with Greece (enosis, which was also the aim of the Greek government), and was linked to many murders, was installed as Cyprus's new president. Kissinger opposed removing the Greek officers who controlled Cyprus's National Guard, which staged the coup, as urged by British Foreign Secretary James Callaghan, though Kissinger opposed enosis. Callaghan wanted to get Makarios back in power. ("If Sampson stays, he would be accused of running a fascist regime," he observed to Kissinger.) Kissinger told Soviet Ambassador Anatoly Dobrynin that he was not disposed to ask for Greek withdrawal in the United Nations until the situation clarified. He opposed reinstating Makarios. He worried that Makarios would look to the Soviet Union for help getting back in power, which, if successful, would lead to the communists becoming "the dominant force" on Cyprus. The United States avoided public backing of either Makarios or Sampson. Kissinger sought to keep his options open.

Several days after the coup, Turkey invaded Cyprus to undo it. Kissinger opposed the invasion. He proposed that Glafkos Clerides, the speaker of the Cypriot House of Representatives who, though a nationalist like Makarios, was seen as more conciliatory and centrist, serve as interim president of Cyprus as a solution to the crisis. Kissinger aimed to prevent war between Turkey and Greece. But he opposed calling a meeting of the UN Security Council because it would "get the Russians involved." To Kissinger's great aggravation, Undersecretary of State Joseph Sisco resisted his order to fly from Turkey to Greece to propose the Clerides solution there because Sisco was sure the Greeks would not accept it since it had been rejected by Turkey. When Sisco did get on a plane to Athens but wanted top Greek officials to meet him at the airport due to possible physical danger, Kissinger couldn't believe it: "He must be out of his goddamn bloody mind." And when an assistant secretary of state did not follow his order to threaten an arms cutoff to Turkey, Kissinger demanded his resignation if he didn't get in line. With nobody at State seemingly inclined to follow his orders, Kissinger threatened "massive changes."

He was also upset with Defense Secretary James Schlesinger, who ordered a temporary suspension of U.S. military aid to Greece against his opposition, advocated a public dissociation from the Greek dictatorship, and supported its replacement. (On top of that, after it was overthrown, Defense issued a statement recognizing its civilian replacement.) "I have been outflanked on the left," Kissinger told Alexander Haig.

On July 23, Kissinger testified to the Senate Foreign Relations Committee at his request to clear himself of charges that he had lied to the committee about his role in the administration's wiretaps during his confirmation hearings to become secretary of state. He was struck by how embarrassingly wishy-washy the committee was—"Their line is that nothing wrong was done," he marveled to Haig. Its whitewash seemed to him a bigger problem than his testimony. He advised Haig, who testified after him, "If you follow the same route, we're home free."

Anatoly Dobrynin
July 15, 1974, 5:30 p.m.
Cyprus President Makarios had been ousted, and while Kissinger knew not only of the Greek dictatorship's plan to overthrow Makarios but that a coup might be imminent, he said later he was taken by surprise by the coup and would have preferred no coup (which is possible). Kissinger apprises Ambassador Dobrynin that the Soviet counselor in Cyprus had reportedly asked Great Britain, one of the guarantors along with Greece and Turkey of Cyprus's independence and the political arrangements agreed upon when it became independent from Britain in 1960, how it would feel if Soviet troops were deployed.[1]

KISSINGER: We just got a message from Cyprus that your counselor asked the British high commissioner how the British would feel about the introduction of Soviet troops to restore order.

DOBRYNIN: Troops? . . . I doubt that very much. . . . To me it sound unbelievable.

KISSINGER: Me too. If you planned something like this you would talk to us.

DOBRYNIN: Yes.

KISSINGER: You know we would not look on it with favor.

DOBRYNIN: I know. . . .

KISSINGER: Let's see if it calms down. . . . The latest report is they are still fighting.

DOBRYNIN: What about Makarios?

KISSINGER: I have a report from Israel. They say they heard him on the radio.

DOBRYNIN: . . . I know this could come about only if Makarios asked for it and then it would have to be discussed. . . .

James Callaghan
July 16, 1974, 10:15 a.m.
Kissinger is against removing the Greek officers who controlled the Cyprus National Guard as British Foreign Secretary Callaghan was demanding. (Callaghan ardently opposed the Greek dictatorship.)[2]

. . . . CALLAGHAN: . . . Makarios has asked for permission to evacuate to our base area. We have done this and we are now thinking of flying him to our carrier. . . .

KISSINGER: If that is the case, we don't want to have him leading an outside movement and ask for Soviet help.

CALLAGHAN: Right. . . . I am going in to make a statement to the House of Commons. I am going to say he asked to be evacuated. . . . I will go on to say the ambassador is informing the Greek government that the government officials of the Cyprus National Guard [i.e., the Greeks] will be replaced at the earliest moment.

KISSINGER: Wait, I think we should stop short on that.

CALLAGHAN: It would reduce tension in the area.

KISSINGER: Once we know there is a clear outcome, fine. But if there is a civil war we would be getting involved.

CALLAGHAN: How do you see it?

KISSINGER: If Makarios is leaving the island I have to make a different assessment than if he is leading a civil war. My main concern is to keep outside powers out of this. . . . We can go along with asking the Greek government to state their intentions. On the remaining Greek officials, we would come to it, but not today. . . . Once there is an outcome, then we can do something. We are not supporting enosis. . . .

Kurt Waldheim
July 16, 1974, 11:50 a.m.
UN Secretary-General Waldheim informs Kissinger of evidence of Greek involvement in the coup and says the UN will protect Makarios.

WALDHEIM: . . . I received from my special representative and commander in chief in Cyprus . . . [a cable saying] Makarios may request a meeting of the Security Council to discuss what he terms Greek military intervention in Cyprus. We know four members of the Greek government are being treated for wounds received during the coup d'état in the last two days, so there was some involvement. I want you to know that we have these indications that the Greek military contingent is involved. . . . The archbishop asked that the British send a helicopter to evacuate him to a British base on the island, and the British high commissioner accepted this on the condition that the archbishop would accept evacuation to the United Kingdom, and in the meantime our commander in chief there has asked for protection. So, Makarios refused to evacuate the island and I have now authorized our commander in chief to grant protection. . . . But for us it will be a problem if the new military government is in control and no president is sworn in, then we have a problem of what to do with Makarios. . . . I think it is important to avoid intervention by the Turks . . . this is the real danger. . . .

Anatoly Dobrynin

July 16, 1974, 12:00 p.m.

Dobrynin reads a message from Moscow calling for an end to Greek intervention in Cyprus and asks Kissinger for the administration's position on going to the UN. Kissinger says it is not prepared to ask for Greek withdrawal and wants to see what the situation is on Cyprus.

DOBRYNIN: Henry, I received another telegram from Moscow.... "They have staged a military coup against the local government. Justice demands for the Soviet Union and the United States and all countries ... to put an end to military intervention in the affairs of Cyprus.... The most urgent task now is the adoption by the Security Council of a decision as to the immediate withdrawal of military personnel and a stop to the intervention by Greece in the internal affairs of Cyprus."...

KISSINGER: We are taking the position that we want more information.

DOBRYNIN: This line and nothing else? ... What about withdrawal?

KISSINGER: I think today we are not going to support a resolution on anything.

DOBRYNIN: On anything? You like to pass a summary of your position?

KISSINGER: You can pass it now. We will oppose enosis between Cyprus and Greece.

DOBRYNIN: Yes, but as for immediate withdrawal, you are not prepared to do it today?

KISSINGER: No....

DOBRYNIN: And if a resolution is introduced, what will you do?

KISSINGER: I do know we will try to avoid taking a vote.

DOBRYNIN: Oh. Well, what is your personal opinion, Henry?

KISSINGER: I want to see what the situation is on the island.

DOBRYNIN: Well, the situation can be helped if you and we would take a stand.

KISSINGER: It depends if there is a government left there.

DOBRYNIN: Well, Makarios is still there on a UN base.

KISSINGER: Well, we are not prepared to do it today....

James Callaghan

July 17, 1974, 2:50 p.m.

Callaghan gives Kissinger the position of Britain and the European Community— to reinstate Makarios—and urges U.S. pressure on Greece. Kissinger says some U.S. officials are mulling a compromise whereby Cypriot Parliament speaker and Makarios's constitutional successor Glafkos Clerides would be appointed interim president, and agrees with Callaghan that Makarios is better than the installed president, Nikos Sampson, who European governments treated as a pariah.[3]

.... CALLAGHAN: ... I'll tell you our position and this is basically the European position.... We think the ideal solution would be to get Makarios back. Whether we can do it by diplomatic means remains to be seen. Makarios asked for diplomatic activity to continue and the need for nonrecognition of the new regime in Cyprus. When you look ahead for six months—will the situation be more or less tense? Our estimation is ... more tense if we can't get Makarios back. But the question is, can we?

KISSINGER: Some of our people are wondering if a compromise [might] not be Clerides.

CALLAGHAN: He couldn't hold it. But the compromise might be an election in three months with Makarios back on the island.

KISSINGER: But how will you get him back?

CALLAGHAN: ... Well, hopefully you would exert your influence on the Greek government about the National Guard officers. . . . We think there is a chance that if there is concerted diplomatic pressure they might calm down by withdrawing some of their officers.... If you think six months ahead, my view is that it is better to have Makarios there than Sampson.

KISSINGER: That is almost certainly true; I agree.

CALLAGHAN: The problem is a three-to-one or five-to-one chance it won't succeed, but it would be worthwhile to do.... If Sampson stays, he would be accused of running a fascist regime, and the Russians are stepping up their activity, so ... it could be that we may crack the regime and get Sampson to withdraw.

KISSINGER: Let me get somebody over to talk to you. We agree on the general approach. We are not too far apart on it.

CALLAGHAN: Well, send somebody, but I don't think we can afford to lose much time to begin pressuring the Greeks....

President Nixon
July 17, 1974, 4:30 p.m.
Kissinger worries that Makarios may look for help from the Soviets to get back in power, which the United States couldn't resist given international support for Makarios, but which would lead to the communists being "the dominant force" on Cyprus; he wants neither Makarios nor Sampson. And if they "rake" the Greek military junta, it might get overthrown and the left could even take over there.

NIXON: How are we getting along with our Greek friends?

KISSINGER: The problem in Cyprus is the Europeans have taken a united position that Makarios ought to be brought back and they want us to bring pressure on the Greeks. My worry is that Makarios now has to lean on the communists and Eastern bloc. All our evidence is that the opposition is in total control of the island. My recommendation is that . . . we work for a compromise in which neither Makarios or the other guy take over. . . . They want us to rake the Greeks, but if they get overthrown then that will jeopardize our whole position.

NIXON: I know that. . . . But not much support from Europe?

KISSINGER: No, but they know we are dragging our feet. But they don't know exactly what we want. . . . If everyone runs to Makarios embracing him as the legitimate head . . . and if the Soviets are the only ones to offer to help restore him, we have no basis for resisting it.

NIXON: I see the danger. We have no support.

KISSINGER: We cannot openly oppose Makarios but we can try to slow it down enough so that perhaps we can crystallize enough support for an internal solution. . . . If the Greeks collapse, then the left wing could take over, or a bunch of Greek colonels who could throw in with the Gaddafi group. . . . My analysis is if Makarios is brought back this way, he will have to kick the Greek officers off the island, and then the communists will be the dominant force, and to balance the Turks he will have to rely on the Eastern bloc. So the coup will have shifted the balance to the left.

NIXON: I get it. Too bad he has to come back. . . .

Jack Kubisch

July 18, 1974, 4:15 p.m.

Kissinger takes exception to U.S. Ambassador to Chile David Popper's admonishment of officials of the brutal Pinochet dictatorship in Chile, and he and Assistant Secretary of State Kubisch discuss giving it military equipment in the face of congressional opposition.

KISSINGER: Do you think our ambassador to Chile could be taught that he is not to reform the Chilean government?

KUBISCH: I think so. What are you referring to?

KISSINGER: To that discussion on military equipment where he lectured them that we preferred democracies and they have to understand that. . . . I prefer them to Allende—old-fashioned as it may be.

KUBISCH: I do too.

KISSINGER: Let's see what we can do on military equipment for them. What is the obstacle?

KUBISCH: We face an imminent problem in Congress. . . . There was a resolution on this last fall. . . .

KISSINGER: We don't have to take it into account.

KUBISCH: We don't want to flout it in such a way they remove our discretion . . . and that they make it mandatory.

KISSINGER: . . . In practice, how do we take this into account?

KUBISCH: We tell them [the Chileans] we will make certain things available—tanks, aircraft. . . . We will not publicize the fact that we have informed them of this. . . .

Robert McCloskey, Robert Ingersoll, Wells Stabler, and William Buffum
July 19, 1974, 9:30 a.m.

Undersecretary of State Joe Sisco was on a mission to Great Britain, Turkey, and Greece to help manage and contain the Cyprus crisis, and Kissinger is adamant with four underlings at State that Sisco receive his marching orders before he talks to anyone. They also take up reports that Turkish naval units were heading toward Cyprus; Kissinger wants Sisco to warn Turkey against invading.

. . . . KISSINGER: . . . Sisco is not to talk to anybody until he gets instructions. Is that clear? . . .

MCCLOSKEY: We sent a flash message out right after I talked to you—the instructions were coming.

KISSINGER: That doesn't mean he will not come back to us and say, "In the absence of instructions I had no choice." You fellows better understand one thing—I am going to do this thing, as long as I am in charge, the way I want it. And Bob Ingersoll, you will see to it that this department is going to do what is needed in this crisis, and I do not give a good god damn about the independence of emissaries and I want to make god damn sure that Sisco knows he is not to talk until he gets instructions, and if [Turkish Prime Minister Bulent] Ecevit climbs down a grease pole, that is going to happen. . . .

MCCLOSKEY: There is a lot of reporting this morning that Turkish naval units are moving out of southeastern Turkey for Cyprus.

KISSINGER: Yeah, I have the impression they are . . . going in tomorrow morning. . . . I want a telegram to Sisco that as soon as he arrives he is to tell Ecevit that we are extremely concerned about unconfirmed reports we have about Turkish military moves. He is instructed to point out to the Turkish government that the U.S. would take the gravest view of a Turkish military move before all diplomatic processes are exhausted. . . . That he must do immediately, because I think we have been waffling and weeping around the place and we have not made clear that we are opposed to military intervention. Secondly, he is to say we are doing this in the Turkish interests, that Turkish intervention will not be the last move, it will be the first of a whole sequence of moves, that in our judgment . . . the government that will emerge out of this cannot be a Greek Cypriot government that will become a Turkish stooge. . . . That therefore if you look for support . . . to the Soviet Union and to its own communist strength on the island . . . what he is starting is a process in which he . . . can easily lose control. . . .

Robert Ingersoll
July 19, 1974, 12:05 p.m.
Kissinger directs Deputy Secretary of State Ingersoll to keep his colleagues under control when Kissinger is in San Clemente and wants to keep the administration's options open on Cyprus.

KISSINGER: Now, Bob, let's get something straight. You're now acting secretary. You're going to shape up this rabble while I'm out of town. . . . And first of all, any press comments on this Clerides thing [serving as interim president], we do not comment on ongoing negotiations. Now you get Stabler and McCloskey under tight control, Bob, or I'm going to clean the whole bunch of them out. . . . This is a goddamn rabble house. Why do I not want to surface Clerides? . . . My nightmare is that we are going to wind up totally isolated. And we will be committed. I wanted us to be in a position where others were committed and we could go either way, depending on the balance of forces. . . . Are you going to take over now? And will you be willing to give orders now? I don't care about their morale. . . . I'm counting on you to keep this thing under control. . . .

Robert Ingersoll
July 19, 1974, 3:40 p.m.
Kissinger complains about a speech by U.S. Ambassador to the UN John Scali, who he despised, that referred to the deposed Makarios as President Makarios.

KISSINGER: I just got the speech of Scali's . . . in which Scali sometimes referred to Makarios as president and sometimes as archbishop. . . . I consider it another example of total indiscipline. . . . Do you suppose our calling him President Makarios is without significance?
INGERSOLL: No. I don't—it is rather significant. . . .
KISSINGER: Did we all agree on that? I mean, is everyone happy with this? I am not.
INGERSOLL: He started out with archbishop—that is what we had in the text. I don't know where he got the President Makarios.

KISSINGER: Well, will somebody call it to his attention? That he is to stick to Archbishop Makarios. . . . If we can interrupt his great flights of policymaking. . . .

Robert McCloskey, Wells Stabler, and Robert Ingersoll
July 19, 1974, 7:30 p.m.
Turkey had begun its invasion of Cyprus, and Kissinger wants Sisco to head from Turkey to Greece and advance their proposal to install Glafkos Clerides as acting president for six months, followed by an election.[4] *He wants to keep Greece from going to war but not via the UN.*

.... KISSINGER: I think Sisco ought to go to Athens. . . . Let him surface the Clerides solution. . . . Secondly, tell them we recommend that they not go to war. That the consequences for everybody including themselves would be disastrous. . . .

MCCLOSKEY: Mr. Secretary, how about our convening an immediate meeting of the Security Council and asking for—

KISSINGER: No, no. God no. . . . I don't want to get the Russians in yet. Let's first get somebody to Greece. . . . Look, to me the Security Council is far down on the agenda. It will make no contribution, it will get the Russians involved, and the best hope is Sisco now. . . .

President Nixon
July 19, 1974, 8:00 p.m.
Kissinger tells Nixon about the Turkish invasion of Cyprus and the Clerides proposal. If Greece doesn't accept Clerides, Kissinger says, there'll be war between Greece and Turkey, in which case they'll have to cut off military supplies to both. Nixon backs the Clerides solution.

KISSINGER: Mr. President, it looks as if the Turks are going to land in Cyprus within the hour if they haven't already landed there. . . . We're going to urge the Greeks to see whether they will accept the solution of the head of the national assembly, Clerides. They'll never accept Makarios without going to war. . . . And the Turks have already told us they will accept anybody, and if they accept Clerides then actually we'll have come out very well. If they don't accept Clerides we're going to have a war between the Greeks and the Turks. . . . Maybe in a few hours we can consider the question of a Security Council meeting. . . .

NIXON: Well, if it gets down to the Greeks and the Turks having at each other . . . we then have to go to the Security Council.

KISSINGER: To the Security Council and NATO and we'll have to stop military supplies to both while they are fighting. There is no sense having an open pipeline to two NATO allies who are fighting each other. . . .

NIXON: I guess there is no way we could have kept the Turks from doing this.

KISSINGER: . . . The only way I suppose we could have done it was by being more threatening, which we weren't. We were maybe too pleading, but frankly we didn't think they'd move this fast. . . . We did send them a very strong note about eight hours ago telling them it would have very grave consequences.

NIXON: Right. Well, don't be concerned about the reaction. The libs and all that sort of thing.

KISSINGER: The libs now having nothing to react to.

NIXON: They're on the side of the Turks, aren't they?

KISSINGER: Well, they're against the Greeks.

NIXON: That's my point. Where do you end up then? Who is their horse?

KISSINGER: Well, we'll be on the side of the Turks by pushing for Clerides. The Greeks won't like that.

NIXON: Okay. Let's push for it all the way.

Robert McCloskey
July 19, 1974, 8:45 p.m.
Kissinger conveys Sisco's mandate (he was resisting going to Greece) and worries about what the Soviets have picked up on McCloskey's open phone line to Sisco.

KISSINGER: Okay. Sisco is to go to Athens. . . . Before he goes to Athens he is supposed [to go] back in to the Turks and he is to tell them, first of all, that we object strongly to their actions, that it has strong consequences for everybody, we now believe that the Clerides solution is the only one, and that he has been instructed to [go to] Athens to propose it, and that we expect the Turks to go along with us. . . . Now, is there anything else on his tortured mind? Has he told you our whole plan on the telephone? . . . What is his reason for not wanting to go to Athens?

MCCLOSKEY: He says there is no way the Greeks will accept the Clerides proposal that has already been rejected by the Turks. . . .

KISSINGER: As to who will be president under those circumstances, Ecevit said the government in Turkey does not care. . . . By now what else have the Russians not picked up? What is there left to say? Okay, we've said so much on the open line we might as well go ahead. But Sisco is going to Athens and he is going to stay there. . . .

Robert McCloskey and Robert Ingersoll
July 19, 1974, 9:25 p.m.
Sisco, who was now on a plane to Greece, wants Greek officials to meet him at the airport.

.... MCCLOSKEY: He called to ask whether he could have instructions that would assure the prime minister or foreign minister would meet him at the airport.

KISSINGER: He must be out of his goddamn bloody mind. Why?

MCCLOSKEY: He feels the sooner he can leave Athens, the better it will be. He fears there may be some internal difficulty, as he put it, develop while he is en route and on the ground. And he thought if he could make his point—

KISSINGER: Oh, don't let's be absurd.

MCCLOSKEY: He asks for authority to go straight away from Athens to Rome or someplace nearby—his first preference would be to return directly to Washington.

KISSINGER: Oh, no, he is going to stay out there—he is going to go to Athens like a good boy, he is going into the town of Athens, and we are not sending instructions to have the prime minister and foreign minister meet him at the airport; there have been other people who have taken risks and Sisco is going to take a few risks. . . . However, if his nerves aren't up to it, let him come home and I'll go out there. How can we ask our ambassador to stay in Athens while our undersecretary is afraid to leave the goddamn airport? . . . He is to go into Athens, he is to carry out his mission, he is to stay there until he is told to leave. . . . And he will not be told to leave until we have a report. . . .

James Schlesinger
July 19, 1974, 9:45 p.m.
Kissinger explains to Defense Secretary Schlesinger his goal of preventing Makarios's return as Cyprus's president and concern that he will turn to the Soviets if he does.

... KISSINGER: ... I believe that what my fellows want to do in my building, of coming all out for Makarios and coming all out against Athens, is very satisfying for the *New York Times* but it develops a legitimacy for Soviet intervention if we can't deliver on it. . . . And it may create an upheaval in Greece in which we will lose the only certain base we have in the eastern Mediterranean. . . . And therefore I want us to move in such a way that if Makarios comes back he will have to deal with us, and secondly, hopefully avoid Makarios coming back and go for some solution like Clerides. . . . But for that we have to produce a temporary stalemate. . . . And this is why we are moving so slowly. Now, the one thing I fear also is this: if the Turks move . . . and Makarios comes back that way, the one thing you can be sure of is that Makarios will not be a Turkish stooge; he will then have to look for support. . . . So he will have to move left domestically and toward the Soviet bloc. . . .

President Nixon

July 19, 1974, 10:06 p.m.

Kissinger reports to Nixon on the Turkish invasion and Sisco's mission to Greece; he advises him not to return to Washington from San Clemente unless the Greeks attack the Turks. Nixon advocates going to the UN for the symbolism. And they need the Greeks to negotiate.

NIXON: Apparently the battle has started, huh?

KISSINGER: Yeah. They are apparently bombing Nicosia and firing on another town, and we haven't had a Greek reaction yet. I've got Sisco going to Athens under protest because he thinks it might be a little dangerous for him there. . . .

NIXON: Dangerous in the sense of anti-Americanism?

KISSINGER: Yeah. That's all right, Mr. President, that's what they pay under-secretaries for.

NIXON: God almighty, that's what they pay us all for. . . . You think this is the kind of a thing that . . . I have to get the hell back there for this thing?

KISSINGER: Not yet, but if the Greeks attack the Turks, Mr. President, then I think you should go back to Washington. If it leads to a major war. . . . But let's see how the Greeks react, Mr. President. There is still a 10 percent chance that this thing will be settled by Monday. . . . If the Greeks accept Clerides as a solution and . . . if the Greeks and Turks then meet in London, I think we could get a cease-fire.

NIXON: And you don't want to go to the UN because that'll get the Russians in it. . . . As you know, Henry, there is always a damn symbolism in the UN. . . . So what would the Greeks do? . . .

KISSINGER: Well, the Greeks will either negotiate or they will attack the Turks in Thrace. . . . If Sisco hasn't lost his nerve completely, I think they can be gotten to negotiate.

NIXON: God, Sisco may lose his nerve, but [U.S. Ambassador to Greece Henry] Tasca won't. Don't underestimate what he can do. He will put the arm on him now. . . .

William Colby

July 19, 1974, 10:35 p.m.

Kissinger and CIA Director Colby discuss the Turkish invasion, the Greek resistance, and the prospect of double enosis on Cyprus (a partition between Turkey and Greece). Colby raises the possibility of Kissinger personally flying Makarios back (an unwelcome idea), but says "you cannot humiliate the Greeks" and that they need a "Greek from the mainland" to be part of the solution on Cyprus.

KISSINGER: . . . Divisions! Are they walking across water?

COLBY: No, they've got about a division afloat and the rest will come in tomorrow.

KISSINGER: But have they got enough equipment for a division?

COLBY: Oh, yeah, they are landing on the north coast, they've landed at Nicosia by airborne and there is a force moving down towards Famagusta that we haven't heard from. . . .

KISSINGER: I don't know where the hell Famagusta is. . . . You mean it is moving overland? Are they going to take the whole island?

COLBY: No . . . they have landed at Kyrenia on the north coast and they have landed some paratroops at Nicosia.

KISSINGER: Why?

COLBY: Because it is the capital and because there is nothing but Turkish population between them and Kyrenia up to the north, so they can link up easily.

KISSINGER: Do you think they'll take Nicosia?

COLBY: Yeah, well there will be some fighting there. But you see what they can do is land there and land at the airport—link up with the people coming in from the sea from the north and then they [can] fight a lot of National Guard in that area—a serious fight will probably develop there. Then they also have a separate landing over [at] Famagusta on the east coast and perhaps one down at Larnaca down on the southeast coast. The object would be then to try to establish themselves in three or four places . . . and then have a basis for negotiation. The problem is the Greeks . . . can't really get much force over there from the mainland because most of the Greek forces are up in the north around Salonica and Thrace.

KISSINGER: You mean they can only defend with what they've got on the island?

COLBY: With the National Guard on the island—that is about 30,000 troops . . . 9,000 plus the mobilization of about 30,000. . . . But then you've got the Makarios problem . . . and there is already a development of some forces going into the mountains with the idea of carrying on a resistance in favor of Makarios. . . .

KISSINGER: I'm assuming Sampson is a dead duck.

COLBY: He'll fight hard and the NG [National Guard] will probably fight with him because these are the extreme Greeks. These guys will fight pretty hard against the Turks.

KISSINGER: Could it wind up with double enosis?

COLBY: It can wind up with the Turks pretty well ensconced on the isle with some forces and establishing themselves . . . on part of the island. So that they cannot be dislodged but not owning the whole island and therefore [have] the basis for a discussion and some diplomacy as to whether it ends up with double enosis or not. . . .

KISSINGER: Is there any sense in pushing for the Clerides solution?

COLBY: The Turks now . . . want double enosis.

KISSINGER: . . . What we told Sisco was to try out the Clerides solution in Athens just to get them to get rid of Sampson.

COLBY: Well, that is still a possibility. But the other possibility is for you to take Makarios back there.

KISSINGER: How will I take him back there?

COLBY: By plane.

KISSINGER: You mean me going with him?

COLBY: Yeah. . . . The only problem in my particular plan is who would be the Greek you would pick up with you, because you'd need a Greek. . . .

KISSINGER: How about [Greek dictator Dimitrios] Ioannidis? . . .

COLBY: No, you would need some other Greek from the mainland. If Makarios goes back, then Ioannidis is discredited, but you cannot humiliate the Greeks, and therefore some Greeks have to have a part of this and it has to be a Greek solution . . . acceptable to the Turks which—all they really don't want is enosis on the Greek side. . . . Meanwhile I think the Turks will establish themselves and have a position from which they will want to bargain. . . . The main problem is to keep the Greeks from starting a fight anywhere else. . . . No movement on the Soviet side at all that we have detected. . . . No fleets or anything else particularly. . . .

KISSINGER: I think they've been too busy monitoring Joe Sisco's phone calls. . . .

Robert Ingersoll

July 20, 1974, 9:30 a.m.

Schlesinger had ordered a temporary suspension of U.S. military aid to Greece, which Kissinger opposed.[5] But Kissinger orders "technical delays." He also wants Assistant Secretary of State Arthur Hartman to threaten an arms cutoff to Turkey absent a cease-fire and demands Hartman's resignation if he doesn't.

KISSINGER: Bob, that was a false alarm you got. . . . There is no cutoff of military aid.

INGERSOLL: Good. They told us unequivocally in the meeting that Schlesinger told them to cut off shipment.

KISSINGER: You'd better go back there . . . and make sure that they get in touch with their secretary and that shipments are not to be cut off, but on the other hand they're not to be delivered either. If you follow me. There should be in the next few days technical delays. There should be no formal announcement of a cutoff. We'll never get it started again.

INGERSOLL: Well . . . they told us that they had already held up—

KISSINGER: It doesn't make a goddamn difference, Bob. You're in charge of this operation until I get back. You just tell them what I agreed with Schlesinger. . . . I just talked to him five minutes ago and he said it's a misunderstanding, but if it's a misunderstanding you'd better make clear it doesn't happen. . . . Has Hartman talked to the Turks? . . . Did we tell him we'd have to cut off aid if there were no cease-fire?

INGERSOLL: I just heard the message described to me and he didn't put that in there. . . .

KISSINGER: What do you mean Hartman didn't put it in there? . . . Well, it's going to be a lonely department when I get back. . . . You get Hartman to call the Turkish ambassador and you tell Hartman that the next time he doesn't carry out instructions I want his resignation. I do not accept the principle that assistant secretaries have a judgment when they're given an order. . . . There could be no misunderstanding. He was on the goddamn phone with me. . . . Tell Hartman to call back the Turkish ambassador. Tell him he did not make himself clear. . . .

Robert Ingersoll
July 20, 1974, 10:15 a.m.
Kissinger is dubious that either Sisco (who was back in Turkey) or Hartman delivered the right message to Turkey.

INGERSOLL: I just talked to Sisco. . . . He has delivered the message. . . .

KISSINGER: Okay. Now, the only question we have in our mind now is what message did he deliver since nobody yet has delivered the message he was ordered to. I don't want him to break the record.

INGERSOLL: Well, Hartman has delivered your message.

KISSINGER: By this point he probably went the other way. My instructions this morning . . . [were that] Hartman should express his personal opinion that having threatened aid cutoffs to Greece it would certainly come to

Turkey if they did not accept a Sisco proposal. It was not to be an official U.S. government threat at that point. It was supposed to be Hartman's personal opinion. I will bet my bottom dollar he didn't do it that way. . . . Bob, you'd better think of whom we put in what places, because I am going to make some massive changes after this crisis. . . .

Bulent Ecevit
July 21, 1974, 10:40 a.m.
Turkish Prime Minister Ecevit (whom Kissinger had known since 1957 when Ecevit was a student at the Harvard International Seminar that Kissinger led)[6] tells Kissinger that Greek navy ships are flying Turkish flags to hide their movement toward Cyprus and that Greek pilots were calling Turkish pilots in Turkish.

> ECEVIT: We are in the middle of a Security Council meeting to discuss this matter. We have a problem. We doubt the reliability of Greece. Ioannidis's word of honor is a joke. We have now figured out what the joke is behind his words. He said we could fire on any ships bearing Greek flags. His ships are [bearing] Turkish flags!
>
> KISSINGER: Well, no one can blame you if you sink your own ships.
>
> ECEVIT: No, Dr. Kissinger, they are not our own ships. They are Greek ships. They are Greek ships [bearing] Turkish flags.
>
> KISSINGER: Yes, Mr. Prime Minister, but you can sink them if they are not your ships but are flying Turkish flags.
>
> ECEVIT: They are using two tricks. We are NATO allies and the Turkish [Greek] pilots know our codes. They speak Turkish. They call our pilots in Turkish using our codewords. We can no longer rely on the words of Greece. . . . They say that they want an armistice. It has become obvious that they want to exploit the cease-fire for massing troops on the island. The Greeks must cease these methods. . . . They have already shown us the tricks that they will use to violate the cease-fire.
>
> KISSINGER: Are you telling me you will not accept a cease-fire?
>
> ECEVIT: We will accept a cease-fire. . . . We have been occupied with the matter of these flags. . . . They had given us their word that no Greek ships would be around Cyprus. We cannot rely on them. . . .

Alexander Haig
July 21, 1974, 10:50 a.m.
Kissinger expresses his indignation that Schlesinger—who advocated a "conspicuous dissociation" from the Greek dictatorship—supported its replacement, opposed a cease-fire, and advised an end to home-porting in Greece of the U.S. Sixth Fleet.[7]

KISSINGER: I have just left the WSAG. We are having a massive problem with Defense. Schlesinger came to the meeting. He is taking an all-out position on the overthrow of the Greeks. He says a cease-fire in Cyprus is not consistent with NATO principles. It is a very clever position. He is willing to give up home-porting. . . . I have been outflanked on the left. . . . I would like to go back into the meeting and tell them that on a number of issues we have no choice. We must insist on a cease-fire. . . . Schlesinger will crucify us. There is a danger of war in Thrace. I want to call the prime minister and tell him that we must have a cease-fire in a matter of hours. . . . I tell you this, we cannot go through another crisis under this man. There is a [*Washington Post*] story today from Michael Getler that all military aid to Greece has stopped. You know where he got that. Schlesinger said to me this morning that the State Department had done it again [i.e., leaked it]. State did not know that we were stopping.

HAIG: I am not sure we can afford this guy anymore.

KISSINGER: This meeting was made entirely for the record. Schlesinger is making the suggestion that the king can substitute for a government that has not even been overthrown yet. [CIA Director William] Colby has now joined Schlesinger. It is the worst I have ever seen. . . .

Alexander Haig
July 21, 1974, 11:35 a.m.
Amid rumors of imminent changes in the Greek military government (its overthrow and replacement by civilian leadership would be announced in Athens in two days), Haig wonders if the CIA is involved.

. . . . KISSINGER: If we don't get a cease-fire today, there's a coup in Greece, this thing is going to go crazy. . . . I mean, there may be a coup anyway whether or not we get a cease-fire.

HAIG: Well, now, are we contributing in any way to that?

KISSINGER: To the coup?

HAIG: Yeah.

KISSINGER: I don't know.

HAIG: That's what worries me about CIA. Are they hacking around there at all?

KISSINGER: I don't think so. . . . I don't think we are behind this. . . .

William Colby
July 21, 1974, 12:00 p.m.
CIA Director Colby suggests fostering a takeover by generals in Greece.

.... KISSINGER: ... What I hope is that this government now does not go into an orgy over the *New York Times*. ... And the way people are talking about Greece, as if you can start a revolution and then control it in this country.

COLBY: Well, that you might be able to do.

KISSINGER: How?

COLBY: By going to the generals. Not the colonels or the captains but the generals.

KISSINGER: And then where will you be?

COLBY: Then you will have the generals running the country, which is essentially the same government but just the generals would be running it instead of the colonels at the moment.

KISSINGER: Well, who is running it now?

COLBY: Ioannidis is running it. ... I am talking about the responsible leadership of the military who have some links with [Konstantinos] Karamanlis [the former and incoming prime minister] and some others, and I don't think you necessarily go for the Gaddafi [type] or the leftists.

KISSINGER: Well, when do we make that decision?

COLBY: Well, I think we ought to make it pretty soon if we're going to do it. ...

James Callaghan
July 22, 1974, 11:25 a.m.
Britain's Callaghan and Kissinger confer on Nikos Sampson, Greece's proxy president, and ousted President Makarios, who Britain still supports but who Kissinger intends to be "noncommittal" with in a meeting. (Sampson was replaced by Glafkos Clerides the next day.)

.... CALLAGHAN: ... We've got to get rid of this fellow Sampson quickly, you know.

KISSINGER: Well, I told you we'd support that. ... I'm seeing Makarios this afternoon. ... And I'm going to play it rather cool.

CALLAGHAN: Don't be too cool. ... You must recognize he's the legitimate president until any other arrangements are made.

KISSINGER: That's right. No, no, I'll be very friendly, but I will be noncommittal.

CALLAGHAN: Yes, that's all right. I tell you, we will have to move very delicately on that one, Henry. ... If we move, we've got to move together.

KISSINGER: No, no, we are not going to make a commitment, but we don't want a final decision made. ... And we will stay loose on it and very friendly. ...

CALLAGHAN: And you must be absolutely filthy to Sampson.

KISSINGER: You can count on that too. [Laughter.]

CALLAGHAN: Very good. I can always count on you being filthy, can I?

KISSINGER: We really have turned nasty on this. . . .

Alexander Haig
July 23, 1974, 2:40 p.m.
Haig, who in 1969–1970 as Kissinger's assistant had passed to the FBI the names of officials and journalists to be wiretapped, consults with Kissinger about their testimony on the wiretaps before the Senate Foreign Relations Committee. Joe Kraft had written a column that morning on Haig's role in the wiretapping, including his request for the tap on William Safire. Kissinger had testified that day, and Haig was scheduled for the next week. They need to be on the same page, Kissinger underscores to Haig. And, he adds, "I wouldn't try to be clever. It's better to say you have no recollection." But the inquiry was a whitewash.[8]

KISSINGER: I had a very good session this morning and if you follow the same route we're home free. Almost everyone agreed to clear us. Starting out on Kraft . . . they asked about that. I said that is all nonsense. Haig never did anything that he was not ordered to do. . . . I said I didn't know about it and I assumed Haig didn't know about the tap. They said, how does Haig's name appear on that request? I said I don't know. . . . That is the only area you have a problem. . . . It was so embarrassingly whitewashy. I don't see how they can publish the transcript. . . .

HAIG: That's good. That Kraft piece came out of Safire. I'm so damn mad.

KISSINGER: In my view, you should stay quiet. If you stick with me on this you can't have any problems because we accounted for all of them. I have not created an independent role for you. . . . I would not get into an independent defense or they'll come after you. . . . You should only function as an appendage to me. . . . The record this morning is embarrassing. It's a total clearing. They cleared the whole process. They started out trying to go the Kraft line and then gave it up.

HAIG: Who's the tough guy on that?

KISSINGER: . . . Well, Symington isn't after you. He's after Haldeman and Ehrlichman. He says these guys always found some legal body to cover up what they did semi-illegally, like the CIA or NSC. That you know is true. [Senator Frank] Church was sort of semi-niggling. They subsided almost immediately. They said, "Is it possible Haig did things on his own?" I said no. They said, "Is it possible he did it on the president's orders?" I said I can't think of a single case. . . . "How do you account for the Safire tap?" I said that the Brandon tap [Safire had been overheard talking to the British journalist Henry Brandon], I know Haig didn't have anything to do with it. . . . [Senator Jacob] Javits was the guy who raised you. But after the first three minutes your name was never raised again. . . . You'll see when you read this thing, if you stick to what I said, it leaves you out totally. In what I said, you're just a transmittal agent. . . . I think the major problem is this is going to be an embarrassment. It was so easy. . . . Their line is that nothing wrong was done. . . . They said, in other words, you gave names that were tapped. . . . Just read what I said. . . . It isn't that they are looking for a villain and thereby clearing me of something. . . . I wouldn't try to be clever. It's better to say you have no recollection. . . .

Dean Rusk
July 23, 1974, 7:20 p.m.
Former secretary of state Rusk had testified to the Senate Foreign Relations Committee on the procedures former FBI director J. Edgar Hoover used when conducting wiretapping.

RUSK: . . . As far as you know, nothing Haig will say will undermine my veracity? I said if you were to say something to me on this subject, I would believe it.

KISSINGER: It is not inconceivable to me that in one or two cases Haig may have received orders from Haldeman or the president, as orders of the president. It's inconceivable to me that Haig did it on his own. There is no possibility that Haig would say I gave him orders to do things beyond what I have testified. . . . It is now clear that the first four cases were done under Hoover's recommendation. It is clear that three of these people I had put on my staff against Hoover's recommendations. . . . And the fourth turned out to be an espionage agent.

RUSK: And the fourth was Henry Brandon. That was ridiculous.

KISSINGER: I know. That was Hoover's view. There were four cases where . . . [I] signed a statement saying I just had a call from Haig who said that he had just been called by the president that the following four names should be put on the list.

RUSK: My guess is that unless Haig's testimony sets them off balance, they are likely to say that after the most careful and meticulous re-examining they have no basis for changing their original judgment and will reaffirm the point that this whole business of wiretapping needs to be looked into by the Muskie subcommittee.

KISSINGER: That doesn't bother me. As a practical matter, there is no possibility for Haig to deviate from my testimony.

RUSK: . . . There was no hostile questioning in terms of you.

KISSINGER: My impression is, in fact, they were a little too easy on me this morning.

RUSK: . . . I wanted to express to you what I said about my confidence in your veracity and make sure that Haig will not undercut me.

KISSINGER: No possibility of that. . . .

Joseph Sisco
July 26, 1974, 4:30 p.m.
Kissinger objects to a statement from Defense recognizing the new Greek civilian government.

. . . .KISSINGER: Schlesinger made a statement yesterday which went beyond what we said. . . . We're not in the business yet where the Defense Department recognizes a government. . . . I'm against this indecent rushing around of the very people who last week were accusing us of being too pro-Greek . . . for whom we can't be too anti-Turkish enough now.

SISCO: Sure, it represents, I'll put it very mildly, a 180 reversal on their part. . .

Nixon's Resignation and Kissinger's Role, and Memoirs

August 1974

On the evening of August 8, 1974, President Nixon, faced with certain impeachment in the House and a long trial and virtually certain conviction in the Senate, announced that he was resigning. Kissinger contested a newspaper column, one with kernels of truth, which argued that he, White House Chief of Staff Alexander Haig, and three Republican senators played critical roles in persuading Nixon to resign. Vice President Gerald Ford became president. Kissinger stayed on as secretary of state and national security adviser. Amid reports that he was planning on writing his memoirs, he exclaimed with considerable exasperation to Random House's president that he was "not in business!"

William Colby
August 2, 1974, 1:00 p.m.
A New York Times *article that morning said top administration officials, reflecting Kissinger's and CIA Director William Colby's thinking that the United States should keep out of other countries' politics, had directed the CIA not to interfere in Greece's internal affairs.*

> COLBY: I hope we can talk about something other than leaks sometime.
> KISSINGER: I was outraged about the story in the *New York Times.* . . . I have been raising hell all over the department. Except for the one quote they swear that it did not come from here. . . . You know my views on this subject and they are not as they are reported. . . . If you ever give me a name—that is asking too much—but if you can ever identify the office I will fire the director. . . . You can be sure, Bill, that I do not deal with you through leaks.
> COLBY: Thanks.

Simcha Dinitz
August 3, 1974, 11:18 a.m.
Kissinger raises with Israeli Ambassador Dinitz Soviet complaints about Israeli harassment of Soviet minesweepers off the Sinai Peninsula.

KISSINGER: We have had a very tough note from the Russians about your buzzing their ships that are engaged in minesweeping. They said two Phantoms took runs at them yesterday simulating attack runs. That if this doesn't stop they will take military action to protect themselves. . . . I do not think this is the time to get into a confrontation. . . . Would you tell them [the Israeli forces] to be careful? The Soviets are looking for some opportunity to show how tough they are. . . . I would like you to urge on your cabinet in the next several weeks not to give them provocation. Normally I would say if the Soviets threaten, one should act brutally.

DINITZ: When they are crossing into our waters and taking photographs with their helicopters, shouldn't we send up planes?

KISSINGER: If they send in helicopters I would not take runs on their ships. Send me a note and say if it happens again we will send planes. Then you will have some cover. . . . I do not want speculation on whether we are staging a Middle East crisis in order to cover up impeachment inquiries. . . .

Gerald Ford
August 8, 1974, 12:30 p.m.
A solemn and tense Nixon had just told Vice President Ford that he would be resigning effective the next day and that Ford would become president.[1]

FORD: I just finished talking with the president and he gave me his decision. . . . I would hope we could get together sometime this afternoon. . . .

KISSINGER: After the president talked to me yesterday I prepared some tentative suggestions for your consideration. . . . They are things that need to be done in the next two days. . . . Can we say to the press that I am coming over to see you or would you rather announce that? . . . I think from the foreign policy point of view it would have a calming effect.

FORD: Why don't you state it or have it released and in any way that you think would be helpful. Don't hesitate to embellish it. . . . As I have inferred in our previous conversations, I really want you to stay and stand with me in these difficult times. . . . I wanted to get that in now so there is no doubt about it. . . .

J. William Fulbright
August 9, 1974, 4:43 p.m.
*Nixon had left the White House for exile in San Clemente, and Senator Fulbright and
Kissinger discuss his departing remarks to his cabinet and staff.*

    . . . FULBRIGHT: . . . I was fascinated by his statement this morning. I saw you
      on television.

    KISSINGER: Well, it was one of the most painful things I've ever witnessed.

    FULBRIGHT: I could tell that. . . . Of course, it was painful and highly emo-
      tional. But nevertheless it was done, and it was very interesting from a purely
      personal point of view.

    KISSINGER: Well, it had almost all the aspects of his personality.

    FULBRIGHT: Yeah . . . and the tragedy and everything else came through in that
      sort of disorganized and rambling way. In a way, it's more impressive than a
      prepared statement of any kind.

    KISSINGER: I agree. It was sort of a faded doom about the man. . . .

Brent Scowcroft
August 10, 1974, 9:05 a.m.
*Rowland Evans and Robert Novak had written in their column that morning about
the key roles of Kissinger, Haig, and three Republican senators in persuading Nixon
to resign.*[2]

    . . . KISSINGER: Have you seen that Rollie Evans article today?

    SCOWCROFT: Yes, I did. Haig is fit to be tied.

    KISSINGER: I'm fit to be tied. . . . With whom was Haig in touch on the Hill?

    SCOWCROFT: I have no idea. . . . I think Haig thinks it came from you.

    KISSINGER: If it came from anyone it came from [Senator] Hugh Scott. . . . It
      didn't come from me.

    SCOWCROFT: It would be useful to chat with Al over here. He's upset about it.

    KISSINGER: I'm upset about it. . . . Hugh Scott told me at a luncheon that Evans
      told him he was going to go on a story like this. . . .

    SCOWCROFT: Would Scott have put you in the key position the way Rollie
      does?

    KISSINGER: No, it isn't true.

    SCOWCROFT: I know. To me, that's the thrust of the article.

    KISSINGER: It could have been Laird. Laird called me.

    SCOWCROFT: . . . You see, the Evans thing, in essence, says you managed the
      whole thing.

    KISSINGER: Do you think I want to be known as the guy who managed
      it? . . .

Hugh Sidey
August 10, 1974, 11:47 a.m.
Kissinger steers Sidey of Time *magazine away from Evans and Novak's thesis.*

KISSINGER: I don't want you to go with that, because that was not my role. . . . I would like to think my role was a comfort and I gave some moral strength when the inevitably of events pushed it in a certain direction. . . . But I was not the guy who threw him over the cliff. . . . It would really mean a lot to me not to be depicted as the ringleader of a coup here. . . .

Arthur Burns
August 10, 1974, 2:33 p.m.
Kissinger and Chairman of the Federal Reserve Burns discuss Nixon's resignation.

KISSINGER: Just about the most heartbreaking thing I've been involved in.

BURNS: Was it difficult?

KISSINGER: Well, it was inordinately painful.

BURNS: I know, but did he understand?

KISSINGER: Yes and no. He understood the arithmetic in the Congress, and he understood what would happen if he fought to the bitter end. . . .

BURNS: I thought until the end that he might keep on fighting. . . . Fortunately, that didn't happen.

KISSINGER: That was awful. . . . I spent three hours with him Wednesday night and it just about tore me up.

BURNS: How was his family?

KISSINGER: They weren't supportive. They wanted him to keep fighting. I would stake my life that he must have authorized clemency. . . . I'm saying what would have happened if he went on?

BURNS: Some of the [House Judiciary] Committee people want this to continue.

KISSINGER: But that can't be permitted. Enough is enough.

BURNS: Exactly. We need to forget. . . .

KISSINGER: I don't want to see a former president of the U.S. in jail or in court. He wasn't a bad president.

BURNS: The idea of equality is ridiculous, after all. Nixon has been punished more than Colson, who gets a year.

KISSINGER: No comparison.

BURNS: He had the most severe punishment.

KISSINGER: A man who spends his whole life getting to where he was.

BURNS: And the only president to leave the office in disgrace. To want blood after that is inhuman.

KISSINGER: I'd go public if it happened.

BURNS: You take the present tapes, to whom do they belong? To Nixon.

KISSINGER: I agree with you. . . .

Robert Bernstein

August 28, 1974, 11:01 a.m.

Kissinger tells Random House's president that a report that someone had called the publisher Farrar, Straus, and Giroux on his behalf about his memoirs was an "outrageous lie" and that he's never had any talks with publishers.

BERNSTEIN: I am calling—our editor got a call from a newspaper yesterday from a reporter . . . saying that somebody in your behalf had called Farrar, Straus and had asked them what they would be interested in—

KISSINGER: That is an outrageous lie!!

BERNSTEIN: I thought so. . . . But I just got nervous.

KISSINGER: It is an outrageous lie! It was in *Newsweek* magazine. I have had no talks. I have never had formal talks with any publishers. . . . I have permitted one or two publisher friends a year and a half ago to tell my lawyer what they thought the situation was at a time when I thought I would leave the government in 1973. . . . I did not permit . . . any publisher to make a formal offer.

BERNSTEIN: I know that.

KISSINGER: You remember it. . . . Because when you talked to me I told you that it was highly inappropriate and you told me it didn't make any sense anyway.

BERNSTEIN: I agree with you. Your memory is 100 percent perfect.

KISSINGER: And therefore it is totally incorrect. . . . Since that time there have been no talks with anybody. . . . I will not discuss publishing contracts while I am in office. . . . I will not entertain offers while I am in office. No one is authorized to negotiate for me. . . .

BERNSTEIN: As I understood it, at such time as you were willing you would let me know, and we would be allowed to make an offer.

KISSINGER: Absolutely, and until then I don't want an offer. . . .

BERNSTEIN: We got a call from a reporter who was evidently trying to find out if we had been approached in any way, and we said no, of course we haven't.

KISSINGER: Well, nobody has ever been approached. Everything has been at the initiative of publishers, and for one two-month period in early 1973 I permitted publishers to write to Carl Maw, who had instructions to file them—not to show them to me. . . . Look, I give you my assurance that when I get ready to write—which will not be until after I have left—

BERNSTEIN: You are not doing it in your spare time now?

KISSINGER: —I will talk to you first.

BERNSTEIN: All right. I really was calling as much to tell you the rumors are around.

KISSINGER: The rumors are outrageous. I am not in business! . . .

ABBREVIATIONS

ABM	antiballistic missile
ACDA	Arms Control and Disarmament Agency
APC	armored personnel carrier
ARVN	Army of the Republic of Vietnam (South Vietnamese army)
CINCPAC	Commander in Chief, Pacific
COSVN	Central Office for South Vietnam
DIA	Defense Intelligence Agency
DMZ	demilitarized zone
JCS	Joint Chiefs of Staff
MACV	Military Assistance Command, Vietnam
NLF	National Liberation Front
NSC	National Security Council
NYT	*New York Times*
POL	petroleum, oil, and lubricants
PRG	Provisional Revolutionary Government
SALT	Strategic Arms Limitation Talks
SAM	surface-to-air missile
WHY	*White House Years* (Kissinger memoir)
WP	*Washington Post*
WSAG	Washington Special Actions Group
YOR	*Years of Renewal* (Kissinger memoir)
YOU	*Years of Upheaval* (Kissinger memoir)

NOTES

Introduction

1. John Osborne interview of Brent Scowcroft, April 10, 1976, Osborne Papers, box 32, folder 8, Library of Congress; Haig deposition in Morton Halperin's wiretapping lawsuit, October 25, 1974, Record Group 460, Plumbers Task Force, Records of the Investigation of the National Security Wiretaps, National Archives and Records Administration; Isaacson, 231; Mardian interview by FBI, May 10, 1973, FBI's "The Vault" online FOIA library, William Safire, part 6 of 6; Blumenfeld et al., 178; https://nsarchive2.gwu.edu/NSAEBB/NSAEBB123/telcon-finding-aid.pdf; Kissinger, *Crisis*, 1; National Security Archive posting, "Henry Kissinger: The Declassified Obituary," November 29, 2023, https://nsarchive.gwu.edu/briefing-book/chile-cold-war-henry-kissinger-indonesia-southern-cone-vietnam/2023-11-29/henry.
2. Isaacson, 230–231; Osborne interview of Scowcroft, op. cit.
3. https://nsarchive2.gwu.edu/NSAEBB/NSAEBB123/complaint.pdf; Wise, 92.
4. Roger Morris email to author; Safire, 169; Isaacson, 233, 388; Haig deposition, op. cit.; Zumwalt, 318; Haldeman, *Ends*, 195; Dallek, 456; Dobbs, 59–60.
5. Safire, 169.
6. Blumenfeld et al., 181.
7. Kalb and Kissinger phone conversation, March 30, 1972, 4:30 p.m.; Ehrlichman, 310.
8. Kimball, 118; Dobrynin and Kissinger phone conversation, November 8, 1972, 9:55 a.m.
9. Carlyle Maw and Kissinger phone conversation, June 22, 1974, 9:40 a.m.
10. Nixon and Kissinger phone conversations, June 11, 1971, 5:48 p.m., and February 11, 1972, 12:00 p.m.
11. Kissinger, *Crisis*, 1.
12. Zumwalt, 309.
13. Kissinger's central role in the wiretapping program, the FBI's many unusual procedures designed to ensure secrecy of the wiretaps, and Hoover's and other FBI officials' and agents' concerns about the wiretapping are documented in the records of the Watergate Special Prosecution Force, Plumbers Task Force, Records of the Investigation of the National Security Wiretaps, at the National Archives (which I examined for a forthcoming book on the wiretaps). Haig's request for the start of the wiretapping on Kissinger's behalf is in a Hoover memorandum for the attorney general, May 12, 1969, in the House Judiciary Committee's impeachment hearings, 1974, Book VII, https://babel.hathitrust.org/cgi/pt?id=umn.31951002171418&seq=9. Kissinger's concern that the wiretapping could be "explosive" and was a "dangerous game" is in a Mitchell interview by the FBI on May 12, 1973, in box 2 of the above Watergate Special Prosecution Force records.
14. Graff, xix; Evans and Kissinger phone conversation, April 24, 1973, 9:30 a.m.; Weinberger and Kissinger phone conversation, August 13, 1973, 6:21 p.m.
15. Van Atta, 183.

16. Kalb and Kalb, 96; Isaacson, 100, 666; Hersh, *Reporter*, 191; Schwartz, 145; Nelson Rockefeller and Kissinger phone conversation, December 26, 1970, 12:35 p.m.
17. Zumwalt, xii, 308, 396–397; Osborne interview of Scowcroft, op. cit.; Isaacson, 190.
18. Nixon and Kissinger phone conversation, June 8, 1971, 6:03 p.m.; Hersh, *Price*, 511.
19. Weiner, 30; Kissinger, *YOU*, 96.
20. Graff, 11; Ehrlichman, 310; Kissinger, *YOU*, 98, 1183, 1212; Weiner, 30; Dobbs, 57; Joseph Sisco and Kissinger phone conversation, January 8, 1974, 9:58 a.m.
21. Dallek, 250–251, 615; Haldeman, *Diaries*, 139, 219, 253; Garment, 186; Ehrlichman, 296–297.
22. https://nsarchive2.gwu.edu/NSAEBB/NSAEBB123/complaint.pdf; Isaacson, 231–232; Hersh, *Price*, 112.
23. https://www.nixonlibrary.gov/finding-aids/kissinger-telephone-conversation-transcripts; Montgomery; Van Atta, 523.
24. Safire, 166–168; "Dr. Kissinger's Role in Wiretapping," Senate Foreign Relations Committee hearings, July 1974, https://babel.hathitrust.org/cgi/pt?id=pur1.32754076921463&seq=3.
25. https://nsarchive2.gwu.edu/NSAEBB/NSAEBB123/carlin.pdf; https://nsarchive2.gwu.edu/NSAEBB/NSAEBB123/complaint.pdf; https://nsarchive2.gwu.edu/NSAEBB/NSAEBB123/mbp.pdf.
26. Kissinger, *Crisis*, 1.
27. Isaacson, 232, 494; Graff, 60; Garment, 279; Haldeman, *Ends*, 210–211.

Chapter 1

1. Kissinger, *WHY*, 245.
2. Haldeman, *Diaries*, 41.
3. Haldeman, *Diaries*, 41; Grandin, 71n.

Chapter 2

1. Haldeman, *Diaries*, 50.
2. The USS *Pueblo* was a U.S. Navy spy ship; North Korea had held its crew hostage for almost a year.
3. Burr and Kimball, 126, 128; Hersh, *Price*, 69–70.
4. Kissinger, *WHY*, 316–319; Van Atta, 185; Hersh, *Price*, 69–73; Isaacson, 181.
5. Haldeman, *Diaries*, 62.
6. Hersh, *Price*, 93–95; Wise, 55.
7. CIA paper, March 10, 1961, https://history.state.gov/historicaldocuments/frus1961-63v10/d54.

Chapter 3

1. Kissinger, *WHY*, 278–282. See Burr and Kimball, chapters 6 and 7, on Duck Hook.
2. Van Atta, 238.
3. *NYT*, September 9, 13, 1969.
4. *NYT*, September 19, 1969; Ehrlichman, 95; *WP*, September 30, 1969.
5. Kissinger, *WHY*, 371; Indyk, 50–51.

Chapter 4

1. Wells, *Within*, 385.
2. Isaacson, 216; Hersh, *Price*, 96–97; Haig, 219.
3. Bilton and Sim, 260.
4. *NYT*, November 26, 1969.
5. Blumenfeld et al., 140.
6. Kissinger, *WHY*, 188–190.
7. Kissinger, *WHY*, 374–375; Garment, 192–193.

Chapter 5

1. *WP*, January 12, 1970.
2. *NYT*, January 10, 22, 27, 1970.
3. Kissinger, *WHY*, 451–452, 453; Hersh, *Price*, 169–170.
4. Kissinger, *WHY*, 333.
5. Kissinger, *WHY*, 452.
6. *NYT*, January 31, 1970.
7. See Hunebelle.
8. *NYT*, February 19, 1970.
9. Weiner, 77.
10. *NYT*, March 21, 1970.
11. Weiner, 79–80.

Chapter 6

1. Kissinger, *WHY*, 473, 487.
2. *NYT*, April 23, 1970.
3. Kissinger, *WHY*, 495.
4. Kissinger, *WHY*, 495–496.
5. Kissinger, *WHY*, 506; *NYT*, May 1, 1970.
6. *NYT*, May 3, 1970; Hersh, *Price*, 193–194; "Dr. Kissinger's Role in Wiretapping," Senate Foreign Relations Committee hearings, July 1974, https://catalog.hathitrust.org/Record/011338566.
7. Haldeman, *Diaries*, 159.
8. Weiner, 90.
9. *WP*, May 8, 1970; Haldeman, *Diaries*, 162.
10. Weiner, 85.

Chapter 7

1. Garment, 251.
2. *WP*, June 5, 1970.
3. *NYT*, June 9, 1970.
4. *WP*, June 18, 1970.
5. *NYT*, July 16, 1970.
6. Quandt, 100–101; Dallek, 221.
7. Quandt, 102; *WP*, August 6, 1970.
8. Kissinger, *WHY*, 585.
9. *WP*, August 8, 1970; Haldeman, *Diaries*, 189; Schwartz, 102.

Chapter 8

1. Kissinger, *WHY*, 673.
2. Hersh, *Price*, 273–274; Kornbluh, 1–2, 7.
3. Kissinger, *WHY*, 610–611; Kalb and Kalb, 199; Indyk, 61; Nixon, 483–484; Hersh, *Price*, 240–241.
4. Hersh, *Price*, 242–244; Nixon, 485; Quandt, 115.
5. Kissinger, *WHY*, 623.
6. Haig, 249.
7. *NYT*, September 26, 1970.
8. Kornbluh, 22–29.

Chapter 9

1 Van Atta, 213.
2. Hersh, *Price*, 305; Van Atta, 213.

3. Haldeman, *Diaries*, 212; Kissinger, *WHY*, 985.
4. *NYT* and *WP*, November 21, 22, 23, 1970.
5. *NYT*, November 28, 1970.
6. *WP*, November 24, 1970.
7. *NYT*, November 29, 1970.

Chapter 10

1. *NYT*, January 7, 1971.
2. Mosbacher and Kissinger phone conversation, January 6, 1971, 4:25 p.m.
3. Kissinger, *WHY*, 997.
4. Kissinger, *WHY*, 995–996, 1000.
5. Sander, 101, 107; Hastings, 575–576; Hersh, *Price*, 308.
6. Kissinger, *WHY*, 1000.
7. *WP*, February 23, 1971.
8. Kissinger, *WHY*, 1003–1006; Weiner, 117; Sander, 3, 86–87; Haldeman, *Diaries*, 250.
9. Kissinger, *WHY*, 1278–1281; Quandt, 135–136.
10. Kissinger, *WHY*, 1279.

Chapter 11

1. *WP*, March 8, 1971.
2. Dallek, 323.
3. Zumwalt, 325–328.
4. Kalb and Kalb, 178, quoting McGrory's column.
5. Kissinger, *WHY*, 1015.
6. *NYT* and *WP*, March 17, 18, 1971; Schwartz, 122.
7. Hastings, 578.
8. *WP* and *NYT*, March 22, 1971.
9. *WP*, March 22, 23, 1971
10. See Bass, 58–59, for Blood's cable.
11. Hastings, 585–593.

Chapter 12

1. Bass, 75–79.
2. Nixon address, millercenter.org.
3. Kissinger, *WHY*, 1005.
4. *NYT*, April 15, 1971; MacMillan, 178, 180; Weiner, 127, 131.
5. *NYT*, April 18, 1971.
6. Kissinger, *WHY*, 714–715; Haldeman, *Diaries*, 282; Isaacson, 339–341; Weiner, 128.
7. Kissinger, *WHY*, 803, 810–820; Dobrynin, 218; Smith, 232–244.
8. *NYT*, May 20, 1971.
9. *WP*, May 20, 23, 1971.
10. Graff, 537.

Chapter 13

1. *NYT*, May 29, June 7, 12, 1971.
2. *NYT*, June 1, 4, 1971.
3. *NYT*, June 13, 1971.
4. Colson, 59–60; Ehrlichman, 301; Isaacson, 329–330.
5. Rudenstine, 70; Wells, *Wild*, 313.
6. Wells, *Wild*, 311–312.
7. Van Atta, 371–372.
8. Wells, *Wild*, 314–315.
9. Kissinger, *WHY*, 756–760; Isaacson, 349; Dallek, 298.

10. Kissinger, *WHY*, 1029–1031.
11. *NYT*, August 5, 1971.
12. Kissinger, *WHY*, 823–831.
13. Hersh, *Price*, 423–438.

Chapter 14

1. William Rogers and Kissinger phone conversation, September 14, 1971, 6:18 p.m.; *NYT*, September 15, 1971.
2. Hastings, 597.
3. *WP*, September 18, 1971.
4. *NYT*, September 19, 1971.
5. *NYT*, September 22, 1971.
6. Kissinger, *WHY*, 769–770; *NYT*, September 22, 1971; MacMillan, 204–207.
7. *NYT*, September 23–26, 1971.
8. *NYT*, September 29, 1971.
9. Quandt, 146; Dallek, 328.
10. *NYT*, October 12, 1971.
11. *NYT*, October 13, 1971; Smith, 319.
12. *WP*, October 15, 1971; AP story, October 16, 1971.
13. Haldeman, *Diaries*, 369.

Chapter 15

1. See Bass, 119–133, on the refugee crisis.
2. Bass, 192–194.
3. Bass, 258–262.
4. Kissinger, *WHY*, 887–890; Bass, 265, 270–271, 445n, 448n.
5. Bass, 268–269; Dallek, 341.
6. Kissinger, *WHY*, 898.
7. Bass, xix–xx, 293–296.
8. Bass, 283–284.
9. Weiner, 145.
10. Isaacson, 373; Hersh, *Price*, 462–463.
11. Kissinger, *WHY*, 900.
12. Bass, 293–298.
13. Kissinger, *WHY*, 907.
14. Bass, 312–313, 318–322; Kissinger, *WHY*, 913.
15. *WP*, December 17, 1971; *NYT*, December 18, 1971.
16. *WP*, December 27–31, 1971.

Chapter 16

1. Hersh, *Price*, 465, 472–475; Weiner, 148–150; Ehrlichman, 306–308; Kissinger, *WHY*, 918.
2. Haldeman, *Diaries*, 394.
3. Hersh, *Price*, 475; Kissinger, *WHY*, 918; Haldeman, *Diaries*, 393, 394; Schwartz, 157.
4. Schwartz, 48–50.
5. Haldeman, *Diaries*, 392, 395.
6. Nixon address, millercenter.org.
7. Walters, 208; Haldeman, *Diaries*, 407.
8. Kimball, 295–296; *NYT*, February 11, 1972.
9. Kissinger, *WHY*, 1079, 1093.
10. MacMillan, 306, 308–312, 322.

Chapter 17

1. *WP*, March 16, 1972.
2. Kissinger, *WHY*, 1111–1113; Weiner, 173.
3. Weiner, 174.
4. *NYT*, April 7, 1972.
5. Kissinger, *WHY*, 1118; *NYT*, April 11, 1972. But it is possible that B-52s were used in southern North Vietnam earlier and never acknowledged or reported.
6. *NYT*, April 15, 16, 17, 1972; Kimball, 305; Haldeman, *Diaries*, 440.
7. Kissinger, *WHY*, 1122.
8. *WP*, April 18, 1972.

Chapter 18

1. Kissinger, *WHY*, 1160.
2. Kissinger, *WHY*, 1169–1174; Nixon, 599–601; Van Atta, 406.
3. Kissinger, *WHY*, 1176–1179; Haldeman, *Diaries*, 454; Weiner, 182; Van Atta, 407.
4. Weiner, 181.
5. *NYT*, May 10, 1972.
6. Nixon and Kissinger phone conversation, June 8, 1972, 12:40 p.m.
7. Kissinger, *WHY*, 1304; *WP*, June 23, 1972; Burr, xv.

Chapter 19

1. Paris peace talks, July 19, 1972, https://history.state.gov/historicaldocuments/frus1969-76v08/d207.
2. *WP*, July 9, 1972.
3. *NYT*, July 25, 1972.
4. *NYT*, July 13, 1972.
5. *WP*, July 29, 1972.

Chapter 20

1. *NYT*, September 10, 16, 1972.
2. Hersh, *Price*, 558.
3. Walters, 230.
4. Berman, 163–171; Kissinger, *WHY*, 1396.
5. Brigham, 222–223; *NYT*, October 25, 1972.
6. Berman, 154, 156, 165; Kissinger, *WHY*, 1344, 1353.
7. Kissinger, *WHY*, 1397; Hersh, *Price*, 604.
8. Transcript of press conference, *NYT*, October 27, 1972; Weiner, 208; Schwartz, 191.
9. Haig, 302; Nixon, 705; Haldeman, *Diaries*, 524.
10. Kissinger, *WHY*, 1404.

Chapter 21

1. *WP*, November 3, 1972.
2. *WP*, November 4, 1972.
3. Kissinger, *WHY*, 1411–1412, 1413–1414.
4. Berman, 184, 187.
5. Brigham, 227–228; Berman, 189–194; Kissinger, *WHY*, 1417–1422; *NYT*, November 27, 1972.
6. Kissinger, *WHY*, 1424.
7. Berman, 205; Kissinger, *WHY*, 1426; Kalb and Kalb, 404.
8. Brigham, 229–234; Kissinger, *WHY*, 1427–1448; Nixon, 733–734; Berman, 215–218.
9. Schwartz, 201.

10. *NYT*, December 19, 1972.
11. *NYT*, December 20, 1972; Brigham, 223, 227; Kissinger, *WHY*, 1417–1418.
12. Kissinger, *WHY*, 1457.
13. Kissinger, *WHY*, 1457–1458.

Chapter 22

1. Kimball, 365; Hersh, *Price*, 625n.
2. Berman, 223–227, 246; Hersh, *Price*, 632; Brigham, 239; Isaacson, 484.
3. Kissinger, *WHY*, 1470.
4. *NYT*, January 27, 1973; Jon Wiener, "When Old Blue Eyes Was 'Red,'" *New Republic*, March 31, 1986.
5. Nixon address, millercenter.org.

Chapter 23

1. *NYT*, February 22, 23, 1973.
2. Haldeman, *Diaries*, 575; Dallek, 459–460; Kissinger, *YOU*, 207.
3. Kissinger, *YOU*, 317; *NYT*, February 27, 1973.
4. *NYT*, February 28, 1973; Weiner, 229n.
5. Graff, 258, 289.

Chapter 24

1. Indyk, 91n; Kissinger, *YOU*, 224.
2. *NYT*, April 28, 1973.
3. Kissinger, *YOU*, 325.
4. Kissinger, *YOU*, 75–76; Garment, 253.
5. Graff, 370.
6. Kissinger, *YOU*, 104–105; *NYT*, May 1, 1973.
7. Graff, 373–374.
8. Kalb and Kissinger phone conversation, May 13, 1973, 11:08 a.m.
9. Hersh, *Price*, 96–97; Lukas, 52–53.
10. Ehrlichman, 301–302; Hersh, "Kissinger and Nixon"; Hersh, *Price*, 391n; Hersh, *Reporter*, 197; Schwartz, 221; Isaacson, 330.
11. *WP*, May 15, 1973.
12. *NYT*, May 16, 17, 1973; Frank Martin to Jay Horowitz, June 16, 1975, Watergate Special Prosecution Force records, https://www.govinfo.gov/content/pkg/GPO-NARA-WSPF-NIXON-GRAND-JURY-RECORDS/pdf/GPO-NARA-WSPF-NIXON-GRAND-JURY-RECORDS-25.pdf; Weiner, 260.
13. *WP*, May 27, 1973.

Chapter 25

1. Frank Martin, "Henry Brandon" (Record Group 460, Plumbers Task Force, Records of the Investigation of the National Security Wiretaps, box 29, National Archives); Director, FBI, to Attorney General, September 12, 1973 (Elliot Richardson papers, box 222, Library of Congress); O. T. Jacobson to the Director, August 6, 1973, FBI document obtained through FOIA; Lukas, 54; Hersh, *Price*, 93–95.
2. Hersh, "Kissinger and Nixon"; Graff, 78.
3. Kissinger, *YOU*, 287–288.
4. *NYT*, September 10, 29, 1972; Garthoff, 305–307.
5. Shultz and Kissinger phone conversation, June 24, 1973, 11:45 a.m.; Weiner, 275.
6. *NYT*, June 15, 1973; *WP*, June 27, 1973.
7. *NYT*, June 30, 1973; *WP*, June 29, 1973.

8. Documents on the wiretapping in the records of the Watergate Special Prosecution Force's Plumbers Task Force's investigation of the wiretaps at the National Archives show Kissinger's central role in Halperin's wiretapping and Hoover's wariness of the secret wiretapping program ordered by the White House, though there was pressure on Kissinger inside the administration to wiretap Halperin, and Hoover, who questioned Halperin's loyalty, probably wanted to tap him. See also Hersh, *Price*, 87.
9. Kornbluh, 97–100, 109, 150–151.
10. Nixon, 900; Graff, 432.
11. Hersh, *Price*, 60–62; Shawcross, 95; Grandin, 54n, 95, 137; Hersh, *Reporter*, 193.

Chapter 26

1. Safire, 166–168; David Wise interview of Safire, 1975 (Wise papers, box 23, Columbia University Rare Book and Manuscript Library); O. T. Jacobson to the Director, August 6, 1973, FBI document obtained through FOIA; *NYT*, August 5, 1973; Wise, 60.
2. Grandin, 54n, 54–55; Hersh, *Reporter*, 193.
3. *NYT*, August 11, 1973. See also Shawcross, 289–290.
4. Isaacson, 502–503.
5. *WP*, August 16, 1973; Isaacson, 212–215; Hersh, *Price*, 87; E. S. Miller to Alex Rosen, October 20, 1971, FBI's "The Vault" online FOIA library, William Safire, part 6 of 6.
6. Wise, 90–91; Hersh, *Reporter*, 187; "Dr. Kissinger's Role in Wiretapping," Senate Foreign Relations Committee hearings, July 1974, https://babel.hathitrust.org/cgi/pt?id=purl. 32754076921463&seq=3; Kissinger, *YOU*, 428–429; Haig deposition in Morton Halperin's wiretapping lawsuit, October 25, 1974, Record Group 460, Plumbers Task Force, Records of the Investigation of the National Security Wiretaps, box 22.
7. Isaacson, 232–233.
8. Kornbluh, 105, 555n; *NYT*, September 13, 1973.
9. McGovern and Kissinger phone conversation, September 17, 1973, 6:03 p.m.
10. *NYT*, September 13, 1973; Wise, 82–83.
11. Isaacson, 228–229; Lukas, 64–65; Nixon, 389; Wise, 3–30.

Chapter 27

1. Quandt, 166; Rabinovich, 100; Kissinger, *Crisis*, 13–14.
2. Kissinger, *YOU*, 454; Quandt, 170; Kissinger, *Crisis*, 33–34.
3. Rabinovich, 357, 358; Garthoff, 362–363, 368–369; Dobrynin, 292.
4. Nixon, 921; Kissinger, *YOU*, 471, 474; Kissinger, *Crisis*, 38, 84–85.
5. Kissinger, *YOU*, 489.
6. Haig, 411; Kissinger, *Crisis*, 147; Indyk, 119, 121.
7. Indyk, 142; Rabinovich, 361.
8. Kissinger, *YOU*, 514–515, 522, 525; Quandt, 180, 183.
9. Kissinger, *YOU*, 552–571.
10. Richardson and Kissinger phone conversation, October 24, 1973, 12:27 p.m.
11. Quandt, 196–197; Dobrynin, 301; Garthoff, 383–384; Kissinger, *Crisis*, 331, 342.
12. Kissinger, *YOU*, 602; Rabinovich, 537, 541–543; Kissinger, *Crisis*, 370–372; Garthoff, 381, 382; Indyk, 5–6, 115–116, 184, 192–193.
13. *NYT*, October 27, 1973.
14. Kissinger, *YOU*, 607–608.

Chapter 28

1. Indyk, 212–226; Kissinger, *YOU*, 619–623.
2. *NYT*, November 17, 1973.
3. Kissinger, *YOU*, 618, 619, 642; Quandt, 213, 214.
4. *WP* and *NYT*, November 21, 1973; Weiner, 289–290.
5. *NYT*, November 25, 1973.

6. Kissinger, *YOU*, 881.
7. *NYT*, December 3, 1973.
8. *WP*, December 28, 1973.

Chapter 29

1. Kissinger, *YOU*, 800–801; Indyk, 294–299.
2. *WP*, January 12, 1974.
3. See Ehrlichman, 302–307; Hersh, *Price*, 471–475.
4. *NYT*, February 7, 1974.
5. *NYT*, February 19, 1974; Dallek, 562.

Chapter 30

1. Schlesinger and Kissinger phone conversation, February 2, 1974, 9:50 a.m.
2. Kissinger, *YOU*, 893.
3. *NYT*, March 23, 24, 25, 1974.
4. *WP*, April 7, 1974.
5. *NYT*, June 7, 1974; Kissinger, *YOU*, 1116; Nixon, 1006.
6. *NYT*, June 19, 1974.
7. *NYT*, June 22, 1974.

Chapter 31

1. Hitchens, 77–89; Kissinger, *YOR*, 199, 204–207; Treaty of Guarantee, August 16, 1960, available online.
2. Kissinger, *YOR*, 209, 210.
3. Hitchens, 85, 86.
4. Kissinger, *YOR*, 216.
5. *WP*, July 21, 1974; Kissinger, *YOR*, 220–221.
6. Kissinger, *YOR*, 217.
7. Kissinger, *YOU*, 1191; *WP*, July 21, 1974.
8. *WP*, July 23, 1974; "Dr. Kissinger's Role in Wiretapping," Senate Foreign Relations Committee Hearings, July 1974, https://babel.hathitrust.org/cgi/pt?id=purl.32754076921463&seq=3.

Chapter 32

1. Ford, 28–29.
2. *WP*, August 10, 1974.

BIBLIOGRAPHY

Bass, Gary J. *The Blood Telegram: Nixon, Kissinger, and a Forgotten Genocide.* Vintage Books, 2014.
Berman, Larry. *No Peace, No Honor: Nixon, Kissinger, and Betrayal in Vietnam.* Free Press, 2001.
Bilton, Michael, and Kevin Sim. *Four Hours in My Lai.* Viking Penguin, 1992.
Blumenfeld, Ralph, and the staff and editors of the New York Post. *Henry Kissinger: The Private and Public Story.* Signet, 1974.
Brigham, Robert K. *Reckless: Henry Kissinger and the Tragedy of Vietnam.* Public Affairs, 2018.
Burr, William, ed. *The Kissinger Transcripts: The Top Secret Talks with Beijing and Moscow.* New Press, 1998.
Burr, William, and Jeffrey P. Kimball. *Nixon's Nuclear Specter: The Secret Alert of 1969, Madman Diplomacy, and the Vietnam War.* University Press of Kansas, 2015.
Colson, Charles W. *Born Again.* Bantam Books, 1976.
Dallek, Robert. *Nixon and Kissinger: Partners in Power.* HarperCollins, 2007.
Dobbs, Michael. *King Richard: Nixon and Watergate: An American Tragedy.* Knopf, 2021.
Dobrynin, Anatoly. *In Confidence: Moscow's Ambassador to America's Six Cold War Presidents (1962–1986).* Times Books, 1995.
Ehrlichman, John. *Witness to Power: The Nixon Years.* Simon & Schuster, 1982.
Emery, Fred. *Watergate: The Corruption of American Politics and the Fall of Richard Nixon.* Times Books, 1994.
Ford, Gerald. *A Time to Heal: The Autobiography of Gerald R. Ford.* Harper & Row, 1979.
Garment, Leonard. *Crazy Rhythm: My Journey from Brooklyn, Jazz, and Wall Street to Nixon's White House, Watergate, and Beyond.* Times Books, 1997.
Garthoff, Raymond L. *Détente and Confrontation: American-Soviet Relations from Nixon to Reagan.* Brookings Institution, 1985.
Gewen, Barry. *The Inevitability of Tragedy: Henry Kissinger and His World.* W. W. Norton, 2020.
Graff, Garrett M. *Watergate: A New History.* Avid Reader Press, 2022.
Grandin, Greg. *Kissinger's Shadow: The Long Reach of America's Most Controversial Statesman.* Metropolitan Books, 2015.
Haig, Alexander M., Jr., with Charles McCarry. *Inner Circles: How America Changed the World: A Memoir.* Warner Books, 1992.
Haldeman, H. R. *The Haldeman Diaries: Inside the Nixon White House.* G. P. Putnam's Sons, 1994.
Haldeman, H. R., with Joseph DiMona. *The Ends of Power.* Times Books, 1978.
Hastings, Max. *Vietnam: An Epic Tragedy, 1945–1975.* Harper Perennial, 2018.
Hersh, Seymour M. "Kissinger and Nixon in the White House." *The Atlantic,* May 1982.
Hersh, Seymour M. *The Price of Power: Kissinger in the Nixon White House.* Summit Books, 1983.
Hersh, Seymour M. *Reporter: A Memoir.* Knopf, 2018.
Hitchens, Christopher. *The Trial of Henry Kissinger.* Verso, 2001.

Hunebelle, Danielle. *Dear Henry*. Berkley, 1972.

Indyk, Martin. *Master of the Game: Henry Kissinger and the Art of Middle East Diplomacy*. Knopf, 2021.

Isaacson, Walter. *Kissinger: A Biography*. Simon & Schuster, 1992.

Kalb, Marvin, and Bernard Kalb. *Kissinger*. Little, Brown, 1974.

Kimball, Jeffrey. *Nixon's Vietnam War*. University Press of Kansas, 1998.

Kissinger, Henry. *Crisis: The Anatomy of Two Major Foreign Policy Crises*. Simon & Schuster, 2003.

Kissinger, Henry. *White House Years*. Little, Brown, 1979.

Kissinger, Henry. *Years of Renewal*. Touchstone, 1999.

Kissinger, Henry. *Years of Upheaval*. Little, Brown, 1982.

Kornbluh, Peter. *The Pinochet File: A Declassified Dossier on Atrocity and Accountability*. New Press, 2013.

Kutler, Stanley I. *The Wars of Watergate: The Last Crisis of Richard Nixon*. Knopf, 1990.

Lukas, J. Anthony. *Nightmare: The Underside of the Nixon Years*. Penguin Books, 1988.

MacMillan, Margaret. *Nixon and Mao: The Week That Changed the World*. Random House, 2008.

Montgomery, Bruce P. "Source Material: Sequestered from the Court of History: The Kissinger Transcripts." *Presidential Studies Quarterly*, December 1, 2004.

Morris, Roger. *Uncertain Greatness: Henry Kissinger and American Foreign Policy*. Harper & Row, 1977.

Nixon, Richard. *RN: The Memoirs of Richard Nixon*. Grosset & Dunlap, 1978.

Quandt, William B. *Decade of Decisions: American Policy Toward the Arab-Israeli Conflict, 1967–1976*. University of California Press, 1977.

Rabinovich, Abraham. *The Yom Kippur War: The Epic Encounter That Transformed the Middle East*. Schocken Books, 2017.

Rudenstine, David. *The Day the Presses Stopped: A History of the Pentagon Papers Case*. University of California Press, 1996.

Safire, William. *Before the Fall: An Inside View of the Pre-Watergate White House*. Belmont Tower Books, 1975.

Sander, Robert D. *Invasion of Laos, 1971: Lam Son 719*. University of Oklahoma Press, 2014.

Schwartz, Thomas A. *Henry Kissinger and American Power: A Political Biography*. Hill and Wang, 2020.

Shawcross, William. *Sideshow: Kissinger, Nixon and the Destruction of Cambodia*. Pocket Books, 1979.

Smith, Gerard. *Doubletalk: The Story of the First Strategic Arms Limitation Talks*. Doubleday, 1980.

Van Atta, Dale. *With Honor: Melvin Laird in War, Peace, and Politics*. University of Wisconsin Press, 2008.

Walters, Barbara. *Audition: A Memoir*. Knopf, 2008.

Weiner, Tim. *One Man Against the World: The Tragedy of Richard Nixon*. Henry Holt, 2015.

Wells, Tom. *The War Within: America's Battle over Vietnam*. University of California Press, 1994.

Wells, Tom. *Wild Man: The Life and Times of Daniel Ellsberg*. Palgrave/St. Martin's, 2001.

Wise, David. *The American Police State: The Government Against the People*. Random House, 1976.

Zumwalt, Elmo R., Jr. *On Watch: A Memoir*. Quadrangle, 1976.

INDEX

Abernathy, Ralph, 193
Abrams, Creighton
  assurance to McGovern that no U.S.
    ground forces would ultimately remain in
    Vietnam, 224, 225–8
  and Cambodia: invasion, 68, 71, 73, 77
  and Cambodia: public bombing, 136
  and Cambodia: secret bombing, 22, 468
  disparaging and replacing, 197, 198, 203, 292,
    299
  and enemy attack on U.S. firebase in South
    Vietnam, 177
  and Green Beret murder scandal, 33
  and Laos: invasion, 148, 154, 156, 162, 163,
    165, 166, 167, 168, 170, 171, 172, 186–7,
    198, 288
  and Laos: statement on another possible South
    Vietnamese move into, 180, 190–1
  and North Vietnam bombing, 276, 289, 292,
    310
  and North Vietnam naval attacks, 284
  and South Vietnam bombing, 56, 57, 269,
    289, 317
  and South Vietnam *versus* North Vietnam
    bombing, 56, 276, 280, 289, 292–3, 303,
    307
  and "supreme commander" in Vietnam, 306,
    307
Abshire, David, 334–5
Afshar, Amir Aslan, 251
Agnew, Spiro
  and Christmas bombing, 388
  and hollering treason at critics, 212
  and McGovern, 338–9, 357
  and North Vietnam bombing, 75–6
  and resignation, 452, 505, 521
  and student protesters, 80, 81
Albert, Carl, 522

Allende, Salvador, 237, 259, 565
  and coup, 1, 472, 495
  and *Enterprise,* 157
  and failed coup efforts, 121, 461–2
  and Korry visit, 120–1
  U.S. undermining of, 1, 7, 103, 156, 461, 462
Alsop, Joseph, 317, 344–5, 427–8
Alsop, Stewart, 226, 344, 345, 379, 387, 449–50
Anderson, Jack
  and Nixon's distancing from Kissinger, 370
  and Plumbers and Pentagon Papers, 450–1
  and Radford leaks, 260, 262, 263, 540
  and Watergate, 446–7
  and Watson, 278, 279
Antiballistic missiles (ABM), 30, 92, 180, 195,
  313
Ash, Roy, 433, 434
Ashman, Charles, 345, 347
Australia, 65, 67

Bangladesh, 243, 256, 259, 261–2. *See also*
  Pakistan
Beecher, William
  and arms to Lon Nol, 65, 69
  and North Vietnam bombing, 66, 73–5
  and secret Cambodia bombing, 443
  wiretapping of, 73, 494, 495
Bell, Beverly, 157
Berger, Marilyn, 4, 534
Berlin, Michael, 548
Berlin talks, 7, 202, 220–3
Bernstein, Robert, 400–1, 436–7, 585–6
Berrigan, Daniel, 144, 159, 160, 161
Berrigan, Philip, 144, 159, 160, 161
Bhutto, Zulfikar Ali, 255–6, 498
Blair, C. Stanley, 81
Blocker, Joel, 44
Blood, Archer, 176–7, 183–4, 262

Blount, Red, 220
Bok, Derek, 405
Braden, Tom, 225, 329–30, 400, 497
Bradlee, Ben, 239
Brandon, Henry, 263, 448–9, 473, 497, 578, 579
Bray, Charles, 204–5
Brennan, Peter, 218
Brewster, Kingman, 79, 80
Brezhnev, Leonid, 268, 442
    and grain deal, 455
    and Jackson SALT amendment, 337, 341, 342
    and Kissinger's secret trip to Moscow, 296
    and Nixon letter, 220
    and summit, 446, 451–2, 453, 455
    and Vietnam peace negotiations, 348
    and Yom Kippur War, 502, 519, 520, 521,
        522, 523, 524–5
Brown, Judy, 239
Bruce, David, 133, 134
Buchanan, Patrick, 166
Buckley, William F., 272, 273, 352–3, 446,
        458–9
Buffum, William, 566
Bundy, McGeorge, 389, 447, 448
Bunker, Ellsworth, 190
    and January 1973 peace agreement, 395
    and Laos invasion, 154, 163, 165, 166, 167,
        168
    and October 1972 peace agreement, 352,
        363–4, 367, 368
    and secret Cambodia bombing, 20, 21
    and South Vietnam bombing, 269
Burns, Arthur, 584–5
Bush, George H. W., 194, 195, 248, 255, 256,
        332
Butterfield, Alexander, 14, 446, 464
Butz, Earl, 454–5
Buzhardt, Fred, 480
    counterattack on Dean by, 445–6, 457–8,
        459–60
    and wiretapping, 488–9, 492

Cahill, William, 41
Caldero, Ray, 328–9
Callaghan, James, 560, 561–2, 563–4, 577–8
Calley, William, Jr., 45, 179, 181, 185–6
Cambodia, 368
    and arms to Lon Nol, 65, 66–7, 69, 82–3
    enemy offensives in, 122, 134–5
    invasion of, 6, 65, 151
    invasion of: compared to Laos, 155, 156
    invasion of: conducting, 72–3, 77–9, 80
    invasion of: planning, 67–8, 69–71
    invasion of: PR and press on, 84, 86, 88,
        89–91, 92
    invasion of: protests against, 72, 76, 78, 79,
        80, 81, 82
    Kompong Speu battle in, 87–8
    public bombing of, 6, 71, 84, 87, 122–3,
        135–8, 155
    public bombing of: after January 1973 peace
        agreement, 6, 389–90, 420, 422–3
    public bombing of: funding cutoff for, 446,
        455–6, 457
    secret bombing of, 6, 16, 17–22, 25, 41, 42,
        58, 63, 70, 290
    secret bombing of: false-reporting system for
        and cover story on, 9, 446, 465–9, 470, 472,
        473, 479–84, 491
    secret bombing of: leaked May 1969 story
        on, 443, 489
    secret bombing of: uncovering of and Senate
        hearings on, 446, 465–9, 472, 479–84, 491
    Snuol retreat in, 201, 203
    South Vietnamese troops in, 84, 88, 134–5,
        136, 149
Capote, Truman, 333
Castro, Fidel, 258, 496
Caulfield, Jack, 474, 499
Cerf, Bennett, 435
Cerf, Phyllis, 435
Chancellor, John, 184, 336
Chandler, Otis, 79
Cheshire, Maxine, 89, 239, 397
Chiang Kai-shek, 187
Chile
    and coup, 472, 495–6, 497–8
    and failed coup efforts, 121, 461–2
    and Korry, 120–1, 156–7
    nationalization of American property in, 237,
        496
    and U.S. support for Pinochet
        dictatorship, 497–8, 565–6
    and U.S. undermining of Allende, 103, 156,
        461, 462
China
    admission to UN of, 240
    and grain, 454
    and India-Pakistan, 243, 251–3, 254, 255–7
    Kissinger's trips to, 7, 202, 213–15, 216,
        217–18, 225, 232–3, 240, 316–17, 403,
        408–11
    and Laos invasion, 147–8
    military aid to Pakistan of, 417–18
    and Nixon's reelection, 362–3
    and October 1972 Vietnam peace
        agreement, 350
    opening to, 1, 7, 180, 187–90, 191–3, 194–5,
        218–20
    political upheaval in, 225, 230–3
    and Soviet Union, 48, 49, 188, 192, 225, 231,
        232, 233, 317, 363, 551, 552

summit, 7, 191, 192–3, 202, 213–15, 216,
217–18, 225, 230–1, 232, 261, 265, 266,
270–4
and warmer U.S. relations, 551–2
and Warsaw talks, 40, 47–8, 49
Chou En-lai, 410
and China opening, 180, 187, 194
and Kissinger's June 1972 visit to
China, 316–17
and political upheaval in China, 231, 233
and summit, 214, 270–1
Christian, George, 365
Church, Frank, 578
CIA (Central Intelligence Agency), 31, 271, 578
and Chile, 461
and Cuba and Cubans, 30, 257
and Greece, 576, 581
and Green Beret murder scandal, 32, 33, 35
and Laos, 51, 60, 61, 202, 204
and Lon Nol, 66
and 1971 South Vietnamese presidential
election, 221
and Yom Kippur War, 512
Clark, Ramsey, 448
Clawson, Ken, 313, 322
Clements, William
and air force planes, 376
and Laos bombing, 423–4
and secret Cambodia bombing, 472, 481–3
and Yom Kippur War, 513, 514, 515
Clerides, Glafcos, 560, 563, 564, 567, 568, 569,
571, 573, 577
Clifford, Clark, 49, 211, 212
Colby, William
and communist aid to North Vietnam, 554
and Cyprus, Greece, and Turkey, 572–3,
576–7, 581
and leaks, 531–2, 581
and Yom Kippur War, 531–2
Cole, Kenneth, 433, 434
Collier, Barnard, 241
Colson, Charles, 218, 264, 311
and Hoffa's POW scheme, 319, 323–6, 327
and January 1973 peace agreement, 391
and Kissinger's "peace is at hand" press
conference, 338, 354–5
and Nixon's reelection, 323, 325–6, 327–8
on Rogers attacking McGovern, 356–7
and SALT and Soviet summit, 313, 322
and Watergate, 438, 447, 460, 584
Connally, John
and Chile, 237
and India-Pakistan, 249, 250, 253–4
and Kissinger's resignation threats, 344–5,
359, 364–6
and mining of Haiphong, 308, 310, 311, 313

and 1971 South Vietnamese presidential
election, 238–9
and Paris peace talks, 318
rumored top position in second Nixon
administration for, 359, 364–6
Cook, Dick, 343–4
Cook, Jess, 467–8
Corday, Eliot, 339
COSVN (Central Office for South Vietnam), 65,
68, 69, 70, 71, 72, 73, 77, 80
Cox, Archibald, 9, 502, 518, 519, 521
Crewdson, John, 473–4, 499–500, 527–8,
532–3
Cromer, George Rowland Stanley Baring, 522
Cronkite, Walter, 337, 345–8
Cuba, 106
alleged Soviet construction of nuclear
submarine base in, 7, 101, 107, 111,
119–20
attack on freighter by gunboat of, 243, 257–9
missile crisis, 107, 256, 524
"provisional government" of, 30
Cubans, right-wing, 96, 97
Cutler, Lloyd, 500
Cyprus
and Clerides solution, 560, 563, 564, 567,
568, 571, 573
Colby on Greek solution, 572, 573
and communists, 560, 564, 565, 567
and double enosis, 572, 573
and enosis, 560, 562, 563
Greek coup in, 7, 559–60, 561, 562
and Greeks posing as Turks, 575
National Guard in, 560, 561–2, 564, 572, 573
Schlesinger on cease-fire in, 576
Turkish invasion of, 7, 560, 566–7, 568–9,
571, 572–3

Davidon, William (Bill), 144, 157
Davidson, Daniel, 44, 421, 437–8, 441, 442
Davidson, Tom, 144, 157, 158
Davis, Nathaniel, 495
Davis, Rennie, 193
Dayan, Moshe
and disengagement after Yom Kippur
War, 536, 537, 548–50
and Israel's shootdown of civilian Libyan
airliner, 407
and Israel's weapons requests, 536, 545, 550
Dean, John
Buzhardt counterattack on, 445–6, 457–8,
459–60
and Hoffa's POW scheme, 327, 328
Kissinger's distancing from, 421, 438, 439,
445, 456
and Watergate, 421, 426, 431, 433, 445
de Gaulle, Charles, 122, 123–4

Dellinger, Dave, 193
DePuy, William, 305, 306, 307
Dinitz, Simcha, 534
    and cease-fire in Yom Kippur War, 519–21
    and disengagement after Yom Kippur
        War, 548–50
    and Egyptian naval blockade, 530–1
    and Israeli harassment of Soviet
        minesweepers, 582
    and Israel's encirclement of Egypt's Third
        Army, 502, 519–21, 523–4, 525–6, 528
    and Israel's weapons requests, 511, 513, 515,
        552, 553
    and Jordan, 511
    and Meir visit, 528–9
Dobbs, Michael, 12
Dobrynin, Anatoly, 26, 77, 236
    and Berlin, 220–1
    and China, 49, 214–15, 273
    and Cyprus, 560, 561, 563
    and Gromyko visit, 36–7
    and Hoffa's POW scheme, 322–3
    Kissinger on "little yellow friends" of, 11
    and Kissinger's appointment as secretary of
        state, 465
    and Kissinger's June 1972 visit to
        China, 316–17
    Kissinger's relationship with, 4–5
    and Kissinger's secret trip to Moscow, 276,
        293, 296
    and Meir visit, 529–30
    and North Vietnam bombing, 350, 360,
        377–8
    Rogers meeting of, 268
    and SALT, 43, 195, 320, 335–6, 342
    and Soviet Jews, 198
    and Soviet pressure on North Vietnamese to
        reduce forces in South Vietnam, 349–50
    and Soviet summits, 276, 293, 303, 451–2
    and statement of Soviet intentions to reduce
        military aid to North Vietnam, 348–9
    and Vietnam peace negotiations, 338, 350,
        351–2, 353–4, 360, 374, 375
    and Vietnam threats, 36, 40, 42
    and Yom Kippur War, 502, 503, 505, 506,
        507, 508–9, 521, 524–5
Dole, Robert, 133
Donovan, Robert, 28
Douglas, Kirk, 333
Duong Van Minh, 216, 221

Eagleburger, Lawrence, 11, 13
Eagleton, Thomas, 320, 334
Eban, Abba, 117, 236
Ecevit, Bulent, 566, 569, 575
Edwards, Agustin, 103
Egypt, 7, 51, 290
    and disengagement after Yom Kippur
        War, 535, 536, 537, 538, 543, 545, 548–50
    and July 1970 cease-fire, 84, 93–4, 95, 96
    and Kissinger's talks with Hafiz Ismail, 420
    military clashes with Israel of, 225, 228–9
    naval blockade at entrance to Red Sea
        of, 530–1
    and 1970 Palestinian insurgency and crisis in
        Jordan, 104, 106, 117
    and 1971 State Department and UN initiatives
        on Middle East, 152, 153, 225, 234, 235–6
    and 1973 State Department initiatives on
        Middle East, 411–13
    Soviet shipment of nuclear weapons to, 531–2
    Third Army of, 7, 502, 519–21, 523–4, 525–6,
        527, 528
    and Yom Kippur War and aftermath, 7, 501–2,
        503–11, 514, 517, 519–21, 522–6, 527, 528,
        531–2
Ehrlichman, John, 4, 12, 123, 265, 408
    and Cambodia invasion, 77, 78
    as "errand boy," 10, 265
    and JCS spying operation and Anderson
        leaks, 263, 535, 539, 540, 541
    and North Korean shootdown of U.S. spy
        plane, 26
    and North Vietnam bombing, 557–8
    and Perot, 52
    recording of conversations of, 2
    resignation of, 431, 433
    and Watergate, 425, 428–9, 430, 431, 433,
        446, 456, 488
    and Watergate: and Plumbers, 438, 439, 450,
        451
    and wiretapping, 500, 578
    and Ziegler after resignation, 486, 488
Eisenhower, Dwight D., 448
Eisenhower, Julie Nixon, 64
Ellsberg, Daniel
    break-in at psychiatrist's office, 421, 438, 439
    and Kissinger, 429, 451
    and Pentagon Papers, 202, 208, 210, 438, 440,
        450
    and Plumbers, 421, 438, 450
    trial of, 429, 434
El-Zayyat, Mohamed, 503–4, 506, 510, 526
Ervin, Sam, 463
Evans, Robert, 239–40, 453
Evans, Rowland, 263, 264, 339
    and Connally, 364, 365
    and Nixon's resignation, 583–4
    and October 1972 peace agreement, 361–2
    report Kissinger would resign by, 341
    and Watergate, 8, 419, 490

Fahmy, Ismail, 527, 538, 549
Faisal, King, 530

Finch, Robert, 185
Fischer, Bobby, 320–1
Fisher, Max, 48
Fitzsimmons, Frank, 218, 322, 324, 325, 326, 327
Flanigan, Peter, 464
Ford, Gerald, 147–8, 343, 521, 522, 581, 582
Fort, David, 15
France, 51, 52–3
Frankel, Max, 264
    article Kissinger fed him, 289, 290
    and Beecher leak on North Vietnam bombing, 73–5
    and Cambodia invasion, 88, 89–90
    and Laos invasion, 148
Freeman, John, 132
Frei, Eduardo, 462
Friedheim, Jerry, 147, 388, 423, 424
Frost, David, 320–1
Fulbright, J. William, 133, 583

Gaddafi, Muammar, 51, 406, 565, 577
Galbraith, John Kenneth, 404–5
Gandhi, Indira
    and cutoff of U.S. aid to India, 249
    and India after Pakistan war, 261
    and Indian refugee crisis, 243
    and India-Pakistan war, 6, 247, 252, 257
    and U.S. relations with India, 498–9
Garment, Leonard
    and Israel, 545, 552–3
    and McDonnell, 85
    and Watergate, 9, 421, 425–7, 428–9, 459–60, 484
    and wiretapping, 469, 476–8
Gelb, Leslie, 10, 207–8, 533, 534
Getler, Michael, 576
Gibbons, Harold, 322, 323–5, 326, 340
Ginsberg, Allen, 180, 193–4
Godley, G. McMurtrie, 139, 145
Goldwater, Barry, 271–2
Graff, Garrett, 8
Graff, Henry, 155
Graham, Katharine, 188, 419, 534
Great Britain, 7, 111, 112, 561–2, 563–4, 566, 577–8
Greece, 108
    Callaghan's opposition to military dictatorship of, 561
    and Clerides, 560, 563, 568, 569, 571, 573
    and Colby's advice and analysis, 572–3, 576–7
    coup in Cyprus of, 7, 559–60, 561, 562
    and Cyprus National Guard, 560, 561–2, 564, 573
    and enosis in Cyprus, 560, 562
    and Greek ships flying Turkish flags, 575

    Kissinger's opposition to "raking," 564, 565
    Kissinger's opposition to withdrawal from Cyprus of, 560, 563
    leak on noninterference in internal affairs of, 581
    overthrow of military dictatorship of, 560, 576
    recognition of new civilian government of, 560, 580
    and Schlesinger, 560, 575–6
    Sisco trip to, 560, 566, 568, 569–70, 571
    temporary suspension of military aid to, 560, 573–4
    and Turkish invasion of Cyprus, 7, 572–3
    and war with Turkey, 560, 568–9, 571
Green, Marshall, 270
Green Beret murder scandal, 6, 32, 33, 35
Greene, Joseph, 420, 422
Gromyko, Andrei, 36–7, 349, 414, 551
Grose, Peter, 31
Gur, Mordechai, 515
Gwertzman, Bernard, 4, 443

Habib, Philip, 20
Haeberle, Ronald, 45
Haig, Alexander, 46, 123, 156, 203, 206, 240, 241, 339, 550
    as "army man," 307
    and Cambodia bombing: public, 123, 138, 423
    and Cambodia bombing: secret, 446, 465, 466, 467, 468, 469, 479, 480, 481, 483–4, 491
    and Chile, 156, 237
    and China, 274
    and Cyprus, Greece, and Turkey, 560, 575–6
    and de Gaulle memorial, 123–4
    and enemy attack on U.S. firebase in South Vietnam, 177
    and Joseph Alsop, 317
    and Kissinger's meeting with purported kidnapping plotters, 158, 160
    and Kissinger's Middle East "shuttle diplomacy," 536–8
    and Kissinger's phone recording system, 2, 3
    and Laos: bombing, 418–19
    and Laos: invasion, 139, 161, 163–4, 167, 169–70
    and Laos: Thai troops in, 61
    and *New York Post* story on Kissinger, 548
    and 1970 Palestinian insurgency and crisis in Jordan, 106–7, 113, 116–17, 118
    and Nixon approaching a nervous breakdown, 532, 533
    and Nixon on Israel and black nuclear bag, 546–7

Haig, Alexander (*Continued*)
  and Nixon's announcement of Kissinger's appointment as secretary of state, 490–1
  and Nixon's resignation, 581, 583
  and Nixon's taping, 14
  and North Vietnam bombing, 73, 293, 557–8
  and oil embargo, 527, 530
  and potential unraveling in Vietnam, 305
  and South Vietnam bombing, 269
  and Teller, 453–4
  and Thieu, 390, 391–2, 393, 394, 396
  and Watergate, 9, 421, 429, 433, 438, 440, 458, 478, 484, 490–1, 517–18, 519
  and wiretapping: allegedly of Kissinger, 493, 532–3
  and wiretapping: and Beecher leak on North Vietnam bombing, 73
  and wiretapping: of Davidson, 44
  and wiretapping: liaison to FBI and requests by, 8, 421, 444, 492, 578
  and wiretapping: 1974 Senate testimony on, 8, 561, 578–9
  and wiretapping: of Safire, 13, 473, 475, 476, 578
  and Yom Kippur War, 502, 505, 507–8, 513, 514–15, 517–18, 522–3, 524–5
Haldeman, H. R., 45, 123, 124, 142, 185, 263, 464
  and Agnew, 81
  and Cambodia invasion, 77, 78
  and China, 213, 215, 273
  and Connally, 364, 365, 366
  and January 1973 Vietnam peace agreement, 398
  and Kent State, 76
  and Kissinger interviews, 402, 410
  and Kissinger-Nixon relationship, 12, 370–1
  and Kissinger-Rogers disputes, 99, 236, 264, 268, 270, 370–1
  and Kissinger's meeting with purported kidnapping plotters, 155, 159–61
  and Kissinger's phone recording system, 3
  and Laos, 61
  and leaks, 28–9
  and McDonnell, 85
  and McGovern, 357
  and Middle East, 99, 236
  and mining of Haiphong, 311
  and Nixon's "end of the war" plan, 126
  and Nixon's January 1972 Vietnam address, 266–7
  and Nixon's tapes, 14
  resignation of, 419, 431, 433
  and SALT and Soviet summit, 313, 322
  and secret Cambodia bombing, 17–18
  Today show remarks of, 261, 267, 268, 270
  and Vietnam peace negotiations, 358

  and Watergate, 425, 427, 428–9, 430, 431, 433, 446, 450, 456, 488
  and wiretapping, 472, 475, 476, 477, 489, 492, 493, 578, 579
  and Ziegler after resignation, 486, 488
Halperin, Morton
  and Beecher story on secret Cambodia bombing, 443
  wiretapping of, 434, 437, 440, 441, 489–90
  wiretapping of: lawsuit over, 446, 458, 459, 472, 488–90
Harlow, Bryce, 35, 472, 486–8, 492–3, 494–5, 496
Harriman, Averell, 52, 211
Harris, Lou, 354, 357
Hartman, Arthur, 573–5
Heard, Alexander, 82, 91
Hebért, Edward, 180, 535, 540
Helms, Richard
  and arms to Pakistan, 254–5, 498
  and Cambodia: arms and support for Lon Nol, 65, 66, 67, 69
  and Cambodia: invasion, 70
  and Cambodia: secret bombing, 19
  and Chile, 103, 461, 462
  firing, 82
  and Ginsberg, 193, 194
  and Laos: bombing, 62
  and Laos: closed Senate sessions on, 202–3, 204
  and Laos: funding for, 216
  and Laos: invasion, 145–6
  and Laos: secret U.S. operations in, 202–3, 204–5
  and leaks, 30–1, 65, 69
  and mining of Haiphong, 308
  and Peru coup plotters, 16–17
  shot in arm from Nixon of, 16
Henkin, Daniel, 73, 74, 75
Hensley, Stewart, 225
Hersh, Seymour, 11
  and Kissinger's lying, 10
  and My Lai massacre, 45
  and secret Cambodia bombing, 4, 465–7, 468–9, 482
  and wiretapping, 4, 440–3
  and Young, 450
Higby, Larry, 493
Hill, Robert, 513
Hoang Duc Nha, 393
Hoang Xuan Lam, 187
Ho Chi Minh, 34, 37
Hoffa, Jimmy, 6, 319–20, 322–5, 326–7, 328, 340
Hoffmann, Stanley, 49–50
Hoover, J. Edgar

and Kissinger's meeting with purported
  kidnapping plotters, 160, 161
and wiretapping, 442, 446, 556, 579
and wiretapping: and blackmail, 2
and wiretapping: of Brandon, 448, 494, 497,
  579
and wiretapping: check on Kissinger's phones
  for, 146–7
and wiretapping: of Halperin, 458, 459, 489,
  490
and wiretapping: sensitivity and secrecy of, 8
House Judiciary Committee, 546, 584
Huang Chen, 216, 454
Hubbard, Henry, 211
Hughes, Harold, 481, 482
Humphrey, Hubert, 5, 190, 318
Hunebelle, Danielle, 10
  Dear Henry by, 299, 315–16, 326
  and French television show on Kissinger, 51,
    57–9, 64, 100
  Walters's advice to Kissinger on, 315–16
Hussein, King, 24
  and Palestinian insurgency and crisis in
    Jordan, 101, 104–5, 108, 112, 113, 114,
    117, 118
  and Yom Kippur War, 511

Idan, Avner, 340–1
India
  and Bangladesh, 259, 261–2
  cutoff of U.S. aid to and PR campaign
    against, 243, 246–7, 248, 249–51, 253, 254
  refugee crisis in, 6, 243
  and UN, 244, 247, 248
  U.S. relations with, 251–3, 261–2, 265–6,
    498–9
  war with Pakistan of, 6, 242–3, 245–57, 523
Ingersoll, Robert, 566–8, 570, 573–5
Ioannidis, Dimitrios, 573, 575
Iran arms to Pakistan, 243, 248, 249, 250, 251,
  254–5, 417–18, 498
Iraq, 101, 104, 105, 106, 118
Irwin, John, 204–5
Isaacson, Walter, 14
Ismail, Hafiz, 411, 420, 422
Israel, 7, 9
  and disengagement after Yom Kippur
    War, 535, 536, 537, 543–4, 545–6, 547,
    548–50, 552–3
  and French jet-fighter sales to Libya, 51, 52–3
  and July 1970 cease-fire, 84, 93–9
  and Lebanon, 340–1, 557
  McGovern emissary to, 338–9
  military clashes with Egypt of, 225, 228–9
  and 1967 Six Day War, 48, 110, 141, 501, 506,
    510, 516
  and 1970 Palestinian insurgency and crisis in
    Jordan, 7, 101, 105–19
  and 1971 State Department and UN initiatives
    on Middle East, 141, 151–3, 225, 234–6
  and 1973 State Department initiatives on
    Middle East, 411–13
  Nixon plan to "lay into," 546–7
  and oil embargo, 527, 533
  and peace negotiations, 7, 37–9, 533–4
  and Rogers Plan, 48
  shootdown of civilian Libyan airliner by, 7,
    403, 405–6, 407–8, 413
  and Soviet minesweepers, 582
  weapons requests of and U.S. military aid
    to, 7, 37–9, 94–5, 502, 509, 511, 512,
    513–16, 517, 536, 545, 550, 552–4
  and Yom Kippur War and aftermath, 7, 501–2,
    503–17, 519–21, 522–6, 527, 528–31
ITT (International Telephone and
  Telegraph), 461, 462, 498, 538

Jackson, Henry, 133, 511, 542–3
  and SALT, 320, 335–6, 337, 341–2, 343–4
Jamieson, John Kenneth, 538
Japan
  and Lon Nol, 66, 67
  and Okinawa, 28
  and textile negotiations, 7, 51, 54, 63–4, 91,
    120
Jarring, Gunnar, 97, 151, 152
Javits, Jacob, 48, 578
Johnson, Lyndon, 59, 68, 127, 182, 325
  and classified documents for his memoirs and
    library, 42–3, 198–9
  Nixon on lying by, 172
  and North Vietnam bombing and shelling, 62,
    284, 289, 295
  and Pentagon Papers, 202, 207, 208, 210–12
  and wiretapping, 447, 448
Johnson, U. Alexis, 54, 63, 119–21, 255
Joint Chiefs of Staff (JCS), 314
  spying operation against Kissinger of, 6, 260,
    262, 535–6, 539–42
Jordan, 94
  and arms to Pakistan, 243, 254–5
  1970 Palestinian insurgency and crisis in, 7,
    101, 104–19
  and Yom Kippur War, 511
Jorden, William, 210–11

Kalb, Bernard, 421, 435
Kalb, Marvin, 523
  as alleged communist, 44
  book on Kissinger by, 421, 435–7
  and January 1973 Vietnam peace
    agreement, 399
  as Kissinger fan, 4

Kalb, Marvin (*Continued*)
  and Kissinger interview, 279, 401–2
  and Nixon's January 1972 Vietnam
    address, 266–7
  wiretapping of, 494
Kane, Joseph, 473
Karamanlis, Konstantinos, 577
Katz, Milton, 80
Keating, Kenneth, 265–6, 498
Kendall, Donald, 51, 63–4, 103, 538
Kennedy, Edward, 26
  alleged lack of integrity of, 10
  and Kissinger's confirmation as secretary of
    state, 496
  and Pakistan, 183
  and POWs, 234
  and Son Tay, 133
  and Watergate, 518
Kennedy, John F., 92, 127, 182, 204–5
Kennedy, Richard, 215
Kennedy, Robert, 199, 416, 447–8, 556
Kent State shootings, 76
Khrushchev, Nikita, 199
Kissinger, Henry
  and Abrams: on another possible South
    Vietnamese move into Laos, 190–1
  and Abrams: criticizing and possibly
    replacing, 203, 292
  and Abrams: his assurance to McGovern that
    no U.S. ground forces would ultimately
    remain in Vietnam, 224, 225–8
  and Berlin, 202, 220–3
  and Cambodia: arms to Lon Nol, 66–7, 69
  and Cambodia: enemy offensives in, 122,
    134–5
  and Cambodia: invasion, 65, 67–8, 69–73,
    76–82, 86, 88, 89–90, 91–2, 155
  and Cambodia: public bombing, 87, 122–3,
    135–8, 389–90, 422–3, 456, 457
  and Cambodia: secret bombing, 16, 17–22,
    42, 290, 478
  and Cambodia: secret bombing: false-
    reporting system and cover story, 9, 446,
    465–9, 470, 472, 473, 479–84, 491
  and Cambodia: secret bombing: leaked story
    on, 443, 489
  and Cambodia: secret bombing: uncovering of
    and Senate hearings on, 446, 465–9, 472,
    479–84, 491
  and Cambodia: Snuol retreat in, 203
  and Chile, 1, 103, 120–1, 156–7, 237, 461–2,
    472, 495–6, 497–8, 565–6
  and China: Kissinger's trips to, 7, 202,
    213–15, 216, 217–18, 225, 232–3, 240,
    316–17, 403, 408–11
  and China: and Nixon's reelection, 362–3
  and China: opening to, 1, 7, 180, 187–90,
    191–3, 194–5, 218–20
  and China: and Pakistan, 243, 251–3, 255–7
  and China: perceived desire for warmer
    relations, 551–2
  and China: political upheaval in, 225, 230–3
  and China: summit, 191–3, 202, 213–15, 216,
    217–18, 225, 230–1, 232, 261, 265, 266,
    270–4
  and China: Warsaw talks on, 47–8, 49
  and Connally rivalry, 318, 344–5, 359, 364–6
  custody and release of phone transcripts
    of, 13–15
  and Cyprus, Greece, and Turkey, 7, 559–60,
    561–5, 566–78, 580, 581
  and Gerard Smith, 43, 195–6, 225, 237–8,
    335
  and Harvard, 5, 10, 47, 181, 182, 404–5
  and hollering treason about critics, 212–13
  and India after Pakistan war, 259, 261–2,
    265–6, 498–9
  and Indian refugee crisis, 243–4
  and India-Pakistan: cutting off aid to India and
    PR campaign against India, 243, 246, 247,
    248, 249–51, 254
  and India-Pakistan: and Raza and Bhutto's
    discussions with Chinese, 255–7
  and India-Pakistan: and Rogers's charge of
    tilting toward China, 252–3
  and India-Pakistan: and UN, 244–5, 246, 247,
    248
  and India-Pakistan war, 242–3, 245–57, 523
  and India-Pakistan war: criticism of Kissinger's
    handling of crisis, 260–1, 262, 263–4, 370
  and intellectuals, 91–2, 155
  and Israel's shootdown of civilian Libyan
    airliner, 403, 405–6, 407–8
  and JCS spying operation and Radford
    leaks, 6, 260, 262–3, 535–6, 539–42
  and journalists, 4, 266–7, 401
  Kalbs' book on, 421, 435–7
  kidnapping plot against (alleged) and meeting
    with plotters, 140, 143–5, 155, 157–61
  and Klein's flacking of his 1973 trip to North
    Vietnam and China, 403, 408–11
  and Laird strains, 6, 46, 140, 141–2, 205–6,
    292–3
  and Laos: bombing, 53–4, 55, 58, 61–2, 155,
    418–19, 420–1, 423–5
  and Laos: closed Senate sessions on, 202–3,
    204
  and Laos: enemy advances and offensives
    in, 60, 259
  and Laos: invasion, 138–9, 140–1, 145–6,
    147–51, 154–6, 161–4, 165–75, 179, 186–7
  and Laos: secret U.S. operations in, 59–60,
    204–5

and Laos: Thai troops in, 61–2, 64
and Laos: U.S. reconnaissance teams in, 147
and leaks, 9, 12, 23, 28–9, 30–1, 46, 73–5,
    225–6, 260, 262–4, 369–70, 450, 546, 581
lying by, 2, 10, 264
and McDonnell, 84, 85–6
and McGovern, 317–18, 320, 329–30, 334,
    338–9, 354, 356–7, 359, 360–1, 496, 497
memoirs of, 2, 10, 44, 320, 332–3, 339,
    400–1, 421, 435, 436, 437, 460–1, 581,
    585–6
and Middle East, 7, 555
and Middle East: Egyptian-Israeli military
    clashes, 228–9
and Middle East: Hafiz Ismail talks, 420, 422
and Middle East: Israeli attacks in
    Lebanon, 340–1, 557
and Middle East: Israeli-Egyptian disen-
    gagement, 535, 536, 537, 538, 545,
    548–50
and Middle East: Israeli-Syrian disengage-
    ment, 536, 543–4, 545–6, 547, 548–50,
    552–3
and Middle East: Israel's weapons requests
    and U.S. military aid, 7, 37–9, 94–5, 502,
    509, 511, 512, 513–16, 517, 536, 545, 550,
    552–4
and Middle East: July 1970 cease-fire, 84,
    93–9
and Middle East: meetings with Saudi and
    Egyptian foreign ministers, 543–4
and Middle East: Meir visits, 37–9, 93, 527,
    528–30
and Middle East: 1970 Palestinian insurgency
    and crisis in Jordan, 7, 101, 104–19
and Middle East: 1971 State Department and
    UN initiatives, 141, 151–3, 225, 234–7
and Middle East: 1973 State Department
    initiatives, 404, 411–13
and Middle East: putting pressure on Israel in
    peace talks, 533–4
and Middle East: Rogers Plan, 48
and Middle East: "shuttle diplomacy," 1, 535,
    536–8, 545–6
and Middle East: Soviet minesweepers in, 582
and mistaken bombing of South Vietnamese
    troops, 149
and My Lai Massacre, 40, 45, 180–1, 185–6,
    197
and 1972 election, 5, 325–6, 327–8
and Nixon relationship, 10, 11–13. *See also*
    Kissinger, Henry, and Nixon strains
and Nixon's resignation, 581, 582–5
and Nixon's speeches and addresses, 43–4,
    181–3, 184–5, 266
and Nixon's tapes, 14, 464

and Nixon strains, 6, 12, 260–1, 262–5,
    370–1, 379, 535, 537–8
on Nobel Prize winners, 86–7
and North Korean shootdown of U.S. spy
    plane, 6, 23–7
and North Vietnam blockade and min-
    ing, 276, 296–7, 299, 305, 306, 307,
    308–11, 312, 313
and North Vietnam bombing: 1970, 55–6,
    57, 60–1, 63, 64, 71–2, 73–6, 122, 123, 125,
    126–7, 128–9, 130–1, 132
and North Vietnam bombing: 1971, 151,
    155, 162–3, 164, 170–6, 225, 228, 230, 231,
    233–4, 259
and North Vietnam bombing: 1972, 275–6,
    277–8, 280–93, 294–6, 298, 299–301,
    303–5, 306, 310, 314, 350
and North Vietnam bombing: 1972: Christmas
    bombing, 360, 374, 375–85, 386, 387–9,
    399–400
and North Vietnam bombing: callousness over
    casualties, 11
and North Vietnam bombing: hydroelectric
    plant and dikes, 314, 320, 330–2, 333–4
and North Vietnam bombing: outside chain of
    command, 557–8
and North Vietnamese offensive in 1972 275,
    277, 280–96, 298–9, 303–5, 311–12
and North Vietnam naval attacks, 276, 280–1,
    283–5
and oil embargo, 527, 530, 533, 534, 537,
    543–4, 547
and Pakistan: arms to, 6, 243, 248, 249, 250,
    251, 254–5, 417–18, 498
and Pakistan: diplomatic dissent over, 176–7,
    179–80, 183–4
and Pakistan: genocide in, 1, 6, 176–7, 183
and Pakistan: U.S. "tilt" toward, 245, 246
"peace is at hand" statement of, 6, 338, 354–5,
    359, 361, 379
and Pentagon Papers, 9–10, 202, 206–13,
    438, 450–1
phone recording system of, 1–3, 5
and POWs, 130, 219, 319–20, 322–5, 340,
    384–5, 413–15. *See also* Kissinger, Henry,
    and Son Tay
and protesters, 48, 76, 80, 81
resignation threats of, 10, 261, 263, 264–5,
    344–5, 359, 364–6, 535, 537, 538
and Resor, 35, 197
and Rogers strains, 12, 84, 92–3, 97–9, 142–3,
    234–5, 236, 240, 246–7, 261, 262, 264–5,
    268, 270, 370–1
and SALT, 43, 180, 195–6, 225, 237–8, 299,
    313, 320, 335–6, 337, 341–2, 452, 551
at Scandia restaurant, 123

Kissinger, Henry (*Continued*)
  and Schlesinger rivalry and strains, 513–16, 545, 546, 551, 558
  secrecy of, 11, 535
  secretary of state appointment and confirmation hearings of, 10, 446, 462–5, 472, 486, 487, 490–3, 494, 496
  and Son Tay, 123, 125–31, 132–4
  and South Vietnam bombing: 1969, 32, 34
  and South Vietnam bombing: 1970, 56, 57
  and South Vietnam bombing: 1972, 261, 268–9, 277, 282–3, 286, 290, 311, 317
  and South Vietnamese 1971 presidential election, 221, 238–9
  and Soviet Union: détente, 1, 273
  and Soviet Union: grain deals, 454–5
  and Soviet Union: Jews in, 198
  and Soviet Union: Kissinger's trips to, 276, 293, 294, 296, 517–18, 551
  and Soviet Union: summits, 188, 192, 219, 220, 231, 237–8, 268, 276, 290, 293, 294, 299, 303, 304, 311–12, 322, 451–3, 455
  and Soviet Union: U.S. relations with, 7, 76–7, 231, 232
  and Sudan killings, 404, 416–17
  and "supreme commander" in Vietnam, 299, 305–8
  and Taiwan, 240, 261, 271–2
  television interviews of, 99–100, 102, 279–80, 336
  and Thieu's possible replacement, 33, 35–6, 202, 216, 217, 218, 221, 300–1, 304
  and Vietnam end date, 185
  and Vietnam peace agreement: January 1973, 386, 389, 398, 403, 406
  and Vietnam peace agreement: January 1973: convincing Thieu to accept it, 386–7, 390–7
  and Vietnam peace agreement: October 1972, 337–8, 348–55, 359, 360, 361–2, 374, 375, 380–1, 383
  and Vietnam peace agreement: October 1972: convincing Thieu to accept it, 338, 348–9, 350, 351, 352–3, 360, 362–4, 366–9, 371–4, 377
  and Vietnam peace talks: 1969, 20, 21–2, 32–3
  and Vietnam peace talks: 1970, 61, 62, 134
  and Vietnam peace talks: 1971, 199–200, 202, 213, 214, 216–18, 259
  and Vietnam peace talks: 1972, 298, 301, 303, 350, 351–2, 353–4, 358, 360, 366–8, 369, 370–1, 373, 374, 380–1, 384
  and Vietnam threats, 32, 36, 40, 41, 42
  and Vietnam troop withdrawals, 28, 45–6, 179, 181
  and Watergate, 440, 505, 537, 543, 546
  and Watergate: advice and discussions on, 8–9, 421, 425–7, 428–34, 457–8, 459–60, 472, 478, 484–8, 518–19, 521–2
  and Watergate: and "bastard traitors," 451, 452
  and Watergate: and Butterfield taping revelation, 446, 464
  and Watergate: and Buzhardt counterattack on Dean, 445–6, 457–8, 459–60
  and Watergate: and FBI leaks, 445, 449–50
  and Watergate: fear of being made a figure in, 556–7
  and Watergate: and foreign policy, 429, 456, 458–9
  and Watergate: and Haldeman and Ehrlichman, 425, 428–9, 431
  and Watergate: and impeachment, 460, 490
  and Watergate: and Nixon's speeches and addresses, 9, 433, 472, 478, 484–8, 517–18
  and Watergate: and Nixon's tapes, 464, 490, 502, 518–19
  and Watergate: and Plumbers and Young, 8, 421, 438, 439–40, 445, 450–1, 474, 532, 536, 541
  and Watergate: and potential resignation, 457, 460, 461
  and Watergate: professed ignorance of and distancing from, 8, 419, 421, 427, 429–30, 438, 439–40, 445, 446–7, 450–1, 456
  and Watergate: and Richardson, 9, 432, 502–3, 521
  and wiretapping, 2, 466
  and wiretapping: allegedly of himself, 8, 146–7, 472, 493–4, 499–500, 527–8, 532–3
  and wiretapping: and Beecher leak on North Vietnam bombing, 66, 73
  and wiretapping: central role in, 1, 8, 421, 441, 489, 492
  and wiretapping: Halperin lawsuit over, 8, 446, 458, 459, 472, 488–90
  and wiretapping: and his confirmation hearings, 10, 472, 492–3, 494, 496–7
  and wiretapping: of journalists, 28, 73, 444, 448–9, 494–5
  and wiretapping: by Kennedy and Johnson administrations, 447–8
  and wiretapping: of Kraft, 440, 472, 500
  and wiretapping: and Kraft disputes, discussions, and columns over, 440, 443
  and wiretapping: minimizing of his involvement in and evasions and lies about, 8, 421, 440, 441–2, 443–4, 445, 446, 448–9, 458, 459, 472, 473–6, 489–90, 492–3, 494–5, 546, 555
  and wiretapping: 1974 Senate testimony on, 8, 560–1, 578–80

and wiretapping: of NSC staff, 28, 44, 421, 434, 437–8, 440, 441, 458, 459, 472, 489–90, 555

and wiretapping: of other officials, 13, 73, 473–8

and wiretapping: and press conference, 546, 555–7

and wiretapping: public revelation of, 7–8, 421, 434

and wiretapping: of Safire and his crusade against the wiretaps, 13, 471–2, 473–8, 479, 497, 578

and wiretapping: and Weicker, 469

and Yom Kippur War and aftermath, 1, 501–2, 503–18, 519–21, 522–6, 527, 528–32. *See also* Kissinger, Henry, and Middle East: Israeli-Egyptian disengagement; Kissinger, Henry, and Middle East: Israeli-Syrian disengagement

See also many other specific topics

Kissinger: The Adventures of Super-Kraut (Ashman), 345–8

Kissinger, Walter, 337, 345–8

Klein, Herb, 263, 370, 403, 408–11

Kleindienst, Richard

  and Hoffa's POW scheme, 327

  and Kissinger's meeting with purported kidnapping plotters, 159, 160

  and Watergate, 431, 432, 433

Klopfer, Donald, 435–6

Korry, Edward, 103, 120–1, 156–7, 461, 462

Kosygin, Alexei, 30

Kraemer, Fritz, 240–1

Kraft, Joseph, 93, 264

  column on Haig's role in wiretapping and request for Safire wiretap, 578

  columns critical of Kissinger over wiretapping, 440, 443

  wiretapping of, 440, 472, 500

Kraslow, David, 4

Krogh, Egil, 438, 439, 451, 499

Kubisch, Jack, 495, 565–6

Laird, Melvin, 41, 134, 190

  and Abrams's assurance to McGovern that no U.S. ground forces would ultimately remain in Vietnam, 225–6, 227–8

  adulatory magazine article about, 205–6

  and biological weapons, 46

  and Cambodia bombing: funding cutoff, 455–6, 457

  and Cambodia bombing: secret, 17, 21, 22, 63

  and Cambodia bombing: secret: false-reporting system, cover story, and Senate hearings on, 467, 468, 469, 472, 479–81, 482, 483, 491

  and Cambodia invasion, 71, 151

and China, 214

and Cuban gunboat attack on freighter, 258

and Defense budget, 143

and government holdovers, 197

and Green Beret murder scandal, 33, 35

and JCS spying operation, 262

and Kissinger's phone recording system and transcripts, 3, 13

and Kissinger strains, 6, 46, 205–6, 292–3

and Laos: bombing, 53–4, 55, 58, 156

and Laos: closed Senate sessions on, 203, 204

and Laos: funding for, 215, 216

and Laos: invasion, 138–9, 146, 149, 150, 167, 168, 173

and Laos: and Kennedy administration, 204–5

and Laos: secret U.S. operations in, 204–5

and Laos: U.S. reconnaissance teams in, 147

and leaks, 9, 27–8, 31, 46–7, 69, 73–4, 225–6, 369–70

lies of, 89–90

and Lyndon Johnson, 42–3, 199

and Middle East, 153

and My Lai massacre, 40, 45, 179, 180–1

and Nixon's "end-of-the-war" plan, 127

and Nixon's resignation, 583

and Nixon's "silent majority" speech, 43–4

and North Korean shootdown of U.S. spy plane, 26, 27

and North Vietnam blockade and mining, 305, 306, 308, 309, 310, 313

and North Vietnam bombing: 1970, 56, 60–1, 73–4, 75, 127, 128, 130, 132

and North Vietnam bombing: 1971, 151, 230

and North Vietnam bombing: 1972, 276, 280–1, 284–5, 288, 289, 290–3, 304, 314, 382

and North Vietnam bombing: 1972: Christmas bombing, 380, 381, 383, 384, 387–8

and North Vietnam bombing: outside chain of command, 557–8

and North Vietnam naval attacks, 281, 284–5

and nuclear weapon test, 215–16

and Pentagon Papers, 202, 209, 210

and plans to keep thousands of civilians in military jobs in Vietnam, 369–70

and Pursley wiretapping, 73

and SALT, 43

and Son Tay, 123, 125, 126, 130, 131, 132, 133

and South *versus* North Vietnam bombing, 56, 276, 280, 290–1, 292, 295

and South Vietnam bombing, 32, 34–5, 269

and South Vietnamese 1971 presidential election, 238–9

Laird, Melvin (*Continued*)
 on South Vietnamese troops and
  commanders, 298–9, 301–2
 and "supreme commander" in Vietnam, 299,
  305, 306, 307, 308
 and threatening Thieu with aid cutoff, 373
 and Vietnam troop withdrawals, de-escalation,
  end of combat involvement, and end
  date, 45–6, 49, 140, 141–2, 185, 205,
  225–6
 and Watergate, 431–2, 456, 457–8, 486, 487,
  518
Lake, Anthony, 441, 442
Landau, David, 435–6
Laos, 368
 Abrams's statement on another South
  Vietnamese move into, 180, 190–1
 bombing in: 1970, 51, 53–4, 55, 58, 62
 bombing in: 1971, 155, 170, 231
 bombing in: 1973, 6, 418–19, 420–1, 423–5
 closed Senate sessions on, 59, 60, 201, 202–3,
  204
 enemy advances and offensives in, 60, 259
 invasion of, 6, 140–1
 invasion of: bullish reports on, 155–6, 161–2,
  170, 172, 173
 invasion of: news blackout on, 148–9
 invasion of: planning of, 123, 138–9, 145–6,
  147–8, 149–50
 invasion of: and press coverage, 141, 154, 155,
  156, 165–8, 174, 181
 invasion of: and PR offensive, 155, 162,
  165–8
 invasion of: and South Vietnamese retreats and
  withdrawals, 154–5, 161–4, 165–73, 174
 invasion of: stalling of, 141, 150–1
 invasion of: and Tchepone, 140, 141, 146,
  151, 154, 155, 156, 163, 164, 169
 invasion of: and Vietnam troop withdrawal
  speech by Nixon, 179, 181
 invasion of: Westmoreland's subsequent
  assessment of, 186–7
 and Kennedy administration, 204–5
 1973 cease-fire agreement in, 6, 418, 420
 secret U.S. operations in, 51, 59–60, 202–3,
  204–5
 Thai troops in, 51, 61–2, 64, 202, 204
 U.S. reconnaissance teams in, 147
Latimer, Tom, 451
Lawrence, Dave, 211
Lazar, Irving "Swifty," 10, 320, 332–3, 339,
  460–1
Leaks
 on arms to Lon Nol, 65, 69
 on biological weapons, 46–7
 on Greece, 581
 to Jack Anderson, 260, 262, 263, 370, 540

 on keeping thousands of civilian personnel in
  South Vietnam in military jobs, 369–70
 against Kissinger, 225, 260, 262–4, 370–1
 and McGrory, 23
 motives and internal machinations over, 9
 on Nixon's Midway announcement, 28, 29
 on North Vietnam bombing, 66, 73–5
 on Okinawa, 28
 and Plumbers, 421, 450
 as problem in Nixon administration, 9
 on SALT, 29, 489, 551
 on Schlesinger-Kissinger divisions, 546
 on secret Cambodia bombing, 443, 489
 on Soviet first-strike nuclear capability, 30–1
 on trading "hardware for software" with
  Israel, 37–9
 on Vietnam withdrawal, 224, 225–6, 227
 on Warsaw talks, 47–8, 49
 and Watergate, 445, 449–50
 and Yom Kippur War, 531–2
 See also Pentagon Papers
Lebanon, 340, 557
Le Duc Tho
 and Christmas bombing in 1972 374, 377,
  382, 384, 389
 and Hoffa's POW scheme, 320, 323, 326
 and January 1973 peace agreement, 386, 389,
  391, 392
 and Vietnam peace talks with Kissinger, 213,
  214, 216, 298, 299, 301, 303, 351, 360, 369,
  371, 374, 380
Lehman, John, 204
Leonard, William, 64, 99–100
Libya
 French jet-fighter sales to, 51, 52–3
 Israeli shootdown of civilian airliner of, 7,
  403, 405–6, 407–8, 413
Lodge, Henry Cabot, 18, 20, 21, 33, 134, 213
Lon Nol, 65, 66–7, 69, 82–3
Lord, Winston, 271, 441
Lowenstein, James, 422, 423
Lucet, Charles, 52–3

MacArthur, Douglas, II, 248, 250
MacCrate, Robert, 181
MacGregor, Clark, 185
MacLaine, Shirley, 85
Maginnes, Nancy, 102
Magruder, Jeb Stuart, 447
Makarios, Archbishop, 568
 actions after Greek coup of, 561–2, 563
 and Callaghan and Great Britain, 560, 561–2,
  563–4, 577
 and Colby's analysis and advice, 572–3
 Kissinger meeting with, 577
 Kissinger's opposition to reinstating, 560,
  564–5, 570–1

overthrow by Greek coup of, 559–60, 561
  and Scali, 567–8
  and Turkey, 571
Mandel, Marvin, 338
Mansfield, Mike, 384, 399
  and China, 191, 214, 552
  resolution on Western Europe of, 196, 197
  Vietnam troop withdrawal amendment
    of, 212
Mao Tse-tung, 187, 225, 230, 231, 232, 270–1
Marder, Murrey, 380–1, 449, 551
Mardian, Robert, 2, 450, 469
Marron, Donald, 399–400
Marshall, Paul, 321
Mathias, Charles, 196–7
Maw, Carlyle, 456, 489–90, 585
McCain, John, 126, 291
McCarthy, Eugene, 193, 431
McCarthy, Joseph, 207
McCloskey, Pete, 213
McCloskey, Robert, 556, 566, 567, 568, 569–70
McCloy, John, 244
McDonnell, Alice, 85–6
McDonnell, Brian
  fast in protest of Cambodia invasion and
    Kissinger's befriending of, 84, 85–6
  and Kissinger's meeting with purported
    kidnapping plotters, 140, 143–5, 157–8,
    159, 160, 161
McGovern, George, 183, 209, 217, 322, 522
  and Abrams's assurance that no U.S.
    ground forces would ultimately remain in
    Vietnam, 224, 225–8
  attacking, 317–18, 356–7
  and Democratic defections, 325
  and Eagleton, 320, 334
  emissary to Israel of, 338–9
  and Haldeman's *Today* show remarks, 267
  and heckler, 360–1
  and Kissinger's "peace is at hand" press
    conference, 338, 354, 359, 361
  and Kissinger's reported fundraising from
    pro-Nixon Democrats, 320, 329–30
  and 1972 election, 359
  and October 1972 Vietnam peace
    agreement, 356–7, 361
  vote against Kissinger's confirmation as
    secretary of state, 496, 497
  See also McGovern-Hatfield antiwar resolution
McGovern-Hatfield antiwar resolution, 208,
  209, 212
McGrory, Mary, 9, 23, 157–8
McNamara, Robert, 172, 199
  and Cambodia invasion, 81–2
  and Christmas bombing of North
    Vietnam, 386, 388–9
  and Hunebelle, 58–9

and Pentagon Papers, 206, 208, 209, 210, 211
Meany, George, 91
Meir, Golda
  and Israeli shootdown of civilian Libyan
    airliner, 405, 406
  and 1970 Palestinian insurgency and crisis in
    Jordan, 111, 113
  and Rogers Plan, 48
  and 1973 State Department initiatives on
    Middle East, 412, 413
  and U.S. military aid, 32, 37–9, 93
  visits to United States by, 32, 37–9, 93, 527,
    528–30
  and Yom Kippur War and aftermath, 503, 526,
    527, 528–30, 534
Meselson, Matt, 443
Meyner, Robert, 41
Middle East
  Egyptian-Israeli military clashes, 228–9
  July 1970 cease-fire, 84, 93–9
  Kissinger's "shuttle diplomacy" in, 1, 535,
    536–8, 545–6
  1970 Palestinian insurgency and crisis in
    Jordan, 7, 101, 104–19
  1971 State Department and UN initiatives
    on, 141, 151–3, 225, 234–7
  1973 State Department initiatives on, 404,
    411–13
  Rogers Plan, 48
  See also Egypt; Israel; Jordan; Syria; Yom
    Kippur War
Mitchell, John, 161, 176
  and Chile, 103
  and Kissinger's battle with Rogers, 234–5, 265
  and leaks, 30–1
  and Middle East, 234–5
  and Pentagon Papers, 206, 208–9
  and Watergate, 355–6, 425, 427, 446, 456,
    457, 464
  and wiretapping, 8, 442, 474, 475, 489, 490,
    556
Mitchell, Martha, 176, 355, 356
Moor, Dean, 44
Moore, George, 416, 417
Moore, Terry, 328–9
Moorer, Thomas, 6, 104
  and Abrams's assurance to McGovern that
    no U.S. ground forces would remain in
    Vietnam, 227
  and Cambodia, 88, 135, 389–90, 481, 483
  and JCS spying operation against Kissinger, 6,
    260, 262, 535, 539–42
  and Laos invasion, 151, 154, 156, 161, 162,
    163–4, 165, 166, 167, 170–1, 172
  and North Vietnam bombing, 11
  and North Vietnam bombing: 1971, 170–1,
    174, 228

Moorer, Thomas (*Continued*)
  and North Vietnam bombing: 1972, 276, 281,
    282–3, 285–6, 287, 300, 310, 382
  and North Vietnam bombing: 1972: Christ-
    mas bombing, 360, 375, 376, 379–80, 381,
    382, 383
  and North Vietnam bombing: outside chain of
    command, 557
  and North Vietnam minesweeping, 406–7
  and North Vietnam naval attacks, 281, 283–4
  replacement of Wheeler as JCS chairman
    by, 56–7
  and Son Tay, 126, 128
  and South Vietnam bombing, 276, 277,
    282–3
  and Vietnam peace agreement violations, 415
Moose, Richard, 422, 423
Moratorium and Mobilization antiwar
    protests, 36, 37, 40, 41, 48
Morris, Roger, 4
Mosbacher, Emil, 142–3
Moyers, Bill, 49–50
Muskie, Edmund, 133, 318, 579
My Lai massacre, 6, 40, 45, 48, 179, 180–1,
    185–6, 197

Nasser, Gamal Abdel, 24
  and July 1970 cease-fire, 84, 93–4
  and 1970 Palestinian insurgency and crisis in
    Jordan, 104, 105, 117
National Liberation Front (NLF), 282
  1972 offensive with North Vietnamese
    by, 275, 280–96, 298–9, 303–5, 311–12
  spring 1969 offensive by, 16, 18
  10-point program of, 389
National Security Archive, 14
Ngo Dinh Diem, 212, 218
Nguyen Cao Ky, 221
Nguyen Phu Duc, 371–3
Nguyen Van Thieu, 219, 361, 415
  consideration of replacing, 33, 35–6, 202,
    217, 218, 221, 300–1, 303, 304
  and January 1973 peace agreement, 386–7,
    389, 390–7
  and Laos invasion, 149, 150, 163, 165, 169,
    172, 187
  and Midway troop withdrawal
    announcement, 28
  and 1971 South Vietnamese presidential
    election, 221
  North Vietnam's demand for removal of, 202,
    216, 217
  and October 1972 peace agreement, 337–8,
    348–9, 350, 351, 352–3, 355, 358, 360,
    362–4, 366–9, 371–4, 377, 383
Nimeiry, Jaafar, 537–8
Nixon, Patricia, 398–9

Nixon, Richard, 43, 49, 193
  and Abrams: on another possible South
    Vietnamese move into Laos, 190–1
  and Abrams: criticizing and possibly
    replacing, 203, 299
  and Abrams: his assurance to McGovern that
    no ground forces would ultimately remain
    in Vietnam, 224, 226–7
  and Berlin, 202, 221–3
  and biological and chemical weapons, 46
  and black nuclear bag, 547
  and Cambodia: arms to Lon Nol, 65, 66, 67,
    82–3
  and Cambodia: enemy offensives in, 122,
    134–5
  and Cambodia: invasion, 65, 69–71, 72–3,
    77–8, 86, 88, 90, 91–2
  and Cambodia: Kompong Speu battle
    in, 87–8
  and Cambodia: public bombing, 87, 122–3,
    135–8, 155
  and Cambodia: secret bombing, 16, 17–22,
    41, 42, 63, 290
  and Cambodia: secret bombing: false-
    reporting system and cover story used, 465,
    482, 483
  and Cambodia: Snuol retreat in, 203
  and Cambodia: South Vietnamese troops
    in, 87–8, 134–5
  and Chile, 103, 121, 237, 461–2, 472, 495–6
  and China: and his reelection, 362–3
  and China: Kissinger's trips to, 202, 213–15,
    216, 217–18, 232–3
  and China: opening to, 7, 180, 187–90,
    191–3, 194–5, 218–20
  and China: perceived desire for warmer
    relations, 551–2
  and China: political upheaval in, 225, 230–3
  and China: summit, 202, 213–15, 216,
    217–18, 225, 230–1, 232, 261, 265, 266,
    270–4
  and China: Warsaw talks on, 47–8
  and Cuba and Cubans, 30, 96, 97, 243, 257–9
  and Cyprus, Greece, and Turkey, 564–5,
    568–9, 571
  and Defense budget, 143
  and de Gaulle memorial, 122, 123–4
  and dovish senators, 27
  and enemy attack on U.S. firebase in South
    Vietnam, 177–8
  and Green Beret murder scandal, 35
  and Heard, 82, 91
  and Helms, 16, 82
  and hollering treason about critics, 212–13
  and impeachment, 502, 518, 581
  and India after Pakistan war, 253, 259, 261–2,
    265–6, 498–9

and India-Pakistan: cutting off aid to India and
PR campaign against India, 243, 246, 247,
248, 249–51, 253
and India-Pakistan: and Rogers's charge of
tilting toward China, 252–3
and India-Pakistan: and UN, 244, 247
and India-Pakistan war, 243, 247–51, 252–3,
257, 523
and India-Pakistan war: criticism of Kissinger's
handling of crisis, 260–1, 262, 264
and intellectuals, 91–2
and Israel's shootdown of civilian Libyan
airliner, 408
and Japanese textile negotiations, 54
and JCS spying operation against
Kissinger, 260, 262
Kissinger on serenity of, 182
Kissinger relationship of, 10, 11–13. *See also*
Nixon, Richard, and Kissinger strains
and Kissinger's appointment as secretary of
state and confirmation hearings, 486, 487,
490–1
and Kissinger's meeting with purported
kidnapping plotters, 160–1
and Kissinger's "peace is at hand" press
conference, 338, 355, 379
and Kissinger's phone recording system, 3
and Kissinger strains, 6, 12, 260–1, 262–5,
370–1, 379, 535, 537–8
and Laos: bombing, 53, 55, 62, 155
and Laos: enemy advances and offensives
in, 60, 259
and Laos: invasion, 138–9, 140–1, 147–8,
149–51, 154–6, 162–3, 165–9, 171–5, 179,
181
and Laos: secret U.S. operations in, 59–60
and Laos: Thai troops in, 61–2, 64
and leaks, 9, 12, 28–9, 30–1, 260
and McGovern, 317–18, 320, 334, 360–1,
497
and Middle East: briefing book for trip to, 555
and Middle East: Israeli bombing in
Lebanon, 557
and Middle East: Israeli-Egyptian
disengagement, 537
and Middle East: Israeli-Syrian
disengagement, 543–4, 547
and Middle East: Israel's weapons requests and
U.S. military aid, 7, 32, 37–9, 512, 517
and Middle East: July 1970 cease-fire, 96–7,
98
and Middle East: Kissinger's meetings
with Saudi and Egyptian foreign
ministers, 543–4
and Middle East: Kissinger's "shuttle
diplomacy," 535, 536–8
and Middle East: Meir visits, 37–9, 529

and Middle East: 1970 Palestinian insurgency
and crisis in Jordan, 101, 104–19
and Middle East: 1971 State Department and
UN initiatives, 152–3
and Middle East: 1973 State Department
initiatives, 411, 412, 413
and Middle East: plan to "lay into"
Israel, 546–7
and Middle East: Rogers Plan, 48
and mistaken bombing of South Vietnamese
troops, 149
and My Lai massacre, 45, 185–6, 197
and nervous breakdown, 532, 533
and Nimeiry, 537–8
and 1972 election, 5, 325–6, 327–8, 359
and Nobel Prize winners, 86–7
and North Korean shootdown of U.S. spy
plane, 23–7
and North Vietnam blockade and mining, 276, 293, 294, 296–7, 299, 305, 306,
307, 308–9, 310–11, 312, 313
and North Vietnam bombing: 1970, 55–6,
57, 63, 64, 75, 123, 125, 126–7, 130–1
and North Vietnam bombing: 1971, 151,
155, 162–3, 164, 171–6, 225, 228, 230, 231,
233–4, 259
and North Vietnam bombing: 1972, 275–6,
277–8, 280–1, 282, 283–4, 285–90, 293,
294–6, 298, 299–301, 303–5, 306, 308, 314
and North Vietnam bombing: 1972:
Christmas bombing, 360, 374, 375–7, 378,
382–5, 387
and North Vietnam bombing: callousness over
casualties, 11, 378
and North Vietnam bombing: hydroelectric
plant and dikes, 314, 320, 333–4
and North Vietnam bombing: outside chain of
command, 557–8
and North Vietnamese offensive in 1972, 275,
277, 280–96, 298–9, 303–5, 311–12
and North Vietnam naval attacks, 276, 280–1,
282, 283–5
November 1 ultimatum of, 6, 32, 40, 41–2
and oil embargo, 527, 530, 533, 535, 537,
543–4, 547
and Pakistan: arms to, 243, 248, 249, 250,
251, 417–18, 498
and Pakistan: diplomatic dissent over, 176–7
and Pakistan: genocide in, 176–7
and Pakistan: U.S. "tilt" toward, 243, 245, 246
and Pentagon Papers, 202, 206–7, 208–9,
211–13
pneumonia of, 462, 463
and POWs, 130, 219, 319, 322, 324, 384–5,
413–15. *See also* Nixon, Richard, and Son
Tay
and protesters, 48, 76, 80, 81

Nixon, Richard (*Continued*)
and resignation, 452, 581, 582–5
and Resor, 35, 197
and SALT, 195–6, 237–8, 335, 337, 341–2
and Schlesinger, 558
and Son Tay, 123, 125–8, 130–1, 132–4
and South Vietnam bombing: 1969, 32, 34
and South Vietnam bombing: 1970, 56, 57
and South Vietnam bombing: 1972, 261, 268–9, 277, 282, 317
and South Vietnamese 1971 presidential election, 221, 238–9
and Soviet Union: grain deals, 455
and Soviet Union: Kissinger's trips to, 293, 294, 296
and Soviet Union: summits, 188, 192, 219, 220, 231, 237–8, 276, 281, 290, 293, 294, 299, 303, 304, 311–12, 451–2, 455
and Soviet Union: U.S. relations with, 76–7, 231, 232
speeches and addresses by, 43–4, 181–3, 184–5, 266
and Sudan killings, 404, 416–17
and "supreme commander" in Vietnam, 299, 305–8
and Taiwan, 261, 272
tape-recording system of, 3, 5, 14, 446, 464
and Thieu's possible replacement, 35–6, 202, 216, 217, 218, 221, 300–1, 303, 304
and Vietnam end date, 185
and Vietnam peace agreement: January 1973, 398–9, 404, 415
and Vietnam peace agreement: January 1973: convincing Thieu to accept it, 386–7, 390–7
and Vietnam peace agreement: October 1972, 360, 375, 382, 383
and Vietnam peace agreement: October 1972: convincing Thieu to accept it, 360, 362–4, 366–9, 371–4, 377
and Vietnam peace talks: 1969, 20, 21–2, 32–3
and Vietnam peace talks: 1970, 61, 62, 134
and Vietnam peace talks: 1971, 199–200, 202, 216–18, 259
and Vietnam peace talks: 1972, 354, 358, 360, 366–8, 370
Vietnam threats by, 27, 40, 42. *See also* Nixon, Richard, November 1 ultimatum of
and Vietnam troop withdrawals, 28, 46, 179, 181
and Watergate, 445, 451, 490–1, 505
and Watergate: and cover-up, 445
and Watergate: and dying, 521
and Watergate: and Haldeman and Ehrlichman, 428
and Watergate: and impeachment, 460, 490
and Watergate: and isolation of, 486–7
and Watergate: and Joseph Alsop's prediction, 427–8
and Watergate: and Kissinger's advice on, 421, 425–7, 472, 485–6, 518–19, 521–2. *See also* Kissinger, Henry, and Watergate: advice and discussions on
and Watergate: perceived deficiency of response to, 430–1, 433–4
and Watergate: and Plumbers, 438
and Watergate: and public confidence and opinion, 527, 531, 552
and Watergate: and Richardson, 432, 502–3, 521
and Watergate: saving and distancing from, 8–9, 425, 426–7, 428–9
and Watergate: speeches and addresses, 9, 433, 472, 478, 484–8, 517–18
and Watergate: and tapes, 446, 464, 490, 502, 517, 518–19
and Watergate: and Theodore White's view, 438–9
and Watergate: and traitors, 451, 452
and Watson, 279
and wiretapping: authorization and ordering of, 441
and wiretapping: and Beecher leak on North Vietnam bombing, 73
and wiretapping: of Halperin, 489
and wiretapping: of Kalb, 494
and wiretapping: by Kennedy and Johnson administrations, 447–8, 556
and wiretapping: and Kissinger press conference, 546, 555–6
and wiretapping: Kissinger's central role in, 441
and wiretapping: and Kissinger's confirmation hearings to become secretary of state, 496–7
and wiretapping: of Kraft, 500
and wiretapping: of NSC staff, 28
and wiretapping: of Safire, 13, 472, 497
and wiretapping: transferring of records of, 2
and Yom Kippur War and aftermath, 502, 505, 506–7, 508, 510–11, 512, 516–17, 523, 524–5, 527. *See also* Nixon, Richard, and Middle East: Israeli-Egyptian disengagement; Nixon, Richard, and Middle East: Israeli-Syrian disengagement
Noel, Cleo, 416
Norman, Lloyd, 470
North Korean shootdown of U.S. spy plane, 6, 23–7
North Vietnam
blockade and mining of, 299, 305, 306, 307, 308–11, 312, 313
bombing of, 6, 11

bombing of: 1970, 51, 55–6, 57, 60–1, 63,
    64, 66, 71–2, 73–6, 122, 123, 125, 126–9,
    130–1, 132
bombing of: 1971, 151, 155, 164, 170–6, 225,
    228, 230, 231, 233, 243, 259
bombing of: 1972, 275–6, 277–8, 282–3,
    285–93, 294–6, 299, 303–5, 306, 310, 314,
    350
bombing of: 1972: Christmas bombing, 360,
    374, 375–85, 386, 387–9, 399–400
bombing of: hydroelectric plant and
    dikes, 314, 320, 330–2, 333–4
bombing of: outside normal chain of
    command, 557–8
bombing of: SAM (surface-to-air missile)
    sites, 55–6, 57, 63, 64, 175
and January 1973 peace agreement, 386, 391,
    392–3, 394, 404, 406–7
Kissinger's 1973 trip to, 403, 408–11
and Laos invasion, 141, 146, 151
military aid to, 348–9, 350, 554
minesweeping in, 406–7, 415
naval attacks on, 276, 280–1, 282, 283–5
1972 offensive of, 275, 277, 280–96, 298–9,
    303–5, 311–12
and North Vietnamese troops in South
    Vietnam, 348, 349, 350, 352, 362, 363, 371
and October 1972 peace agreement, 338,
    351–2, 353–4, 355, 358, 360, 366–8, 369,
    374, 380–1
and POW releases, 413–15
spring 1969 offensive of, 16, 18
See also Nixon, Richard, November 1
    ultimatum of; Son Tay prison camp raid;
    Vietnam peace negotiations; Vietnam War
Novak, Robert, 339, 583–4

Oil embargo, 513, 527, 530, 533, 534, 535, 536,
    537, 543–4, 545, 547
Operation Duck Hook, 32, 36, 41–2
Osborne, John, 192, 443–4, 463–4
Osmer, Margaret, 102, 316

Packard, David, 34, 142
and Cambodia bombing: public, 87
and Cambodia bombing: secret, 16, 17, 18, 19
and Cambodia invasion, 86, 88
and Cuba, 119
and Kompong Speu battle, 87
and Middle East, 95, 104
Pakistan
diplomatic dissent over, 176–7, 179–80,
    183–4
genocide in, 1, 6, 176–7, 183
and UN, 244, 246, 247
U.S. "tilt" toward, 6, 243, 245, 246, 260
and U.S. arms to, 6, 243, 248, 249, 250, 251,
    254–5, 417–18, 498
war with India of, 6, 242–3, 245–57, 523
Palmer, Bruce, 169
Passman, Otto, 249, 331
Peers, William, 179, 180, 181
Pentagon Papers, 262
and court injunction, 208
and Ellsberg, 202, 208, 210, 438, 450
and Kennedy and Johnson
    administrations, 202, 206, 212–13
Kissinger's denials of awareness of existence
    of, 202, 207–8, 209–10, 211
Kissinger's distancing from, 9–10, 202
and Lyndon Johnson, 9, 202, 208, 210–12
and Plumbers, 438, 450–1
publication of, 9, 202, 206–7, 450
suspicion Laird leaked them, 209, 210
Peres, Shimon, 558
Perot, Ross, 52
Petersen, Henry, 447
Peterson, Peter, 359, 364–5, 447
Pham Van Dong, 410
Pineau, Julie, 141
Pinochet, Augusto, 1, 497, 565
Plumbers. *See* Kissinger, Henry, and Watergate:
    and Plumbers and Young; Watergate, and
    Plumbers
Pompidou, Georges, 52, 53, 124
Popper, David, 565
Price, Ray, 478
Pueblo, USS, 24
Pursley, Robert, 73, 151, 241, 491
Pusey, Nathan, 82, 91

Quinn, Sally, 326

Rabasa, Emilio, 497–8
Rabin, Yitzhak, 93
and Egyptian-Israeli military clashes, 228–9
and Israel's shootdown of civilian Libyan
    airliner, 403, 405, 407, 408
and July 1970 cease-fire, 94–5, 96, 97, 98
and 1970 Palestinian insurgency and crisis in
    Jordan, 101, 111–12, 113–14, 115, 116,
    117–19
and report Kissinger would resign, 344
Radford, Charles, 262, 540
Random House, 10, 421, 435–7, 585–6
Rather, Dan
and Kissinger's appointment as secretary of
    state, 446, 462–3, 464–5
and Kissinger's meeting with purported
    kidnapping plotters, 158
on Kissinger's reputation that he never lied, 10
and Nixon's January 1972 Vietnam
    address, 267

Raza, N. A. M., 245, 254, 255–6
Reagan, Nancy, 272–3
Reagan, Ronald, 272–3, 284
Rebozo, Bebe, 161, 328
Resor, Stanley, 35, 197
Reston, James, 23, 401, 443, 523, 546
Rheault, Robert, 33
Riad, Mahmoud, 236
Richardson, Elliot, 382
    appointment as attorney general, 432
    and Cambodia bombing, 422–3
    and Cambodia invasion, 73
    and China, 49, 194, 273
    and Cuba, 30
    and Kissinger's confirmation hearings, 494
    and Laos bombing, 58, 421, 424–5
    and leaks, 29
    resignation of, 9, 502–3, 521
    and South Vietnamese 1971 presidential
        election, 238, 239
Rivero, Horacio, 305, 307
Roberts, Chalmers, 99
Rockefeller, David, 65, 78, 542–3
Rockefeller, Nelson, 181, 279
    and China, 194–5, 218
    and criticism of Kissinger over
        India-Pakistan, 264
    and Gandhi meeting, 243–4
    and Kissinger's battle with Rogers, 264–5
    and Kissinger's phone transcripts, 5, 13
    and Kissinger's talk of resigning, 261, 264–5
    and military equipment for South
        Vietnam, 362
    and Mosbacher, 142
    and North Vietnam bombing, 281, 284
    and Pentagon Papers, 209–10
    and Waldheim, 320, 330–1
    and wiretapping, 472, 493–4
Rodino, Peter, 33
Rogers, William (Bill), 26, 41, 134, 141, 199,
        205, 406, 534
    and Berlin, 202, 220–1, 222–3
    and cable on East Germany, 270
    and Cambodia: arms to Lon Nol, 65, 67, 69
    and Cambodia: invasion, 65, 71, 72, 73, 78,
        80, 89–91
    and Cambodia: secret bombing, 17, 18, 19, 21
    and China, 194, 213, 215, 240, 270–1, 272,
        273–4
    and Cuban gunboat attack on freighter, 258
    Dobrynin meeting of, 268
    and French plane sales to Libya, 52–3
    and India-Pakistan war, 243, 246–7, 251–2
    and India-U.S. relations, 243, 246–7, 266
    and international conference on Vietnam and
        POWs, 413–14, 415
    and January 1973 Vietnam peace
        agreement, 390, 398
    and Jill St. John, 89
    and Kissinger's memoirs, 44
    and Kissinger's secret trip to Moscow, 296
    and Kissinger strains, 12, 84, 92–3, 97–9,
        142–3, 246–7, 261, 264–5, 268
    and Korry, 156–7
    and Laos: bombing, 53–4, 55
    and Laos: funding for, 216
    and Laos: invasion, 145, 161–2
    and Laos: secret U.S. operations in, 59–60
    and leaks, 29, 31, 69
    and McGovern, 356–7, 359, 361
    and Middle East, 38, 268
    and Middle East: July 1970 cease-fire, 84, 93,
        95, 97–9
    and Middle East: 1970 Palestinian insurgency
        and crisis in Jordan, 104, 105–6, 107–8,
        109, 112–13, 115–17
    and Middle East: 1971 State Department and
        UN initiatives, 152, 153, 225, 234–6
    and Middle East: 1973 State Department
        initiatives, 404, 411–12
    and Middle East: Rogers Plan, 48
    and mining of Haiphong, 308, 310–11
    and Mosbacher, 142–3
    and My Lai massacre, 181
    and Nixon's "silent majority" speech, 43–4
    and North Vietnam bombing, 61, 73–4, 122,
        128–9, 130
    and pacifying South Vietnamese on October
        1972 peace agreement, 370–1
    and Pakistan, 6, 180, 183–4, 243, 246
    and Pentagon Papers, 202, 207–8
    and replacement by Kissinger, 446, 462–3,
        465
    and report Kissinger would resign, 344, 345
    and SALT, 180, 195, 196
    and Son Tay, 125, 126, 128–30
    and Soviet summit, 278–9
    and Taiwan, 240
    and Vietnam peace negotiations, 92
    and Watson, 278, 279
Rostow, Walt, 47, 50, 208, 209, 211–12
Rowen, Harry, 210
Rowley, James, 447
Ruckelshaus, William, 223, 437
Rumsfeld, Donald, 185
Rush, Kenneth, 375
    and Berlin, 202, 220, 222–3
    and Chile, 472, 495
    and Greene cables, 422
Rusk, Dean, 199, 579–80
Russell, Richard, 70

Sadat, Anwar
  and disengagement after Yom Kippur
    War, 537, 547, 548–50
  and Egyptian naval blockade, 530
  and Israeli shootdown of civilian Libyan
    airliner, 406
  and Yom Kippur War, 520–1, 523, 524
Safire, William
  and alleged wiretapping of Kissinger, 472, 499
  and criticism of Kissinger over
    India-Pakistan, 263–4
  and Kraft column on Haig's role in
    wiretapping, 578
  wiretapping of and crusade against administra-
    tion's wiretapping, 13, 471–2, 473–8, 479,
    496–7, 500, 578
SALT (Strategic Arms Limitation Talks), 92,
    188, 276
  agreement, 7, 299, 313
  announcements, 180, 195–6
  and Jackson amendment, 320, 335–6, 337,
    341–2, 343–4
  and Kissinger-Gerard Smith tensions, 43, 195,
    225, 237–8, 335
  and leaks, 29, 30, 489
  SALT II, 551
  and Soviet summits, 237–8, 452
Sampson, Nikos, 560, 563, 564, 573, 577
Sato, Eisaku, 54, 63, 66, 91
Saudi Arabia, 527, 530, 533, 543–4, 555
Saunders, Harold, 107, 555
Scali, John
  and China summit, 273–4
  and Edward Kennedy, 234
  and India-Pakistan war, 248
  and Laos, 204
  and leaks against Kissinger, 225
  and Makarios, 567–8
Schecter, Jerrold, 4
Schlesinger, James
  and Cyprus, Greece, and Turkey, 560, 570–1,
    573–4, 575–6, 580
  and Israel's weapons requests, 502, 511, 512,
    513–16, 536, 545, 550
  and Kissinger rivalry and tensions, 513–16,
    545, 546, 551
  and oil embargo, 534
  and possible Peres meeting, 558
  and SALT II, 551
  and secret Cambodia bombing, 472, 479,
    480, 481, 482, 484
  and Yom Kippur War, 502, 511, 512, 513–16
Schneider, René, 121
Schreiber, Taft, 391
  and Judy Brown, 239
  and Kissinger's reported fundraising from
    pro-Nixon Democrats, 329, 330

and Lazar, 339, 460
  and potential Kissinger position at
    MCA, 456–7
  and Watergate, 460
Schulberg, Stuart, 315, 316
Scott, Hugh, 133, 583
Scowcroft, Brent
  and Israeli bombing in Lebanon, 557
  and JCS spying operation against
    Kissinger, 539
  and Kissinger's Middle East "shuttle
    diplomacy," 538
  on Kissinger's secretiveness, 11
  and Nimeiry, 537
  and Nixon's resignation, 583
  and oil embargo, 533
  and Schlesinger, 558
  and Yom Kippur War, 525
Semenov, Vladimir, 238
Semple, Robert, 311, 425
Sevareid, Eric, 266
Shakespeare, Frank, 106
Shalev, Mordechai, 504–5, 557
Shepley, James, 35–6
Sherman, George, 434
Shriver, Sargent, 361
Shultz, George, 223
  and administration's credibility gap, 82
  and Defense budget, 143
  and Kissinger's phone recording system, 3
  and Soviet grain deal, 455
  and Watergate, 421, 430–1, 433–4, 488
Sidey, Hugh, 4, 35, 215, 584
Sihanouk, Norodom, 65, 66, 465
Sinatra, Frank, 4, 397–8
Sirhan, Sirhan, 416, 417
Sirica, John, 502, 518, 519, 521
Sisco, Jean, 534
Sisco, Joseph
  and Cyprus, Greece, and Turkey, 560, 566,
    568, 569–70, 571, 573, 574–5, 580
  and India-Pakistan, 245
  and Israeli shootdown of civilian Libyan
    airliner, 403, 405–6
  and Kissinger strains, 404, 411–13
  and Middle East: Greene cables, 422
  and Middle East: July 1970 cease-fire, 93–4,
    95–6, 97, 98
  and Middle East: Meir visits, 93
  and Middle East: 1970 Palestinian insurgency
    and crisis in Jordan, 104, 105, 108, 109,
    111–13, 115–16, 117, 118–19
  and Middle East: 1971 State Department and
    UN initiatives, 151–3, 234, 235–6
  and Middle East: 1973 State Department
    initiatives, 404, 411–13

Sisco, Joseph (*Continued*)
  and Middle East: putting pressure on Israel in peace talks, 533–4
  and Middle East: U.S. military aid to Israel, 38, 39, 553–4
  and proposed Kissinger-Gromyko meeting in Syria, 551
Sitton, Ray, 465, 467, 479
60 Minutes, 64, 99–100, 102
Slater, Jim, 321
Smith, Gerard, 43, 180, 195, 196, 225, 237–8, 335
Smith, Hedrick
  and Cambodia invasion, 88, 90
  and Okinawa and Midway leaks, 28
  wiretapping of, 28, 449, 494, 495
Smith, Howard K., 182
Sonnenfeldt, Helmut, 10
Son Tay prison camp raid, 6, 122, 123, 125–31, 132–4
South Vietnam
  bombing in: 1969–1970, 32, 34, 56, 57
  bombing in: 1972, 261, 268–9, 277, 282–3, 286, 290, 299, 311, 317
  enemy attack on U.S. firebase in, 177–8
  and January 1973 peace agreement, 386–7, 390–7
  lack of military initiative of, 302
  military capability of and military equipment for, 150, 301–2, 362
  1971 presidential election in, 221, 238–9
  and October 1972 peace agreement, 348–9, 350, 351, 352–3, 360, 362–4, 366–9, 371–4
  and peace agreement violations, 415
  threatened U.S. aid cutoff during peace negotiations, 371–3, 387, 391, 392, 393, 394, 396
  See also Cambodia, South Vietnamese troops in; Laos, invasion of; Nguyen Van Thieu; Vietnam peace negotiations
Souvanna Phouma, 139, 145, 205
Soviet Union
  alleged construction of nuclear submarine base in Cuba by, 7, 101, 107, 111, 119–20
  and Cambodia invasion, 76–7
  and China, 48, 49, 188, 192, 225, 231, 232, 233, 273, 317, 551, 552
  and Cyprus, 560, 561, 563, 564, 565, 567, 568, 569, 570–1, 573
  and détente, 1, 273
  and first-strike nuclear capability, 30–1
  and grain deals, 454–5
  and India-Pakistan, 243, 244, 247, 248, 249, 250, 252, 253, 254, 255, 256, 257, 261
  and Jewish emigration and Soviet Jews, 7, 198
  and Middle East: Egyptian-Israeli military clashes, 229
  and Middle East: July 1970 cease-fire, 94, 96
  and Middle East: minesweepers, 582
  and Middle East: 1970 Palestinian insurgency and crisis in Jordan, 101, 104, 105, 106–7, 108, 109, 110, 111, 113, 116, 117, 118
  and Middle East: 1971 State Department and UN initiatives, 152–3
  and Middle East: SAMs in Suez Canal zone, 96
  and Middle East: shipment of nuclear weapons to Egypt, 531–2
  and military aid to North Vietnam, 348–9
  and North Vietnam bombing, 276, 289, 290, 291, 294, 295, 377–8
  and summit: 1972, 188, 192, 219, 220, 231, 237–8, 268, 276, 278, 281, 290, 293, 294, 299, 303, 304, 311–12, 313, 322
  and summit: 1973, 446, 451–3, 455
  tanker of threatened by right-wing Cubans, 96, 97
  and Yom Kippur War and aftermath, 501–2, 503, 505, 506, 507–9, 516–17, 519–21, 522–5, 527, 528, 531–2, 549
  See also Dobrynin, Anatoly; Kissinger, Henry, and Soviet Union: trips to; SALT (Strategic Arms Limitation Talks)
Spassky, Boris, 320
St. John, Jill, 89
Stabler, Wells, 566, 567, 568
Stans, Maurice, 464
Stein, Howard, 431
Stennis, John
  and Cambodia invasion, 69–70
  and JCS spying operation against Kissinger, 535, 539–40, 541–2
  and Meir visit, 528–9
  and My Lai massacre, 180
Stevenson, Adlai, 188, 189
Stoessel, Walter, 47
Sudan diplomatic killings, 7, 404, 416–17
Suharto, 82–3
Sullivan, William C., 492
Sullivan, William H., 204–5, 413
Sumner, Gordon, 515
Swank, Emory, 423
Symington, Stuart
  and Laos, 59, 60, 202–3, 204
  and secret Cambodia bombing, 481, 482, 491
  and wiretapping, 578
Syria, 340, 551, 555
  and disengagement after Yom Kippur War, 536, 543–4, 545–6, 547, 548–50, 552–3
  and 1970 Palestinian insurgency and crisis in Jordan, 7, 101, 104, 105, 106, 107, 108, 109, 110, 111, 112, 113, 114, 115, 116, 117, 118–19

State Department statement on restoring
relations with, 554–5
and Yom Kippur War, 7, 501–2, 503–17

Taiwan, 187, 188, 194, 240, 261, 271–2
Tasca, Henry, 571
Taub, William, 319–20, 323–5, 326–7, 328, 340
Teller, Edward, 453–4
Thomas, Helen, 449
Timmons, William, 341–2, 343, 391, 531
Toth, Robert, 429–30, 540–1
Tran Kim Phuong, 371
Tran Van Lam, 396
Truman, Harry, 452
Turkey, 108, 561, 562
and Clerides, 560, 568, 569
and double enosis in Cyprus, 572, 573
invasion of Cyprus by, 7, 560, 566–7, 568–9,
571, 572–3
and Makarios, 571
Sisco trips to, 566, 569, 574–5
threatened arms cutoff to, 560, 573–5
and war with Greece, 560, 568–9, 571
Turnbull, John, 85

Ulasewicz, Anthony, 474
Unger, Leonard, 58
United Nations
and China and Taiwan, 240
and Cyprus and Greece, 560, 562, 563,
568–9, 571
and India-Pakistan, 243, 244, 246, 247, 248
and Middle East, 48, 118
and Middle East: Yom Kippur War, 501, 502,
506, 507, 508, 509, 519, 522–3

Van der Beugel, Ernst, 47
Vietnam peace negotiations, 6
and January 1973 peace agreement, 386–7,
389, 390–7, 398, 403, 406
in 1969 16, 20, 21–2, 32–3
in 1970 61, 62, 92, 134
in 1971 199–200, 202, 216–18, 259
in 1972 300–1, 303, 348–55, 358, 360, 366–8,
369, 373, 374, 380–1, 384
and North Vietnam's demand that Thieu be
replaced, 33, 202, 216, 217
and October 1972 peace agreement, 337–8,
348–55, 360
Vietnam War, 1, 6
1968 bombing halt, 66, 73, 92, 125, 259
1969 enemy-declared cease-fire, 34
and prisoners of war (POWs), 6, 133
and prisoners of war (POWs): and Hoffa
scheme. *See* Hoffa, Jimmy
and prisoners of war (POWs): and peace
negotiations, 133, 134, 234, 384–5

and prisoners of war (POWs): releasing, 52,
130, 134, 184, 219, 398, 404, 413–15
protests against: 1969, 36, 37, 40, 41, 48
protests against: 1970, 65, 72, 76, 78, 79, 80,
81
and troop withdrawals, 28, 37, 179, 181
and U.S. casualties, 11, 40, 42
See also Cambodia; Laos; My Lai massacre;
North Vietnam, blockade and mining
of; North Vietnam, bombing of; North
Vietnam: 1972 offensive of; Operation
Duck Hook; South Vietnam, bombing in;
Vietnam peace negotiations
Vogt, John, 164, 283, 310
Vorontsov, Yuli, 105, 106

Waldheim, Kurt, 320, 330–2, 562
Wallace, Mike, 100, 102
Walters, Barbara
and Haldeman's *Today* show remarks, 261,
267, 268
and Hunebelle, 299, 315–16
and interview with Kissinger, 401–2
and Martha Mitchell, 355, 356
and press linking her to Kissinger, 4, 343, 355,
356
Warren, Gerald
and Abrams, 191
and alleged wiretapping of Kissinger, 528,
532, 533
and JCS spying operation and Radford
leaks, 262–3
and Syria, 554–5
Wasserman, Lew, 457
Watergate, 440, 442, 456, 505, 527, 537, 543
break-in, 421, 425, 426
and Butterfield taping revelation, 446, 464
and Buzhardt counterattack on Dean, 457–8,
459–60
and foreign policy, 429, 456, 458–9
Kissinger's advice and discussions about, 8–9,
421, 425–7, 428–34, 457–8, 459–60, 472,
478, 484–8, 518–19, 521–2
Kissinger's fear of becoming figure in, 556–7
Kissinger's professed ignorance of and
distancing from, 8, 419, 421, 427, 429–30,
438, 439–40, 445, 446–7, 450–1, 456
leaks on, 445, 449–50
mushrooming of and revelations on, 421, 425,
445
and Nixon speeches and addresses, 9, 433,
472, 478, 484–8, 517–18
and Nixon's tapes, 464, 502, 517, 518–19
and Plumbers, 8, 421, 438, 439–40, 445,
450–1, 499, 536
and political damage around country, 431–2

Watergate (*Continued*)
  saving and distancing Nixon from, 8–9, 425, 426–7, 428–9
Watson, Arthur, 278, 279
Weicker, Lowell, 469
Weinberger, Caspar, 8
Weiner, Tim, 11, 12
Welander, Robert, 542
Westmoreland, William, 67–8, 186–7, 197, 198
Wheeler, Earle, 20
  and biological weapons, 46
  and bombing suspension in South Vietnam, 34
  and Cambodia invasion, 70, 71, 78
  and Laos bombing, 55, 58
  and North Vietnam bombing, 63, 71–2, 73, 75
  and Operation Duck Hook, 41
  replacement by Moorer, 56, 57
  and secret Cambodia bombing, 22, 467, 468, 469, 480
White, Bill, 211
White, Theodore, 421, 438–40
Williams, John, 199
Wilson, Earl, 356
Wiretapping, 2
  allegedly of Kissinger, 8, 146–7, 472, 493–4, 499–500, 527–8, 532–3
  of Beecher, 73, 494, 495
  and Beecher leak on North Vietnam bombing, 66, 73
  of Brandon, 448–9, 473, 494, 497, 578, 579
  of Davidson, 44, 421, 437–8, 441, 442
  of Halperin, 8, 434, 440, 441, 446, 458, 459, 472, 489–90
  and impeachment investigation, 8, 546
  of Kalb, 494
  by Kennedy and Johnson administrations, 447–8
  and Kissinger press conference, 546, 555–7
  Kissinger's central role in, 1, 8, 421, 441, 489, 492
  and Kissinger's confirmation hearings to become secretary of state, 10, 472, 492–3, 494, 496–7
  Kissinger's minimizing of his involvement in and lies and evasions about, 8, 421, 440, 441–2, 443–4, 445, 446, 448–9, 458, 459, 472, 473–6, 489–90, 492–3, 494–5, 546, 555
  Kissinger's 1974 Senate testimony on, 8, 560 1, 578 80
  of Kraft, 440, 472, 500
  of Lake, 441, 442
  of Lord, 441
  Nixon's authorization of, 441
  and Okinawa and Midway leaks, 28
  public revelation of, 7–8, 421, 434

of Pursley, 73
of Safire and his crusade against the wiretaps, 13, 471–2, 473–8, 479, 496–7, 578
secrecy and extreme sensitivity of, 8
of Smith, 28, 449, 494, 495
unconstitutionality and illegality of, 7–8
and Weicker, 469
Woods, Rose Mary, 537
Wouk, Herman, 333
Wright, Charles, 485, 487

Xuan Thuy, 32–3, 40, 350, 380

Yablans, Frank, 453
Yahya Khan, 177, 248
Yom Kippur War and aftermath, 1, 7, 501–2, 503–18, 519–21, 522–6, 528–32
Yoshida, Mr. (pseudonym), 54, 63–4, 91, 120
Yost, Charles, 197
Young, David
  and JCS spying operation against Kissinger and Anderson leaks, 536, 540–1
  and Plumbers, 438, 439–40, 445, 450–1, 499, 536, 541

Ziegler, Ronald, 74, 124, 185
  and Cambodia, 66
  and China, 213, 214, 272
  and Christmas bombing of North Vietnam, 377, 378–9
  and Connally, 318
  and Haldeman and Ehrlichman after their resignations, 486, 488
  and Hunebelle, 326
  and India-Pakistan, 249–50
  and January 1973 Vietnam peace agreement, 398
  and Jill St. John, 89
  and *Kissinger: The Adventures of Super-Kraut*, 347–8
  and Kissinger at Scandia restaurant, 123
  and Kissinger interviews, 279, 402
  and Kissinger's meeting with purported kidnapping plotters, 155, 158–9
  and Kissinger's parents, 276–7
  and Klein's selling of Kissinger's 1973 trip to North Vietnam and China, 408–9
  and Laird's statements on end of combat involvement in Vietnam, 141–2
  and Laos, 61, 62, 168
  and Middle East, 99
  and Nixon's distancing from Kissinger, 370
  and restoring relations with Syria, 554–5
  and Rogers, 92, 99
  and Watergate, 458, 502, 519
  and wiretapping, 472, 479, 556–7
Zumwalt, Elmo, 11